STILWELL'S MISSION TO CHINA

GENERAL JOSEPH W. STILWELL

UNITED STATES ARMY IN WORLD WAR II

China–Burma–India Theater

STILWELL'S MISSION TO CHINA

by

Charles F. Romanus

and

Riley Sunderland

MILITARY INSTRVCTION

OFFICE OF THE CHIEF OF MILITARY HISTORY

DEPARTMENT OF THE ARMY

WASHINGTON, D. C., 1953

Library of Congress Catalog Card Number 53–60349

Reprinted 1970

UNITED STATES ARMY IN WORLD WAR II

Kent Roberts Greenfield, General Editor

Advisory Committee

Office of the Chief of Military History

Maj. Gen. Orlando Ward, Chief

The History of

THE CHINA–BURMA–INDIA THEATER

Stilwell's Mission to China

This volume, one of the series UNITED STATES ARMY IN WORLD WAR II, is the first to be published in the subseries THE CHINA–BURMA–INDIA THEATER.

The volumes in the over-all series will be closely related and will present a comprehensive account of the activities of the Military Establishment during World War II. A tentative list of subseries is appended at the end of this volume.

. . . to Those Who Served

Foreword

Reading the history of the China–Burma–India Theater will be an eye opener and a lesson to those who, in the future, have to deal with allies in far distant lands about whom so much should be known and so little is.

Contemporary history is limited in its vision, as indeed is all history, insofar as the records are limited. This history is no exception; the records used are mainly of U.S. Army origin. However, time flies and experience of the past is essential to wisdom in the future. To wait for additional evidence might deny pertinent information to those who need it now. Moreover, the records turned up by the authors of this book are exceptionally rich.

A careful reading of this volume will emphasize the necessity on the part of the leading participants in a combined venture to understand the characteristics and over-all objectives of the nations as well as the individuals concerned in the endeavor. If such an understanding is present, and if due weight is given it by those involved in negotiations as well as in the execution of the plans, the better will be the result. The degree to which this understanding was achieved by the leading participants is left for the reader to decide.

Decisions, to be sound, must perforce be based on up-to-date facts. The danger of making them from information supplied from not too well informed sources, and without information that could readily have been brought to bear, is self-evident.

While still in the service, the authors were sent to Asia in the summer of 1945 to join the Historical Sections of the India–Burma and the China Theaters. Riley Sunderland went to New Delhi, India, and Charles F. Romanus to Chungking, China. Each spent about a year in his respective post before work was begun on this volume.

Washington, D. C.
10 March 1952

ORLANDO WARD
Maj. Gen., U.S.A.
Chief of Military History

Preface

The United States Army Forces in the China, Burma and India Theater were originally planned as a task force to support China. They were largely based on India; only a small fraction of their strength was in China itself. In China, the Generalissimo, Chiang Kai-shek, was Supreme Commander, China Theater. In India, Gen. Sir Archibald P. Wavell had a comparable role and title. The two portions of the U.S. forces—in India and China—were separated by Japanese-occupied Burma. The U.S. theater commander had two major roles, in that he was an American theater commander and also chief of the Generalissimo's Allied staff for China Theater. The command situation was thus most complex. More complications were provided by the differing views on strategy held by the United States, the Republic of China, and the British Commonwealth.

After a few months' research, the authors concluded that, without some understanding of the roles played by the President and the Joint and Combined Chiefs of Staff, the full story could not be told. They therefore examined the relevant files of the Chief of Staff of the U.S. Army, of the Joint and Combined Chiefs of Staff, of the Secretary of War, of the Operations Division of the War Department, and of the War Department Classified Message Center.

The authors are greatly indebted to many of the participants in the events described in the text who were willing to offer comment and criticism on several drafts of the manuscript: Col. Harry S. Aldrich, Brig. Gen. Edward H. Alexander, Col. Haydon L. Boatner, Lt. Gen. George H. Brett, Col. Frank Dorn, Lt. Gen. Hugh A. Drum, Col. Henry W. T. Eglin, General of the Army Dwight D. Eisenhower, Col. Benjamin G. Ferris, Col. Arcadi Gluckman, Maj. Gen. Thomas G. Hearn, the Hon. Nelson T. Johnson, Maj. Gen. Edward E. MacMorland, Brig. Gen. John Magruder, Maj. Gen. Frank D. Merrill, Maj. Gen. Sherman Miles, Lt. Gen. Eugene Reybold, Col. Frank N. Roberts, Maj. Gen. Franklin C. Sibert, Gen. Brehon B. Somervell, Admiral Harold R. Stark, and Lt. Gen. Albert C. Wedemeyer. These men are of course not responsible for any errors of fact or interpretation in the pages following.

The authors have been greatly aided by and are grateful for the opportunity to discuss the history of the China–Burma–India Theaters with Colonel Aldrich, Colonel Dorn, General Drum, Colonel Gluckman, General Hearn, Maj. Gen. Patrick J. Hurley, Mr. Johnson, General MacMorland, General Magruder, General of the Army George C. Marshall, General Merrill, Mr.

William D. Pawley, Colonel Roberts, Admiral Stark, and General Wedemeyer.

The authors have pitched their narrative at the level of the U.S. theater headquarters. As such, it is a contribution to a better understanding of the American effort in Asia, 1941–1946, and to the study of Sino-American relations in the same period; it is not a definitive history of the war in Asia. The U.S. Air Force is telling its story in many volumes written from its own point of view. So, too, are the technical services, such as the Quartermaster, Ordnance, Transportation, Medical, etc. The British official history is being prepared. The Chinese may someday give their side. From these several sources, some historian may ultimately produce a fairly complete history of the war in Asia. The present volume initiates a reconnaissance of part of the area the future historian must cross.

The authors' decision to prepare their history in this manner reflects their mission, that of preparing the history of a U.S. Army theater of operations, a decision further reinforced by the nature of the available sources and the limits of time and funds.

As the authors' familiarity with their subject increased, and as more and more papers of the most private nature were opened to them, they concluded that the relations of the theater commander to the Chinese were central to any story of the U.S. Army's efforts in China, Burma, and India. Thanks to Mrs. Joseph W. Stilwell and Mr. Robert E. Sherwood, a great quantity of material from the Stilwell and Hopkins Papers for the period in which General Stilwell commanded the China, Burma and India Theater was made available. Much of the material in Book VII of the Hopkins Papers, though it goes far to explain President Roosevelt's attitude toward China in 1942 and 1943, has not been included in this volume, because the subject seems one for historians of the Presidency.

The authors have been greatly assisted by collections of private papers made available by General Drum, General MacMorland, Colonel Aldrich, Mr. Pawley, and General Hurley.

Treated at length in this volume are the proposals of General Stilwell to the National Government of the Republic of China in the execution of his orders from the War Department to "support China" and to assist in "improving the combat efficiency of the Chinese Army." Such Chinese replies as were given to Stilwell are also included. Other volumes will cover in full the 1944 command crisis and the work of General Wedemeyer as Commanding General, U.S. Forces, China Theater, 1944–1946.

Nothing pertinent to General Stilwell's conduct of his mission has been omitted. The authors are aware of the issues presented by the civil war in China. On the question of General Stilwell's relations to the Chinese Communists the evidence is almost entirely negative. After examining Stilwell's papers both private and public the authors are convinced that his interest in

xii

the Chinese Communists was minor and his relations with them casual and incidental. General Stilwell's interests in China centered on his attempt to carry out the War Department orders to reform the Chinese Army to a passable level of efficiency. His differences with other personages in China revolved around the issue of Army reform. That portion of Stilwell's wartime journals published as *The Stilwell Papers* and this and the succeeding volume, with but two exceptions, tell the full story of Stilwell's relations with and opinions of the Chinese Communists so far as it has been preserved by the documents and the persons consulted by the authors.

The exceptions, omitted from the text only because they contribute nothing new to an understanding of Stilwell's mission to China, are these. (1) At the Washington Conference of May 1943 General Stilwell wrote a note to himself .to the effect that the United Front of Chinese Nationalists and Chinese Communists should be restored. The context suggests, though not strongly, that Stilwell meant a political united front. The topic then disappears from his writings. (2) On the same visit to Washington he described the Chinese Communist to the then Army Chief of Staff, General Marshall, as a man who wanted taxes cut to a bearable level.

Like most professional soldiers of the major powers, Stilwell had little interest in political and social problems, foreign or domestic. From a most conservative background in upstate New York, Stilwell entered the U.S. Military Academy, after which he spent his life in the regular service. He detested sham and pretense of whatever variety, but he was not a radical, and his efforts to reform the Chinese were limited to "improving the combat efficiency of the Chinese Army," as the War Department had ordered him.

Among the authors' professional colleagues, special thanks are due to Lt. Grace Person Hayes, USN, of the Joint Chiefs of Staff Historical Section. Lieutenant Hayes read and commented on almost every page of the manuscript. Capt. Tracy B. Kittredge, USN, of the same office, was most helpful. Dr. Lee Bowen, of the Air Force historians, gave generously of his time and effort. Maj. Charles F. Byars, USAF, gave the first chapters his careful attention. Miss Alice Miller, formerly of the Registered Documents Section, Plans and Operations Division, guided the authors through the intricate record of the war's higher direction. Miss Miller gave many hours of her time to the authors and they are greatly indebted to her. The authors are grateful to Miss Margaret E. Tackley for the excellent work she did in selecting the photographs for the volume. The editor of the volume, Miss Ruth Stout, performed her task with high professional skill. The copy-editing duties were discharged most capably by Miss Gay Morenus.

From September 1948 to October 1950 the authors were aided by Mrs. Jacqueline Perry Griffin, research assistant. Mrs. Griffin assembled the apparatus of documentation and citation and prepared the manuscript of the first seven chapters. In research, she studied the operations of Southeast Asia Command. Her good judgment, narrative skill, and editorial touch have greatly improved the text.

Mrs. Dorothy Campbell Liles, research assistant, prepared the manuscript of Chapters VIII, IX, and X and verified quotations and citations. Mrs. Elaine Conroy Deane assumed many of the duties of research assistant in addition to normal secretarial tasks. Miss Mildred Bucan, Miss Kay Atema, Miss Alfa Staken, Miss Margaret Reardon, and Miss Marion R. Reidy gave invaluable secretarial and stenographic help.

Washington, D. C.
10 March 1952

CHARLES F. ROMANUS
RILEY SUNDERLAND

Contents

PART ONE

The United States and China Become Allies

PART TWO

Plans for Breaking the Blockade of China (May 1942–March 1943)

PART THREE

U.S. Air Power Given the Stellar Role in China Theater

Charts

Tables

Maps

Illustrations

The *Frontispiece* is a photographic copy of an oil
painting by Howard E. Smith.   The painting is
a part of the memorial collection at West Point.

The photographs are from the files
of the Department of Defense.

PART ONE

THE UNITED STATES AND CHINA
BECOME ALLIES

CHAPTER I

Aid to China Involves the U.S. Army

The geographic circumstance that placed China across the Pacific Ocean from the United States, the history and culture that gave it some 400,000,000 industrious, clever, prolific people of an ancient civilization, and the disorders that vexed the Chinese land as its people sought to adapt themselves to the industrial ways and materialist culture of the West long combined to make China an object of peculiar interest and concern to the people and Government of the United States. Itself the outstanding example of revolt against European colonialism, the United States of America was sympathetic to the efforts of the Chinese to work out their destiny in their own way and supported them as the situation permitted.

The United States could not believe that the possession of modern industrial techniques by European states and the one Oriental nation successfully imitating them, Japan, conferred the right to dispose of the freedom and patrimony of Asia and considered that the long-range interests of the United States were best served by the support of Asiatic nationalism. As the twentieth century progressed, Asiatic nationalism began to rise ever closer to the flood stage. Large-scale fighting threatened Asia as Japan, the latecomer to industrialism, started to repeat, at China's expense, the imperialist behavior of her Western tutors. Japan's actions seemed contrary to the course and spirit of international political developments of the 1920's; they threatened to upset the *status quo* in the Pacific in a manner dangerous to American security, and so the United States, fearing the ultimate menace, moved ever closer to open support of China, which was immediately menaced.

The history of Japanese efforts to establish a special position for the Japanese Empire in China is far too long to detail here. China's markets and resources and the absence for many years of a strong central government seemed to the Japanese to offer natural and obvious opportunities, while the undisciplined troops of Chinese war lords on occasion subjected Japanese citizens to treatment of the sort to which, fifty years before, Japan's western mentors had habitually responded by the dispatch of gunboats. So there were incidents, diplomatic notes, and diplomatic crises. Lending hope for the future, the period 1922–1930 after World War I brought forth liberal cabinets in Japan which signed treaties pledging their nation to allow China the chance to work out her destiny in her own way. Then came the Great Depression of the thirties. Japan's overseas markets contracted and unrest grew. The most powerful voices of protest in Japan came from factions allied to, or even part of, the Japanese Army. These sought a remedy for Japan's troubles at home in seizing the raw materials and monopolizing the markets of China and her northern possession, Manchuria.

The Japanese Army's continental adventure began 18 September 1931 when a carefully staged incident near Mukden, Manchuria, offered the pretext under which the Japanese Army, while the Japanese Foreign Office offered polite regrets and promises that soon proved empty, soon overran all Manchuria. (*Map 1*)* The United States was then under Republican administration. President Herbert C. Hoover was a man of peace, profoundly adverse to the United States' taking any course in the Pacific, in restraint of Japan, that might mean war. The rest of the Great Powers, for diverse reasons, were equally reluctant to undertake vigorous action.

Faced with a situation in which military and economic sanctions, by European powers or the United States or both, were out of the question, Mr. Hoover's Secretary of State, Henry L. Stimson, suggested that the United States adopt a policy of not recognizing the legality of any changes in Asia that the Japanese might effect by force. To Mr. Stimson, announcement of the policy on 7 January 1932 was a reassertion of cherished American convictions and a notice to the Chinese that the United States would not condone violations of China's sovereignty and territorial integrity.[1] The note had no discernible effect on the Japanese, but it placed on record for all to see that American and Japanese interests, as defined by the two governments, were clashing and identified Stimson as a firm opponent of Japanese aggression in the Far East.

Having separated Manchuria from China the Japanese found themselves faced by a Chinese boycott. One of the few means of retaliation open to China, the boycott was a severe blow to Japan's trade in one of her principal markets. Chinese indignation was steadily rising and there were attacks on Japanese residents in China. The Japanese had occupied Manchuria on less provocation. On 28 January 1932 they landed an expeditionary force in Shanghai. Heavy fighting followed in which for the first time the Chinese gave a good account of themselves against the Japanese. World opinion, governmental and public,

---

[1] Henry L. Stimson and McGeorge Bundy, *On Active Service in Peace and War* (New York, 1947), Ch. IX.
* Inside back cover.

quickly hardened, and in May 1932 the Japanese withdrew their forces from Shanghai. An uneasy peace followed in Asia.

In the years that followed there were great changes in China and the United States. In the United States, the Democratic administration of Franklin Delano Roosevelt took office in March 1933. In China, the Chinese gave the appearance of rapidly and steadily coalescing into a unified state. Their finances improved, their manufactures increased, and peace and stability gradually spread through the land as the Nationalist Government of the Republic of China, controlled by the Kuomintang Party under Generalissimo Chiang Kai-shek, brought one after another of the war lords to heel and attracted more and more Chinese to its banner. By 1937 there was but one major dissident element, the Chinese Communists. Possessed of their own small army, they were compressed into the far northwest of China. Generalissimo Chiang was bitterly opposed to them and by one expedition after another had steadily whittled away their territory.

The Japanese did not watch the unification and progress of China with complacence. In the four and a half years from 1932 to summer 1937 there were incidents on China's Manchurian and Mongolian frontiers; Japanese troop movements and maneuvers involved the Japanese garrisons, which treaty rights permitted in north China; Japanese naval landing parties went ashore at Hankow, Pakhoi, Tsingtao, and a suburb of Shanghai; and within Japan the forces favoring aggressive policies in Asia grew steadily in strength. The behavior of the Japanese toward China greatly irritated Chinese opinion, which was growing ever more nationalistic, and there was increasing popular pressure on the Chinese Government to resist Japan.

Japanese imperialists and Chinese Communists posed a grave problem for the Generalissimo. The resources of China's new government did not permit him to deal with both simultaneously. The solution that he preferred, and that he sought to follow, was to crush the Communists while opposing Japan by diplomacy alone. This did not meet with general approval. Chinese opinion generally was outraged by the Japanese, and since the articulate elements in China were either sincerely nationalist or thought it politic to profess such sentiments, it may well be that many Chinese overrated their resources and underestimated their enemy's. Be that as it may, in December 1936 a group of Chinese led by Marshal Chang Hsueh-liang kidnapped the Generalissimo. To their captive, they insisted that he lead both Nationalists and Communists into a United Front, which would stand firm against the Japanese. The Generalissimo won his freedom by agreeing, and honored his bargain. The next Japanese move meant large-scale hostilities.

On 8 July 1937 Japanese troops attacked a Chinese garrison near Peiping, in north China. At first a local incident, it spread as the Japanese manifested an aggressive, intransigent attitude, while the Chinese, having already lost

Manchuria and seen their control of north China whittled away, showed no disposition to yield further. Military operations on the grand scale were soon under way with the national forces supporting the provincial troops who were first involved. The Nationalist Government of the Republic of China had tried to create a modern army, for only thus could it continue to dominate China's factions and provinces and hope to resist further Japanese encroachments on Chinese territory.

For military advice and martial gear the Kuomintang had turned to Germany, Italy, and Russia, not to the United States, whose Army in the thirties was unimpressive. By 1937 the skilled and highly regarded German Military Mission (1928–38) had brought about thirty divisions, loyal to Chiang Kai-shek, to a standard of efficiency never before known in China.[2] These troops fought in the defense of the lower Yangtze valley, but by 1939 the Japanese possessed the lines of communications, the seaports, and the key cities of China, including the capital, Nanking.

As the Chinese fell back into the interior, the Chinese and sympathetic observers released accounts to the Western world claiming that the Chinese had lost only because they lacked modern arms. Neither the German Mission, which had trained and advised the best Chinese divisions, nor Col. Joseph W. Stilwell, the American Military Attaché (1935–39), agreed with the press releases. According to their reports, the Chinese committed basic military errors: neglect of fundamental principles of strategy and tactics; improper use of supporting weapons; indifference to military intelligence; inability to adopt sound command and staff procedures; failure to establish a communications net; and failure to keep vehicles and weapons in operating condition.

After the capture of Canton and Hankow in October 1938, the Japanese paused to consolidate their positions. The Chinese seized the opportunity to raise a series of obstacles ahead of the river lines and mountain barriers of west and south China. Roads were trenched, railways dismantled, bridges removed, ferry sites destroyed, and mountain passes barricaded to give the Chinese a buffer from fifty to one hundred miles wide. Walled towns attracted remnants of the national divisions and housed makeshift arsenals. Chungking became the seat of the Generalissimo's wartime government. A stalemate settled over the vast front, broken by sporadic Japanese forays to disperse Chinese troop concentrations and, in 1939, by two abortive Chinese offensives which could not gain enough momentum. Both sides engaged in diplomatic maneuvering, with each other and with possible allies. Nationalist China sought closer ties with Britain, France, the Soviet Union, and the United States. Japan drew closer

---

[2](1) MA Rpts: Maj John Magruder, 20 Dec 26–15 Mar 30; Col Nelson E. Margetts, 16 Mar 30–2 Mar 32; Lt Col Walter S. Drysdale, 3 Mar 32–7 Jul 35; Col Joseph W. Stilwell, 8 Jul 35–30 Apr 39; Maj William Mayer, 13 Jun 39–18 Aug 42. National Archives. (2) Selected papers of the German Military Mission. Folder 2009–255, National Archives.

to heavily armed and increasingly aggressive Fascist Italy and Nazi Germany, the Axis Powers. Opportunities for Japanese aggrandizement in Asia at the expense of European colonial powers developed steadily as war clouds in Europe gathered. In China, the Japanese reorganized their twenty-three divisions and twenty independent mixed brigades on a garrison basis in order to free mobile troops for service elsewhere. In March 1940 the Japanese installed Wang Ching-wei's puppet regime in Nanking, but his defection from the Nationlist cause had no decisive result.[3]

China Seeks U.S. Aid

War in Europe after September 1939 made it unlikely that European powers friendly to China could spare arms and technical assistance, so the Chinese Government approached the United States, whose sympathy for it was openly manifested by government and people alike, though not on a scale to commit the United States to intervention in the Sino-Japanese conflict. In two loans the American Export-Import Bank lent the Chinese-owned Universal Trading Corporation $45,000,000, its use restricted to purchase of civilian supplies.[4]

Following the occupation of Poland by German and Russian armies in September 1939 there was a period of undeclared truce in Europe, called at the time the "phony war." War was real enough at sea, but on land, save in Finland where the Russians struck to extend their borders, there was quiet. Then on 9 April 1940, without warning, the Germans attacked Norway and Denmark. The long training and preparation of the Germans carried all before them, and the campaign in Norway was obviously in its final stages when on 10 May 1940 the Germans struck again, this time against Holland, Belgium, and France, the first two of them declared neutrals. Being then at the peak of their power, the German Army and Air Force overran France and the Low Countries in six weeks. The British Expeditionary Force, plus a considerable number of Frenchmen, was successfully withdrawn through Dunkerque harbor, but this deliverance, though hopeful for the future, could not obscure the fact that Adolf Hitler's Germany was master of Europe from the Pyrenees to North Cape, from the Atlantic to the Polish marshes, on the far side of which Russia stood in strange, uneasy partnership. Italy joined Germany in the closing days of the fight, and there seemed every prospect that Japan might soon do the same and seize the chance of taking French, British, and Dutch

---

[3] (1) Rpts and selected papers cited n. 2. (2) MA Rpts, Stilwell. Folders 2657–H–439, 2279–I–4, National Archives. (3) Japanese Studies in World War II (hereafter, Japanese Study −), 76, China Expeditionary Army Operations in China and Manchuria, 1937–45, and 70. Gen Ref Br, OCMH. (See Bibliographical Note.)

[4] Background on Chinese loans as well as a summary of Sino-American agencies involved in the transactions in Memo, BR 7, Far Eastern Sec, Co-ordinator of Information, sub: American Aid to China. (Hereafter, American Aid to China.) AG(AMMISCA) 400.3295, Job–11, HRS DRB AGO.

possessions in Asia. Britain stood alone, and the United States had to make decisions of the utmost gravity.

In June 1940 Mr. T. V. Soong [5] visited the United States to ask for arms and more credits. Two factors weighed heavily in favor of a loan to China for arms. U.S. sympathy lay with China's cause and American planners, in appraising the possibility and probable course of a conflict with Japan, recognized the advantages for the United States in having China's manpower and geographic position as an aid. However, the United States was most anxious not to provoke Japan to ally herself with Germany since that alliance would further jeopardize England's already desperate position. Moreover, since Germany had just overrun western Europe to the English Channel, the United States itself seemed in danger, and the American munitions stock was not great enough to provide for China after American needs were met and after the United States supported Great Britain, whose plight seemed most directly to affect the United States. Furthermore, it was not feasible to diminish the U.S. stockpile in order to send supplies to China since matériel previously sent was not reaching the fronts because lines of communications were inadequate for forwarding it.[6]

Two blows fell hard on Chinese morale with the advent of autumn. The first was the entrance of the Japanese into northern Indochina on 23 September, by agreement with the Government of Unoccupied France. Then, four days later, Japan, Germany, and Italy signed a pact whose wording suggested they would join in offensive action against the British Commonwealth and the United States. To encourage the dejected Chinese, the United States gave a third credit of $25,000,000 to China. But the loan did not answer China's pleas for arms, and in October the Chinese renewed their requests. They were spurred on by the fact that the Japanese occupation of northern Indochina closed the Yunnan–Indochina Railway, leaving the Burma Road, which extended from Chungking to the terminus of the Burma Railways, Lashio, Burma, as China's sole supply link with the outside world. The Burma Road, though maladministration and corruption had reduced its inherently low capacity, now had great symbolic value as China's last tie with freedom. That summer the sorely tried British had closed the Lashio terminal for three

---

[5] Mr. Soong, brother-in-law of the Generalissimo, received his bachelor's degree from Harvard in 1915. Following graduate work at Columbia, he returned to China. Showing great aptitude for finance, Soong became Minister of Finance in the Sun Yat-sen regime in Canton in 1925. From 1930 to 1933 he was governor of the Central Bank of China. Soong then became chairman of the Board of Directors of the National Bank of China. Shortly after the beginning of war in the Pacific on 23 December 1941, he became Minister of Foreign Affairs.

[6] (1) Capt Tracy B. Kittredge, USNR, draft MS, United States–British Naval Co-operation, 1940–1945, III, D, 87; III, D, 302–03; IV, D, 247, n. 1; IV, A, 297. JCS Hist Sec. (2) Studies of China's geographic position and manpower as early as January 1940 appended to JB Paper 355 (Ser 691), 9 Jul 41. AG (AMMISCA) 336.2. (3) WPD Study 4389, Cases 1–28, Sec 1, A47–30, contains staff papers on which the Joint Board Paper is based. (4) Robert E. Sherwood, *Roosevelt and Hopkins: An Intimate History* (New York, 1949), p. 150.

months to placate the Japanese. Although the Burma Road was reopened on 10 October 1940, the Chinese and British saw the events of September bringing the Japanese ever closer to it, and there was little Britain could do to keep the Japanese out of Burma.[7]

On 18 October 1940 the Generalissimo described his problems and made his proposals to the U.S. Ambassador, Mr. Nelson T. Johnson. The Generalissimo admitted that the Japanese blockade had weakened China's economy and hurt public morale. The Chinese Communists were taking advantage of the situation, and by his own admission the Generalissimo feared them more than he feared the Japanese. (It must be recalled that this was the era of the Russo-German nonaggression pact of 1939, and that the Russian and German Foreign Ministers were soon to meet and debate the parceling out of the Middle East.) The Generalissimo was anxious lest the Japanese seize Singapore or cut the Burma Road. Before either of these disasters, China must have economic aid plus numbers of U.S. aircraft manned by American volunteers. Unless this aid came soon, China might collapse. If it came in time, the internal situation would be restored and the Japanese forestalled. The aircraft would also permit the Generalissimo to effect a "fundamental solution" of the Pacific problem by destroying the Japanese Navy in its bases.[8] Proposed a month before British carrier aircraft attacked the Italian Navy at Taranto, the Generalissimo's plan might indeed have been the fundamental solution, but in the irony of history it was the Japanese who attempted the method at Pearl Harbor.[9]

Mr. Johnson considered this a time for decision and urged the State Department to effective action to uphold the U.S. position in the Far East. The Department's reply on 23 October was guarded in tone.[10] It reassured the Generalissimo by observing that both Singapore and the Burma Road appeared safe for the present, and went on to describe Chinese and American interests as parallel, even though the traditional U. S. policy was one of shunning alliances. It concluded with the statement that the U.S. Government would continue to study the matter to see what could be done within the framework of existing law. Every reader of the press knew that the United States had found it legally possible to ship large quantities of arms to the British, and

[7] (1) For an analysis of the pact by the U.S. Ambassador to Japan, see the State Department's *Papers Relating to the Foreign Relations of the United States, Japan: 1931–1941* (Washington, 1943), Vol. II, pp. 169–70. (2) The Chinese requests are in Rads, Chungking 524, 526, Johnson to STATE, 17, 18 Oct 40. Dept State 793.93/16241, 793.94/16245. (3) Prime Minister Churchill's explanation to Mr. Roosevelt of the British decision to close the Burma Road in Winston S. Churchill, *Their Finest Hour* (Boston, 1949), pp. 497–98.

[8] Rads Chungking 528, 529, Johnson to STATE, 20 Oct 40. Dept State 793.94/16249, 793.94/16251.

[9] On 12 November 1940 British torpedo-carrying planes sank the battleship *Cavour* and grounded two other Italian warships at Taranto.

[10] (1) Rad 529 cited n. 8. (2) Rad STATE 181, Washington to Johnson, 23 Oct 40. Dept State 793.94/16245.

therefore, although the Generalissimo did not say so specifically, he impressed Ambassador Johnson as being pleased with the American reply. He asked the American envoy to convey his deep gratitude to President Franklin D. Roosevelt.[11] After the American note of 23 October, the Chinese closed their ears to offers of mediation from Japan's ally, Germany.[12]

The fear of the Chinese Communists that the Generalissimo communicated to Ambassador Johnson may have reflected awareness of a widening breach between the Nationalists and Communists, which became evident a few months later in January 1941. No outsider could hope to untangle the rights and wrongs of the incident that marked the end of the United Front, but in January 1941 the Nationalists and the Communist New 4th Army clashed. When the battle ended, the New 4th Army headquarters staff were dead or captive, together with their troops. Thereafter, many Nationalist divisions were deployed against the Communists, who, for their part, were quite willing to join in fratricidal war. This meant that the Generalissimo had another factor to consider in the shifting political balances within China.

In November 1940 the Generalissimo sent a mission under Maj. Gen. Mao Pang-tzo, Director of the Operations Division, Chinese Air Force, to the United States. With him was an American citizen, Capt. Claire L. Chennault (USA-Ret.), who had been an articulate and forceful advocate of fighter aviation vis-à-vis the bomber and a daring and skillful pilot. After his retirement from the U.S. Army Air Corps in 1937 for physical disability, Chennault had gone to China, where he had won the confidence and affection of the Chinese. As one of their technical advisers he had become a colonel in their Air Force. Studying Japanese equipment, tactics, and military potential, Chennault had devised a plan to defeat Japan with a small air force, operating under a tactical system designed by him to exploit the relative strengths and weaknesses of American and Japanese aircraft and pilots.[13]

Since 1937 the Chinese had been discussing with two other Americans the possibility of using their influence and business organizations in placing American air power in China. Mr. William D. Pawley and Lt. Comdr. Bruce Leighton (USNR-Ret.) were asked by Soong and Mao to co-operate in giving air support to the Chinese.[14]

The Mao mission presented its request on 25 November 1940 to the President's Liaison Committee, the civilian agency co-ordinating foreign arms purchases in the United States. The Chinese wanted 500 combat planes

[11] Rad Chungking 551, Johnson to STATE, 31 Oct 40. Dept State 793.94/16277.
[12] Rad Chungking 581, Johnson to STATE, 22 Nov 40; Rad Chungking 587, Johnson to STATE, 27 Nov 40. Dept State 793.94/16345. Ambassador Johnson summarized his October and November conversations with the Generalissimo in the latter message.
[13] Maj. Gen. Claire L. Chennault, USA-Ret., *Way of a Fighter: The Memoirs of Claire Lee Chennault* (New York, 1949), pp. 59, 90–104.
[14] Ltr, W. D. Pawley, Pres, Intercontinent Corp., to Romanus, 6 Jul 50. HIS 330.14 CBI 1950. (See Bibliographical Note.)

delivered to China in 1941. They also wanted crews to fly them since, despite the efforts of successive European and American air missions, the Chinese had been unable to train a body of pilots. One hundred and fifty basic trainers and ten transports would complete a small but balanced air force. Twenty percent spare parts were requested, plus matériel to build 14 major airfields and 122 landing strips, and ammunition and ordnance requirements for one year's operation.[15]

Concurrently with Mao's aircraft proposal came a Chinese bid for $30,000,000 worth of ground force matériel. This first bid was on a scale appropriate to the equipping of thirty Chinese divisions. Extension of a $100,000,000 credit on 1 December 1940 became the first step toward initiating military aid for China. Of the total sum, 25 percent could be used to purchase arms. Obviously this amount was insufficient to finance either Mao's aircraft program or the Chinese bid for ground force matériel. Nor was the U.S. Army able to find facilities to manufacture the caliber of weapons which the Chinese requested. The Chinese were also told that the U.S. Army had no authority to sell ordnance from its own stocks to China.[16]

With $25,000,000 available, Mao's aircraft requests fared better. On 4 December Dr. Stanley K. Hornbeck of the State Department hinted that military aid to China would start with aircraft and that no objection would be raised to the American volunteer scheme. On 19 December 1940 Mr. Roosevelt approved military aid for China and asked the State, War, Navy, and Treasury Departments to find ways of implementing a program.[17]

Fearing Japan's intentions since the Japanese sank the USS *Panay* in December 1937, the Navy Department closely studied the Mao proposals. Secretary of the Navy Frank Knox, assisted by his aide, Capt. Morton L. Deyo (USN), discussed both the strategic implications and the Chinese ability to use and maintain 500 modern aircraft with Mr. Pawley and Commander Leighton. Both had had years of experience in selling transport and combat aircraft to the Chinese Government. Having served on the U.S. Navy's Yangtze River patrol, Commander Leighton had acquired a deep appreciation

[15] (1) Specifically, the Chinese asked for 250 Brewster 4F–4's or Grumman 36A's, 100 Curtiss-Wright P–40's, which were considered a match for the new Japanese Zero fighter, 50 Douglas B–23's, and 100 Lockheed Hudsons. The Mao-Chennault specifications in Ltr, Soong to Maj Gen James H. Burns, Executive Off, Office, Div of Def Aid Rpts, 31 Mar 41. Exhibit A, Sec II, ASF (DAD) ID, A46–299, Folder, China—Requirements Presented by the Chinese Representatives. (Hereafter, Soong Requirements.) (2) Ltr, Philip Young, Office of Production Management, to Harry Hopkins, 21 Apr 41, sub: Rpt on China Requests for Lauchlin Currie. China Pre-Pearl Harbor Folder, Hopkins Papers, Franklin D. Roosevelt Library, Hyde Park, New York.

[16] Ltr, Archie Lockhead, Pres, Universal Trading Corp., to Philip Young, Chairman, President's Ln Com, 8 Jan 41; Memo, Lt Col Edward E. MacMorland, Secy, Army-Navy Munitions Bd, for ACofS, G–4, WDGS, 17 Jan, sub: Chinese Ordnance Reqmts; Memo, Maj Gen James H. Burns, U.S. Army member, President's Ln Com, for Young, 28 Jan 41. China Folder, ASF (DAD) ID, A46–299.

[17] Kittredge, draft MS, Evolution of Global Strategy in World War II, Ch. 11, p. 119. JCS Hist Sec.

of the strategic importance of China-based air power to deter further Japanese aggression, but he was quick to point out its limitations in the hands of the Chinese. He insisted that American technicians would have to assist in all phases of the 500-plane air force scheme, otherwise there would be failures and waste. Though proceeding with caution, Mr. Knox soon became a leading advocate of aircraft and volunteers for the Chinese Air Force.[18]

Unfortunately, the Mao program conflicted with American and British requirements, whose high priorities were to keep this matériel from China until June 1942.[19] The thought behind aid to China was to keep the Japanese fully occupied there beginning in the last six months of 1941, not twelve months later, and the time lag suggested this could not be done. The size of the program was quite acceptable, for the policy then was to accept foreign orders which would lead to enlargement of the U.S. munitions plant.[20] The initial step in resolving priority conflicts was the agreement of the British purchasing mission to let the Chinese have 100 P–40B's allocated to Britain, if the Chinese in turn would yield their priority rights to 100 later model fighters.[21] The British assumed responsibility for completing the armament of the P–40's. In their haste to get fighters, the Chinese agreed and accepted the first thirty-six P–40's without essential combat gear.

While the various bureaus worked on these proposals, which Chennault had prepared with expert care, Mr. Soong and his Chinese colleagues laid before the President a scheme to bomb Japan from Chinese bases with B–17's manned by American volunteers. This proposal won considerable attention, unlike the Generalissimo's proposal to sink the Japanese fleet. Gen. George C. Marshall, Chief of Staff of the U.S. Army, said it had the approval of the Secretary of State, Cordell Hull, and his colleague, Secretary of the Treasury Henry Morgenthau. Appearing at the War Department with that august support, the plan underwent a more searching examination, during which it appeared that the Chinese had already expended a group of Martin bombers without result by operating them without fighter cover or antiaircraft support, just as they proposed to operate the B–17's. Trained American crews were as scarce as B–17's. Permitting them to volunteer would greatly handicap the Army Air Corps' expansion program. Moreover, because it was most difficult to ship spare parts to airfields within bombing range of Japan, maintenance problems

[18] (1) Memo, Leighton for CNO, 17 Jan 41. Incl B, JB Paper cited n. 6(2). (2) Ltr, Leighton to Deyo, 20 Jan 41. Leighton Folder 1–9, W. D. Pawley Papers, Intercontinent Corp., 30 Rockefeller Plaza, New York, N. Y.

[19] Memo, Col Charles Hines, Chairman, Clearance Com, Army-Navy Munitions Bd, for President's Ln Com, 6 Dec 40, sub: Chinese Aircraft and Antiaircraft Reqmts. China Folder, ASF (DAD) ID, A46–299.

[20] Memo, Hines for President's Ln Com, 3 Feb 41, sub: Chinese Aircraft and Program. China Folder, ASF (DAD) ID, A46–299.

[21] Memo, Burns for Lt Col Andrew J. McFarland, 23 Dec 40, sub: Conf re Allocation of P–40 Aircraft, AG 400.3295 (4–14–41) Sec 1A, Tab C.

for the B–17's would be insoluble. Although the War Department did not grant the request for B–17's and volunteer crews, the discussions showed that at this early date the Department entertained the idea of containing Japan by putting air power into China.[22]

Origins of Lend-Lease Aid for China

After the purchase of 100 P–40's, the Chinese were in need of more credits to complete the Mao air program and to contract for matériel for the Chinese Army. Early in January 1941 the War Department told the Chinese to await developments on both of their projects since the American aid program was about to undergo a profound change.[23] Because of the pending exhaustion of British dollar resources, President Roosevelt in December proposed the device of removing the "dollar sign" by lending or leasing arms to Great Britain or any other nation whose defense was thought vital to American security.[24] Lend-lease was a tremendous weapon in the bloodless struggle then under way between the United States on the one hand and Germany and Italy on the other, because it put the prodigious resources and industry of the United States behind Great Britain and China.[25]

The Lend-Lease bill went before Congress on 6 January 1941. In comparison with Great Britain, China played a very minor role in the planning of lend-lease legislation. One reason was that, apart from the Mao program, Washington had little specific, itemized information as to what China's overall needs were, for Soong's staff had offered only vague generalities.[26] The British, on the other hand, had presented concrete programs on which the estimate of the first lend-lease appropriation was based. A second reason lay in the fact that, though the War Department wanted Japan to be contained in China, the British Commonwealth with its vast holdings in the Orient was considered to have a predominant interest in maintaining China as a belligerent.[27] The Commonwealth would have received U.S. approval of any reasonable program of transfers to China.

At this point the Generalissimo asked that Dr. Lauchlin Currie, one of the President's administrative assistants, be sent to China to examine the military and economic situation. Dr. Currie subsequently visited China from 28 January to 11 March 1941. Without, it would seem, having actually explored the scope

---

[22] Min, Conf in OCofS, 0830, 23 Dec 40. Vol I, Conferences, A47–68.

[23] (1) Memos cited n. 16. (2) Memo, Col Hines for Ray A. Graham, President's Ln Com, 3 Feb 41. China Folder, ASF (DAD) ID, A46–299.

[24] Sherwood, *Roosevelt and Hopkins,* p. 225.

[25] For details on the background of the Lend-Lease Act see Richard M. Leighton and Robert Coakley, Logistics of Global Warfare: 1941–43, a forthcoming volume in this series.

[26] J. Franklin Ray, Jr., Notes on History of Lend-Lease Aid to China, prepared for Hist Sec, Hq, U.S. Forces, India–Burma Theater, 1945. Gen Ref Br, OCMH.

[27] JB Paper cited n. 6(2).

and degree of completion of the various projects presented to him by the Chinese, Currie returned to tell the President that in anticipation of increased U.S. support the Generalissimo was rushing completion of airfields for B–17's, making plans to centralize administrative control of the Burma Road, and assembling troops at strategic points to receive American weapons. Currie also presented Chinese requests for technicians, advisers, and further credits for currency stabilization.[28]

The President signed the Lend-Lease Act on 11 March 1941. On 31 March Soong presented China's requirements to Maj. Gen. James H. Burns, Executive Officer of the Division of Defense Aid Reports, the forerunner of the Office of Lend-Lease Administration.[29] This and subsequent Chinese requests were considered in the light of the availablity of matériel and of the already formulated policy of making the major American effort in the Atlantic or European area.[30]

Soong's first request for supplies and services fell under seven heads, but close analysis revealed it centered about three related projects. These were:

1. An enlargement of the Mao-Chennault proposals, calling for a modern air force of 1,000 aircraft, with American training and technical help.

2. Arms which, if issued on the basis of organization finally presented by the Chinese in March 1942,[31] would equip thirty divisions.

3. An efficient line of communications between China and friendly powers, with:

    a. A narrow-gauge railway from Yunnan to the Burma Railways.

    b. A highway from Sadiya, India, across north Burma to China.

    c. Trucks, repair shops, and resurfacing for the Burma Road.

    d. Transport aircraft to supplement the road and railways.

Scattered through the request were indications of the strategy behind them, which suggested a Chinese hope that the air force would protect China's airfields and cities and their approaches. With these secure, the lines of communications to them could operate efficiently. Expanded lines of supply would then support the newly equipped divisions, some of whose requirements would be supplied from China's arsenals. Soong believed that a revitalized Chinese Army could not only hold key defensive points, thereby forcing Japan to keep troops in China, but could ultimately assume the offensive. He estimated that with adequate lend-lease aid these strategic aims might be achieved in two years' time.[32]

---

[28] (1) American Aid to China, pp. 17–18. (2) A part of Currie's findings is set forth in Résumé of the Economic and Political Situation in China and Suggestions for Action, 14 Apr 41. Dept State 893.50/245.

[29] Soong Requirements.

[30] Sherwood, *Roosevelt and Hopkins,* pp. 272–73.

[31] See pp. 25, 42–43, n. 24 on p. 159, and p. 235, below.

[32] Soong Requirements.

On his return from Chungking, Dr. Currie had received from Mr. Harry L. Hopkins, the President's confidential adviser, the task of expediting Chinese lend-lease aid.[33] Currie found Soong's program faring badly in the initial confusion of setting up lend-lease machinery.[34] Powerful impetus toward expediting aid to China came from the signature on 13 April of the Russo-Japanese neutrality pact, which stunned the Chinese. The Chinese had found the USSR willing to sell them small quantities of arms, and now this source had dried up. So the Generalissimo again appealed for help, while Washington was eager to find means to offset the pact's effect on world public opinion.[35]

Dr. Currie rushed Mr. Soong's program to the War Department,[36] where it received searching analysis. The consensus at the Department was that the Chinese were not prepared to take full advantage of the Lend-Lease Act because they did not know what they needed. Requirements for ordnance and aircraft were in specific quantities and understandably identified, but engineering and medical requirements were in "general statements . . . to be followed by detailed information as soon as available."[37] For the Yunnan–Burma Railway they asked 30,000 tons of rails but omitted specifications. In asking for trucks, Soong gave elaborately worked out tables, all on the basis of 4-ton trucks, which were not available in quantity in the United States and which would have torn the unimproved Chinese roads to pieces. The spare parts problem for these vehicles was met by the simple request for some, with no estimate based on operating experience as to what quantity might be needed. To be sure, the program promised "future details" on these matters, but this was March 1941 and Soong had been asking aid ever since the previous June. Every day of delay in giving the specifications meant a day of delay in procurement, while the general air of vagueness and unreality about these requirements made an unfavorable impression on the War Department.

On 22 April the War Department gave Currie a preliminary report on Soong's program and a list of matériel which if available could be supplied to China without interfering to any appreciable extent with U.S. Army and British programs.[38] (*Table 1*) Scarcity of trucks and road-building machinery forced

---

[33] Memo, Hopkins for Burns, 4 Apr 41. Folder, China Personnel, ASF (DAD) ID, A46–299.

[34] Ltr, Young to Hopkins, 21 Apr 41, sub: Rpt on China Requests for Laughlin Currie, with comments and atchd tables. China Pre-Pearl Harbor Folder, Hopkins Papers.

[35] (1) Memo, Sumner Welles for Hopkins, 21 Apr 41; Cables, Roosevelt to Chiang Kai-shek, 26, 28 Apr, 2 May 41. Record Room, Dept State. (2) Summaries on Russian Aid to Nationalist China in Ltr, Louis Johnson, Actg SW, to Secy State, 15 Jun 38, sub: Rpt on Equipment Coming into China. Item 563, Secy War, A46–215. (3) U.S. Embassy Rpt 14, Clarence E. Gauss to Hull, 6 Jun 41. AG (AMMISCA) 334.8. (4) MA Rpt 13 (China), IG 5610, 16 Sep 41, sub: Mun, Imports and Exports from Russia to China. MID Library.

[36] Ltr, Currie to Stimson, 14 Apr 41. AG 400.3295 (4–14–41) Sec 1A.

[37] (1) Soong Requirements. (2) Rpt 1, signed MacMorland, Def Aid Div, 30 Apr 41, sub: Rpt of Accomplishments, Functionings, etc., of Def Aid Div, OUSW. ASF (DAD) ID, A46–299.

[38] Memo, Stimson for Currie, 22 Apr 41, sub: Aid Program to China—Lend-Lease Act. AG 400.3295 (4–14–41) Sec 1A.

Currie to cut the list, and the President earmarked $45,100,000 to initiate China's lend-lease program.[39] (*See Table 1.*) Since funds were available, Soong's

TABLE 1—INITIAL PROGRAMING OF LEND-LEASE FUNDS FOR CHINA: APRIL 1941

Type	Soong Program		Initial Approval	
	Quantity	Estimated Cost	Quantity	Estimated Cost
Total..................	....	$76,100,000	....	$45,100,000
War Department Procurement	....	56,600,000	....	28,600,000
Trucks, Commercial........	7,300	21,000,000	2,000	6,000,000
Trucks, Military	6,500	19,000,000	2,000	6,000,000
Railroad Equipment.........	....	15,000,000	....	15,000,000
Communications Equipment.	....	1,000,000	....	1,000,000
Tractors...................	150	300,000	150	300,000
Passenger Cars............	300	300,000	300	300,000
Treasury Department Procurement...................	....	19,500,000	....	16,500,000
Arsenal Materials..........	....	10,000,000	....	10,000,000
Cotton Blankets............	3,000,000	4,500,000	3,000,000	4,500,000
Road Machinery...........	....	3,000,000	....	....
Gasoline (gallons).........	5,000,000	1,000,000	5,000,000	1,000,000
Grey Sheeting (yards).......	10,000,000	700,000	10,000,000	700,000
Lubricating Oil (tons)......	2,500	250,000	2,500	250,000
Diesel Oil (tons)..........	5,000	50,000	5,000	50,000

Source: Memo, Stimson for Currie, 22 Apr 41, sub: Aid Program to China—Lend-Lease Act. AG 400.3295 (4-14-41) Sec 1A.

initial requisition on 1 May (as against a requirement) for 300 2½-ton trucks was speedily approved by Mr. Roosevelt on 6 May.[40] Within a fortnight this first lend-lease equipment left New York bound for Rangoon, Burma. Meanwhile, the War Department completed its estimate of availability, dollar costs, and shipping data for the whole Soong program. This study laid the basis of all Chinese lend-lease programing before Pearl Harbor. Singling out ordnance items, Currie secured War Department and presidential approval for funds to start the ground force project. (*Table 2*) Currie learned that the War Department's approval of funds for the production of any item on a Chinese program did not make its delivery to China a sacred commitment. The War Department

[39] Memo, Currie for Roosevelt, 23 Apr 41, sub: Prelim Aid Program for China—Lend-Lease Act. AG 400.3295 (4-14-41) Sec 1A. Mr. Roosevelt placed his familiar "O.K.–F. D. R." on this memorandum.

[40] (1) Folder, China Requisition, AG (AMMISCA) 400.312. (2) Ltr, Currie to Hopkins, 25 Apr 41. China Pre-Pearl Harbor Folder, Hopkins Papers. (3) AG 400.3295 (4-14-41) Sec 1A contains Mr. Roosevelt's original signature to the statement that China was vital to the defense of the United States and was eligible for lend-lease aid. (4) AG (AMMISCA) 523.02 and 611 contain sailing data and cargo content for the first twelve lend-lease shipments to Rangoon.

emphasized that emergencies might force shifting priorities when the weapons were ready for distribution.[41]

By late spring 1941 an additional $100,000,000 of lend-lease funds was divided between Soong's communications and air force projects.[42] (See Tables 1 and 2 for first grants.) Since he had been given little hope that ordnance and communications items would be available for China in any quantity before mid-1942, Currie concentrated his efforts on a more promising air program.

TABLE 2—ESSENTIAL ORDNANCE REQUIREMENTS REQUESTED AS LEND-LEASE FOR CHINA: MAY 1941

Item	Requirements		Availability
	Quantity	Estimated Cost	
Total........................	....	$49,341,000	
Pack Howitzer, 75-mm............	600	9,200,000	Mid-1942.
Ammunition, 75-mm. (rounds)....	1,200,000	19,128,000	Mid-1942.
Gun, 75-mm. motorized..........	144	3,007,000	On receipt of 105-mm. replacements.
Shell, 75-mm. (rounds)..........	144,000	1,866,000	On receipt of 105-mm. replacements.
Tank, Light, with machine guns...	360	15,000,000	Immediate order.
Truck, ¼-ton (jeep).............	1,000	1,140,000	Immediate order.

Source: Ltr, Stimson to Currie, 16 May 41. WD 400.3295 (5-14-41) MC, China Lend-Lease, ASF (DAD) ID, A46-299.

Putting Air Power in China: The AVG and Currie's Lend-Lease Program

Two air programs were clearly emerging from the original Chinese 500-plane proposal by the early spring of 1941. The availability of 100 Curtiss P-40B's in January and February 1941 afforded an opportunity that Chennault and Soong had exploited, with powerful and essential aid from the services. Soong's aim was to rush the organization of a fighter group for earliest possible service in China. Currie, on the other hand, was eager to secure lend-lease funds to fill a larger long-range air program, which, if successful, would have created a potent Chinese Air Force. While both programs developed concurrently, the P-40 project outdistanced its lend-lease counterpart in the period before Pearl Harbor.

On 15 February 1941, General Marshall told the Acting Secretary of State, Mr. Sumner Welles, that a man had been found who was willing to take a

[41] Ltr, Robert Patterson, Actg SW, to Currie, 3 May 41. AG 400.3295 (4-14-41) Sec 1A. The War Department's review of Soong's entire program is dated 30 April 1941 and is appended to Patterson's letter. The War Department estimated that Soong's requirements, at a cost of $1,067,000,000, would take eighteen months to fill.

[42] Memo, Patterson for Marshall, 19 Jul 41, sub: Relative Co-ordination of Chinese Def Aid. AG 400.3295 (4-14-41) Sec 1A, Tab H.

chance on recruiting pilots for the P–40B's in spite of existing neutrality legis-lation.[43] This was the same Mr. Pawley who had been conferring with Secretary Knox since December 1940 on a volunteer scheme. Two months later Pawley signed a nonprofit contract with Soong to equip, supply, and operate the American Volunteer Group (AVG), as it was to be known. Under the contract, Colonel Chennault bore the unmartial title of supervisor. To insure co-ordination between the different branches of the organization setting up the AVG, the contract required Chennault to maintain close liaison with Pawley's organization in the Far East and in New York.[44]

Although the AVG was not supported by lend-lease funds, the War and Navy Departments, giving effect to the President's policy, were soon involved. Both services extended facilities to Pawley's recruiting agents and released pilots and crews for service in China's Air Force.[45] Pawley's agents toured Air Corps and Navy training fields everywhere save in Hawaii and the Philippines, offering big salaries and hinting of bonuses for victories confirmed. Administrative and technical staffs were complete on 9 August, but pilot recruiting was not complete for another month. There were 101 pilot volunteers, 63 from the Navy and 38 from the Army, each with a one-year contract dating from the time the volunteer reached the Far East.[46] Overseas movement began on 9 June with the first pilots sailing later on a Dutch vessel escorted through the Japanese mandate islands by American warships. Though contrary to the neutrality laws, the escort was considered by Admiral Harold R. Stark, Chief of Naval Operations, to be essential to U.S. support of China.[47]

Having signed a contract with Soong on 15 April 1941 to secure volunteers for the 100 P–40's (which had already been put on board ship for Rangoon), Mr. Pawley sent his brother Edward to Chungking to check the preparations the Chinese had promised to make to receive the American Volunteer Group in China. Edward Pawley reported that the Chinese had not begun their preparations to receive the volunteers. Consequently, Pawley told his brother to ask the British military authorities in Burma for training facilities. At Lashio, Mr. Edward Pawley was so fortunate as to encounter Air Chief Marshal

[43] Min, Standing Ln Com, 15 Feb 41. A48–139.

[44] (1) Interv with Pawley, 24 May 51. (2) Ltr, with atchd Central Aircraft Mfg Co. contract, Soong to Pawley and Leighton, 15 Apr 41. Contract Folder, Pawley Papers.

[45] Numerous folders in the Pawley Papers show the official relationship between the services and Mr. Pawley's organization. Through unofficial correspondence with many friends in the serv-ices, former Army and Navy officers on the staff of Pawley's company adopted current Air Corps Tables of Organization and Equipment for the organization of the AVG. The extent of this contri-bution is revealed in the Leighton and Aldworth Folders, Pawley Papers.

[46] (1) Letters of introduction to Pawley's agents at Navy and Army installations are in the W. D. Pawley Folder, Pawley Papers. (2) Rad, Chennault to Soong, 8 Feb 42. CDS Folder 2–10, Pawley Papers. This message verifies that on 2 April 1941 Chennault received approval from Soong to pay a 500-dollar bonus to AVG pilots. (3) Ltr, Capt Richard Aldworth (USA-Ret.) to Capt F. E. Beatty (USN), Aide to Secy Knox, 24 May 41. Navy Dept Folder, Pawley Papers. (4) Progress reports on personnel for the AVG are in the Pawley Papers. (5) Contract cited n. 44(2).

[47] Interv with Admiral Stark, 26 Apr 49, Washington, D.C.

Sir Robert Brooke-Popham, the British commander-in-chief in the Far East, who numbered the defense of Burma among his many responsibilities. Sir Robert was most helpful, and obtained permission of the British War Office to offer facilities at Toungoo and Magwe to the American Volunteer Group.[48]

When the first contingent of volunteers arrived on 28 July, they were promptly sent to a recently completed Royal Air Force (RAF) airdrome in the midst of a pestilent jungle six miles from Toungoo. This airfield was turned over to the AVG by London for full combat training with the proviso that the Burmese airfields would not be used as a base to attack the Japanese, for Britain was anxious to avoid war with Japan. Administrative difficulties with the British and Burmese civil authorities resulted from the arrangement. Having been forbidden to use American armed guards or to employ the Burmese as guards, the AVG felt its security jeopardized and was finally able to obtain Gurkha guards. The AVG could make no additions or changes in airfield construction without the official permission of the RAF. The position of the American volunteers training in Burma was anomalous, for the AVG was part of the Chinese Air Force, and, until war between the United States and Japan broke out, they had no official connection with the United States Army Air Forces.

At Toungoo the volunteers for three squadrons of P–40's were trained in Chennault's system of tactics, which was based on years of study and observation of the Japanese Air Force. Chennault's men used a two-ship element, always flying and fighting in pairs, diving in, making a quick pass, and then breaking away, thus exploiting the superior diving speed of the P–40 and refusing the turning combat for which the frail, maneuverable, Japanese aircraft were designed. Gunnery was stressed, that the brief contact might be lethal. As a unit, the AVG was trained to break up the Japanese formations, confront their pilots with unexpected situations, and exploit the resulting confusion.[49]

The training in these tactics took a heavy toll of the planes, which were badly in need of proper and complete equipment. In the haste to obtain fighters, the P–40's had been accepted without necessary equipment and spare parts, on the understanding that the British would release guns and ammunition from their lend-lease stocks. This division of responsibility produced much debate in the days ahead, with the principal Chinese purchasing and supply agency, China Defense Supplies, Inc., arguing that if the British could not equip the aircraft the War Department had to.[50] The latter was not eager

[48](1) Pawley Interv cited n. 44(1). (2) Air Marshal Sir Robert Brooke-Popham, "Operations in the Far East, from 17th October 1940 to 27th December 1941," *Supplement to The London Gazette,* January 22, 1948, par. 26.

[49](1) Chennault, *Way of a Fighter,* pp. 107, 117–19. (2) Robert B. Hotz, *With General Chennault* (New York, 1943), pp. 112, 115–17, 125.

[50] Ltr, David M. Corcoran, Pres, CDS, to Burns, 10 May 41. Folder, China Lend-Lease Corresp, Apr–Oct 41, ASF (DAD) ID, A46–299.

to be charged with support of a fighter group so far from U.S. bases, and was further embarrassed by the current grave shortage of .30- and .50-caliber ammunition. Though the War Department approved the concept of keeping the Japanese contained in China, when faced with the concrete problem of creating and supporting the AVG some of its senior members had misgivings. Fully admitting that the details of logistical support made "the whole thing so confusing" and convinced that the sober facts of inadequate ordnance and signal equipment had not been brought to Mr. Roosevelt's attention, Secretary of War Stimson refused to entertain any claim that the Department was not responsible for the AVG. "Unfortunately, it is," was his comment. Ultimately, Currie had to take the matter to the President with the pertinent remark that if the fighters were sent to China without ammunition, there would be an international scandal and the rest of the lend-lease program might as well be forgotten. The President ordered the release of ammunition, and 1,500,000 rounds came from Army stocks. Spare parts were just as hard to find, for the factory no longer made many of them for the outmoded P–40B. The larger question of the War Department's relation to the AVG was not settled before war commenced.[51]

Though involved in the effort to rush creation of a fighter group Dr. Currie was also at work on his larger program. After considering U.S. aircraft production figures and bearing in mind that China received but $53,000,000 for aircraft out of the first lend-lease allocations, Currie outlined his program on 28 May 1941.[52] To supplement the AVG's 100 fighters, he arranged with the British to release 144 Vultee P–48's. At the Republic aviation plant he found 125 P–43's. In addition he located 66 Lockheed and Douglas bombers under British contract for which the RAF lacked pilots. These he proposed to obtain by transfer from the British. Placing his program before Secretary Knox, Currie argued: "If this program were adopted China would possess, in early 1942, a respectable air force, judged by Far Eastern standards, which should be sufficient to (a) protect strategic points, (b) permit local army offensive action, (c) permit the bombing of Japanese air bases and supply dumps in China and Indo-China, and the bombing of coastal and river transport, and (d)

[51] (1) Quotations from Min, Conf in OSW, 0915, 10 Jun 41. OSW Conf, A45–466. (2) Ltr, Marhall to Currie, 16 Jun 41. AG 400.3295 (4-14-41) Sec 1A. (3) Memo, Currie for Hopkins, 3 Jul 41; Memo, Hopkins for Burns, 12 Jul 41. China Pre-Pearl Harbor Folder, Hopkins Papers. (4) Memo, Maj Gen Leonard T. Gerow, Actg CofS, WPD, for Maj Gen R. C. Moore, DCofS, 1 Aug 41, with accompanying Ltrs from JSM in Washington; Ltr, Young to Stimson, 8 Aug 41. AG 400.3295 (4-14-41) Sec 1A.
[52] (1) Memo, Robert A. Lovett, ASW for Air, for Stimson, 14 Jun 41, sub: Status of Chinese Requests for Air. Stimson Papers in temporary custody of Dr. Rudolph A. Winnacker, Office, Secy Def. (2) Memo, Maj Patrick W. Timberlake, recorder, Jt Aircraft Com, for Burns, 19 Apr 41, and Burns' reply to Timberlake, 23 Apr 41. Folder, China Lend-Lease Corresp, Apr–Oct 41, ASF (DAD) ID, A46–299. (3) WPD 4389, Cases 1–28, Sec 1, A47–30. (See Bibliographical Note.) (4) Because Currie's program involved diversion of lend-lease aircraft, the Joint Aircraft Committee had to seek policy guidance from the Joint Board. Joint Board Paper 355 (Ser 691) contains Currie's Short-Term Aircraft Program for China.

permit occasional incendiary bombing of Japan." [53] Currie set 31 October 1941 as the date for the completion of the program, and claimed that such a force would be "a powerful means to check a Japanese attack on Singapore and the South Seas." [54] Studying these proposals, the highest joint service echelon, the Joint Board, raised no objections to their strategic concepts.[55]

The Indochina Crisis and Aid to China

During the winter of 1940–1941 the greatest military events took place on the shores of the Mediterranean. The German armies placed ever more men opposite the Russian frontier, but in the Mediterranean only their air arm was active. There the Germans had to support Fascist Italy, which in fall 1940 proved incapable of overrunning Greece and in December 1940 lost its military reputation at the hands of Gen. Sir Archibald P. Wavell, the British commander in the Middle East. This German air support was not enough, while the German southern flank opposite Russia needed strengthening. Germans in various guises moved into the Balkans in ever greater numbers. The Yugoslav people in March 1941 revolted against an attempt to bring them into the German camp as a satellite. It was the first spontaneous popular defiance of Germany's "new order" in Europe.

The Germans could not let the challenge pass. By a great feat of rapid planning and logistical improvisation they so quickly altered their dispositions in the Balkans that on 6 April 1941 they could attack Yugoslavia and Greece. The events of spring 1940 were repeated as the perfectly equipped, splendidly trained German veterans overran the Yugoslavs who tried to defend their borders, while the inability of the Greeks to withdraw their best troops from Albania made futile Wavell's attempts to support the Greeks with a small air contingent and a task force of some 60,000 men, of whom about 33,000 came from Australia and New Zealand. The evacuation under the blows of the Germans, whose air superiority could not be disputed in the campaign's later phases, was a painful experience.

After Greece surrendered on 24 April 1941, the Germans organized an airborne attack on the island of Crete. The Germans began their operation on 20 May and after a week's hard fighting had another victory, for Crete was

---

[53] Ltr, Currie to Knox, 28 May 41. Incl, JB Paper 355 (Ser 691). In addition to the proposal on combat aircraft, Currie incorporated a plan to place ten DC–3 transport planes in service with the China National Aviation Corporation for hauls between Lashio and Kunming. In July the Joint Board found that no transports were available, but in the fall lend-lease funds to buy ten DC–3's, with a promise that all would be in service by March 1942, were given to the Chinese. Currie's program also covered the training of 500 Chinese airmen on lend-lease funds. Training of the Chinese began on 1 October 1941 with a group of fifty pilots followed each week by a class of fifty new candidates.

[54] Incl to JB Paper 355 (Ser 691).

[55] Stark and Marshall approved JB Paper 355 (Ser 691) on 12 July 1941, followed by Knox on the 15th and by Acting Secretary of War Patterson on the 18th.

theirs. But the triumph, though technically of great interest, was as costly to the Germans as to the Allies for the German airborne units which took part were thoroughly shaken up and the Germans never tried to duplicate Crete. Much of the burden of Crete's defense was borne by Dominion troops; their losses in Crete and Greece had effect on the policies of their governments.

Then the German divisions moved back north and east, leaving garrisons in the Balkans. In May and June they rejoined the principal German forces, which for months past had been quietly gathering along the Russian frontier. The Russians were alarmed; the Germans, enigmatic. The Russians attempted various forms of appeasement, but the Germans were bent on their project and crossed the Soviet frontier on 22 June 1941. Like Napoleon, Hitler had turned his back on the Channel and was marching to Moscow. It appeared certain that the German armies would be occupied for some weeks to come. A few even hoped the Russians might last out the winter.

About 4 July 1941 British and American intelligence agencies became aware that the Japanese were on the verge of a major move. The United States had broken the Japanese diplomatic code, and so the President and Cabinet in early July had the full revelation of how Japan would react to the situation created by the German attack on Russia on 22 June 1941. They learned that Japan would not attack Russia, but would try to end the undeclared war in China and prepare for a southward advance, toward the oil and rubber of British Malaya and the Netherlands Indies. As a first step, Japan would occupy southern French Indochina and Thailand, even at the risk of war with Great Britain and the United States.[56] This was alarming news, for the British might not survive the loss of their Far Eastern possessions. Furthermore, the motorized American economy, now pledged to support Britain's cause, depended on Malayan rubber.

The Japanese steps were soberly and earnestly debated by the President, his Cabinet, and at the highest service levels during July's summer heat. An oil embargo, striking at the weakest spot in the Japanese economy, was proposed, but Admiral Stark and General Marshall opposed it, warning that it might mean war, for such an embargo would offer Japan the somber choice of surrender or striking for the oil of the Indies.[57] Diplomatic warnings over the next few days failed to stop the Japanese, and the United States was confronted

---

[56](1) Rad 255, Canton to Tokyo, PURPLE Code, 14 Jul 41, *Hearings of the Congressional Joint Committee Investigating the Attack on Pearl Harbor* (Washington, 1946), Pt. 12, Exhibit 1, p. 2. (2) Memo, Notes on Cabinet Mtg, 18 Jul 41, Stimson Papers. (3) Ltr, Stark to Admiral Thomas C. Hart, 24 Jul 41, *Hearings of the Congressional Joint Committee . . .*, Pt. 16, Exhibit 106, p. 2173. (4) Memoirs of Prince Konoye, *Hearings of the Congressional Joint Committee . . .*, Pt. 20, Exhibit 173.

[57](1) Memo, Capt Kittredge to authors, 4 Apr 50. HIS 330.14 CBI 1950. (2) Japanese attempts to create a synthetic oil industry were an admitted failure by mid-1941. U.S. Strategic Bombing Survey [USSBS], Over-all Economic Effects Div, *Effects of Strategic Bombing on Japan's War Economy* (Washington, 1946), p. 9. (3) Jerome B. Cohen, *Japan's Economy in War and Reconstruction* (Minneapolis, Minn., 1949), p. 137.

with Japanese occupation of southern French Indochina on 21 July 1941.[58] Following as it did on the seizure of northern Indochina in September 1940 and Hainan in February 1939, the Japanese advance southward was an ominous step.

The American reaction was strong and culminated in a decisive step that set a time limit within which the Pacific problem would inevitably be brought to the crisis stage and which would greatly affect any long-range program of aid to China. On 23 July the President approved a Joint Board paper which recommended that the United States equip, man, and maintain the 500-plane Chinese Air Force proposed by Currie. The paper suggested that this force embark on a vigorous program to be climaxed by the bombing of Japan in November 1941. Joint Board Paper 355 also defined the strategy behind aid to China: "The continuation of active military operations by the Chinese is highly desirable as a deterrent to the extension of Japanese military and naval operations to the South."[59]

The general concept of giving China lend-lease aid, as distinguished from any specific program that might be submitted, was approved because at this time in Washington there was a myth and a hope about China. An ardent, articulate, and adroit Sinophile faction claimed that the Chinese were courageously and competently resisting the Japanese and needed only arms to drive them into the sea. The services were too well informed to share that belief, but they hoped that if the Chinese were rearmed, reorganized, and trained they might cause the Japanese such concern as to bar any adventures in the South Seas. So the myth and the hope converged, and lend-lease aid to China found increased support in high places.[60]

A presidential proclamation calling the armed forces of the Philippine Commonwealth into the service of the United States was issued, and Lt. Gen. Douglas MacArthur became head of a new army command in the Far East. Plans were set in motion to reinforce the Philippines. General Marshall and Admiral Stark believed it was understood that economic sanctions would not go beyond the licensing of Japanese trade, to control all exports to Japan. On 26 July an order was issued from the summer White House at Hyde Park freezing Japanese assets. Press and public hailed it as an "oil embargo," and when no licenses for the purchase of oil were ever issued to the Japanese under the executive order, it became in effect the decisive step of embargo, setting

[58] U.S. Department of State, *Peace and War: U.S. Foreign Policy, 1931–1941* (Washington, 1942), pp. 696, 699.
[59] The President initialed a covering letter to JB Paper 355 (Ser 691) on 23 July 1941. This letter, dated 18 July, is from Patterson and Knox to the President and was returned to the Joint Board in the form of a memorandum by Lt. Col. William P. Scobey, Secretary of the Joint Board, for General Marshall on 23 July 1941. These covering papers head the Army's copy of JB Paper 355 (Ser 691) in G–3 Registered Documents Section.
[60] (1) Sherwood, *Roosevelt and Hopkins*, p. 405. (2) Memo, Brig Gen Sherman Miles, Actg ACofS, G–2, WDGS, for CofS, 26 Mar 41, sub: Chinese Power of Resistance. MID 381.2, China (3–26–41). (3) Memo, Patterson for Marshall, 19 Jul 41, sub: Relative Co-ordination of Chinese Def Aid. AG 400.3295 (4–14–41) Sec 1A, Tabs A–H.

about a twelve-month limit within which the Japanese would have to reach an understanding with the United States or attack the Netherlands Indies.[61]

The Joint Board recommendations approved by the President on 23 July were that (a) 269 fighters and 66 bombers be furnished for "effective action against Japanese military and naval forces operating in China and in neighboring countries and waters"; (b) the United States provide means to train Chinese to fly and maintain these aircraft; (c) the United States send a military mission to China to advise the Chinese on the proper use of the large amount of arms being furnished by the United States. Aircraft allocations were left subject to U.S. and British requirements; most of them would have to be transferred from British allocations. Thus, the Joint Board accepted Currie's aircraft program.[62]

Immediately after the President's approval of these recommendations, Soong and Pawley initiated plans for a second American Volunteer Group, based on American concepts of a light bombardment unit, with American pilots for the thirty-three Lockheed Hudson bombers and Chinese pilots for the thirty-three Douglas.[63] Hiring began on 1 November, but Pawley had difficulty in finding trained bombardiers. On 21 November forty-nine ground personnel for the second AVG left for China. The outbreak of the war stranded them in Australia.[64]

In November and December 1941 there was a distinct possibility that the AVG might become an Anglo-American organization. Following a warning from the British Ambassador to China on 31 October 1941 that the situation

---

[61](1) In the margin of a draft manuscript of this chapter, Admiral Stark wrote: ". . . statement about oil is correct—but I understood at the time—it was not an oil embargo though it ultimately did develop into it." HIS 330.14 CBI 1950. (2) In commenting on a draft manuscript for this portion of the text, Admiral Stark and Captain Kittredge, Joint Chiefs of Staff Historical Section, outlined the following Joint Board recommendations of 25 July 1941 which the Chief of Staff and the Chief of Naval Operations thought had been approved by the President:

"1 A Presidential proclamation calling the Philippine forces in U.S. service, with the appointment of Gen. MacArthur as Commanding General of a new army command, 'U.S. Army Forces in the Far East' (USAFFE) with proposals for immediate strengthening of U.S. forces in the Philippines.

"2 Approval of the program for aid to China, including the CAF [Chinese Air Force] project, the AVG program, the supply of further ordnance material for the 30 division program, and the sending of a U.S. military mission.

"3 Approval of proposals for release of munitions for Russia, including items from the Army and Navy and future production previously allocated to the U.S. and British forces.

"4 Maintenance of the closing of the Panama Canal to Japanese ships, with provision for co-operation with British and Allied forces in the Southwest Pacific for reduction of shipments to Japan.

"5 No general embargo on Japan, but introduction of a licensing system for exports, assuring U.S. control of all shipments to Japan."

(3) For data on Japan's oil situation, see sources cited in note 57(2) and (3).

[62] JB Paper cited n. 6(2).

[63] Initial plans for a Chinese-American composite unit were laid in the Soong-Pawley-Aldworth-Chennault correspondence of fall 1941. Captain Aldworth drafted Tables of Organization and Equipment to meet the needs of the 66 bomber and 269 fighter allocations. Chennault approved these tables for the second AVG on 29 September 1941. Ltr, Aldworth to Soong, 17 Aug 41; Ltr, signed "Ken", to Aldworth, 24 Aug 41; Ltr, Soong to Chennault, 15 Aug 41; Rad, Chennault to Soong, 29 Sep 41. Soong-Pawley Folder, Pawley Papers.

[64] 2d AVG Folder, Pawley Papers.

in China was very grave, Air Chief Marshal Brooke-Popham's headquarters began preparations to place a volunteer fighter squadron and, if possible, some bombers in China to operate with the American Volunteer Group. William D. Pawley strongly urged the British project and co-operated in the logistical preparations.[65]

The aircraft procurement recommended by the board went more slowly. When the complicated details of transferring aircraft from British to Chinese allocations had been completed and Currie had been rescued from the embarrassment caused by his having promised aircraft to China before the British consented to release them, it appeared that deliveries could not start until November 1941 and would not be complete until April 1942.[66] So went another hope of containing the Japanese in 1941.

The Thirty Division Program

Mr. T. V. Soong's requirements of 31 March for artillery and arsenal materials clearly implied a plan to rearm thirty divisions. He gave priority to thirty battalions of 75-mm. pack howitzers, with 2,000 rounds per piece, and thirty battalions of 37-mm. antitank guns, with 1,500 rounds each. The War Department understood this artillery was organic to the Chinese division, but Mr. Soong did not elaborate the point. Lower priority went to thirty battalions of 105-mm. and eight battalions of 155-mm. howitzers, with ammunition. For the Chinese infantry, Soong asked 15,000 7.92-mm. machine guns with 500,000,000 rounds of ammunition. China had perhaps 200 obsolete tanks, and Soong wanted 360 light tanks and 400 scout cars to replace them.[67]

As the War Department studied Soong's proposals, it found there was little that it could spare from existing stocks or current production. However, if the President was to allocate $184,000,000 from lend-lease funds, future production might meet China's ordnance needs by mid-1942. In mid-May 1941 the Secretary of War agreed with Dr. Currie that the Chinese might begin their rearmament with $50,000,000 of lend-lease funds and that $23,000,000 worth could be from U.S. Army stockpiles or current production. From the latter sources the War Department hoped to find before mid-1942: 144 75-mm. guns, 235 75-mm. howitzers, 265 scout cars less armament, 360 light tanks

---

[65] (1) Brooke-Popham Despatch, *Supplement to The London Gazette*, par. 26. (2) Pawley Interv cited n. 44(1).

[66] (1) Ltr, Currie to Soong, 23 Jul 41. Item 13, AG (AMMISCA) 336.2. (2) Min, JB Mtg, 4 Sep 41. G–3 Registered Documents Section. (3) Ltr, Currie to Hopkins, 20 Aug 41. China Pre-Pearl Harbor Folder, Hopkins Papers. (4) Ltr, Soong to Col William J. Donovan, 16 Aug 41. Folder, China–Howitzers, ASF (DAD) ID, A46–299. (5) Memo, Currie for Roosevelt, 26 Aug 41; Cable 4166, Ambassador John Winant to Hopkins, 9 Sep 41. China Pre-Pearl Harbor Folder, Hopkins Papers. (6) Memo, Maj Gen Henry H. Arnold for Marshall, 9 Sep 41. ASF (DAD) ID, A46–299. (7) Schedules for the release of the P–43's and P–66's in Rad, Col H. W. T. Eglin, Chief, AMMISCA Washington Detail, to Magruder, 15 Oct 41. Item 25, AG (AMMISCA) 336.2.

[67] Soong Requirements.

with machine guns, and 1,000 ¼-ton trucks (jeeps). Ammunition would be included. Additional lend-lease funds were set aside for an arsenal program and signal, engineering, and medical items.[68]

In May 1941 the Chinese purchasing and supply authority in the United States, China Defense Supplies, began to present its detailed requisitions against the approved thirty division program.[69] Although China Defense Supplies' officials could call on War Department personnel to assist them in preparing these requisitions, complaints soon arose that these Chinese agents not only had no idea of what was actually needed for war in China but were ignorant of the inherent limitations and qualities of the weapons desired. One example was the story of the Chinese requisition for 50,000 .30-caliber rifles, M1917–A (Enfield), with bayonets, scabbards, and accessories. The War Department had some on hand in mid-1941, though 1,000,000 had already gone to Britain. The weapon compared very well with the standard Japanese piece, and the Chinese and their sympathizers represented their need for arms as desperate. The War Department considered making these rifles available to the Chinese even before their request was received, though there was no .30-caliber ammunition immediately available. On 17 June Soong bid for 50,000 Enfield rifles, but when a sample was delivered to his ordnance expert the latter said "it would jeopardize his reputation" to send the Enfields to China and demanded 50,000 Garand semiautomatics. Supply of the Garand was quite inadequate for the U.S. Army at this time, and none were available. There was the further problem of finding enough ammunition for this weapon, with its high rate of fire. Later the War Department learned in confidence that the Chinese were negotiating with a small New York manufacturer to convert the Enfields into semiautomatics, a difficult and most unsatisfactory operation. Still later, China Defense Supplies urged that the 50,000 rifles be sent to China, there to be converted to 7.92-mm., a task which would have absorbed the energies of the Chinese arsenals for months on end. In February 1942, after some had been shipped to Great Britain and others issued to the state militias, the War Department still had 20,000.[70] These Enfields went to India and ultimately were used by the Chinese to retake north Burma.

In their requisitions for tanks, the Chinese again revealed ignorance of what was possible for operations in China. Soong asked for the standard U.S. light tank, a 13-ton model. Since it was pointed out repeatedly that this tank could not cross the majority of bridges in China and Burma, Chinese insistence on the 13-ton type until as late as November 1941 typified something that appeared over and over again—Chinese demands for the biggest and newest equipment regardless of availability or practicality. The story of the Marmon-

---

[68] Memo, Patterson for Marshall, 19 Jul 41, sub: Relative Co-ordination of Chinese Def Aid. AG 400.3295 (4–14–41) Sec 1A, Tabs A–H.
[69] *Ibid.*
[70] (1) AG (AMMISCA) 474. (2) Folder, China Rifles, ASF (DAD) ID, A46–299.

Herrington 7-ton tanks was very like that of the Enfields. The tank was in production, it was available in quantity, and it could be used on the primitive Chinese road net. The Chinese objected to its armament of one .50- and two .30-caliber machine guns and demanded it carry three .30-caliber machine guns, a flame thrower, and a 37-mm. antitank gun, an impossible problem in design and production on a 7-ton chassis. When the Chinese had been persuaded to accept the standard armament, it then developed there was a shortage of .50-caliber machine guns, so Marmon-Herrington was told to use three .30-caliber pieces. When the tanks began coming off the assembly line in December 1941, it was found the turrets would not permit replacing the .30's with .50's when the latter became available. The Chinese at once charged bad faith and refused to take delivery. Excited tempers were cooled when arrangements were made at London to supply the Chinese with 1,200 Bren gun carriers from British and Canadian production in place of the tanks, which the United States accepted and used for guarding airfields.[71] Such action by China Defense Supplies resulted in increased and irresistible pressure within the War and Treasury Departments to secure a greater measure of control over the whole process of rearming the Chinese Army.[72]

Creation of the American Military Mission to China (AMMISCA)

China's military problems were not new to the War Department. Military attachés and the recent air mission to China (17 May–6 June 1941) of Brig. Gen. Henry B. Clagett, commanding the Philippine Department Air Force, reported on those problems.[73] Other officers, including General Marshall, had served in China with the tiny garrisons that the United States maintained there as a symbol of its support of Chinese nationalism against the several European and Asiatic imperialisms. Twenty-eight officers had been in China (1923–37) as language students. There was, therefore, a group of men in the War Department well able to interpret press dispatches from China and to appraise Chinese requests for aid.

The difficulties that arose in processing Chinese requests for lend-lease arms suggested to several officers that the War Department take some positive

---

[71] (1) Folder, China Tanks, ASF (DAD) ID, A46–299. (2) Folder, Marmon-Herrington Co., Inc., AG 095, ASF (DAD) ID, A46–299. (3) AG (AMMISCA) 400.312. (4) AG (AMMISCA) 470.8. (5) Ltr, Col Haydon L. Boatner to Chief, HD SSUSA, 14 Nov 47. HIS 330.14 CBI 1947. (6) Memo for Record by Boatner, 7 Oct 41. Folder, China Lend-Lease Corresp, Apr–Oct 41. ASF (DAD) ID, A46–299.

[72] Memo, Burns for Hopkins, 14 May 41, with Incl, Ltr, J. P. Sanger, Asst Dir of Purchases, to C. E. Mack, Dir of Procurement, Treasury Dept, 8 May 41. China Pre-Pearl Harbor Folder, Hopkins Papers.

[73] During Currie's mission to Chungking, the Generalissimo had requested that a high-ranking air officer come to China. Mr. Roosevelt approved the request. Seeing that Soong's program of air power in China was obviously going to claim a large share of American resources, Marshall sent Clagett to China. Clagett's report of the Chinese Air Force and its installations in Rpt, Clagett to Marshall, 12 Jun 41, sub: Air Mission to China. AG (AMMISCA) 336.2.

action to improve the handling of lend-lease by China. The current military attaché in Chungking, Lt. Col. William Mayer, recommended on 15 June 1941 that his successor be a general officer charged with advising and assisting the Generalissimo. He observed that both Joseph W. Stilwell and John Magruder had attained general officer's rank, had been attachés in China, and so either would be qualified.[74] On 16 June G–4, War Department General Staff, suggested a lend-lease mission of Army personnel.[75]

Memoranda began to pass back and forth, from which these arguments for the dispatch of a mission emerged: (1) preliminary plans and moves for aid to China had not been meshed with the over-all lend-lease program, with strategic estimates, or with national policy; (2) Soong's strategic goals would be more easily reached if American personnel, acting with China's leaders, could advise and assist the Chinese; (3) since China Defense Supplies had no competent military advice, it had asked for far more equipment (and brought pressure to bear to get it) than the Chinese could use or even transport to China; (4) China's history provided many instances of the waste of foreign loans and gifts; (5) the work of the German Military Mission, which had greatly assisted the Generalissimo's rise to power, could be excelled by American officers profiting by the Germans' experiences; (6) the American Volunteer Group and its logistical problems were not receiving proper attention; (7) if war came, a basis for Sino-American military co-operation would have been laid.[76]

Further support for the mission came from the foreign scene. Knowledge that if war came the British Military Attaché to China, Maj. Gen. L. E. Dennys, would emerge as chief of a military mission sponsoring guerrilla and RAF activities suggested an American mission.[77] The fear that the Soviet Union might be defeated also expedited the formation of an American mission to China as a reassuring diplomatic gesture, for the Chinese feared Russian collapse would release Japanese troops in Manchuria for adventures elsewhere.[78] On 3 July 1941 General Marshall approved the American Military Mission to China (its short title, AMMISCA, will be used hereafter).[79] Eight days later the Acting Chief of Staff, G–2, Brig. Gen. Sherman Miles, wrote a personal

---

[74] Rad, Mayer to AGWAR, 15 Jun 41. AMMISCA Rad File, Job–11.

[75] Memo, Brig Gen Eugene Reybold, Actg ACofS, G–4, WDGS, for CofS, 16 Jun 41. Folder, Mission to China, ASF (DAD) ID, A46–299. Maj. Haydon L. Boatner prepared this paper for Reybold's signature.

[76] (1) Memorandum cited note 68 contains various staff studies for initiating AMMISCA for the Office, Under Secretary of War, to consider. (2) Memo with Incls, MacMorland, Def Aid Div, OUSW, for WPD, 20 Jun 41, sub: Organization of Mil Mission to China. WPD 4389–7, Sec 1. (3) The Assistant Secretary of War, John J. McCloy, supported AMMISCA since he had been disturbed over the lack of planning for the AVG. Memo, McCloy for Miles, 21 Jul 41. G–4, 32192/1, A43–3.

[77] American reports on the scope and mission of the British Military Mission to China in Rad, MA Chungking to AGWAR, 25 Jun 41; Rad, MA Chungking to WPD, 6 Jul 41; Rad, STATE 82, Gauss to Hull, 24 Jul 41. AG (AMMISCA) 334.8 and WPD 4389–11, Sec 1.

[78] Memo, Welles for Hopkins, 7 Jul 41. WPD 4389–7, Sec 1.

[79] WPD 4389–17.

letter to Brig. Gen. John Magruder, commanding Fort Devens, Mass., to inform him he was being considered to head a lend-lease mission to China, which in the event of war would be "the liaison for strategic planning and cooperation with our ally, China."[80] Magruder reported to Washington soon after and began his studies of the China problem.[81]

As was noted previously, the Joint Board paper approved by the President on 23 July called for a military mission to China, which thus put the final seal on the project, and the bureaucratic struggle to write the directive, fix the jurisdiction, and prescribe the composition of AMMISCA began. There were long discussions with the State Department, which wanted the mission to be controlled by the new American Ambassador to China, Mr. Clarence E. Gauss.[82] The War Department carried its point with the contention that AMMISCA was "operational" in the highest sense, so that Magruder was merely attached to the Embassy to assure what was called "the coordinating jurisdiction of the Ambassador."[83]

AMMISCA Receives Its Orders

The Chinese were told of AMMISCA's coming on 20 August 1941,[84] four days before the British Prime Minister, Mr. Winston S. Churchill, revealed that conversations were under way between the American and Japanese Governments on the gravest issues of Pacific diplomacy. The question of Magruder's directive became an immediate issue. For a while it was felt that Magruder should be authorized to conduct staff talks with the Chinese on co-operation between the two Allied Powers should war arise in the Pacific between America and Japan.[85] If adopted, this provision would have helped fill one of the gaps in prewar planning, but it was never authorized. When the issue came to a head in November, the War Department told Magruder to express no opinions of his own on the employment of U.S. Forces in China, nor to discuss any Chinese proposals, but simply to transmit the latter to Washington.[86]

The orders given General Magruder faithfully reflected the growing War Department convictions about China. He was told to:

[80] Memo, Miles for Magruder, 11 Jul 41. AMMISCA Folder 1, Gen Ref Br, OCMH. (See Bibliographical Note.)

[81] Magruder's planning papers in AMMISCA Folder 1.

[82] As a Foreign Service officer at Shanghai, Gauss had had long experience in dealing with the Chinese. As it worked out, Gauss had no control over AMMISCA, which, since the latter appeared to control lend-lease aid, created a situation not lost on the observant Chinese. Gauss was Ambassador to China until November 1944.

[83] The exchange of planning papers is in AMMISCA Folder 1.

[84] (1) Ltr, Roosevelt to Soong, 20 Aug 41. Folder, Mission to China, ASF (DAD) ID, A46–299. (2) Sherwood, *Roosevelt and Hopkins*, p. 404.

[85] WPD 4389–17.

[86] Rad, AMMISCA 40, AGWAR to Chungking, 15 Nov 41. WPD 4389–30.

(1) Advise and assist the Chinese Government in all phases of procurement, transport, and maintenance of materials, equipment, and munitions requisite to the prosecution of its military effort.

(2) Advise and assist the Chinese Government in the training of Chinese personnel in the use and maintenance of materials, equipment, and munitions supplied as defense aid material by the United States.

(3) When requested, assist personnel of other Departments of the [United States] Government in carrying out their respective duties in furtherance of the objectives of the Lend-Lease Act pertaining to China.

(4) Assist the Chinese Government in obtaining prompt and co-ordinated administrative action by the United States authorities necessary to insure the orderly flow of materials and munitions from lend-lease agencies to the Chinese military forces.

(5) Explore the vital port, road, and railroad facilities with a view to the establishment and maintenance of an adequate line of communications.[87]

Magruder was further instructed to negotiate only with the Generalissimo, and to refrain from dealings with the war lords and cliques.

Diplomatically, the dispatch of AMMISCA may be classed with other measures taken at this time as warnings or deterrents to Japan, such as the oil embargo, stern notes, and the reinforcement of the Philippines. Though AMMISCA was primarily intended to see to it that lend-lease aid was effectively applied, the Joint Board was well aware that it had great, possibly dramatic, potentialities since the ultimate objective of all this was "Chinese military self-sufficiency."[88] Magruder told Marshall that "implementation in China of this policy in counterbalancing Japanese military capacity, if successfully carried out, can be measured militarily in terms of army corps."[89]

During the first two weeks of September, AMMISCA took hold among the swarming bureaus of Washington. It had two functional subgroups, one to operate in China and on the line of communications up from Rangoon, and the other in Washington to deal with China Defense Supplies, the Treasury, the rest of the War Department, and other government agencies. Magruder also received approval of his plan to form groups of specialists who would go to China from time to time "in connection with vital road and railroad problems, training in new equipment as it is made available, motor and armament maintenance problems, etc."[90]

[87] (1) Memo, Patterson for Magruder, 27 Aug 41, sub: Instructions for Mil Mission to China. AMMISCA Folder 1. (2) Points 4 and 5 in JB Paper 354 (Ser 716), 19 Sep 41.

[88] JB Paper 354 (Ser 716).

[89] Memo, Magruder for Marshall, 11 Aug 41, sub: Mil Mission to China. AMMISCA Folder 1.

[90] (1) *Ibid.* Approval came in Memo cited n. 87(1). (2) Three valuable diaries record AMMISCA activities. The official diary, recorded and numbered by weeks, not only contains a daily summary, but has appended to it the most important papers and staff studies which were sent by pouch to Washington. AMMISCA Weekly Rpts in AG (AMMISCA) 319.1. The weekly diary of the Washington Detail of AMMISCA is in the same file. The other two diaries are unofficial. One is the work of Col. Edward E. MacMorland, Chief of Staff, AMMISCA, and it provides background information on conferences and policy radios reported to Washington. Another diary was kept by Col. Harry S. Aldrich, who recorded day-by-day events in Burma before Pearl Harbor. Aldrich's diary later records the activities of the Joint Allied Military Council located in Chungking. Notes from the MacMorland and Aldrich Diaries are in Gen Ref Br, OCMH. (See Bibliographical Note.)

Before he left for Chungking, Magruder was quickly initiated into the problems of his new role. The composition of his staff was affected by the Generalissimo's desire, expressed through Soong, that certain technicians be included.[91] This was an opportunity to acquire valuable experience for the War Department, which therefore sent several reserve officers to cope with technical problems peculiar to the Orient. Magruder also found that the Chinese expected him to have great weight in War Department discussions of lend-lease arms.[92] When Mr. Soong complained to Col. William J. Donovan, Co-ordinator of Information, that the United States was not keeping its promises to China, the matter was promptly referred to Magruder. In suggesting an answer, Magruder told Marshall that "since the will of Chiang Kai-shek almost alone fixes the will of the Chinese people, the morale of this leader should be supported in every practicable way."[93] He asked Marshall to approve shipment of matériel for two battalions of field artillery, to accelerate the delivery of 144 P–43 fighters, to arrange for immediate procurement of the thirty-three Lockheed Hudsons, and to ship ordnance and ammunition for the American Volunteer Group at once. This time Marshall's reaction was immediate and favorable, for the War Department released its first shipment of ammunition to the Chinese as August 1941 ended. The release of yet more aid was an imminent prospect and China's lend-lease funds were scheduled for a sharp increase in the planning for a second lend-lease appropriation bill (later passed in October 1941).[94]

On 13 September 1941 the first group of AMMISCA personnel flew to Chungking via Manila and Hong Kong. Before their arrival, the Japanese forces in China opened a drive on Changsha. This offensive brought new appeals for aid from the Generalissimo, for any Japanese activity forced him to expend some of his carefully husbanded stocks.[95] Japanese extremists, on their side, could persuade themselves further that Washington was merely trying to gain time before attacking them, because Magruder stopped at Manila on 3–4 October to confer with senior American and visiting British officers from Singapore.[96] Moreover, Japanese agents at Rangoon could count every ton of aid going over the docks.

General Magruder's arrival in Chungking coincided with the ceremonies commemorating Double Ten Day (10 October), the thirtieth anniversary of

[91](1) Memo, Eglin for Co-ordinator of Information, 12 Nov 41. AG (AMMISCA) 334.8. (2) Ltr, Soong to Donovan, 16 Aug 41. Folder, China—Howitzers, ASF (DAD) ID, A46–299.
    [92] AG (AMMISCA) 210.
    [93](1) Ltr cited n. 91(2). (2) Quotation in Memo, Magruder for Marshall, 18 Aug 41, sub: Release of Equipment for China. AMMISCA Folder 1.
    [94] G–4/32192, A43–3.
    [95] Ltr, Soong to Hopkins, 24 Sep 41. China Pre-Pearl Harbor Folder, Hopkins Papers.
    [96](1) On 19 September 1941 Magruder was instructed to stop in Manila to confer with MacArthur who had been charged "for all strategic planning involving U.S. Army Forces in the Far East." Both officers were told to maintain correspondence and liaison on this subject. Ltr, Marshall to MacArthur, 19 Sep 41, sub: Mil Mission to China. WPD 4389–19. (2) MacMorland Diary, 3 Oct 42.

the Chinese Republic, and enthusiasm for AMMISCA's arrival was unconcealed. Though the Generalissimo was absent from Chungking when
AMMISCA arrived, and for a fortnight more, Magruder lost no time in going
to work. Officers were assigned to five major projects: communications, aviation, military supply, arsenals, and military training.[97] Their work deployed
some of them along the line of communications from Rangoon north, sent
some to observe the front at I-chang and on the Yunnan–Indochina border,
and retained the rest around Chungking. Magruder told his officers these duties
would involve work in widely separated areas, often out of touch with
Chungking, so that they would have to show initiative and good judgment.
Under no circumstances were AMMISCA officers to exceed their authority by
negotiating or making commitments to British and Chinese officials or
American agencies until such matters had been approved through diplomatic
channels.[98] They were reminded that they could hardly hope to change characteristics which the centuries had implanted in the Chinese, that AMMISCA's
"effectiveness will depend not on our efforts to change or reform the Chinese,
but upon our ability to put our advice and aid in such forms as to make it
practical."[99]

The Chinese Army, Fall 1941 [100]

The state and nature of the Chinese Army in the fall of 1941 were no surprise to Magruder and many of his staff who had served in China before. From
personal observations Magruder's staff were able to bring their recollections up
to date and to send back to the War Department a series of reports on the
Chinese Army. From military attaché reports of the twenties and thirties, from
the reports of AMMISCA officers, and from the reports of observers who saw
the Chinese Army at first hand, the War Department received the impression
of a heterogeneous force that had considerable potentialities but that was not
yet an effective, well-trained, well-disciplined army.

[97](1) MacMorland Diary. (2) Memo, Magruder for AMMISCA Personnel, 25 Oct 41.
AMMISCA Folder 5.
[98] Memo, Magruder for Stf Off, 7 Nov 41. AMMISCA Folder 5.
[99] Memo, Magruder for all AMMISCA Offs, 18 Sep 41. AG (AMMISCA) 210.
[100](1) Unless indicated otherwise, this section is based on the following sources:
(a) AMMISCA rpts and files in Job-11; (b) AMMISCA radio files incorporated with Hq, U.S.
Forces, China Theater, records at KCRC; (c) AMMISCA Folder 1; (d) MA Rpts cited n. 2(1);
(e) WPD 4389-15, 102; (f) GHQ, Far East Comd, Mil Hist Div, *Imperial General Headquarters*
Army Orders, Vol. I, Army Directives, Vol. I. Gen Ref Br, OCMH. (2) Additional background
material on the Chinese Army is given in the following secondary works: (a) Graham Peck,
Two Kinds of Time (Boston, 1950); (b) *The China Year Book,* H. G. W. Woodhead, ed. (Shanghai
and London, 1941); (c) Evans F. Carlson's *The Chinese Army: Its Organization and Military
Efficiency* (New York, 1940) treats of the Chinese Army before the Japanese blockade;
(d) Theodore H. White and Annalee Jacoby in their *Thunder Out of China* (New York, 1946)
present their view of the Chinese Army; (e) Gerald K. Winfield's *China: The Land and the
People* (New York, 1948) has a chapter, "War and the People of China," which discusses Chinese
popular attitudes toward their Army; (f) David Morris' *China Changed My Mind* (Boston, 1949)
is a candid opinion of a wartime observer.

During the 1930's, newborn Chinese nationalism and recurrent waves of anti-Japanese sentiment brought a number of war lords to the Generalissimo's Nationalist banners. There was a brief United Front period when the Chinese Communists recognized the Generalissimo's leadership in resisting the Japanese. The result was a coalition army but not a unified national force as Westerners conceived an army to be. Its German-trained divisions, and those of the more progressive and capable war lords, would be classed as mediocre by Western standards. These divisions numbered perhaps forty in all, but were under-strength, lacked heavy equipment, and were widely dispersed. The balance of the Chinese "divisions" were in reality large bands of lightly armed and poorly trained men, whose allegiance enabled their commanders to dominate the peasantry. These troops were not in contact with the Japanese, and could not have been maintained in battle against them. The greatest asset of the Chinese Army was the hardihood and valor of the peasant soldier, fighting in defense of the familiar things of his province. Its greatest liability was the failure of its war lord commanders to see their soldiers as anything more than counters in the unending game of Chinese politics.

In terms of formal structure, the Generalissimo, presiding over the National Military Council, commanded this coalition army. He maintained this command by seeing to it that, so far as Chinese domestic politics permitted, only men loyal to himself held positions of consequence. Loyalty to the Generalissimo rather than success in battle was the secret of a brilliant military career in China. The Chinese Army was deployed over twelve war areas and received orders through the Generalissimo's Chief of Staff, General Ho Ying-chin, working with the National Military Council. What effective fighting China had done since 1939 had been done within one particular war area at a time. In most cases, war area boundaries conformed to the ancient provincial boundaries. Often the war area commander doubled as provincial governor and exercised both military and political control. In the rear of each war area were a few of the Generalissimo's loyal divisions to guarantee the fidelity of the war area commander.

This decentralized regional defense system was primarily intended to keep the Japanese from ending the war with one blow. It also tended to keep dissident or traitorous elements (puppets) from taking advantage of a military crisis to seize control of an unoccupied area. The system had two major drawbacks. The wide dispersion of the better troops left the Generalissimo no mass of maneuver. And, the creation of twelve war area commanders with military and political power resulted in the creation of as many semi-independent satraps. Under these circumstances, the Generalissimo's greatest contribution to China's war of resistance lay not in his military skill, but rather in his political talents in keeping the war area commanders loyal to China.

Each war area commander recruited, trained, and partially equipped his own men. If a Japanese foray threatened more than one war area, the National

Military Council tried to co-ordinate the efforts of the menaced war areas. Consequently, a species of coalition warfare, involving all the attendant difficulties that the United Nations met in their attempts to wage it on the global scale, was to be met within China. Japanese expeditions often moved along war area boundaries, strongly suggesting that they were taking advantage of Chinese politics to cause their opponents the maximum of political embarrassment.

On paper, the Chinese division included all the arms and services it needed to make it a self-sufficient combat team. Division strength was nominally 9,529, but divisions averaged from six to seven thousand, some of them, of course, far understrength. Aside from lacking competent and trained commanders and staff officers and having only the rudiments of a supply system, the Chinese division had no artillery and was understrength in heavy weapons and rifles. The 800-odd pieces of Chinese artillery, a heterogeneous assortment from the arsenals of Europe and Japan, were hoarded by the war area commanders and the Generalissimo, to be doled out a piece at a time on great occasions. Their employment was extremely inefficient. For artillery support the division relied on its trench mortars, of which it had eighteen to thirty. On paper the division had 324 light and heavy machine guns (7.92-mm.) but the average was 200, of which 36 were heavy. China had perhaps 1,000,000 rifles. Its arsenals could make field artillery, mortars, machine guns, and rifles plus ammunition, but the general shortage of nonferrous metals and explosives kept output to a trickle.[101] Added to the general concept of the division as the personal property of its commander and to the inherent thrift of the Chinese, this shortage of matériel for 300-odd divisions made the Chinese extremely reluctant to use or expend any item of equipment.

That the division was its commander's property affected all Chinese tactics and strategy. The division was a military and political asset, not to be expended, for no replacements of men or matériel would be forthcoming. American observers believed that the divisional commander who lost one third of his men lost one third of his power and income. Consequently, though there were shining and valiant exceptions, most Chinese commanders would not dream of leading their troops as would their Japanese opponents, who, with their men, thought dying for the Emperor the goal of a soldier's life. Moreover, Americans who worked closely with Chinese divisions discovered that in those units, which they had no reason to consider atypical, the soldier's pay was among the perquisites of the commander. It was therefore to the commander's interest to keep his unit somewhat understrength.

The location of divisions in the Chinese order of battle does not suggest that China had traded space for time. The Chinese divisions had not retired into western China there to mass and wait the arrival of arms from the West.

---

[101] Description of a Chinese division in AG (AMMISCA) 371.

Instead, the greater part had fallen back from the big cities and railway lines into the countryside, while the Japanese flowed round and past them. Nor had the Generalissimo concentrated any of his better troops in areas where they might hope to receive U.S. arms. Had there been a plan to receive such help and then prepare for a great effort to drive the Japanese into the sea, the chosen troops would have been designated and a portion of them would be in training centers eagerly waiting the arms and instructors. On the contrary, years passed before the Chinese finally settled on the divisions they wanted to re-equip, while the American experience with training centers for Chinese troops in China paralleled that of the man who led his horse to water, but could not make it drink.

The nomenclature of units in the Chinese Army resembled the Japanese system rather than the American. The Chinese used the now familiar triangular (three-regiment) division, but had no army corps. Instead, they had armies, each consisting of three divisions plus army troops. Three Chinese "armies" in turn made a "group army," which was analogous to the American army. Thus the Chinese built their Army up by dividing each successive higher echelon by three—three regiments to a division, three divisions to an army, and three armies to a group army. Most Chinese war areas had three group armies.

China had about 3,819,000 men under arms. Of these, 2,919,000 were formed into 246 divisions classed by the Chinese as "front-line" troops, plus 44 "brigades" (a term loosely applied to men organized on military lines). In rear areas were another 70 divisions plus 3 brigades, or 900,000 more. Except for the Generalissimo's personal troops, estimated at about 30 divisions, the loyalties of China's troops lay with their war area commanders.[102]

The whole tangled structure of Chinese politics, culture, and society was reflected in the question of what troops would obey whom under what set of circumstances. Loyalty being a conditional virtue in most men, only an observer gifted with clairvoyance could state with accuracy that such and such a division would obey the orders of Chungking under all circumstances. Thus, the Chinese Ministry of War would not attempt to order certain Yunnanese and Szechwanese divisions[103] to leave their native provinces. On another occasion, a very senior general officer of the Chinese Government bitterly protested giving lend-lease to the troops of a certain war area commander, of unchallenged loyalty to Chinese nationalism and the Allied cause, at a time when those troops were hotly engaged with the Japanese.[104] The war area commander was then out of favor in Chungking, and only a very few insiders would have known why.

---

[102](1) Orders of Battle as assembled from Chinese and American sources in AG (AMMISCA) 336.2, 371. (2) MA Rpts, MID 2009–198, 2271–I–36, 2657–H–439, 2271–L–19, 2347–I–44, 2271–I–33, 2279–I–14, 2009–255. National Archives.
[103] See Ch. IX, below.
[104] MS, History of ZEBRA Force, pp. 6–7. Gen Ref Br, OCMH.

Staff and command procedures were peculiar to the Chinese Army. Orders given through a staff officer meant nothing. Orders had to come from the commander personally, and, if written, bear his seal or *chop*. Transport was not something to be carefully provided for in advance but was commandeered, often at gun point, or else was an object of barter and diplomatic negotiation between the commanders. Diversion of transport to haul loot and commanders' personal property was one of the more noticeable abuses.

The maintenance of this huge mass was a fearful drain on the Chinese economy. The number of Chinese divisions was more than three times as many divisions as the United States had in the field in 1945. A veritable flood of lend-lease equipment, in hundreds of thousands of tons every year, would have been needed to arm 316 divisions and 47 brigades, after they had been taught how to use and maintain it. A small amount, spread over all these units with a nice eye to face and patronage, would have been spread so thin as to have no effect on the situation. Thus, 1,080 75-mm. howitzers would give a modest artillery complement, not far below Japanese standards, to thirty divisions. Spread evenly over 316 divisions it would amount to about three new pieces for each division, which would leave each unit only nominally less ineffective than before.[105]

From 19 October to 10 November 1941, two of AMMISCA's officers inspected the I and V War Areas, which swung north and east of Chungking in a broad arc across the natural avenues of a Japanese approach to Chungking. These officers reported:

V. CONCLUSIONS:

1. The training in the artillery is very poor. A certain amount of technique is taught in the schools regarding indirect fire, but in actual practice the greater use is in direct fire, with axial methods for indirect fire being used where an obstacle provides protection for the guns.

2. The officer personnel in batteries is poor. How poor is difficult to visualize without seeing. In the battery specially selected for our inspection at Laolokow [Lao-ho-kou] the battery commander was not of a very high order of intelligence. He was barefooted except for sandals. It would probably be very difficult to teach modern artillery methods to men of this type.

3. The entire military system, being built on personal loyalty, prevents it being possible to train artillery officers and send them to units indiscriminately as we do in the States.

4. There is very little activity along the front. Either side could probably push in a salient at any point they throught it profitable to do so. No contact between Chinese and Japanese troops at the front was observed.

5. The interest of the Chinese towards any agressive action appears to be quite negligible, regardless of their statements that all they need is airplanes, tanks, and artillery in order to drive the aggressor from their shores.

[105] Maj. Gen. Yu Ta-wei's ordnance inventory distributed on current U.S. Army Tables of Organization and Equipment forms the basis of this computation. General Yu's inventory of Nov 41 in Memo, Lt Col Arcadi Gluckman, AMMISCA Supply Specialist, for Magruder, 17 Nov 41, sub: Ordnance Equipment for Thirty Assault Divisions, AG (AMMISCA) 319.1. The latter survey is in Stilwell Numbered File (hereafter SNF —) 52. Stilwell Documents, Hoover Library. (See Bibliographical Note.)

6. The small amount of artillery available in the past has resulted in artillery not being present in most divisions, but being held centrally under army or higher control.

7. The maintenance of motor transport is very faulty and makes the use of mechanized units a matter of doubtful advisability.[106]

The Generalissimo Warns of Peril

Shortly after General Magruder and his staff arrived at Chungking the Chinese through AMMISCA warned of an imminent Japanese attack on Kunming and asked for more arms in accents of urgency that caused grave concern on the highest levels in Washington. The President, the State Department, and the Joint Board were all involved in deciding how the United States should act, while in Chungking Magruder was drawn into those discussions of strategy and policy which his directive had sought to prevent. The Generalissimo's warnings seem in retrospect to have originated before Magruder reached Chungking.

In the fall of 1941 the Chinese made two requests for an emergency issue of arms. Neither was related to the initial Soong requests of March 1941. In the first, the Generalissimo asked Soong to arrange a complete revision of existing lend-lease delivery schedules, saying that he needed 1,000 antiaircraft guns by 31 October, and a number of pack howitzers by the end of the year. The Generalissimo explained he wanted these weapons for the central China front. Moreover, he was greatly disappointed that the 13-ton tanks "originally promised us" could not be shipped in the near future. With the supply line so congested, it was manifestly impossible to have these weapons in China by 31 October, but the request was promptly forwarded to the War Department, which had to explain that the munitions stockpile would permit only 61 howitzers and 285 .50-caliber machine guns to go by the end of 1941.[107]

The War Department's reply distressed Currie, who wrote Hopkins on 6 October: "Aside from 500 Bren guns with ammunition which I got from Canada, we haven't shipped one gun yet to China on Lend-Lease." [108] The Generalissimo's plea brought results. The outcome was that almost a year after the Chinese first asked for arms, China Defense Supplies shipped the first weapons for the Chinese Army on the SS *Tulsa* on 22 October. The cargo was a most valuable one, with 48 75-mm. howitzers, 11,000 Thompson submachine guns, 500 more Bren guns, 100 .50-caliber machine guns, ample ammunition, and 35 scout cars.[109] Sent at a time when American forces in the Philippines

---

[106] Rpt, Lt Cols George W. Sliney and Edwin M. Sutherland. Item 87, AMMISCA Folder 4.

[107] Ltr, Soong to Currie, 24 Sep 41; Ltr, Currie to Patterson, 29 Sep 41; Ltr, Patterson to Currie, 1 Oct 41; Ltr, Currie to Hopkins, 6 Oct 41. China Pre-Pearl Harbor Folder, Hopkins Papers.

[108] Ltr, Currie to Hopkins, 6 Oct 41. China Pre-Pearl Harbor Folder, Hopkins Papers.

[109] History of the China–Burma–India Theater, 21 May 1942–25 October 1944 (hereafter, History of CBI), Sec. III, App. III, Item 1. OPD 314.7 CTO, A47–30. (See Bibliographical Note.)

were soon to enter battle with obsolete 2.95-inch howitzers, vintage of '98, the shipment was a real sacrifice.

The Generalissimo's first request may have been a testing of the American position, for he promptly followed it by sounding the alarm in the strongest manner. The Generalissimo and Madame Chiang Kai-shek welcomed Magruder and AMMISCA to Chungking at a conference on 27 October 1941. Magruder presented his five-point program for the Generalissimo's considera- tion.[110] The Chinese leader was satisfied with Magruder's approach to the issues but singled out aviation for the top priority, for he was expecting early arrival of the promised lend-lease aircraft. The Generalissimo proposed that AMMISCA assume control of and develop the AVG, even at the cost of sep- arating it from the Chinese Air Force. Before Magruder could comment on these points the Generalissimo introduced grave issues of high policy into the conference.

The Chinese Government feared that Japanese troops from Indochina were about to attack Yunnan Province and seize Kunming. This action would close the Burma Road and destroy China's last link with the outside world. Actually, the seeming threat was but part of a Japanese cover plan to draw attention from projected operations elsewhere.[111] To meet this disturbing prospect the Generalissimo asked that air support be detached from the RAF at Singapore, and that Anglo-American diplomatic pressure be placed on the Japanese.[112] Magruder concurred in the Generalissimo's views and sent them on to Washington,[113] where they resulted in grave concern during October– November 1941. The Generalissimo and Magruder met again on 31 October, and the Chinese leader again stressed his fear of a Japanese drive on Kunming.[114] Magruder sent these warnings as well to Washington. His radios asked for guidance, saying that, as far as the U.S. effort in China was concerned, the heart of the matter was the Generalissimo's intention of using the AVG, without regard to its state of training and equipment, against the Japanese if they should attack Yunnan.[115] Thus, despite the precautions of those who drew up Magruder's directive, the Chinese had immediately involved him in a discussion of major points of U.S. Pacific policy.

The Chinese reasons for doing so seem clear. Immediately after the dis- closure on 24 August 1941 that Japanese-American diplomatic conversations of the greatest importance to the peace of the Pacific were under way, the Generalissimo had taken diplomatic action to defend China's interests. He told

---

[110] See p. 32, above.

[111] *Imperial General Headquarters* Army Directive 969, 20 Sep 41, GHQ, Far East Comd, Mil Hist Div, *Imperial General Headquarters* Army Directives, Vol. II. Gen Ref Br, OCMH.

[112] Memo, Conf with Generalissimo Chiang Kai-shek, 27 Oct 41. AMMISCA Folder 3.

[113] Rad AMMISCA 28, Magruder to Marshall and Stimson, 28 Oct 41. Bk A (1941), Folder 8, Executive Office Files, OPD. (Hereafter, OPD Exec –.) (See Bibliographical Note.)

[114] Memo, Conf with Generalissimo Chiang Kai-shek, 31 Oct 41. AMMISCA Folder 3.

[115] Rad AMMISCA 32, Magruder to Marshall and Stimson, 31 Oct 41. Bk A (1941), OPD Exec 8.

the President that China's failure to win an ally had given the Chinese a feeling of isolation. The Generalissimo suggested that Mr. Roosevelt take the initiative in arranging either of two alternatives: (1) the Soviet Union and Great Britain propose an alliance to China; (2) the United States, Great Britain, and the Netherlands Indies include China in their discussions.[116] This latter was a clear reference to the staff talks that the latter three powers had conducted intermittently since January 1941. The President did not accept either of the alternatives, but sought to reassure the Generalissimo by announcing AMMISCA's creation.[117] The Generalissimo was not told that Magruder was forbidden to engage in staff talks; very likely he assumed that was one major reason why Magruder was in Chungking. The Generalissimo could also remember the success of his recent plea for arms.

The Generalissimo's conversations with Magruder were followed shortly by a note that came from T. V. Soong, giving China's requirements in munitions if Yunnan was to be held.[118] Mr. Roosevelt gave the Generalissimo's note to Secretary of State Hull, and Soong's note went to Hopkins. Conferences followed between the State, War, and Navy Departments, and in the Joint Board. The radios from AMMISCA and the Chinese notes received the most earnest and searching examination.

The War Plans Division of the War Department, at Marshall's request, examined the problem posed by the Chinese and concluded that aid for Kunming could come only from the Royal Air Force at Singapore or the American air garrison of Manila.[119] The latter would weaken Manila and risk war with Japan; "no involvement should be risked which would lessen the main effort against Germany." [120] G–2, War Department General Staff, strongly doubted the likelihood of a Japanese attack on Kunming. The Joint Board met on 3 November and reaffirmed the desire and the necessity of avoiding Pacific commitments so as to concentrate on the Atlantic. A note embodying the views of the military went to the State Department, which shortly after thanked the services for their "lucid" analysis, saying that AMMISCA had caused the State Department more worry than was necessary.[121]

---

[116] Sherwood, *Roosevelt and Hopkins,* p. 404.

[117] Though Mr. Roosevelt informed Soong of AMMISCA's creation on 20 August 1941, the President did not issue a press release on AMMISCA until 26 August 1941. See n. 84.

[118] Memo, Soong for Roosevelt, 31 Oct 41. Folder, China 2, ASF (DAD) ID, A46–299.

[119] Memo, Gerow for Marshall, 1 Nov 41, sub: Far Eastern Situation. Bk A (1941), OPD Exec 8.

[120] Memo, Gerow for Marshall, 1 Nov 41, sub: Immediate Aid to China. Bk A (1941), OPD Exec 8. Table A of this memorandum contains the G–2 estimate.

[121] (1) Memo for Record, Col C. W. Bundy, Chief, Plans Gp, WPD, 1 Nov 41, sub: Immediate Aid to China. Bk A (1941), OPD Exec 8. (2) Memo for Record, Bundy, 2 Nov 41, sub: Notes on Conf with Mr. Currie at State Dept, 1245, 1 Nov 41. Bk A (1941), OPD Exec 8. (3) Admiral Royal E. Ingersoll reminded the Joint Board of the decision to make a major effort in the Atlantic and pointed out that a major effort in the western Pacific, or a shift of the major effort to that ocean to rescue China would force a tremendous shift of merchant ship tonnage. Statement of Ingersoll before the JB, 3 Nov 41. Bk A (1941), OPD Exec 8. (4) Dr. Hornbeck called General Marshall on the evening of 4 November 1941. Memo, Marshall for Gerow, 5 Nov 41. Bk A (1941), OPD Exec 8.

Roosevelt had asked the Chief of Naval Operations and Chief of Staff for their views on the AMMISCA and Chinese messages. Their reply defined the highest service views on aid to China on the eve of Pearl Harbor. On 4 November Stark and Marshall told the President that they did not think the United States would be justified in undertaking an offensive war against Japan to keep her from cutting the Burma Road and taking Kunming. "The only existing plans for war against Japan in the Far East are to conduct a defensive war, in co-operation with the British and Dutch . . . ." [122] By mid-December 1941, there would be added U.S. strength in the Philippines, but even so, until February or March 1942, intervention against Japan, save in defense of the Philippines or Malaya, would be futile. Military counteraction against Japan should follow only if Japan attacked the United States, the Netherlands Indies, or British Commonwealth, or moved into west or south Thailand, or Timor. The Atlantic First policy should be adhered to. With respect to the AMMISCA and Chinese notes, they recommended that no U.S. armed forces be sent to China; that reinforcement and equipment of the AVG be expedited; that aid to China be accelerated; and that no ultimatum be sent to Japan. [123] The State Department thoroughly approved of these views. [124]

Meanwhile, Churchill had received a similar appeal from the Generalissimo and, fearing that the Japanese might "drift" into war, suggested on 5 November that another strong warning be sent from Britain and the United States. Churchill observed that the policy of gaining time had worked so far, "but our joint embargo is steadily forcing the Japanese to decisions for peace or war." [125]

Soong appealed directly to Roosevelt on 8 November, asking that the U.S. Navy release one-third of its dive bombers to China, to be delivered to the Philippines by aircraft carrier and ferried from there to China. On arrival there they would be manned by Chennault's pilots. [126] Soong's proposal was another indication that the Chinese found it very difficult to understand the organizing, training, and equipping of military units. On the eve of Pearl Harbor they were proposing to deprive the U.S. Navy's carrier air groups of their most effective weapon and themselves of what proved the best fighter group in Asia, to produce an extemporized and untrained dive-bomber unit which would then be sent into battle without fighter cover. With this scheme went a restatement of Chinese ordnance requirements without whose satisfaction, Soong

---

[122] (1) Memo, Marshall and Stark for Roosevelt, 4 Nov 41, sub: Far Eastern Situation. Bk A (1941), OPD Exec 8. (2) *Report of Congressional Joint Committee on Pearl Harbor Attack* (Washington, 1946), p. 342.

[123] Memo cited n. 122(1).

[124] Currie and Hull concurred in the views of the War Department. Memo cited n. 121(2).

[125] (1) *Report of Congressional Joint Committee . . .,* p. 340. (2) Rad, Churchill to the Generalissimo, undated. Bk A (1941), OPD Exec 8.

[126] Ltr, Soong to President, 8 Nov 41, sub: China and Impending Attack on Burma Road. China Pre-Pearl Harbor Folder, Hopkins Papers. The President sent Soong's letter to Hopkins with a typed note dated 12 November 1941: "What can we do about this?"

stated, the Chinese could not hope to resist a Japanese attack on Kunming.

The President and Hopkins sent Soong's note to the War Department. Marshall and Stimson personally reviewed the ordnance situation and found the cupboard almost bare. In effect, Soong was told that he would have to be content with what was already earmarked for China, plus some 2.95-inch howitzers and 3-inch antiaircraft guns that would be rushed from the Philippines when their replacements arrived. The Generalissimo was reminded through Soong that twenty-four nations in all were clamoring for lend-lease aid, and that the United States, in addition, had its own forces to equip. The best the United States could do in response to Soong's appeal was to speed the flow of lend-lease aid and facilitate the building-up of the American Volunteer Group. Soong was further informed that the United States was reinforcing the Philippines, whose garrison, with the Pacific Fleet, would be a significant factor in the situation.[127]

In mid-November, General Marshall prepared a reply to Magruder's queries of 28 and 31 October. An exchange of memoranda in July 1941 with the State Department on a lend-lease training program for Chinese airmen influenced Marshall's answer that the Chinese would have to decide when the AVG was to be used. At that time General Marshall, who had experience of Chinese methods and temperament, proposed to Currie that as a *quid pro quo* the United States receive certain guarantees from the Chinese regarding the command and staff functions of the Americans with the AVG, and that Magruder have the responsibility of fixing the date the AVG entered combat.[128] Such a proposal was an attempt by Marshall to use lend-lease as a bargaining device toward gaining greater efficiency and a degree of self-help from the Chinese. The State Department and Currie had demurred, the latter writing, "In view of the dependence by China upon us for continued aid, it is not anticipated that any difficulty of non-co-operation will be experienced." [129]

AMMISCA's Appraisal of the Thirty Division Program

Among the orders Magruder took with him to Chungking was one to report as soon as possible on the Chinese capabilities for offensive action in

---

[127](1) These curt summaries should not be taken as indicating any brusqueness in the letters themselves, which were sympathetic and friendly. The items desired by the Chinese were those desperately needed by all. (2) Sherwood, *Roosevelt and Hopkins,* pp. 408–09. (3) Ltr, Soong to Stimson, 6 Nov 41; Ltr, Stimson to Soong, 12 Nov 41, sub: Def of Yunnan and Burma Road. AG 400.3295 (4–14–41) Sec 1A. (4) *Report of Congressional Joint Committee . . .,* p. 343.

[128](1) Ltr, Marshall to Currie, 5 Jul 41, sub: Aviation Aid to China. Item 10, AG (AMMISCA) 336.2. (2) Ltr, Marshall to Currie, 15 Jul 41. AG 400.3295 (4–14–41) Sec 1A. (3) Min, Conf in OSW, 0915, 21 Jul 41. OSW Conf, A45–466. (4) Ltr, Currie to Soong, 23 Jul 41. Item 13, AG (AMMISCA) 336.2. (5) Ltr, Currie to Marshall, 6 Aug 41; Ltr, Marshall to Currie, 30 Aug 41. AG 336.2 (7–30–42). (6) WPD 4389–15. (7) Rad AMMISCA 82, Marshall to Magruder, 15 Nov 41. AG 400.3295 (4–14–41) Sec 1A.

[129] Ltr, 6 Aug 41, cited n. 128(5).

1941. [130] From surveys of China's twenty arsenals, from observer reports of the central China and Indochina border fronts, and from studies of Chinese service schools, Magruder concluded that, if the Chinese were given arms and were willing to use them effectively, a considerable number of divisions could execute diversions or even substantial local offensives.[131] Subsequent events showed that the War Department concurred.

But on what basis were these arms to be distributed? Soong's programs of March 1941 had implied thirty divisions, but final confirmation did not come until 17 November when Maj. Gen. Yu Ta-wei, head of the Chinese ordnance departments, told Lt. Col. Arcadi Gluckman of AMMISCA that for some time the National Military Council had planned to create thirty *kung chen tui* (or assault-on-fortified-position) divisions. Ten thousand strong, the new units were to be organized into ten armies and located in strategic defensive positions. At the same time, General Yu stated that twelve divisions had been designated and the remainder were under consideration. General Yu told Gluckman that Chinese arsenals could furnish rifles for the thirty divisions plus many of their infantry weapons, but that powder and metals for ammunition were nonexistent in China. He claimed that most of the 800-odd pieces of field artillery were being distributed among the twelve divisions, but that spare parts and ammunition for them, especially for those brought from the Soviet Union, were almost exhausted. This plan was still tentative, for the Generalissimo had not yet approved it.[132]

Realizing that Soong had already submitted most of General Yu's needs for procurement, Magruder radioed Stimson that little more could be done on matériel until the Thirty Division Program had the Generalissimo's unqualified approval. For future guidance of the War Department Magruder recommended that ground force matériel be released to the Chinese on the following priorities: (a) arsenal metals, explosives, and machinery; (b) finished small arms ammunition; (c) infantry weapons; (d) organic division artillery; (e) corps artillery. Furthermore, he urged the War Department to remove the Chinese supply agencies in Washington from the lend-lease field.[133]

AMMISCA learned too that the Generalissimo contemplated establishing two training centers, one near Kunming, the other near Kweiyang where cadres of the thirty divisions might learn to use lend-lease arms. During October and November 1941, however, the National Military Council hesitated to locate the centers or name their commanders. Despite this procrastination, Magruder

---

[130](1) JB Paper 354 (Ser 716), 19 Sep 41. (2) JB Paper 325 (Ser 729), 25 Sep 41.
[131](1) Weekly AMMISCA Diary (Nov 41). AG (AMMISCA) 319.1. (2) AMMISCA Folder 5.
[132] Memo, Gluckman for Magruder, 17 Nov 41, sub: Ord Equipment for Thirty Assault Divs. AG (AMMISCA) 319.1. Magruder's first indorsement was dated 7 March 1942. The long delay reflects the fact that Chinese Government agencies in Chungking did not until then come to a very tentative agreement on the Thirty Division Program's various aspects, such as the choice of the divisions to be re-equipped.
[133] Rad AMMISCA 12, Magruder to AGWAR, 20 Nov 41; Rad AMMISCA 45, Magruder to AGWAR, 11 Nov 41. AMMISCA Radio File, Job–11.

asked AMMISCA's Washington office to dispatch "task force specialists" to aid the Chinese in setting up tank, infantry, and artillery schools.[134] These requirements were being studied when war came.

Before Pearl Harbor, AMMISCA personnel expressed two differing views on China. Familiar with China, Magruder was neither surprised nor depressed by the contrast between Chinese propaganda in the United States and Chinese action in China. By estimating what might still be done by tactfully applying American technique, Magruder reported to the Secretary of War and the Chief of Staff in tones of mild optimism regarding the creation of an effective Chinese Army. Magruder considered he was not there to describe or expose China to his superiors, many of whom had served in China, but rather to aid China in helping itself.

Nevertheless, many of Magruder's assistants were surprised and disillusioned by what they saw in China. As these officers traveled about China, visited Chinese headquarters, chatted with Chinese officers, and inspected Chinese establishments they saw for themselves the manner in which the Chinese were resisting Japan. Inevitably, they appraised the Chinese war effort as would professional soldiers, and their letters began to flow back to friends in the War Department and to families at home couched in terms of angry disillusion.[135] Typical of many such was a report to General Magruder by Lt. Col. George W. Sliney, summing up the impressions of his inspection trips in October and November:

The following general impressions were gained through conversations with Chinese officers and by observations of conditions of front-line activity and of training, during my visits to the 1st, 5th, and 8th War Areas, to the Training Center at Cha Tso, and to the Field Artillery School at Tuyin. Such matters are not subject to proof, but should receive consideration in deciding any Allied plan of action.

(a) Several Chinese officers have stated to me that they believed China might be able to win this war without further fighting. They expected international diplomatic pressure to force Japan out of China. I feel that this attitude combined with many months of inactive defense has created a non-aggressive attitude in the soldiers that will take time to overcome.

(b) The general idea in the United States that China has fought Japan to a standstill, and has had many glorious victories, is a delusion. Japan has generally been able to push forward any place she wanted to. She has stopped mostly because of the fact that a certain number of troops can safely hold only a certain number of miles of front without allowing dangerous holes to exist in it. The will to fight an agressive action does not yet exist in the Chinese Army. If the Government of the United States is counting on such intent it should be cautioned against being too sure of any large-scale offensive action at present. This attitude is being changed by diplomatic persuasion from without, but it will require well-

[134] (1) Rad AMMISCA 60, Magruder to AGWAR, 20 Nov 41. Job–11. (2) Memo, Eglin for G–1, WDGS, 22 Nov 41, sub: Task Off for U.S. Mil Mission to China. AG (AMMISCA) 319.1. (3) Rad AMMISCA 76, Magruder to AGWAR, 3 Dec 41. Job–11.

[135] Not only do the reports and letters in AG (AMMISCA) 319.1, AMMISCA Folder 1, and WPD 4389–102 present these two differing views, but interviews with Magruder and former officers in AMMISCA support these statements. Correspondence with former AMMISCA officers in HIS 330.14 CBI 1950.

directed propaganda from within to give the proper mental attitude to the soldiers who are to do the fighting.

(c) Many small things all pointing in the same direction have caused me to have a feeling, stronger than a suspicion, that the desire of the Chinese for more modern matériel was not, before December 8th, for the purpose of pressing the war against Japan, but was to make the Central Government safe against insurrection after diplomatic pressure by other nations had forced Japan out of China.

(d) The method of employment of artillery by the Chinese is very inefficient due to the poor standard of education of the officer personnel. In releasing American artillery to the Chinese this fact should be considered, as well as the relative likelihood of its actually being employed by the United States or by China.

It is recommended that the above ideas be considered by the American Military Mission in making plans, and be presented to the War Department for consideration in connection with other available opinion in planning any War Department action in this hemisphere.[136]

AMMISCA, Lend-Lease, and the Line of Communications

Following his initial conferences with the Generalissimo, Magruder flew between Chungking, Kunming, Lashio, Rangoon, and Singapore, acting as trouble shooter for his five projects.[137] His chief concern, however, was the line of communications to Kunming, since all AMMISCA's projects depended on a flow of matériel from the port of Rangoon, up the Burma railway and highway to Lashio, and then over the road to China. This problem of the line of communications was to vex all Magruder's successors as it vexed him; in many ways it was the principal problem of the American effort in China, Burma, and India.

Like the Chinese Army, the port of Rangoon and the Burma Road had been fully described in reports from U.S. representatives in Burma and Yunnan. By fall 1941 local American representatives believed that the Burma Road was the worst logistical bottleneck in aid to China. There were physical limitations because it was not an all-weather highway and so suffered during the monsoon rains. Communications along its length were woefully inadequate. There were sanitary limitations because it passed through a malarial belt. Since the road's 715 miles were the last route over which goods could move to a starving Chinese economy, the Burma Road was the center of interest to speculators and traders, and a battleground for politics—national and local, Burmese, Chinese, and British.[138]

Attempting to control the road's traffic, the Generalissimo had piled agency on agency, over which his cousin, General Yu Fei-peng, presided.[139] Summarizing this situation, a military attaché report of August 1941 remarked:

[136] Memo, Sliney for Magruder, 10 Dec 41. AMMISCA Folder 4.
[137] Weekly AMMISCA Diary (Nov 41). AG (AMMISCA) 319.1.
[138](1) Ltr, Lt Col David D. Barrett, Asst MA Chungking, to G–2, WDGS, 6 Apr 41, sub: Burma Road. AG (AMMISCA) 611. (2) Rpt, Austin C. Brady, American Consul, Rangoon, Burma, to Secy State, 14 June 41, sub: Gen Transportation Conditions Affecting Shipt of Supplies through Burma into China. Item 2, Port of Rangoon Folder, CT 42, Dr 4, KCRC.
[139] American Aid to China.

The foreigner who surveys the Road is inclined to jump to the conclusion that a competent man, backed by the Generalissimo, can administer it efficiently without much difficulty. He forgets that the Generalissimo is not the absolute dictator of China, and that even if he himself were to devote all of his time to the efficient administration of the Road, he might not be able to overcome the myriad difficulties which would face him in the way of vested interests, political intrigues, distrust, jealousy, and even enmity of important subordinates, and above all, the general inability of the Chinese efficiently to administer anything through centralized control.[140]

Surveying the problem, lend-lease officials in Washington learned that British traffic figures for Lashio were greater than Chinese border figures at Wanting, which in turn were 50 percent more than at Kunming. The unmistakable inference was that goods brought over what was then termed by the press "China's life line" were simply vanishing into the countryside for private profit. Customs figures indicated that, in May 1941, 25 percent of the tonnage arriving at Kunming was yarn and piece goods, 27 percent military goods and metals, and 39 percent was spare parts and gasoline exclusive of what the trucks carried for their own use. The last was a most important item, for trucks had to carry their own fuel. As a result, one estimate was that to lay down 5,000 tons at Chungking, 14,000 had to leave Lashio. When it is recalled that Chungking in turn was many hundreds of miles from the Chinese lines, which meant a further immense effort to move supplies eastward, it can be seen that the road was hardly China's life-line. But it offered the hope that under competent and honest management it might be made to carry 30,000 tons a month of ordnance, nonferrous metals, explosives, and gasoline, as against a trickle of oil and cloth for the bazaars, and a few arms for the war lords' praetorian guards.[141]

In August of 1941 Mr. David G. Arnstein and two associates prepared a report for the Generalissimo (copies sent to Mr. Roosevelt and Mr. Hopkins) which summarized the impressions made on them by an inspection of the Burma Road and the Chinese agencies operating on it. Arnstein reported that no less than sixteen Chinese agencies operated on the Burma Road. All were heavily overstaffed with inexperienced executives, their relatives, hangers-on, and so forth. No central authority regulated traffic or controlled drivers. Trucks were overloaded, recklessly driven, and given no systematic maintenance. Vehicles moved in convoys of fifteen to twenty-five, which would all halt when one truck was stopped for repairs or to have its papers checked. Lucrative private trucking crowded the road as speculators in Rangoon bought trucks, loaded them with bazaar goods, and after two or three trips sold them in Kunming at a great profit. The profits of private trade and employment made government drivers quit unless they too could smuggle goods and passengers into

---

[140] MA Rpt (China) IG 4610, 23 Aug 41, sub: Present Status of Burma Road. AG (AMMISCA) 611.

[141] (1) Ltr, Currie to MacMorland, 7 Jul 41; Memo, Miles for MacMorland, 8 Jul 41, sub: China Aid Program; Memo (unused), MacMorland for Miles, 10 Jul 41. Folder, China Lend-Lease Corresp (Apr–Oct 41), ASF (DAD) ID, A46–299. (2) American Aid to China.

China. Arnstein's report, which the Generalissimo carried about with him for some days, and by which he was most impressed, recommended sweeping changes, including the significant one that arms have priority over consumer goods and that a foreigner be appointed to run the road with full powers.[142] Putting the final seal on his work by declining such a post, Arnstein then left China.

The port of Rangoon itself was no bottleneck, but administrative difficulties in Rangoon wasted time.[143] Customs regulations were sources of infinite difficulty, for the transit of lend-lease supplies and of goods bought by the Chinese with pre-lend-lease credits involved importing and re-exporting. The semi-autonomous Government of Burma had a 1-percent transit tax on all items bound for China which of course included lend-lease aid. Arnstein's report, and later communications from AMMISCA, directed such attention to this tax on the American effort to support China and divert the Japanese from Malaya and the Netherlands Indies that the British Foreign Office finally announced Great Britain would assume the tax burden by giving the Burmese an equivalent subsidy.

The formalities of compliance with customs and the transit tax were time wasting. For example, each vehicle assembled had in effect to be checked into Burma at Rangoon and checked out again at the border. Chinese and Burmese Government agencies were suspicious of each other and filled the ears of AMMISCA personnel with tales of what they suffered at the hands of their opposite numbers. All this tended to slow the movement of goods through Burma.

The major physical bottleneck in the Burma line of communications was the Gokteik gorge between Mandalay and Lashio. There the Burma Railways climb 3,000 feet in twenty-seven miles, about half the distance at a grade of 1 foot in every 25. Trains had to be broken into sections and hauled by hill-climbing locomotives. Because of this, and because the Burma Railways also had to serve the needs of the Burmese economy, Burmese rail officials could promise the Chinese but 550 tons a day to be laid down at Lashio in November. Deliveries in that month suggested the performance would not match the promise. There was also a road from Mandalay to Lashio; it, too, had a very limited capacity, thanks to one particularly bad stretch.

The result of this maladministration and limited capacity was a massive congestion of the line of communications to China. Lend-lease material was pouring into Burma via Rangoon far faster than it moved up the Burma Road

---

[142] Rpt, Arnstein, Harold C. Davis, and Marco F. Hellman, to the Generalissimo, 9 Aug 41, sub: Present Trucking Opns as Conducted on Burma Road and Recommendations for Their Improvement. AG (AMMISCA) 231.5. Arnstein completed his survey as an employee of the Chinese Government.

[143] Sources consulted for this section: (1) American Aid to China. (2) Rpt cited n. 138(2). (3) Rpt, Maj John E. Russell, AMMISCA Specialist, to Magruder, 12 Nov 41, sub: Lend-Lease Supply and Transportation in Burma. Port of Rangoon Folder, CT 42, Dr 4, KCRC.

from Lashio. At Lashio it was added to a stockpile of arms and raw materials purchased by the Chinese with credits granted earlier. In July 1941, of the 79,000 tons of Chinese goods stored in Rangoon, only 22,000 tons were truckable. At that month's rate of moving goods, eight months would have been needed to clear the stockpile, yet more was coming in constantly. At the end of the rail line, Lashio, 30,000 tons were stored, a four month's backlog.

Soong's March 1941 lend-lease program had faced the line of communications problem.[144] The program included trucks, road-building matériel, spare parts, and maintenance facilities for the Burma Road, and matériel for the projected narrow-gauge Yunnan–Burma Railway. This latter would have made a dramatic improvement in the situation could it have been completed. Currie had laid the scheme before the President, and the Chinese Government had presented it to British authority, which had been interested in such a railway since 1938. Both the British and the President approved the idea, and the Chinese began their section in April 1941. Lend-lease funds introduced an American interest, and the War Department sent Maj. John E. Ausland, a former official of the Chicago, Burlington & Quincy Railroad, to Burma. The Government of Burma assigned Sir John Rowland as Director of Construction and the Chinese provided the services of Brig. Gen. Tseng Yang-fu, Vice-Commissioner of Communications. Though their responsibilities cut across international lines, the triumvirate co-operated in a wholehearted fashion.

By September 1941 the Office of the Chief of Engineers had 90 percent of the required equipment and supplies for the Yunnan–Burma Railway on order. The War Department bought an abandoned 125-mile stretch of narrow-gauge line from the Denver and Rio Grande Western Railroad and began dismantling it for shipment to Burma. Shipments of supplies for the line increased as autumn wore on. But greater familiarity with the terrain and with the project began to reveal discouraging obstacles. The War Department found that procurement of diesel locomotives and rolling stock would delay the project until late in 1942. Meanwhile, Major Ausland's report suggested that bridging the Salween River and completing certain tunnels in Yunnan would also delay the railway until the winter of 1942–43. In addition to these problems, Ausland reported that the British feared the monsoon rains would make the Yunnan–Burma Railway a six-year effort. There was also a problem of health, for the 200,000 conscripted Yunnanese laborers were working in areas where a deadly form of malaria was endemic. To alleviate this, Currie and Hopkins sent a Public Health commission to aid in mosquito control.[145] When war came, shipments of railway matériel for Burma ceased; shipments en route were diverted to India, where they found use in other transportation projects in support of China.

---

[144] Folder, China Railways and Railway Requirements, ASF (DAD) ID, A46–299. This folder and AG (AMMISCA) 453 and 611 outline the scope and size of the Yunnan–Burma Railway project.
[145] American Aid to China.

Surveying this often depressing scene, AMMISCA urged the War Department to send matériel and experts to increase Burma Road capacity. The Department did its best to comply. General Motors was given a contract to assemble trucks in Rangoon. Forty-five technicians left on 10 November to help with supply and maintenance problems. Within the United States, warehouse facilities were expanded to speed movement of lend-lease to shipside. In November 14,561 tons left Newport News, Virginia, and more was piling up to await shipping space. But these measures were at best palliatives, and AMMISCA warned that tighter controls over lend-lease purchases would have to be established and maintained until all Chinese stockpiles in Burma had been cut to more manageable proportions. In October 1941 more goods moved from Lashio to China than arrived from Rangoon. This was not, however, all lend-lease aid, most of which was held in Rangoon by the congested lines of communication.[146]

Recommendations to Washington on the logistics problem were made on 12 November and had conclusive effects when the Chinese lend-lease program was appraised after Pearl Harbor. AMMISCA suggested that there be no more purchasing or shipping of goods for China until the Burma stockpile was inventoried to see what was actually at hand. When purchasing was resumed, AMMISCA suggested it should not be done by Chinese agencies in Washington, which were ignorant of the real supply situation in China, but by the War Department in accord with AMMISCA recommendations. Other suggestions were that ship sailings from Newport News be staggered to avoid choking Rangoon with undeliverable goods; that title to lend-lease be kept in U.S. hands until it was actually delivered to the Chinese in China, so that it should not be the object of squabbles and corruption among outside parties; and that, as a matter of policy, goods procurable locally should not be sent on lend-lease, so as to end, among several other objectionable practices, that of sending lead to one of the world's greatest sources of nonferrous metals.[147]

Summary

As November passed into December, and the Japanese task force drew closer to Pearl Harbor, the status of the American effort to aid China was:

1. A clearly defined concept of the reasons for giving arms to China had been framed by the military and approved by the President.

2. The War Department had weighed its resources against world-wide demands on them, and had programed a series of shipments to China on which to base procurement. (Table 3 includes 1941 shipments.)

3. In framing this program the War Department had implicitly accepted the Chinese proposals to (a) create a modern Chinese Air Force, (b) institute

---

[146] AG (AMMISCA) 319.1.
[147] Rpt cited n. 143(3).

and maintain an efficient line of communications into China, and (c) arm thirty divisions.

4. A military mission had been sent to China to aid the Chinese in asking for and using American matériel and services.

There was, however, one gap in this program. There was no planning to meet the effect of war in the Pacific by a combined Sino-American effort. Such staff talks had been held between British and Americans, but there had been none between Chinese and Americans. Partly as a result of this, Magruder had no directive as to what his mission would be were war to result from the current Japanese-American crisis in the Pacific.

TABLE 3—LEND-LEASE SUPPLIES SHIPPED TO CHINA: MAY 1941–APRIL 1942 [a]

[In Long Tons]

Type	Total	1941								1942			
		May	Jun	Jul	Aug	Sep	Oct	Nov	Dec	Jan	Feb	Mar	Apr
Total.....	110,864	7,552	4,917	5,452	8,099	9,146	9,803	14,561	7,145	9,920	6,487	20,343	7,439
Arsenal.....	24,703	3,125	5	3,112	82	250	1,807	4,661	1,804	2,388	256	7,121	92
Aviation....	2,533	0	0	0	0	0	246	144	6	264	58	1,123	692
Airplanes.....	1,657	0	0	0	0	0	53	130	0	200	44	687	543
Airplane Parts.	876	0	0	0	0	0	193	14	6	64	14	436	149
Medical....	1,138	0	0	0	22	0	6	120	0	50	28	228	684
Motor Transport	33,536	1,998	1,512	0	5,346	6,643	4,153	5,701	1,468	2,477	1,871	2,158	209
Vehicles......	29,081	1,930	1,287	0	4,440	6,473	3,826	4,906	1,252	1,754	1,367	1,671	175
Spare Parts...	4,455	68	225	0	906	170	327	795	216	723	504	487	34
Ordnance...	11,398	0	0	0	91	30	784	18	364	1,044	496	3,571	5,000
Weapons.....	1,286	0	0	0	0	0	114	14	9	297	23	635	194
Ammunition..	8,725	0	0	0	91	30	625	3	347	461	469	2,129	4,570
Miscellaneous.	1,387	0	0	0	0	0	45	1	8	286	4	807	236
Petroleum..	14,927	2,404	1,970	728	15	1,500	0	1,931	9	195	837	4,929	409
Aviation......	5,562	1,155	0	0	0	1,500	0	1,931	9	0	5	553	409
Motor Transport......	9,365	1,249	1,970	728	15	0	0	0	0	195	832	4,376	0
Road Building.......	19,365	0	1,410	1,605	2,496	665	2,125	1,351	2,543	2,801	2,938	1,078	353
Materials.....	12,593	0	1,410	1,605	1,461	615	919	996	1,967	1,547	1,550	523	0
Machinery....	1,398	0	0	0	40	0	570	21	53	199	0	191	324
Tools and Equipment.....	5,374	0	0	0	995	50	636	334	523	1,055	1,388	364	29
Signal......	651	0	0	0	0	0	105	21	106	281	3	135	0
Textiles....	2,613	25	20	7	47	58	577	614	845	420	0	0	0

[a] Loss of Burma prevented delivery of some of this tonnage.

Source: Memo, 1st Lt William S. Brewster for Lt Col Lucien C. Strong, 20 May 42. AG(AMMISCA) 319.1.

CHAPTER II

War Creates a China Theater and a U.S. Task Force to China

When the Japanese attacked Pearl Harbor on 7 December 1941, the Republic of China, the British Commonwealth of Nations, the Netherlands Indies, and the United States found themselves allies at war with Japan. To make their joint effort effective called for co-operation and mutual assistance in the highest sense. The United States had engaged in strategic planning with the British and Dutch and some arrangements for co-operation with them in the event of war had been made. There had been nothing like that with the Chinese, and, as has been noted, General Magruder, Chief of the American Military Mission to China, was ordered by the War Department not to engage in staff talks with them. The United States, however, was committed to equip a modern Chinese Army and Air Force. Logic suggested that the next step was to reach a satisfactory working relationship with the Chinese and to develop an understanding on what the Chinese would do with the lend-lease they received. For their part, the Chinese were actively interested in taking the role of a great power beside their new-found allies.

On 8 December 1941 the Generalissimo made the first of a series of proposals to create an over-all plan for the conduct of war in the Pacific and, assuming an early entrance of Russia into the war against Japan, to make an alliance of the United States, the Soviet Union, the Republic of China, and the British Commonwealth. He convoked a meeting of General Magruder; the British Envoy, Sir Archibald Kerr Clark Kerr; the British Military Attaché, General Dennys; China's Minister of Defense, Gen. Ho Ying-chin; and a senior Foreign Ministry officer, Dr. Quo Tai-shi. Madame Chiang was also present.[1] At this 10 December meeting the Generalissimo presented his pro-

---

[1] Madame Chiang, sister of Mr. T. V. Soong, had spent many years in the United States. After being privately tutored in Macon, Ga., Madame Chiang entered Wellesley College, from which she graduated with honors. As the Generalissimo's wife, she entered actively into public life, both in China and on the world stage. In China, she held many governmental posts, among them that of secretary-general of the Chinese Commission on Aeronautical Affairs and that of chairman of the Women's Advisory Council of the New Life Movement. During the war she became a patroness of the International Red Cross and in the United States was honorary chairman of United China Relief. Madame Chiang received many awards from philanthropic societies in the United States for her charitable work in China.

posals for Allied unity and a four-power pact. The Generalissimo suggested:

1. The United States should propose a comprehensive plan for joint war action for America, Britain, China, Netherlands East Indies, and Russia.
2. Immediately and before Russia participates in the [Pacific] war, the United States should take the leadership in initiating a comprehensive plan for action of the United States, Britain, Netherlands East Indies, and China in the western Pacific.
3. The locale for joint working out of details of the ABCD Plan should be Chungking.
4. There should result a military pact among the ABCDR for mutual assistance.[2]

In representing the United States in discussions of these matters with the Generalissimo, Magruder was handicapped because his directive said nothing of what line he should take in the event of war. His solution was to draft a proposed directive over 10 and 11 December and to radio it to Washington for approval.[3] Until that approval came on 21 December, he acted in accordance with his own best judgment, which suggested to him that he impress on the Chinese the urgent necessity of China's taking vigorous action to contain as many Japanese troops as possible. Because of his connection with lend-lease, Magruder occupied a most important position in the eyes of his Allied colleagues, but his discretion was strictly limited by his prewar directives. The British representatives were principally interested in transfers from the Chinese lend-lease stockpile in Burma to strengthen the small, poorly equipped garrison of that vital area and in having the American Volunteer Group made part of Burma's air defense. Thus, there was little the British and American representatives in Chungking could do on their own authority with the Generalissimo's proposals.[4]

Notes from the Chinese Government carried the Generalissimo's plan to Moscow and Washington. The first Soviet reaction was not unfavorable, the only condition being that a joint plan for co-operation by the Great Powers must precede any declaration of war by the USSR against Japan. The Soviet military attaché told the Generalissimo that there must be such a plan already and that the Generalissimo was surely aware of it. Then a few days later a note from Marshal Stalin to the Generalissimo dismissed the project for the time being. China was assured that the Soviets would eventually fight Japan, but it was explained that the war against Germany had overriding priority and that preparation for war against Japan would take time.[5]

On the 15th came Roosevelt's reply, suggesting conferences at Chungking, Singapore, and Moscow to arrive at preliminary plans to pass on to Washing-

[2] Memo, Confs with Generalissimo, MacMorland, recorder, 8, 10 Dec 41. AMMISCA Folder 7.
[3] Rad AMMISCA 94, Magruder to AGWAR, 11 Dec 41. AMMISCA Radio File, Job–11.
[4] MacMorland Diary, 10, 16, 18 Dec 41.
[5] (1) Rad AMMISCA 95, Magruder to Marshall, 11 Dec 41; Rad, Stalin to Chiang, 12 Dec 41. Bk 1, OPD Exec 8. (2) Stalin's message was by no means the first indication that the Soviets would fight Japan. On 13 October 1941 the Soviet Union "suggested preliminary staff discussions for military action against Japan. This proposal was never acted upon by our government." Memo, Brig. Gen. Raymond E. Lee, Actg ACofS, G–2, WDGS, 12 Feb 42, sub: Int Estimate. Item 5, Bk V, Hopkins Papers.

ton by 20 December. The President expressed the hope that this might lead to a permanent organization.[6] Churchill and the British Chiefs of Staff were expected in Washington in late December to revise existing plans and prepare new ones; the President's deadline was obviously related to that. The Generalissimo responded by calling a conference to meet at Chungking on 17 December.[7]

The Chungking Conferences

The gathering did not convene in the way the Generalissimo intended, because the two senior Army officers who were to represent the British Commonwealth and the United States were unable to arrive on 17 December. General Wavell, the British delegate, was Commander-in-Chief, India, and from 12 December responsible for Burma as well as India. He was pressed for time in trying to organize his new command for defense against the Japanese, and so unable to attend. The American delegate, Maj. Gen. George H. Brett, an air officer, had been ordered to China to investigate the possibility of basing heavy bombers there, and the War Department took advantage of this circumstance to make him its representative.[8] He was then in Burma.

Magruder feared to betray the conference by references in a radio, and so Brett did not know why he was so urgently wanted in Chungking. Realizing the strategic importance of Burma, Brett devoted himself to trying to solve the problem created by the presence of Chinese stockpiles adjacent to defenders badly in need of arms. Brett suggested that they be transferred to the British, urging Magruder to go to Rangoon, even as Magruder was urging Brett to fly to Chungking.[9]

So the Generalissimo's 17 December conference saw only the formal presentation of the Generalissimo's plan for Allied unity in the Far East, a plan which provided for an Allied general staff at Chungking. Magruder and his British colleagues approved in principle but could do nothing more pending the arrival of Generals Wavell and Brett for the postponed major conference.[10] There the question of providing central direction for the Allied war in the Pacific rested until the conferences of 22 and 23 December.

Simultaneously with Chinese efforts to make of the United States, Great Britain, China, and the Netherlands Indies (for that portion of the Dutch possessions was taking vigorous naval action in support of Britain and America) a real coalition in which they would share on equal terms, there were in Chungking discussions on offensive action by the Chinese armies, the

[6] Rad, Roosevelt to Chiang, 14 Dec 41. Item 8, Conf File, Dec 41, CT 23, Dr 2, KCRC. The message arrived in Chungking on 15 December 1941.
[7] Memo, Conf with Generalissimo, MacMorland, recorder, 16 Dec 41. AMMISCA Folder 7.
[8] Rad, Consul Gen, Cairo, to Consul Gen, Chungking, 12 Dec 41. Conf File, Dec 41, CT 23, Dr 2, KCRC.
[9] MacMorland Diary, 17, 18, 20 Dec 41.
[10] (1) Memo cited n. 7. (2) Memo, Conf with Generalissimo, MacMorland, recorder, 17 Dec 41. AMMISCA Folder 7.

use of the AVG in Burma, lend-lease transfers, and the reinforcement of Burma by the Chinese. Hong Kong was now under heavy Japanese attack, and both AMMISCA and the War Department believed that the Japanese attacks on Allied Far Eastern territory were made by troops drawn from China. To repeated representations, including some very frank remarks by Magruder to General Yu, head of China's ordnance establishment, the Chinese made no concrete response. The impression of AMMISCA's chief of staff was that the Chinese would shun offensive action, wait until their allies had won the war, and then use their jealously husbanded supplies for the solution of the Communist problem.[11]

In response to suggestions from Dennys that the Chinese do something to relieve the pressure on Hong Kong, the Chinese said that they intended to use seven armies in the relief, with small-scale activities by 17 December and effective operations by the end of the month. Instead of holding its mainland positions for thirty days as Dennys promised, the Hong Kong garrison was forced from them in three.[12] Indiscreetly, the British told the Chinese Minister of War that they planned to employ two bomber squadrons in China if the Commander-in-Chief, Singapore, could spare them.[13] Asked later if he could relieve Hong Kong without support from these twenty-four aircraft, General Ho seized on the remark to say his troops could at least distract the Japanese. On or about the 22d the Chinese felt that a Japanese threat to Changsha forced them to abandon their operations in support of Hong Kong.[14] Hong Kong fell on Christmas Day. (For Japanese plans in China see Map 2.)

The Chinese were generous with the AVG, which was a part of their Air Force. Initially, they agreed to put part of it in Burma; the air warning net there was known to be poor. When, in the early days of the Pacific war, Allied aircraft were destroyed on the ground at Pearl Harbor and at Clark Field in the Philippines, the Chinese were disturbed and changed their minds, saying that Colonel Chennault (Chinese Air Force) had decided the inadequate net would force him to withdraw from Burma to Yunnan. Dennys observed that Chennault had probably been spoiled by the excellent warning net in China, that the ample warning given there could hardly be expected in Burma. To this the Generalissimo retorted that he did not want his aircraft destroyed on the ground. Despite his apprehensions he finally committed the AVG to the defense of Burma and kept it there throughout the First Burma Campaign.[15]

The questions of Chinese reinforcements and lend-lease transfers for Burma reached the crisis point on 23 and 25 December. Each was some weeks in developing. From the day the war began the Chinese offered to send a large

[11] MacMorland Diary, 16, 18 Dec 41.
[12] Rad, AMMISCA to MILAD, Washington, 14 Dec 41. Int Summary 2, AMMISCA Folder 7.
[13] (1) Memo, Conf with Chinese Minister of War, Gen Ho, MacMorland, recorder, 16 Dec 41. AMMISCA Folder 7. (2) MacMorland Diary, 13, 14 Dec 41.
[14] Rad, AMMISCA to MILAD, 22 Dec 41. Int Summary 9, AMMISCA Folder 7.
[15] (1) AMMISCA War Diary, Ser 37, 14 Dec 41. AMMISCA Folder 2. (2) Memos cited n. 10(2) and n. 13(1).

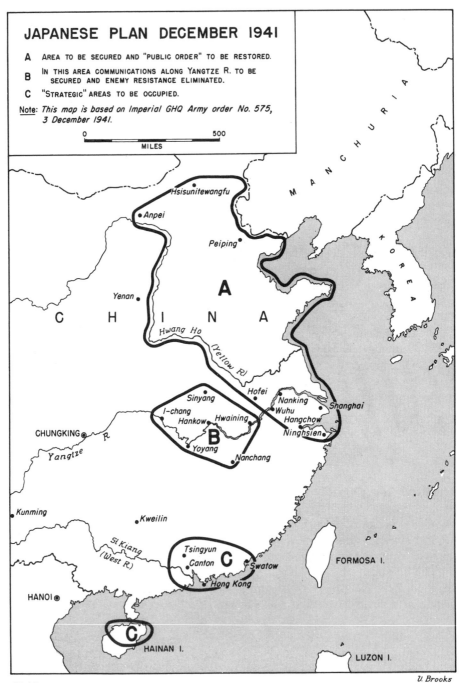

JAPANESE PLAN DECEMBER 1941

A AREA TO BE SECURED AND "PUBLIC ORDER" TO BE RESTORED.

B IN THIS AREA COMMUNICATIONS ALONG YANGTZE R. TO BE
SECURED AND ENEMY RESISTANCE ELIMINATED.

C "STRATEGIC" AREAS TO BE OCCUPIED.

<u>Note</u>: *This map is based on Imperial GHQ Army order No. 575,
3 December 1941.*

0   500
MILES

U. Brooks

MAP 2

number of troops to share in Burma's defense. However, they insisted that the troops enter en masse, that they occupy a definite sector, and that they operate under a comprehensive plan. The Generalissimo explicitly and forcefully objected to any piecemeal commitment of his troops. To these Chinese offers Dennys always replied that the rice supply would permit accommodating only one regiment or, at most, two.[16]

There the matter stood when on 22 December Generals Wavell and Brett finally arrived in Chungking to talk with China's leaders, with the British Ambassador, and with Magruder. Brett's orders, as he received them on his arrival, were to encourage the conferees to take every advantage of Japan's "present over-extension" (an echo of the prewar underestimate of Japanese capabilities) and to put maximum pressure on every part of the Japanese front. He was to assure the others that the United States would do its part, was taking prompt measures to reinforce the Philippines by air, and was determined to insure their successful defense.[17]

Wavell, like Dennys, Magruder, and the War Department, thought the Japanese overextended. He was not alarmed by the evidence of Japanese activity reported by Burma Army headquarters. But if worst came to worst and Burma was invaded, Wavell, as of 23 December, expected it to be reinforced by the British 18th Division, the 17th Indian Division, and two East African brigades. There were also diplomatic considerations in his mind. He wrote later that it was desirable for Burma to be defended by imperial troops rather than foreign.[18] Moreover, the Sino-Burmese boundary was in dispute, and Chinese claims went far into north Burma.[19] While in Burma Brett had observed Chinese methods of operating the line of communications from Rangoon northward and had received a very bad impression of Chinese ability and integrity, an impression he believed Wavell shared.[20]

Therefore, when the Generalissimo repeated his earlier offers by stating his willingness to send the Chinese 5th and 6th Armies to the defense of Burma, Wavell replied that he needed one AVG squadron, supplies of various sorts from the Chinese lend-lease stockpiles in Burma, but of troops only the whole of the Chinese 93d Division, if it could be supplied from China, and a regiment of the Chinese 49th Division to be kept in reserve just across the border. To Wavell this was a "qualified acceptance" of the Chinese offer to send troops, but the qualifications were precisely those to which the Chinese had earlier

---

[16](1) Memo, Confs with Generalissimo, 8, 15 Dec 41. AMMISCA Folder 7. (2) Memo cited n. 13(1). (3) MacMorland Diary, 15 Dec 41. The British Ambassador was present at the 15 December conference.

[17] Rad WAR 71, Marshall to Brett, 15 Dec 41. AG 381 (11–27–41).

[18](1) Wavell candidly owns to a miscalculation. *Despatch by the Supreme Commander of the ABDA Area to the Combined Chiefs of Staff in the South-West Pacific: 15 January 1942 to 25 February 1942* (London, 1948). (2) Gen. Sir Archibald P. Wavell, "Operations in Burma from 15th December, 1941, to 20th May, 1942," *Supplement to The London Gazette*, March 11, 1948, par. 5.

[19](1) End-paper map, *China's Destiny*, by Generalissimo Chiang Kai-shek (New York, 1947). (2) Brig. Gen. [Dr.] Ho Yung-chi, *The Big Circle* (New York, 1948), pp. 89–90, 130–32.

[20] Ltr, Brett to Sunderland, 10 Mar 50. HIS 330.14 CBI 1950.

objected.[21] Brett and Magruder each reported to the War Department that Wavell had refused the Chinese offer. Magruder thought Wavell's refusal inconsistent with the picture of Burma's defenseless state, presented to justify requests for the transfer of China's lend-lease. The Chinese thought it a refusal and were bitterly angry.[22]

Complying with Mr. Roosevelt's suggestions of 15 December, the Chungking Conference on 23 December created a permanent group to act as the local war council. Its members were: Dennys (Wavell's nominee); Ho (the Generalissimo's); and Magruder (ex officio). Having set up its part of the machinery, the meeting then launched into a long discussion of the plan to be sent to Washington. The thread of discussion was frequently broken as various of the conferees began on topics that were important but irrelevant. Madame Chiang entered freely into the exchange, stressing China's need for help. The session ended with a decision to send Roosevelt some proposals phrased by Brett, but the Generalissimo indicated his dissatisfaction by saying that he would forward a plan of his own.[23]

The Generalissimo's proposals were the first Chinese plans to evict the Japanese ever laid before China's allies. They may never have reached Washington either through Chinese or American channels though copies were given to the conferees. The Generalissimo proposed that the Allies, including the Soviet Union, make their main effort in Asia with the aim of defeating the Japanese in 1942. The first step, said the Chinese, was to rush air and naval reinforcements to hold Allied positions in the South Pacific. That done, the Allies should concentrate on gaining the mastery of the air. Air power was to be placed in Alaska, the Maritime Provinces, and China's coastal provinces. Japan would be blockaded. Then, when the Japanese armies in China were

---

[21] (1) Memo, Conf with Generalissimo, 23 Dec 41. AMMISCA Folder 7. (2) Wavell Despatch, December 15, 1941, to May 20, 1942, *Supplement to The London Gazette,* par 11. (3) MacMorland Diary, 23 Dec 41. (4) Rad DBA/10, CCS to Wavell, 5 Feb 42. War Office Folder, Earliest Messages to and from General Wavell and other Commanders in the ABDA [American-British-Dutch-Australian] Area, January–February–March 1942, A48–179. (Hereafter, Earliest Messages Folder, A48–179.)

[22] Rad AMMISCA 124, Magruder to President, 25 Dec 41; Rad, Brett to AGWAR, 27 Dec 41. History of CBI, Sec. III, App. III, Item 1, Tab D.

[23] The six points of General Brett's plan were:

"1. As a first essential to secure against enemy attack Rangoon and Burma, both of which are vital for China's continued resistance and any extension of joint action from China. Meanwhile to take offensive air action against Japanese bases and installations to the greatest extent that resources permit.

"2. Maintain China's resistance by continued supplies of matériel to enable Chinese armies to prepare and train for the ultimate offensive against Japan.

"3. Meanwhile the Chinese armies should continue to occupy the Japanese forces on their front by attacks or threats of attacks and by action against their vulnerable lines of communication.

"4. As soon as resources permit, to pass to an offensive against Japan with all forces available, Chinese, British, and American.

"5. This Joint Military Council sitting in Chungking will meet and submit information and proposals to enable the Allied Supreme War Council to work out strategy for East Asia.

"6. Hope is expressed that a permanent organization to be set up in the United States will soon materialize."

Memo cited n. 21(1).

isolated, the Chinese would move to crush them. If the Japanese were to seize the great area between Singapore, Rangoon, and Manila, then the Allies should prepare a pincers attack from north Burma and the Australian area.[24]

The plan included no discussion of command, of supply problems, or of what each partner would offer. It proposed that the Chinese armies move only after Japan had been successfully isolated from the mainland by the efforts of China's allies. The great weaknesses of the plan lay in its casual dismissal of Germany and its complete failure to realize that massive air power could not be sustained in China at the end of the inefficient and congested Burma Road. Had every ton over the Burma Road, at its December performance, gone to the air force, only eight squadrons of B–17's could have been supported in China, and those without fighter support.[25] Appraising the Chungking Conference a few weeks later, the War Department concluded that "very little, in a way of concrete results" was achieved.[26] The Generalissimo's announced willingness to let the British share in lend-lease stockpiles and to let the AVG stay in Burma was a slender counterweight to the animosity Wavell aroused.[27]

The Tulsa Incident

Almost immediately afterward Sino-British relations were strained still more by the incident of the ship *Tulsa* and her cargo of valuable munitions at Rangoon. The British forces in Burma, guarding the last line of communication between China and the outside world, were badly in need of equipment. Space-time factors suggested the Chinese lend-lease stockpiles as the logical means of adding to the defenses of an area in whose safety China was so vitally interested. The War Department was sympathetic to the suggestion that lend-lease be transferred to Burma's garrison, because now it fully appreciated the importance of Burma and feared an emergency might soon develop there. Accordingly, Magruder was asked to persuade the Chinese to the most strategic use of the matériel. This was the central point, for the Chinese acquired title to lend-lease goods as they left the United States and so there could be no transfer without their consent. Therefore, on 16 December Magruder received War Department permission to transfer Chinese lend-lease to the British, if the Chinese consented, with orders to report any such transaction later to the War Department.[28]

The responsible American officer at Rangoon, Lt. Col. Joseph J. Twitty,

[24] Proposal, The General Scheme for the Associated Operation of United States, Great Britain, Union of Socialist Soviet Republics of Russia, Netherlands, and China. Item 39, Conf File, Dec 41, CT 23, Dr 2, KCRC. The Generalissimo's comments on the proposal are in the memorandum cited note 21(1).

[25] A B–17 squadron required 1,000 tons a month. Memo, Col Clayton L. Bissell for Lt Gen Henry H. Arnold, CG AAF, 20 Feb 42. AG (AIR) 381 China.

[26] *Aide-Mémoire,* Notes on China, Brig Gen Dwight D. Eisenhower, WPD, for Lt Gen Hugh A. Drum, 2 Jan 42. History of CBI, Sec. III, App. III, Item 2.

[27] For an expression of the ill will, see Rad cited n. 21(4).

[28] Rad, Gerow to Magruder, 14 Dec 41. AG 400.3295 (4–14–41) Sec 1A. Magruder received this message on 16 December 1941.

was aware that the momentarily expected Japanese bombing of Rangoon might destroy the docks and warehouses and with them most of the accumulated lend-lease supplies. The ships in the harbor, among them the *Tulsa,* were extremely vulnerable, and the stevedores were deserting. Colonel Twitty was also under heavy pressure from the Governor-General of Burma, Sir Reginald Hugh Dorman-Smith, and from General Brett, then in Burma en route to China. Sir Reginald hinted at confiscation of the stocks in order to get the equipment which Burma's defenders so badly needed, while Brett told Twitty that American heavy bombers might be in Burma in thirty days and strongly recommended (though he never ordered) that Twitty safeguard the U.S. interest in this matter.[29]

Communications with Chungking were very bad; therefore, Twitty turned to the War Department for guidance, telling AMMISCA of his step on 16 December. Washington replied that Magruder had authority to act and would guide Twitty. Colonel Twitty once again turned to General Magruder and, while he was waiting for an answer, very strong hints came from sources close to the Governor-General of Burma that the stocks were about to be confiscated. Twitty, therefore, formally asked the Government of Burma on 19 December to impound and safeguard all lend-lease stocks until their ultimate use could be decided. Of these, the *Tulsa*'s cargo was the most valuable, and so the whole affair became known as the *Tulsa* incident.[30]

Colonel Twitty then broke the news to Gen. Yu Fei-peng, the Generalissimo's cousin and the senior Chinese representative in Burma. Yu appeared reassured by Twitty's statement that this was emphatically not a confiscation but merely an impounding until a decision could be reached on emergency use. Indeed, far from seeming angered, Yu suggested that a committee of experts from the three powers be set up to decide on the best division of the stocks; Twitty agreed at once. Brett reported the impounding to AMMISCA in Chungking, saying that he had suggested it and that the whole situation waited on Magruder's arrival at Rangoon. This message reached Magruder on 21 December. At first Magruder thought of flying to Rangoon, but when he found no aircraft available he sent a radio to Twitty saying that the lend-lease material could neither be impounded nor transferred without the consent of both the Chinese and the War Department. Magruder's intention was to settle the matter at the forthcoming 23 December conference.[31] Magruder's order was not received in Rangoon until the 23d.

[29] Ltr, Twitty to Magruder, 16 Dec 41, sub: Conf with Gov-Gen; Field Msg 10, Twitty to SW, 12 Dec 41. Items 20, 23, Port of Rangoon Folder, CT 42, Dr 4, KCRC.
[30] Rad, WAR to Rangoon, 17 Dec 41; Memo, sub: Record of Events at Rangoon, 7–31 Dec 41. Items 24, 43, Port of Rangoon Folder, CT 42, Dr 4, KCRC.
[31](1) Rad, Brett to Arnold and Magruder, 19 Dec 41; Rpt, Maj John E. Russell, AMMISCA's Rangoon Off, to Twitty, 19 Dec 41, sub: Rpt of Conf Held With Gen Yu This Morning; Paraphrase of Msg, U.S. Embassy, Chungking, to U.S. Consulate, Rangoon, 21 Dec 41; Memo for Record by Magruder, 21 Dec 41, sub: Notes on Retransfer of Lend-Lease Matériel to British in Burma, Items 30, 29, 38, 17, Port of Rangoon Folder, CT 42, Dr 4, KCRC. (2) Memo, Hq 204 Mission for AMMISCA, recd 16 Dec 41. Conf Files, Dec 41, CT 23, Dr 2, KCRC.

Meanwhile, the Rangoon committee formed at Yu's suggestion began its work, examining the stocks and deciding what could be released for immediate shipment to China and what should be kept for possible future use in Burma. In the course of these efforts the committee released far more supplies to the Chinese than could possibly be trucked up the road in the near future. There was one unfortunate incident when, on 20 December, a group of British soldiers seized 150 trucks from a Chinese Government agency without reference to the committee, but this seemed to be smoothed over with apologies to General Yu and promises from Brett and Twitty that the committee's prerogatives would be respected.[32]

During his visit to Chungking for the 23 December conference, Brett discussed the lend-lease transfers with Magruder, as Magruder promptly told Twitty by letter. They must have discussed it in the light of General Yu's apparent acquiescence in the procedure and the Generalissimo's willingness to share with the British. They "agreed that it is a matter for the British and Chinese to settle in conference here [Chungking]."[33] The phrase suggests a hope that the *fait accompli* of Rangoon would be accepted in Chungking, if the British saved Chinese face by presenting a detailed list of their needs even as those were being met in Rangoon. There seems to have been no discussion with the Chinese of the fact that the stocks actually had been impounded.

On Christmas Day the Joint Military Council of Dennys, Ho, and Magruder met at the Bureau of Foreign Affairs to pass on the requests for lend-lease transfers that had been made by British representatives in Chungking. General Ho began the meeting amiably enough by saying the Generalissimo had agreed to release twenty machine guns for the defense of Burma. Then Ho stunned Magruder and Dennys by reading a telegram from General Yu which accused the British of seizing China's lend-lease stocks with Twitty's connivance. He further charged that Twitty had rejected Yu's protest on the ground that the seizure was in line with U.S. policy. Therefore, Ho continued, the Generalissimo had decided that the seizure of the *Tulsa*'s cargo was an unfriendly act and that all lend-lease at Rangoon should be given to the British or returned to the Americans. All Chinese military personnel would return to China and co-operation between Britain and China would cease, because it was impossible for them to fight Japan side by side.[34] The Chinese obviously assumed that American lend-lease was a proper subject of contention between themselves and the British Commonwealth.

[32] Memo, R. C. Chen, Secy, Rangoon Com, 20 Dec 41, sub: Memo of First Mtg of Com for Survey of Chinese Govt Supplies in Burma; Incl to Ltr, R. C. Chen, Officiating Mgr, Southwest Transportation Co., Rangoon, to Twitty, 21 Dec 41; Min, Second Mtg of Com for Survey of Chinese Govt Supplies in Burma, 22 Dec 41. Items 32, 33, 35, Port of Rangoon Folder, CT 42, Dr 4, KCRC.
[33] Ltr, Magruder to Twitty, 23 Dec 41. Item 18, Port of Rangoon Folder, CT 42, Dr 4, KCRC.
[34] (1) Memo, Gluckman for Magruder, 25 Dec 41, sub: Rpt on Conf Held 25 Dec. Item 19, Port of Rangoon Folder, CT 42, Dr 4, KCRC. (2) MacMorland Diary, 26 Dec 41, 20 Jan 42. (3) Aldrich Diary, 26 Dec 41. Aldrich was told that the Generalissimo had refused to see the British Ambassador.

Magruder and Dennys made conciliatory replies, and Ho agreed to arrange an audience with the Generalissimo for Magruder. Because of Yu's telegram, Chinese anger was directed toward the British though the latter had been acting on Twitty's request. Magruder, at least, among the conferees had been informed that all the while Yu was amicably joining in the division of the lend-lease stocks. Yu's motives for sending the telegrams are unknown. It is possible that the seizure of the 150 trucks led him to repay in kind what he took to be bad faith; equally possible, that he was moved to act by the prospect of losing control of the immensely profitable traffic in lend-lease.[35]

Magruder found the Generalissimo in a friendly mood on 26 December. Remarking that he had already approved the initial British list of requests, he accepted Magruder's politic assurances and agreed that AMMISCA might send an officer to Rangoon to regularize the transaction. Very considerable amounts of lend-lease were afterward transferred to the British in Burma, but at Chinese insistence Colonel Twitty was relieved of his post and succeeded by Lt. Col. Adrian St. John. The War Department approved Magruder's conduct of the affair and warned St. John against any transfers not approved by the Chinese.[36]

In Washington, Hopkins called the matter to the attention of British authority on the cabinet level. The explanation that was returned was accepted, Hopkins being satisfied, apparently, with indicating White House interest where the Chinese were involved. The Rangoon committee survived Yu's telegrams and continued its work into 1942. The incident later caused several changes in lend-lease procedure, intended to eliminate the possibility of such disputes in the future.[37]

---

[35](1) Ltr cited n. 33. (2) Concerning Chinese corruption in the handling of lend-lease, Mr. Roosevelt was told:

"On the issue of whether or not any of the 'goods and munitions purchased for China never gets to China—but not for military reasons' our check to date indicates that (a) Some of the goods presumably destined for the Chinese Government are in fact purchased for private account through various corporations in the United States. These goods, upon arrival on the Burma Road, were picked up by the private individuals or firms for whom they were really destined; (b) There is some evidence of minor pilfering on the Burma Road with the resultant effect that some of the goods have been put to private rather than military use; (c) After December 7th, some pilfering has taken place at the docks at Rangoon because the material was not adequately guarded; (d) By far the major part of the goods which did not get put to military use was either destroyed or lost at Rangoon or on the Southern part of the Burma Road by reason of conditions prevailing after December 7th and the inefficiency of the port, customs, and military officials in Burma."

Ltr, Thomas B. McCabe to President, 13 May 42. Bk V, Hopkins Papers.

[36](1) Rad AMMISCA 129, Magruder to Stimson, 28 Dec 41. AG 400.3295 (4–14–41) Sec 1A. (2) Memo, Conf with Generalissimo, 26 Dec 41. AMMISCA Folder 7. (3) Rad, WD to St. John, 30 Dec 41. AG 381 (11–27–41) Sec 1A. (4) Rad AMMISCA 158, Magruder to Stimson, 4 Jan 42; Rad, Stimson to St. John, 10 Jan 42. Items 205, 575, Msg File 5, A47–136.

[37](1) Ltr, Lord Beaverbrook, Minister of Supply, to Hopkins, 31 Dec 41; Ltr, Hopkins to Beaverbrook, 1 Jan 42. Hopkins Papers. (2) "General Magruder trying hard to have Rangoon board of three given enough authority to settle allocations on the spot and avoid misunderstandings that arise due to distance and slowness of communications," wrote Aldrich in his diary on 2 January 1942. (3) Memo, Col Henry S. Aurand, Def Aid Dir, for Edward L. Stettinius, Jr., Office, Lend-Lease Administration, 15 Dec 41. AG (AMMISCA) 400.3295.

The Creation of an Allied China Theater

Immediately after the outbreak of war, Churchill and Roosevelt agreed it was necessary to examine strategy and policy anew in the awful light cast by the now world-wide conflagration. The ARCADIA Conference of the two statesmen and their service advisers convened in Washington on 22 December. There they formed a committee of the British and American Chiefs of Staff, henceforth to be called the Combined Chiefs of Staff, or CCS, to advise them on the conduct of the war.

A rapid survey of the situation when the conference convened would have revealed a scene whose externals were discouraging but which included the three greatest of the Great Powers, the United States of America, the British Commonwealth, and the Soviet Union, allied at last, a tremendous concentration of force, actual and potential. In the Pacific, the surprise Japanese blow at Pearl Harbor left 2 battleships sunk and beyond salvage, 2 more resting on the bottom but salvable, 3 more badly damaged, and the last of the 8 lightly so. It would be some months before the Pacific Fleet could intervene in force. In Asia, Japanese land operations were under way at Hong Kong, in the Philippines, and in Malaya. Two British capital ships were lost off Malaya. The Japanese were advancing steadily and smoothly.

In the Mediterranean, since 18 November 1941 the British Eighth Army under Gen. Sir Claude J. E. Auchinleck had been attacking the German and Italian forces in an attempt to retake Cyrenaica, lost at the time of Greece and Crete, and if possible drive on to Tripoli. The battle was hard and well fought by both sides, but at length the Eighth Army had moved forward deep into Cyrenaica, unfortunately without cutting off any considerable body of the enemy. Though defeated, the German and Italian forces were intact.

The Russian armies had surprised both friend and foe. Since 22 June 1941 they had lost great stretches of territory and suffered heavy casualties, but no German victory was decisive. On 4 December 1941 the Germans launched one last attack in a desperate effort to reach Moscow. It failed, and Hitler was now left to face the Russian winter, for which he had not prepared his armies. The German armies in late December were at the gates of Leningrad; they had recoiled at Moscow, but lay within sixty miles of it; and in the south the Russians had driven them from Rostov and forced a retreat of some forty miles.

Among the pressing problems created by the war was that of China, and considerable attention was given to it. The ARCADIA conferees had begun to apply the principle of unified Allied command and set up such a headquarters under General Wavell for the area of Southeast Asia. Mr. Roosevelt's concern for China was shown at a White House conference on 28 December with the American delegates to ARCADIA. There he ordered that something be done to establish a committee in Chungking to help the Generalissimo's morale. The President's first proposals for a grand council in Washington had yielded

to the more compact and workable CCS, but he still liked the idea of a subordinate council in Chungking. The establishment of Wavell's headquarters,
ABDACOM (American-British-Dutch-Australian Command), had left one
area in the Far East not included in the scheme of unified command. This was
China, for it was agreed that the Chinese would never consent to any portion
of their country being placed under foreign command.[38]

Therefore, on 29 December the CCS suggested the creation of a China
Theater under the Generalissimo, to include also northeast Burma and such
parts of Thailand and Indochina as might be occupied by what were now
called the United Nations. Northeast Burma was deleted, but the announcement of the Generalissimo's theater, over which he would preside as Supreme
(Allied) Commander, assisted by an Allied staff, was made on the 29th, coinci-
dentally with that of General Wavell's appointment to his difficult post. The
Generalissimo as Supreme Commander, China Theater, was in no way subordinate to the Combined Chiefs of Staff, nor was any portion of China's
territory then or ever under the jurisdiction of any other officer of the United
Nations. Though an Allied commander, the Generalissimo was responsible
only to himself, which made him unique among those who afterward held
similar posts.

Burma was placed under Wavell's command rather than that of General
Headquarters (India) and India Command, its natural base, because Churchill
thought it well to give the impression that Wavell was stretching out his hand
to help the Generalissimo. Roosevelt agreed, saying it was particularly important to restore the Generalissimo to a good frame of mind. He added bluntly
that Generals Wavell and Brett had made a very poor impression at Chungking, partly because of the coincident requisitioning of Chinese lend-lease at
Rangoon and partly because Wavell had refused the Chinese offer to reinforce
Burma. The President displayed great concern over the Chinese attitude and
suggested to Churchill that Wavell be ordered to go out of his way to placate
the Generalissimo and bring him to a more co-operative mood.[39] Behind
Roosevelt's expressions of concern over the Generalissimo lay his policy
toward China, which his Army Chief of Staff defined after the war as "to treat
China as a Great Power."[40] Asking the Generalissimo to accept the post of

[38] Sherwood, *Roosevelt and Hopkins,* p. 458.

[39] (1) Memo, Conf at White House, 28 Dec 41, 1145, Folder, Notes on Informal Conferences
Held during Visit of British Chiefs of Staff to Washington; Notes taken by British Secretariat,
Washington War Conf, Record of a Meeting Held at the White House on Thursday, 1st January
1942 at 6:30 P. M. WDCSA 334, A45–466. (2) Sherwood, *Roosevelt and Hopkins,* pp. 445, 458.
(3) Rad, SN to Naval Attaché, Chungking, 31 Dec 41. Item 46, Conf File, Dec 41, CT 23, Dr 2,
KCRC. Transfer of communications facilities from a Yangtze gunboat to a station at Chungking
afforded the U.S. Navy an excellent contact with Washington. The Generalissimo was notified of
his Allied role through this channel much to the embarrassment of AMMISCA, which did not
include Navy personnel. Throughout the history of the U.S. theater of operations in China,
Burma, and India the Navy channel on certain occasions was a source of concern to Headquarters,
U.S. Army Forces, in Chungking.

[40] Asked in so many words, "What was the President's policy toward China? Did he ever
explain it to you?" General Marshall replied after some reflection that the policy was to treat
China as a great power. Interv with Gen Marshall, 6 Jul 49.

Supreme Commander, China Theater, so great in potential importance, the President added that to make his command effective it was believed a combined planning staff of British, Chinese, and American officers should be set up at once.[41]

The U.S. Role: A Second Mission or a Theater?

Prewar planning of proposals for strategic action by the United States in relation to China, should hostilities arise, had not progressed beyond the staff study phase. There were no comprehensive plans, like the RAINBOW series, setting forth in detail what the United States would propose to the Chinese and be prepared to attempt in company with them.[42] When on 2 January the officer tentatively selected by the War Department and approved by the President to go to China arrived in Washington, the question of that wartime relationship became immediate and pressing. The initial choice was Lt. Gen. Hugh A. Drum, suggested for the post by Stimson. General Drum was then the senior line officer in the United States Army and one of the very few with combat experience in general officer's rank.

As he left his First Army headquarters in New York, General Drum believed he was being summoned to Washington to receive a mission of transcendent importance—in Europe. From a conversation with Roosevelt in the summer of 1939, when the European situation was growing ever more ominous, he had received the impression that, should there be another war and should the United States be involved, Drum would command a new American expeditionary force to Europe. Drum's expectations and their subsequent disappointment were a factor in his reactions, for to his surprise he was offered a post in China.

The scene in the War Department as General Drum arrived was dominated by the effort to deploy inadequate American resources to best effect in meeting a number of grave dangers. The effort was being made by a small group of men in the Department who had to improvise and adjust under appalling pressures. The speed and weight of the Japanese drive in the Pacific were upsetting all prewar concepts. If, on the one hand the defense of Southeast Asia and Australasia was necessary, on the other, the long-run strategic advantages of making the principal U.S. effort in the Atlantic could not be overlooked.

---

[41] Rad cited n. 39(3). This message was prepared in the Office of the Secretary of War on 29 December. Hopkins, Stimson, Marshall, Col. De Witt Peck, USMC, Col. Thomas T. Handy, Comdr. Bertram J. Rodgers, USN, and Lt. Col. Willard G. Wyman, WPD, drafted the final memorandum for the President. WPD 4389–61.

[42] For a discussion of the RAINBOW plans, see Mark Skinner Watson, *Chief of Staff: Prewar Plans and Preparations,* UNITED STATES ARMY IN WORLD WAR II (Washington, 1950), pp. 103–04.

In response to these strategic necessities there were troop and aircraft movements toward the Southwest Pacific to succor Australia and New Zealand and defend the Malay Barrier. To seize the initiative in the main theater, the Atlantic, efforts were being made to prepare for the occupation of French North Africa (GYMNAST). Maj. Gen. Joseph W. Stilwell arrived in Washington on 25 December as U.S. commander-designate of GYMNAST.[43] To accomplish these two efforts would force the Army to scrape the bottom of the barrel of available resources. Moreover, the Anglo-American agreement that the Atlantic should be the main theater was now on record, and General Marshall was resolved that the U.S. effort should be concentrated in that area.[44]

The day he arrived in Washington, General Drum conferred with Secretary of War Stimson; with General Marshall; with Lt. Gen. Henry H. Arnold, who in fact if not in name commanded the air arm; with the Assistant Secretary of War, Mr. John J. McCloy; and with Brig. Gen. Dwight D. Eisenhower, Deputy Chief of the War Plans Division for the Pacific and Far East. From these discussions with General Drum it soon appeared that the War Department was not agreed within itself on what should be done for China, that some favored a mission with command responsibilities not accorded to Magruder's, while others contemplated an American theater of operations in China from which to operate against the mainland of Japan.

Stimson told General Drum that China was in bad shape and might accept a separate peace. On the other hand, it was the best theater and offered the best bases from which to operate against Japan. Difficulties over command problems had arisen because the Generalissimo, somewhat against his will, had been limited to China proper as his sphere of operations, and because the British had insisted that Chinese troops stay out of Burma. Stimson said that the British had no respect for Chinese fighting ability and had angered the Chinese by lend-lease diversions. He saw two great objectives: (1) to secure China as a base for early operations against Japan; (2) to keep China in the war. He went on to say that some strong U.S. officer was needed in China to handle the British; to bring them to a proper feeling about Chinese military forces, about Burma Road problems, and about the handling of lend-lease supplies destined for China. The Secretary, as a final consideration, gave as the main objective steps and plans to secure China as a main theater of operations. It was mentioned in passing that T. V. Soong had suggested that the presence in Chungking of a high-ranking officer would be beneficial, that he might command the Chinese Army, and that General Stilwell had been considered for the post but

---

[43] (1) In 1941–1942 *Malay Barrier* was the term commonly applied to the Malay Peninsula and the Netherlands Indies, which were viewed as protecting the Indian Ocean and Australasia against attack from the north. (2) Sherwood, *Roosevelt and Hopkins,* p. 460. (3) Joseph W. Stilwell, *The Stilwell Papers,* Theodore H. White, ed. (New York, 1948), p. 11.

[44] (1) Stimson and Bundy, *On Active Service,* pp. 415, 528. (2) Sherwood, *Roosevelt and Hopkins,* p. 445.

rejected, because it was feared that he would not have enough face with Chinese officials who would remember him as an attaché.[45]

General Drum next talked with General Marshall. Although Stimson had been talking in terms of a theater of operations, General Marshall seemed to think along the lines of a mission. Air power in China was the theme of much of Marshall's discourse. He saw Cairo and the supplies there as a base to support air power in China, though Drum would have to use great tact and diplomacy in getting the British to transfer lend-lease stores in the Middle East for use in China. After interviewing Marshall, Drum talked to Arnold, Eisenhower, and McCloy, each of whom gave him still another viewpoint, ranging from McCloy's description of a great Allied front stretching from Gibraltar to Canton, to Arnold's modest plans to operate a few air squadrons in China.[46]

The differing points of view given to Drum, particularly the wide gap between those of Stimson and Marshall—the former speaking again and again of a theater, the latter, of a mission and air power—made Drum feel that the War Department had not settled on what he was to do in China. His impression of divergent views in high places was confirmed by a War Department paper entitled Notes on China, which had been given to him by Eisenhower as he waited in Stimson's anteroom and which gave the War Departments' intentions as:

(1) To provide equipment to the Chinese Army to enable it to continue operations against the Japanese. This includes assistance in the maintenance of communications.

(2) Instigating Generalissimo Chiang Kai-shek to intensify Chinese effort and to restore the waning spirit of the Chinese in carrying on the conflict.

(3) To secure, maintain, and operate air bases for air operations against the Japanese.

(4) To organize various types of American units by enlistment in the American Army to carry on guerrilla warfare.[47]

Notes on China very closely paralleled a British staff study, Aid to China, British Policy in Support of China, which had been received by the War Department in September. The emphasis which Notes on China gave to guerrilla warfare as one of the principal U.S. activities in China was at complete odds with existing U.S. policy, i.e., the Thirty Division Program, and was quietly forgotten in a few weeks.[48]

[45] (1) A memorandum for the record prepared early in 1942 by General Drum, entitled The China Proposal, pp. 4–9. Drum Papers, Empire State Building, New York, N. Y. (See Bibliographical Note.) (2) Diary kept by Col. Charles E. Rayens, a member of the Drum party, entry of 9 January 1942. Drum Papers.

[46] (1) The China Proposal, pp. 9–14. Marshall's views of 2 Jan 42 on pp. 19–25. (2) Memo, Drum's conversation with Marshall, 2 Jan 42. History of CBI, Sec. III, App. III, Item 3.

[47] Aide-Mémoire, Notes on China, cited n. 26.

[48] (1) Aid to China, British Policy in Support of China, 5th September, 1941. AG (AMMISCA) 351. (2) At one time, Drum's role was seen as simply liaison with the Generalissimo and organizing Sino-American guerrilla units. It was so described in an undated memorandum to Roosevelt, signed by Stimson, which, since it is an original copy, presumably never left the Chief of Staff's office. The next paper in the file is dated 12 December 1941. Nothing on the Stimson letter suggests Roosevelt ever saw it. Memo, Stimson for President, WDCSA, Far East (1941–1942), A46–523.

There was a conflict between Stimson's theater and Marshall's mission views as thus presented. General Drum felt that this had to be resolved if he were to understand his task, and so, utilizing a staff hastily assembled for him, many of whom had had long experience in China, he prepared a memorandum whose acceptance or rejection would clarify the position of the War Department. After surveying the current situation in China, Burma, and India, Drum's paper characterized the objective of the proposed mission as "nebulous, uncertain, and indefinite." He felt that sending one more mission would be an empty gesture. Drum suggested instead that the government "decide on a policy and arrange the means" before sending him to China. Though he did not ask for troops or tonnage, Drum still felt that the officer sent should be able to hold out a fairly definite indication to the Chinese of what the United States would do. He suggested that first priority be given to improving the Burma Road and that the main effort in China should be toward building up a strong air force.[49]

General Drum at once discussed the memorandum with Stimson and General Eisenhower, who represented the War Plans Division. Then, Stimson, expressing his views, gave Marshall and Drum a note which confirmed the impressions that Drum had received in his interview with the Secretary. Stimson wrote that his talk with Drum had helped "to clarify some inchoate ideas which I already had about the China Theatre" and commented favorably on Drum's project for an offensive from Burma into Thailand.[50] General Drum considered the note as an approval of the views that he had stated, a feeling strengthened by an order from the Chief of Staff's office saying that Drum would be on an extended absence and would be allowed to retain his quarters on Governor's Island. He returned to New York on 5 January to arrange his domestic affairs and prepare for China duty.[51]

In Chungking, the Chinese had been weighing the nomination of the Generalissimo to be Supreme Commander of an Allied China Theater. They accepted about 5 January and asked that the President send a high-ranking U.S. officer to be chief of the Generalissimo's joint (or Allied) staff. The Chinese letter had an interesting provision: ". . . That this officer need not be an expert on the Far East; on the contrary, he [the Generalissimo] thinks that military men who have knowledge of Chinese armies when China was under war lords, operate at a disadvantage when they think of the present Chinese national armies in terms of the armies of the war lords." [52] Though in Drum's interview with Stimson he had been assured that his ignorance of the Chinese language would not handicap him, this suggestion from the Chinese—that ignorance of

[49] Memo, Drum for Stimson and Marshall, 5 Jan 42, sub: Mission to China. History of CBI, Sec. III, App. III, Item 1.
[50] Memo, Stimson for Marshall, 6 Jan 42. History of CBI, Sec. III, App. III, Item 11.
[51] The China Proposal, Exhibit Ia.
[52] Ltr, Soong to McCloy, 6 Jan 42. History of CBI, Sec. III, App. III, Item 17. In the early days of the war, the terms *joint, allied,* and *combined* were used interchangeably.

China's very recent military past would be an advantage—may have been disquieting to the War Department. Read in the light of AMMISCA radios, it suggested that the Chinese wanted a senior American officer in Chungking who would accept what he was told by the Chinese at face value and in effect be another Chinese envoy to the United States.[53]

While in New York, Drum learned that his orders were about to be discussed with the British. Desiring to be sure that his views were represented, since in certain areas he would serve under Wavell, Drum hastily returned to Washington. On arrival he spoke to Stimson. The two men were in accord about the desirability of a thrust across Thailand and Indochina to take the Hanoi-Haiphong area and open a supply line to China, but when the Secretary turned the conversation to the larger aspects of the war, he puzzled Drum. Some of Stimson's comments recalled the picture McCloy had painted of a vast Allied front from Gibraltar to Canton, and General Drum wondered why he was not told of such a project clearly and plainly. The Secretary did make clear that Drum was not to hurry to China but was to study conditions in the Middle East en route. On reflection, Drum was still further mystified by this comment and felt the interview did not make Stimson's wishes clear.[54]

General Drum returned to his office in the War Department and there learned that a draft of his instructions, prepared in the War Department, was being submitted to the British Joint Staff Mission for their comments. Drum believed that the precedent of Gen. John J. Pershing in World War I, whom the then Secretary of War, Newton D. Baker, had allowed to draft his own instructions, ought in some measure to apply to him in taking over such an important assignment, and so Drum hastily prepared another memorandum to Stimson and Marshall, expanding and clarifying his views. While this paper was being typed in final form, Eisenhower showed him a copy of the War Department draft. The title, Immediate Assistant [sic] to China, strengthened Drum's impression that a post comparable to that of the chief of a military mission was being prepared as the American answer to China's problems. Further examining the paper, General Drum took exception to the complete absence of Stimson's views. He also felt that the paper would place the officer sent to China in a poorly defined command relation to the Generalissimo and General Wavell.[55]

The Drum memorandum may be summarized in his own words as "a plan of operations, mainly American, from without China to within China for the purpose of securing adequate lines of supply by which to build up in China a

[53] Ltr, Wyman to Rayens, 21 Jan 42. Drum Papers. (2) On the letter, Soong to McCloy, 6 January 1942, Colonel Wyman penned this note: "This letter brought to the attention of General Drum, 23 January." History of CBI, Sec. III, App. III, Item 17.

[54](1) The China Proposal, pp. 47–49, 53–61. (2) Diary, 7 Jan 42, cited n. 45(2). Made just after the interview, this entry repeats Stimson's injunction that Drum should take his time.

[55](1) Memo for COS, 8 Jan 42, sub: Immediate Assistance to China. ABC 4 CS2, A48–224. General Drum's copy was headed Immediate Assistant to China. (2) The China Proposal, pp. 55, 56–61, 62–63.

theater with adequate bases, air and ground, from which to attack Japan. Every
indication and study convinced me that the first problem was to establish lines
of supply into China." For personnel, Drum recommended only that a general
program be drawn up as a basis for planning and negotiations with the British
and Chinese.[56] These concepts were markedly similar to the future development of the China–Burma–India Theater. At this time they did not meet with
General Marshall's approval.

The divergence between the theater concept, shared by Drum and Stimson,
and the mission concept, advocated by the War Plans Division and the Chief
of Staff, was now so apparent that General Drum considered he would have
to make an effort to resolve the conflict if he was to have a workable directive.
Therefore, he secured appointments with Marshall on 8 and 9 January.

In the first interview with General Marshall, at which General Eisenhower
was also present, General Drum pointed out the difference in viewpoint
between the various papers that had been circulated—the Notes on China
given him as he waited in Stimson's office, Stimson's approval of Drum's 5
January 1942 memorandum, and Immediate Assistant to China. His own
views, Drum remarked, followed those of the Secretary, which he thought
sound. He then "pointed out the inconsistency and impracticability of my
serving three masters—the War Department as U.S. representative in China,
under command of Chiang in China, and under Wavell both inside and outside
of China." [57]

General Marshall then stated his views. In explaining them, he defended
the proposed command organization under which the officer representing the
United States in China was to operate in accordance with Marshall's master
design of securing unity of Allied command in all theaters.[58] Marshall had
not used Drum's 8 January memorandum because he had no intention of sending large forces to China or making an effort (in the foreseeable future?) to
open supply lines to China. U.S. air units would be sent to China after more
pressing problems, mainly defense of the Malay Barrier, had been solved.
Marshall's immediate concern in China was to build up the American Volunteer Group. His main objective for China was to "arm, equip, and train
Chinese forces in China," and he wanted Drum to take with him some officers
who could act as commanders of Chinese army corps. When Drum objected
that the limited capacity of the Burma Road made such a project as rearming
Chinese forces impracticable, Marshall replied that "more of the equipping of
the Chinese forces could be done with resources within China proper." [59]

Drum believed such a project was impracticable, that resources within

---

[56](1) Memo and Annex 1, Drum for Stimson and Marshall, 8 Jan 42, sub: Strategic and
Operational Conception of U.S. Effort to Assist China. History of CBI, Sec. III, App. III, Item 12.
(2) The China Proposal, pp. 56–61.
[57] The China Proposal, pp. 63–66.
[58](1) *Ibid.* (2) Sherwood, *Roosevelt and Hopkins*, p. 455.
[59] The China Proposal, pp. 63–66.

China were too limited. He then raised the issue of what he could really hope to accomplish in China with the resources Marshall seemed willing to allot him. It was still obvious that the Marshall and Stimson views on what should be done for China were far apart. Drum stated that, if Marshall's approach were adopted, Drum would be involved in a minor effort with no possibility of tangible or decisive results.[60]

Feeling that the issue of a U.S. mission to China or a U.S. theater in China was still unsettled, General Drum saw General Marshall again on 9 January. Unfortunately, in this interview, the discussion drifted away from the attempt to settle the strategic question involved and became confused with the issue of whether the proposed post was suitable for a general officer of Drum's experience. When Marshall repeated that there would be no large U.S. forces for China but some aircraft and munitions if they could be transported, Drum remarked that this meant that he, as one of the three senior officers of the Army who had combat experience with major units, would be wasted in a minor post at a time of grave crisis. This General Marshall took as a lack of enthusiasm for the task. General Drum demurred, explaining that he would be happy to go if Stimson's views prevailed. Marshall concluded the interview by saying that large U.S. forces would not be sent to China, and therefore he must recommend against Drum's assignment.[61]

After his interview with Marshall, Drum was left in an embarrassing position because of divided counsels in the War Department. Though Drum was not aware of it at the time, his appointment had been approved by the President before Drum had been called to Washington and a staff had been assembled for him by the War Plans Division. The studies prepared by his staff had suggested an approach to the China problem that Mr. Stimson had approved. But this approval had not been enough to clarify the picture.

Although other officers called to Washington in those days to assume field command were also meeting divided counsels and administrative confusion, as General Stilwell so picturesquely set forth in his diaries,[62] it is not strange that General Drum felt that he, as one of the senior officers in the Army, was entitled to more consideration. Moreover, he believed that his views on China were shared by Stimson, the highest authority in the War Department.

On 10 January Drum restated his views and the outcome of his interviews with Marshall in another memorandum and again referred the matter to Stimson, saying that if Stimson's views prevailed, he would be happy to go but feared that he was about to be wasted in a minor post, far from the main effort. Then General Drum returned to New York, expecting an early reaction. When none was forthcoming, he sought and obtained an interview with Stimson on 13 January, in which Stimson agreed to read Drum's 10 January

---

[60] *Ibid.*
[61] The China Proposal, pp. 69–71.
[62] *The Stilwell Papers,* pp. 15–17.

note. Later, Drum heard that Stimson felt Drum had refused to go to China. This was very disturbing to Drum, who promptly obtained a further interview with Stimson. Stimson now remarked that Drum had knocked down his plans like a house of cards, a vivid phrase which illuminated the situation where the prolonged earlier presentations by the Secretary had not.

General Drum replied that—now he understood Stimson's desire to have him in China—he was anxious to go, whether China was to be an active theater or not, and reaffirmed his position in a letter to Stimson from New York on 15 January. But Stimson did not change his mind, and a brief reply on 17 January closed the episode. Not until 23 January did Drum learn of the Generalissimo's willingness since 5 January to accept an American officer as his chief of staff.[63]

Selection of Stilwell and His Directive for China

When it became apparent that Drum was not going to China, Marshall on 14 January 1942 proposed the name of General Stilwell.[64] They had served together at the Infantry School and in China. The Chief of Staff had the highest regard for Stilwell's ability as a tactician and a trainer of troops, and his star had risen with Marshall's. Great things were expected of Stilwell, as shown by his nomination for command of the North African expedition then being planned in Washington.[65] Born in March of 1883, Stilwell was no longer young, but he was energetic and indefatigable. As military attaché in China, he had examined the mechanism of the Chinese Army and meticulously studied every Sino-Japanese battle of the 1937–38 period.[66] Marshall knew that Stilwell was not a diplomat,[67] but the mission that was about to be offered Stilwell called for a great many other qualities. The situation in Burma was appearing ever more ominous. As early as 28 December 1941, G–2, War Department General Staff, had warned that the Japanese would be in Rangoon in five weeks unless Burma was heavily reinforced.[68] During General Drum's visit to Washington the War Department had shown itself well aware of the friction among Burma's defenders. Therefore a skilled field commander from a third party might be acceptable to British and Chinese as a solution of the

---

[63] (1) Memo, Drum for Stimson and Marshall, 10 Jan 42, sub: Vital Considerations Relative to My Proposed Trip to China. WPD 4389–71. (2) The China Proposal, Exhibit N(1) and pp. 73–78, 81–89. (3) Ltr, Drum to Stimson, 13 Jan 42. History of CBI, Sec. III, App. III, Item 15. (4) Ltr, Drum to Stimson, 15 Jan 42; Ltr, Drum to Knox, 16 Jan 42; Ltr, Stimson to Drum, 17 Jan 42, Drum Papers. (5) Stimson and Bundy, On Active Service, p. 529. (6) Penned Note cited n. 53(2).

[64] (1) The Stilwell Papers, pp. 25–26. (2) Stimson and Bundy, On Active Service, pp. 529–30.
[65] Interv with Gen Marshall, 6 Jul 49.
[66] (1) Stilwell's tactical studies of the Sino-Japanese hostilities are with his personal papers. (2) MA Rpts, Stilwell, 8 Jul 35–30 Apr 39. National Archives.
[67] Interv cited n. 65.
[68] Memo, Lee for WPD, 28 Dec 41, sub: Japanese Attack Against Burma. WPD 4544–35.

local command problem and might be able to organize successful resistance to the Japanese. Moreover, the Chief of Staff was most interested in reform of the Chinese Army, as his talks with Drum had shown. The discussions between Marshall, Stimson, and Stilwell between the 14th and 23d of January 1942 strongly suggest that events had now persuaded Marshall and Stimson to choose the man who had impressed Marshall as being a gifted field commander and trainer of troops with the added qualification of being thoroughly acquainted with China and the Chinese soldier. In any event he decided to send Stilwell with all haste to Burma and China after the U.S. Government had made the necessary diplomatic arrangements.[69]

The situation was changing from day to day as the Japanese surged on, and AMMISCA radios were painting an ever blacker picture of conditions in China. They reported that China was not keeping significant Japanese forces in check, and that war-weariness and passivity pervaded the nation and the army. For the present, the best that could be hoped was that an area in China suitable for air attacks on the Japanese lines of communications and homeland might be kept free. The United States should not look for much in the way of military results from its lend-lease to China; the benefits should be measured in diplomatic terms and as such they were a necessary expenditure. If the Generalissimo and his supporters were kept in power China would remain at least formally belligerent, but if the regime fell the peoples of Asia would gravitate toward Japan. Describing Burma as an indispensable air base, AMMISCA suggested its primary task should be to obtain proper ground facilities, communication nets, and antiaircraft cover for American air units in Burma.[70]

Between the 14th and 23d of January, Stimson, Marshall, and Stilwell discussed sending Stilwell to China and Burma with the mission, as Stilwell saw it, to "coordinate and smooth out and run the road, and get various factions together and grab command and in general give 'em the works. Money no object." [71] Stimson began on the 14th by stating on Soong's authority that the Chinese Army would accept an American commander.[72] Asked if he would take the post of senior U.S. officer in the China Theater (nothing being said about the post of chief of staff to Chiang Kai-shek), Stilwell replied that he would go where he was sent. Asked his requirements for success in China and "especially in the Burma theatre," Stilwell listed them as "executive control,

[69](1) Interv cited n. 65. (2) On 16 January Marshall authorized Stilwell to draft proposals for final agreement with the Chinese Foreign Minister. After this was accomplished Stilwell prepared his own directive for the mission to China. Memo, Marshall for McCloy, 16 Jan 42. WDCSA, Far East (1941–42), A46–523.

[70](1) Rad AMMISCA 163, AMMISCA to AGWAR, 5 Jan 42. AG 381 (12–19–41). (2) WPD 4389–58.

[71] The Stilwell Papers, p. 26.

[72] Stilwell Black and White Book (hereafter, Stilwell B&W), 14 Jan 42. (See the Bibliographical Note for an explanation of these copybooks, in which Stilwell recorded his reflections on the day's events.)

GEN. GEORGE C. MARSHALL *conferring with Henry L. Stimson, Secretary of War, in the Munitions Building, Washington, January 1942.*

(or?) command." [73] Marshall told Stilwell to phrase the desired agreement, and the letter went over McCloy's signature to Soong for concurrence on behalf of the Chinese Government.[74] On the 21st the Chinese Government agreed to Stilwell's having executive authority over British, Chinese, and American units, especially in Burma, and to his being chief of the Generalissimo's Allied staff.[75] In the light of this, Marshall again spoke to Stilwell

[73] (1) *The Stilwell Papers,* p. 25. (2) Stilwell Diary, 15, 16 Jan 42. (See Bibliographical Note for an explanation of Stilwell's day-by-day diary.)

[74] (1) Memo cited n. 69(2). Appended to Marshall's memorandum was a letter ready for McCloy's signature and dated 15 January. In this letter McCloy told Soong:

"In our [Marshall, Stimson, McCloy, Stilwell] opinion, the services of such an officer could be of far greater value, especially in the Burma Theater, where Chinese, American, and British factors are all present, if he were given executive power to coordinate these factors. This, of course, amounts to command power over Chinese units, as well as British and American, but there is no other way to get the same results. Also in his capacity of Chief of Staff for the Generalissimo, such an officer would be fully cognizant of all matters of policy. An expression of feeling of the Generalissimo on this matter would be appreciated."

[75] (1) The Generalissimo concurred in full with the War Department's proposals. Rad, Chiang to Soong, 21 Jan 42. OPD Exec 8. (2) Ltr, McCloy to Soong, 23 Jan 42. WDCSA, Far East (1941–42), A46–523.

on the 23d: "(Marshall): 'Will you go?' (Stilwell): 'I'll go where I'm sent.' " [76] That was Stilwell's attitude as revealed in his private papers. He did not seek the post; he did not reveal any joy in it; he would go where he was sent.

The mission proposed for Stilwell, because of the warnings from AMMISCA and the demonstrations of Japanese prowess in Malaya, and possibly because of the influence of Drum's studies of the China problem, was very different from that suggested to Drum. Stilwell was told to go at once to the Far East. On arrival at Chungking he would become chief of the Generalissimo's as yet nonexistent Allied staff. Stilwell would then go to Burma where it was hoped he would take command of the Allied forces there, smooth out the bickerings and rivalries, and save Burma for the United Nations. Stilwell's expectation of command in Burma began to fade almost as soon as he accepted his new post, for he learned that the British had named an officer senior to him to command their forces in Burma.[77]

Stilwell's duties as one of the Generalissimo's chiefs of staff—the other being Gen. Ho Ying-chin, Chief of Staff of the Chinese Army—were established in an exchange of letters between China's Foreign Minister and the Secretary of War. The Chinese diplomat described the Chinese understanding of them as: "To supervise and control all United States defense-aid affairs for China; under the Generalissimo to command all United States forces in China and such Chinese forces as may be assigned to him; to represent the United States on any international war council in China and act as the Chief of Staff for the Generalissimo; to improve, maintain, and control the Burma Road in China." [78] The Soong–Stimson letters also provided that Colonel Chennault (Chinese Air Force) would be the highest ranking air officer in China.[79] Stilwell noted in his diary: "The 'control of defense-aid clause' is to give it to me and not Magruder." [80]

---

[76](1) Stilwell Diary and Stilwell B&W, 23 Jan 42. (2) Stimson cleared Stilwell's appointment to China on 23 January 1942. Memo, Stimson for Marshall, 23 Jan 42. WDCSA, Far East (1941–42), A46–523.

[77](1) *The Stilwell Papers,* p. 26. (2) On 2 February 1942 Stimson regarded Burma as being in such peril that it was first on his list for personal attention. On the 16th he insisted that an American must command in Burma, because of the United States' relations with China. He was willing to go to the President and fight for it, if General Marshall wanted to make it an issue (presumably if the British sent someone of higher rank to Burma). War Council Mtgs, 2, 16 Feb 42. WDCSA, Notes on War Council, A48–139. (3) Stilwell B&W, 24 Jan 42.

[78](1) Ltr, Soong to Stimson, 30 Jan 42. U. S. Department of State, *United States Relations with China: With Special Reference to the Period 1944–1949* (Washington, 1949), p. 469. The exchange of letters between Stimson and Soong on 29 and 30 January 1942 is on pages 468–69 of this book. (2) Ltr, Stimson to Soong, 29 Jan 42, based on Memo, Stilwell for Marshall, 28 Jan 42, sub: Suggested Ltr of Instructions. WPD 4389–64. (3) Soong's original letter of agreement on Stilwell's role and authority in the China Theater in WDCSA, Far East (1941–42), A46–523.

[79] In replying to Stimson's letter of 29 January, Soong stated that it was the Generalissimo's desire to retain "Colonel Chennault as the highest ranking American Air officer in China." Soong's acceptance, however, did not close the agreement as far as the War Department was concerned. On 3 February, Soong learned that Colonel Bissell, not Chennault, was to be the senior United States aviation officer in China. Ltr, McCloy to Soong, 3 Feb 42. WDCSA, Far East (1941–42), A46–523.

[80] Stilwell Diary, 26 Jan 42.

Stilwell's relations with the British were defined by a Combined Chiefs of Staff paper which was a revised version of the proposed instructions to Drum. Stilwell's (Chinese) forces if they entered Burma would come under ABDACOM, which would issue the necessary directives for his co-operation with the British. He would be allowed to establish and use bases, routes, and staging areas in India and Burma to support his operations, and he could make every effort to increase the capacity of the Burma Road from Rangoon to Chungking. To that end, the Burmese authorities would be instructed to make all possible improvements. Stilwell could build and operate airfields in Burma. He would be the principal liaison agency between Wavell and the General-issimo.[81] As for the feelings with which he approached his British and Chinese allies, when he took up his work, Stilwell observed: "The Burmese hate the British and Chinese; maybe they are partly right." [82]

Stilwell's orders assigning him to duty in China read:

1. By direction of the President, you are detailed as a member of the General Staff Corps, assigned to General Staff with troops, and designated as Chief of Staff to the Supreme Commander of the Chinese Theater and upon reporting to the Supreme Commander, you are, in addition, appointed Commanding General of the United States Army Forces in the Chinese Theater of Operations, Burma, and India.

2. You will assemble in Washington, D. C. immediately such staff as you may select, and be prepared to depart, with your staff, at an early date for Chungking, China, where you will assume the duties set forth in a letter of instructions to be issued.[83]

The War Department orders to Stilwell were to "increase the effectiveness of United States assistance to the Chinese Government for the prosecution of the war and to assist in improving the combat efficiency of the Chinese Army." [84] These words, or a close paraphrase of them, he put at the head of each of the private analyses of his mission that he wrote in the years to come. The phrase in Stilwell's War Department orders "to assist in improving the combat efficiency of the Chinese Army" presumably meant that he was to assist the Generalissimo in such an effort. Formal notification of Stilwell's mission was given on 23 January, and he took over Drum's office and part of his staff.

Looking over Drum's staff studies, his first reaction was unfavorable.[85] As he reflected on Drum's papers over the next few days and talked repeatedly to Chinese officials in Washington, Stilwell's views on what he needed began to change and jell. His conferences with personnel of China Defense Supplies, who were to be his colleagues in lend-lease affairs, gave a bad impression of

[81] U.S. ABC–4/9, 10 Jan 42, sub: Immediate Assistance to China. History of CBI, Sec. III, App. III, Item 18.

[82] Stilwell B&W, 25 Jan 42. Stilwell's phrase is not "pretty right," as in the printed text of *The Stilwell Papers,* page 32.

[83] Ltr Order, TAG to Stilwell, 2 Feb 42. AG 210.311 (2–2–42) OD–E.

[84] Ltr, Marshall to Stilwell, 2 Feb 42, sub: Instructions as U.S. Army Representative to China, with 4 Incls. History of CBI, Sec. III, App. III, Item 36A.

[85] (1) Diary and B&W entries cited n. 76(1). (2) *The Stilwell Papers,* pp. 31, 32, 34.

their approach to China's problems.[86] In the course of his study Stilwell also heard of a developing project for bombing Japan. Review of Magruder's requests for specialists to train and equip a certain number of Chinese divisions enabled Stilwell to determine his personnel needs.

Putting all of this together in a note to Marshall, Stilwell estimated his needs and type of organization on the eve of his departure for China. Stilwell asked Marshall to approve the following: (1) that his staff and such forces as might join him be called a task force, thus permitting nomenclature more appropriate to an organization larger than a military mission; (2) that, as available, equipment for thirty Chinese divisions be sent to him; (3) that this force be supported by U.S. service units and aviation as they became available; (4) that, if Rangoon fell, the flow of supplies would not be stopped but would be continued and be diverted to a suitable base in India, preferably Calcutta; and (5) that transport aircraft would be allocated to speed the movement of supplies to China. The long-range objective of Stilwell's plans was to build up the combat efficiency of the Chinese Army and to prepare a land base of operations for a final offensive against Japan, in which at least one U.S. corps would join.[87]

So that he might arrive with something tangible to cheer the Chinese, Stilwell produced a shopping list of ordnance items, which with the air support then under consideration, he called the "minimum essential." He asked immediate shipment of 500 heavy machine guns, 30,000 Enfield rifles and 10,000,000 rounds of small arms ammunition. The manufacture of 7.92-mm. ammunition was requested. For artillery, Stilwell wanted 70 75-mm. howitzers with 500 rounds each, and 36 old-style (horse-drawn unmodernized) 155-mm. howitzers with 1,500 rounds each.[88]

The War Department examined Stilwell's requests, and a few were approved. Significantly, the long-range objective was not. There was agreement to keeping up the flow of supplies to Rangoon, to sending transport aircraft as they became available, and to permitting General Stilwell to call his group The U.S. Task Force in China. It was stated that 100 75-mm. howitzers were on the way and that raw material for China's arsenals was at

[86] Stilwell Diary, 24, 27–31 Jan 42. Stilwell remarked: "Chow at Soong's. . . . Talk about freight transport if Rangoon falls. No thought of fighting. The Chinese 'can't do this or that'—just a flat statement. Their transport man, C. S. Liu, now has a scheme for getting in via the Persian Gulf, Iran, Caspian Sea, Turkestan, Sinkiang, etc!!!! Soong wants dive bombers for the Yangtze, and tanks, and planes, and this, and that. He can't get the fundamental picture, of course." Stilwell B&W, 27 Jan 42. Beginning on 24 January Stilwell conferred for a week with China Defense Supplies officials.
[87] (1) Memo, Stilwell for Marshall, 31 Jan 42. History of CBI, Sec. III, App. III, Items 23, 24. (2) "A task force consists of those units (combat and service) necessary to carry out certain planned operations (task). It has no fixed organization." FM 101–10, WD, 21 Dec 44. Staff Officer Field Manual, Organizational, Technical, and Logistical Data, p. 19.
[88] Draft Memo, Stilwell for Marshall, 31 Jan 42, sub: Aid to China. History of CBI, Sec. III, App. III, Item 23. Though unused, this draft memorandum elaborates Stilwell's requests and explains reasons for each request. Stilwell wanted the items to be shipped to Calcutta without delay.

Rangoon. Shipping machine guns would complicate the problem of ammunition supply, but a few 155-mm. pieces could be sent. The final list included 200 machine guns and 20,000 rifles; 5,000 rounds for the 155's; light artillery as requested with 148,000 rounds.[89]

In organizing the personnel of his group before leaving for China, Stilwell gave its members assignments based on those in a corps headquarters. This suggested that he was preparing to assume command responsibilities in Burma, "over such Chinese Forces as may be assigned" to him. For personnel, he drew on the staff he had had as III Corps commander in California and inherited others from Drum's group of advisers. With the concurrence of War Plans Division, Stilwell named his headquarters, plus such U.S. forces as might come under his command, The United States Task Force in China.[90]

Moving Toward a Larger Concept

The War Department concept of aid to China went through a very considerable evolutionary process in January and February. In retrospect, it seems that so many U.S. projects to aid the Chinese were set afoot in those months as to make it obvious that a mission could not co-ordinate and control them all. Something closer to an American theater of operations was more and more plainly indicated. When General Drum first came to Washington, the solution had seemed to be a more impressive mission to the Generalissimo, largely diplomatic, with lend-lease, guerrillas, and a minute air force as tokens of good will. But the day before General Drum arrived, the Chinese made proposals that, when joined with others, ultimately made an American theater of operations essential. On New Year's Day they requested lend-lease matériel to build a road across north Burma to tap the Burma Road. The route would be Ledo (India)–Fort Hertz–Myitkyina–Lung-ling. The slow mills began to grind and the proposal went to AMMISCA, which in reply outlined the pros and cons, pointing out that despite the Generalissimo's optimistic figure of five months, two and one half years would be a better estimate of the construction time. Support quickly came to the project from high places in Washington.[91]

Lauchlin Currie told the President on 24 January that a road from India to

---

[89] Memo with 4 Incls, Col Benjamin G. Ferris, G-4 Stilwell Mission, for G-4 WDGS, 6 Feb 42. History of CBI, Sec. III, App. III, Item 37. On 7 February Eisenhower wrote on Ferris's memorandum that the list "has been approved by the C/S for the W. D., and by Gen. Somervell as Acting D C/S."

[90] WPD 4389–64.

[91] (1) *The Stilwell Papers,* pp. 26, 38. (2) Ltr, William S. Youngman, Executive Vice-Pres, CDS, to Stettinius, 1 Jan 42. AG 400.3295 (4–14–41) Sec 1A. (3) Ltr, Lt Col John E. McCammon to Currie, 13 Jan 42. AG (AMMISCA) 611. (4) Ltr, Magruder to Rear Echelon, AMMISCA, 30 Jan 42, sub: Rpt on Szechwan–Assam Highway, AG (AMMISCA) 611. (5) Aldrich Diary, 13, 18, 20 Jan 42. (6) Rad AMMISCA 201, Magruder to AGWAR, 19 Jan 42. AG 400.3295 (4–14–41) Sec 1A. (7) Magruder sent Maj. Paul L. Freeman, Jr., to Calcutta to reconnoiter its use as a port to receive diverted lend-lease cargoes from Rangoon. MacMorland Diary, 19 Jan 42.

China across north Burma would do much to compensate for the incidents which had disturbed Sino-American relations. Currie feared they would be further upset by the probable fall of Rangoon.[92] Following a memorandum from the War Plans Division to Marshall, which urged such a road, plus another from Imphal to Kalewa, as an "urgent military necessity," the War Department sent a radio to AMMISCA to hammer home the importance attached to building such a road as soon as possible.[93] Visiting India, the Generalissimo reached agreement with the Government of India on a road from Ledo as well as another from Imphal, plus road, port, and railroad facilities for lend-lease in India. In early February the Chinese statesman announced that a road from Assam to China would be built. The Allied military representatives in Chungking concurred, and Washington gave its blessing with lend-lease. So, before Stilwell ever saw the road that was to bear his name, it was formally agreed on by the three powers, and the United States was committed to procure lend-lease aid, though the project was not yet a U.S. responsibility.[94]

The airline over the bottlenecks of the Burma Road was viewed as a recourse that could be applied immediately by sending transport aircraft to India. At the most optimistic rational estimate the Imphal Road would take seven months, but the transports could fly at once. T. V. Soong sent a memorandum to the President on 31 January 1942 forecasting the imminent closure of the Burma Road. In it he made the memorable statement that only 700 miles of "comparatively level" stretches lay between Sadiya, India, and Kunming, China. This was the famous Hump, as villainous and forbidding a stretch of terrain as there was in the world.[95] One hundred DC-3's on this route, Soong assured the President, could fly 12,000 tons a month into China. Roosevelt approved and told the Generalissimo, "Definite assurance

[92] Memo, Currie for Roosevelt, 24 Jan 42, sub: Chinese Situation. History of CBI, Sec. III, App. III, Item 19.
[93] (1) Gerow's memorandum gave the Chinese figure of five months as the time to build the Ledo Road, via Fort Hertz and Myitkyina. Memo, Gerow for Marshall, 11 Feb 42. AG (AMMISCA) 611. (2) Rad, Eisenhower to Magruder, 22 Feb 42. AG 400.3295 (4–14–41) Sec 1A.
[94] (1) AG (AMMISCA) 611. (2) On 14 February Currie suggested that copies of correspondence on the new roads be made available to the U.S. Army Engineers because of future responsibilities that might be involved. The War Plans Division stated that it knew of no projects in the China–Burma area for which the Chief of Engineers was responsible and recommended filing Currie's memorandum. Memo, Currie for TAG, 14 Feb 42; Memo, Brig Gen Robert W. Crawford, sub: Information for Chief of Engrs, 23 Feb 42. AG (AMMISCA) 611.
[95] (1) Memo, Soong for Stilwell, and Incl, Memo for President, 31 Jan 42. History of CBI, Sec. III, App. III, Item 22. (2) Though a reconnaissance of the Imphal Road by an AMMISCA officer in mid-March 1942 revealed it could not be completed in seven months, and then could be used only to support the Allied forces in Burma, Soong told the War Department that it would be open to traffic on 1 April and urged that Chinese lend-lease equipment be stockpiled in India to be sent over it. In spring 1942 he suggested a line of supply from the Arctic Circle south across Siberia and northern China to Chungking. Sherwood, *Roosevelt and Hopkins,* p. 529. Meanwhile, matériel was requisitioned by China Defense Supplies to be sent over these nonexistent supply routes. See AG (AMMISCA) 611, the best single source on this period and subject.

can now be given you that the supply route to China via India can be maintained by air even though there should be a further set back in Rangoon." [96] Before his departure for China, Stilwell was told to set up the airline to China even though the Burma Road was held.

Therefore, the day he met the President for an interview and final word, Stilwell could write in his diary, "Events are forcing all concerned to see the importance of Burma. We must get the air line [the Hump] going at once, and also build both the back-country roads [Ledo Road; Imphal Road]." [97] A mission could not handle this, an American task force was required. That night, Stilwell recorded in his diary that the President had told him that the war would be over in 1943, that one year hence would see the turn. Stilwell was to tell the Generalissimo that Germany was not the number one enemy, that all enemies were equally important. The United States was in to see it through, and would fight until China regained "*all* [Stilwell's italics] her lost territory." He saw Harry Hopkins too, and Hopkins stated flatly that Stilwell was going to command troops, that the Generalissimo might in addition offer him command of the whole Chinese Army.[98]

The Generalissimo's chief aide-de-camp told Magruder:

> Just received a telegram from Generalissimo Chiang saying: "The telegram from Mr. Stimpson [*sic*] as forwarded by General Magruder on February 9th was respectfully acknowledged. General Stilwell's coming to China and assuming duty here is most welcome." The Generalissimo further said: "I am deeply gratified in learning of the American War Department's help in supplying arms and equipment for the AVG." In notifying you of this matter I wish you the best of health.[99]

Stimson's agreements with Soong and the growing threat in the Middle East expedited War Department plans to give Stilwell the means to establish, maintain, and protect the roads and airlines, and to implement his mission to China. Designated as The United States Task Force in China, Stilwell and his staff left for Chungking on 11 February.[100] War Department directives streamed out to various officers, detailing them to duty in several projects scheduled to join Stilwell in the Far East. Most advanced were the China air projects under the supervision of Col. Clayton L. Bissell. Force AQUILA (code designation for the Tenth Air Force) was soon to leave the United States under Col. Caleb V. Haynes with orders to report to Maj. Gen. Lewis H. Brereton upon arrival in India. Brereton was already en route to India from Java with remnants of a small air force. Haynes carried instructions for Brereton to be prepared to keep open the supply route between India and China and, if

---

[96](1) Rad, Roosevelt to Generalissimo, 9 Feb 42. Bk VI, Sec 3, Hopkins Papers. (2) Sherwood, *Roosevelt and Hopkins,* p. 513.

[97] *The Stilwell Papers,* p. 38.

[98] Stilwell Diary, 9 Feb 42. Compare the above with page 36 of *The Stilwell Papers.*

[99] Ltr, Gen Ho Yao-tzu, Chief, Generalissimo's Aide-de-Camp Office, to Magruder, 14 Feb 42. SNF–56.

[100] WPD 4389–64.

ordered, to conduct offensive missions from China Theater. Though this latter was set forth as a goal of his labors, Brereton was also told that Stilwell could order him to conduct such missions from India and Burma as Stilwell thought necessary. These orders made Brereton, rather than Bissell or Chennault, responsible to Stilwell for establishing U.S. air power in Asia.

Task Force AQUILA, containing the Headquarters and Headquarters Squadron, Tenth Air Force, was the heart of the China aviation project. Other elements of the project were: (a) Col. Leo H. Dawson's flight of 33 A–29's, designed to deliver the lend-lease planes to the Chinese Air Force while the pilots would join the Tenth Air Force; (b) Col. Harry A. Halverson's flight of B–24's, known as the HALPRO Group and destined for the Tenth; (c) a group of 51 P–40E's at Takoradi, West Africa, for delivery to the AVG; (d) Col. James H. Doolittle's mission of medium bombers (later 16 B–25's), destined for the Tenth; and (e) a block of 35 DC–3's for transport duty with the Tenth. On 22 February, Colonel Bissell left for China to co-ordinate the China aviation projects.[101]

General Brereton plunged at once into his task of reorganization, reporting that he would set up a service command area and a combat area. The Ferry Command headquarters were to be at Karachi rather than Bangalore. He would put Tenth Air Force Headquarters at New Delhi to be near General Headquarters (India), the highest command echelon in the Indian Army. Brig. Gen. Earl L. Naiden would be chief of staff of the Tenth Air Force and Brig. Gen. Francis M. Brady would run the Ferry Command. In order of priority Brereton asked Washington to send air warning equipment and personnel, a P–38 reconnaissance squadron, fighter units, and antiaircraft.[102]

In Iran, Brig. Gen. Raymond A. Wheeler was informed that he was now commanding general of the Services of Supply in China, Burma, and India, and that his mission was to do whatever was necessary to rush equipment and supplies through to Stilwell. For this, he could assume any necessary supply and administrative functions in India. To guide his planning, Wheeler was told that a major convoy had been diverted from Australia to India, and that 120 fighter aircraft would arrive soon after. For the American forces in India, Wheeler was to keep a six months' level of supply, for the 1,000 men to be in China, a nine months' level.[103] Naming the commander of a Services of Supply

[101] (1) Memo, Bissell for Arnold, 20 Feb 42, sub: China Aviation Projects, AG (AIR) 381 China. (2) Memo, Col Harold L. George, ACofS Air, WPD, for CofS USA, 24 Feb 42, sub: Establishment of an American Air Force in India. Item 2, OPD Green Book (Asiatic Sec), Gen Ref Br, OCMH. (3) Ltr, Arnold to Haynes, 21 Feb 42, sub: Ltr of Instructions. Item 24, OPD Green Book. (4) Rad WAR 637, Hq AAF to American MA, Cairo, for Haynes, 21 Feb 42. AG 400.3295 (8–9–41) Sec 8. (5) Rad WAR 239, Marshall to Stilwell, 28 Feb 42. AG 381 (2–24–42) 2.
[102] Rad WAR 239, Marshall to Stilwell, 28 Feb 42; Rad AMSEG 516, Brereton to Arnold, 2 Mar 42; Memo, Eisenhower for Secy WDGS, 25 Feb 42, sub: Comd in India. AG 381 (2–24–42) 2.
[103] (1) Memo, Maj Gen Brehon B. Somervell, G–4, for TAG, 27 Feb 42, sub: Designation of CG SOS USAF in India. AG 381 (2–24–42) Sec 2. (2) Rad AMMISCA 239, Marshall to Stilwell, 28 Feb 42. AMMISCA Radio File, Job–11.

for Stilwell's task force is a far cry from the concepts of the hastily assembled Notes on China that Drum was given as he waited in Stimson's anteroom.

Stilwell was brought into this redirection of policy and planning with a clarification of his powers and mission. With the rank of lieutenant general he was directed to assume command of all U.S. forces in India on his arrival there, as against the earlier order making the effective date his arrival at Chungking.[104] After giving notice of his intentions to General Wavell, Stilwell could move any of his men from India or Burma to China in line with his "primary mission," laid down anew in terms of classic simplicity: "Support China!" [105]

Summary

In February 1942 the United States thus took a major step forward in carrying out its historic attitude toward China. China and the United States were now more closely associated than ever before in their history. China had come so far from the days of her nineteenth century impotence that a Chinese leader, Chiang Kai-shek, was the Supreme Commander of an Allied theater of war, which meant that any British or American forces to enter it would be under his orders. To carry on his duties as Supreme Commander he had asked for and had been given an American general to serve as chief of the Generalissimo's Allied staff. This officer, General Stilwell, had in turn been given a task force with which to sustain the Chinese. Thus, the beginnings of a mechanism to solve the problems of Sino-American co-operation in warring on Japan had been assembled. The problems of that co-operation remained to be solved. AMMISCA's radios had given clear warning of what they would be, that the Chinese war effort was in the realm of politics and propaganda rather than on the field of battle. How could the Chinese be induced to pull their weight in the common struggle? Stilwell's task would be a heavy one and it would require the full support and encouragement of his government if he were to succeed in it.

---

[104] (1) Memo cited n. 102. (2) Stilwell's date of rank as Lieutenant General, AUS, was 25 February 1942. Rad AMMISCA 230, AGWAR to Magruder, 26 Feb 42. AMMISCA Radio File, Job–11.
[105] CM–OUT 247, Marshall to Stilwell, 3 Mar 42. Original draft of this radio with note, "O.K., G.C.M.," in AG 381 (2–24–42) Sec 2.

CHAPTER III

Stilwell Begins His Mission

When General Stilwell landed in India, he stepped upon a stage whose dimensions were gigantic. The area of China, Burma, and India was about equal to that of the United States, but its population of nearly 900,000,000 was almost seven times that of Stilwell's nation. The human scene in China, Burma, and India was as complex as the geographic. Here were two of the world's oldest and greatest civilizations, the Indian and the Chinese. Politically, Chinese nationalism was triumphant and Indian nationalism was growing ever stronger. India was part of the British Commonwealth and British administrators and soldiers had to consider grave problems of imperial policy. In China, Generalissimo Chiang Kai-shek had to take the long view, had to make momentous decisions. No statesman in Asia could think that simple victory was the goal of war. Asia and its problems had been in the world for a long time. The day after the war ended the problems would still be there.

Two spurs of the Himalaya Mountains sharply divide the three nations of India, Burma, and China. Between India and Burma are the Naga Hills, Chin Hills, and the Arakan Yoma, some of them as high as 10,000 feet. They curve in a great arc from near Tibet down to the Bay of Bengal. In early 1942 this barrier was crossed by nothing more than jungle trails, though the Governments of India and Burma were hard at work on a road linking the two states. The hills and valleys are covered with tropical forest, and in many areas pestilence is endemic. Between Burma and China is another rampart behind which lies an immense plateau on the China side. This mountain barrier, too, comes very near the sea so that Burma, lying as it does among the mountains, is something like a long blind alley, most easily reached by sea.

Communications in China, Burma, and India were poor. China had been isolated by a Japanese blockade. She had few trucks, for a nation of 400,000,000, and the Japanese in China had been at pains to take the few key rail centers in China's simple rail net. The Chinese were amazingly ingenious at maintaining wire and radio communication, but the net was not adequate for heavy traffic. The Indian rail system was very heavily burdened by the demands of war, production, and the growing Indian economy, as India was the arsenal for the Allied effort in the Middle East. Indian telephone and telegraph communications seemed rather inefficient to those Americans who used them.

To make matters still more difficult for Stilwell, Indian ports were 12,000 miles from the United States, so that it took a cargo ship almost two months to make the voyage. For a final complicating factor, there was the sheer physical problem of exerting effort in a subtropical climate where malaria and intestinal diseases were endemic.[1]

The theater of military operations, Burma, was 261,610 square miles in area, about as big as Texas. Within Burma, three great rivers run north and south, their valleys dividing the land into corridors. (*Map 3*)* From east to west, these are the Salween, Sittang, and Irrawaddy. With its mouth at Moulmein, the Salween River descends from the mountain mass along the Sino-Burmese border, where it flows through a mighty gorge. The Sittang and Irrawaddy Rivers are separated by the Pegu Yoma which, save for an isolated peak to the north, rarely rises above 2,000 feet in height and is often dissected by river valleys. Nevertheless, these hills effectively divide lower Burma into the Irrawaddy and Sittang valleys. If a defender of Burma falls back from the sea coast to the north, he finds the Irrawaddy valley grows wider because the arc of the Arakan Yoma and the Chin Hills (Burma's western wall) swings towards the west and India; then as he falls back still farther north the defender finds himself in the plain of central Burma as the Pegu Yoma ends.

The climate of Burma is an important military feature, for during the rainy season fighting is almost impossible. Burma lies in the monsoon belt. The rains come in mid-May and last till mid-October. In all sections of Burma, saving only the dry zone of the Irrawaddy from Prome to Mandalay, the rainfall is extremely heavy, averaging about two hundred inches a year along the frontiers and in the north. In the dry zone, but thirty inches of rain fall in the year. The best of the year in Burma is said to be the cool, dry season from November to February.

The principal lines of communications were the rivers and the Burma Railways. The great Irrawaddy River is navigable for 900 miles, its tributary, the Chindwin, for 350 miles, and fleets of river steamers carried tons of cargo from Rangoon to Bhamo, which lies almost on the Chinese border. The Salween River, because of its rapids, is only navigable for short stretches, and a tidal bore in the Sittang limits the river's use to small craft.

The military situation which Stilwell faced in China and Burma was a somber one. Thirty days before Stilwell's arrival, General Magruder described the Chinese situation of February 1942 in blunt terms. He told the War Department that Chinese and Sinophile propagandists had painted a grossly misleading picture of China's war effort, which if accepted at face value would

[1] History of Services of Supply, China, India, Burma Theater, 28 February 1942–24 October 1944, pp. 2–7. Gen Ref Br, OCMH.
* Inside back cover.

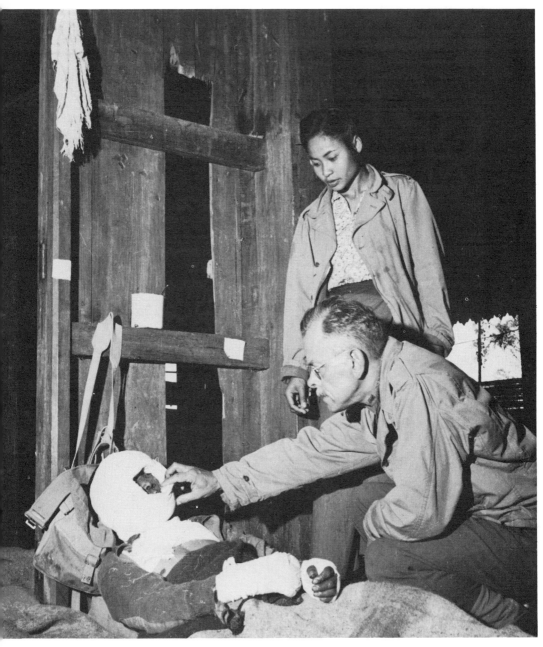

DR. GORDON SEAGRAVE *and a Burmese nurse examine a wounded Chinese soldier. (Photograph taken after Seagrave was commissioned in the U.S. Army.)*

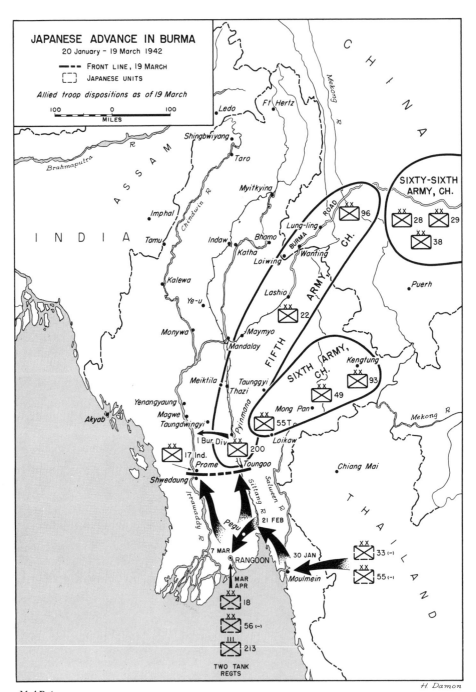

JAPANESE ADVANCE IN BURMA
20 January - 19 March 1942

▬ ▬ ▬ FRONT LINE, 19 MARCH
⌐ ┐ JAPANESE UNITS
└ ┘

Allied troop dispositions as of 19 March

100   0   100
MILES

MAP 4

H. Damon

gravely impair future American planning. Magruder recommended credits and lend-lease aid to China, not because they would increase China's potential offensive strength, but because they would keep the Generalissimo in power, prevent the end of China's passive resistance, and retain the possibility of using Chinese territory to base air attacks on Japan. Offensives in China, said Magruder, would have to be made by foreign units while Chinese manpower simply flowed into the military vacuum that might thus be created (as the Japanese massed their garrisons to meet the threat). The Japanese forces allegedly contained by the Chinese numbered twenty-eight inferior divisions, many of them really held by fear of the Soviet Union. The Chinese had no intention of taking offensive action, which would inevitably dissipate the economic and political value of their troops.[2]

Dealing with Chinese officials was extremely difficult, Magruder went on, because of their utter disregard for logistics. They had no idea of the capabilities of sea and air transport, and they made extravagant demands which they wanted fulfilled immediately. Their pet strategic cure-all was air power, and they were unmoved by the fact that their transport system would not support a tenth of the aircraft that they wanted to have in China. Magruder was convinced that some plain, blunt speaking would be necessary in dealing with the Generalissimo. He was a great man, Magruder conceded; he held China's factions and provinces in the semblance of nationality, but the fact had to be driven home to him that China was making a minimum effort though it stood to lose everything if the United Nations failed. In reply the War Department stated that it was aware of the situation within China and that Magruder's remarks confirmed its opinions. Steps were being taken to curb the propaganda extravagances of which Magruder complained.[3]

The First Burma Campaign began when the Japanese attacked southern Burma from Siam on 20 January 1942 with about 18,000 men. (*Maps 3 and 4*) Their purpose in occupying Burma was to cut the line of communications from Rangoon to Kunming and then to hold Burma as the southwestern anchor of a great defense perimeter swinging from Southeast Asia through the Southwest and Central Pacific Areas.[4] Moving almost straight across south Burma from east to west toward Rangoon, the Japanese *55th* and *33d Divisions,* of two regiments each, had gone from victory to victory over Indian, British, and Burmese troops, who were inexperienced, untrained in jungle warfare, and overly dependent on motor transport. The Japanese successes had been crowned by the Battle of the Sittang Bridge on 22–23 February, when the Japanese succeeded in ambushing two Indian infantry brigades of the 17th

[2] Rad AMMISCA 256, Magruder to Marshall, 8 Feb 42. AMMISCA Radio File, Job–11.
[3] (1) *Ibid.* (2) Rad AMMISCA 192, Marshall to Magruder, 15 Feb 42. AMMISCA Radio File, Job–11.
[4] USSBS, Naval Analysis Div, *The Campaigns of the Pacific War* (Washington, 1946), pp. 3, 43.

Indian Division on the east bank of the Sittang River. The two brigades were cut to pieces. On 2 March the Japanese crossed the Sittang River, moved past Pegu, and swung south on Rangoon.[5]

When after the Battle of the Sittang Bridge the menace to Rangoon became obvious and imminent, the AMMISCA personnel in Rangoon on Magruder's orders destroyed all movable lend-lease stores. Much equipment had been sent north, the rate hitting 1,000 tons a day as disaster neared, but it was necessary to burn 972 trucks in various stages of assembly, 5,000 tires, 1,000 blankets and sheeting, and a ton of odds and ends. A great deal of lend-lease was transferred to the imperial forces in Burma: 300 Bren guns with 3,200,000 rounds, 1,000 submachine guns with 180,000 rounds of ammunition, 260 jeeps, 683 trucks, and 100 field telephones.[6]

The Japanese took Rangoon on 6 March, while the 17th Indian Division fought its way out of a possible Japanese encirclement and fell back north up the Irrawaddy valley. The Japanese *33d Division* began to follow the 17th Indian Division up the Irrawaddy valley. The *55th Division* in the Sittang valley was facing the 1st Burma Division, which latter had not been engaged as a unit. The orders from General Wavell to the British defenders were to hold upper Burma as long as possible to cover the oil fields at Yenangyaung, to keep contact with the Chinese, and to protect the road being hastily built from Assam to Burma.[7]

As of early March, the Japanese plans for the next phase of the Burma campaign seem to have been elastic, and still in process of formulation. They suggest an intention to make the main Japanese effort via Rangoon–Toungoo–Mandalay, which if successful would isolate Burma from China and thus cut off any Chinese troops who might come to the aid of Burma's defenders. Japanese reinforcements arriving through Rangoon would be committed to the Japanese right.[8]

The most hopeful note in the Burma military situation was that Chinese troops were moving in, in force. Shortly after the "qualified acceptance" of Chinese reinforcements and the injury to Chinese pride caused by the *Tulsa* incident it became necessary for the British to ask China's aid in defending Burma. It was then apparent to them that the "violence, fury, skill, and might

---

[5] (1) Japanese Study 88. (2) Interrogs, Lt Col Minoru Kouchi, Lt Gen Yutaka Takeuchi. Gen Ref Br, OCMH. (See Bibliographical Note.) General Takeuchi places the Japanese strength at 16,000.

[6] There were, however, 19,052 tons of lend-lease materials in dead storage which were left behind: "miscellaneous light loads for dead storage, 903 tons; industrial machinery, 3,030½ tons; electrical equipment, 686 tons; and construction materials, 14,432½ tons." Rpt, St. John to Stilwell, 10 Mar 42, sub: Rpt on Rangoon Opn from 1 Jan 42 to Evacuation Date. Item 47, Port of Rangoon Folder, CT 42, Dr 4, KCRC.

[7] (1) "Report by General the Honourable Sir Harold R. L. G. Alexander, K.C.B., C.S.I., D.S.O., M.C., on Operations in Burma from 5th March, 1942, to 20th May, 1942," *Supplement to The London Gazette,* March 11, 1948, pars. 3, 15, 16. (2) Japanese Study 88.

[8] Japanese Study 88.

of Japan has far exceeded anything we had been led to expect." [9] The original deployment in Burma, which was effected before hostilities began, was based on the prospect of a Japanese drive through the Southern Shan States via an existing and presumably inviting road. Subsequent events in Malaya, however, showed that the mobility of the Japanese forces had been underestimated. The Malaya operations revealed that the enemy were not tied to roads, and might, therefore, be capable of moving directly across south Burma on Rangoon. Therefore British and Indian battalions had to move from the Shan States and Mandalay to around Moulmein and were replaced with the Chinese 5th and 6th Armies. [10]

Since transport was scarce, troop movements were made slowly. Moving the balance of the Chinese 93d Division (6th Army) into Burma was agreed to by General Wavell on request from Burma Army headquarters on 19 January. Two days later he agreed to the 49th Division. The Chinese Ministry of War issued orders to move the last of the 6th Army's three divisions on 3 February. The General Officer Commanding, Burma, Lt. Gen. T. J. Hutton, discussed the matter with the Generalissimo when the latter visited India and reached an understanding. On 31 January Hutton asked Wavell's permission to admit the 5th Army, the Generalissimo concurred on 3 February, and movement began on 28 February. General Wavell's action preceded the intervention of Churchill and Roosevelt. Prompted by the Joint Chiefs of Staff, who thought no political or administrative difficulties should be allowed to prevent the Chinese from joining in the defense of Burma, Roosevelt had personally raised the matter with Churchill. [11]

So began China's share in the First Burma Campaign. There was no difficulty in supplying the 93d Division because its arrival had been anticipated. The 49th Division was something of a problem, but by mid-March it was comfortably settled in huts. The Temporary-55th Division was the last of the 6th Army to arrive—a new unit, badly led, meagerly equipped, and poorly trained. [12]

---

[9] Reprinted from Winston S. Churchill, *Secret Session Speeches,* compiled with introductory notes by Charles Eade (New York, 1946), p. 54. Copyright, 1946, by Simon and Schuster, Inc.

[10] (1) Col E. C. V. Foucar, M. C., Draft Narrative of the First Burma Campaign (December 1941–May 1942), 23 Sep 43, pp. 38, 48. Gen Ref Br, OCMH. (Hereafter, Foucar.) (2) Ltr and Incl, Maj Gen S. W. Kirby, Cabinet Office, Hist Sec, London, to Sunderland, 21 Nov 51, HIS 330.14 CBI 1951.

[11] (1) Foucar, pp. 131–32. (2) Rad, MA London, 19 Feb 42. Item 1377, Msg File of Feb 11–20, 1942, A47–36. (3) "Report by Lieut.-General T. J. Hutton, C.B., M.C., on Operations in Burma from 27th December, 1941, to 5th March, 1942," *Supplement to The London Gazette,* March 11, 1948, pars. 21–24. (4) Memo, Gerow for U.S. Secy for Collaboration, 20 Jan 42. ABC 336 China (26 Jan 42) Sec 1A, A48–224. (5) JCS 1, 31 Jan 42, sub: Co-operation with Chiang Kai-shek. (6) CCS 22, 2 Feb 42, sub: Co-operation with Chiang Kai-shek. (7) Memo, Gerow for TAG, 22 Jan 42, sub: Far Eastern Situation. AG 381 (11–27–41) Sec 1. (8) Rad, Churchill to POTUS (President Roosevelt), 7 Feb 42. Bk VI, Sec 3, Hopkins Papers.

[12] Brig John F. Bowerman, British Ln Off with 6th Army, Notes on Duties with Chinese Expeditionary Force, Combat Rpts and Misc Ln Off's Rpts. ALBACORE Hist File, Northern Combat Area Command Files, KCRC.

The Command Situation, China–Burma–India, March 1942

The rapid Japanese successes were forcing an alteration in the system of unified Anglo-American command set up at ARCADIA. Possibly foreshadowed by Churchill's comment of 10 February that he clearly understood the President would have the primary responsibility in dealing with China in all cases, and following soon after Wavell's ABDACOM was dissolved on 25 February, a CCS proposal of 8 March 1942 suggested a triple division of strategic responsibility. The whole Pacific, including China, would be under American direction though local operational control in China would be with the Generalissimo. The United States would make decisions on broad strategy, which would include offensives in a northwesterly direction from the main U.S. bases and attacks on Japan proper from China. From Singapore to and including the Middle East would be the British sphere of responsibility though the United States would continue lend-lease support. The Atlantic theater would be an area of combined responsibility. Co-ordinating operations between the areas would remain the subject of study and recommendation by the CCS. In accepting the CCS's proposal, Churchill assumed that any large-scale operations to seize the initiative would be discussed by the CCS in Washington and not ordered by the Joint Chiefs of Staff (JCS) unilaterally.[13]

In compliance with this arrangement, Stilwell was told by the War Department on 15 March that Wavell was now "Supreme Commander, India," that the CCS had made Wavell responsible for operations in Burma, and was reminded that any of his forces operating in India or Burma would be under Wavell's command.[14]

There were many implications in this division of responsibility as regarded Burma, all containing seeds of future trouble. The Generalissimo's concurrence was not invited, which angered him.[15] Nor was it suggested to him that he was exercising "local operational command" under the Joint Chiefs of Staff. A major campaign was under way in Burma, which lay on the border between

---

[13] (1) On 2 February 1942 the Joint Staff Planners of the JCS could state academically that agreed Anglo-American strategy was to hold the areas from which future offensives might be launched. Twelve days of Japanese advances forced revision of this paper. JPS 4, 2 Feb 42, sub: Agreed Concepts of Grand Strategy. (2) Japanese success was directly responsible for its successor, JPS 4-A, 14 Feb 42, sub: Agreed concepts of Grand Strategy. (3) Memo for Record, signed HLH, on telephone talk with Churchill, 1 Feb 42; Cable 527, Hopkins to Churchill, 11 Feb 42; Rad 28, London to POTUS, 12 Feb 42. Hopkins Papers. The point at issue was the Chinese sitting with the Pacific War Council in London, but the adjective "all" in the phrase "dealing with China in all cases" seems governing. (4) Sherwood, *Roosevelt and Hopkins,* p. 502. (5) Cable, Roosevelt to Hopkins, 16 Feb 42, Roosevelt and Hopkins MS, VI, 87. (6) Cable 115, Roosevelt to Churchill, 8 Mar 42. Bk V, Hopkins Papers. (7) The proposal was carefully worked out by the CCS machinery and drafted by Eisenhower. At the 3 March 1942 meeting the CCS agreed to an Anglo-American operational boundary roughly along the line of the Malay Barrier. CCS 9th Mtg, 3 Mar 42. (8) Cable 46, Churchill to Roosevelt, 18 Mar 42. WDCSA 381, A46–523.

[14] Rad AMMISCA 247, Marshall to Stilwell, 15 Mar 42. SNF–56.

[15] History of CBI, Sec. III, Ch. IV, The First Campaign in Burma, p. 10. (Hereafter, The Campaign in Burma.)

the Middle Eastern and Pacific spheres of responsibility. Any Sino-British operation in Burma would thus be based on two separate areas of strategic responsibility. Moreover, according to the CCS proposal, a British subject commanded in Burma. Six Chinese divisions, as against two British, would shortly be in that area. What would happen if the Generalissimo insisted that, as China supplied the men, it should also supply the commander? General Stilwell had been sent to Asia with the thought, among others, that he would command in Burma, but this was now impossible. (*Chart 1*)

Below the CCS level, but independent of its direction, came the Generalissimo's China Theater, as created at ARCADIA. There were five elements in the command structure at Chungking: the Generalissimo, the Chinese Army, the Joint Military Council, AMMISCA, and Stilwell as chief of the Generalissimo's joint staff. Because of the decisions of ARCADIA, the Generalissimo had a dual status, as the Chinese leader and as an Allied commander. The Generalissimo was Commander in Chief of the Chinese Forces and Chairman of the Supreme National Defense Council, a post like that of Prime Minister. As Supreme Allied Commander, he was in command of all Allied forces in China, precisely as MacArthur and Eisenhower were to be in their theaters. They, however, were under the CCS, whose task it was to reconcile national differences and recommend directives in the common interest, whereas the Generalissimo was accountable to himself alone, free to act as he thought China's interest might require, and free to order his two chiefs of staff, Stilwell and Ho Ying-chin, accordingly. When the Generalissimo's co-operation was desired by the United States, it had to be obtained by diplomatic processes.

As Supreme Commander of the China Theater, the Generalissimo was responsible for operations carried on in it. It was the Generalissimo's responsibility to make decisions and to lay down the broad lines of policy he desired to have followed. Both as Supreme Commander and as Generalissimo he had to supervise the training, equipping, and supplying of his troops, and the performance of duty by his subordinates. His chiefs of staff were advisers only, not executive officers.

Stilwell, as the Generalissimo's chief of joint staff, was placed in a difficult position from the beginning. He was sent to China to aid the Generalissimo in discharging the duties of Supreme Commander of an Allied theater. In this role he was assistant to a commander who was a free agent and whose conceptions of China's interests did not always agree with those of the CCS. But Stilwell had three other roles. He was commanding general of the American forces in India and Burma as well as in China; he was the military representative of the President of the United States in Chungking; and he was dispenser of lend-lease matériel for the United States. His roles would be workable while the Republic of China and the United States agreed. When they disagreed or when they were seeking an agreement, Stilwell was automatically placed in a dilemma, uncertain whether to comply with the wishes of the man who was

CHART 1 — DIVISION OF ALLIED COMMAND RESPONSIBILITIES IN SOUTHEAST ASIA: MARCH–APRIL 1942

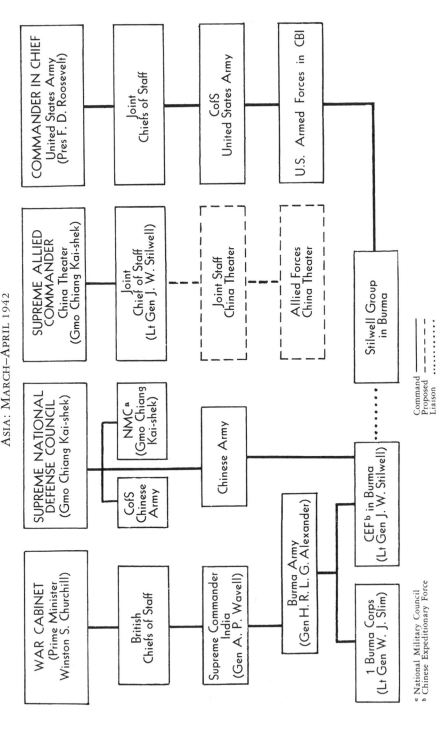

Command ————
Proposed – – – – –
Liaison ·········

[a] National Military Council
[b] Chinese Expeditionary Force

his immediate superior and Allied theater commander or to follow the directives of the Joint and Combined Chiefs. Ideally, his Chinese and American superiors should have agreed on and issued him a combined directive. In practice, Stilwell's American superiors would order him to secure the assent of his Chinese superiors, a process vexing to the Chinese, who would have greatly preferred the reverse. Stilwell recognized his predicament and, as will be noted, offered several solutions to those in authority, which they did not accept.

Stilwell's plight would have been eased had the Generalissimo's joint staff—representing the United States, Great Britain, China, and the Netherlands—ever been organized. The Joint Military Council in Chungking was in existence when he arrived and offered the possibility of being elevated into a joint staff by a few changes in assignment and terminology. Organized on 31 December 1941, the council had never grown in stature and authority because the governments represented thereon had never acquiesced in, if indeed they were fully aware of, its possibilities. After the first fortnight, Magruder's membership on the council was overshadowed by the general knowledge that another and senior American officer was coming to China. China's representative, General Ho, could do nothing without consulting the Generalissimo, while the British apparently were content to let the Chinese and Americans offer a lead. The Netherlands' member, added later, soon represented only a government in exile but distinguished himself on one occasion by an outburst of frank and excellent advice. On 24 April he pleaded for an Allied staff and some kind of co-ordinated strategy. That night Magruder's chief of staff wrote in his diary that if an Allied plan for the Pacific existed, AMMISCA knew nothing of it and the same might be said for the Generalissimo.

The council recommended the construction of the Ledo and Imphal Roads and the transfer of lend-lease matériel to the British (13 January), but its sessions usually appeared futile to Cols. Harry S. Aldrich and Edward E. MacMorland, who often served as U.S. representatives.[16] The key to this innocuous desuetude probably lies in the rapid emergence of the Combined Chiefs of Staff as the principal agency for the direction of the Anglo-American war effort. The Combined Chiefs of Staff were the superiors of the British and American representatives on the council, who could hardly advocate views of which their superiors disapproved or supervise the execution of policies for which their superiors would not provide resources. Consequently, the Chinese found it more convenient to deal with higher authority in London and Washington.

The Chinese Army and its Chief of Staff, General Ho, contributed more complexities. As has been noted, the Chinese Army was a coalition of armed factions and provincial levies, whose loyalties were local and personal rather than national, plus a hard core of about thirty divisions personally loyal to the

[16](1) Aldrich Diary, 31 Dec 41, 2, 8, 9, 13 Jan 42. (2) MacMorland Diary, 1, 6, 13 Jan, 17 Feb, 24 Apr 42.

Generalissimo. This situation created many delicate problems of domestic politics for the Generalissimo, which he was not disposed to brush aside. Rather, he often seemed preoccupied with them.[17] For Stilwell to persuade the Generalissimo to commit the Chinese Army or any major portion of it to offensive action was not easy. "It would be naive in the extreme to suggest that all [Stilwell] had to do to make China an agressive factor in the war against Japan was to place lend-lease arms in Chinese hands and, in consultation with the Generalissimo, issue orders for the attack."[18] General Ho's actions soon suggested to Stilwell that he saw in the arrival of an American as chief of staff of the Generalissimo's joint staff the introduction of a rival center of power and influence and a direct challenge to his own position. This rivalry, tempered by the requirements of the military situation, produced a state of affairs in which Ho and Stilwell sometimes co-operated amicably and sometimes sought each other's removal.[19]

AMMISCA might have acted as an energizing and unifying force but, though it had been given very broad powers, it never had a clear indication as to what the War Department wanted done with those powers.[20] As has been noted, the Department was attacking the China problem, but the process of solving it took time.[21] After 9 February, when Colonel Aldrich had a secret interview with the Generalissimo's military secretary, the Chinese were formally aware that Stilwell was coming.[22]

Early U.S. Logistical and Administrative Problems

General Magruder's wartime directives ordered him to persuade the Chinese to contain as many Japanese forces as possible and to speed the flow of arms through Burma to China. Repeated attempts to persuade the Chinese to action had brought no results.[23] As for increasing the quantity of lend-lease aid moving through Burma, AMMISCA reconnoitered alternative routes across Burma to India, one of its officers driving by jeep from Lashio to Calcutta across the 8,000-foot Chin Hills on the trace of the Imphal Road.[24] AMMISCA sent its officers to Burma to fight the administrative ineptitude and confusion that slowed traffic there. One of them, Maj. James Wilson, rendered distinguished

---

[17] See Ch. I, pp. 32ff., above.
[18] History of CBI, p. 94.
[19] For an attempt at removal see Memo, Stilwell for Soong, 27 Dec 42. This memorandum bears Stilwell's note: "Gist to T. V. verbally." Stilwell Documents, Hoover Library.
[20] MacMorland Diary, 3 Jan 42.
[21] See Ch. II, pp. 63–70, above.
[22] The urgent secrecy of this meeting was rather spoiled when a suddenly drawn portiere revealed four Chinese servants eavesdropping. Aldrich Diary, 9 Feb 42.
[23] Rad AMMISCA 94, Magruder to AGWAR, 11 Dec 41; Rad AMMISCA 95, Magruder to AGWAR, 11 Dec 41; Rad AMMISCA 140, Magruder to SW and AGWAR, 31 Dec 41; Rad AMMISCA 84, Gerow to Magruder, 4 Jan 42. AMMISCA Radio File, Job–11.
[24] AG (AMMISCA) 611.

service in moving lend-lease equipment north from Rangoon and died in the bombing of Mandalay by the Japanese.[25]

AMMISCA was authorized immediately after Pearl Harbor to induct the AVG into U.S. service if the Chinese agreed, but AMMISCA found the Chinese determined to bargain and Chennault "vigorously opposed." The Chinese agreed in principle but found endless reasons to delay induction. On one occasion they demanded a greatly increased allotment of lend-lease arms as a precondition; on another, that all U.S. air units in China be placed under Chinese command and that Chinese citizens be allowed to join any such unit sent there. When, on 1 January 1942, the question of induction had seemed settled on every point but one, Hollington Tong, Vice-Minister of Information, brought forth a fresh set of demands from the Generalissimo.[26]

The proposal for an international guerrilla force in China, mentioned in the Notes on China which Drum had been given and included in directives to AMMISCA, was quietly forgotten. No Americans, therefore, shared the heartbreaking experiences of those British commandos who came to China to destroy bridges and to harass the Japanese in the guerrilla manner so colorfully described in the press, only to find that the last thing the Chinese desired was to provoke the Japanese into reprisal raids.[27]

AMMISCA had tried to improve the Chinese Air Force and Chinese Army. After a careful study based on the work of earlier U.S. missions, Magruder gave the Generalissimo a plan to reorganize the Chinese Air Force. The Generalissimo approved it and issued orders to place it in effect, but nothing happened. Colonel Sliney, Magruder's artillery specialist, instructed Chinese artillerymen in the use of 75-mm. pack howitzers that arrived from Burma. Colonel MacMorland suggested that AMMISCA personnel go to Burma as liaison officers with the Chinese 5th and 6th Armies, but General Magruder demurred, saying no one was available.[28]

The command situation in China as of Stilwell's arrival was therefore very different from that contemplated when his orders were issued. There was no joint staff of which he might at once become chief, and circumstances suggested that there never would be one. For several reasons AMMISCA had not created a smoothly running organization which he might take over. The War Department had not made its desires clear. The reluctance of the Chinese to let the AVG be inducted as the 23d Pursuit Group until China had gained

[25] MacMorland Diary, 25 Jan 42.

[26](1) MacMorland Diary, 29 Dec 41, 1, 7 Jan 42. (2) Aldrich Diary, 1 Jan 42. (3) Chennault, *Way of a Fighter,* p. 170. (4) Ltr and Notes, Aldrich to Sunderland, 18 Feb 50. HIS 330.14 CBI 1950. (5) The proposal for integrated Sino-American units, which would pose baffling problems in command assuming that the language barrier could somehow be surmounted, was Madame Chiang's. Rad AMMISCA 140, Magruder to AGWAR, 31 Dec 41. WPD 4389–64.

[27](1) Morris, *China Changed My Mind,* pp. 109–10. (2) In the AMMISCA files, Job–11, is a ballad written by a member of this unit describing his Chinese experience in blunt soldier language. (3) History of CBI, p. 92.

[28] MacMorland Diary, 4, 11 Mar 42.

every possible diplomatic advantage from the situation kept the most effective Allied air unit in Southeast Asia from the control of the potential U.S. theater headquarters, AMMISCA. Operating the line of communications through Burma was another major task for a theater headquarters, but the Japanese cut that line with their capture of Rangoon.

In India the picture was more hopeful; present there were the beginnings of the Tenth Air Force and of the airline from India to China (though a Services of Supply did not begin work until April). The real growth of the Tenth Air Force began with initiatives by Generals Marshall and Brett. Recognizing the strategic implications of the probable loss of Java to the Japanese, on 11 February Marshall suggested to Wavell that the 19th Bombardment Group (H) be sent from ABDACOM to Burma, assuring him further that fighter cover for Burma was en route.[29]

Independently, General Brett had arrived at similar conclusions. He hoped ultimately to establish a force of U.S. heavy bombers in the general area of Akyab–Calcutta. The first essential was fighter cover, so, going from Burma to join Wavell's command in the Netherlands Indies, Brett had diverted a convoy from Australia to India for Burma duty. In it was the old carrier USS *Langley*, with thirty-two P–40's set up on deck and plenty of pilots and ground personnel. A few days later Wavell overruled him and decided to send the USS *Langley* to Java after all. She was sunk en route and all that reached India from the convoy in the way of air power was the ground echelon of the 7th Bombardment Group (H), 51st Air Base Group, personnel of the 51st Pursuit Group, and ten P–40's.[30] Also present were seven radio teams and Detachment, Company B, 52d Signal Battalion, originally intended to provide communications in Java.[31]

In accordance with the War Department directives of February 1942, on 5 March, General Brereton, as Commanding General, Tenth Air Force, assumed command of this effort to put U.S. air power in India. General Stilwell was told by the War Department that the Tenth would operate offensively in China under his direction. In addition to the 10 surviving P–40's, 51 fighters and 12 B–17's for the American Volunteer Group were en route and 33 more heavies would be allocated as soon as possible. A further increment would be 37 B–24's for the express mission of bombing Japan from Chinese bases, the HALPRO project.[32]

[29] Rad, Marshall to Wavell, 11 Feb 42. AG 381 (11–27–41) Sec 2B.

[30] Rad ABDA 395, Brett to AGWAR, 17 Feb 42; Rad, Brett to AGWAR, 20 Feb 42; Rad ABDA 492, Brett to AGWAR, 21 Feb 42; Rad ABDA 530, Brett to Arnold, 23 Feb 42. AG 381 (11–27–41) Sec 2B, Sec 2C.

[31] Sgts John and Ward Hawkins, History of the 835th Signal Service Battalion, pp. 1–4. Gen Ref Br, OCMH.

[32] (1) Wesley Frank Craven and James Lea Cate, eds., *The Army Air Forces in World War II: I, Plans and Early Operations, January 1939 to August 1942* (Chicago, 1948), p. 484. (2) Rad WAR 239, Marshall to Stilwell, 1 Mar 42. Item 3, Bk 1, JWS Personal File, A48–102. (See Bibliographical Note.) (3) Dispatch 308, Eisenhower to Stilwell, 21 Mar 42. Item 21, OPD Exec 10.

Organization of the airline to China was under way concurrently with Stilwell's first surveys of his new position. In January and February 1942 Chinese and American authorities contemplated an airlift from Assam, India, to Myitkyina in north Burma, a barge line from Myitkyina to Bhamo, and a truck haul from Bhamo to China. Stilwell was told of the project before he left Washington, and on 21 March the President ordered activation of the Assam–Burma–China Ferry Command. General Naiden, chief of staff of the Tenth Air Force, surveyed the projected air route and concluded that the normal run should be from the Royal Air Force base at Dinjan to Myitkyina. To meet the complex inadequacies of the Indian transport net, Naiden also proposed another airline connecting the seaport of Karachi with Dinjan. To fly these routes, twenty-five aircraft were diverted from commercial airlines in the United States, and ten came from Pan American Airways' trans-African line. The latter began the service, arriving at Karachi on 5 April.[33]

Stilwell's First Problems

General Stilwell's aircraft touched Indian soil at Karachi on 24 February 1942. The next day he and his staff were in New Delhi, India's capital, to confer with General Headquarters (India). There he learned that only one Indian infantry brigade could be spared to reinforce Burma.[34] From India he went to Lashio in Burma where he was introduced to the Generalissimo and to Colonel Chennault. Chennault was now a world figure in his own right. His skillful and prescient training of the American Volunteer Group, the devoted leadership of the squadron commanders, and the skill and courage of the pilots and ground crew had resulted in an imposing number of Japanese aircraft shot down in Burma. The Japanese had been kept from closing the port of Rangoon by air action, and Chennault's Flying Tigers for many weeks had supplied the Allied public with the only good news from the Far East. Chennault and Stilwell spoke together at Kunming on 4 March, where Chennault agreed to serve under Stilwell and further consented to induction of the American Volunteer Group into the Army Air Forces (AAF). "A big relief," wrote Stilwell, who had feared Chennault might object on both points.[35]

When Stilwell arrived in China, the question of AMMISCA's command relation to him arose at once. The War Department solved it by superseding Magruder's directive and placing all AMMISCA personnel at Stilwell's disposal. Using AMMISCA's officers and men, together with the personnel arriving in the China–Burma–India area, for his United States Task Force in China, Stilwell integrated all into a Headquarters, American Army Forces, China, Burma and

---

[33] MS, History of the India–China Ferry under the Tenth Air Force. USAF Hist Div, Air University Library, Maxwell Air Force Base, Ala.
[34] *The Stilwell Papers,* pp. 45–47.
[35] Stilwell B&W, 4 Mar 42.

India. This headquarters was established at Chungking on 4 March 1942. Significant of the approach General Marshall had desired, the new title excluded the word *theater*.[36]

The first conference between Stilwell, the Generalissimo, and Madame Chiang was held on 6 March 1942 in Chungking. Stilwell delivered the President's oral message,[37] explained the orders under which he was to operate, and described the help en route to China. The Generalissimo was concerned about command in Burma and about Sino-British relations. His comment on Stilwell's status was: "I told those Army commanders [in Burma] not to take orders from anybody but you and to wait until you came." [38] That was good news to Stilwell, for it seemed a clear indication that Stilwell would command the Chinese troops in Burma. The Generalissimo showed no hesitation over the proposed joint staff which Stilwell was to lead and assured him it would be set up the next day. The one problem seemed to be Sino-British relations, for the Generalissimo strongly objected to British command in Burma.[39]

When the Chinese staff proposals came on the 9th, they were a subtle repudiation of the Soong-Stimson agreements of January. The understanding reached by the two governments through Soong and Stimson had been that Stilwell would be chief of staff of the combined Sino-British-American forces in the China Theater, an Allied chief of staff under a Supreme Allied Commander. The Chinese proposed to make Stilwell chief of staff of the Allied (*i.e.,* Anglo-American) forces only, which were then the American and British military missions, together with Stilwell's task force in China—perhaps 300 men and nothing more. By writing in one of his copybooks, "At least Chiang Kai-shek is sticking to one part of the agreement [command]," Stilwell implied his awareness that the Chinese had already defaulted on the other, a joint staff for China Theater.[40] However, that same night, 9 March, the Generalissimo talked with Stilwell until midnight and said he was radioing Washington that Stilwell should command both British and Chinese in Burma.[41]

Since the Generalissimo had earlier promised to place the Chinese 5th and 6th Armies under British command, AMMISCA personnel were dismayed

[36](1) Rad AMMISCA 355, AGWAR to AMMISCA, 11 Mar 42. AG 400.3295. (2) Stilwell's task force staff formed the nucleus of Headquarters, American Army Forces, China, Burma and India. Nevertheless, staff assignments in the new headquarters on 15 March 1942 did not suggest that this staff would channel Stilwell's orders to a theater-wide organization. At this time most of the personnel in Stilwell's task force were not in Chungking. They were either waiting assignments in India for duty in Burma or were en route to the Far East. SO 1, Hq, American Army Forces, CBI, 4 Mar 42; SO 2, Hq, American Army Forces, CBI, 15 Mar 42. (3) MacMorland Diary, 20 Mar 42.
[37] Ch. II, p. 78, above.
[38] Stilwell Diary, 6 Mar 42. Gen. Shang Chen, Director of the Foreign Affairs Bureau, National Military Council, told Stilwell that he was now "No. 2 in China."
[39] *The Stilwell Papers*, pp. 50–51.
[40](1) Stilwell B&W, 9 Mar 42. (2) Stilwell Diary, 9 Mar 42. The diary entry is: "Shang came in with the diagrams for the staff. Just stooge stuff." (3) *The Stilwell Papers*, p. 55.
[41](1) Stilwell Diary, 9 Mar 42. (2) Min (Chinese version), Conf, Stilwell and Generalissimo, 9 Mar 42. Folder 2, Stilwell Documents, Hoover Library.

when they learned that the Generalissimo now objected to British command in Burma. He announced that he distrusted them after their recent setbacks, while Madame Chiang was violently anti-British in talking to MacMorland, AMMISCA's chief of staff.[42]

The Chinese radioed Washington in strong terms that Stilwell should lead in Burma. They seemed quite serious in their insistence, telling Stilwell that if the British tried to give orders, the Chinese would withdraw from Burma.[43] Certainly this was consistent with their earliest utterances; on 16 December 1941, General Ho told the British military attaché that if the Chinese were to be effective in Burma, they would have to operate independently in their own assigned sector.[44] In replying on 10 March, the President temporized, saying he hoped that Stilwell would be allowed to work out the very difficult and involved command problem on the spot without the need of placing it formally before the British. The Generalissimo read the President's reply, then turned to Magruder and MacMorland, who delivered the message on 13 March, and said that there must be unified command in Burma, either under the Chinese or the British. He preferred Stilwell, because he did not trust the British in the light of their Far Eastern record.[45]

The British were not pleased with Stilwell's presence in Burma, because their Gen. Sir Harold R. L. G. Alexander (now commanding Burma Army) had expected to command the Chinese, and because Stilwell had neither a staff nor knowledge of the local situation. Churchill added that the British had prepared a supply service for the Chinese, together with a liaison net down to the division level. He suggested to the President that Stilwell be under Alexander's command.[46] The President and Marshall answered much as they had to the Generalissimo. They assured Churchill that Stilwell wanted to solve the command problem by co-operating with Alexander until the Chinese came into line. They described Stilwell as immensely resourceful and capable, informed on Chinese matters, and devoid of thoughts of personal aggrandizement. Though ordered by the Generalissmo to take no orders from the British, he could co-operate if the Generalissimo was pleased with the supply arrangements that the British made for his troops. The President and Chief of Staff

[42] (1) *The Stilwell Papers*, p. 53 (2) MacMorland Diary, 9 Mar 42.

[43] (1) Rad, Chiang Kai-sek to Soong, for Roosevelt, 10 Mar 42. Item 19A, OPD Exec 10. (2) Rad AMMISCA 349, Stilwell to AGWAR, 11 Mar 42; Rad AMMISCA 342, AGWAR to AMMISCA, 1 Apr 42. AMMISCA Radio File, Job–11.

[44] (1) Memo, Confs with Generalissimo, 8, 15 Dec 41; Memo, Conf with Chinese Minister of War, Gen Ho, MacMorland, recorder, 10 Dec 41. AMMISCA Folder 7. (2) MacMorland Diary, 15 Dec 41.

[45] (1) Memo, Eisenhower for Marshall, 11 Mar 42. Item 19A, OPD Exec 10. When Eisenhower gave the draft memorandum to the President he explained that it was just a temporizing measure. Roosevelt included this passage in his message: "I realize the above sounds like temporizing . . . ." (2) Memo, Magruder for Stilwell, 13 Mar 42, sub: Views of Generalissimo on Comd in Burma. SNF–56. This memorandum repeats the Generalissimo's proclaimed desire that Stilwell command all Allied forces in Burma.

[46] Rad, Churchill to Roosevelt, 17 Mar 42. ABC 311.5 (1–30–42), A48–224.

added the very pointed comment that a Chinese commander might make things impossible for Alexander.[47]

Meanwhile, in Chungking Stilwell was trying to solve the command problem and free himself of the tactical and personnel restrictions imposed by the Generalissimo. For a short-term solution of the Sino-British impasse Stilwell favored co-operation, and for the long run he had no objections to serving under Alexander; indeed, when on one occasion a translator's error made it appear for a while that, at Stilwell's urging, the Chinese had accepted British command, he wrote in his diary: "Suddenly the sun breaks through."[48] Stilwell worked earnestly to smooth over the situation, for two divisions of the 5th Army were being held at the Burmese border until the command and supply questions were settled to the Generalissimo's satisfaction. Stilwell knew that the Chinese reinforcements were needed in Burma and had suggested sending in still another Chinese army. He was satisfied with British handling of the supply question, and Alexander and he had agreed to handle the command question for the present by close co-operation.[49] On 27 March, after Alexander visited Chungking and saw the Generalissimo, the Chinese reversed themselves again on the command question. Madame Chiang sent a casual little note to Stilwell, saying, "At your suggestion, pending further developments from Washington, the High Command of Burma will rest in General Alexander's hands. . . ."[50] The concession proved meaningless, and in his report on the campaign Alexander called his command nominal.[51]

Stilwell's own command position was settled on 11 March after the Chinese gave many hints, which Stilwell recorded with care:

Chinese *fa tzu* [method]—they don't say to me—"you will command the 5th and 6th Armies under such and such conditions." Instead, it sort of slips out after a lot of talk. Of course, I couldn't ask outright. "I told them to take orders from the British until you get there"; "when you go down to Burma"; "Gen. Shang Chen will introduce you"; "I don't ask for a Chinese commander; I just want them to include the British in your command."[52]

When the Generalissimo finally gave the word he was quite clear:

I wish to inform you that this morning I issued orders to place the 5th and 6th armies under your command. . . . General Ling Wen-wei has his headquarters at Lashio, and in the rear you can use his. I have ordered him to give you all assistance, and you can use his staff officers, and in the rear he can act as your chief of staff. Generals Ling, Tu, and Kan (commanders-in-chief of the 5th and 6th army [*sic*]) have been ordered to take orders from you absolutely. . . .[53]

[47] Memo, Marshall for Field Marshal Sir John Dill, JSM, 19 Mar 42. Item 62, OPD Exec 10. Marshall's description of Stilwell was: "an immensely capable and remarkably resourceful individual, but he is not in any degree a 'pusher' for himself and he possibly understands more of how to do business with the Chinese, particularly in regard to military matters, than any other individual in this country."
[48] Stilwell Diary, 11 Mar 42. (2) Stilwell B&W, 11 Mar 42.
[49] History of CBI, Sec. III, Ch. IV, pp. 9–10.
[50] Handwritten Ltr, Mayling Soong Chiang (Mme. Chiang) to Stilwell, 27 Mar 42. Stilwell Documents, Hoover Library.
[51] Alexander Report, *Supplement to The London Gazette*, pars. 19, 22.
[52] Stilwell B&W, 10 Mar 42.
[53](1) Min (Chinese version), Conf, Stilwell and Generalissimo, 11 Mar 42. Stilwell Documents, Hoover Library. (2) Stilwell B&W, 11 Mar 42.

The restrictions which the Generalissimo now proceeded to place upon Stilwell's use of his new command were hard on an aggressive soldier. Stilwell tried to have them lifted and thought he succeeded, only to conclude in time that the Chinese concessions on strategy as on command were purely formal. In the initial conference of 6 March the Generalissimo stated accurately that there was no plan for the campaign in Burma. In succeeding talks he tried to make his views clear to Stilwell. These discussions revealed the Generalissimo's belief that his 5th and 6th Armies were the best he had, that they should not attack the Japanese, but that, if the Japanese attacked them and were repulsed, then they might attack. He expressed extreme distrust of the British. More specifically, the Generalissimo stated: "My idea ultimately is to hold a line east and west through Thazi if the Chinese troops are to defend Mandalay. In that case, should the British troops at Prome retreat, then we hold a slanting line with Mandalay as the pivot point in order to protect Myitkyina and Lashio, our railway and highways in order to keep communications between China and India uninterrupted." [54] A day later he remarked, "As long as the British hold Prome, we hold Toungoo." [55]

When it came to tactics, the Generalissimo severely restricted Stilwell. The latter was to put his forces in a column of divisions about fifty miles apart. The 200th Division of the 5th Army was to stay at Toungoo as long as the British held Prome. The 6th Army was to hold fast in the Shan States. The remaining two divisions of the 5th Army were to enter Burma when supplies were satisfactorily arranged and then advance as far as Mandalay. Caution and the defensive were enjoined over and over again though Stilwell suggested an offensive to retake Rangoon. [56]

Three things fitted together in Stilwell's mind: the Generalissimo's injunction to hold north Burma in order to cover the route to India; the approach of the monsoon rains which would probably begin about 15 May; and the terrain of Burma from Mandalay and above, with a steep escarpment rising dramatically from the plain just east of Mandalay. Stilwell's intentions for the campaign in Burma were to work toward the recapture of Rangoon because he thought that the Japanese might be weak and that boldness might pay big dividends. If this plan failed then the Chinese would fall back toward the north and, from positions on the high ground east of Mandalay, offer a flanking threat to any Japanese drive northward. The monsoon rains were expected to complicate the Japanese task enormously. [57]

[54] Min (Chinese version), Conf, Stilwell and Generalissimo, 9 Mar 42. Stilwell Documents, Hoover Library.
[55] Min (Chinese version), Conf, Stilwell and Generalissimo, 10 Mar 42. Stilwell Documents, Hoover Library.
[56] (1) Ibid. (2) Min, Conf, Stilwell and Generalissimo, 9 Mar 42. Stilwell Documents, Hoover Library.
[57] (1) Interv with Col Frank Dorn, 2 Oct 47, at Carlisle Barracks, Pa. Interview Folder, Gen Ref Br, OCMH. (2) Min, Confs, Stilwell and Generalissimo, 9, 10 Mar 42. Stilwell Documents, Hoover Library. (3) Handwritten Paper by Stilwell, sub: General Plan. SNF-56.

Stilwell's larger plans were:

General Plan: (1) Complete communications with India, and operate against the Japs at Rangoon. Whether or not we use the port, it must be denied to the Japs for use as a base. Reinforce the 5th and 6th Chun [armies], first with the 71st. Move other units into the Kunming area, where they can train, as a preliminary to moving them into Burma. After making Rangoon safe, concentrate at Kunming–Kweiyang for an offensive to Hanoi (1), or to clear the Hankow area (2).

(1) The Hanoi plan would give us a base for aviation to work on the Jap communications, but it would not decide anything. The Japs would by-pass it. Hankow would have to be taken, anyway. (2) Clearing the Hankow area would put us within striking distance of Japan. The Japs would be backed up to Nanking and Suchow, and a push north through Kaifeng would force the evacuation of South Shansi and the Chengchow area. By this time aviation should be available to support all ground operations.

Hankow could be isolated by a holding attack in West Hupeh and a double envelopment—through Sinyang and north of the Tai Pieh Shan and from the Changsha–Hengyang area on Nanchang and Kiukiang.

The 30 divisions to be equipped and armed should be designated at once [in the 9 March conference, the Generalissimo said it would be easy to designate them when the arrival date of the lend-lease was known] and brought to the Kweiyang–Kunming area for training and as a preliminary concentration for possible use in Siam and Indo-China. Thought should be given to the use of guerrillas there; it would be helpful to have them established well inside the borders before troops move in. They should take the attitude that the Chinese are liberating the natives and establish friendly relations if possible.

Everywhere in occupied China, regular forces and guerrillas should increase their activity, and at the very least, constantly harass the Japs and keep them from mutual support. The weak points will be disclosed and we will know what, if any, air strength can be pushed in to help them.

Work on all roads should be pushed. Sooner or later they will be needed for heavy motor traffic. Work should be pushed on all airfields that need it.

A general plan for location of dumps, etc., should be prepared, based on a basic plan for future operations.[58]

Immediately after the Generalissimo stated on 11 March that Stilwell would command in Burma, Stilwell left to meet with his new subordinates, Lt. Gen. Tu Yu-ming (5th Army), Lt. Gen. Kan Li-chu (6th Army), and Lt. Gen. Lin Wei (the Ling Wen-wei of the conference minutes, Chinese General Staff Mission). They all agreed with Stilwell that the way to defend north Burma was to stand at Toungoo; Lin Wei and Tu agreed to start the two remaining divisions of the 5th Army to Burma. Then Stilwell went back to Chungking to see if the rest of the Army hierarchy would join him in asking the Generalissimo's consent to Stilwell's orders for a concentration around Toungoo. Stilwell felt optimistic; Tu and Kan made a good impression on him and he felt the Chinese accepted him.[59] The War Department was told that there were restrictions on him but that he hoped to do something if the Japanese were not reinforced.[60]

[58] Paper cited n. 57(3).
[59] The Stilwell Papers, pp. 62–64.
[60] (1) Rad AMMISCA 377, Stilwell to AGWAR, 18 Mar 42; Rad AMMISCA 379, Stilwell to AGWAR, 19 Mar 42. AG 381 (12–19–41).

Under Stilwell's persuading, the Generalissimo somewhat relaxed his restrictions on tactics. In an emergency the 22d Division, 5th Army, might help the 200th Division, 5th Army, at Toungoo, but the 96th Division, 5th Army, was to stay in Mandalay. The attitude was to be strictly defensive, and General Alexander was to be helped only in an emergency. Three more divisions (66th Army) were promised, one of them to Mandalay, two to stay on the border. The Generalissimo observed that three Chinese divisions were needed to match one Japanese division and odds of five to one for an attack.[61]

Darkening Prospects for Burma's Defenders

Far to the south of Chungking, Mandalay, and Toungoo, a series of naval disasters in the Indian Ocean left Burma's defenders without British or American reinforcements in the closing days of the campaign because they aroused the gravest apprehensions for the safety of India. Even before action was fairly joined in the Far East, the loss or disabling in November–December of 4 Royal Navy battleships, 1 battle cruiser, and 1 aircraft carrier severely handicapped the Royal Navy. In March 1942 the Admiralty was able to spare for operations in the Indian Ocean 5 old battleships, 3 carriers, 14 cruisers, and 16 destroyers. Their commander, Admiral James Somerville, R.N., expected the Japanese to appear with a few carriers supported by three of the ubiquitous *Kongo*-class battle cruisers, a force he could meet with reasonable chance of success. When the Japanese were sighted, Somerville decided to try for a night air strike, like that which had been so successful at Taranto. In the maneuverings preliminary to that attempt, he lost two heavy cruisers, a destroyer, and an auxiliary cruiser to the Japanese carrier aircraft, which also raided Ceylon. There was a large-scale flight of refugees from Ceylon, and essential services were dislocated.[62]

Somerville missed his attempt at a night contact and, as he now believed the Japanese carrier force was present in strength, he did not risk a daylight encounter but withdrew his carrier division plus the *Warspite* to Bombay and sent the battleships to Kilindini on the African coast, thus acknowledging that for the time at least Japan controlled the Bay of Bengal. Sweeping the bay, the Japanese sank the old light carrier H.M.S. *Hermes,* a destroyer, and a corvette. Then they sank 100,000 tons of merchant shipping, and withdrew to the east on the long voyage that ended at Midway. Somerville was justified in his apprehensions; present were six Japanese carriers plus four *Kongo*'s with

---

[61] Stilwell Diary, 19 Mar 42.
[62](1) Churchill, *Secret Session Speeches,* pp. 57–58, 74–75. (2) Lt. Col. Frank Owen, *The Campaign in Burma* (London, 1946), pp. 167–72. (3) Admiral Sir William James, *The British Navies in the Second World War* (New York, London, 1946), pp. 149–51. (4) Ltr, CinC, Colombo, to CinC, India, information copy to SEAC, 22 Nov 43. SEAC War Diary, A46–217. (See Bibliographical Note.) (5) Ltr cited n. 10(2).

cruisers and destroyers. It was the Japanese naval air arm in the days of its greatest power.[63]

These successes suggested that Japan and Germany might be on the way to linking their forces in the Middle East, leading inevitably to the loss of India and China, a most alarming prospect to American leadership. Faced with the grave concern that the British Chiefs of Staff felt for India, General Marshall stated that American air power in India [64] would support General Wavell. There were no AAF aircraft available to reinforce India, but with British consent a considerable number of U.S. aircraft earmarked for the RAF were released to American use and sent to India. To the Prime Minister's appeal for naval aid Roosevelt replied that a major Anglo-American concentration off Ceylon was not as workable a solution as the replacement of the Royal Navy's Home Fleet units by American ships, thus releasing British craft for service in a homogeneous British Eastern Fleet. This was speedily done, and the British accelerated long-standing arrangements for the occupation of Madagascar to prevent an expected Japanese landing. Operations began on 5 May and firmly established Allied power on that island, which lay athwart the principal Allied line of communications to the Middle East.[65]

Fears for India's safety had their effect on the defense of Burma. In spring 1942 India had 984,514 men under arms. Eight brigades (2 divisions) were lost in Malaya; 5 Indian brigades were in Burma. Six divisions were in the Middle East. That left 4 in India, 1 in Ceylon—all of them new with far less training than the units lost in Malaya. Establishments in India had been drawn on heavily to equip the Middle East and, to a lesser degree, Malaya. With the needs of defense against the turbulent tribes of the Northwest Frontier Province, this left one brigade which was marching in overland when the end came. On 7 March General Wavell told the British Chiefs of Staff his "grave doubts" of his ability to hold Burma and urged a concentration in northeast India. The War Cabinet ruled that Ceylon should receive reinforcements rather than northeast India, so air and land reinforcements from India went to Ceylon rather than to Burma. Within India, Madras, Bengal, and Orissa had to be garrisoned against Japanese attacks, and in mid-March the first two were held

---

[63] USSBS, *Campaigns of the Pacific War,* pp. 31, 36.

[64] See Ch. II, above.

[65] (1) Memo, Marshall for Roosevelt, 18 Mar 42. Attached to the original, according to a note at the bottom, were a memorandum from roving Ambassador William C. Bullitt, Proposal for Establishment of U.S. Air Units in Cairo, and a memorandum from the President to Marshall. AG 381 (2–24–42) Sec 2. (2) Eisenhower called defense of the India–Middle East area the most important problem demanding immediate solution by the CCS. Memo, Eisenhower for Marshall, Apr 42, sub: Strategic Conceptions and Their Application to Southwest Pacific. ABC 381 (9–25–41) Sec 1, A48–224. (3) *The Memoirs of Cordell Hull* (New York, 1948), Vol. II, p. 1,482. (4) DO (42), 10th Mtg, Minutes of Meeting Held on Tuesday, 14th April (42), at 10:00 P.M. WDCSA 381, File I, A46–523. (5) Sherwood, *Roosevelt and Hopkins,* pp. 523–38. (6) Samuel E. Morison, *The Rising Sun in the Pacific: 1931–April 1942* (Boston, 1948), p. 167. (7) Rad, Churchill to Roosevelt, 7 Feb 42. Bk VI, Sec 3, Hopkins Papers. (8) Rad 134, Roosevelt to Churchill. Hopkins Papers. (9) Rad, Roosevelt to Hopkins, for Churchill, 14 Apr 43. Bk VII, Sec 1, Hopkins Papers. (10) Rad 320, Maj Gen Joseph T. McNarney to Marshall, 14 Apr 42. WDCSA 381 (Middle East), A46–523.

by two Indian divisions. The British 70th Division (less one brigade) was in Orissa and was expected to be reinforced in the summer by the British 5th Division and two Indian armored brigades. Ceylon was garrisoned by the 16th and 17th Australian Brigade Groups, the 34th Indian Division, and the 16th Brigade Group, 70th Division, supported by 3 fighter squadrons, 1 light bomber squadron, and 1 torpedo squadron. Surveying the Indian strategic picture in the House of Commons, Churchill remarked that General Wavell "is not therefore at present in a position to denude himself to any large extent and he must not cast away his resources." [66] With naval control of the Bay of Bengal lost to the Japanese, with grave concern felt that the Japanese might bypass Burma and land on the Bengal coast, other considerations had to yield. That Burma was written off is implied by Churchill's admission on 18 April that he did not know of anything more to be done for Alexander.[67]

German naval records reveal that on several occasions the Japanese gave their allies reason to think they were contemplating a move toward the Suez Canal. In conversations between German and Japanese officers in the spring of 1942, India was rarely mentioned. On one occasion the Japanese told the Germans they planned to take Madagascar, and on another asked for information on the beaches of Ceylon. On 19 April the Japanese Foreign Minister told the German Ambassador that Japanese actions would eventually extend to the western part of the Indian Ocean. Unhappily for those members of the Operations Division of the German Naval Staff who favored operations in the Mediterranean toward the Middle East, on 15 May the Japanese finally told the German Naval Staff that their next major effort would be made east, toward Hawaii and Midway, rather than west toward Suez. On the German side there were differences of opinion about a drive toward Suez and the naval operations staff could never persuade higher authority to give its views the necessary support that might have led to serious discussions with the Japanese. Axis unity was not what it appeared to be, for probably as early as January 1942 Japanese *Imperial General Headquarters* had decided to make the next major effort in the Pacific.[68]

---

[66](1) Field Marshal Viscount Wavell, "Operations in Eastern Theatre, Based on India, from March 1942 to December 31, 1942," *Supplement to The London Gazette,* September 18, 1946. (2) Churchill, *Secret Session Speeches,* pp. 68–70. (3) Because of the dissolution of ABDACOM, Burma was back under General Headquarters (India). Rads DBA 17; TOO 1927Q/17; DBA 20; ABDACOM 01623, 19 Feb 42; DBA 21; ABDACOM 02397, 25 Feb 42. Earliest Messages Folder, A48–179. (4) Rad New Delhi 47, 2 Apr 42. Item 1461, Folder 9, A47–136. (5) Hist Sec (India), India at War, 1939–1943, pp. 10, 11, 27, 34, 39, 44–45, 59, 64, 137. Gen Ref Br, OCMH. (6) Ltr (copy 1787/H), Brig W. E. H. Condon, Combined Inter-services Hist Sec (India), to Col the Nawabzada Mohammed Sher Ali Khan, Indian Embassy, Washington, 1 Feb 47, sub: Hist Information on Indian Army. HIS 330.14 CBI 1947.

[67] Rad, Churchill to Roosevelt, 18 Apr 42. ABC 381, Burma (3–10–42), A48–224.

[68](1) Office of Naval Intelligence, War Diary of the German Naval Staff, Operations Division. Pt. A, Vol. 28, entries of 19, 21, 22 Dec 41; Pt. A, Vol. 29, p. 117, entry of 13 Jan 42; Pt. A, Vol. 30, p. 175, entry of 17 Feb 42, p. 218, entry of 20 Feb 42, p. 221, entry of 21 Feb 42, p. 172, entry of 17 Feb 42, p. 240, entry of 23 Feb 42; Pt. A, Vol. 32, p. 70, entry of 3 Apr 42; Pt. A, Vol. 33, p. 24, entry of 2 May 42, p. 120, entry of 9 May 42, p. 195, entry of 15 May 42. (2) Japanese Study 72, History of the *Army Section, Imperial General Headquarters.*

Whatever the Japanese intended to do in the Pacific, they were far from idle in Burma. Exploiting the advantages of sea power to the utmost, they were reinforcing faster than the Allies. Originally they had planned to take Burma with four regiments, but the fear of heavy Chinese reinforcements made added strength seem desirable, while the fall of Singapore on 15 February made it available. The *18th* and *56th Divisions* (less the *146th Regiment* of the *56th*), the *213th Regiment* of the *33d Division,* plus the *1st* and *14th Tank Regiments,* arrived at Rangoon by sea during March and April. The *18th* and *56th* went to the Sittang valley, while the *213th* rejoined its division.[69]

1 BURMA CORPS [70]	JAPANESE *15TH ARMY*
(Lt. Gen. William J. Slim)	(Lt. Gen. Shojiro Iido)
7th Armored Brigade Group	*33d Division* (Lt. Gen. Genzo Yanagida)
1st Burma Division (Maj. Gen. J. Bruce Scott): 1st Burma Brigade, 2d Burma Brigade, and 13th Indian Infantry Brigade	*213th Regiment* *214th Regiment* *215th Regiment*
17th Indian Division (Maj. Gen. David Cowan): 16th, 48th, and 63d Indian Infantry Brigades	*18th Division* (Lt. Gen. Renya Mutaguchi)
	55th Regiment *56th Regiment* *114th Regiment*
CHINESE EXPEDITIONARY ARMY IN BURMA [71]	
(Lt. Gen. Joseph W. Stilwell)	*55th Division* (Lt. Gen. Yutaka Takeuchi)
5th Army (Lt. Gen. Tu Yu-ming): 22d, 96th, and 200th Divisions	*112th Regiment* *143d Regiment*
6th Army (Lt. Gen. Kan Li-chu): 49th, Temporary-55th, and 93d Divisions	*56th Division* (Lt. Gen. Sukezo Matsuyama)
66th Army (Lt. Gen. Chang Chen): 28th, 29th, and 38th Divisions	*113th Regiment* *146th Regiment* (Arrived May 1942) *148th Regiment*

[69] (1) SEATIC Bulls 244, 245. MID Library. (2) Japanese Study 88, Ch. IV.

[70] Following the Battle of the Sittang Bridge, 23 February, 46th Indian Infantry Brigade was broken up to provide replacements. During the campaign, the Army in Burma had a total of 30 battalions, Burmese, Indian, and British. These were attached to and detached from brigades as the tactical and administrative situation required. Only those battalions of the Burma Rifles which engaged in combat are included in this total. Present in Burma were a number of paramilitary formations such as the 6 battalions of the Burma Frontier Force, the 5 battalions of the Burma Auxiliary Force, and 5 100-man columns of mounted infantry. These five columns gave good service, but the Burma Frontier Force and Burma Auxiliary Force did not have such capabilities as would justify listing them in an order of battle. There were also four more battalions of Burma Rifles (11th, 12th, 13th, 14th) of which the first two were employed chiefly on interior guard duty and the latter two proved unreliable and never entered combat.

[71] The numbered designations of the three regiments in a Chinese division can be determined by multiplying the division's designation by three. The product is the number of the third regiment. Thus, the regiments of the 22d Division are 64th, 65th, and 66th.

Information on Burmese, Chinese, and Japanese forces from:

(1) Foucar. (2) Japanese Study 88. (3) SEATIC Bulls 244, 245. MID Library. (4) The Campaign in Burma.

Burma's defenders, badly handicapped throughout the six-month campaign by utterly inadequate information on the enemy, did not know that the Japanese strength had almost doubled. The G–2 journal of Stilwell's headquarters quoted a British report that forty Japanese transports landed troops at Rangoon on 12 April. The official theater history of the campaign, prepared after its close, put the *33d* and *55th Divisions* in Burma and the *17th* and *18th* in northern Thailand as of March–April 1942. Actually, northern Thailand was empty of Japanese, while there were four divisions in Burma proper, three of them in the Sittang valley.[72]

The Japanese headquarters, *15th Army,* planned to complete the campaign by late May by surrounding and annihilating the British and Chinese force in the vicinity of Mandalay. The *33d Division* would drive north up the Irrawaddy valley through Prome and Yenangyaung; the *55th,* up the Rangoon–Mandalay Road through Meiktila; the *56th,* wide to the east through Taunggyi and then northward. The *18th* would be in reserve in the Sittang valley.[73]

The Chinese Expeditionary Force

The Chinese divisions entering Burma, though with one exception fairly representative of the better Nationalist divisions, still had weaknesses that put heavy burdens on the skill of their leaders and the devotion of their troops. They varied greatly in size. The 200th Division began with about 8,500 men. It was fully motorized and had a small armored component. The other two divisions of the 5th Army, the 96th and 22d, had about 6,000 men each. The 6th Army divisions averaged 5,700 in strength. These were not all combat troops by any means; each division included coolie labor units for transport and replacements.[74]

The 5th Army originally had twelve 75-mm. pieces, some of which were lend-lease howitzers. By 5 April, twenty-four lend-lease 75-mm. howitzers had been added to that modest store. A motorized battalion of 105-mm. howitzers was present during the campaign. Medical supplies were almost nil, and the Chinese medical organization was largely on paper. Very valuable aid was given by Dr. Gordon Seagrave, an American medical missionary later famous as the Burma Surgeon, his few doctors, American and British ambulance

---

[72](1) MA Rpt IG 6910, in Opns Jour, Burma, 16 Mar–2 May 42, Col Frank N. Roberts, G–2, p. 18. MID Library. This report contains daily G–2 information of Stilwell's headquarters. (2) Notes by Colonel Roberts, as collated by Capt. John LeR. Christian. MIS Folder, Burma Campaign, MID Library.

[73] Japanese Study 88, Ch. IV.

[74](1) Memo, sub: Chinese Organization. MIS Folder, Burma Campaign, MID Library. (2) Memo, Col Rufus S. Bratton, Chief, Int Gp, WDGS, for Chief, Strategy Sec, OPD, sub: The Recent Campaign in Burma. MID Library. (3) Memo of Conf with Minister of War, 23 Dec 41, AMMISCA Folder 7. (4) Foucar, pp. 133, 164. (5) Aldrich Diary, 11 Jan 42. (6) The Campaign in Burma, p. 25. (7) Rad AMMISCA 256, Magruder to AGWAR, 13 Feb 42. AG 400.3295 (4–14–41) Sec 1A.

drivers, Burmese nurses, and British medical units supplied by Alexander from his own meager resources. Commissioned as a major in the Medical Corps, Seagrave was aided by Capt. John H. Grindley, and Capt. Donald M. O'Hara. Though a dental surgeon, Captain O'Hara tirelessly assisted in the treatment of Chinese wounded. The bulk of medical supplies came from the American Red Cross stocks at Lashio.[75]

Logistics was a source of concern, though the supply and maintenance of the Chinese were assumed by the British. Southward movement of Chinese troops and supplies, on the Chinese side, was the responsibility of that same General Yu Fei-peng with whom Colonel Twitty had attempted to deal. Yu was also charged with moving Chinese Ministries' and China Defense Supplies' stocks to China. The opportunities of commercial profit from transporting rice, gasoline, and consumer goods to China were enormous, and many Americans who dealt with Yu believed he was diverting trucks and fuel from military movements to take the fullest advantage of these commercial opportunities.[76]

Officials of the Government of Burma and Army in Burma headquarters were well aware of this and resolved that their resources should not be used by the Chinese to compensate for, or to expedite, Yu's transactions. Consequently, even legitimate Chinese requests for supplies and trucks were met with suspicion. These bickerings tended to distract attention from the real needs of the front. Nor was the Government of Burma helpful. All Chinese troops moving to the Sittang and Irrawaddy fronts had to pass through Mandalay, and the Government of Burma ruled that only one Chinese division at a time could be in that city. Therefore, each division in turn had to clear Mandalay completely before the next entered. Concentration was hampered by this and, because the 38th Division was several weeks in clearing the Mandalay area, the final collapse found the other two divisions of the 66th Army hopelessly strung out along the road from China.

The Burma Railways were poorly managed by the Government of Burma, and they were not at their best under Japanese bombing. They were not militarized until late in the campaign. Efforts to stiffen their personnel—many of whom deserted their posts—with veteran Chinese railway men, as requested by the British military attaché in China, were temporarily defeated by the railway management with the statement that nothing was known in Burma of such arrangements. Many of the Americans concluded that the Government of

---

[75](1) Foucar, App. (2) Memo cited n. 74(1). (3) The Campaign in Burma, p. 24. (4) First Burma Campaign, a diary of the campaign kept by Col. Willard G. Wyman, 5 April 1942. Gen Ref Br, OCMH. (5) Ltr, Boatner to authors, 4 Apr 50. HIS 330.14 CBI 1950. (6) Captain O'Hara's service was rendered under a peculiar physiological difficulty—he was allergic to rice. Ltr, Lt Col Felix Nowakowski, Records Administration Center, St. Louis, Mo., to Sunderland, 13 Feb 50. HIS 330.14 CBI 1950.

[76] (1) See Ch. II, pp. 57–60, above. (2) The Campaign in Burma, pp. 12–13. (3) Ltr, Boatner to Chief, HD SSUSA, 14 Nov 47. HIS 330.14 CBI 1947. (4) Ltr, Boatner to Stilwell, 13 May 42, sub: Anglo-Chinese Relations at Lashio. SNF–21. Boatner, then a lieutenant colonel, commanded Stilwell's rear echelon at Lashio.

Burma would not recognize the existence of an emergency but adhered to the leisurely, settled routines of peace, regardless of consequences.[77]

The command technique Stilwell used in Burma is revealed by passages in his writings, in addition to the procedures he followed. To help him command the 5th and 6th Armies through Chinese channels Stilwell used a personal staff and a liaison system. This staff, plus senior Chinese officers, aided him in preparing plans, staff studies, and orders. Orders went to the Chinese General Staff Mission to Burma, which translated them into Chinese and arranged them in the accepted form. The General Staff Mission passed the orders through Chinese channels to the Army commanders concerned. Stilwell's American liaison officers informed him of the execution of the orders in the field. Stilwell expected the main burden of command to be borne by the Chinese themselves. Their commanders were men of long experience in fighting the Japanese; the troops, though lightly equipped, were many and were veterans. Stilwell could not be on every front and expected the Chinese commanders to show a degree of initiative.[78]

The American personal staff and liaison system had its headquarters at Maymyo. Brig. Gen. Thomas G. Hearn was chief of staff; Lt. Col. Frank N. Roberts, G–2; Col. Frederick McCabe, G–3; Col. Benjamin G. Ferris, G–4. Stilwell's aide was Lt. Col. Frank Dorn. The forward command post, under Maj. Gen. Franklin C. Sibert, assisted by Lt. Col. Willard G. Wyman, was initially near General Tu's headquarters. General Sibert doubled as liaison officer with Tu's 5th Army and as tactical adviser to the Chinese. Colonel Sliney was artillery adviser to the 5th Army. Colonel McCabe was also liaison officer with the Chinese 6th Army, as was Colonel Aldrich of AMMISCA. Maj. Frank D. Merrill, who had come to Burma from the Philippines prior to the outbreak of the war to join AMMISCA and who had been with the British during the opening phases of the campaign, was liaison officer with the British. Capt. Paul L. Jones acted as transportation officer and cut across command channels and red tape in the attempt to move supplies forward. Supply officer and headquarters commandant for Stilwell's modest establishment was Maj. Felix Nowakowski.[79]

The Chinese Begin Their Fight

The concentration of the 200th Division about Toungoo in the Sittang valley was covered by the 1st Burma Division. On 1 March this formation

[77] (1) Ltr cited n. 76(4). (2) Hutton Report, *Supplement to The London Gazette,* par. 44. (3) The Campaign in Burma, p. 13. (4) Notes on First Burma Campaign by Maj. Frank D. Merrill. Gen Ref Br, OCMH.

[78] Stilwell's liaison system in Burma in 1942 was very similar to the one the French used during World War I. By their system, General Headquarters (Grand Quartier Général) continuously and swiftly informed of events in the field. Stilwell's knowledge of the French system came from a volume by Edward L. Spears, *Liaison, 1914: A Narrative of the Great Retreat* (Garden City, N. Y., 1931), in his Carmel, Calif., library.

[79] Ltr, Merrill to Maj Gen Harry J. Malony, Chief, HD SSUSA, 10 Jul 47, p. 6; Ltr, Maj Gen W. G. Wyman to Malony, 27 Jun 47; Ltr, Nowakowski to Sunderland, 13 Feb 50. HIS 330.14 CBI 1947, 1950.

scored one of the rare Allied tactical successes of the campaign by recovering two Burmese villages from the Japanese in an attempt to close on the 17th Indian Division. Then it halted, for the decision had been reached to mass the British (or imperial forces, as they will be called henceforth, because most of them were Indian and Burmese) in the Irrawaddy valley while the Chinese gathered around Toungoo.[80] On the 15th, Alexander promised Stilwell that the Burma Division would hold its position below Toungoo until Stilwell could move up another Chinese division to support the 200th.[81] Before that stage was reached, General Tu asked General Alexander to move the Burma Division "out of his way." Alexander was willing, for he was concerned about the Irrawaddy valley and wanted to hasten his concentration there. At this point, Stilwell intervened through Major Merrill and, reminding Alexander of his promise, secured a delay in the Burma Division's withdrawal. The 5th Army's concentration was still incomplete when the Japanese began to drive north. The Burma Division fought several rear guard actions before it passed through the Chinese lines and began to entrain for its trip to the Irrawaddy.[82]

After Stilwell established himself in Burma on 21 March, he sent out Battle Order 0001, through the Chinese General Staff Mission to Burma, to Headquarters, Chinese Expeditionary Force, thus proclaiming his intention of using the normal Chinese command channels. The chief of the mission, General Lin Wei, reported the order had gone at once to Generals Kan and Tu and should reach them on the 22d. Further, added Lin, he had alerted Tu by telephone, so that the 5th Army could go to work at once. The order attached the Temporary-55th Division of the 6th Army to the 200th Division and directed the 55th to close on the 200th. Both forces were to be under General Tu, who was made responsible for Toungoo's defense. The 22d Division, under Stilwell's control, was to move to Taungdwingyi, at the rear and center of the Allied line from Prome to Toungoo, and be prepared to assist the British in the Prome area. The 96th Division, also in army reserve, would move to Mandalay.[83]

This attempt to do China's share in holding the line Toungoo–Prome, as the Generalissimo had directed, resulted in the stubborn twelve days' defense of Toungoo by the 200th Division against repeated attacks by the *55th Division*. The walled town of Toungoo was a railroad station and road junction on the Mandalay–Rangoon road, and from it there was a road east into the Shan

---

[80] Foucar, pp. 96, 109–12, 125–26.
[81] Stilwell Diary, 15 Mar 42.
[82] (1) Diary, 18 Mar 42, cited n. 75(4). (2) Ltr, Col Frank D. Merrill, Notes on Burma Campaign. History of CBI, Sec. III, Ch. V. (3) History of CBI, Sec. III, Ch. IV. (4) The Campaign in Burma, pp. 10–11. (5) Rad MA London, 13 Mar 42. Item 1469, Folder II, A47–136. (6) Foucar, pp. 125–30. (7) Burmarmy Sitrep, 23 Mar 42. All Burmarmy Sitreps are in Operations Information Telegrams, A48–179. (8) Memo, Merrill for Stilwell, 20 Mar 42. SNF–56.
[83] (1) Battle Order 0001, 21 Mar 42, Lashio, Gen Stf Mission to Burma, NMC of Republic of China, Hq, Chinese Expeditionary Force, to Lt Gen Y. M. Tu, CO 5th Army, and to Lt Gen L. T. Kang [*sic*], signed Joseph W. Stilwell, Lt Gen, USA, Commanding; Ltr, Lin Wei to Stilwell, 21 Mar 42. Stilwell Misc Papers, 1942. (See Bibliographical Note.)

States that connected with the several roads from south to north that ultimately joined the Burma Road. There was an airfield adjacent to Toungoo, where the AVG trained before the war. The town itself was one of the larger population centers in the area. Almost due west of it on the Irrawaddy River was Prome, a rail terminus and river port. Prome was held by elements of 1 Burma Corps (17th Indian Division, 1st Burma Division, 7th Armored Brigade Group) under Lt. Gen. William J. Slim. Slim's men faced the Japanese *33d Division (213th, 214th, 215th Regiments)*.[84]

There was no line in the sense of a continuous fortified position, for the smallness of the force, the distance, and the intervening hill mass prevented that, but if either partner fell back the other would be concerned about his exposed flank, so each anxiously eyed the other. Toungoo's garrison, the 200th Division, was led by Maj. Gen. Tai An-lan, a man of "ability and force, and considerable courage." [85] General Tai had two regiments in Toungoo, less detachments on an outpost line to the south, with his third regiment guarding the airfield to his rear.

The Japanese wanted to take the airfield and also uncover the road to Taunggyi. Orders for an attack by the *55th Division* with two regiments were issued on 12 March, and the operation began on the 19th when the *112th Regiment* hit Tai's outposts. The Chinese held stoutly south of Toungoo on the five succeeding days, and the Japanese decided to try encirclement, sending their *143d Regiment* around the Chinese west flank. The *143d* surprised the airfield garrison about 0700 on 24 March and cut the road and rail line to the north.[86]

With the Chinese regiment holding the airfield were a mountain battery and some mounted infantry of the Burma Division en route to the Irrawaddy front. There must have been some choice as to a line of retreat, for the imperial units managed to make their way to the Irrawaddy, while the Chinese fell back on Toungoo. The town was then besieged, though it was incompletely encircled and open to the east. Fortunately, the Chinese had prepared it for all-around defense, with brick pillboxes and carefully arranged fields of fire.

Stilwell arrived at the front on 22 March. Over the next two days he and Tu reached a tentative agreement to bring the 22d Division as near as possible to Toungoo and prepare to counterattack with it in support of the 200th.[87] The Temporary-55th Division would be in reserve near by. On the 25th, the Chinese 1st and 2d Reserve Regiments arrived north of the city, were ordered to retake the airfield, but failed to move. To the south the *112th Regiment* launched one strong attack after another into Toungoo, broke into it, and by the evening of the 26th held it to the line of the railroad. The valor of the

---

[84](1) Rad AMMISCA 371, Stilwell to AGWAR, 18 Mar 42. AG 400.3295 (4–14–41) Sec 1A. (2) Japanese Study 88, Ch. IV.
[85] The Campaign in Burma, p. 93.
[86] Japanese Document 3562, Vestiges of War, a history of the *55th Division*, pp. 6–9. Gen Ref Br, OCMH.
[87] The Stilwell Papers, p. 69.

Chinese soldiery, stubborn and tenacious in defense, asserted itself in those close quarters, and for three days the struggle rocked back and forth within the walls. Though Stilwell's command post believed it had identified all three of the 55th's regiments in action at Toungoo, which would make the Japanese force a powerful one, Stilwell nevertheless thought the situation hopeful.[88]

The Government of Burma, whose attitude toward the southward movement of the Chinese troops seemed to Stilwell's staff to lie somewhere between the apathetic and the hostile, was shocked by the encirclement of Toungoo and bestirred itself to speed the 5th Army's concentration.[89] The 22d Division was in place and ready to attack south to relieve the 200th Division, an attack which would have caught the 143d Regiment between two fires and confronted two Japanese regiments with two divisions plus two regiments of the Generalissimo's best troops. "Here's our chance," wrote Stilwell on 26 March.[90]

The next day Stilwell began to learn that, despite the Generalissimo's statements in Chungking and the seeming acquiescence of the Chinese headquarters and the Chinese General Staff Mission to Burma, he did not command. The 22d Division failed to move, and Tu was prolific with excuses as to why an attack was impossible. On the 28th, Tu again agreed to move, as the chief of the Chinese military delegation to India and Burma told Stilwell, "I have just received a telegram from Lt. Gen. Tu Yu-ming, Vice-commander, CEF [Chinese Expeditionary Force] in Burma, which states: 'Your order dated 28 March 1942 has been received. I had circulated it [sic] to all the troops under my command. I feel, sir, I have the honor to transmit it to you.' "[91]

Stilwell now began to fear that the Japanese were reinforcing on his front with troops from the Irrawaddy and so on 28 March he asked Alexander to attack. Next day Major Merrill and Lt. Kenneth G. Haymaker left for Prome to seek Alexander's and Slim's co-operation. Though Alexander thought nothing useful could be accomplished by the operation he agreed and the attack was delivered as promised. On the Sittang front the 22d Division again did nothing, so on 30 March Stilwell faced the command issue squarely and resolved to confront the Generalissimo with the facts.[92]

While Stilwell was arguing and pleading with Tu Yu-ming to attack one Japanese regiment with five Chinese regiments, the Japanese were vigorously at work in Toungoo, and on 30 March the 200th Division began to retire. The withdrawal was well handled, and the 200th Division got away intact. The stubborn defense of Toungoo by the 200th Division was the longest defensive stand made by any of Burma's defenders and reflected great credit on the

---

[88](1) *The Stilwell Papers,* pp. 69–71. (2) Ltr, Boatner to Chief, HD SSUSA, 30 Jul 47, p. 20. HIS 330.14 CBI 1947.
[89] Ltr cited n. 76(4).
[90] Stilwell Diary, 26 Mar 42.
[91] Ltr, Fisher T. Hou, Chief, Chinese Mil Delegation to India and Burma, to Stilwell, 31 Mar 42. SNF–56.
[92] *The Stilwell Papers,* pp. 74–75.

division and its commander. Five years after, the Japanese looked back on it as the hardest fighting of the campaign.[93]

Merrill and Haymaker returned from their trip to Slim's headquarters to report that Slim had ordered one armored and two infantry brigades to attack the Japanese flank on the Irrawaddy. "In case of a breakthrough," they added, "objective is Rangoon." [94]

Alexander greatly restricted the number of troops to be used in the attack. The Burma Division, now reduced to seven battalions, was not drawn on. For the first phase a task force of three battalions plus one company of infantry, a tank battalion, a battery of artillery, and a company of sappers and miners was assembled. A reinforced battalion was ordered to protect the flank on the Irrawaddy.

The operation began the evening of 28 March, sorely hampered by the lack of air reconnaissance. Next day the British task force found the Japanese active on its eastern flank and became involved in a struggle with road blocks in trying to cope with this situation. Word then came that the Japanese (*215th Regiment*) were in Shwedaung, behind the task force. The British commander elected to cut his way out through the town, having already tried and failed to budge the Japanese on his eastern flank. The fighting on the outskirts of Shwedaung that afternoon and night was heavy, for the Japanese were continually reinforced from across the Irrawaddy. The detachment placed to guard against this had been ambushed and overwhelmed. The task force fought its way into Shwedaung during the day but could not get its vehicles through the town. They were abandoned at 1800 hours and the men retreated on foot. Ten tanks were lost, and units for which figures were available in 1943 reported 371 casualties. As a result of this action, the general fatigue of the troops, and the nature of the terrain, Wavell and Alexander agreed that a retreat of some fifty miles should begin "forthwith." [95]

The Loss of Air Cover

Having been driven from the Irrawaddy valley on 21 and 22 March, the Allied air units were unable to influence the campaign. Shortly before the loss of Rangoon the RAF and AVG withdrew to Magwe. For an air-warning net that field depended on two lines of Observer Corps telephones down the Sittang and Irrawaddy valleys. Nothing had been done to give the field accommodations, revetments, or dispersal facilities. The Japanese *5th Air Division,*

[93] (1) Japanese Study 88. (2) CM–IN 0262, Stilwell to AGWAR, 1 Apr 42. (3) Ltr, 10 Jul 47, pp. 23–24, cited n. 79. (4) The Campaign in Burma, pp. 15–23. (5) Jour., pp. 3–9, cited n. 72(1). (6) Diary, 28 Mar 42, cited n. 75(4). (7) Jack Belden, *Retreat with Stilwell* (New York, 1943), p. 43. (8) Interrog, Colonel Kouchi, Stf Off, *15th Army,* 8 Jan 48. Gen Ref Br, OCMH.

[94] Diary, 29 Mar 42, cited n. 75(4).

[95] (1) Foucar, pp. 112–23, 138. (2) Burmarmy Sitreps, 31 Mar, 1 Apr 42. (3) Alexander Report, *Supplement to The London Gazette,* par. 29.

the Japanese air headquarters in Burma, surmised the existence of another Allied air base in the Irrawaddy valley after Rangoon's fall and began the search. The find was actually made by the *33d Division* on 9 March, probably by agents attached to that unit.

With the completion of the Japanese campaign in Java the arrival of six more Japanese air regiments was expected by *5th Air Division,* and the blow on Magwe was held back till their arrival.[96] Meanwhile, discovering some fifty Japanese aircraft on Mingaladon field near Rangoon, the RAF mustered 9 Blenheim light bombers and 10 Hurricane fighters for a profitable attack on 21 March. While these aircraft were refueling and rearming in leisurely fashion that afternoon, the Japanese retaliated with the full weight of ten air regiments, perhaps 200 aircraft, all they had in Burma. Two more heavy attacks were made on the 22d.[97] When the Japanese finished, 9 Blenheims and 3 P–40's were counted as destroyed on the ground; 3 Hurricanes destroyed in the air; 5 Blenheims left unserviceable. As a result of this crippling blow the RAF aircraft withdrew to Akyab on the Arakan coast, while the ground personnel went to Lashio. Japanese bombings on 23, 24, and 27 March made Akyab untenable, and the few RAF surviving aircraft went to India from where they made some fifty-eight attacks in support of Alexander's withdrawal. The AVG displaced to Kunming to refit and reorganize.

Having forced the Allied air arm beyond the borders of Burma, the methodical Japanese now turned to the bombardment of the Burmese cities. They were largely unopposed, and their attacks usually ended the normal life of whatever town they chose to assault—Prome, Meiktila, Mandalay, Thazi, Pyinmana, Maymyo, Lashio, and Taunggyi.[98]

At Magwe the tactical results of the disaster were serious. There was no fighter cover for Allied troop movements. Allied commanders had only sporadic and inexpert air reconnaissance. The Japanese exploited the advantages of air reconnaissance to the utmost. The absence of air cover and reconnaissance on the Allied side was further aggravated by the sentiments of the Burmans. The countryside was now passively hostile, occasionally flaring into overt violence. Thanks to sympathetic Burmans, Japanese knowledge of the dispositions and movements of the Allies was detailed and exact, while the Japanese themselves seemed to melt into the background. Bullock-cart transport and native dress aided greatly in this. The Allies felt themselves constantly observed, while their stragglers were sniped or butchered, their wounded mutilated, and their buildings burned. There is no evidence that this guerrilla activity affected the course of the campaign or could not have been disregarded by a vigorous commander who took routine precautions, but it weighed on the spirits of the Chinese, Indian, and British soldiers.

[96] (1) Foucar, pp. 219–21. (2) Japanese Study 94, Ch. VI.
[97] (1) Jour, p. 3, cited n. 72(1). (2) The Campaign in Burma, pp. 15–16. (3) Japanese Study 94, Ch. VI.
[98] Alexander Report, *Supplement to The London Gazette,* par. 26.

SURVIVORS OF JAPANESE AIR ATTACK *are helped from collapsed shelters in Maymyo, Burma, April 1942.*

Many high functionaries of the Burman independence movement visited Japan in 1940–41, and the Japanese later stated that information was received from them. Very probably arrangements were made then to arm and train Burmese patriots when the Japanese attacked. Such an "army," perhaps 1,000 strong, was actually organized during the campaign. In addition to volunteer informants, the Japanese made good use of aerial reconnaissance and information patiently gathered from commercial sources.[99]

Stilwell's G–2, Colonel Roberts, had no means to cope with such a situa-

---

[99] (1) Wavell Despatch, December 15, 1944, to May 20, 1942, *Supplement to The London Gazette,* par. 32. (2) Hutton Report, *Supplement to The London Gazette,* par. 55. (3) Alexander Report, *Supplement to The London Gazette,* par. 31. (4) Interrog of Lt Gen Shinichi Tanaka, 13 Jan 48. Gen Ref Br, OCMH. General Tanaka was chief of operations of the General Staff in Tokyo; with Headquarters, *Southern Army,* in Singapore; commanded the *18th Division* in the North Burma Campaign (1943–44); and ended the war as chief of staff of the *Burma Area Army.* (5) Interrog cited n. 93(8). (6) Interrog, Lt Col Masahiko Takeshita, Stf Off, *15th Army,* 8 Jan 48. Gen Ref Br, OCMH. Colonel Takeshita claimed that the Japanese had not had a very exact knowledge of Burma's terrain before the war, and so spent one month in intensive study of material captured at Rangoon. He also referred to the services of Japanese living in Burma.

tion. His G–2 Section was simply himself, with occasional aid in translation from Merrill, who had been a language student and lived with the Japanese Army. In Roberts' opinion, the British tended to concentrate on a network of informants and to neglect ground reconnaissance, so that only rarely did they know where the Japanese were prior to the next Japanese attack. Their interest was directed toward material of value to the War Office. The Chinese, though willing to help Roberts, seemed to him not very interested in military intelligence, and their combat reports were unreliable. The result was that Burma's defenders did not know the strength or disposition of the Japanese and were "practically blind." Searching for some remedy, Roberts persuaded Chennault to assign two fighters a day to reconnaissance, for he could not obtain such help from the Royal Air Force. The effect of these dangerous and seemingly futile missions was very bad on pilot morale.[100]

The AVG Keeps Up the Fight

From the Chinese side of the fighting in Burma, Chennault retaliated swiftly for the attack on Magwe. Flights of the 1st and 2d AVG Squadrons were staged through forward airstrips to attack the Chiang Mai airfields on 24 March. The 2d Squadron attacked successfully, but the strike was marred by the loss of two pilots, one of them Jack Newkirk, of Scarsdale, N. Y., who with ten and a half victories was one of the leading American aces of the war's early days. On 10 April Chennault personally led twelve fighters to Loiwing, just over the border from Burma, and resumed operations from there. He had a grand total of 35 fighters in commission (including 13 new P–40E's) and 20 deadlined. To receive P–40E's the AVG had had to detach some of its pilots and send them to Takoradi in Africa to ferry them back to China. Twenty-six were on hand there by 23 April.[101] With their better equipment and performance they were a godsend to the AVG. Medium bombers would have been extremely useful to Chennault. He understood there were some in India and in April tried to obtain them from Brereton and Bissell, but none could be made available until June, long after the campaign was over. If the B–25's led by Lt. Col. James H. Doolittle in the first air attack on Tokyo on 18 April had made good their landing in China, they would have joined Chennault, but bad weather and poor communications, plus a flight longer than planned, resulted in the loss of all sixteen.[102]

---

[100] Ltr, Roberts to Malony, 21 Jul 47. HIS 330.14 CBI 1947.

[101] (1) Robert B. Hotz, *With General Chennault* (New York, 1943), pp. 199–200. (2) Chennault was ordered to active duty (he was until then a retired officer) on 9 April 1942 as a colonel and almost immediately afterward was promoted to brigadier general. (3) Memo 2, Bissell for Generalissimo, 14 Apr 42, sub: AVG; Ltr to CO, First AVG, 23 Apr 42. Ltrs to Generalissimo (Apr 42–Apr 44), CT 23, Dr 1, KCRC.

[102] (1) Ltr, Chennault to Bissell, 21 Apr 42; Ltr, Chennault to Brereton, 23 Apr 42, sub: Employment of B–25's. AVG File, Gen Ref Br, OCMH. (2) Craven and Cate, eds., *The Army Air Forces*, I, pp. 438–44.

Most of the AVG missions flown in April were patrol and reconnaissance, many of them low-level, three-ship flights over the Chinese lines to "show the flag" and "build morale." These latter missions were heartily disliked by the pilots, who considered themselves entirely vulnerable to the Japanese. Because they reported negative information on Japanese troop movements, they came to feel that their lives were being needlessly risked on futile reconnaissance missions. Actually, the information was useful to Stilwell, because it established the fact that there was no threat to Meiktila from a Japanese flanking movement as was feared for a time.

Two Japanese attempts to destroy the AVG at Loiwing resulted in the damage of 9 parked aircraft, while the Japanese lost 11. After the second Japanese raid on 10 April there was no major aerial combat until the 28th, when 14 or 15 P–40's met a force of escorted bombers near Lashio. Calculating that the Japanese would try to make a burnt offering of the AVG for the Emperor's birthday, Chennault emptied the Loiwing field and disposed his fighters to intercept. Thirteen Japanese fighters were downed for one AVG fighter damaged in landing.[103] On the basis of statistics April was a good month. The AVG tallied 33 Japanese aircraft as certain and 10 probable, for the loss of 1 aircraft destroyed and 9 damaged by strafing, with one pilot wounded.[104]

The type of mission flown, the cumulative strain of months of combat against heavy odds, the mounting discontent over the lack of aircraft and pilot replacements, the feeling of isolation and sacrifice, finally took concrete form among members of the AVG in a refusal to obey orders. A plan to fly escort for RAF Blenheims after the RAF had failed to keep an earlier rendezvous lit the fuse. Three or four pilots assigned to the mission refused to go. A group meeting only increased the tension and twenty-four pilots, the overwhelming majority of those present, offered their resignations. This crisis was met when Chennault told his pilots their action would be considered desertion. All but a few took back their resignations and the affair was smoothed over.[105]

Knowing the causes of the outbreak, Chennault tried to remove them. He suggested four immediate steps to Colonel Bissell of Stilwell's staff, who was also Army Air Forces representative at Chungking. These were: an appeal from the President to the AVG to stay in action; the immediate transfer of 30 fighter pilots and 50 to 100 crewmen from those then present at Karachi; early transfer of increments of the 23d Pursuit Group so the AVG could be reconstituted as a U.S. fighter group under that unit designation; relief from low-level, ground-support missions. A message from Roosevelt to the group was speedily sent. The progress of the campaign soon made it impossible to fly

[103] Ltr, 10 Jul 47, cited n. 79.
[104] (1) Chennault, *Way of a Fighter,* pp. 149–50. (2) Hotz, *With General Chennault,* pp. 201–06. (3) Int Summary, AVG Activities for Apr 42, Hq AVG. AVG File, Gen Ref Br, OCMH.
[105] (1) Hotz, *With General Chennault,* pp. 207–16. (2) Ltr, Chennault to Bissell, 19 Apr 42. AVG File, Gen Ref Br, OCMH.

the sort of missions objected to. The other suggestions were not acted on. Loiwing was evacuated on 4 May with the approach of the Japanese Army.[106]

The Attempts To Reinforce

Though these events meant the loss of air cover in Burma, the failure to remedy the situation did not mean lack of interest at the highest level. President Roosevelt, General Marshall, and Dr. Currie resembled men frantically working at a fire engine who see only a few drops of water trickle out at the end of a very long and leaky hose. Aircraft and pilots were allocated in quantity to Stilwell's air force, but nothing seemed to emerge in the Burmese skies.

Presumably, there were very considerable reinforcements for the AVG on the way. Marshall heard a month later that fifty-five pilots were set up for the 23d Pursuit Group on the assumption that the AVG would be inducted and redesignated as the 23d Group. Thirty-three of them were to fly over in A–29's for the Chinese Air Force; the other twenty-two pilots were designated already. The situation looked even brighter with regard to aircraft for the AVG and Chinese Air Force. There were 13 P–40E's east of Karachi, 6 there, and 29 on the way; 34 P–66's were on ship; 30 P–43's at Karachi, 57 at sea, and 21 in the United States ready to go.[107] On paper this seemed an imposing aggregation, and so Stilwell was asked by the War Department to find out if the Generalissimo would part with any of them for Brereton's use since no other fighters were readily available.[108]

The proposal came at a singularly poor time. The Generalissimo had complained to the President of the poor support China was receiving. Shortly after, there came a reply over Roosevelt's signature saying that the United States was stretched to the utmost. The menace to India, and so to the life line to China, was very grave, and immediate support had to be given to the British. This would have to come from the aircraft intended for the AVG, so after that unit had been brought back to strength the difference would go to Brereton for the defense of India. Coming only a few days after Stilwell's Chungking headquarters had promised that no aircraft would be diverted without the Generalissimo's consent, this was too much for the Chinese. The Generalissimo was "angry and excited." He told Bissell the action was a breach of faith which would adversely affect the good relations between China and the United States. Madame Chiang sent a very strong message to the President, bitterly protesting any such diversion from China's meager allocations. Plainly there had been administrative confusion in Washington, and Currie rushed off a cable, reaffirm-

---

[106](1) *Ibid.* (2) Memo, Col John R. Deane, Secy, WDGS, for, President, for CofS, 23 Apr 42. WDCSA (China), A45–466. (3) Chennault, *Way of a Fighter,* Chapter XI, gives Chennault's side of the story. The Air Forces' attitude is given in *The Stilwell Papers,* page 37.

[107] Memo, Brig Gen John H. Hilldring for CofS, 3 Apr 42, sub: Induction of AVG; Tab C, sub: Matériel and Personnel Status of AVG Replacements. WDCSA (China), A45–466.

[108] CM–OUT 2348, Arnold to Stilwell, 14 Apr 42.

FIGHTER PLANES, P–43'S, *receiving line service at an airfield in China, 1942.*

ing the old policy of making no diversions without China's consent. The Generalissimo was told that 456 aircraft were definitely allotted to China and would be sent in haste. The War Department query on the possibility of diverting Chinese aircraft was promptly shelved by Stilwell's headquarters.[109]

But there was no relief for the AVG in any of this, either with regard to personnel or matériel. Without informing Stilwell or Chennault, the Air Ferry Command canceled the forward movement of the replacements, so that two months after the first P–40's landed at Karachi, Chennault received only thirty-two aircraft and no personnel replacements.[110] No pilots reached him before the loss of Burma. Of the lend-lease fighter aircraft over which the Chinese were so concerned, ten P–43's were borrowed by Chennault from the Chinese Air Force and used in the summer of 1942. The remainder of those ferried to China were never used in combat. Those in India were, with Chinese consent, returned to U.S. custody in July and salvaged, for after the Chinese had insisted on receiving them and accepted delivery they then stated the P–43's

[109](1) Memo 4, Col Bissell for Generalissimo, 18 Apr 42. Ltrs to Generalissimo (Apr 42–Apr 44), CT 23, Dr 1, KCRC. (2) Memo, Marshall for President, 22 Apr 42, sub: Airplanes for China. WDCSA (China), A45–466. (3) Rad, Marshall to AMMISCA, 15 Apr 42. AG 381 (12–19–41). This radio put Brereton under British command for the time being and repeated that all aircraft over the authorized strength of the AVG would go to him. (4) Rad, personal from President to Generalissimo, 21 Apr 42. Bk V, Hopkins Papers.

[110] CM–IN 0955, Stilwell to AGWAR, 4 May 42.

were unfit for combat.[111] In India, Brereton was struggling to assemble his Tenth Air Force with plenty of fuel and pilots but no aircraft. The Chinese would not consent to his having "their" fighters, while the B–17's were helplessly strung out over the long ferry route from Miami, victims of a spare parts shortage and poor maintenance. Four months of unremitting effort from March to June 1942 brought no increase whatever in the size of Brereton's force.[112]

Brereton was more than willing to use what he could against the Japanese. This was 8 heavy bombers—6 of them from Java and 2 that had struggled across Africa—none in good condition. Conferring with Stilwell in Burma on 24 March, Brereton set 1 May as the approximate date that the Tenth could go into action. When he returned to Delhi three days later, Wavell told him that there was a strong possibility of a "combined sea-air attack in the near future on Calcutta or Colombo, possibly both," because the Japanese were accumulating shipping at Rangoon and at Port Blair in the Andaman Islands, which they had occupied shortly before. This and a "query from Wavell" led Brereton to rush preparations and attack Rangoon and Port Blair. The Rangoon mission was a failure, but eight tons of bombs were laid on Port Blair. Stilwell was surprised and angered, for he wanted the heavy bombers used against hostile aviation in Burma, and Brereton appeared close to disobedience.[113]

Brereton, however, as Stilwell soon learned, was acting in accord with the wishes of the President and Chief of Staff. The Tenth's commander also sent Stilwell a detailed, candid explanation of his problems and his actions, which revealed he had 7 B–17's, 1 B–24, 1 B–24D, and 7 P–40E's. His bombers could not operate in daylight, because the gunners were not trained and would not be so for another fortnight. The readiness of more squadrons depended on the receipt of aircraft, a matter over which he had no control and little information. His bombing missions had been flown on moonlit nights which was a good way to train raw crews. To operate in Burma he needed fighter cover and air-warning services, which were not then available.[114]

In answer, Stilwell expressed complete faith in Brereton as a commander and as a fighter. He added that he knew crossed radios and poor communications might cause misunderstandings. He wanted his U.S. forces to work as a team, and of his subordinates he asked only a prior look at major matters of policy and enough advance warning to co-ordinate the American effort. The tone was cordial and suggested that Stilwell regarded the incident as closed.[115]

[111] (1) Chennault, *Way of a Fighter,* p. 178. (2) Memo 26, Bissell for Generalissimo, 2 Jul 42. Ltrs to Generalissimo (Apr 42–Apr 44), CT 23, Dr 1, KCRC. (3) CM–IN 05412, Stilwell to Arnold, 13 Oct 42.
[112] Craven and Cate, eds., *The Army Air Forces,* I, pp. 494–95.
[113] Lt. Gen. Lewis H. Brereton, *The Brereton Diaries* (New York, 1946), pp. 113, 116–17. (2) Wavell Despatch, December 15, 1941, to May 20, 1942, *Supplement to The London Gazette,* par. 24. (3) Rad cited n. 109(3). (4) Rad AMMISCA 463, Stilwell to Brereton, 5 Apr 42. Item 6, Bk 1, JWS Personal File.
[114] Rad 21, Brereton to Stilwell, 9 Apr 42. Stilwell Misc Papers, 1942.
[115] Rad, Stilwell to Brereton. Stilwell Misc Papers, 1942.

On 15 April the War Department told Stilwell that until further notice, the Tenth Air Force would support Wavell and the defense of India. The B–17's struck the Rangoon docks on 16 and 29 April. [116]

Summary

March closed with Stilwell's central problem clear to him and the importance of its solution growing more urgent by the day. The military situation was bad enough, with the Toungoo–Prome line falling and air support lost. The only possible American contribution was more air support, and that was failing to arrive. These circumstances Stilwell apparently saw as subordinate to the one great question of command. He saw three possible courses open to him: (1) to accept his situation and do nothing about it; (2) to resign his command; and (3) to demand complete freedom of action in Burma with a force of Chinese under his command. He decided to proceed to Chungking, describe the situation to the Generalissimo, and then suggest that the Generalissimo either relieve him or give him independent command. With this resolve Stilwell left Burma for Chungking on 31 March 1942.[117]

[116](1) CM–OUT 2708, Marshall to Stilwell, 15 Apr 42. (2) Rad 134, President to Former Naval Person. Hopkins Papers. (3) Craven and Cate, eds., *The Army Air Forces,* I, p. 501.
[117](1) Stilwell Diary, 1 Apr 42. (2) *The Stilwell Papers,* pp. 75–78.

CHAPTER IV

China's Blockade Becomes Complete

When Stilwell conferred with the Generalissimo and Madame Chiang on 1 April he could not charge a clear, apparent repudiation of the Soong-Stimson accord on command, for he was faced with something else. The Generalissimo had given Stilwell command of the Chinese Expeditionary Force in Burma and then treated Stilwell exactly as he did his other army commanders. The Generalissimo believed in exercising the most detailed command from Chungking, on the basis of information which he received days late over an uncertain communications net.[1] And so he had sent radio after radio and letter after letter to his commanders in Burma—some bypassing Stilwell, some going to him. The Generalissimo's March 1942 letters to Stilwell have not survived, but Stilwell's description of them suggests they were like those of April and May 1942, which are available: "They direct all sorts of action and preparation with radical changes based on minor changes in the situation."[2] The result was that Tu had ignored Stilwell's orders, and that Alexander, to whose supreme command in Burma the Chinese had agreed, was in fact unable to exercise that command.

At the conference with the Generalissimo and Madame Chiang on 1 April, Stilwell asserted that the Chinese commanders had failed to obey and did not indicate his belief that in reality they were obeying the Generalissimo. (Stilwell took the same line with his superiors in Washington, in that he did not put the

[1] The Generalissimo described his system of command to Stilwell some months later in a conference, 24 June 1942. See Min (Chinese version), Conf, Stilwell and Generalissimo, 24 Jun 42. Stilwell Documents, Hoover Library. Stilwell's appraisal of the system, based on experience of it, is on pages 77–78 of *The Stilwell Papers*.

[2] (1) Quotation from *The Stilwell Papers*, p. 76. (2) Upon his return to the United States in 1944, Stilwell filed the Generalissimo's letters of April and May 1942 in three folders which are now in the Hoover Library. One group is in SNF–12; one is a folder labeled CKS Correspondence; and the third is an inclosure to General Lo Cho-ying s account of the First Burma Campaign in SNF–12. (3) "The Generalissimo, however, is the military commander in chief of the Chinese forces and it is his custom to give direct instructions to his divisional commanders. He sees no impropriety in this. In fact he actually gave me some of his communications to his divisional commanders in Burma, obviously expecting me to concur in their propriety and reasonableness. These communications, however, were direct orders and had the effect of completely undermining Stilwell's position as Commander-in-Chief in the field." Rpt, Dr. Lauchlin Currie, sub: Rpt on Visit to China, 24 Aug 42. OPD 336 China (24 Aug 42) F/W 111, A47–30.

CONFERENCE AT MAYMYO, BURMA. *Generalissimo and Madame Chiang Kai-shek with Lt. Gen. Joseph W. Stilwell, 9 April 1942.*

principal blame on the Generalissimo but rather on the division and army commanders.) Stilwell asked the Generalissimo to relieve him, adding that since the Chinese had accepted British command his presence was no longer necessary. If the Generalissimo was dissatisfied with Stilwell, certainly here was the opportunity to send him home. On that note Stilwell returned to his quarters.[3]

Next day he was invited back to Huang Shan, the Generalissimo's country estate, to learn that the Generalissimo was ready to take steps to confirm Stilwell's full authority. This the Generalissimo proposed to do by appointing Lt. Gen. Lo Cho-ying as Stilwell's executive and by personally visiting Burma to make Stilwell's status clear to the latter's subordinates. Quickly taking advantage of the more favorable atmosphere, Stilwell asked for the services of British-trained guerrilla units from Kiangsi Province. The Generalissimo at once agreed. Stilwell felt the request appealed to the Generalissimo, that he had been irked by British control over Chinese units.[4]

Sometime between the 2d and 4th of April Stilwell asked for the seal of authority. The Generalissimo agreed. On the 15th General Shang Chen sent the *chop* to Magruder:

> Acting under the instructions of the Generalissimo, I am sending you, by special messenger, an official seal bearing in Chinese the following inscription:
> "Chief of Staff, Headquarters of the Supreme Command of the Allied Forces, China War Theater."
> You are kindly requested to hand the seal over to Lt. Gen. Joseph W. Stilwell for his personal use.[5]

The Generalissimo then flew to Burma for conferences with the Chinese and British commanders over the 6th and 7th of April. There he lectured the Chinese generals and made it clear that Stilwell commanded. He told Alexander that the British must stand firm where they were, that there must be no more withdrawals. Stilwell was also encouraged by his own government. Roosevelt was very pleased by the frankness of Stilwell's report on the Toungoo fiasco and especially with his prompt measures to correct the situation. Apparently established in command beyond doubt, Stilwell prepared an ambitious plan for the discomfiture of the *55th Division* and began to busy himself with its execution.[6]

[3](1) *The Stilwell Papers,* pp. 76–80. (2) Stilwell Diary, 1 Apr 42. (3) Stilwell B&W, 1 Apr 42.

[4](1) Stilwell Diary, 2 Apr 42. (2) Stilwell B&W, 2 Apr 42. The British-trained Kiangsi troops were in the 32d Group Army under the command of Lt. Gen. Li Mo-an.

[5](1) Ltr FAB 66, Gen Shang to Magruder, 15 Apr 42. Stilwell Folder, China 1942, Stilwell Personal Papers. (2) Stilwell Diary, 4 Apr 42. Editor White's passage on page 116 of *The Stilwell Papers* omits Stilwell's recording on page 49, Stilwell B&W, of the fact that he received the *chop* as chief of staff instead of one proper for the commander in chief of the Chinese Expeditionary Force in Burma.

[6](1) *The Stilwell Papers,* pp. 82–83. (2) CM–IN 2406, Stilwell to AGWAR, 7 Apr 42. (3) The Campaign in Burma, p. 30. On 8 April 1942 Tu was at pains to announce that Lo now commanded. (4) Rad, Marshall to Stilwell, 3 Apr 42. AG 381 (12–19–41).

Stilwell asked the War Department to send an American infantry division to India, saying its presence would greatly strengthen his hand even if it could not be brought to Burma at once.[7] When it soon became obvious that no U.S. division would be assigned to him, Stilwell remarked in casual conversation with his staff that he wished he had some Chinese Communist troops in Burma, that he was sure they would accept orders from him. His G–2, Colonel Roberts, deprecated the suggestion, observing that since the Chinese Communists were not fighting the Japanese in China they were not likely to be willing to fight them in Burma. In 1944, Stilwell told Marshall that the Chinese Communists would have been willing to fight under him in 1942, and a passage in one of his analyses of the situation implies that in that year he had sought to use them somewhere but had been refused permission by the Generalissimo.[8]

The Pyinmana Plan and the Irrawaddy Front

General Stilwell's plan to defeat the Japanese at Pyinmana called for the 96th Division to concentrate in defensive positions there. (*Maps 3 and 5*) The 200th Division was to be poised and ready north and northeast of Pyinmana. The 22d Division was to fall back slowly on Pyinmana. On reaching its vicinity, the 22d was to fall back rapidly to the northwest, allowing the Japanese to come into contact with the 96th Division. Two weeks were allowed for this. As soon as the Japanese were well involved, a heavy counterattack was to be launched with all three divisions. "For the sake of policy," this emerged as "General Tu's Plan" for a counteroffensive. To the Chinese right, it would be essential for the British to hold in the Irrawaddy valley. They doubted their ability to do this and, when the Generalissimo visited Burma, Army in Burma headquarters asked for a Chinese division. One division was promised on condition that the British hold just north of Allanmyo.[9]

Deployment of the Chinese forces for the Pyinmana battle began on 3 April, and the 200th and 96th Divisions were in place by 6 April. The 22d Division executed its delaying mission successfully. The Japanese were still to

[7] Rad AGWAR 448, Stilwell to Stimson and Marshall, 3 Apr 42. Item 5, Bk 1, JWS Personal File.

[8](1) Interv with Brig Gen Frank N. Roberts, 25 Apr 51. (2) Rad CHC 1241, Stilwell to Marshall, 3 Jul 44. SNF–131. (3) Stilwell's cryptic comment is: "Use of Reds: 1942—No. Later attempts. No. Use of Cordon troops (Hu /Tsung-nan?/). No. Finally 1944—a few units grudgingly moved through fear for Kunming." The passage is from a paper found among his miscellaneous writings, which begins with the passage, "Mission.—Raise efficiency of Chinese Army for participation in the war. Chiang Kai-shek failure to carry out . . .," and ends, "No support anywhere. Chinese could not believe Chinese troops could fight the Japanese. No interest in Ramgarh or in Burma." Stilwell Papers, Hoover Library. (4) No other references to this episode have been found by the authors in any source examined by them.

[9](1) Notes by Col. Frank N. Roberts, as collated by Capt. John LeR. Christian. MIS Folder, Burma Campaign, MID Library. (2) Foucar, pp. 202, 224. (3) The Campaign in Burma, pp. 30, 31.

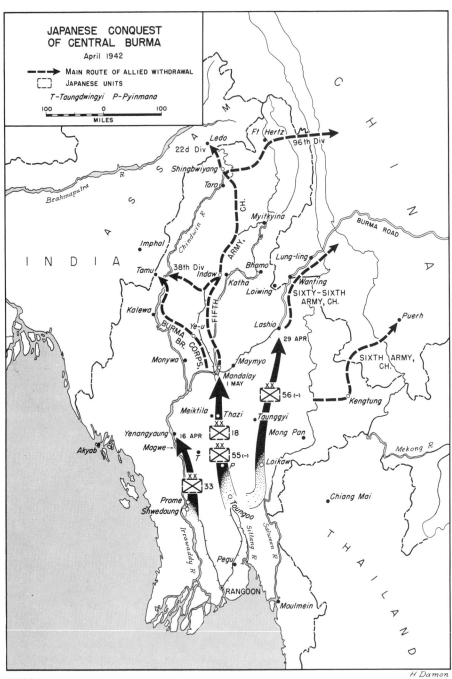

JAPANESE CONQUEST
OF CENTRAL BURMA
April 1942

- - - - ➤ MAIN ROUTE OF ALLIED WITHDRAWAL
⊏⊐ JAPANESE UNITS
T-Taungdwingyi P-Pyinmana

100   0   100
MILES

MAP 5

H Damon

be delayed as late as 17 April, for when the Chinese battalion on the outpost line withdrew prematurely, the officer responsible was sentenced to be shot. The Pyinmana trap was ready to be sprung, but events forced its dismantling before the intended victim was fairly ensnared. General Stilwell had ordered the 22d Division to delay for two weeks. It had done that but as the Chinese and Stilwell waited for the Japanese, events along the Irrawaddy had, by the 17th, made it impossible to execute the Pyinmana plan.[10]

An ultimate withdrawal from Prome to Allanmyo had been agreed on by Generals Wavell and Alexander, but the 63d Indian Infantry Brigade holding Prome, when attacked by the Japanese on the night of 30–31 March, withdrew after brief and desultory fighting, leaving 17th Indian Division's right flank exposed. On learning that the Japanese were passing through the gap, thus raising the possibility of a road block in his rear, the division commander after a consultation with corps headquarters ordered a retreat to the Allanmyo area. The movement was made speedily and without enemy interference.[11]

While the Chinese were insisting on the holding of Allanmyo and Stilwell at Pyinmana was awaiting the chance to launch his attack, the British commanders in Burma had been thinking of still further withdrawals. On 3 April Wavell radioed the War Cabinet that 1 Burma Corps would probably have to fall back to Magwe, about twenty miles up the river beyond Minhla, because the position they held was untenable. He was not hopeful of the situation in Burma and was considering the various evacuation routes. Next day, at Wavell's request, Alexander submitted his own estimate in equally dark terms, for he thought a gradual withdrawal northward inevitable, with the Allies covering Mandalay as long as possible. To complete the picture, Brereton submitted a similar estimate.[12] Since Wavell and Alexander took this attitude, it is hardly surprising that, though there was no Japanese pressure, between 3 and 8 April 1 Burma Corps fell back from about Allanmyo to the line Minhla–Taungdwingyi. Though the Japanese Air Force was usually much in evidence in those dark days, there was no contact with their ground forces.

This withdrawal was announced to Stilwell's and the Chinese 5th Army headquarters on 6 April. The British liaison officer painted a depressing picture, saying that as a result of previous battles their battalions were down to 300 or 400 men each and tanks could not operate off the roads without careful prior reconnaissance. The Chinese were upset by the news and caustic in their comments. General Sibert told the British liaison officer that the Chinese were

---

[10](1) The Campaign in Burma, pp. 30, 42. (2) Opns Jour, Burma, 16 Mar–2 May 42, Col Roberts, G–2, p. 11. MID Library. (Hereafter, Roberts' Journal.)

[11](1) Foucar, pp. 140–44. (2) Roberts' Journal, p. 11. (3) Burmarmy Sitrep, 4 Apr 42.

[12](1) Rads London 2312, 2337, 3, 6 Apr 42. A47–136. (2) Speaking to MacMorland on 10 April, Col. Orde Charles Wingate, later the famous Chindit commander, forecast a withdrawal to northern and eastern Burma. MacMorland Diary, 10 Apr 42. (3) CM–IN 2166, Brereton to AGWAR, 7 Apr 42.

extremely disappointed in British withdrawals and that continued withdrawal would have a serious effect on the attitude of the Chinese. On the 10th Lo and Tu presented Stilwell with a letter, dated 9 April, from the Generalissimo, saying there would be no Chinese division to aid the British; a battalion was enough.[13]

This letter began a series of references to the Irrawaddy front in communications from the Generalissimo that go far to illustrate his method of long-range command and his bypassing Alexander, to whose over-all command in Burma he had recently agreed. On 10 April the Generalissimo reversed his stand of the 9th and wrote:

> . . . According to our original plans a strong division must speedily be sent to support the British forces in meeting the northward advance of the enemy along the Irrawaddy. This is a strategic move which can by no means be neglected. It is my fundamental plan for the destruction of the enemy forces in Burma. It is imperative that, be the circumstances what they may, a division or more of our strength be so dispatched, as I directed in the first place. . . .[14]

On the 12th he again ordered the reinforcement of two key points within the British sector.[15] On the 15th the Generalissimo wrote:

> . . . The British force moreover are now in a hopeless position and to reinforce them by a division will not avail to maintain their lines. They will not wait until our forces have fought a decisive action at Pyinmana but will voluntarily abandon their positions and retreat to the Western bank of the Irrawaddy river. In view of this certainty our forces must quickly frame new plans for independent action without reference to the movements of the British forces. . . .[16]

This passage is certainly clear enough even if contradictory of the order three days before. On 20 April the Generalissimo reversed himself once again and ordered Stilwell to rescue the British.[17] As a result of these reversals and the physical impossibility of moving divisions about at that rate, when the British did take their stand on the line Minhla–Taungdwingyi to the right flank of the Chinese, there were no Chinese to help them in their attempt to hold a forty-mile front with 10,000 men and thirty-six guns.[18]

---

[13] (1) Roberts' Journal, p. 21. (2) First Burma Campaign, a diary of the campaign kept by Col. Willard G. Wyman, 6 April 1942. Gen Ref Br, OCMH. (Hereafter, Wyman Diary.)

[14] Ltr, Generalissimo to Stilwell, Lo, and Tu, 10 Apr 42. SNF–12.

[15] Ltr, Generalissimo to unnamed addressee [Lin Wei], 12 Apr 42. SNF–12.

[16] Ltr, Generalissimo to Lo, 15 Apr 42, Incl to Lo's account of the Burma Campaign. SNF–12.

[17] Ltr, Generalissimo to unnamed addressee [Lin Wei], 20 Apr 42. Folder, CKS Corresp, First Burma Campaign, Stilwell Personal Papers.

[18] Normal divisional organization called for 9 infantry battalions; at this time the 17th Indian Division included the remnants of 17. The 1st Burma Division with 7 weak battalions was badly understrength, but received 3 battalions from the 17th and 1 from the 7th Armored Brigade before it reached the Yenangyaung oil fields. Rad, New Delhi 49, 31 Mar 42. Stilwell Documents, Hoover Library. The Japanese had three regiments plus artillery, perhaps 15,000 men. Though the odds were not impossible, the defenders did not yet appreciate the importance of aggressive patrolling and co-ordinated attacks. Consequently, the Japanese could move almost at will through the gaps on the long front.

The Collapse of the Irrawaddy Front

The 17th Indian Division, less the 48th Brigade, held Taungdwingyi, a prepared position. At the other end of the line the 2d Burma Brigade was in Minhla, and four brigades in the center were to operate as a striking force. By a clever ruse, the Japanese opened a hole near the western end of the line. In trying to plug that breach, the imperial forces in the center of the line inclined westward, also opening a hole. This was very apparent to British commanders on the spot, who decided to accept the gap, to move the 1st Burma Division back on the great Yenangyaung oil fields, but at all costs to hold Taungdwingyi, the link with the Chinese. On the night of the 15th word was received that some 2,000 Japanese were bypassing the 1st Burma Division and heading north, undoubtedly toward Yenangyaung.[19]

Moving unobserved by the 1st Burma Division, the *214th Regiment,* plus the *2d Mountain Artillery Battalion,* established itself around the ford of the Pin Chaung, north of Yenangyaung, believed to be the only suitable exit for motor transport in the area. Beginning at 0100 on 15 April, shortly before the Japanese revealed their presence, the great Yenangyaung oil fields were burned on General Slim's order. At midnight of the 16–17th the Japanese opened fire on advanced elements of the Burma Division, whose main body was then twelve miles to the south, making the dreaded road block again a grim reality. The block was reported to corps headquarters, and arrangements were made through corps headquarters on the night of the 17th for co-operation with the Chinese 38th Division, 66th Army. Once the 38th Division was intended for the defense of Mandalay. But in compliance with the Generalissimo's 10 April order, it had moved toward the Irrawaddy as of 12 April to strengthen the link between the two armies, and so its 113th Regiment was now within marching distance.[20]

Maj. Gen. Sun Li-jen, the 38th Division commander and a graduate of the Virginia Military Institute, took personal command of the operations, supported by the tanks and artillery of the 7th Armored Brigade Group that had crossed the Pin Chaung Ford before the Japanese opened fire. The first phase of the Burma Division's attack on 18 April went according to plan and carried it to the outskirts of the little suburb north and east of Yenangyaung where the roads of the area converge for the ford. There the attack bogged down, with the Indian, Burmese, and British troops exhausted by days of marching and fighting in heat of over 110° F. Sun left Kyaukpadaung the night of the 17th to relieve the trapped Burma Division. Unfortunately for hopes of a

---

[19](1) Foucar, Ch. 17. (2) Roberts' Journal, pp. 14, 18–21. (3) The Campaign in Burma, pp. 36–43. (4) SEATIC Bull 245, 5 Oct 46, sub: History of Japanese *15th Army*, pp. 24–25.

[20](1) Foucar, p. 158. (2) Belden, *Retreat with Stilwell*, p. 107. (3) Roberts' Journal, pp. 21–22. (4) Alexander Report, *Supplement to The London Gazette,* App. A. (5) Wyman Diary, 16 Apr 42. (6) *The Stilwell Papers,* p. 83. (7) Stilwell Diary, 12 Apr 42.

speedy rescue, he had been informed it was in a perimeter on the main high-way just north of Yenangyaung. The Chinese attack of the 18th cleared a large section of the Pin Chaung by 1000 but went no further. At 1700 Slim urged the 38th Division to attack again, but it refused to do so without further recon-naissance. Sun remarked to Merrill at the time that every Allied action in Burma to date had failed for lack of proper reconnaissance and that he was not minded to repeat the error.[21] Far to the south the 17th Indian Division demon-strated against the rear and flank of the Japanese force, sending out two columns, each of a battalion of infantry and a squadron of tanks, which the Japanese ignored. Within the perimeter of the Burma Division, the situation was now grave, and late on the 18th General Scott asked permission to abandon his transport and to make his way across country, a request refused on the grounds that the Chinese would soon appear.[22]

The Chinese attacked into Yenangyaung at 0800 on 19 April, expecting to meet the Burma Division there. Instead, they found the Japanese entrenched in five strong points. By 1130 three were taken, but there was no contact with the exhausted Burma Division. That force had managed to hold during the night of the 18–19th, though to the south it was now in contact with elements of the *215th Regiment*. An attack toward the ford in the morning made little progress, and some of the troops were demoralized. Another attack planned for later in the morning was canceled for fear it might lead to an inadvertent clash with the Chinese. Unknown to the Burma Division, a renewed Chinese attack by 1500 was making steady progress. To meet it, the Japanese shifted some of their men, leaving a gap. Consequently, when the tanks with the Burma Divi-sion were finally ordered to leave the road and look for a way out to the east over the oxcart tracks, at about 1300 they reported an unguarded track, and by using it, a part of the Burma Division with some tanks and vehicles was able to escape to the north. About 1600 under the force of the Chinese attack the Japanese fell back to the south and east, and the rest of the division was with-drawn over the black-top road. For its escape the division paid with most of its motor transport, its 40-mm. antiaircraft guns, most of its 3-inch mortars, eight cannon, four tanks, and 20 percent casualties.[23] Stilwell's action in send-ing the 38th Division to aid the British and guard his flank satisfied the Generalissimo: "I have received the news of the Yenangyaung trouble. The oil fields are lost. We must make our own plans—immediately move the best troops to crush the enemy's left. . . ."[24]

As a result of these setbacks along the Irrawaddy, which threatened his right

---

[21](1) Foucar, pp. 161–64. (2) Belden, *Retreat with Stilwell*, pp. 133–51.

[22](1) Foucar, pp. 164, 168. (2) The Campaign in Burma, p. 48. (3) Stilwell understood the 17th Division's demonstration to be a major thrust against the *33d Division's* rear. Stilwell Diary, 18 Apr 42.

[23](1) The Campaign in Burma, pp. 48–50. (2) Belden, *Retreat with Stilwell*, pp. 152, 160–64. (3) Roberts' Journal, pp. 21–22. (4) Foucar, pp. 164–65, 167.

[24] Ltr, Generalissimo to unknown addressee, 20 Apr 42. Stilwell Personal Papers.

flank, Stilwell had to abandon his cherished plan for the Pyinmana battle though he hoped the Allies could reorganize their forces and form new lines. The Irrawaddy defeats were no surprise to him; several days before the Battle of Yenangyaung he reported the British forces were near exhaustion and collapse, but if they could hold a few days more he would counterattack from Pyinmana. He thought the general situation critical and the British command discouraged. Stilwell thought it probable the Allies would be "back in the hills" by 10 May.[25] The mishaps of the 1st Burma Division and the resulting threat to Stilwell's flank and rear required immediate emergency measures, so he ordered the Chinese 200th Division to Meiktila (18 April) to fill the 60-mile gap to his right and rear. Tu accepted the order; then he did nothing to execute it. Not yet aware of this, Stilwell concluded that the Japanese had overextended themselves in the Irrawaddy and decided that he might make a virtue of the necessity by falling on the *33d Division* with his 22d, 200th, and 38th Divisions while the 17th Indian Division attacked Magwe. He also thought only two enemy regiments were on the Sittang front. After being quickly worked out with Alexander, Slim, and Tu, the plan was ordered on the 19th with great hopes of a real success. On the 20th it was canceled, and Tu's action forgotten for the time, because it became clear that one more disaster had befallen the Allies in Burma.[26]

The Japanese Drive to Lashio

In the account of the campaign so far, the two great corridors into northern Burma have figured prominently. There were still other routes to the north which Stilwell's staff described as permitting a Japanese attack directly on Lashio. These were the many tracks and the principal road north through the Shan States. Here the Chinese 6th Army (General Kan) was deployed, with the Temporary-55th Division (1st, 2d, 3d Regiments) along the Mawchi–Htuchaung–Bawlake–Loikaw Road, the 49th Division at Mong Pan, and the 93d Division at Kengtung. As yet there had been only border skirmishes, though on occasion they made screaming headlines in the American press, and the 6th Army had contributed nothing to the campaign in central Burma despite attempts by Stilwell to use the Temporary-55th Division at Toungoo. What held the 6th Army in the Shan States was the belief that there were some 50,000 Siamese and Japanese troops in northern Thailand, including two Japanese

---

[25] (1) Stilwell told the Generalissimo that Yenangyaung was the sole cause of the abandonment of the Pyinmana plan and the subsequent Chinese withdrawal, not any action of the Chinese. Madame Chiang to Currie, quoting Stilwell's radio, Maymyo 68, 19 April 1942, verbatim. WDCSA 384 (4–28–42). The message is also quoted in The Campaign in Burma, p. 44. (2) CM–IN 4660, Stilwell to Marshall, 15 Apr 42. (3) Rad, Stilwell to SEGAC (The Generalissimo's radio call station Chungking), 18 Apr 42. Stilwell Personal Papers.

[26] (1) The Campaign in Burma, pp. 45–46. (2) Alexander Report, *Supplement to The London Gazette,* pars. 36, 45, 46. (3) Wyman Diary, 19 Apr 42. (4) *The Stilwell Papers,* pp. 89–90. (5) Stilwell Diary, 17, 18, 19 Apr 42.

divisions.[27] Actually, the only major Japanese unit in the whole of Indochina and Thailand was the *21st Division,* at Hanoi, French Indochina. In early 1942 the Japanese held those countries with small garrison forces.

The British liaison officer with the 6th Army invited Kan's attention to the scattered state of his divisions and the absence of a central reserve. The proposal to remedy these defects bogged down in administrative formalities, Kan saying that higher authority had made the dispositions, which he could not change, and when he agreed that the matter should be referred to Headquarters, Army in Burma, that body replied no Japanese threat was anticipated. This was an unfortunate state of affairs because the Temporary-55th Division was the principal obstacle to the revised Japanese plan for the encirclement and annihilation of Burma's defenders.[28] Since a Chinese document taken at Toungoo said the principal Chinese forces would seek a decisive engagement south of Mandalay, the Japanese decided to make a final revision of their operational plan to aim at a gigantic encirclement of Burma's defenders south of Mandalay and Lashio. The revised *15th Army* operational plan, issued at Toungoo on 3 April, called for the use of all its divisions, directing the *56th* on Lashio, the *18th* and *55th* on the east and west suburbs of Mandalay respectively, and the *33d* up along the Irrawaddy's banks, sending one element to the Mandalay plain and another to Bhamo. For its mission the *56th Division* was heavily reinforced with the *14th Tank Regiment* and two battalions of artillery and was made mobile by the attachment of ample motor transport. If weather permitted, airborne troops would seize Lashio.[29] The Japanese thus aimed at a double envelopment. Lashio was the goal, for its capture, cutting the Burma Road, would go far to isolate China and to prevent a retreat by the Chinese forces in Burma.

When the Chinese company garrisoning Mawchi was driven out during the first week in April, the encircling Japanese column moved on in its attempt to cut the Burma Road and force on Burma's defenders the alternatives of surrender or flight through the jungles and mountains. At first there was no great concern felt; the Japanese force seemed small. But it moved east and north steadily, defeating a Chinese regiment, which had to be ordered to withdraw and reorganize.[30]

---

[27](1) The Campaign in Burma, pp. 30, 33, 28, 11. (2) *The Stilwell Papers,* pp. 69, 71, 74. (3) Colonel Aldrich, the American liaison officer with the 6th Army, tells of attempting to persuade Kan to move. (4) Supply and Evacuation Plan for a Withdrawal, 4 Apr 42. Stilwell Misc Papers, 1942. This paper lists a drive through the Shan States as second among Japanese capabilities.

[28](1) French Indochina and Thailand Order of Battle Review, 1 Oct 45. MID Library. (2) *The Stilwell Papers,* pp. 85–87. (3) Brig John F. Bowerman, British Ln Off with 6th Army, Notes on Duties with the Chinese Expeditionary Force, Combat Rpts and Misc Ln Off's Rpts. (Hereafter, Bowerman.) ALBACORE Hist File, Northern Combat Area Command Files, KCRC. (4) Interv with Col Aldrich, 1948. HIS 330.14 CBI 1948. Colonel Aldrich knew Brigadier Bowerman, whose report is cited above, and considered him an excellent soldier and a careful observer.

[29](1) Japanese Study 88, Ch. IV. (2) Japanese Study 94, Ch. VI.

[30](1) Wyman Diary, 6 Apr 42. (2) Bowerman. (3) The Campaign in Burma, pp. 34–35. (4) Roberts' Journal, pp. 13–14. (5) Foucar, pp. 198–99.

The Generalissimo was disturbed when he received word of this, and wrote Stilwell on 8 April:

Special attention must be given to the enemy forces in the Mawchi sector. If they are a regiment in strength it would seem that our division under Gen. Ch'en Mien-wu will not be equal to the task of repulsing them single-handed. It is my view that if the enemy is not genuinely taking the offensive against the center of the 5th Army a detachment of mechanized troops with tanks and mounted artillery [sic] should be despatched to assist General Ch'en's division in destroying the enemy forces at Mawchi. The security of our rear may thus be safe-guarded. This will certainly be the soundest course.

The effect of this was lost by his writing the following day:

. . . At the moment we must give our whole attention to the concentration of the 5th Army's strength in preparation for a decisive battle at Pyinmana. It would be best for whole or half of the British tank strength to be moved to support our center. In this way we could be sure of success. . . .[31]

At Stilwell's headquarters, his G–2, Colonel Roberts, had been for some days concerned over his inability to locate the third regiments of the *33d* and *55th Divisions.* When the Chinese reported this series of contacts on the east flank of the Allies' central concentration, Roberts was alarmed. Because of the pressure under which Stilwell was then working, Roberts had to raise the issue at mess, suggesting that this was one of the missing regiments and that its goal was Lashio. Stilwell immediately appreciated the menace and called a conference with Tu and their staffs on 9 April.

. . . The estimate of the Japanese strength and plans was that Japs would advance in 3 columns from West and East: Prome–Magwe; Toungoo–Pyinmana; and Bawlake–Taunggyi, with Mandalay as their objective; flank columns to provide double pincers. . . .[32]

It was an excellent estimate of the Japanese plan. To counter it, the 93d Division less one regiment would close on the Temporary-55th Division; the 49th Division plus one regiment of the 93d Division would continue to watch the Thailand border; the 66th Army would mass below Mandalay as rapidly as possible, and the Pyinmana plan would go on as before. Orders for the concentration were put into the cumbrous and unwieldy Chinese staff machine.[33]

[31](1) Ltr, Generalissimo to Stilwell, 8 Apr 42, appended to Lo's account of the First Burma Campaign. SNF–12. (2) Ltr, Generalissimo to Stilwell, 9 Apr 42. SNF–12.

[32] Wyman Diary, 9 Apr 42.

[33](1) Interv with Col Roberts, 4 Dec 46. (2) The Campaign in Burma, p. 39. (3) Foucar, p. 198. (4) After the war the Japanese gave their plan as:

"The *56th Division* will leave Loikaw on 20 April and advance through Laihka to the vicinity of Lashio in order to cut off the enemy retreat and prepare for the next operation. . . . The *18th Division* will start from the east side of the Toungoo–Mandalay railway and advance to the eastern part of Mandalay and cut off the Mandalay–Lashio road. . . . The *55th Division* will advance to the southwest part of Mandalay by first defeating the enemy west of the Toungoo–Mandalay railway, to smash the enemy main force at the Irrawaddy River. . . . The main body of the *33d Division* will advance from the east bank area of the Irrawaddy River to the vicinity of Myingyan. It will then advance to defeat the enemy main force in the vicinity of Mandalay by outflanking the right wing of the enemy."

Japanese Study 88.

On 11 April Stilwell visited the 6th Army, where it was now known a Japanese blow would fall though incomplete order of battle data on the Japanese led to a very serious underestimate of its weight.

> Chen Li-wu "just pulling back, of course (Better place to fight)." Jap strength can't be greater than 2,000. 55th is to *fight* in Bawlake area, seriously. 3d Regt to come down at once. By PM, 11th, one regiment in Bawlake (less one bn and one co) and one regt in position at Mei Chaung. Ch'en says he will counterattack from west . . . 55th has about 6,500 men. 200th has 6,125. 38th has 7,500—1,750 per regt plus 2,500. 55th has ten TM's [trench mortars] per regt plus 50 rds.[34]

After Stilwell's visit to the 6th Army front and at his insistence Lo reprimanded Kan. Stilwell also wanted General Chen relieved. Drafting his notes to Lo, Stilwell wrote:

> I recommend that General Kan, CG, 6th Army be reprimanded.
> 1. He does not control the actions of his division commanders.
> 2. He has moved, without orders, units under the control of the Zone Commander.
> 3. He does not keep sufficiently informed about the military situation, or the care and supply of his troops.
> I recommend that Gen. Ch'en Li-wu, CG of the 55th Division, be relieved of command at once.
> 1. He has no control over his division.
> 2. He has already withdrawn, without orders, before an inferior Jap force, and needlessly given up vital ground.
> 3. He has shown no disposition to obey his strict orders to attack and re-take Mawchi, but instead has taken a defensive stand with six battalions opposed by only one battalion of the enemy.[35]

Though the Temporary-55th Division was in a poor state, untrained, poorly organized and disciplined, its units strung out along the road in bivouac areas with no preparations for defense, Chen was not relieved.[36]

Stilwell apparently checked the 6th Army sector still further by calling in the commander of the 49th Division for consultation. The Chinese reported his front quiet, and Stilwell noted: "Front apparently well covered. . . ."[37] AVG aircraft and pilots were brought up for an attempt at reconnaissance.[38]

When the movement orders finally were delivered on 13 April, the 93d Division would not obey them and was supported in this by Kan, both insisting that trucks be furnished. Vehicles were so few, and the drivers so terrified of the Chinese, that thirty days would be needed to move the division a distance it could march in eight. Area headquarters for the Southern Shan States was not helpful, refusing to give troop movements priority over back-

---

[34] Stilwell Diary, 11 Apr 42.
[35] (1) These recommendations are undated and are in Stilwell Misc Papers, 1942. (2) *The Stilwell Papers*, p. 87.
[36] (1) Bowerman. (2) Interv with Aldrich. HIS 330.14 CBI 1948.
[37] Stilwell Diary, 12 Apr 42.
[38] Wyman Diary, 12, 14, 15 Apr 42.

loading rations until Alexander's headquarters approved. Subsequent negotiations were complicated by the diversion of trucks by still other Chinese authorities. Compounding the failure, Stilwell's headquarters and liaison officers were unaware that the 93d Division was not moving.[39] When the 93d Division finally began to move, it was too late to affect the issue. The 49th Division was not ordered west until the 20th.[40]

While these attempts were being made to bring aid to the Temporary-55th Division, its 1st Regiment, which was falling back after its earlier defeat by the Japanese, was overtaken by them and further punished, while the 2d Regiment, Temporary-55th Division, which had been moving south, was taking up defensive positions on the Htu Chaung Creek. Here followed a brief pause in which the Temporary-55th Division was content to remain passive in bivouac along the road. The Chinese troops were suffering severely from thirst, and the energetic British liaison mission with the 6th Army tried to bring down truckloads of fresh water. This ended when the Chinese promptly confiscated the trucks. Colonels McCabe and Aldrich, Stilwell's liaison team with the 6th Army, pleaded with Kan to counterattack, or at least to patrol aggressively. They had no success, and a strange sort of truce settled on the battlefield. The Japanese put it to good advantage.[41] While the Temporary-55th remained passively in bivouac, the *56th Division* sent company after company toiling through the woods parallel to the road on which the Chinese camped.

A frontal attack on the Htu Chaung on 16 April was followed on the 17th by attacks from the flanking companies along the full forty miles of road from the Htu Chaung north. By morning of the 19th one Japanese element was a few miles south of Loikaw and was joined in an hour by a battalion which had marched diagonally across the mountains from Toungoo.[42] Under these attacks from front, side, and rear, the Temporary-55th Division simply disintegrated, its soldiers fleeing to the hills. The two battalions of the 93d Division, the first part of the long-awaited reinforcements from the east, turned about and returned whence they had come. The road to Lashio was open to the exultant Japanese. Communication between the Temporary-55th Division and the 6th Army ceased on the night of 18 April; the division was no longer a fighting unit.[43] Unaware as yet of the Temporary-55th Division's collapse, Stilwell wrote, "Col. Chiang will start them if they have not yet jumped off. 1st objective, Mawchi; 2d objective, Toungoo." [44]

---

[39] (1) Bowerman. (2) The Campaign in Burma, pp. 39, 53, 63. (3) McCabe's and Aldrich's reports reached Stilwell through British signals to Maymyo. (4) Memo, Boatner, 30 Jul 42, sub: Rpt on Some Activities of 93d Div in Burma. SNF–21.
[40] (1) The Campaign in Burma, pp. 53, 63, 50. (2) Foucar, p. 199. (3) Memo cited n. 39(4).
[41] Bowerman.
[42] (1) Japanese Study 88, Ch. IV. (2) Map, Japanese Study 100, Annex 5.
[43] (1) The Campaign in Burma, pp. 40, 52. (2) The Chinese Army in Burma. MIS Folder, Burma Campaign, MID Library. (3) Foucar, p. 199. (4) Roberts' Journal, p. 23. (5) Ltr, Aldrich to Sunderland, with notes, 18 Feb 50. HIS 330.14 CBI 1950.
[44] Stilwell Misc Papers, 1942.

Attempts To Prevent the Debacle

The collapse of the Temporary-55th Division and the failure to stem the Japanese in the Irrawaddy forced the complete recasting of Allied plans. One last attempt was made to save north Burma. Surveying the problems involved in trying to command part of a coalition army of races and nationalities drawn from the British Isles, India, Burma, and China and highly frustrated by the difficulties he faced with the Chinese, Stilwell tore off a page of copy paper and appraised his situation as follows:

Yesterday, April 19, Lo Cho-ying went up to Maymyo without notifying me. Lin Wei had phoned him that he had an important letter (CKS, of course). Lo did not dare hesitate. We had just arranged the general plan of attack and everything was apparently agreed upon. (Incidentally, all of our measures conformed to the provisions of the letter.) Today we learned that the 55th was smashed and the Japs already far north of Loikaw. I directed Yang to order Kan to bring up a regiment of the 49th to Loilem and block off, also to order the 22d to the Pyawbwe–Thazi area, with one regiment directed on Kalaw (the 22d has not yet appeared at Yamethin). Tonight, news comes that the 96th is in trouble at Kyiddaunggan. I am sending Sibert down to investigate. The 200th is moving to Kyaukpadaung. The 114th Infantry [Regiment, 38th Division] is moving to Taungtha. The 113th [Infantry Regiment, 38th Division] is coming back to Kyaukpadaung. Slim wants to withdraw the Burdiv [1st Burma Division] and the Mcz Brig [7th Armored Brigade]. (I am objecting to latter save piecemeal.)

Meanwhile, Tu goes to Kyaukpadaung, and there is no one to direct the 96th and 22d. Lo goes to Maymyo and there is no one to direct the 6th Army. Lo confers with Alexander and Lin Wei and I do not know what they have decided to do. Slim wants to turn the whole thing over to *Tu,* and so does Alexander. Somebody has to control the mess and I am the goat. Lo sends word by Chiang that he has decided to go to Kyaukse because the phone service is good, and asks me to go up there, *tomorrow night.* He may not or does not know even now what is happening to the 6th Army and the 96th Division. What I have ordered may be the exact opposite of instructions he may be putting out. I have sent Chiang to get him and bring him back here at once, *urgent.*

This is another sample of long-range command and army politics. If CKS continues his tactical masterpieces, the mess will merely get worse. It is an impossible situation, which I will have to see through as best I may. CKS has made it impossible for me to do anything, and I might as well acknowledge it now.[45]

Stilwell's countermeasures to block the Japanese drive to Lashio should be appraised against the persistent belief that the Japanese task force was a small one. As late as 21 April, Stilwell's G–2 considered it was a reinforced battalion of the Japanese *55th Division* that had moved on Mawchi. Colonel Roberts further believed that the *18th Division* was in Thailand (whereas it was now on the Sittang front). It was more than ever probable, Colonel Roberts thought, that the Japanese in Burma had been reinforced, but he admitted that he did not know if the *18th Division* had moved.[46]

Stilwell's further reaction was to order the 200th Division to Taunggyi

---

[45] *Ibid.*
[46] Memo, Roberts for Stilwell, 21 Apr 42. Stilwell Misc Papers, 1942.

to attack the Japanese in the Loikaw–Loi-lem area. This forced the abandonment of the attempt to hit the Japanese *33d Division* at Yenangyaung. "First priority, plug the Loikaw break!" [47] A concentration of the 49th and 93d Divisions on the Temporary-55th Division had already been ordered. In the Sittang valley the 96th Division was ordered to delay the Japanese for one week. The 17th Indian Division was now falling back on Meiktila. Three days later, on the 25th, a conference was held between Alexander, Stilwell, Lo, and Slim, at which they laid plans for a concentration before Lashio and for the motorized 200th Division to sweep up behind the Japanese task force that was racing for Lashio. This plan accorded well with Stilwell's earlier orders and was based on them. The Mandalay concentration was successfully completed.[48] The 96th Division continued in the delaying role earlier intended to cover the counterattack at Yenangyaung, and it held back the Japanese while the 17th Indian Division, 7th Armored Brigade, and the 22d Division took positions around Meiktila and Thazi. In so doing, the 96th Division suffered heavy losses in a series of actions climaxed when Japanese tanks caught the whole division on the road on 24 April. From Meiktila north to the Mandalay area, the several brigades of the 17th Indian Division, the 22d Division, and a regiment of the 38th Division, with invaluable assistance from the 7th Armored Brigade, covered one another in a series of leapfrogging movements under pressure from both the *18th* and *55th Divisions*.[49]

To the east four Chinese divisions were maneuvering, and to the south the Chinese 5th Army Command (200th Division, reinforced) was on its way to Taunggyi. Two of the four divisions (49th, 93d) had been in the Shan States when the first attempts to keep the Japanese from Lashio were being made. The 93d, as noted earlier, began its march west after some delay but on learning of the defeats in the west turned about and returned to Kengtung. The 49th Division was sent west on 20 April from its post ninety miles from Taunggyi and moved so fast that on the 21st it was in contact with the Japanese. The subsequent engagement, of minor nature, did not affect later events.[50]

On 23 April the 6th Army's commander forbade the now-assembled 49th Division to attack and ordered it withdrawn. The 49th Division commander, Gen. Peng Pi-shen, was infuriated by the order. He was ready to attack, knew that the 200th Division was attacking Taunggyi from the west and that it was to go on to Loi-lem. A juncture of the 200th and 49th Divisions behind the Japanese Lashio-bound task force could have great results. Peng and his chief of staff discussed open disobedience, tried for three hours to reach General

[47] Stilwell Diary, 21 Apr 42.
[48] (1) The Campaign in Burma, pp. 52–55, 63–64. (2) *The Stilwell Papers,* pp. 90–92.
[49] (1) Roberts' Journal, pp. 22, 24–26, 27–30. (2) The Campaign in Burma, pp. 54, 57, 59, 60–71. (3) Burmarmy Sitrep, 29 Apr 42. (4) Japanese Study 88, Ch. IV. (5) Foucar, pp. 173–80.
[50] (1) The Campaign in Burma, pp. 53, 64, 74. (2) Foucar, p. 201.

Kan by radio, and, finally, slowly complied with the order. This excellent division never had a chance to display its worth in battle, but it retreated to China in good order.[51] At the time this withdrawal was not known to Stilwell or Lo.

Of the three divisions of the 66th Army then entering Burma, the 38th Division had already been in combat and done very well. The 29th Division was marching in down the Burma Road and its leading regiment entered Lashio on 29 April, the day the city fell. The 28th Division was in the Mandalay area and on 22 April was ordered to take positions across the roads south of Lashio. There was confusion on the railways, confusion further compounded by changes in the movement orders of the 28th Division. As a result, six days later on the night of 28–29 April, the three regiments of the 28th Division were strung out all the way from Maymyo to a point just south of Lashio. Thus, of the nine Chinese divisions in Burma, several took very little part in the operations culminating in the fall of Lashio. But at the time this was not reported to Stilwell and Lo, who accordingly could not intervene and complete the concentration to defend Lashio. One reason for the failure to move divisions was that Stilwell could not get lend-lease trucks from the Chinese authorities in Lashio with which to move troops. Asked to provide 150 trucks of the 850 then in Lashio, they sent 22.[52]

Colonel Boatner called on the AVG to help stem the Japanese rush to Lashio. In response, they flew strafing missions on the 24th and 25th, burning a number of gasoline trucks caught on the open road and attacking a Japanese troop convoy. Through an error later attributed to General Lin Wei of the Chinese General Staff Mission to Burma, who was believed to have furnished the AVG with inaccurate data on the location of Chinese troops, the AVG also strafed some Chinese units.[53]

Generals Stilwell and Lo were with the 200th Division when it was rushed from the Meiktila area to retake Taunggyi. For this operation the 1st and 2d Reserve Regiments were attached; the task force was designated 5th Army Command and placed under General Tu. The critical importance of speed had been stressed, but when the 5th Army Command encountered the Japanese outposts near Taunggyi, it promptly halted. These were the security detachments of the Taunggyi garrison, one Japanese battalion. On arriving next morning, the 25th, at 1030, Stilwell found the 5th Army Command still halted and ordered an immediate attack. Contact was made with a few more Japanese at 1130, and by afternoon a little more distance had been gained, whereupon Lo ordered Tu to take Taunggyi that day or suffer the consequences, with a reward of 50,000 rupees to the troops if the town fell. In the late afternoon of

---

[51] Memo cited n. 39(4).

[52](1) The Campaign in Burma, pp. 41, 53, 54, 64, 74. (2) Roberts' Journal, pp. 24–26. (3) Foucar, pp. 171–201. (4) *The Brereton Diaries*, p. 124. (5) Wyman Diary, 26 Apr 42.

[53](1) The Campaign in Burma, p. 64. (2) Int Summary, AVG Activities for Apr 42, AVG Hq. AVG File, Gen Ref Br, OCMH.

the 25th Taunggyi was finally taken from its small Japanese garrison. Gathering momentum, the 200th Division reached Loi-lem on the 29th. From that area it later began its retreat to China.[54]

Lashio fell in the early afternoon of 29 April to the *148th Regiment* after a 5-hour battle. Another Japanese regiment quickly followed into the city. Colonel Boatner had tried to slow the Japanese by destroying the bridges to the south. Two Chinese battalions had made a stand across the roads below Lashio, but these efforts only gained a few hours. Boatner and his British colleagues had destroyed what they could, but the Japanese gained 44,000 tons of arsenal stores, some of which were repossessed three years later. As many women and children as possible were flown out.[55]

Plans for the Future

Alexander's and Stilwell's problems at this point in the campaign fell naturally into three parts. Only the first two were similar for both commanders. Each had to conserve his forces as far as possible. Both were ordered to protect communications across north Burma from India to China. But Alexander's further responsibilities lay toward India, whereas Stilwell's mission was to support China. Stilwell's thoughts in the latter days of the campaign, up to the time when the Japanese cut him off from the north, were shaped by the concerns he shared with Alexander, plus the plan he conceived in early April to carry out his mission to China.

On 16 April Brig. Gen. William R. Gruber, who had been representing Stilwell in India in conferences with Brereton and with Wavell's headquarters, received from Stilwell an order to go from Burma to Chungking to present Stilwell's Proposal to Organize and Train a Chinese Force in India.[56] Framed during the perils and problems of the First Burma Campaign, the plan molded all of Stilwell's later proposals. The project was presented to the Generalissimo on 27 April.[57]

Acting as the Generalissimo's chief of staff, Stilwell warned the Generalissimo in his proposal that the Japanese would probably interrupt any road or airline across north Burma that might become operative in the near future. This would isolate China from the lend-lease stores accumulating in India. To counter this, Stilwell proposed moving about 100,000 Chinese soldiers to India to equip them with lend-lease and train them into an élite corps from

---

[54] (1) The Campaign in Burma, pp. 52, 58, 62, 67, 75, 83. (2) Stilwell Diary, 23, 25 Apr 42.
[55] (1) The Campaign in Burma, p. 74. (2) Foucar, p. 74. (3) Ltr, Boatner to CG AAF CBI, 13 May 42, sub: Incidents Prior to and Immediately Following Fall of Lashio (April 20–29, 42). HIS 330.14 CBI 1950. (4) Ltr, Boatner to Chief, HD SSUSA, 14 Nov 47. HIS 330.14 CBI 1947.
[56] Stilwell Diary, 16 Apr 42.
[57] Memo, Stilwell for Generalissimo, 27 Apr 42, sub: Proposal to Organize and Train a Chinese Force in India. Stilwell Documents, Hoover Library. General Gruber opened and ended the proposal with a note that this was not presented as coming from the U.S. or British Governments.

which an improved Chinese Army could grow. The Chinese force would be organized into two corps of three divisions each.

Stilwell's command provisions were interesting:

5. *Selection of Commanders and Personnel.*—Selection of Chinese officers up to the grade of regimental commander, non-commissioned officers, and men to be made in accordance with policies personally dictated by the Generalissimo so as to insure the availability of personnel of the highest type suitable to handle the technical equipment involved. Carefully selected Chinese officers will be used from the outset in all grades up to and including regimental commander. Higher commanders and principal staff officers initially to be American officers until such time as Chinese officers can be substituted.

To move these men to India, Stilwell proposed they be concentrated about Kunming in order to begin their move about 15 May 1942. From Kunming they would march or be flown across north Burma via Myitkyina–Mogaung–Shingbwiyang to Ledo. The immediate and obvious objection to the plan as it appears is the difficulty of moving the Chinese troops from China to India. Stilwell wrote: "Movement to railheads in India to be made by marching with such assistance from highway transport organizations and the U.S. Air Freight Line as may be practicable. . . ." Any such marching would have to be done during the monsoon rains over dry-weather roads and pack-horse trails.

How he would use the 100,000 soldiers was tersely stated:

8. *Operation Objectives.*—Upon completion of the training of this force estimated between 4–6 months, operations to be undertaken in the following phases:
1st Phase—Recapture Burma; the decisive effort to be made from India, a secondary effort to be made from China and the northern Shan States.
2nd Phase—Eject the enemy from Thailand.

After conferring with General Gruber, the Generalissimo agreed to the plan "in general," with a few modifications. The Chinese leader wanted half of the senior officers to be Chinese, plus formal assurance from the British and U.S. Governments that his troops would not be used to maintain the British position in India in the event of civil disturbance there. Gruber concluded his message by saying he would fly to Delhi on 3 May to present the project to Wavell and Wheeler.[58]

Alexander's plans on 23 April were:

1. . . . to cover the communications between India and China. A withdrawal North of Mandalay will cut the LOC [Line of Communications] via the Chindwin, Mandalay, and Lashio. In the event of such a withdrawal it will be necessary to cover the broken ends of the communications with India and China via the above route and also to cover the projected route between India and China via the Hukawng Valley.
2. In the event of a withdrawal North of Mandalay, all Chinese forces east of the railway Mandalay–Pyawbwe are to withdraw to the North and NE for the defence of the Lashio Road under the direction of the GOC, Chinese Armies.[59]

[58](1) Gruber told Stilwell of this by a penciled note on lined paper with no date or sender's number. Stilwell Misc Papers, 1942. (2) ". . . Gruber reports complete success of his job. We to have complete direction of move (the staff is squabbling a bit)." Stilwell Diary, 29 Apr 42.
[59] Operational Instruction 46, Army in Burma, 23 Apr 42. Stilwell Misc Papers, 1942.

The order stated that because of the bottleneck in communications at Mandalay and the need to protect the Chindwin and Shwebo routes, British forces and the Chinese 38th Division would not become involved in close defense of Mandalay. It further directed that Headquarters, Army in Burma, would move on the axis Shwebo–Mandalay.

Below Mandalay the course of the Irrawaddy River placed it directly across the Allied line of retreat, and only the Ava Bridge offered a ready crossing, a situation which, as the Allied forces crowded against the river, must have seemed uncomfortably like that on the Sittang in February. So, on 25 April after a conference with Stilwell, Alexander ordered a withdrawal to the north bank of the Irrawaddy, to begin that night. On the same day tanks and trucks of the 5th Army could be seen moving north through Lashio to China, passing troops of the 66th Army stolidly moving into Burma. The evacuation of the 5th Army was without Stilwell's orders and was the beginning of the collapse that rendered futile any hopes of holding Myitkyina and the trace of the Ledo Road.[60] On 26 April Alexander decided that the fall of Lashio would be a matter of days. A Japanese thrust from Lashio via Bhamo to Myitkyina would make any stand north of Mandalay futile, and so the defense of India would have to be his major consideration.

At a conference on 29 April between Alexander, Stilwell, and Lo, Alexander decided to hold the line Kalewa–Katha–Bhamo–Hsenwi; failing that, he would move the bulk of his troops to India. The 5th Army troops, with the 22d and 38th Divisions, would delay along the Mandalay–Myitkyina railway, while the 96th Division would go directly to Myitkyina. When and if necessary, Alexander would move his headquarters to Myitkyina as well. Necessary supply arrangements were begun.[61] It was Stilwell's intention at the time to make his next stand in north Burma, so he wrote in his diary on 30 April, "Our crowd direct to Myitkyina." He himself planned to go to Loiwing to direct the fight to keep some sort of communications open to China. To the War Department he reported on 4 May that Chinese control of their troops was weak and collapse seemed near. General Lo and the Chinese quartermaster had left Stilwell and his staff to their own devices. He said that he would try to move to Myitkyina, but if that failed, he would go west to Imphal in India.[62] Team I (or Item) of the seven radio teams that had reached India in March from the Java convoy was in Burma, part of it with Stilwell's personal staff, from about 27 April 1942 to the end of the campaign. This handful of radiomen and

---

[60] (1) Alexander Report, *Supplement to The London Gazette,* pars. 47–49. (2) Bowerman. (3) The Campaign in Burma, p. 73.

[61] (1) On 27 April 1942 the Chinese received orders from the Generalissimo to fight a mobile battle, to stay in Burma, and to hold Kengtung and the Bhamo–Myitkyina area. Lo's account of the Burma Campaign. SNF–12. (2) Ltr, Generalissimo to unknown addressee, undated. CKS Corresp, Stilwell Documents, Hoover Library. (3) *The Stilwell Papers,* p. 93. (4) Alexander Report, *Supplement to The London Gazette,* par. 54. (5) Wyman Diary, 30 Apr 42. (6) Stilwell Diary, 29, 30 Apr 42.

[62] Rad, Stilwell to AGWAR, 4 May 42. Stilwell Documents, Hoover Library.

Brereton's few B–17's were the only American reinforcements to reach China, Burma, and India in time to play any part whatever in the lost campaign.[63]

The Evacuation of Burma

The withdrawal to the north of the Irrawaddy was covered in its initial stages by the 48th Indian Brigade at Kyaukse. Skillful use of artillery and armor held off elements of the *18th Division* in a well-fought action, and the Japanese were kept below the Myitnge River until the bridges were blown. There was no Japanese pressure on the 63d Indian Brigade and the Chinese 22d Division along the river line, but it was felt that they could not withstand a heavy attack, and so they were withdrawn across the Irrawaddy the night of 30 April. The great Ava Bridge was destroyed at midnight. Central Burma was now firmly held by the Japanese.[64]

The general withdrawal to the line indicated by Alexander on 29 April was ordered for 2 May; the Chinese forces in the eastern half of Burma were already in full movement back to the Salween River, whose mighty gorge was the natural defense line of southwestern China. Stilwell's and Alexander's hopes of a stand across north Burma began to vanish as the Chinese streamed out of Burma. The aircraft that was to take Stilwell to eastern Burma failed to arrive on time, and Loiwing, his intended destination, was evacuated that same day. Gradually, Stilwell was being driven to the conclusion that he could exercise no control over the Chinese armies and that evacuation of his personal staff was his next problem.

Nevertheless, as of 5 May Stilwell still intended to go to Myitkyina and was just a few hours ahead of the 5th Army. On the 4th he had learned that the railway was blocked, so he took his party north by motor convoy. On 5 May, halting his convoy near Indaw, a railroad station, he and his aides went on ahead to inquire about the railway. They were told it was blocked north and south of Indaw. Because Japanese were reported at Bhamo, within easy striking distance of Myitkyina, Stilwell decided then and there on 5 May not to attempt to make his way by car to Myitkyina but instead to take his party due west to India, as it would be impossible to reach Myitkyina before the Japanese, who occupied it on 8 May.[65]

In marching out to the west, Stilwell could make arrangements for the reception in India of his Chinese troops. Stilwell, Lo, and Alexander agreed on

---

[63] Sgts John and Ward Hawkins, History of the 835th Signal Service Battalion. Gen Ref Br, OCMH.

[64](1) Foucar, pp. 175–80. (2) The Campaign in Burma, pp. 74–75. (3) CM–IN 7935, Stilwell to AGWAR, 30 Apr 42.

[65] The entry of 5 May in the Wyman Diary, "Possible presence of Japs at Bhamo dictated movement out of Burma via Imphal," with Stilwell's action of the same day in asking about a train to Myitkyina, seems to fix 5 May as the date that Stilwell elected to move out of Burma to the west. Had he made the decision on the 4th of May, he would not be asking about trains north on the 5th. *The Stilwell Papers*, pp. 96–98.

30 April that if the plan to hold the line Kalewa–Katha–Bhamo–Hsenwi failed, the 5th Army troops plus the 38th Division would march from Katha to Imphal. This withdrawal would be the beginning of the plan to put Chinese divisions in India and bring them up to strength with replacements and supporting troops. The 30 April understanding that the Chinese would march out to India should now have been in effect, but orders from the Generalissimo sent the 96th and 22d Divisions wandering through northern Burma.[66]

The War Department approved Stilwell's withdrawing to India on the assumption it was related to his training plan.[67] Indeed, Stilwell's conduct of the whole campaign received the approval of the American and Chinese Governments. On 18 April he received a formal commendation from the Secretary of War and warm personal greetings came from General Marshall on the 29th when the campaign was nearing its dismal close. Madame Chiang sent a long cable to Currie saying that the Generalissimo had "entire confidence" in Stilwell.[68] In Cabinet session Roosevelt "expressed great satisfaction over Stilwell's handling of the whole situation," a sentiment Marshall relayed to Stilwell on 12 May.[69]

For the Chinese divisions that went east, the campaign in Burma merged into a fight to keep the Japanese out of China; but the Allied forces that withdrew into India could halt there without an invading army on their heels. An invasion of India was not scheduled, and the *15th Army* halted its pursuing forces on the borders of India. Alexander's hopes of keeping a foothold in Burma had to yield to India Command's belief that it could not maintain his forces there. The withdrawing imperial forces had to fight two engagements as they fell back. The *215th Regiment, 33d Division,* occupied Monywa, across the withdrawal route, on 1 May, overrunning the Burma Division headquarters and taking all its code books. The 63d, 13th, and 1st Burma Brigades fought their way into town so that the transport could bypass the town on cart tracks and head north to Ye-u, where all the tracks for the Chindwin River began.[70] The 1st and 2d Burma Brigades made their separate ways to the Indian frontier. The rest of the army marched to the river port at Shwegyin where it fought off the pursuing *213th Regiment,* which came up while embarkation was in progress.

There were no further interruptions, and the force reached Tamu on 14 May

---

[66](1) See n. 57. (2) CM–IN 7490, Stilwell to AGWAR, 28 Apr 42. (3) MacMorland Diary, 25 Apr 42. (4) *The Stilwell Papers,* p. 94. (5) The Campaign in Burma, pp. 74, 75. (6) Memo, Gruber for Stilwell, 12 May 42. Folder, Operations–Burma Evacuation, Gen Ref Br, OCMH.

[67](1) Rad WAR 575, Marshall to Stilwell, 30 Apr 42. Paraphrased in Folder cited n. 66(6). (2) CM–IN 1606, Stilwell to Marshall, 6 May 42.

[68](1) Rad, Marshall to Stilwell, 18 Apr 42. AG 381 (12–19–41). (2) Rad WAR 570, Marshall to Stilwell, 29 Apr 42. (3) Rad WAR 336, Marshall to AQUILA, 12 May 42. Paraphrased in Folder, cited n. 66(6). (4) Cable, Mme. Chiang to Currie, 6 May 42. Folder 19B, OPD Exec 10.

[69] Notes after Cabinet Mtg, 1 May 42. WDCSA 334–M, A46–523.

[70](1) Alexander Report, *Supplement to The London Gazette,* pars. 55, 61, 62. (2) Japanese Study 88, Ch. IV. (3) *The Stilwell Papers,* p. 97.

as the first rains were falling. It had been a hard march, aggravated by the accumulated fatigues of the campaign, by the forbidding terrain, and by the presence of refugees fleeing the Japanese terror. The Burma Corps was in no shape to withstand an attempted invasion of India. It brought out 10 25-pounders, 4 antitank guns, 14 3.7-inch mountain guns, and about 80 vehicles. Of 31 infantry battalions, 5 mountain batteries, 1 field regiment, and assorted line of communications troops, some 12,000 exhausted and malarious survivors reached India. These units had suffered 13,000 casualties, with 9,000 missing in action.[71] Unfit for combat as they were, these troops, plus the 1st Indian Infantry Brigade and one other battalion and the Chinese 38th Division, were all that guarded the 500-mile frontier of Assam. In Bengal there were only the very new 14th and 26th Indian Divisions.[72]

The Chinese Withdrawal

Of the Chinese divisions, the 22d and the 38th, plus fragments of the 28th, 96th, and 200th, made their way westward to India. The 5th Army and the 38th Division moved north together from Mandalay until they reached the Indaw–Katha area. On 4 May General Lo received orders from the Generalissimo sending the 5th Army to Myitkyina. Lo himself had sought to persuade Tu to retreat on India. General Sun took counsel of himself, concluded the supply situation would be impossible in north Burma, and after making a vain appeal to Chungking for guidance, sent his 38th Division to India. After a brief engagement with the Japanese, the 38th Division detached the 113th Regiment to act as a rear guard. The 113th Regiment seemed trapped for a few days but made its way across the Chindwin on 30 May. Of this regiment, Colonel Wyman, of Stilwell's staff, wrote: "The story of the 113th is really an epic." Its companion regiments, in good condition, reached India on 25 May. An incident might have been precipitated by an excitable refugee who advised the Governor of Assam that the 38th Division was a "mere rabble" who should be disarmed and confined. The governor endorsed this proposal, and General Gruber was forced to intercede with General Wavell to prevent such an affront to Chinese pride. The Assam tea planters received the Chinese with great coolness, and there was mutual relief when the 38th Division was sent to permanent quarters in Bihar Province. From the First Burma Campaign the

---

[71] (1) Foucar, Ch. 21, p. 241. (2) Owen, *Campaign in Burma,* p. 26. (3) The Campaign in Burma, p. 76. (4) *The Stilwell Papers,* p. 97. Many of the missing were dead, who under conditions of jungle warfare had simply disappeared. Some 3,000 were members of Burmese units, many of whom had probably deserted. British and Indian units reported 6,000 missing in action. Of these, many were undoubtedly prisoners of war, and a great number of these unfortunates must have died in Japanese custody. The enemy was not meticulous in reporting such matters.

[72] Hist Sec (India), India at War, 1939–1943, p. 113. Gen Ref Br, OCMH. The 2d and 5th British Divisions arrived in India from the United Kingdom that summer. The latter went to the Middle East after a brief stay. A great deal of ordnance was also received from the United Kingdom.

38th Division and its brilliant commander emerged with their reputations established. To the tactical feat of Yenangyaung, the gallant and capable Sun Li-jen added the unique achievement of bringing his division through the Chin Hills as an intact fighting unit with discipline and morale unimpaired.[73]

The Generalissimo's orders for the 5th Army changed again on 18 May, and the 5th was ordered to "take position" between Myitkyina and Fort Hertz. At one time it had been within a few days' march of the Indian border (Manipur State) and safety, before veering north toward China.[74] At this time the 5th Army was the 22d and 96th Divisions, headquarters and army troops, and assorted stragglers. The two divisions parted company. Survivors of the 22d Division emerged in the Ledo area in July and August, having made good their withdrawal over the ghastly "refugee trail." The local British area commandant estimated that about 30,000 persons essayed the refugee trail, of whom 23,000 succeeded. Months later the bones of those who failed were whitening the trail, in many places literally so.

The first civilian refugees and Chinese troops lived off food stores accumulated for coolies working on the Burma side of the Ledo Road. The local Kachin tribesmen were very charitable and gave freely of their stores. When these were gone, looting by the refugees began. The American and Royal Air Forces dropped food in the Hukawng and Mogaung Valleys on a large scale. One hundred and fifty tons of supplies were dropped at Shingbwiyang between 29 June and 12 August and a total of 132 tons at other points along the trail for the 5th Army and 22d Division alone. Colonel Boatner, who surveyed the area, believed there was no shortage of food after the Chinese reached Taro.

The struggle to reach Taro took a heavy toll, and the evacuation of the Chinese was caught up in the flood of civilian refugees leaving Burma. Boatner reported that Chinese soldiers of the 96th Division looted and murdered among the refugees and Kachin tribesmen and that many Chinese officers made their men stagger out under useless equipment and displayed incompetence and callousness in handling the food dropped to them. The discipline of the 38th Division and the professional skill of its commander were a striking contrast. To alleviate the situation along the refugee trail, Indian authority sent officers into Burma from Ledo who improvised crude refugee camps and did their best to keep the stream of soldiers and civilian refugees flowing steadily into India. Sheer physical exhaustion, heartbreak at the loss of family and livelihood, intestinal disease, raw food, and malaria were the principal killers. The camp administrators, knowing that the apathetic and indifferent

---

[73] (1) Ltr, Brig Cawthorn, Dir of Mil Int, GHQ (India), to Gruber, 15 May 42; (2) Ltr, Gruber to Wavell, 16 May 42. Folder, Chinese Army, Trek from Burma, Gen Ref Br, OCMH. (3) History of CBI, Sec. II, Ch. V, p. 3. (4) Foucar, pp. 189, 201, 203. (5) The Campaign in Burma, pp. 82–87. (6) Wyman Diary, 8 Jun 42. "Gen. Sun's constant supervision of all matters pertaining to his troops is of the highest type." In a letter, Wyman to Stilwell, 17 June 1942, the former calls General Sun "a top soldier." Gen Ref Br, OCMH. (7) Lo's account of the Burma Campaign. SNF–12.

[74] Chih Hui Pu Diary, p. 2. Folder, Chinese Army (Ramgarh), Gen Ref Br, OCMH.

would die on the road, bullied and beat the laggards into moving on and encouraged and fed the stouthearted.[75]

All that the small group of Americans who had been flown from Burma to India could do was act as liaison between the Chinese and British, and Brereton's air force. Lacking resources of their own the Americans sometimes felt that they were contributing nothing. The AAF could consider it had kept the Chinese from perishing miserably in the northern Burma jungles. It alone had made possible the amazing march of the 96th Division, which made its way to Taro, then turned north to Shingbwiyang and Fort Hertz, from whence it made its way through the largely unknown country of northern Burma back to China. By its endurance the 96th Division showed some of the very best qualities of the Chinese Army, as it had earlier shown some of the worst.[76]

Moving directly to India to arrange for the reception of the Chinese divisions which he expected to follow him, Stilwell led a heterogeneous group: the small staff which he had kept after moving the bulk of his headquarters out to China and to Calcutta, the Seagrave ambulance unit with its nineteen gallant Burmese nurses, the Friends Ambulance Unit, a Chinese general with his bodyguard, a group of British officers, a newspaperman, nine mechanics, and three civilian refugees. Stilwell had undisputed command and used it to bring his people through the jungles quickly and in good health. No detail of command was too small for his attention.

Stilwell abandoned his motor transport on 6 May and engaged porters from a village near by. His plan was to go west for two days on foot. This march would place his party on one of the tributaries of the Chindwin, flowing west and south in the direction of India. The stream would in turn carry them near the village of Homalin, very close to India. Over the 6th, 7th, 8th, and 9th the party, with Stilwell always in the lead, marched westward. Heat exhaustion took its toll. Several people fell out and had to be revived. High above, the monkeys grimaced and chattered as the khaki snake wound slowly west along the trails and in the shallow streams. At the village of Maingkaing a day was spent building rafts. While the rest of the party moved westward by raft, traveling night and day, 1st Lt. Eugene P. Laybourn took the mules and a group of Chinese overland to Homalin. The mule train was met on schedule. The Chindwin was crossed on 13 May. The next day there was clear indication that the journey was nearly over, for the trails began to incline upward and the air to cool. India's guardian mountains were near. The march of the Stilwell party was not like the purgatory suffered by those who perforce came out through

---

[75] (1) Ltr, Boatner to Stilwell, 23 Aug 42, sub: Rpt on Activities in Dibrugarh–Ledo–Tipang Area from 20 Jun to 16 Aug; MS, Evacuation of Burma, Folder, Chinese Army, Trek from Burma. Gen Ref Br, OCMH. Evacuation of Burma appears to be a fragment of a long report by one of the officers sent up the trail. It gives the impression of a flood of horrors, perils, and adventures on such a scale that the author had neither the time nor inclination for fear or disgust. The extraordinary became commonplace, and he strove with it and recorded it as a matter of routine. (2) MA Rpt 655, 21 Sep 42. MID Library.
[76] (1) The Campaign in Burma, pp. 86–87. (2) History of CBI, p. 35.

north Burma but the general loss of weight and fatigue revealed the strain endured. Capt. Roscoe L. Hambleton, who tried to make his way out with the Chinese 5th Army, died of privation before reaching India.[77]

Stilwell's safe arrival on Indian soil 15 May created a new figure in contemporary American legend: "Vinegar Joe" Stilwell, the acid-tongued, indomitable, gruff-voiced, kindhearted old soldier who could make his way through any jungle. Stilwell offered no alibis, sketched no soothing picture of a triumphant withdrawal, but flatly stated: "We got a hell of a beating. It was as humiliating as hell. We ought to find out why it happened and go back!" [78]

Akyab, on the Bay of Bengal, was evacuated on 4 May by the 14/7 Rajputs, placed there in late January to keep the Japanese from using its airfield as a base from which to bomb Calcutta. Two more battalions went there on 18 March and were taken out shortly after because of the Japanese occupation of the Andamans. Heavy Japanese bombings in late March affected civilian morale, malaria began to make serious inroads on the garrison, and nationalist sentiment was increasing sharply. A strong force of Japanese-led Burmans with artillery was reported on the mainland at the end of April, and this, added to the other circumstances, made withdrawal of the battalion appear advisable. Akyab was occupied soon after.

While the remnants of four imperial and Chinese divisions were struggling through the mountains into India, on the other side of Burma six Chinese divisions were returning over the paths they had taken so hopefully three and four months before. All but the Temporary-55th and 28th Divisions were in relatively good order; behind them the *18th* and *56th Divisions* were pressing rapidly north and east. Here there could be no disappearing into the jungle. The Japanese exploited their success energetically, and for a time it appeared they would not be halted short of Kunming itself. Several months before, Churchill gave his opinion that the Japanese would not invade India when they had conquered Burma but that they would attempt an invasion of Yunnan Province, so the Japanese might take the terminus of the Burma Road and complete the isolation of China. When the pilots of the AVG destroyed a Japanese truck convoy with pontoon equipment and mightily harassed the *56th Division*'s truck convoys, they considered they had halted a possible Japanese invasion of China. Further support to this view comes from the fact that the Japanese did attempt to infiltrate across the Salween and sent patrols and swimmers across it just as they had in February before Martaban. On the other hand, six years later the commanding general of the *18th Division,* a staff officer of the *56th Division,* and a staff officer of the *15th Army* denied that there was

[77] (1) *The Stilwell Papers,* pp. 99–103. (2) Wyman Diary, 1–20 May 42. (3) Ltr, Nowakowski to Sunderland, 13 Feb 50. HIS 330.14 CBI 1950.
[78] (1) *The Stilwell Papers,* pp. 96–104. (2) Wyman Diary, 1–20 May 42. (3) Though Stilwell did not reach Imphal, capital of Manipur State, until 20 May, his party crossed the border at Saiyapaw on the 15th. History of CBI, p. 26.

WITHDRAWAL FROM BURMA. *Convoy on the road en route to India, above. Below, the Stilwell group walk up a river after abandoning their vehicles.*

WITHDRAWAL FROM BURMA. *General Stilwell, followed by two aides, Lt. Col. Frank Dorn and 1st Lt. Richard Young, leads the way through the jungle, above. Below, a brief rest is taken at a campsite. Left to right, Capt. Paul L. Jones, Lt. Col. Frank D. Merrill, Col. Robert P. Williams, and Col. Adrian St. John.*

any plan to invade Yunnan. Their statements are supported by an order of 26 April from *15th Army* directing pursuit to the line of the Salween. Whatever the recollections of Japanese officers six years later, the Chinese Government and General Chennault, having witnessed the debacle in Burma, were thoroughly alarmed and did their best to make invasion of Yunnan impossible.[79]

The Japanese occupied eastern Burma along four lines. One column thrust along the Burma Road, one went straight east from Loi-lem, and the two columns of Siamese plodded north from Chiang Mai. The *Reconnaissance Regiment* of the *56th Division* left Lashio on 30 April and went on up the Burma Road, scattering a battalion of the Burma Frontier Force, taking the suspension bridge over the Shweli west of Namhkam, and going on to Bhamo. On the way they had a brush with the Chinese 29th Division and thrust them aside. The *148th Regiment* went straight up the Burma Road to the hills near the Salween. On 4 May they were relieved by a smaller unit, retraced their steps, and went on to take Myitkyina on the 8th. The unit which had relieved them pressed on to the Salween River and was halted there by the Chinese, who wrecked the bridge. The Japanese delay to permit the relief of the *148th Regiment* may have been a great blunder, for a bridgehead over the Salween gorge would have been of tremendous value.[80]

Around and between these racing columns with their infantry in trucks and with tank spearheads, the 28th, 29th, and 200th Divisions were fighting and marching their way to the Chinese border. The adventures of the 200th Division were especially notable. Its successes in the Taunggyi area were made futile by the capture of Lashio, but the 200th Division, plus half of the 2d Reserve Regiment and two battalions of the Temporary-55th Division, was still in Taunggyi on 6 May. That day the 200th Division received conflicting orders from the Generalissimo and General Tu. The division commander obeyed General Tu's order and marched on Myitkyina, which lay many miles to the north.[81] While trying to make its way through a mountain pass, the division came under Japanese rifle fire. The commander, the same General Tai who fought so well at Toungoo, was wounded and died soon after. The division turned back and took an easier route.[82] This led the 200th Division toward Bhamo, in which vicinity it turned sharply east and made its way over the mountain paths to China. In effect, the 200th had cut right across the Japanese lines of communications and made its long journey behind Japanese task forces that were fanning out along the Yunnan border, many miles to the east.

As for the 28th and 29th Divisions, the former as of 4 May had two regi-

[79] (1) Foucar, pp. 206–08. (2) Statements of General Tanaka, General Takeuchi, Lt Col Taro Hayashi, and Col Motohisa Yoshida. Gen Ref Br, OCMH. (3) Japanese Study 88, Ch. IV. (4) MacMorland Diary, 8 May 42. MacMorland quotes Chennault as saying that the AVG had stopped an invasion.

[80] (1) Japanese Study 88, Ch. IV. (2) The Campaign in Burma.

[81] The preceding passage on the withdrawal of the Chinese Expeditionary Force from Burma is based on Japanese Study 88, and the Campaign in Burma, pp. 24, 80–89, 91.

[82] Rpt, With the 200th Division Withdrawing into China, translated by "P. F." SNF–21.

ments scattered between Lashio and Lung-ling, with the rest of its personnel north of Lung-ling. By 15 May it had collected itself and moved east of the Salween. The terrain in this section of the world lent itself well to such cross-country escapes, for by moving at night, troops could escape aerial observation, and the Japanese by day could not see through the sheltering mountains. Moreover, the Japanese could not be present in great force everywhere, and there must have been many gaps through which hardy and determined men could find a path. The 29th Division on 4 May was badly defeated at Wanting and soon had one regiment and two battalions scattered south of Wanting, with the rest of the division north of Lung-ling.

The lower Salween country was occupied by Japanese and Thai troops—the *56th Regiment, 18th Division,* from Loi-lem in Burma, the others north from Chiang Rai in Thailand. There was some fighting in the Kengtung area. After three days the Generalissimo intervened and ordered the Chinese 6th Army, of which only the 49th Division was fighting, to fall back on Puerh, China. This it did at once, thus bringing the 49th and 93d Divisions back to Chinese soil. The Japanese followed, taking Kengtung on 28 May, and advancing on Mong Yawng, fifty miles east, on 30 May. On the southern Salween front the Japanese were thus moving on in the full tide of hot and successful pursuit, but on the northern portion of that enormously long front, 250 miles away, the Chinese had halted, rallied, and mounted a counteroffensive with six divisions.

The curtain went up on the last act on 9 May. The Chinese 71st Army opened an attack toward Lung-ling, committing its 87th and 36th Divisions, keeping the 88th Division in reserve at Pao-shan.[83] The attempt failed, and the 87th was driven back, the Japanese following and attacking Hongmoshu, just northwest of the Hwei-tung Bridge over the Salween River. The Chinese counterattacked on the 15th. On 23 May the fighting took a favorable turn for the Chinese, and they captured Hwangtsoapa (sixteen miles northeast of Lung-ling on the Burma Road) and Fangmakiao (about ten miles south of Lung-ling). Heavy fighting developed next day at Shatzupo to the north, and the Chinese were well into an attack on a considerable scale, headed just south of west. Shatzupo was taken the next day. The inevitable Japanese counterattacks were repulsed, and by the end of May there was general and confused fighting throughout the Teng-chung–Lung-ling–Hwei-tung Bridge area. The situation was in hand, and the Japanese made no grand break-through into Yunnan Province.[84]

The AVG took part in these actions, first by helping to halt the Japanese advance and then by aiding the Chinese counteroffensive. Chinese bombers attacking Lashio were escorted on 2 May, and on the 7th and 8th enemy col-

[83] Sources cited n. 81.

[84] Japanese Study 88 speaks of fighting the 71st Army (heroes of Shanghai fighting in 1937) along the Salween. It states the Chinese counterattacked, and that the *56th Division* "checked" these attacks.

umns west of the Salween were bombed and strafed. One Japanese air raid on Pao-shan, the new AVG base, was successful because of surprise; for the second, the defenders were aloft and ready, destroying seven Japanese fighters. The monsoon rains shielded the Japanese ground forces in the middle of May. From 25 May on the AVG could and did attack steadily, the effort varying from 5 P–40's on 25 May to 12 on 29 May. Hanoi airfield was raided, too. Such was the opulence of Japanese air power in that region that some 60 aircraft were seen on the field, of which 1 transport and 15 fighters were claimed as destroyed. For the month the AVG could claim 24 fighters, 1 bomber, and 57 trucks as destroyed, for a loss of five pilots killed in action and 6 aircraft destroyed.[85] The Tenth Air Force from its bases in India attacked Mingaladon field, Rangoon, on 4 and 5 May, Myitkyina airfield on the 12th and 13th, and the Rangoon docks and Myitkyina on 29 and 30 May.[86]

Summary

At the end of May 1942 the Japanese held most of Burma with its rice, oil, tungsten, manganese, and 16,000,000 people. They had completely isolated China by land and could reasonably hope to isolate it by air. From Burma they could launch their attacks into China or India as they chose. From Burma they could bomb Calcutta and its neighboring cities, the very center of the Indian war effort, or they could reach far into western China. In taking Burma, they outfought and outmaneuvered 9 Chinese divisions, 5 Indian infantry brigades, 2 Burmese infantry brigades, 1 British armored brigade, and 6 British infantry battalions, totaling perhaps 81,000 men, supported by a modest complement of artillery, an American fighter group, and several Royal Air Force squadrons. In winning this victory, the Japanese used 10 infantry and 2 armored regiments with ample air support and claimed to have lost 1,280 dead and 3,158 wounded.[87]

Writing at the end of the third volume of his diary and dating his remarks 10 May, which meant he wrote them on the march out, Stilwell poured his bitterness into a scathing analysis of the campaign:

Hostile population; no air service; Jap initiative; inferior equipment (arty, tks, MG, TM): inadequate ammunition (50 rds [per] TM, 100 rds [per] arty [piece];) inadequate transport (300 trucks, mostly in 5th A;) no supply set-up; improvised medical service; stupid, gutless command; interference by CKS; Br. mess on R.R.; rotten communications; Br. defeatist attitude; vulnerable tactical situation; knew it was hopeless.[88]

[85] Int Summary, AVG Activities for May 42, Hq AVG. AVG File, Gen Ref Br. OCMH.
[86] The New York Times, May 15, 16, June 2, 1942.
[87] (1) Japanese Study 100, sub: Summary of Progress of Operations by 15th Army. (2) In a postwar survey, U.S. Strategic Bombing Survey Report 64d, Ground Logistics, (9) Statistics of Losses, the Japanese losses show 9,600 battle casualties including 7,400 killed in action and 500 dead from wounds received in action. This report is in the National Archives. (3) The Campaign in Burma, pp. 90–91.
[88] Stilwell Diary, 10 May 42.

PART TWO

PLANS FOR BREAKING THE BLOCKADE OF CHINA (MAY 1942–MARCH 1943)

CHAPTER V

Stilwell's Mission Interrupted by an Ultimatum

General Stilwell arrived in New Delhi on 24 May. The march out had been grueling, but Stilwell lost no time in preparing his proposals for Stimson, Marshall, and the Generalissimo. Those to his American superiors were a logical development of the 27 April 1942 proposals to the Generalissimo. The ones he sent the Generalissimo were the first of their series.

Stilwell asked Marshall and Stimson to send him one or more U.S. divisions for a major Allied operation toward the South China Sea. If American combat troops were sent to India, he would add them to the retrained and re-equipped Chinese veterans of Burma. With that force he would retake Burma and drive the Japanese from Thailand, and then from within China he would force an entry into the triangle Hanoi–Hainan–Canton. A foothold there would permit attack on major Japanese sea and air routes. Moreover, U.S. troops in India, as both token and example, were the surest way to keep the Chinese co-operative.

As for the Chinese Army, Stilwell told Stimson and Marshall that it was weak because its matériel was thinly spread over its 300-odd divisions. These supplies should be pooled and redistributed to a smaller number of divisions to make them an effective fighting force. A purge of the higher-ranking Chinese officers was required. They were physically brave, but they had no moral courage, never went to the front, never reconnoitered, and never supervised their troops. The Generalissimo should choose a man in whom he had confidence (Stilwell did not suggest that he be the man) and give him the field command with full responsibility, untrammeled by wires and letters from Chungking. Supply, communication, and medical services all needed revitalization. In a private letter to Stimson, Stilwell surveyed the defeat in Burma. Stilwell did not place the blame for the debacle on any one individual or set of circumstances. In the letter he mentioned that he had recommended the Chinese execute the commanders of the 6th Army, of the Temporary-55th and 96th Divisions, and one regimental commander of the 28th Division.[1]

General Marshall sent Stilwell's plea for American troops to the President

[1] (1) CM–IN 7037, Stilwell to Marshall, 25 May 42. (2) Ltr, Stilwell to Stimson, 25 May 42. Stimson Papers. (See Bibliographical Note.)

but with the comment that the personnel and shipping situation would not permit an affirmative answer. Instead, Marshall suggested a plan submitted by the Operations Division (OPD) of the War Department on 26 May 1942 with the significant title, Keeping China in the War. OPD told Marshall that the airfreight line could never deliver enough supplies to China and that the Burma Road would have to be reopened. Because India and Burma were in the British sphere of strategic responsibility, the action to reopen the Burma Road, OPD went on, had to be primarily British, assisted by the U.S. means at hand, which were the Tenth Air Force and Chinese lend-lease. This would go far to arm 250,000 Indian troops, who would then descend on Burma. The Generalissimo's approval of this transfer of Chinese lend-lease was of course required, and Marshall proposed to the President that Stilwell be asked to obtain it. Stilwell's role in the command or direction of this Allied attempt to reoccupy Burma could be determined after he had reported on his success with the Generalissimo.[2]

The President approved Marshall's suggestion, and the radio went to Stilwell for comment. Stilwell in reply urged Marshall to make no final decision until the proposal to train Chinese troops in India had been worked out. Moreover, both he and the Chinese believed that though General Headquarters (India), Wavell's headquarters for India Command, was contemplating the reconquest of Burma, no plans had been made and no date set. The Chinese would not give arms to an enterprise that to them appeared so indefinite.[3]

In a cordial radio on 16 June Stimson and Marshall reaffirmed their faith in Stilwell and told him they were trying to get the Generalissimo's consent to conditions which would make Stilwell's task easier. If they failed in this, they would send him to another theater where his talents might be applied. Thus, Stilwell's first approach to the War Department for tools to do the job had run hard aground on the rocks of the troop and shipping shortage.[4]

Stilwell's Proposals To Reform the Chinese Army

From New Delhi Stilwell flew to Chungking, arriving there on 3 June, the brief delay caused largely by bad weather. The general was ill. Defective yellow fever serum brought on a debilitating attack of yellow jaundice, which made it very hard for Stilwell to be up and about. Despite this, the day after his arrival he forced himself to keep an appointment with the Generalissimo

[2](1) Memo, Gen Crawford, Actg ACofS OPD, 26 May 42, sub: Keeping China in War. OPD 381 CTO (5–26–42), A47–30. OPD was the wartime successor to War Plans Division (WPD). (2) Memo, Marshall for President, 28 May 42. WDCSA (China), A45–466.
[3](1) CM–IN 1878, Stilwell to Marshall, 6 Jun 42. (2) Min, War Council Mtg, 8 Jun 42. WDCSA, Notes on War Council, A48–139. (3) Stilwell was unaware that in June 1942 Wavell had submitted outline plans for Burma's reconquest to the British Chiefs of Staff. Wavell Despatch, March 1942 to December 31, 1942, *Supplement to The London Gazette*, pars. 27–30.
[4] CM–OUT 3751, Stimson to Stilwell, 16 Jun 42.

and Madame Chiang at which he "gave them the full story [of Burma], pulling no punches, and naming names." [5] He also presented his proposals for the reform of the Chinese Army:

MAY 26, 1942.

NOTES FOR THE GENERALISSIMO

The Chinese Army is weak partly because of lack of equipment, but mostly for other reasons. It is too large to equip properly with the matériel now available, but a reduced number of divisions could be furnished with suitable weapons, including artillery, if a determined effort were made to get it together. A reorganization should be commenced at once with this end in view. A few dependable, well-equipped, well-supported divisions would be worth far more than double the number of the present average. The lack of artillery, A.A. guns, tanks, and planes has been evident for a long time. There is no use in continuing this complaint. The question is what can be done now with what we have.

(1) I recommend the merging of divisions to bring all units up to full strength, and the assignment of all available weapons to these divisions as far as they will go. Our available striking force will then be concentrated, and usable, as it is not now.

The average of the rank and file is willing, disciplined, inured to hardship, and responsive to leadership. The junior officers respond readily to direction. Battalion and regimental commanders show considerable variation, but there are many good ones. It would be easy to sift out the inefficient in these grades, and the resulting promotion would have a good effect on morale. Division and Army commanders are a great problem. Very few of them are efficient. They seldom get up to the front and they very rarely supervise the execution of their orders. Reports from the front are accepted without check, and very often prove exaggerated or entirely false. The vital necessity of continuous reconnaissance and security is commonly ignored, often with fatal consequences. The average division commander seems to feel that issuing an order from a point sometimes 50 miles from the front is all that is required of him. Many of these officers are personally brave, but most of them lack moral courage.

(2) I recommend a rigid purge of inefficient high commanders. This could be accomplished partly by the training section, which could require field tests, and partly on recommendations from officers in whom the Generalissimo has the highest confidence. Without a clearing out of the inefficient, the Army will continue to go down hill, no matter how much matériel is supplied for it.

The system of command must be clarified and unity of command insisted upon. The Generalissimo must pick some one man in whom he has confidence, give him a general directive, and then let him handle the troops without interference from anyone whomsoever. This man must not only control the tactical direction of the troops, but also their transport, supply, communications, and medical service. During the Burma campaign letters and instructions from various sources reached various commanders who as a result were

[5] *The Stilwell Papers*, pp. 110–13.

confused as to their action. The Generalissimo himself writes to various commanders making suggestions based on his knowledge of the situation, and giving advice as to courses of action in certain contingencies. These commanders, in their high regard for the Generalissimo's experience and ability, invariably interpret these suggestions and this advice as orders and act on them as such. (The Generalissimo gets unquestioned loyalty from his officers.)

(3) I recommend that in future operations one man be chosen with complete authority to direct the action with complete control over the services, and with no staff other than his own present. Liaison officers from the War Ministry can check all his orders and actions, as well as his reports, but his absolute control of the troops must not be infringed upon.

The above recommendations cover the main points which observation convinces me are essential if the Chinese Army is to remain an efficient fighting force. There are other things that must be attended to. A better system of supply and transport must be set up. Communications must be improved. The medical service must be organized in units that can move at once to serve any theater of operations. Rewards for gallant conduct should be made promptly. Punishment must be prompt and ruthless, no matter what the rank of the offender. The situation looks dark, but it can be saved by a vigorous and immediate overhaul of the entire organization. The Army will be smaller, but it will be far more efficient and easier to supply and handle. China can even now produce, with the meager resources available, a striking force that can hold the Japs off until the growing offensive powers of the Allies turns [*sic*] the scales toward complete victory.[6]

Glancing quickly at the paper, Madame Chiang remarked that this was what his German advisers had told the Generalissimo. Twenty days later at another conference she said that the drastic measures advocated by General Stilwell could not be taken. It was necessary to be "realistic," Madame Chiang went on, "heads cannot be lopped off otherwise nothing would be left." [7] This was the only Chinese reaction to Stilwell's proposals of 26 May. In his files Stilwell kept an envelope with his memoranda to the Generalissimo for the period 26 May–1 August 1942. On the cover he tabulated and summarized them by date, and after each he gave the Chinese reaction. For ten of the thirteen memoranda, including his 26 May proposal, he gave the Chinese response as, simply, "No answer." [8]

Stilwell's jaundice greatly restricted his activities until late June but he was able to meet twice with the Generalissimo. At the first conference on 15 June the Generalissimo scoffed at any suggestion that the British might drive back into Southeast Asia. He revealed his belief that masses of the latest and best

----

[6](1) Notes for Generalissimo, 26 May 42. Stilwell Documents, Hoover Library. (2) Stilwell summarized these proposals for Marshall in CM–IN 5665, Stilwell to Marshall, 18 Jun 42.

[7](1) *The Stilwell Papers,* p. 113. (2) Min (Chinese and American versions), Conf, Stilwell, Generalissimo, and Mme. Chiang, 24 Jun 42. Stilwell Documents, Hoover Library. Stilwell and Mme. Chiang started their conference at 5:00 P.M. and their talks ended at 7:00 P.M. The Generalissimo was present from 5:30 to 6:30 P.M. Nowhere in the public or private papers of General Stilwell could there be found a proposal "that all Chinese Armies be reorganized with American officers holding all posts of colonel and above." From *Way of a Fighter,* p. 167, by Claire L. Chennault. Copyright, 1949, by Claire Lee Chennault. Courtesy of G. P. Putnam's Sons.

[8] See illustration on opposite page.

matériel would win the war. Stilwell retorted that the only way was to reorganize thoroughly the Chinese Army. His point then, and later, was that it was fatuous to give a medium tank or a howitzer to a peasant soldier who had never seen anything more complex than his father's wheelbarrow; that the Chinese Army had to be trained and reorganized before it could profitably be given new equipment. To this belief the Chinese never subscribed. Madame Chiang's comment to Stilwell's retort was that the Generalissimo had to consider "certain influences." [9]

The conferences of 24 June revealed that Madame Chiang wanted General Tu to command the Chinese troops in India, who were simply to rest there and not undergo training. Then the Generalissimo entered and stated (according to the Chinese minutes) that the Chinese in India were to be trained. After two hours Madame Chiang herself raised the command point again, and this time the Chinese agreed that Tu would be relieved and that Lo Cho-ying would command, though Stilwell would have preferred either an American, General

[9](1) *The Stilwell Papers*, p. 115. (2) CM–IN 5665, Stilwell to Marshall, 18 Jun 42.

986352 O—52——12

Sun (38th Division), or Maj. Gen. Liao Yao-shiang (22d Division), in that order.[10]

When the Generalissimo was present at the conference, Stilwell was able to raise the question of the joint staff. This body, which was to have been set up in March, was still not created in June.[11] Proposals had been exchanged, though it seemed to the Americans that General Ho, the Chinese Chief of Staff and Minister of War, had not read those sent by the Chinese staff to Stilwell. General Ho, however, shared his subordinates' belief that the joint staff should be under the Chinese General Staff.[12] This would produce an arrangement similar to that which would have obtained if General Eisenhower and his Allied staff in England had been placed under the British Imperial General Staff. In the discussion it appeared that the Generalissimo's views on the joint staff agreed exactly with Stilwell's; that the Generalissimo as Supreme Commander, China Theater, should issue orders to Stilwell, his Allied chief of staff. The joint staff would then prepare orders accordingly, whose execution would be through the Chinese General Staff for the Chinese Army, and through General Stilwell for Allied Forces in China Theater. It appeared to Stilwell that the Generalissimo also had not seen the Chinese proposals.[13]

The Generalissimo went on to say, at the 24 June conference, that a headquarters for China Theater should be established and a comprehensive plan drawn up. This plan should have two phases—the first being to maintain the *status quo* in China, the second to prepare for the counteroffensive. As theaters for the counterblow the Generalissimo mentioned Burma, Thailand, Indochina, and China itself. Stilwell replied that his plan would be ready either that day or the next. The Generalissimo then turned to lend-lease equipment and aircraft, saying that once a plan had been made to bring in 5,000 tons of supplies a month and to maintain 500 aircraft in China, then attention could be directed to training troops.

Coming back to command problems, the Generalissimo explained his system:

. . . I cannot overemphasize the need of a general plan for the whole of the China Theater of War. It will have a great effect upon the morale of not only the army but also the people of China. I can send representatives from various military organizations to your office once it comes into existence thereby increasing the effectiveness of the work. I want you to be very close to me and to serve as an important member of the brain trust. I want you to know what is going on and to see me very frequently.

There is a secret for the direction of Chinese troops unlike the direction of foreign troops. I am well aware of the fact that our senior officers do not possess enough education and suffi-

---

[10] Min (Chinese version), Conf, Stilwell, Generalissimo, and Mme. Chiang, 24 Jun 42. Stilwell Documents, Hoover Library.

[11] Ch. III, pp. 87–89, 94–96, above.

[12] (1) Stilwell Diary, 15, 16, 24 Jun 42. (2) Min (Chinese and American versions), Conf, Stilwell, Generalissimo, and Mme. Chiang, 24 Jun 42. Stilwell Documents, Hoover Library.

[13] Memo 161, Stilwell for Shang Chen, 27 Jun 42. Stilwell Documents, Hoover Library.

cient capacity for work. Anticipating them to make mistakes, I often write to them personally so that timely warned they might avoid them. Knowing their limited capacity I plan ahead for them. We have been carrying on the war of resistance for five years in such conditions.

At the outbreak of the war, Japan announced that in three months the war would be over and friends of China believed this, but we are still able to continue it, because of the understanding of the limitations of our senior officers and the resort to timely warnings. In other words prevention is better than cure. The German officers who had been employed by China for their training were unable to get along with Chinese officers. It would be necessary to think in terms of their mentality. If you are with me closely for a few months, you will understand the psychology of Chinese officers, and I will tell you more about their peculiarities. . . .[14]

Stilwell's proposed plan for China Theater, as requested by the Generalissimo, was then in course of preparation. Phase I of the plan has not survived, but Phase II, the Counteroffensive, a study of an operation to seize the Hankow area, shows his attempt to comply with the orders of the Supreme Commander, China Theater.[15] Before these plans could be presented, word came of a crisis in the Middle East that left Stilwell writing: "Now what can I say to the G-mo? We fail in *all* our commitments and blithely tell him to just carry on, old top." [16]

Beginnings of Trouble

On 23 June the War Department notified Stilwell that Brereton was to take the Tenth's heavy bombers and a number of the Assam–Burma–China airline's transport aircraft, with necessary personnel, and go to the Middle East.[17] The British forces in that area had been severely shaken and driven from Cyrenaica into Egypt by Italo-German forces under the leadership of Gen. Erwin Rommel. The Suez Canal, the Middle East, and the lines of communication to India and China via the Cape of Good Hope all seemed in danger, and help had to be sent. In June 1942 Churchill was present in Washington to discuss strategy with Roosevelt and the Combined Chiefs of Staff.

News of the Axis successes in North Africa, which included the stunning surprise of Tobruk's fall on 21 June, made Churchill favor an attack on North Africa to relieve the pressure in the Middle East.[18] This attack might have meant the end of preparations for the cross-Channel assault by the Anglo-American forces on northern France (code name, BOLERO). However, as a result of a series of compromises the basic plan for BOLERO was preserved. To achieve the plan the United States made certain concessions, among which was

---

[14] Min (Chinese and American versions), Conf, Stilwell and Generalissimo, 24 Jun 42. Stilwell Documents, Hoover Library. Quotation from the Chinese version.

[15] (1) Preliminary Estimate, II, The Counteroffensive. SNF–14. (2) Gen Hearn, A Critique of the Hankow Operation. SNF–14.

[16] *The Stilwell Papers,* p. 119.

[17] CM–OUT 5699, OPD to Stilwell, 23 Jun 42.

[18] (1) CM–IN 6008, Col Bonner F. Fellers, Cairo, to AGWAR, 17 Jun 42. (2) CM–IN 6491, Fellers to WD, 19 Jun 42. (3) Sherwood, *Roosevelt and Hopkins,* pp. 590–99.

the transfer of General Brereton with all of his available aircraft from India to the Middle East and the halting in Africa of a shipment of Lockheed Hudson (A-29) bombers intended for China. The immediate result of Brereton's transfer was, as Marshall recognized, serious trouble with the Generalissimo.[19]

But Marshall pointed out only the proximate cause of American difficulties with the Generalissimo, because trouble had been brewing for months. Three important points were vexing the Chinese: China was not admitted to membership in the Combined Chiefs of Staff; since January 1942 the Generalissimo's Foreign Minister had been sending him inflammatory reports about the way lend-lease was being administered by the Americans; and the several aviation projects for China were very slow in materializing.

For a brief period after Pearl Harbor things had gone very well on the diplomatic front. After the ARCADIA Conference Roosevelt had insisted that China be treated as a Great Power. The Generalissimo had become Supreme Commander of China Theater. He had convened an Allied military council in Chungking; he had accepted an American as his Allied chief of staff; he had sent three armies and the American Volunteer Group to the defense of Burma. Possibly impressed by China's new status as a Great Power (certainly a triumph for Chinese diplomacy and propaganda), the Generalissimo had been late in seeking a place for China with the emerging Combined Chiefs of Staff and their subordinate body, the Munitions Assignments Board.

Not until 19 April 1942 did the Generalissimo bid for CCS membership for China.[20] A negative reply was sent on 13 June 1942; it politely recognized China's importance in the war, but it was still a refusal. One reason behind the refusal lay in the fact that CCS membership would have entailed membership in the Munitions Assignments Board, whose function was to allocate the pooled exportable Anglo-American munitions production. China could contribute nothing to such a pool and would only make demands for a greater share in it.[21]

The strength of the Generalissimo's feelings had been shown by his quoting the Indian nationalist leader, Mohandas K. Gandhi: "Why, they [the British and the Americans] do not even admit your country to their staff talks!" The Generalissimo had gone on to tell T. V. Soong: "If we are treated thus during the stress of war, what becomes of our position at the peace conference? You

---

[19] Statement of Marshall, Notes on War Council Mtg, 29 Jun 42. WDCSA, Notes on War Council, A48-139. Also notes of 22 June 1942. Same file.

[20](1) Sherwood, *Roosevelt and Hopkins*, pp. 515-16. (2) Telg, Chiang to Soong, 19 Apr 42; Ltr, Soong to Hopkins, 20 Apr 42. Bk VI, Hopkins Papers.

[21](1) Ltr, Field Marshal Dill, Gen Marshall, and Admiral Ernest J. King, CinC, U.S. Fleet, to Lt Gen Hsiung Shih-fei, Chief, Chinese Mil Mission to U.S., 13 Jun 42. ABC 384 (China), 29 May 42, A48-224. (2) CCS 74, 29 May 42, sub: Chinese Concept of Conduct of Present War. (3) JCS 17th Mtg, Notes (Tab A), 1 Jun 42. ABC 384 (China), 29 May 42, A48-224. (4) CCS 22d Mtg, 2 Jun 42. (5) Ltr, Hsiung to CCS, 26 Jun 42. ABC 336 (China), 26 Jan 42, Sec 1A, A48-224.

must insist that we have our own stand, and we have our own independent position to uphold." [22]

China's share in lend-lease had been shrinking. When actual war broke out between the United States and the Axis powers, every weapon and every pound of supplies had to be used. By late spring 1942 the Chinese had accumulated 149,000 tons of lend-lease in the United States and 45,000 tons in India, for which prospects of delivery after the loss of Burma were dim indeed. Strongly and eloquently opposed by Soong and his associates, the Munitions Assignments Board of the Combined Chiefs of Staff moved steadily toward repossessing the Chinese stockpiles and cutting new allocations of Chinese lend-lease to what might be expected to be flown to China in the near future. As the War Department's representative in Chungking, charged with supervising and controlling China's lend-lease, Stilwell was inevitably brought into this delicate and, for the Chinese, irritating situation.

Asked by Dr. Currie in March for his opinions on the then billion-and-a-half-dollar Chinese lend-lease program, Stilwell agreed with Currie to reduce it to arms for thirty divisions, aircraft for the 500-plane air force, and road-building machinery.[23] Consistent with this, Stilwell recommended that the War Department procure and ship arms for the Thirty Divisions and the Chinese Air Force.[24] That Stilwell should comment on Chinese bids for lend-lease aid, as he was obliged by his orders to do, soon angered the Generalissimo.

Before Pearl Harbor lend-lease had been allocated among the several sovereign Allied states on a quasi-diplomatic basis. After Pearl Harbor the Munitions Assignments Board allocated it among theaters of operations in accordance with CCS strategic concepts. The Generalissimo's China Theater was not under the Combined Chiefs, but his share of lend-lease after Pearl Harbor was set by the Munitions Assignments Board, which was under the CCS. Ultimately, the Generalissimo realized that the only way he could increase his share was to appeal directly to the President.[25]

At the end of April, the War Department suggested that Stilwell and the Generalissimo agree on China's lend-lease, then forward a series of periodic

[22](1) Telg, Chiang to Soong, 19 Apr 42. Bk VI, Hopkins Papers. (2) China sought representation on the CCS until V-J Day. Ltr, Shang Chen, Chief, Chinese Mil Mission to U.S., to CCS, 3 Jul 45, Incl to JCS 1407, 5 Jul 45, sub: Chinese Representation on CCS.

[23] Rad AMMISCA 261, Currie to Stilwell, 7 Mar 42. AMMISCA Radio File, Job–11.

[24] Stilwell recommended that the prewar communication projects be cut, but he asked the War Department to fill Chinese lend-lease requisitions on the basis of a new Chinese Table of Organization and Equipment that was handed to him on 9 March 1942. The request was granted. (1) Stilwell Diary, 9 Mar 42. (2) Rad AMMISCA 345, Stilwell to AGWAR, 10 Mar 42. AMMISCA Radio File, Job–11. (3) Memo, Eisenhower for Aurand, 15 Mar 42, sub: Priorities to China. OPD 400.3295 (China), 11 Mar 42, A47–30. (4) Memo, Eisenhower for McCloy, 31 Mar 42. Same file.

[25](1) CCS 50/2, 23 Mar 42. (2) Leighton and Coakley, Logistics of Global Warfare: 1941–43. (3) Memo, Soong for Hopkins, 22 Apr 42; Ltr, Burns to Hopkins, 22 Apr 42, sub: Shipts to China; Memo, Soong for Hopkins, 1 May 42; Memo, Hopkins for Malony, 30 Apr 42, and Malony's reply, same date; Memo, Soong for Hopkins, 1 May 42. Bk V, Hopkins Papers.

agreed-on requisitions. Magruder answered for Stilwell, who was at that moment on the ox roads toward Myitkyina. Magruder dismissed the suggestion as nothing but a treatment for symptoms and proposed the *quid pro quo* policy which was to dominate the War Department's views for months to come. Magruder acknowledged that the Chinese had been led to expect more lend-lease than they could ever receive. He recommended for a first step to get the Generalissimo to agree to a specific and limited organization of ground and air forces which could be supplied partly by lend-lease.[26]

The trend toward greater control over Chinese lend-lease by the Munitions Assignments Board was dramatically highlighted in May by the repossession of the 149,000-ton stockpile at Newport News, Virginia, to which Soong reluctantly assented.[27] Moreover at this same time, in response to a request from its Ground Committee, the Munitions Assignments Board studied a new lend-lease program for China. On 8 May a China Defense Supplies official had given Brig. Gen. Henry S. Aurand, Chairman of the Munitions Assignments Committee (Ground), an emergency air transport program, which the official said was the result of a White House conference. The China Defense Supplies official also said that Soong considered the program as an ultimatum. The Chinese program called for the air delivery of 7,500 tons a month. The Munitions Assignments Committee (Ground) selected a figure which was approximately half of the Chinese demand. Concurrently, the Munitions Assignments Committee (Ground) requested a decision from the Munitions Assignments Board on a tonnage figure to be used as a basis for assignment and asked for authority to negotiate a six months' program (May to October) and to recommend assignments for May and June. The Munitions Assignments Board assigned 3,500 tons (items for the Chinese Army) for May and June respectively and projected a program for July through October 1942. (*Table 4*) Mindful of putting more air power in China, the Munitions Assignments Board set aside an additional 1,500 tons a month for Chennault on the same basis as the 3,500-ton program for the Chinese Army. During the duration of the emergency air transport program, the board named Stilwell as its agent to receive the lend-lease in India for China and to name the time and place for delivery to China.[28]

In June this prospect of 5,000 tons, already drab beside the transferred 149,000 tons, grew even more so as Soong learned that the War Department

[26](1) Memo, Aurand for McCloy, 27 Apr 42. ASW 400.366 (China). (2) CM–OUT 5680, Marshall to Stilwell, 29 Apr 42. (3) CM–IN 0513, Magruder for Stilwell to AGWAR, 2 May 42. (4) Memo, Magruder for Stilwell, 18 May 42, sub: Some Observations on Present Situation in China. AMMISCA Folder 7.

[27](1) The battle over the lend-lease stockpile at Newport News and at other depots in the United States is contained in a series of letters between McCloy and Soong from 19 to 21 May 1942. ASW 400.336 (China). (2) One hundred thousand tons of the Chinese lend-lease stocks were War Department procured and the remainder were Treasury stocks. This 149,000 tons excluded 10,317 carloads of steel rails and accessories for the Yunnan-Burma Railway. See Ch. I, above. Memo for Record. ASW 400.336 (China).

[28](1) Min, MAC(G) 27th Mtg, 11 May 42. (2) Min, MAB 15th Mtg, 15 May 42, Item 6.

TABLE 4—ACTUAL AND PROJECTED DELIVERIES OF LEND-LEASE EQUIPMENT UNDER THE CHINESE EMERGENCY AIR TRANSPORT PROGRAM: MAY–OCTOBER 1942 [a]

[In Long Tons]

Type of Equipment	Actual [b]		Projected [c]			
	May	June	July	August	September	October
Total..........	3,500	3,500	3,506	3,522	3,489	3,458
Ordnance............	2,865	2,744	3,168	3,130	2,570	2,943
Signal..............	200	321	188	242	169	165
Medical..............	235	235	150	150	150	150
Motor Transport......	200	200	0	0	600	200

[a] Exclusive of air corps fuel.
[b] Lend-Lease commitment to China as of 19 May 42.
[c] For planning purposes only, July through October.

Source: Min, MAC(G) 28th Mtg, 14 May 42, Tab B; Min, MAC(G) 29th Mtg, 18 May 42, Tab B. CCS 334.8 MAB (5–15–42).

regarded only the May and June 3,500-ton allotments as a firm commitment. Soong learned further that Stilwell was now the Munitions Assignments Board's agent in setting the date and place at which lend-lease titles passed to Chinese hands, a response to the *Tulsa* incident. It is worthy of note that not then or ever was Stilwell given power to say how much lend-lease China should receive. He might propose, but the Munitions Assignments Board disposed. Unfortunately, Soong did not tell the Generalissimo about Stilwell's new powers. For his part, Stilwell quickly saw that he had received lend-lease duties of baffling complexity. In the light of the events described above it would seem that the Chinese failure to grapple realistically with the transportation of lend-lease matériel and their preoccupation with simply staking out a claim to large portions of American production, both military and commercial, and then defending it tooth and nail were responsible for this development.[29]

Besides the difficulties over lend-lease supplies and China's lack of CCS membership there were others on the handling of U.S. air power in China, Burma, and India.[30] On 2 April the Generalissimo agreed to dissolve the AVG in exchange for Stilwell's promise of a complete U.S. fighter group (the 23d Pursuit Group) by 4 July when most AVG pilots' contracts with Pawley's company would expire.[31] The bitterness of AVG personnel, which caused the

[29](1) CM–OUT 6222, Somervell to Stilwell, 29 May 42. (2) Ltr, MAC(G) to CDS, 16 Jun 42, sub: Chinese Emergency Air Transport Program. Folder, China Requirements, ASF (DAD) ID, A46–299. (3) Rad, Marshall to Stilwell, 9 Jun 42. (4) *The Stilwell Papers*, pp. 126–27, 130–31. (5) CM–IN 1942, Stilwell to AGWAR, 5 Jun 42. (6) History of CBI, Sec. II, Ch. XI.
[30] See Ch. II, above.
[31](1) CM–IN 0629, Stilwell to AGWAR, 2 Apr 42. (2) Chennault, *Way of a Fighter*, pp. 170–72. (3) See Ch. I, p. 18, above. (4) AVG contracts would start expiring by 4 July 1942, since the first pilots had reached the Far East on 3 July 1941 to begin their one-year contract with Pawley's company. AVG Contract Folder, Pawley Papers.

mutiny described in Chapter III, was not diminished by Brig. Gen. Clayton L. Bissell's lack of success in handling the problem of induction, and only five pilots agreed to accept Army Air Forces commissions.[32] Though Bissell repeatedly urged the War Department to send the men and the aircraft needed for the new fighter group and for added bomber and fighter strength, as 4 July drew near, it was ever more apparent they would not be on hand.[33]

Despite Stilwell's directives, Headquarters, Tenth Air Force, gave him little aid in his attempts to cope with the problems of establishing U.S. air power in China. The Tenth's attention was centered on India. The burden of negotiations with the Chinese and of making arrangements for basing more U.S. aircraft in China fell on Stilwell, who necessarily delegated the task to his air officer, Bissell. To Stilwell, the slowness with which the Tenth moved men and aircraft to China contrasted unfavorably with the speed with which the Tenth sent its heavy bombers, transports, and key staff personnel to Egypt. The failure of Headquarters, Tenth Air Force, to issue a directive to Chennault for China operations forced that task on Bissell. Bissell also had to "make all arrangements for receiving, housing, and feeding 10th Air Force [in China]."[34] All this embarrassed Stilwell in his relations with the Generalissimo and Chennault, who mistakenly believed that Stilwell was indifferent to the possibilities of China-based air power.[35]

A further complication was created by the Chinese agreement to furnish ground facilities plus fuel and bombs from their meager stores to the new 23d Pursuit Group on the understanding that the United States would replace them. The Chinese were manifestly living up to their promise. These arrangements had of course been made without foreknowledge of the Middle East crisis, which transformed what had been an amicable arrangement into what the Generalissimo probably thought one more failure to make good on a U.S. promise.[36]

To the irritating AVG problem was added the Doolittle raid on Tokyo. Bombers surviving the raid were expected to land in China, where they would join Chennault. The Generalissimo did not want the B-25's landing in China after bombing Tokyo, for he feared a violent Japanese reaction. He had only been apprised of the project at the last minute, and his wishes were in effect

---

[32] See Ch. III, pp. 112–13, above.

[33] (1) CM–IN 1226, Bissell to AGWAR, 5 May 42. (2) CM–OUT 2275, Marshall to Stilwell, 12 May 42. (3) CM–IN 5194, Bissell to AGWAR, 19 May 42. (4) CM–IN 8047, Stilwell to AGWAR, 28 May 42.

[34] (1) Stilwell denounced Headquarters, Tenth Air Force, on eighteen separate counts. Documents entitled Case, Obstacles. SNF–12. (2) *The Stilwell Papers,* pp. 139–40.

[35] Chennault, *Way of a Fighter,* Ch. 12.

[36] (1) Ltr, Bissell to Maj Gen Chou Chih-jou, Dir Commission of Aeronautical Affairs, NMC, 10 Jun 42. Item 128, Corresp Folder (Jul 42–Nov 43), CT 23, Dr 2, KCRC. (2) CM–IN 9114, Stilwell to Marshall, 27 Jun 42. (3) Memo 24, Bissell for Generalissimo, 23 Jun 42. Corresp Folder, Memos for Mme. Chiang (May–Sep 42), CT 23, Dr 2, KCRC. (4) Rpt of Conf with Mme. Chiang, 24 Jun 42, sub: Opns of American Aviation in China. Corresp Folder (May–Sep 42), CT 23, Dr 2, KCRC.

overruled.[37] Marshall apologized to the Generalissimo for the failure to consult him.[38]

As the Generalissimo had feared, fifty-three Japanese battalions drove through Chekiang Province, whose people had received the wrecked American crews. Issued 30 April 1942, the orders of *Imperial General Headquarters* to *China Expeditionary Forces* were to "thwart the enemy's plans to carry out air raids on the homeland of JAPAN from the Chekiang Province area. To accomplish this mission he [the Commander-in-Chief, *China Expeditionary Forces*] will annihilate enemy forces in said area and destroy the area's principal air bases." Thus was plainly evidenced the extreme sensitivity of the Japanese to any American move which threatened aerial bombardment of Japan proper, and in moving through Chekiang the Japanese did what ingenuity and malice suggested to persuade the hapless peasants that hospitality to Americans was inadvisable. To the eternal credit of the Chinese, they spurned both the lesson and its teacher.[39]

The Japanese sweep through Chekiang Province ended still another air project. The plan to bomb Japan with China-based B–24's, HALPRO, in which the Generalissimo had been greatly interested, was canceled and the B–24's stopped in Egypt because Stilwell felt that the loss of the Chekiang bases and the lack of transports made the effort impossible.[40]

Air Transport Disappoints the Chinese

Activated on 21 March with Pan American Airways' twenty-five transports, the Assam–Burma–China Ferry Command hardly began operations before it was forced to take its aircraft off the run to China in order to drop supplies to the soldiers and refugees streaming out of Burma. In mid-May came the monsoon, causing round trips to China to average only fifty-seven each in May and June. Twenty-one flying days were lost to the rains. As a result, only a few score tons were flown into China.[41]

The United States in spring and summer 1942 did not have transport aircraft to spare for the airline to China. In April 1942 first priority for transports went to aircraft for the airborne components of the projected cross-Channel

[37] (1) Rad AF3/294, Arnold to Stilwell, 18 Mar 42. (2) CM–IN 3130, AMMISCA to AGWAR, 11 Apr 42. (3) Memo 3, Bissell for Generalissimo, 16 Apr 42. Ltrs to Generalissimo (Apr 42–Apr 44), CT 23, Dr 2, KCRC. (4) Memo, Gen McNarney, DCofS, for Roosevelt, 16 Apr 42, sub: First Sp Bombing Mission (China). AG 381 (16 Apr 42).

[38] Marshall's apologies were conveyed to the Generalissimo by Bissell in Memo 5, Bissell for Generalissimo, 19 Apr 42. Ltrs to Generalissimo (Apr 42–Apr 44), CT 23, Dr 2, KCRC.

[39] (1) *Imperial General Headquarters,* Army Order 621, 30 Apr 42, GHQ, Far East Comd, Mil Hist Div, *Imperial General Headquarters* Army Orders, Vol. II. Gen Ref Br, OCMH. (2) Japanese Study 77.

[40] (1) CM–OUT 1929, Arnold to Stilwell, 9 May 42. (2) Memo 14, Bissell for Generalissimo, 11 May 42, sub: Second Sp Aviation Project; Memo 17, Bissell for Generalissimo, 26 May 42. Ltrs to Generalissimo (Apr 42–Apr 44), CT 23, Dr 2, KCRC.

[41] (1) History of the India-China Ferry under the Tenth Air Force. USAF Hist Div. (2) Craven and Cate, eds., *The Army Air Forces,* I, pp. 497–502. (3) See Ch. III, p. 93, above.

assault; second priority to the Air Ferry Command of the AAF, which was charged with flying men and supplies to the different war fronts; and third priority, to Stilwell's China–Burma–India (CBI) command. The value of the Ferry Command's second priority may be judged by the number of aircraft on its roster in April 1942 — 57. Stilwell's command was allotted 75 aircraft, of which 34 were en route. A week later at the next CCS meeting it was announced that CBI would be cut to 57 aircraft, including those of China National Aviation Corporation. For the present no more were available.[42]

The most common Washington estimate was the erroneous one that seventy-five aircraft could fly 5,000 tons a month to China, which would provide 3,500 tons of lend-lease matériel and 1,500 tons of supplies for a U.S. air force in China. The Chinese applied the heaviest diplomatic pressure to have this tonnage reached; the President in turn interested himself directly in the Ferry Command's operations and equipment. He told General Arnold on 5 May:

> I gather that the air ferry route to China is seriously endangered [by the loss of Burma]. The only way we can get certain supplies into China is by air. I wish you and Mr. Lovett would confer immediately with Dr. Soong and General Shen on alternative air routes. I want you to explore every possibility, both as to airplanes and routes. It is essential that our route be kept open, no matter how difficult.[43]

With the Chinese and the President both demanding action, Arnold suggested that fifty B–24's be converted to transports and based on Allahabad in India, far from the vulnerable airfield in Assam from which aircraft were then flying to China. OPD argued that converting fifty B–24's would be a heavy drain on BOLERO. OPD thought the airline to China merely a token operation, not worth a heavy commitment. In the light of the OPD comments Arnold then recommended, and the President agreed, that the airline should be kept open as long as possible with commercial types only. Stilwell did not participate in this correspondence, but the Chinese blamed him for the War Department's stand.[44]

Unable to get the B–24's, the Chinese then wanted four-motored transports. The Generalissimo personally appealed to Roosevelt. When consulted by Hopkins, the Army replied that only twenty-seven C–54's would be produced in 1942 and that they could not be supported in India.[45]

[42](1) CCS 17th Mtg, 28 Apr 42, par. 1. (2) CCS 18th Mtg, 5 May 42, par. 1.

[43](1) Ltr with Incl, McCloy to Hopkins, 4 May 42, Bk V, Hopkins Papers. (2) Ltr, President to Arnold, 5 May 42. Bk V, Hopkins Papers. (3) Memo, Col Deane for Marshall, 27 Jul 42. WDCSA, Notes on War Council, A48–139. (4) Rad, Stilwell to Marshall, 28 Sep 42. Item 41, Bk 1, JWS Personal File, A48–102, Record Group 800, HRS DRB AGO. (See Bibliographical Note.)

[44](1) Ltr, Arnold to DCofS, 12 May 42, sub: India-China Ferry Route; Memo, Eisenhower, ACofS, for DCofS, 14 May 42; Notes for Record on Memo, McNarney for Arnold, 18 May 42. WDCSA (China), A45–466. (2) The Stilwell Papers, p. 120. (3) Rpt, Currie to Roosevelt, 24 Aug. 42, sub: Rpt on Visit to China. OPD 336 China (24 Aug 42), A47–30.

[45](1) Telg, Chiang to Roosevelt, 1 Jun 42; Ltr, Malony to Hopkins, 13 Jun 42. Bk V, Hopkins Papers.

Inability to support more transports in India was the other half of the Army's problems in expanding air tonnage into China, the first being the world-wide shortage of transports and crews. Since 4 May the War Department and the White House had been aware of the logistical problem in India. The only Assam field for the air ferry was Dinjan. Shared by the transports, AAF and RAF fighters, and transient craft, it was saturated. Worse yet, Dinjan had no warning net, and lack of spare parts grounded ten of the thirty-five transports available in July. A further obstacle to flying lend-lease tonnage into China was the priority of Chennault's air force on whatever was flown into China. Therefore, Stilwell warned that for months to come not more than 5 or 10 percent of the monthly allotments of lend-lease material the War Department was discussing with the Chinese would be airlifted. It was a grave error, he wrote, to build Chinese hopes with promises that could not be fulfilled.[46]

Even War Department efforts to bring the Chinese to a more realistic appraisal of the airline's problems were useless, for the Chinese answer to objections and arguments was always simply: "More aircraft!" They told the President and Hopkins that four-motored aircraft were much more airworthy than twin-engined, able to fly when the twin-engined could not, and therefore the answer to the problem of monsoon weather.

There was a price attached to assignment of transport aircraft to the CBI, for they were in great demand in other theaters, a factor sometimes overlooked in the heat of controversy. If the choices before the War Department had been only two, either to place transports and crews on the Hump or to use them on domestic airlines, then there could have been no further argument. But this was not the case. The CCS, the President, and the Prime Minister were now on record that the main effort should be made in Europe. Airborne operations could, and did, play a great role in the projected cross-Channel assault. Every transport sent to the CBI area was a diversion from the main effort, and the War Department so regarded the matter all during the war.

In June 1942 Stilwell and Arnold joined to ask that 75 transports be placed *in service* (as against the 100 *projected*) on the airline to China, or Hump, as it was coming to be called from the massive hump of mountains crossed by the transports on their way to China. Stilwell wanted the 75 transports by August 1942, but OPD again pointed out the diversion from BOLERO, and so the target date was deferred to March 1943.[47]

[46](1) History cited n. 41(1). (2) Ltr, McCloy to Hopkins, 4 May 42. Bk V, Hopkins Papers. (3) CM–IN 6354, Chungking to AGWAR, 18 Jun 42. (4) CM–IN 6551, Karachi to AGWAR, 19 Jun 42. (5) CM–IN 2686, Naiden to Marshall, 7 Jul 42.

[47](1) Ltr, Soong to Hopkins, 15 Jun 42; Ltr, Hopkins to Arnold, 15 Jun 42; Ltr, Roosevelt to Arnold, 15 Jun 42; Memo, Arnold for Hopkins, 18 Jun 42. Bk V, Hopkins Papers. (2) Memo, Handy for Marshall, 14 Aug 42, sub: Three Minimum Reqmts for China Theater Submitted by Generalissimo. WDCSA (China), A45–466. (3) Stimson and Bundy, *On Active Service*, p. 538. (4) Rad, Stilwell to Marshall, 28 Sep 42. Item 41, Bk 1, JWS Personal File. (5) JCS 30th Mtg, 25 Aug 42, par. 7.

SNOW-CAPPED MOUNTAIN PEAKS OF THE HIMALAYAS *on the airline to China. Photograph, taken in 1944, shows a C–46 transport plane flying over the Hump.*

As a result of these difficulties, plus some administrative ineptitude, the Ferry Command flew 80 tons to China in May, 106 in June, and 73 in July. Chinese dissatisfaction was unconcealed. Stilwell was very critical, writing:

1. Tents, tent-pins, GI cans, and field ranges coming in to Kunming via transport plane.
2. No attention to capacity. CNAC [China National Aviation Corporation] 4,700 lbs, USA, 3,500 lbs.
3. Many incomplete loads in and out. Crew chiefs riding. Why not group them for maintenance on the ground?
4. Pilfering going on along the line.
5. CNAC flying regularly when weather keeps us [AAF] grounded. . . .[48]

Soong's Warning

The hardening U.S. attitude on lend-lease, coming as it did during the disastrous Burma campaign and at the start of the Japanese Chekiang drive, disturbed the Chinese. As a remedy the Chinese asked that Hopkins, who was head of the Munitions Assignments Board and a good friend of China, fly to Chungking to review Sino-American relations. Hopkins' health and his great responsibilities would not permit him to go, and the President decided to send Dr. Currie instead. Currie began his preparations for the long trip.[49]

On 20 June Stilwell reported to the War Department that the air ferry line could not bring a tenth of what the Chinese expected to China. He was not complacent about it, for when a garbled radio two days before had distorted his position and said he wanted only "10" transports on the Hump, he hastened to clarify it by telling General Arnold that he understood 100 transports were to be available for ferry service, that this number would be "sufficient under present conditions." [50]

The Munitions Assignments Committee (Ground) knew that there were 45,000 tons of Chinese lend-lease stockpiled in India and that the May and June shipments would add another 7,000 tons. In the light of this, and knowing that only a few hundred tons would be flown to China in the next few months, the committee contemplated releasing but 400 tons as the July assignment. On 22 June General Aurand, Chairman of the Munitions Assignments Committee (Ground), recommended that no assignment to China be made for July. The OPD member of the committee, Brig. Gen. Thomas T. Handy, objected on the ground that Stilwell's position in getting the Generalissimo to place Chinese

---

[48](1) SNF–12. (2) History cited n. 41(1). (3) MS, History of the India Burma Theater, 24 Jun 45–31 May 46, Chart facing p. 300. Gen Ref Br, OCMH.

[49] Rad, Chiang to Roosevelt, 27 May 42, including Note from Soong to Hopkins, 1 Jun 42; Memo, Currie for Hopkins, 1 Jun 42, including Msg from Mme. Chiang to Currie, 31 May 42. Bk V, Hopkins Papers.

[50](1) Memo, Wheeler for Sibert, 4 Jun 42, sub: Emergency Air Transport Program for China; 1st Ind, Naiden to Stilwell, 7 Jun 42. Item 159, Corresp Folder (Jul 42–Nov 43), CT 23, Dr 2, KCRC. Naiden said delivery of 150 tons a day for the next six months was an impossibility. (2) Rad AD 122, Stilwell to Arnold, 18 Jun 42. SNF–12. (3) CM–IN 6354, Stilwell to Marshall, 20 Jun 42.

troops in India would be compromised by Aurand's recommendation. The case was referred to the Munitions Assignments Board and the CCS. Meanwhile, Soong somehow managed to keep informed of the U.S. attitude and action on China's July assignment.[51]

Soong's understanding of what Stilwell was telling his American superiors is given in a radio from him to Stilwell on 17 June 1942:

> Following message for General Stilwell through Madame Chiang Kai-shek from Minister T. V. Soong:
> Have been following with admiration your valiant exertion. Trust you are recovering rapidly from arduous trip. We have been much encouraged by your advocating of rearmament plan for thirty divisions and wish to thank you. I have put up to the President most effectively [sic] immediate aids to China are:
> 1. American air force unit operating in China.
> 2. Large scale air transport from India to China.
> In this connection I wish to observe that American production of combat and transport airplanes has amazingly increased since your departure for China. U.S. War Department is acting on our request but in the absence of supporting telegram from you rather slowly. You must realize miraculous hold you have in this country from President, Secretary, and Chief of Staff downward and that any request from you will be supported even including the despatch of American division to India for the recovery of Burma. Kindest regards.[52]

On learning of the Munitions Assignments Committee's attitude toward the July assignment, Soong sent scathing memorandums to Hopkins and McCloy, in which he charged that Stilwell inspired the committee's viewpoint.[53] Ignoring the Indian stockpile, Soong stated that China wanted 3,500 tons a month assigned to her or nothing at all, an implied threat to abolish the China Theater. On 20 June Soong pleaded his case in a note to the President and Prime Minister, then meeting in Washington. Reminding them through Hopkins of past commitments to China, Soong delivered his *démarche,* the prediction that inter-Allied co-operation in the form of China Theater would cease if the United States abrogated the 3,500-ton emergency air transport program.[54]

Telephone calls, reassuring letters, and friendly conversation from American officials during the next few days were only mild sedatives for the angered Soong, who for weeks had been reporting every adverse development to his

---

[51] (1) Ltr, Soong to McCloy, 18 Jun 42. ASW 400.336 (China). (2) Min, entry 515, MAC(G) 35th Mtg, 22 Jun 42. (3) Min, MAB 21st Mtg, 24 Jun 42.

[52] Rad, Soong to Mme. Chiang for Stilwell, 17 Jun 42. SNF–12.

[53] (1) Ltr cited n. 29(2). (2) Ltr, Soong to McCloy, 18 Jun 42. ASW 400.336 (China). (3) Ltr, Soong to Hopkins, 20 Jun 42. Bk V, Hopkins Papers.

[54] Ltr, with Memo, Soong to Hopkins, 20 Jun 42; Ltr, Soong to Hopkins, 23 Jun 42; Ltr, Currie to Hopkins, 23 Jun 42, with atchd Msg from J. Franklin Ray, Jr., Office of Lend-Lease Administration, 21 Jun 42, on status of Chinese lend-lease stockpile in India; Note, Hopkins to Currie, 24 Jun 42, in which Hopkins said that he was taking immediate steps to halt the Munitions Assignments Committee (Ground) recommendation to stop the July assignment; Memo, Hopkins for Burns, 24 Jun 42; Memo, Burns for Hopkins, 25 Jun 42, sub: Mun to China; Memo, Soong for Hopkins, 25 Jun 42. Bk V, Hopkins Papers.

government.[55] Then came the climax. As early as 17 June American observers in Cairo had warned that the Allied position in the Middle East was deteriorating, that reinforcements were needed if Egypt and the Suez Canal were to be held. There was especial need of heavy bombers to cut the Axis supply route from Italy to Africa. Heeding these warnings, Marshall asked Stilwell to survey the B-17 position in India. On 23 June came the order sending Brereton, the B-17's, and the transports to Egypt. Brereton's removal was called a temporary diversion after which the aircraft would return to Stilwell's command. Simultaneously, Stilwell was told that a flight of A-29's en route to China would be held up at Khartoum, Egypt.[56]

The decision to move Brereton and to hold the A-29's was made at a White House conference, and the decision's possible consequences had been considered. Afterward, it was conceded in OPD that the Chinese, both in Washington and in Chungking, had not been approached tactfully, nor had Stilwell been brought into the situation in a manner appropriate to his delicate and complex position. Though Marshall said that sending Brereton to Egypt caused difficulty with the Generalissimo, in retrospect it appears as merely the last of a long series of irritants and disappointments.[57]

The Generalissimo's Anger

Stilwell now had the painful duty of presenting the bad news of Brereton's transfer and the A-29 situation to the Generalissimo. The Chinese minutes record:

The Generalissimo saw General Stilwell at 11 a.m. on June 26th, 1942. Present were Madame Chiang, General Grober [*sic,* Gruber] and General Bissel [*sic*]. Following is the gist of the conversation:
STILWELL: I greatly regret that I have to report some bad news, though it is of temporary nature. General Brereton has been ordered by Washington to proceed to Egypt immediately with the heavy bombers from India. He would be given all transport planes which he needs for the transportation of the personnel and outfit for the bombers. This would reduce the tonnage of material sent from India to China.
GISSIMO: What is the number of heavy bombers sent from India to Egypt, and what is the number of transport planes required for carrying the personnel and outfit?

[55](1) Memo, Brig Gen St. Clair Streett for Gen Handy, 29 Jun 42, sub: Restrictions on Movement of Dawson Mission [A-29]. OPD 452.1 (Middle East) Sec 2, A47-30. (2) The Generalissimo mentioned Soong's reports to Stilwell on 26 June 1942. Min, Conf, Stilwell and Generalissimo, 26 Jun 42. Stilwell Documents, Hoover Library. (3) Burns called Soong to reassure him that the Munitions Assignments Committee (Ground) decision was being altered. Memo, Burns for Hopkins, 25 Jun 42. Bk V, Hopkins Papers. (4) In a telephone conversation with Brig. Gen. Walter B. Smith, General Handy explained that it had been difficult to contact Soong and members of the Chinese Embassy staff in Washington. Tp Conv record, Handy with Smith, 29 Jun 42. Bk 6, OPD Exec 8.
[56](1) CM-IN's cited n. 18. (2) CM-IN 6689, AQUILA to AGWAR, 20 Jun 42. (3) CM-OUT 5699, OPD to Stilwell, 24 Jun 42. (4) CM-IN 7816, Stilwell to AGWAR, 24 Jun 42. (5) CM-OUT 6075, AGWAR to Stilwell, 24 Jun 42.
[57](1) Sherwood, *Roosevelt and Hopkins,* pp. 598–99. (2) Memo cited n. 55(1). (3) Tp Conv record cited n. 55(4). (4) *The Brereton Diaries,* 9 Aug 42, p. 145.

STILWELL: I have received no information concerning the number of heavy bombers that are being sent to Egypt. The number of transport planes to be required will depend upon the number of heavy bombers to be sent. I have still another bad news to report. A squadron of light bombers, A–29, which were on their way from America to China, have been diverted at Kaharitum [*sic*, Khartoum], south of Cairo, for use in Egypt. I believe that the situation in the Near East must be very critical.

GISSIMO: How many of the A–29 light bombers have been so diverted?

STILWELL: I do not know. However I do know that the number of A–29 bombers being sent by America to China is 33. I am unable to tell how many of them have been diverted for use in Egypt. The telegram from Washington did not mention whether there would be replacements for them or whether those A–29 bombers which would arrive in Egypt later would continue their journey to China. I do not like this news. The third matter which I wish to report concerns a telegram received from New Dehli [*sic*] in which General Wavell inquired whether you would approve of Ramga [*sic*, Ramgarh] as the site for the quartering of Chinese troops in India, and if you should approve of this site, he would assign it to the Chinese troops. In my opinion Ramga is the best place to quarter the Chinese troops. The climate there is good.

GENERALISSIMO: Exactly what is the status of the 10th U.S. Air Force in India from which heavy bombers are being detached for use in Egypt.

STILWELL: The 10th U.S. Air Force has been assigned for use in the China Theater of War and Burma and placed under my command.

GENERALISSIMO: Since you are my chief of staff, my approval should be secured of the disposition of the 10th U.S. Air Force.

STILWELL: You are right. I have made repeated efforts to bring the 10th U.S. Air Force to China as early as possible. [The American minutes do not record Stilwell's agreeing or even responding to the Generalissimo's observation.]

GENERALISSIMO: President Roosevelt in his telegram to me stated that he had ordered the transfer of the 10th U.S. Air Force from India to China for use. His order cannot be lightly changed. If it were contended that the situation in Egypt is grave, I must point out that the Chinese situation in Chekiang and Kiangsi is no less critical.

MADAME: Every time when the British suffered a defeat, they took away our war equipment or that which had been promised to us. Such being the case there is no need for China to continue the war.

STILWELL: I myself have objected to this diversion of war material from China. At one time, when Washington intended to assign the 10th U.S. Air Force to General Wavell for control, I raised strong objection and made it clear that if I could not get back the air force for use in China I prefer to be relieved of my duties in this country. What has now happened is a great surprise to you as well as to me [*sic*].

MADAME: What are we going to do about this? Can we stop the movement of heavy bombers to Egypt?

STILWELL: The bombers are already on their way to Egypt and I do not think their movement can now be stopped. The news about the sending of heavy bombers to Egypt is bad enough, but what is even worse in the diversion of A–29 light bombers from China. Heavy bombers are not suitable for the Libya campaign. All the pursuit planes and medium bombers of the 10th U.S. Air Force however remain in India.

GENERALISSIMO: I am unhappy about this development. The China Theater of War is lightly regarded. Naturally I wish to know whether America and Britain consider it as one of the Allied Theaters.

MADAME: You should send some important member of your mission to Washington and place the matter before the high authorities there.

STILWELL: I am sending General Grobel [*sic*] to Washington on such a mission.

GENERALISSIMO: All I wish to know is whether they don't care about the China Theater of War. I would like you to get a clear-cut answer on this point. In the past China has done her very best in upholding the Allied cause, and has fulfilled her obligations faithfully. For five years she has fought not only for herself but also for the Allies. If America and Britain felt the need of maintaining her strength for resistance, they should not continuously pay scant attention to her. The way China is now being treated shows that she is out of the picture altogether.

STILWELL: This is not so. We attach much importance to the China Theater of War. What has been done is out of ignorance on the part of American officers in Washington concerning the situation in China.

GENERALISSIMO: Since President Roosevelt in his telegram promised to supply China with planes and war materials she needs, what is being done amounts to disobedience of his orders. I do not suppose that President would approve of all this change. Less than ten per cent of what he had agreed to give to China has been supplied. I do not entertain any doubt that the President is sincere. What has been done is perhaps without his consent or knowledge. As chief of staff to me, you are responsible for seeing to it that the promised material is forthcoming.

STILWELL: I have tried my very best in getting the people in Washington to supply China with more planes, ground troops, more war material, and even with one American division. All that Washington replied is that there is a great lack of shipping space for sending them to China.

GENERALISSIMO: Telegrams which I have received from Dr. T. V. Soong stated that the War Department told him that they are waiting for your recommendations which have not yet been sent by you.

STILWELL: It is absurd. This is not the case. The War Department has a list of priorities to supply.

MADAME: Another telegram from Dr. Soong states that replying to the War Department's inquiry whether you needed more transport planes, you said that you do not need any more.

STILWELL: In regard to this, I remembered having wired that for the present we can make use of 100 transport planes although as a matter of fact the fields here in China can accommodate only 50 planes.

GENERALISSIMO: In one of his telegrams to me President Roosevelt mentioned that he had already handed over 425 or 440 planes (I cannot remember the exact figure), but I do not know where they are.

STILWELL: These planes must be between America and India.

MADAME: Have any of them been diverted?

BISSELL: I understand we have 20 B–17, or Flying Fortresses, in India, which either wholly or partially are being sent to Egypt.

The Chinese minutes end here; the American version of the conference closes on a dramatic note supplied by Madame Chiang Kai-shek:

The Generalissimo must make a speech at the end of the fifth year [of the Chinese war] on 7 July. He must tell the Chinese people the truth at that time. The pro-Japanese element is very active. The Generalissimo wants a yes or no answer to whether the Allies consider this theater necessary and will support it.[58]

[58](1) Min (Chinese version), Conf, Stilwell and Generalissimo, 1100, 26 Jun 42. Stilwell Documents, Hoover Library. (2) Memo of Conf at 1100, 26 Jun 42, Bissell, recorder, for Stilwell and Mme. Chiang. Memoranda for Mme. CKS Folder (May–Sep 42), CT 23, Dr 2, KCRC. (3) The Generalissimo's frequent references to telegrams from the President cannot be documented from War Department files. These assurances of support possibly could have been transmitted to Chungking via Navy or State Department channels and not communicated to Stilwell. It is more probable that the Generalissimo is referring to radios received from Soong's transmitter in Wash-

The contrast between Soong's 17 June radio, with its acknowledgment of Stilwell's recommending arms for the Thirty Divisions, and the Generalissimo's statement that Soong was charging Stilwell had sent no recommendations and desired no more transports for the Hump, implanted in Stilwell an immediate distrust of the Chinese Foreign Minister that he never quite lost.[59]

Stilwell quickly advised Marshall of this virtual ultimatum from the Chinese.[60] Appraising the situation to himself, Stilwell concluded that the crisis was simply a larger version of the tense period following the diversion of the Tenth Air Force to Wavell's support in April. Stilwell believed that because of the President's reaction to the Generalissimo's message the Chinese had concluded that "violent protests" would give them the "upper hand" where the allocation of U.S. resources was concerned.[61]

Stilwell's radio to Marshall stirred official Washington, and Currie's trip to China was expedited.[62] When the President's reply was sent on 27 June, it was, as Stilwell noted, "quiet and dignified and promised nothing." [63]

Stilwell received an appointment with the Generalissimo and met with him and Madame Chiang on 29 June. The President's message was delivered, and Stilwell received from the Generalissimo the "three minimum requirements essential for the maintenance of the China Theater of War." They were:

1. Three American divisions should arrive in India between August and September to co-operate with the Chinese Forces in restoring the line of communication through Burma.
2. Beginning from August the Air Force in the China Theater of War should consist of 500 planes continuously fighting at the front. This strength must be maintained without interruption by necessary replacements.
3. Beginning from August, the monthly aerial transportation should be 5,000 tons.[64]

In the conference the Chiangs made it abundantly clear that the 28 June note was an ultimatum. Indeed, Madame Chiang made delivery of the A–29's the test of whether the Allies wanted China Theater.

These were what came to be called, simply, the Three Demands. The second and third were already familiar, and Stilwell had previously urged that

ington, allegedly quoting the President. Thus, on 1 July 1942 Madame Chiang stated that "she had received, under date of June 18th, from Soong, a statement that the President had made available for the Generalissimo the 10th Air Force for employment in China." Memo of Mtg, Stilwell and Mme. Chiang Kai-shek, 1 Jul 42. Memoranda for Mme. CKS Folder (May–Sep 42), CT 23, Dr 2, KCRC. No communication to that effect was ever received by Stilwell from higher authority. Soong's statement is completely inconsistent with the White House decision to send the Tenth's B–17's to Egypt.

[59] *The Stilwell Papers*, pp. 120, 123, 126, 130–31.

[60] (1) CM–IN 8586, Stilwell to Marshall, 26 Jun 42. (2) CM–IN 8933, Stilwell to Marshall, 27 Jun 42.

[61] (1) The diversion of the Tenth Air Force is in Chapter IV, above. (2) History of Blackmail, Stilwell B&W. Probably written on 22 July 1942, judging by dates on succeeding entries.

[62] (1) Memo, Moore for Marshall, 27 Jun 42. WDCSA (China), A45–266. (2) Memo, Deane for Marshall, 28 Jun 42. Statement, Marshall before War Council, 6 Jul 42. WDCSA, Notes of War Council, A48–139.

[63] (1) CM–OUT 7014, Roosevelt to Chiang, 27 Jun 42. Stilwell delivered this message in person on 29 June 1942. (2) Quotation from *The Stilwell Papers*, p. 121.

[64] Ltr, Generalissimo to Stilwell, 28 Jun 42. SNF–12.

the War Department provide them, plus one or more American divisions, though with a great deal more thought to their logistic implications. Consistent with his previous practice, the Generalissimo had not mentioned what his matching contributions to China Theater would be. Though Stilwell could not concur in the time limits the Generalissimo had set, he was convinced the War Department should adopt the Three Demands as a goal to be met when the air ferry was fully operational. The Three Demands went to Washington, which began to weigh them and prepare an answer.[65]

Stilwell's Staff and Command Roles Upheld

Having tried to test the U.S. attitude toward China with the Three Demands, the Chinese moved on to test Stilwell's authority. They asked Stilwell if two lend-lease transports operating for China National Aviation Corporation could be reassigned to the Generalissimo.[66] "Feeler," wrote Stilwell, "I can't duck that one." [67] He met it by answering that while the Generalissimo might have the transports as lend-lease essential for the prosecution of the war, he could not obtain U.S. munitions by ordering Stilwell as his chief of staff to procure them.[68] Then, to avoid future misunderstandings and attempts at the extension of the Generalissimo's powers, such as the Chinese leader's belief that he controlled the Tenth Air Force, Stilwell spelled out his several roles:

(1) I am the United States Government representative on any war council held in China. . . . I present and maintain the policy of the United States as it is communicated to me. . . .[69]

(2) I am in command of U.S. Forces in CBI and therefore have the responsibility beyond the limits of China Theater. Since Burma and India are not in the China war theater, I have to co-operate with the British in those areas. In China . . . the Generalissimo is Supreme and commands all forces that operate there.[70]

(3) I am charged with the supervision and control of lend-lease material and am to decide the place and time that title passes. After title passes, the Generalissimo controls the disposition of material. I was given to understand that lend-lease equipment would be employed in the effective prosecution of the war and in such matters I act as the representative of the President who can under law recall lend-lease materials at any time prior to delivery.[71]

---

[65](1) CM–IN 0560, Stilwell to Marshall, 1 Jul 42. (2) CM–IN 2385, Stilwell to Marshall, 3 Jul 42.

[66](1) *The Stilwell Papers,* p. 121. (2) "The Madame (Chiang) also raised the question of the Generalissimo's authority to divert CNAC lend-lease planes to the Chinese Air Force. General Stilwell was requested to render an opinion on the Generalissimo's authority." Memo of Mtg, Stilwell with Mme. Chiang, 1 Jul 42. Stilwell Documents, Hoover Library.

[67] Stilwell B&W, 1 Jul 42.

[68] Ltr, Hearn to authors, 12 Feb 50. HIS 330.14 CBI 1950. Hearn urged Stilwell and Bissell to adopt this answer to the Generalissimo's challenge.

[69] See Soong-Stimson accord, 23–30 January 1942, Chapter II, above.

[70] See 2 February 1942 presidential directive, and ARCADIA paper, ABC 4/9, Chapter II, above.

[71] See Soong-Stimson accord, 23–30 January 1942, MAB Directive, 14 May 1942, and McCloy letter to Soong, June 1942, Chapters II and V, above.

(4) I am Chief of Staff of the Generalissimo's Joint Staff which functions when forces of the Allies carry on operations in China war theater in connection with the Chinese Army. As Chief of Staff my duties are concerned with planning, organization, training, and operation in the field and do *not* extend to procurement of materials. I prepare plans as directed by the Generalissimo and when they are approved by him transmit them to various contingents for execution.[72]

(5) And intrinsically I have my basic status as an officer of the United States Army sworn to uphold the interests of the United States.

(6) Within the above limitations my only objective is the effective prosecution of the war. . . .[73]

Pondering the techniques of negotiation he met, Stilwell wrote:

Next thing will be: "Can the G-mo order transports off the freight line?" We'll have to stop him there, and claim it's an SOS function, so Wheeler, who has the responsibility for delivery, must also have undivided authority. Same old story—edge in on one thing at a time, and every time you get it ask for the next one. Never by any chance say "thank you." For instance, we charter the CNAC at big prices to get [personnel for two squadrons of] the 10th AF moved. They listen without a word and pass to something else.[74]

The Generalissimo's strong reaction to Stilwell's note of explanation of his staff and command roles suggested he was testing not only Stilwell's position but the whole fabric of U.S. lend-lease policy. He at once protested to the President about the two transports, complaining that Stilwell had forced the Supreme Commander of the China Theater to "beg" for lend-lease supplies already delivered to China. He claimed, "Clearly . . . this could not have been the original intention of the U.S. Government." If it was, the Generalissimo asked that Stilwell's dual responsibility to the American and Chinese Governments be ended; "otherwise both military and political relations will be adversely affected. . . ."[75]

Obviously, the Generalissimo's anger and bitterness over the events of the past four months were now focused on Stilwell, who could only comment that he was the executor of U.S. policy toward China, not its author. From this time forward it was clear that Stilwell's recall would please the Generalissimo. For his part, Stilwell wrote presciently that the Generalissimo risked two things by persisting in his complaints and importunities: "(1) The definite loss of all supplies he was counting on from the U.S. and the big money that would be withdrawn, and (2) the loss of the sympathy of the American people, who are with him while he fights, but who won't back a quitter."[76]

The official position Stilwell took was that "it's [the Three Demands] still an ultimatum from the Generalissimo to the President, and so beyond my

[72] See Soong-Stimson accord, 23–30 January 1942, Chapter II, above.
[73] (1) Memo, Stilwell for Generalissimo, 2 Jul 42. Item 19, OPD Exec 10. (2) *The Stilwell Papers*, p. 121.
[74] Stilwell B&W, 1 Jul 42.
[75] Soong delivered the Generalissimo's message to President Roosevelt on 5 July 1942. Memo, Chiang for Roosevelt, 5 Jul 42. Item 19, OPD Exec 10.
[76] (1) Quotation from *The Stilwell Papers*, pp. 125–26. (2) CM–IN 7340, Stilwell to Marshall, 21 Jul 42. (3) CM–IN 9072, Stilwell to Marshall, 24 Jul 42.

province"— an obvious attempt to preserve his future usefulness by relegating discussions of Sino-American relations to those who controlled them, the President and the Generalissimo.[77] Since Stilwell took that stand, there was every reason why he should emphasize his position outside the conflict of policy by acting as the Generalissimo's chief of staff. So he continued, in early July, to send memorandums to the Generalissimo.

Having received the Generalissimo's challenge to Stilwell's lend-lease authority, the President asked Marshall to draft a reply. Approved by the President, Marshall's answer to the Generalissimo was given to Soong on 14 July. The sum of it was that even though Stilwell might be recalled, any successor would have exactly the same powers over lend-lease arms to which the Generalissimo objected in Stilwell and the same primary responsibility to the United States. Soong did not transmit this vital message in full but gave the Generalissimo his own expurgated version, plus the gist of a conversation with the President. Marshall sent Stilwell an information copy of the President's message to the Generalissimo, which Stilwell delivered to the Chinese leader. The correct text of the President's reply was displeasing to the Generalissimo, who retorted that if the President intended to send such a message, China Theater would go. Immediately, Soong was called to the White House and told that Stilwell's dual roles would be unaltered.[78]

The memorandums Stilwell sent to the Generalissimo in early July illustrate his attempt to function as the chief of staff of China Theater, despite the Three Demands crisis. In the first, he surveyed the military situation in China, estimated Japanese capabilities in every major sector, and concluded that Kunming was the logical target of the next Japanese effort and so should be more heavily protected by Chinese reinforcements.[79] Five days later he warned that an attack on Kunming airport by Japanese paratroops could disrupt the air transport line and Chennault's air operations. He asked that a Chinese regiment be stationed in Kunming to guard against such a thrust.

He sent the Generalissimo comments on the belief among Chinese officers that "If China had enough planes and tanks and guns, it would be a simple matter to defeat the Japanese." First, Stilwell gave his views on the potentialities of air power:

[77] *The Stilwell Papers,* p. 121.
[78] (1) Memo, Hopkins for Marshall, 9 Jul 42. Item 19, OPD Exec 10. (2) Memos, Deane for Marshall, 13, 19 Jul 42. WDCSA, Notes of War Council, A48–139. (3) CM–OUT 4444, OPD to Stilwell, 16 Jul 42. (4) CM–OUT 6863, Marshall to Stilwell, 24 Jul 42. (5) Memo, McCloy for McNarney, 27 Jul 42. Item 19, OPD Exec 10. (6) CM–OUT 8454, Marshall to Stilwell, 29 Jul 42. (7) This incident did not mark an end to the Chinese practice of altering the President's messages to the Generalissimo to make them read more agreeably to their recipient. It was to continue until the President ordered in May 1944 that notes to the Generalissimo be delivered personally by the senior U.S. officer in Chungking. Memo, Roosevelt for Marshall, 3 May 44. Folder 1, Generalissimo Chiang Kai-shek (GMO CKS), Item 58, OPD Exec 10.
[79] Memo, Stilwell for Generalissimo, 2 Jul 42, sub: Prelim Estimate of *Status Quo* in China. Stilwell Documents, Hoover Library.

. . . In every case [Stilwell listed China, Britain, Germany, Malta], the damage has been severe, but no decision has been gained. This is because of the limitations of the airplane; it can do a great deal of damage, but it is still only an auxiliary of the ground forces, indispensable if a decision is to be reached, but incapable of reaching that decision by itself. The great limitation is that although it can neutralize an area, or deny it to the enemy for a time, it cannot hold ground. Only the troops on the ground can do that, and only by so doing can a decision be reached.

Then, after discussing the capabilities of artillery and armor, Stilwell gave his analysis of German successes, 1939–42:

All the foreign powers have come to the conclusion that the German successes so far are due mainly to three very fundamental things. These are:
  1. Excellent physical training. Basic stamina.
  2. The ability to use their weapons intelligently and efficiently under any circumstances.
  3. Excellent tactical instruction in the small units.
These three things are placed first, ahead of special provision in the way of big guns, tanks, dive bombers, flame-throwers, and all the mechanical contrivances that the Germans have produced. They are even put ahead of the excellent German organization, system of command, the wide initiative allowed subordinates, and mere numbers. It is an illuminating commentary on the tremendous value of a solid foundation, on which an immense organization can be built and operated successfully.

What did all this mean to China? Stilwell asked.

China has in the field some 300 divisions. They cannot possibly be supported in the air by the proportion of planes considered necessary in Europe. Instead of 10,000 planes, we should be glad to have 500 available for combat. Neither is it possible to deliver or maintain the mass of tanks that a European army would consider necessary. Neither is the artillery available in types or numbers that would be considered necessary for such a force. But there does exist a large reservoir of man power, armed fairly well with rifles, machine guns, and mortars. If the number of divisions could be reduced by 50 percent, the weapons available would go far toward fully equipping them, and the undesirable and physically unsuitable soldiers would be weeded out. By combining the available artillery, a large number of these divisions could be given effective fire support, and in action, the infantry of a division could be relieved, leaving its artillery in to support the new one. Artillery losses being small in proportion to infantry casualties, this doubling of artillery duty has been frequently practiced.

This reduction of the total number of divisions, and amalgamation into complete units, with a normal complement of rifles, machine guns, and mortars, plus the improved artillery support contemplated would in my opinion greatly increase the combat strength of the Army. Much of the reorganization could be accomplished within the war zones where the troops are stationed, without too much displacement of units. It could be done progressively and quietly. A course of field training for small units could be carried out at the same time, and when completed the Generalissimo would have a well-equipped, mobile force in every war zone, ready to move at short notice, easily handled, and of far greater combat strength than before.

I realize and appreciate the objections that are raised when changes in command are advocated. The Generalissimo alone can decide whether changes are worth while, and since I have already brought up the subject, I will not repeat it here, except to reiterate that an efficient unit deserves to have an efficient and capable commander.

With no chance to train a relatively large force in India, where we have access to stocks of weapons and munitions, and with supplies in China reduced to the point where they must be conserved, the above procedure is strongly recommended as the most workable plan by which the combat efficiency of the Chinese Army can be raised to the point where it can meet successfully any crisis that may confront it.[80]

A memorandum from Stilwell on the joint staff for the China Theater of war told the Generalissimo that the proposal passed between the War Ministry and Stilwell "seems to be acceptable in general outline. . . . There is close enough agreement on the general plan to proceed with it." [81] The only major point not clarified by the plan was the circumstances under which it would come into operation. On this, however, Stilwell believed himself in agreement with the Generalissimo, so he suggested the Generalissimo proceed to designate the Chinese officers to serve on the staff.

To these memorandums, the Chinese made no answer.[82]

Moving Toward a Compromise

While waiting for Washington's reply to the Three Demands, Stilwell did what he could in China to lay the groundwork for a solution. He was convinced that the Generalissimo's hints of a separate peace were simply diplomatic maneuverings, a belief shared by Ambassador Gauss.[83]

On the sensitive question of lend-lease, Stilwell had, as he told the Generalissimo, sent General Gruber back to the United States in haste. Gruber was ordered to plead for the restoration of the 3,500-ton emergency air transport program, with the argument that the saving to American arms supplies resulting from cutting this program was insignificant compared to the resulting damage to Sino-American relations. Before Gruber reached Washington, Anglo-American differences on the July assignment of 3,500 tons to China had been resolved. The CCS continued the program only through July. So small a share of lend-lease was not in line with Stilwell's attitude as reflected in this diary entry: ". . . How can China do it alone? We are reduced to holding Yunnan and playing it out with the Tenth Air Force, and a trickle of 3,500 tons a month kept up only by my screaming. I can have this much as long as it strengthens my hand, but otherwise they'll cut even this dribble off." [84]

Working to find a solution of the Three Demands on which he, the Generalissimo, and the CCS might agree, Stilwell surveyed the future of China Theater. Because of the shipping situation, he did not expect U.S. infantry in CBI before summer 1943. If the War Department and the CCS intended China Theater ultimately to be developed, then Stilwell and his staff could continue

---

[80] Memo, Stilwell for Generalissimo, 7 Jul 42. Stilwell Documents, Hoover Library.
[81] A second Memo, Stilwell for Generalissimo, 7 Jul 42. Same file.
[82] See Illustration, p. 155.
[83] *The Stilwell Papers,* p. 126.
[84] (1) CCS 90, 90/1, 2, 10 Jul 42, sub: Jul Asgmt for China. (2) CCS 31st Mtg, 16 Jul 42, Item 4. (3) CM–OUT 5475, Marshall to Stilwell, 18 Jul 42. (4) Quotation from Stilwell Diary, 23 Jul 42.

as before, coaxing and persuading the Chinese into going on another year. On the other hand, he feared that the War Department might not have any serious plans for China Theater. Once the Chinese learned this, Stilwell's usefulness was gone. There was only one way out which did not depend on large resources obtained from the United States. The solution was to persuade the British and Chinese to join in retaking Burma. This might be done if the situations in North Africa, then menaced by the Axis, and in Yunnan, then threatened by the Japanese from Burma and Indochina, were cleared up. Once Rangoon was reopened, thought Stilwell, surely some shipping would be assigned to CBI and lend-lease would again flow into China. "Under the circumstances that prevail at present, this is the first step towards a sustained counter-offensive, and only when the Yunnan threat is removed and the African crisis passed can it be set up." [85]

Having analyzed the situation in China Theater, and having concluded that reopening the line of communications from Rangoon to Kunming was the essential preliminary to a solution of strategic problems in China, Stilwell proceeded to prepare a detailed memorandum on operations to reoccupy Burma. The memorandum he drafted 10 July, therefore, followed several days of intense intellectual effort in which Stilwell considered every aspect of his problems in attempting to support China. Stilwell's approach was objective and coldly professional, with nothing to suggest he was obsessed by a spirit of revenge for the defeat in Burma. [86]

Acting as chief of staff to the Generalissimo, Stilwell submitted his memorandum to the Supreme Commander, China Theater, on 19 July. In so doing, he had two motives: to afford the Generalissimo a dignified solution to the Three Demands crisis, and to commit the Chinese to a course of action. If the Generalissimo displayed a willingness to engage the enemy, Stilwell reasoned, the War Department could hardly refuse him the means. With respect to the Chinese, the plan gave Stilwell a way to secure from them an indication of what they would do with the lend-lease they so eagerly sought. The plan also gave the War Department a chance to bargain with the Chinese, to propose that if the Chinese reformed a number of divisions to Stilwell's satisfaction, the United States would then arm them. [87]

In his black book Stilwell outlined the basis of his action:

The only way I see now is to force the W.D.'s hand—(Burma)—and then get them to force CKS' hand, by making conditions for the help they would supply. I would ask for three Chinese divisions that I would pick, for each U.S. division supplied; complete command of the mixed force, with power to punish and reward, promote and demote, and progressively increased authority and control of added units in case of success—five for one

[85] Memo, Stilwell, 10 Jul 42, sub: What is Future of China War Theater? SNF–12.
[86] (1) Memo, Stilwell, 10 Jul 42, sub: Plan for Retaking Burma. SNF–12. (2) For another view of Stilwell's motivation, see Chennault, *Way of a Fighter*, pp. 210, 270–76.
[87] (1) Stilwell B&W, 20 Jul 42. (2) Memo, Stilwell for Marshall, 30 Jul 42. CCS 381, Burma (8–25–42), Sec 1. (3) CM–IN 0789, Stilwell to Marshall, 2 Aug 42.

if we could get Burma back, ten for one if we took Hankow; twenty for one if we took Hsuchow. Then we *would* have something.[88]

He also explained his motives to the War Department:

In order to carry out my mission of increasing the combat efficiency of the Chinese Army, trading must be the basis of action. Logic and reason, or personal influence, will not produce satisfactory results. Pressure and bargaining are the means that must be relied on. . . . If it is considered important to keep pressure on the Japanese, in spite of tremendous demands on our resources in other theaters, the War Department should know what the Chinese are prepared to contribute to the effort. The only way to be sure is to propose a plan under which they would have to commit themselves.[89]

Distinctly foreshadowed by Stilwell's April 1942 proposals, and reminiscent of the Generalissimo's 23 December 1941 paper, the 18 July memorandum called for Allied co-operation in retaking Burma.

If the Japanese make no attempt to invade Yunnan this summer, a plan should be set up to retake Burma. Unless some preparations are made, the fall months will be lost and the arrival of material will be further delayed. It is of the utmost importance to again start a flow of munitions through Rangoon into China.

1. The plan depends on the decision of the War Department. If shipping can be allotted to bring into Rangoon 30,000 tons a month for six months, the situation will be eased materially. (This supply will be principally artillery and small arms ammunition, bombs, guns, gasoline, trucks, tanks, etc.)

2. Without British help, the project is not practicable. Washington should be asked to use its influence to get them to cooperate, and the value of a U.S. ground unit in India should be emphasized. If Chinese and American units are ready to move, the British could hardly fail to act to regain their own territory.

3. The Chinese approach should be a statement of the case, and an offer to furnish an army of twenty picked divisions well backed up by artillery, if London and Washington will cooperate. The British should (a) put enough naval strength in the Bay of Bengal to control it, (b) invade Burma via the Chindwin toward Shwebo and Mandalay, and (c) make a landing at Rangoon. The Chinese should attack towards Lashio, and from there towards Loilem and Mandalay. If U.S. units are available, they should either come in with the British along the Chindwin, or join in seizing Rangoon. The attacks toward Shwebo and Mandalay should get well under way before the attempt on Rangoon is made, and the Andamans should be occupied immediately before the attack at Rangoon. Enough aviation should be built up in India to cover these operations strongly. A parachute unit should be made available for the Rangoon operation.

4. Unless positive action is taken to re-open Burma, the offer of U.S. help to China is meaningless. If the Chinese show a desire to do their part fully, the War Department can hardly disregard the request. . . .[90]

There were indications from the Chinese side that the Generalissimo was not averse to compromise and reconciliation. The most encouraging sign was the appointment of Stilwell as commander in chief of the Chinese Army in India, with Lo Cho-ying as his deputy. Stilwell's power was limited to re-

[88] Stilwell B&W, 20 Jul 42.
[89] Memo cited n. 87(2).
[90] (1) Memo with Incl, Stilwell for Generalissimo, 18 Jul 42, sub: Suggested Ltr from General-issimo to President. Stilwell Documents, Hoover Library. (2) Ch. II, pp. 56–57, Ch. IV, pp. 135–36, above.

organization, training, and "directing." [91] But the picture was not growing uniformly brighter for on 10 July one of the ablest Chinese officers told Stilwell that the Generalissimo had ordered his war area commanders to "conserve their strength." [92]

The Generalissimo Modifies His Demands

Therefore, when Dr. Currie arrived on 20 July he found considerable progress had already been made toward a solution of the Three Demands. By summer 1942 Currie had had a year of dealing with the Chinese and was conversant with their methods and attitudes. He was therefore not unprepared for what he saw in Chungking though he had not been thoroughly briefed beforehand on the local command situation. Currie attacked his problems vigorously, talking with Stilwell and the Chinese. In the course of these exchanges the fact emerged that Soong had not presented the President's 12 July message to the Generalissimo but only his own highly expurgated version. Moreover, the Chinese claimed Soong had never explained the Soong-Stimson accord of 23–30 January 1942 to his government. Currie immediately realized the effect of Soong's actions on Stilwell's and the President's relations with the Generalissimo.[93] Currie also found the First Burma Campaign embittering Stilwell's relationship with the Generalissimo. Currie considered that Stilwell was at "no particular pains" to hide his resentment at having been handicapped by the Generalissimo's letters to the Chinese commanders, while the Generalissimo resented what he considered Stilwell's failure to obey his orders. In analyzing this situation, Currie made no mention of General Alexander, the Supreme Allied Commander in Burma, but described Stilwell as "Commander-in-Chief in the field," reported the issue as lying between Stilwell and the Generalissimo, and expressed his opinion that Stilwell had "illusions" about his ability to command Chinese troops.[94]

Weighing his observations of Stilwell and the Chinese, Currie decided to back Stilwell's conceptions. He recommended the full restoration of the 3,500-ton emergency air transport program, subject to Stilwell's periodic reviews. He also urged that the President give Stilwell a copy of every presidential message to the Chinese. The President agreed. The War Department helped with the news that China's lend-lease requisitions would be fitted into the 3,500-ton program, which might even be increased.[95]

In one phase of the negotiations Currie attempted to clear up the confusion

[91](1) Memo, FAB/NMC 60, Shang Chen for Stilwell, 2 Jul 42. SNF–12. (2) Translation of Ltr O, Chiang to Stilwell, 14 Jul 42. SNF–77 Generals Liao, Sun, and Lo were placed under Stilwell.
[92] Stilwell Black Book, 10 Jul 42.
[93](1) *The Stilwell Papers,* pp. 128–31. (2) Stilwell Diary, 25, 27, 31 Jul 42. (3) CM–IN 9776, Currie to Roosevelt, 28 Jul 42. (4) Rpt, Currie to Roosevelt, 24 Aug 42, sub: Rpt on Visit to China. OPD 336 China (24 Aug 42), A47–30.
[94] Rpt cited n. 93(4).
[95](1) CM–OUT 8122, Gruber to Stilwell, 28 Jul 42. (2) CM–IN 9776, Currie to Roosevelt, 28 Jul 42. (3) CM–OUT 8454, Marshall to Stilwell, 29 Jul 42.

caused by Soong's alleged failure to explain Stilwell's status to the Chinese Government along the lines of the Soong-Stimson accord of January 1942. While so engaged Currie told General Ho that, because no Allied staff had yet been set up for China Theater, Stilwell's role as Chief of Staff, China Theater, was confined to those sections of China Theater which lay outside the territorial boundaries of the Republic of China. Since, as of July 1942, the boundaries of China Theater and the Republic of China coincided exactly, Stilwell's role inside China thus appeared to be eliminated.[96]

The Chinese quickly saw the difference between Stilwell's and Currie's description of Stilwell's powers, and Soong at once brought the matter to Marshall's attention. McCloy answered for the War Department:

It is our understanding that General Stilwell is the Chief of Staff to the Generalissimo's Joint Staff which functions when forces of the Allies carry on operations anywhere in China Theater. As Chief of Staff his duties are concerned with planning, organization, training, and operations in the field. He prepares plans as directed by the Generalissimo and when they are approved by him transmits them to various contingents for execution.[97]

Responding to Currie's visit, the Generalissimo gave concrete indication of conciliatory feelings by agreeing orally on 27 July to Stilwell's 18 July proposals for a Burma campaign.[98] Stilwell immediately submitted to the Generalissimo on 29 July an ambitious proposal for a general Pacific offensive in which the now-approved Burma operation took its proper place. If the Generalissimo approved, the Chinese leader could then send this Pacific Front plan to the President and Prime Minister as China's suggestion for Allied operations in the Pacific. In a covering letter Stilwell made it clear that his proposal was in the nature of a suggestion for possible future planning. Stilwell explained he was in no position to commit the United States to any course of action.[99]

The formal approval of Stilwell's 18 July memorandum came from the Chinese on 1 August. It modified the Three Demands in that one U.S. division, 500 planes, and 5,000 tons would be acceptable to the Chinese without specifying a deadline for fulfillment. The Generalissimo clearly described China's contribution to a future Burma operation. The memorandum read:

In acknowledging the receipt of your Memorandum, dated July 18th, the Generalissimo directs me to inform you that the Chinese Government is in full agreement with your proposed plan to retake Burma and appreciates its significance both from the political and military points of view. But in order to insure that the campaign will be successfully carried out, your attention is particularly invited to the following three points:

[96] CM-IN 9776, Currie to Roosevelt, 28 Jul 42.
[97] (1) Ltr, McCloy to Soong, 18 Aug 42. ASW 400.336 (China). (2) CM-OUT 5982, Marshall to Stilwell, 19 Aug 42. (3) See p. 156, above.
[98] Stilwell Diary, 27 Jul 42.
[99] (1) Memo, Stilwell for Generalissimo, 29 Jul 42, sub: Pacific Front Proposal. Stilwell Documents, Hoover Library. (2) After Currie's return the Stilwell proposal became CCS 104, 29 Aug 42, sub: Pacific Front Plan Presented by Generalissimo. (3) Memo, Stilwell for Marshall, 30 Jul 42, with Incl A, Memo, U.S. Secy, CPS, for Brig Gen Albert C. Wedemeyer, JPS, 16 Mar 43, sub: Plan for Retaking Burma. ABC 384, Burma (8-25-42), Sec 2, A48-224.

1. The occupation of the Andamans, the giving of support to the armed forces to land at Rangoon and, later on, the controlling of the Bay of Bengal, as well as the giving of support to transports to unload supplies at Rangoon;—the accomplishment of all these depends on the British Navy and Royal Air Force in making their greatest effort. Whether Great Britain can really make such an effort, only the British Government is in a position to say. It is therefore deemed necessary that the attitude of Great Britain in this case should first be ascertained and that she be urged to act.

2. Regarding the suggestion that one to three divisions of U.S. ground units should assist the British to attack Shwebo and Mandalay via the Chindwin, it is imperative that the time required for the building of the road between India and Burma should be figured out well in advance and road construction be pushed with all speed. Otherwise, to launch an attack merely with light arms will have little chance of success.

3. China is able with effort to concentrate in Western and Southern Yunnan an army of twenty picked divisions backed up with necessary artillery . . . (there are at present 36D, 87D and 88D of 71A; 49D, 93D and N28D [New 28th Division] of 6A; 82D, 139D and 141D of 32A; and 2RD [2d Reserve Division]; to which may be later added 9D, 76D and N33D of 2A; 24D, 196D and T57D [Temporary-57th Division] of 76A; and also 54A when necessary) . . . and to attack from Lashio. Judging from our equipments and experiences in the past, the Chinese troops can be expected to hold up the enemy's main force in Burma and eventually to deal him a decisive blow. But to attain the military objective of storming the enemy's strongholds and capturing strategic points, no success can be achieved without the effective assistance of the air force. This is not possible with the minimum of air force that has recently been decided upon to be put into operation in the front. Furthermore, the concentration of armed units, the establishment of supply depots and the transportation of supplies are also difficult problems which must be satisfactorily solved in order to meet the exigencies of war.[100]

Accepting Stilwell's Pacific Front proposals of 29 July, the Generalissimo asked Currie to bring them before the President and the Combined Chiefs of Staff. (*Map 6*) The Pacific Front plan called for the retaking of Burma by 12 divisions from Yunnan, and 1 U.S. and 3 British divisions, with the 2 divisions of the Chinese Army in India driving from Manipur State. These Allied forces would converge above Mandalay, then fan out across south Burma, Thailand, and to the coast of Indochina. The Allied advances from India called for no grandiose road construction since the Imphal–Tamu–Kalewa–Shwebo roads could be used. In Yunnan, the Chinese would establish a troop reserve at Kunming and would use 9 divisions along the Indochina border for offensives aimed at Hanoi and Haiphong or at Canton and Hong Kong, or eventually at both areas. Outside the Asiatic theater, there would be an Allied offensive north from Australia, and the U.S. Navy would make an all-out attack on Japanese communications.

On 4 August Stilwell's artillery officer, Colonel Dorn, sent an outline of the Pacific Front plan to the War Department and added a personal note for General Handy of OPD:

We all believe that the Generalissimo must be handled on an "ultimatum basis"; be told in plain language what he must do and be given a very short time in which to decide and

---

[100] Ltr, FAB/NMC 82, Shang Chen to Stilwell, 1 Aug 42. SNF-73.

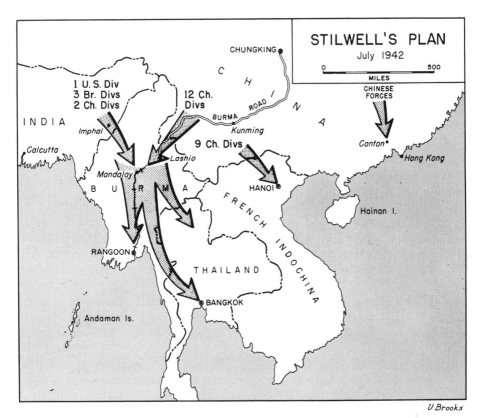

MAP 6

reply. If he threatens to make peace with Japan, tell him to go ahead. In all probability the Japanese would laugh at him now. Besides there exists what amounts to an undeclared peace anyway, with mail and a considerable trade going back and forth between occupied and unoccupied China. That is why tungsten shipments have not been as large as had been expected. The Japs pay a little better price. . . .

Until we re-take Burma, and re-open the port of Rangoon, all talk and planning to aid China are utterly meaningless. But all aid to China must have a string which demands action from them, or Rangoon or not, the present regime will do nothing but hoard the matériel in order to perpetuate itself after the war. It is short-sighted, but the regime itself is short-sighted or it would not need to worry about its own position in China after the war. In other words they expect an upheaval or revolution of some kind. In fact T. V. Soong in Washington expressed the opinion that the present regime would be out of a job six months after the war was over. He ought to know. . . .[101]

On 6 August Currie left Chungking to lay the Pacific Front plan (also called the Generalissimo's plan) before the President and the CCS.[102]

[101] Ltr, Dorn to Handy, 4 Aug 42. OPD 381 CTO, Sec 3, A47–30.
[102] (1) Memo, Stilwell for Generalissimo, 29 Jul 42, sub: Pacific Front Proposal. Stilwell Documents, Hoover Library. (2) *The Stilwell Papers*, pp. 131–33.

Seeking to take advantage of the more aggressive Chinese attitude, Stilwell immediately submitted a suggestion that the Chinese raid Indochina to "determine the intentions of the Japanese in that vital area," from which an attack might easily be launched on Kunming. He suggested that two divisions then in south Yunnan make the attack. ". . . If the enemy is contemplating an action in this area, such an attack would begin it under very favorable conditions for us. The Japanese would have lost the initiative, and the Chinese would be farther forward on ground favorable for defense in case the enemy is strong there. If he is weak, reserves could follow immediately to exploit any success that might be obtained." [103] No answer or comment was ever received from the Chinese.

Giving tangible proof of interest in the project for retaking Burma, the Generalissimo ordered the National Military Council to discuss the assembling, training, and equipping of the Thirty Divisions (twenty of them were designated on 1 August) with Stilwell, eighteen months after Soong first requested U.S. arms for them. The Generalissimo had given a tentative list of the thirty in March, then withdrawn his support from the plan as the Burma campaign grew steadily worse for the Allies. The Generalissimo also ordered, in the same first week of August, that the highest Chinese staff echelon, the National Military Council, should inform Stilwell of the Chinese order of battle, the various fronts in China Theater, and what the Chinese strategic concepts were in each war area. Within a fortnight all these were revealed to Stilwell's staff. Passive defense was the order of the day in each war area from Sian to Indochina. Even the sixteen armies charged with preventing the Chinese Communists from taking Sian were awaiting the end of the Pacific war. No offensive against the Japanese was contemplated, not even guerrilla action.[104]

For their part, the Japanese made an unwitting contribution to Sino-American amity by ending the Chekiang expedition on 28 July, thus removing pressure on the Generalissimo to seek immediate, massive U.S. help.[105] Examination of the Japanese supply plan for 1942, which *Imperial General Headquarters* issued 20 March 1942, suggests the Japanese were quite content to let the *status quo* prevail in China. For example, but 5,000 rounds of 150-mm. high explosive would be shipped to China from the homeland. Approximately 60,000,000 rounds of type 38 rifle ammunition would be kept on hand in China; if less were needed, even that modest stock would be reduced. As replenishment, 20,000,000 rounds of rifle ammunition would be shipped to *North China Area Army*, and them alone. For the whole Japanese establishment in China, there would be shipped 10,900,000 rounds of practice

[103](1) Memo, Stilwell for Generalissimo, 1 Aug 42, sub: Proposed Raid Into Indochina. Stilwell Documents, Hoover Library. (2) Stilwell B&W, 1 Aug 42.
[104] Notes of Mtg with NMC, Aldrich, recorder, 20 Aug 42. Item 225, Corresp Folder (May–Dec 42), CT 23, Dr 2. KCRC.
[105] (1) Japanese Study 77. (2) See p. 163, above.

ball ammunition, and 6,200,000 blank cartridges. Food would be procured in China. The picture painted by the Japanese supply arrangements is of an army of occupation, with training duties, living off the country, and launching occasional punitive expeditions.[106]

On 29 August Stilwell asked the War Department to provide weapons for the American portion of the Thirty Divisions, stressing artillery, automatic weapons, and ammunition. The War Department answer was favorable.[107]

Stilwell responded to the Generalissimo's more co-operative attitude by encouraging the Chinese in regard to the Hump:

1. Information has just been received that the War Department will furnish up to the 75 army transports and the total of 25 transports for CNAC as fast as airplanes are available.

2. I have requested that 2½ full crews for each transport airplane be provided to secure the maximum hours flying from each transport and have been informed that beginning the first of October additional pilots will be provided at the rate of 30 each month.

3. On my recommendation the War Department has directed General Brereton to return to India any transports not urgently needed in the Middle East. . . .[108]

While his superiors pondered their next moves, Stilwell spent a week in India. He visited Ramgarh and ordered officers to get supplies moving from Karachi to the Chinese troops that had withdrawn from Burma. He also talked with Wavell and informed him that the Generalissimo was contemplating a major operation for retaking Burma.[109]

Stilwell's suggestion that the United States reach a clear understanding with the Chinese on what they would do with the lend-lease they received was not accepted by Currie. Adhering to the views he had expressed in the fall of 1941, Currie thought it unwise to put any pressure on the Chinese since the United States was not planning to meet the Three Demands in full. The President approved and adopted this line in framing his final reply to the Three Demands note.[110]

---

[106] The Japanese stocks in China were kept at a level estimated as enough for one battle; the resupply factor for rifle ammunition was 0.3. See *Imperial General Headquarters* Army Directive 1122, 20 Mar 42, GHQ, Far East Comd, Mil Hist Div, *Imperial General Headquarters* Army Directives, Vol. II. Gen Ref Br, OCMH.

[107] (1) CM–IN 11061, Stilwell to Gruber, 29 Aug 42. (2) CM–IN 11380, Stilwell to Marshall, 29 Aug 42. (3) CM–OUT 5287, Marshall to Stilwell, 17 Aug 42. (4) CM–OUT 2055, Marshall to Stilwell, 6 Sep 42. (5) CM–OUT 1047, Marshall to Stilwell, 3 Oct 42.

[108] Memo, Stilwell for Generalissimo, 6 Aug 42, sub: Opn of Transport Airplanes. SNF–21.

[109] (1) *The Stilwell Papers*, p. 139. (2) Stilwell B&W, 10 Nov 42.

[110] (1) Memo, Stilwell for Currie, 1 Aug 42, sub: Gen View of Chinese Situation. Stilwell Documents, Hoover Library. (2) CM–IN 0433, CM–IN 0789, Stilwell to AGWAR, 2 Aug 42. (3) Currie's view on Chinese co-operation is in Chapter I, page 41, above. (4) As early as 4 September 1942, at the President's request relayed through Marshall, OPD drafted a message for the President to send to the Generalissimo, informing him of the U.S. answer to the Three Demands and asking in return for the development of the Thirty Division Program and the reorganization of his army with Stilwell as adviser. Currie objected to the draft reply. It was modified before being sent to Stilwell for comment. Memo, Handy for Marshall, 4 Sep 42, sub: Support of China, with Incl, Memo, Marshall for President, 11 Sep 42, sub: Support of China. OPD 381 CTO, Sec 2, A47–30. (5) Memo, Currie for Marshall, 12 Sep 42, sub: Cable from You to Generalissimo. WDCSA 381, File I, A46–523. (6) Ltr, Currie to Marshall, 14 Sep 42. Item 22, OPD Exec 10.

On his return to Washington Currie supported Stilwell's projects but suggested that Stilwell be sent to another theater.[111] Marshall could see that the Generalissimo had convinced Currie of Stilwell's unpopularity with the regime, but even a presidential query about moving Stilwell to another theater did not persuade Stimson and Marshall to do so.[112] Upon his return Currie asked Marshall to consider Stilwell's transfer. Marshall desired to know if Currie was acting on the President's behalf. When the negative reply came, Marshall dismissed the topic from their conference.[113] Not pressing the issue, Roosevelt for the moment gave Stilwell his support, but not to the extent of requiring reform of the Chinese Army in exchange for lend-lease aid.[114] This policy was in accord with the recommendation Currie made to the President in his report on his trip to Chungking: "I do not think we need to lay down any conditions or tie any strings to our support."

Before supporting Stilwell so firmly, Marshall had consulted him. The Chief of Staff told Stilwell that he was fully aware of Soong's attitude and activities and of the effect of Soong's actions on Sino-American relations and on Stilwell's position. He added that Stimson and he were disturbed over Stilwell's delicate situation and knew they had been able to give Stilwell but little support. The issue was becoming more acute because the Combined Chiefs of Staff were considering the reoccupation of Burma after the monsoon rains. Marshall asked what the prospects for a combined Sino-British effort in Burma were and whether the Generalissimo's attitude toward Stilwell would permit the latter's taking a leading role in such a venture.[115]

In reply Stilwell summarized the progress he had made in plans to retake Burma but cautioned that the Chinese showed a clear disposition to coast and to let others finish the war. He repeated the AMMISCA warning—that the Chinese wanted to finish the war with their arsenals stocked and their armies well equipped, by implication, to handle domestic disturbances. He was not concerned about his relations with the Generalissimo and did not understand Currie's references to "strongly antagonistic feelings." Stilwell believed that the Generalissimo knew what had happened in Burma as well as he did, that any feeling on the Generalissimo's part about Stilwell's status in China could

[111](1) On 24 August Currie recommended to the President that Soong, Gauss, and Stilwell be replaced. He argued that Stilwell and the Generalissimo had had a basic misunderstanding over the chief of staff role since January 1942. Rpt cited n. 93(4). (2) Memo and Ltr cited n. 110(5), (6).
[112](1) Interv with Marshall, 6 Jul 49. (2) Memo, Roosevelt for Marshall, 3 Oct 42. Marshall discussed Stilwell's transfer with Stimson. They agreed that no one could be found to replace Stilwell. Ltr, Marshall to Roosevelt, 6 Oct 42, sub: Situation Relative to Stilwell. OPD 381 CTO, Sec 2, A47-30.
[113] Interv cited n. 112(1).
[114](1) Rpt cited n. 93(4). (2) Memo, Marshall for Roosevelt, 2 Oct 42, sub: Support of China. The President approved this memorandum on 10 October 1942 and it went to Stilwell as WAR 1469, Marshall for Stilwell, 12 Oct 42. OPD 381 CTO, Sec 2, A47-30. (3) Item 54, OPD Exec 10. (4) Memo, Roosevelt for Chiang, 12 Oct 42. Item 71, Bk 1, JWS Personal File.
[115] Rad, Marshall to Stilwell, 1 Sep 42. WDCSA 381, File I, A46-523.

be traced to Soong. Stilwell's last meetings with the Generalissimo had been pleasant and he hoped something could be done. Stilwell closed his reply by offering an acid test of Chinese intentions—progress on the Thirty Division scheme. If the Chinese had any thought of taking an active part in the war, they would certainly want to rebuild their armies. If they wanted to be only formally belligerent, then the Thirty Division scheme would continue to creep forward.[116]

Planning the Air War in China Theater

Immediately after Currie's departure, Stilwell pressed his air officer to study the immediate use of American air power in China. One may surmise that, by preparing a suitable plan, Stilwell desired to commit the Generalissimo as Supreme Commander, China Theater, to making defense of the Hump air terminal the primary mission of China-based air power, thus precluding development of a China Theater in which U.S. air power did the work and the Chinese reaped the benefits. Stilwell also desired a program in which requirements in Hump tonnage would balance 3,500 tons of air cargo a month for the Thirty Division build-up with tonnage to support the China Air Task Force.[117]

In compliance with Stilwell's wishes his staff submitted their study, the China Air War Plan, on 8 September. The paper divided the major tasks between the China Air Task Force and the Chinese Air Force. The former was charged with protecting the air ferry line; the latter, Chungking and the Yangtze valley. Of the two missions given above, the China Air Task Force's mission defending the air transport route was rated as the first objective of the China Air War Plan.

The study proposed to accomplish the defense of the airline and of Chungking by offensive operations against hostile air concentrations. These offensive operations would be mounted from a perimeter line of bases from Heng-yang to Meng-tzu. After defense of the airline and China's capital came missions against "targets of opportunity and war industries within the radius of action of our air force." Among these, shipping had highest priority. As for ground operations, these were covered with the provision, "The Chinese Air Force and the American Air Force will afford support to ground operations of the Chinese Army when sufficient strength is available after accomplishment of the primary mission of these air forces (defense of the air ferry route)."[118]

This plan was formulated after submission of General Chennault's views which had been placed before Stilwell in July. Activated on 6 July, the China

---

[116] Rad, Stilwell to Marshall, 4 Sep 42. Item 35, Bk 1, JWS Personal File.

[117] (1) The inference is based on Stilwell's August–September radios, warning Marshall that the Chinese wanted U.S. air power to assume the major burdens in China Theater. (2) Memo, Col Edward H. Alexander for Stilwell, 8 Sep 42, sub: China Air War Plan. Item 15, Bissell Corresp Folder (Jul–Sep 42), CT 23, Dr 2, KCRC.

[118] Memo cited n. 117(2).

Air Task Force had continued the AVG's successes.[119] Contemplating the potentialities of China-based air power, Chennault told Stilwell that if he were given 100 of the then new P-51 fighters and 30 B-25 medium bombers he would accept "responsibility" for:

(a) Destruction of Japanese aircraft in much greater number than CATF's entire strength.
(b) Destruction of enemy military and naval establishments in China to encourage Chinese resistance.
(c) Disruption of Japanese shipping in the interior of China and off the coasts of China.
(d) Interdiction of Japanese air concentrations being ferried from Chinese bases across Indochina and Thailand into Burma.
(e) Destruction of Japanese air force morale by destroying its rear depots and production facilities.[120]

The whole bent of Chennault's plan was aggressive. Stilwell modified it to the extent that he desired Chennault to make defense of the Hump his primary mission.

Stilwell sent to the Generalissimo on 13 September a second plan for operations of the China Air Task Force alone:

2. The primary mission of the United States China Air Task Force is to defend the ferry route from India to China. The secondary mission is to conduct operations to destroy hostile aircraft, shipping, and installations in other areas when such operations do not jeopardize the primary mission and when munitions are available for such operations.
3. The plan to accomplish the mission of the United States China Air Task Force contemplates offensive operations for the destruction of aircraft and installations on hostile airdromes within striking distance of the air freight route; the destruction of hostile aircraft operating against air transports or the terminal facilities of the air route, and the attack on communications necessary for the support of such hostile air operations. In addition occasional air attacks on favorable targets of opportunity are envisioned.
4. Your approval of the above for future planning and execution is requested.[121]

For whatever reason, the plan of the China Air Task Force's commander for his unit's operations was submitted three days later, but it was consistent with the above. As did his July paper, Chennault's September proposals stressed aggressive action against Japanese shipping, but he accepted Stilwell's views by suggesting Hump defense as his primary mission. Chennault also proposed the most vigorous action against Japanese air power, which was also in line with Stilwell's thinking. Significantly, Chennault asked that his command become independent of Bissell's Tenth Air Force and operate directly under Stilwell. For his operations, Chennault requested 1,986 tons a month. There was a serious flaw in his logistical planning. His study placed on the Tenth's Air Service Command the responsibility of supplying and supporting the

---

[119] At midnight on 4 July 1942 the AVG had become a legend. On 6 July the China Air Task Force was activated. On 8 July Chennault assumed command of the CATF. History of the CATF, 1942–43. File 830.01, USAF Hist Div.
[120] Memo, Chennault for Stilwell, 16 Jul 42. Item 23, Corresp Folder (Jul 42–Jan 43), CT 23, Dr 2, KCRC.
[121] Memo, Stilwell for Generalissimo, 13 Sep 42, sub: Employment of U.S. CATF. SNF-53.

BRIG. GEN. CLAIRE L. CHENNAULT

China Air Task Force at its forward fields. To discharge this responsibility, the Air Service Command in China would require a certain amount of Hump tonnage to support either trucks or transport aircraft. Yet Chennault was asking every ton of Hump tonnage for tactical operations of the China Air Task Force. This posed a dilemma for Stilwell's headquarters. Stilwell approved Chennault's September proposals, save the paragraph on command, yet until ways were found to bring more tonnage over the Hump and then move it forward to Chennault's fields, such approval was academic.[122]

As his memorandum of 7 July 1942 [123] to the Generalissimo made clear, Stilwell was far from underestimating the potentialities of China-based air power. His diaries for September and October faithfully record the box score of every air engagement with the Japanese and reveal that he prodded Bissell and Chennault to seize opportunities for aggressive air action against major

---

[122] Memo, Chennault for Bissell, 16 Sep 42, sub: Plan for Employment of CATF and Atchd Servs; 1st Ind, Bissell for Stilwell, 17 Sep 42 (approved); 2d Ind, Stilwell for Bissell, 21 Sep 42 (approved); Memo, Chennault for Bissell, 22 Sep 42, sub: Plan for Tactical Employment of CATF; 4th Ind, Stilwell for Chennault, 3 Oct 42 (approved). Item 304, U.S. Opns in China Folder (Sep 42–Jul 43), CT 23, Dr 2, KCRC.
[123] See pp. 175–77, above.

Japanese targets. There is no suggestion in the diaries that he sought to hamper Chennault or felt hostility toward him or his views. Stilwell told Marshall he felt it necessary to avoid provoking a Japanese reaction until gasoline stocks for Chennault's air force had been built up.[124]

In late September, speaking on the larger aspects of China Theater, he warned Marshall that the Chinese wanted the China Air Task Force strengthened to a point where it could fight the Japanese by itself, leaving the Chinese free to rest on their oars until their Allies defeated the Japanese. He reported that the Chinese ignored the ground aspects of war in China. The Thirty Division plan, Stilwell remarked, was the real reason for the existence of the airline to China. He told Marshall that even though it was now impossible to fly in all the American weapons originally contemplated, great progress toward a better Chinese Army still could be made by reorganization, filling the Thirty Divisions to full strength, equipping them with the weapons available in China, and concentrating them in strategic positions. He reported that the Chinese were doing nothing to accomplish the Thirty Division plan, and that American pressure was needed. The Chinese were meeting all of Stilwell's arguments, he told Marshall, with demands for more transports on the Hump.[125]

Summary

June and July saw a false start toward carrying out Stilwell's mission to support China and reform its Army. Immediately after Stilwell had presented his proposals to the Generalissimo his mission was gravely compromised by the order to move Brereton's B-17's to the Middle East. Following a number of disappointments in regard to lend-lease, aviation projects, and diplomatic status, the step angered the Chinese. Since it was diplomatically inadvisable for the Chinese to blame Stilwell's superiors, their disappointments were thereafter charged to Stilwell, as though he were a free agent.

After the U.S. Government reacted coolly to Chinese hints of a separate peace, the expressions of the Chinese moderated, and in succeeding weeks it was possible for Stilwell and the presidential emissary, Mr. Currie, to prepare the way for Chinese acceptance of something less than full compliance with the Three Demands.

---

[124](1) Stilwell Diary, 10–12 Oct 42. (2) CM–IN 10959, Stilwell to Marshall, 24 Sep 42.
[125] CM–IN 12306, Stilwell to Marshall, 28 Sep 42.

CHAPTER VI

U.S. Forces Organize and Prepare for New Tasks

If Stilwell succeeded in persuading the Chinese to co-operate in retaking Burma, and if the forthcoming reply to the now-modified Three Demands strengthened their resolve to proceed along the lines of the Pacific Front and the China Air War Plan, then Stilwell's chief concern would be American support of the Chinese effort. "Support China" would be an injunction to be interpreted in the most literal terms and to be carried out by a U.S. Army organization modeled to that end.

Although the loss of Burma left Stilwell's Task Force in China, plus the Tenth Air Force and the infant Services of Supply, without a specific immediate mission, the Pacific Front and the China Air War Plan obviously involved future tasks of considerable magnitude for the U.S. Army. Therefore, while waiting for the final settlement of the Three Demands crisis, Stilwell expanded his modest organization into a larger one which, with the tacit approval of the War Department, became known as the China, Burma and India Theater of Operations. It will be recalled that Stilwell had left the United States as a task force commander, indeed, that his willingness to accept that status was one of the reasons he had been given his mission to China. Now, that was to change, and Stilwell, his superiors, and his subordinates soon referred to his position as that of U.S. theater commander in China, Burma, and India.

Apart from setting up his widespread CBI command, Stilwell worked at his three other command and staff assignments. As chief of staff to the Generalissimo, he created an office at Chungking and secured clerical help for preparing his proposals for reform of the Chinese Army and operations in China Theater. This post he kept most meticulously separate from his U.S. Army command, and members of his American staff were not aware of his plans and projects for China Theater. Stilwell sometimes called on individual American officers to prepare staff studies on China Theater problems; at other times, staff sections sent memorandums to their Chinese counterparts, but only with Stilwell's approval. Occasionally Stilwell detailed American officers to confer with Chinese on matters of mutual concern. Until the Chinese would agree to set up a joint staff for China Theater as promised by them in January

1942, Stilwell proposed to discharge his staff responsibilities in China Theater by himself with the aid of a liaison officer, Col. John Liu of the Chinese Army, who also served as a translator, and a few enlisted clerks.

In the conduct of two other responsibilities, Stilwell made free use of American personnel. As the Munitions Assignments Board's agent, he supervised and controlled lend-lease in China, although he never bore a formal title, such as Lend-Lease Administrator for China. As commanding general of the Chinese Army in India, Stilwell staffed a headquarters with Chinese and American officers who would, he hoped, work harmoniously in creating a new army.

Expansion of Headquarters, U.S. Army Forces, CBI, July–December 1942

The command of Chinese troops given by the Generalissimo, the desire to anticipate the arrival of a U.S. corps for which Stilwell's staff was hoping, and finally a War Department directive led directly to the metamorphosis of Stilwell's task force into a theater of operations. When Stilwell reached New Delhi at the end of May 1942, he arranged for General Sibert and a small staff including Colonel Ferris to work with the British in finding a concentration area for the Chinese straggling out of Burma. The Services of Supply (SOS) was spreading across India. The Tenth Air Force was organizing itself for expansion. Sibert, Ferris, and their staff began to look ahead toward the reception of a U.S. corps in India. As the number of Americans in CBI and the extent of their responsibilities grew, the mental horizon of those who commanded them broadened, and so the Stilwell group in New Delhi more and more thought of themselves as acting in the capacity of a theater headquarters. Though the hope of receiving a corps from the War Department lasted for some months, it soon became apparent to the embryonic theater headquarters staff in New Delhi that the Chinese 22d and 38th Divisions if trained, re-equipped, and brought to strength might substitute for an American corps.[1]

June passed before the Generalissimo charged Stilwell with the task of feeding and caring for his troops in India. The British were finally persuaded to offer Ramgarh, Bihar Province, as the Chinese training center, and on 2 July the Generalissimo gave Stilwell command of the Chinese Army in India. This step passed almost unnoticed, however, so overshadowed was it by the Middle East and Three Demands crises.

On 22 June 1942 the War Department ordered Stilwell to issue orders relieving all units and individuals under his command from assignment to Army Group, Washington, D. C., and to assign them under a permanent change of station to the American Army Forces in "India, China, and Burma." [2]

[1] (1) CM–IN 7262, Stilwell to Marshall, 25 May 42. (2) Memo, Hearn for Maj Gen J. C. Bruce, British Mil Mission to China, 19 Jun 42. Item 151, Misc Corresp Folder (May–Dec 42), CT 23, Dr 2, KCRC. (3) Interv with Col Ferris, 1 Dec 48.
[2] (1) CM–IN 0570, Stilwell to Marshall, 2 Jul 42. (2) CM–OUT 5537, AGWAR to Stilwell, 22 Jun 42.

The War Department's radio went to Stilwell's staff in Chungking which promptly relayed it to General Sibert in New Delhi. The latter headquarters at once relieved the personnel of the several troop movements which had arrived in China and India from their assignment to Army Group, Washington, D. C., and reassigned them to "this theater of operations." There were no more radios on this point between Washington and Chungking, but thereafter communications from Stilwell's headquarters to the War Department, and from the War Department to Stilwell, referred to him as theater commander, to his headquarters as theater headquarters, and to his command as the China, Burma and India Theater of Operations.[3] In the absence of further, conflicting evidence, it must be assumed that both the War Department and General Stilwell regarded the Department's 22 June radio as sufficient authority for the establishment of an American theater of operations in China, Burma, and India.

The next step in the evolution of the CBI Theater was a letter of instructions from Stilwell on 6 July 1942 setting up the command structure for his theater. Stilwell made his headquarters at Chungking the office of record of his command, under the name "Headquarters, American Army Forces, China, Burma and India." The New Delhi headquarters was titled "Branch Office, Headquarters, American Army Forces, China, Burma and India." New Delhi was specifically authorized to issue directives in line with established policies in the name of the "Theater Commander."[4] Henceforth, the U.S. Army correspondence and orders within CBI Theater clearly differentiated between the functions and personnel which were assigned to Headquarters, CBI, to the SOS, and to the Tenth Air Force.

A few days later Stilwell established a branch office in Kunming to make the city's shift from a Burma Road terminal to an air ferry discharge point and a major base for Chennault as smooth as possible. Colonel MacMorland, who had suggested the step, commanded the new U.S. Kunming Area Command. MacMorland was to relieve Chennault of housing, mess, supply, and communications responsibilities and to give the Chinese a central American agency with which to deal on supply matters for that area.[5] Thus with two branch offices under way at mid-July Stilwell awaited the outcome of his Pacific Front proposals before undertaking any more expansion in his theater.

It was not until Currie was off for Washington with the Generalissimo's set of modified demands and the Pacific Front plan that Stilwell left to inspect his new theater organization. During August he traveled from Kunming to

[3] (1) SO 25, India Hq, Stilwell Mission, 16 Jul 42. This special order indicates that it was issued pursuant to a 25 June 1942 radio from Stilwell in Chungking. (2) CM–IN and CM–OUT messages in the Staff Communications Office, Department of the Army, for the period after 16 July 1942 refer to Stilwell, his headquarters, and his command as being a "Theater of Operations."

[4] Ltr of Instructions, Stilwell to Sibert, Wheeler, and Naiden, 6 Jul 42. Corresp Folder (May–Nov 42), CT 23, Dr 2, KCRC. The abbreviation AAF conflicted with Army Air Forces, so it became the accepted practice to use U.S. Army Forces, China, Burma and India.

[5] (1) Memo, MacMorland for Stilwell, 9 Jul 42, sub: Liquidation of Kunming Office. AG 500, Hq USAF CBI, KCRC. (2) GO 5, Hq USAF CBI, 18 Jul 42.

Karachi, stopping at Chabua, New Delhi, and Calcutta, and spending a week at Ramgarh.[6] Command and organizational problems received personal attention at each place. On 18 August the War Department approved Stilwell's candidate for command of the Tenth Air Force, General Bissell. On 26 August the Ramgarh Training Center for Chinese troops was activated with Colonel McCabe as commandant.[7] Chart 2 shows the command and staff structure of Stilwell's theater at the end of 1942.

During his tour Stilwell acquainted his officers with the progress of negotiations in Chungking and New Delhi and asked them to relate their activities to that progress. They were told to report difficulties encountered and anticipate the need of staff studies.[8] As Stilwell traveled about CBI, wherever he worked was a third theater headquarters, in fact if not in name, New Delhi and Chungking being the other two. Inevitably, a certain amount of confusion resulted in Chungking or New Delhi until Stilwell's decisions reached them by courier or radio and were relayed throughout the command. On occasion it became exceedingly difficult for Stilwell's chief of staff, General Hearn, to determine which headquarters spoke for the commanding general at any one time.[9]

Hearn's difficulties increased as Stilwell conducted talks first with the Chinese and then with the British and reversed the process for agreements on the Pacific Front and the China Air War Plan. Frequent trips between Chungking and New Delhi gave Stilwell an opportunity to see Bissell, Wheeler, Sibert, Ferris, Chennault, and MacMorland in person. In consequence, Hearn's staff had a difficult job in keeping abreast of orders and policy announcements. Stilwell's many conferences with commanders resulted in a multiplication of staff studies, and the amount of staff work gradually forced the Chungking and New Delhi headquarters to assume staff responsibility for the U.S. Army units within the country of their location.[10]

Branch Office, New Delhi, soon outstripped its parent headquarters at Chungking both in personnel and activity. In terms of strength, it was the larger of the two by November 1942. New Delhi had better facilities, reflecting the greater resources of India and the fact that the major U.S. effort would be exerted from there. Present in Branch Office until the end of 1942 were the theater finance, inspector general, judge advocate general, surgeon, and quartermaster officers. To these Special Staff Sections, the theater ordnance officer was added in November 1942. On 6 October Branch Office lost Sibert as a commanding general, and Stilwell put a deputy chief of staff, Brig. Gen. Benjamin

[6](1) *The Stilwell Papers,* pp. 135–41. (2) CM–IN 0789, Stilwell to Marshall, 2 Aug 42.
[7](1) Rad 1133, Marshall to Stilwell, 4 Aug 42. Item 27, Bk I, JWS Personal File. (2) GO 1, Hq Ramgarh Training Center, 26 Aug 42. (3) MS, History Ramgarh Training Center, 30 Jun 42–15 May 45. Gen Ref Br, OCMH.
[8](1) CM–IN 10959, Stilwell to Marshall, 23 Sep 42. (2) Memo with Incl, Sibert for Stilwell, 19 Oct 42, sub: Bimonthly Stf Rpts. Corresp Folder (Mar–Dec 42), CT 23, Dr 2, KCRC.
[9] Ltr, Boatner to authors, 4 Apr 50; Ltr, Hearn to authors, 16 Feb 50; Ltr, Ferris to Sunderland, 21 Feb 50. HIS 330.14 CBI 1950.
[10](1) *Ibid.* (2) Interv cited n. 1(3).

CHART 2—ORGANIZATION OF U.S. ARMY FORCES IN CHINA–BURMA–INDIA:
DECEMBER 1942

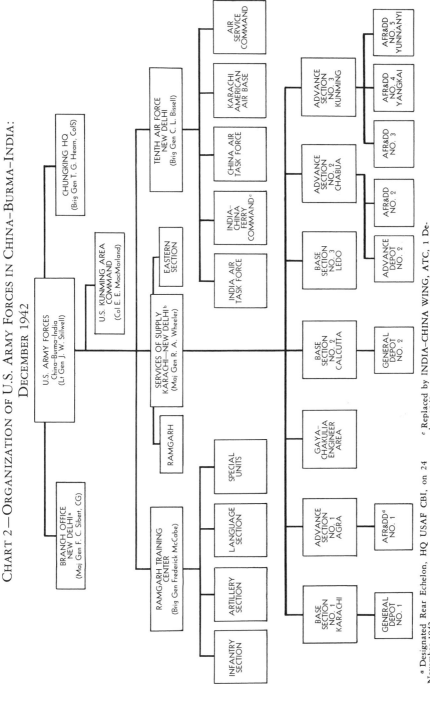

[a] Designated Rear Echelon, HQ USAF CBI, on 24 November 1942.
[b] Karachi (23 Apr–27 May 42), New Delhi (27 May 42–15 Apr 46).
[c] Replaced by INDIA–CHINA WING, ATC, 1 December 1942.
[d] AIR FREIGHT RECEPTION AND DISCHARGE DEPOT.

G. Ferris, in charge of the office. Ferris also became Stilwell's principal liaison officer with General Headquarters (India). On 24 November Branch Office got a more appropriate title for the scope and size of its activities: Headquarters, Rear Echelon, United States Army Forces, CBI.[11]

The new organization merited its title because of the extent of its contacts with the Chungking headquarters, with General Headquarters (India), and with the War Department. Ferris kept the Chungking headquarters in touch with the expansion of his special staff through bimonthly reports. The absence of an approved Allied operational plan, while a serious drawback to normal functioning, gave each officer an opportunity to do a great deal of anticipatory planning for Stilwell. If Stilwell or his headquarters staff was dissatisfied with the performance of any function by SOS, the tendency was to place that responsibility under theater headquarters. Thus by the end of 1942 signal, post exchange, malaria and venereal disease control, military police, mail, and censorship were theater functions, which meant that Headquarters, U.S. Army Forces, CBI, exercised SOS functions to a considerable degree.[12]

Apart from theater staff work, such officers as the theater quartermaster, judge advocate general, postal inspector, and surgeon had many contacts with General Headquarters (India). As a result of co-ordinating their staff work, several international agreements were reached.[13] For example, the judge advocate general aided in getting the United States and Indian Governments to agree that "the American military authorities in India had exclusive jurisdiction over criminal offenses which might be committed in India by members of U.S. forces." [14] Rear Echelon's necessary contacts with the War Department on "technical or administrative matters" forced Ferris to organize his own office of record.[15] The radio teams of the 835th Signal Service Company tied together these several American installations.

The G-1 Section in Chungking attempted to direct personnel matters for the theater until June 1943. Throughout this period the G-1 officer was handicapped by the lack of personnel statistics available to his assistant in New Delhi.[16] The G-2 Section in Chungking was rudimentary, with two officers and one enlisted man, one officer being the Order of Battle Section. As plans for the Burma operation progressed, G-2 in Chungking was compelled to rely heavily on General Headquarters (India), which was very helpful.[17] It was not possible for Stilwell to set up his own intelligence net in China Theater, for there the Generalissimo was Supreme Commander, and a chief of staff

[11] Memo cited n. 8(2); Memo with Incl, Ferris for Stilwell, 18 Dec 42. Corresp Folder (Mar–Dec 42), CT 23, Dr 2, KCRC.
[12] *Ibid.*
[13] *Ibid.*
[14] Memo, Stilwell for his Comd, 19 Nov 42. Corresp Folder (Mar–Dec 42), CT 23, Dr 2, KCRC.
[15] History of CBI, Sec. III, Ch. XIII, Administration.
[16] History of CBI, Sec. III, Ch. XIII, G-1 Section.
[17] History of CBI, Sec. III, Ch. XIII, G-2 Section.

does not set up an intelligence system in rivalry with his commander. The same situation obtained in India, where Wavell was Supreme Commander.

The G-3 Section in New Delhi continued to work on plans for the recapture of Burma, which Ferris had started immediately after the evacuation of Burma. G-3 was also concerned with procuring, moving, and training troops. It was initially handicapped by the absence of any directive for troop deployment to CBI. There were no American combat troops in CBI, so it was not possible for G-3 to say: "We have fifteen divisions allotted to us, therefore we need so many service troops, making our grand total 750,000 men."[18] Rather, troops were needed and allotted as successive projects were added to support China or Pacific operations. Until May 1943 Stilwell's headquarters, SOS, and the Tenth Air Force each submitted requisitions for troops directly to the War Department. In connection with forward planning of supply and construction requirements, the G-3 Section in New Delhi was called on to prepare estimates of troop strengths, so that the Government of India and General Headquarters (India) could have a basis for estimating American requests for supplies and labor. Under the circumstances suggested above, in 1942–1943 these estimates were little better than educated guesses, always likely to be overturned by the next great international conference.[19]

The G-4 Section in Chungking was small and often inadequate to cope with its tasks. The Delhi section worked under better conditions, disposing of more ample resources, and it was able to plan and carry out the re-equipping of the Chinese forces that retreated on India. The Chungking G-4 Section was the liaison with the Chinese Government for supplies for the Thirty Divisions and for the AAF installations in Yunnan and the east. Though the Chinese intent often seemed good, American staff officers found their administrative practices hard to bear and administrative problems were many.[20]

Transportation and related problems, such as procurement of gasoline and alcohol for motor fuel, road building, and maintenance, were the subjects of many conferences and many American promptings. Insufficient Chinese appropriations, the Chinese policy of meeting budgetary deficits by printing money, and price control regulations that made the cost of the raw materials greater than the price of the finished product kept Chinese industrial production at a fraction of capacity. Generally, at any given point in China, Chinese contributions to the war effort were limited to what the local countryside could spare.[21]

During the fall of 1942, lend-lease requisitions came to the War Department from Chinese agencies and from the Chungking and New Delhi head-

---

[18](1) Ltr, Ferris to Sunderland, cited n. 9. (2) History of CBI, Sec. III, Ch. XIII, Administration.
[19] History of CBI, Sec. III, Ch. XIII, G-3 Section.
[20] History of CBI, Sec. III, Ch. XIII, G-4 Section.
[21] *Ibid.*

quarters for the units to be equipped in India and China. There was no theater effort to co-ordinate or screen these requests on behalf of Stilwell as lend-lease representative.[22]

By the end of September 1942 Stilwell received preliminary indications of what the War Department's reply to the modified Three Demands would be. While there was no immediate hope for U.S. ground troops, a 500-plane air force was promised, and the 3,500 tons a month lend-lease program for the Chinese Army would continue. These resources, plus those that could be procured locally, were all that would be at Stilwell's disposal. Nevertheless, he had deployed his U.S. forces from Karachi to Kunming to assist the Chinese in getting ready for the first phase of the proposed offensive. Of necessity, the creation of two headquarters, of an enlarged Services of Supply with three base sections and three advance sections, and of the Tenth Air Force, had been ordered in advance of approved War Department Tables of Organization and Equipment. To man his theater, Stilwell endeavored to keep his staff small since all personnel so far had come from the casual movements sent to the CBI in the spring of 1942. At the beginning of October only one major head-quarters, Tenth Air Force, had a Table of Distribution, and even its subordinate commands were created and operated without such tables.[23] On 5 October, as a result of a conference among the New Delhi headquarters, Tenth Air Force, and the Services of Supply, tentative Tables of Distribution for a theater headquarters, a rear echelon, and both major operating commands were forwarded to Stilwell. He studied them carefully in the light of future necessity as suggested by the progress of his negotiations with Chinese and British authority, but it was not until 21 January 1943 that the War Department was willing for the tables to take effect in the CBI Theater.[24]

Tenth Air Force Plans and Organization

The only U.S. combat unit at Stilwell's disposal was the Tenth Air Force with its subordinate China Air Task Force. Brereton's absence in Egypt left the Tenth with only an acting commanding general until 18 August. The War Department had hesitated to approve Stilwell's candidate, General Bissell, because of Chinese opposition. Bissell's appointment, however, had merit as far as Arnold and Stilwell were concerned. He had been Stilwell's staff air officer since February; he had weathered the Generalissimo's disappointment

---

[22] *Ibid.*

[23] (1) Notes, Conf, Br Office with CGs, SOS and Tenth Air Force, 3 Oct 42. Corresp Folder (Mar–Nov 42), CT 23, Dr 2, KCRC. (2) CM–OUT 8582, Marshall to Stilwell, 25 Sep 42.

[24] (1) Memo, Sibert for Stilwell, 5 Oct 42, sub: Sp T/O Theater Hq. Item 289, Corresp Folder (1941–42), CT 23, Dr 2, KCRC. "A presumption [*sic*] was made in this study that a Head-quarters would be maintained in both Chungking and New Delhi; also that the theater com-mander would become the field commander. This would necessitate an adequate mobile Head-quarters which would in turn include a very mobile small command group." (2) GO 4, Forward Echelon, Hq USAF CBI, 21 Jan 43.

on each of China's aviation projects, and he had laid the basis for deploying part of the Tenth Air Force to China Theater. Bissell was well aware of the logistical problems of putting and maintaining air power in the CBI Theater. He was also coping daily with the political problems involved.[25]

Almost immediately after Brereton's departure the British Joint Staff Mission in Washington (British liaison with the Joint Chiefs of Staff) proposed that the Tenth be placed at the disposal of and under the control of the Air Officer Commanding-in-Chief (India). In the light of the Three Demands crisis such action would have had a bad effect on the Chinese. The Joint Chiefs of Staff, therefore, assured the British that, if a threat to India developed, Stilwell would co-operate with Wavell in meeting it. In accordance with this policy, co-ordination between the Tenth and the Royal Air Force was maintained by liaison and daily conferences.[26]

To strengthen Stilwell's hand in getting the Chinese to moderate their demands and to proceed along the lines of Stilwell's proposals to the Generalissimo, the War Department during July outlined the aircraft strength that the Tenth would have by 30 September. It would be brought to 160 fighters, 57 medium bombers, 35 heavy bombers, and 13 P-38's.[27] Assuming this combat strength, plus the long-standing promise to put 75 C-47's with the Tenth and 25 transports in the China National Aviation Corporation, Stilwell's air planners envisaged a balanced air force for the CBI Theater. Aware of British concerns in India, but with his 18 July proposal to the Generalissimo more in mind, Stilwell told the War Department about his plan for using the Tenth Air Force.[28]

Basically, Stilwell's air plan envisaged support for the Chinese ground effort into Burma, operation and defense of the Hump in order to bring 3,500 tons a month to the Yunnan build-up, and aviation gasoline and spare parts for Chennault. This last objective was already being developed, and the Tenth's units were being deployed accordingly. On 6 July the China Air Task Force, consisting of the 23d Pursuit Group (74th, 75th, and 76th Squadrons), with

[25](1) Rad 921, Marshall to Stilwell, 29 Jun 42; Rad 892, Stilwell to Marshall, 30 Jun 42; Rad 976, AGWAR to Stilwell, 8 Jul 42; Rad 942, Stilwell to Marshall, 14 Jul 42; Rad 1020, Arnold to Stilwell, 17 Jul 42; Rad 967, Stilwell to Arnold, 20 Jul 42; Rad 1133, Marshall to Stilwell, 4 Aug 42. Bk 1, JWS Personal File. (2) Craven and Cate, eds., *The Army Air Forces,* I, pp. 508–13. (3) MS, History of the Tenth Air Force Headquarters for the Calendar Year, 1942, and from 1 January to 31 May 1943. USAF Hist Div. (4) SO 41, Br Office, Hq USAF CBI, 18 Aug 42.

[26] Ltr with Incl, Air Marshal Douglas C. S. Evill to Arnold, 3 Jul 42; Ltr, Arnold to Evill, 14 Jul 42. WDCSA (China), A45–466.

[27](1) On 18 August the War Department again proposed to place the above planes in the Tenth Air Force. Moreover, Stilwell was promised 1,700 men a month to bring the Tenth to full strength by January 1943. Ltr, Streett to Stilwell, 18 Aug 42, sub: Status of Units of Tenth Air Force. Item 271, Misc Corresp Folder (Jul 42–Nov 43), CT 23, Dr 2, KCRC. (2) On 12 October 1942 the President assured the Generalissimo that the Tenth Air Force would contain the above strength. Item 54, OPD Exec 10.

[28](1) CM–OUT 6392, Marshall to Stilwell, 22 Jul 42. (2) CM–IN 8729, Stilwell to Marshall, 25 Jul 42. (3) The China Air War Plan, discussed in Chapter V, above, concerned the Tenth's role in China Theater where Stilwell was under the Generalissimo. Stilwell's plan in CM–IN 8729 was also concerned with India and Burma.

the 16th Fighter Squadron attached, plus the 11th Bombardment Squadron (B-25's), was activated. On 8 July Chennault assumed command. He had 56 P-40's (only 30 were operational) and 8 B-25's (7 operational). The small size of Chennault's force was often mentioned in the U.S. press.

To balance the China Air Task force, Stilwell planned to place similar fighter and medium bomber forces in upper Assam. (The India Air Task Force was activated formally on 3 October with Brig. Gen. Caleb V. Haynes commanding.) With a task force at either end of the Hump the newly activated India–China Ferry Command (15 July 1942) could operate with greater security. The B-24's promised by Marshall were to be based in India, where they could bomb strategic targets in Burma or move into China Theater, if and when they could be supported there. At the air gateway to the CBI Theater, the Tenth set up a Karachi American Air Base Command under the command of General Brady. His mission was primarily to receive and train crews for combat and transport operations. Logistical support for the Tenth came from its own Air Service Command, which got a new Commanding Officer, Col. Robert C. Oliver, on 14 August 1942.[29]

Oliver continued to build on the organization which he inherited from Brig. Gen. Elmer E. Adler, who had activated the Tenth's Air Service Command on 1 May 1942 with headquarters at New Delhi. Service command personnel came from the 51st Air Base Group, which on 12 March became the first troop unit to reach the CBI. Headquarters and Headquarters Squadron and the 54th Air Base Squadron of the 51st Group remained at Karachi. The 59th Matériel Squadron was divided into detachments and deployed at airfields across India and in China. On 16 May the 3d Air Depot Group disembarked at Karachi and soon moved to Agra. When Oliver assumed command, the Air Service Command had base units operating at Agra, Allahabad, Chakulia, Bangalore, Dinjan, and Chabua, in India, and at Kunming, China.[30]

The Air Service Command worked with and through Wheeler's SOS in the procurement of common usage items, and in transportation, except by air, required for movement of all supplies. Quartermaster supplies for the Tenth Air Force came from Wheeler. In addition to supplying and transporting supplies for the Tenth, the Air Service Command repaired, overhauled, salvaged, and manufactured aircraft. An outstanding result of this effort was the activities of the Hindustan Aircraft Corporation at Bangalore. The company was owned

---

[29](1) CM-IN 1403, Stilwell to AGWAR, 4 Jul 42. (2) By merging the Trans-India and Assam–Burma–China Ferry Commands on 15 July, the India–China Ferry Command under General Naiden was activated. Ltr Order, signed Naiden, Hq Tenth USAF CBI, 9 Jul 42. AG 320.2. (3) Ltr, Bissell to Chennault, 25 Sep 42, sub: CATF. Item 268, Misc Corresp Folder (May–Dec 42), CT 23, Dr 2, KCRC. (4) Rad 401, Naiden to Chennault, 7 Jul 42. AG (Tenth AF 322. (5) Ltr, Naiden to CO, Trans-India Ferry Comd, and CO, Assam–Burma–China Ferry Comd, 9 Jul 42. Item 221, Misc Corresp Folder (May–Dec 42), CT 23, Dr 2, KCRC. (6) *Time*, July 20, August 3, 18, 24, 1942. (7) Craven and Cate, eds., *The Army Air Forces*, I, p. 495. (8) History of CBI, Sec. II, Ch. VI, Air Service Command.

[30] History of CBI, Sec. II, Ch. VI, Air Service Command.

by Mysore and the Government of India. In addition to manufacturing and repairing planes for its owners, the plant was committed to manufacture fifty single-engined Vultees for the Chinese Republic. On 5 August the Hindustan Aircraft Corporation agreed to service, repair, overhaul, and fabricate all necessary parts of American-produced aircraft, engines, and equipment "regardless of use." At first the venture looked promising for the Tenth.[31]

Although the logistical situation in India was potentially better, Chennault had some local resources to operate on until the Hump could expand. A June survey of Chinese stocks, which the Generalissimo said could be used but would have to be replaced, revealed that (a) 72 P-40's could fly 18 missions a month for three and a half months, (b) 11 B-25's could fly 8 missions during the same period, and (c) 12 B-24's could stage 2 missions over the same period. Spare parts, ammunition, and personnel supplies, however, were in very short supply.[32]

During the fall of 1942 the Tenth Air Force could not reveal its full potentialities. It was a time of preparation and orientation. The Tenth was dependent on the 12,000-mile supply route from the United States. Often there were diversions of aircraft and supplies along the way. The Indian transportation system between Karachi and the Assam fields was inefficient and was heavily burdened by the needs of the Indian divisions (4 Corps) and the Royal Air Force squadrons concentrating in northeastern India to guard against a possible Japanese invasion. The Indian environment was bad for both the Americans and the aircraft; heat and disease racked the aircrews and abrasive dust ground down the engines. General Arnold believed that there had been lack of proper attention by the Tenth's senior officers to the requirements of their men.[33]

But over and above its logistic difficulties the Tenth Air Force faced basic problems of strategy and command. If the Allies agreed, the Tenth was in position to play its tactical role. Each day of delay in agreeing on strategy meant that the Tenth would continue to fight on the principle of co-operation with the British and Chinese rather than in an Allied command with them. Difficulties and differences continued to breed as long as this condition existed. Airfield construction, deployment of units, operation of a transport line, selection of targets, allocation of aircraft and air forces supply, and related problems necessarily moved from both Bissell and Stilwell for higher authority to solve.[34]

[31] Ltr, Bissell to Stilwell, 3 Sep 42. Item 249, Misc Corresp Folder (May–Dec 42), CT 23, Dr 2, KCRC.
[32] CM–IN 9114, Stilwell to Marshall, 27 Jun 42.
[33] (1) Ltr, Arnold to Bissell, 12 Sep 42. Incl to Item 206, Bk 3, JWS Personal File. (2) Craven and Cate, eds., *The Army Air Forces,* I, pp. 510–12. (3) Hist Sec (India), India at War, 1939–1943, pp. 107–08. Gen Ref Br, OCMH. (4) Brief History of the AAF in India and Burma, 1941–43. File 825.01, USAF Hist Div. (5) RAF Narrative, The Campaigns in the Far East, III, India Command, September 1939 to November 1943, p. 82. USAF Hist Div.
[34] See Ch. VII, pp. 250ff., Ch. VIII, pp. 266–92, Ch. IX, pp. 313–27, below.

The Services of Supply: The Indian Base

The original War Department directive on 28 February to General Wheeler ordered him:

> To take necessary action required to push equipment and supplies through to General Stilwell and to assume all supply and administrative functions in India necessary to successful functioning of his command.
> To investigate and report upon special supply requirements; supplies locally procurable; special supply difficulties and the availability of storage space.[35]

The mission received more precise definition in April 1942:

> 1. Operate the Services of Supply from base ports in India forward to include the railheads, river heads, and air line terminal in Assam. [*Map 7**]
> 2. Supply all U.S. ground forces in this theater of operations and the U.S. Air Forces to the extent requested by the Commanding General, American Air Forces in India.
> 3. Receive, warehouse, assemble and transport Chinese lend-lease and other government supplies.[36]

The scene of Wheeler's principal activities, India, was 12,000 miles from his port of embarkation, Los Angeles. The round trip by sea required about four months. India's military resources were at the disposal of General Headquarters (India), whose attention was largely fixed on the Middle East. Though the Indian Army and the Government of India were very generous, still, the American military were as guests in another's home; the Americans could ask but could not command. Nationalist sentiment and Japanese successes greatly affected the Indian mind in summer 1942. The Government of India saw the Americans with their needs as another factor in a complex and unstable situation, while Gandhi feared that the Americans were there simply to assist British rule. It is an irony of history that the soldiers brought to Asia to support Chinese nationalism were suspect to its Indian counterpart.[37]

India was not a perfect base. Some 400,000,000 Indians weighed heavily on the agricultural resources of a land just entering upon the industrial revolution. There was no surplus capacity for unproductive military effort; Indian contributions were sacrifices. The climate and sanitary conditions were especially bad in those portions of India nearest to China, where the major part of the U.S. effort would necessarily be exerted. More than one hundred inches of rain a year fell in many places in Assam, one spot receiving more than 1,000 inches. Intestinal disease, malaria, plague, and smallpox were endemic. The difficulty of obtaining good fresh food in Assam made it worth while to fly perishables

---

[35] History of Services of Supply, China, India, Burma Theater, 28 February 1942–24 October 1944, p. 1. Gen Ref Br, OCMH. (Hereafter, SOS in CBI.)

[36] MS, History of SOS, USAF CBI, 42–43. Gen Ref Br, OCMH.

[37] (1) Memo, John P. Davies, Jr., Second Secy of U.S. Embassy, atchd to stf of CG, USAF CBI, for Stilwell, 14 May 42, with Incl, "Foreign Soldiers in India," by M. K. Gandhi, *Harijan,* April 26, 1942. History of CBI, Sec. III, Ch. X. (2) CM–OUT 1740, Marshall to Stilwell, 6 Aug 42.

* Inside back cover.

from China to India occasionally on returning transport aircraft. Soldiers lost weight and grew tired and listless because of vitamin deficiency.[38]

Shipping was always the sovereign influence on Allied strategy and to economize it the U.S. forces were directed to make the maximum possible use of local resources. The port situation added weight to this policy. Bombay, then the best port in India, was "hopelessly clogged with mismanaged Allied shipping."[39] Calcutta, the second best, was so exposed to enemy air attack in 1942 as to be thought unusable. And Karachi, the third choice, was separated from the Assam air bases by the whole width of India.[40] This expanse was inadequately bridged by the Indian rail net. From Karachi to Delhi, rail traffic passed over a broad-gauge line, part of it double-tracked, that linked Karachi with the hinterland north of Delhi. From Delhi eastward connections were good until Assam was reached, where the real bottleneck was to be found in the Assam line of communications. As the SOS history describes it:

> The Assam LOC [Line of Communications] consisted of broad gauge lines of the Bengal and Assam Railway northward from Calcutta to Santahar and Parbatipur; meter gauge lines of the Bengal and Assam railway running eastward from Santahar and Parbatipur to northern Assam; meter gauge lines of the B & A Railway in east Bengal running eastward from a Brahmaputra River ferry connection with the Santahar Branch and northward from Chittagong to a junction with the main lines at Lumding; barge lines on the Brahmaputra River; combinations of rail and barge lines utilizing various transshipment points along the river.[41]

The broad-gauge section of the line seemed more than able to carry all the traffic that the meter-gauge section could take. The meter-gauge lines had been laid out to support the vast tea gardens of Assam, whose demands were light, and the intermediate managerial staff found it hard to cope with the growth of traffic from three or four trains a day to fourteen. Added to the inherent limitations of meter gauge and inexperienced personnel were the lack of adequate transshipment facilities from broad to meter gauge; the absence of a bridge across the Brahmaputra, which made ferries necessary; the heavy grade between Lumding and Manipur; the general shortage of rolling stock; and the frequent interruptions of traffic by the monsoon.[42]

General Headquarters (India) had been well aware of this, and in summer 1942 suggested that U.S. railway troops operate key sections of the line. In compliance with the War Department's desire that they function with a minimum of U.S. troops, Stilwell and Wheeler declined the invitation. It may also be surmised that they were reluctant to assume added responsibility in an area that a few months before had been designated one of British responsibility.

---

[38](1) SOS in CBI, pp. 3–4, 425. (2) SOS in CBI, App. 16, Medical Section, p. 16.

[39] SOS in CBI, pp. 3–4, 123, 131.

[40] MS 428, Army Service Forces Activities in the Supply of China, Burma, and India, 1942–1943, p. 20. Gen Ref Br, OCMH.

[41] SOS in CBI, p. 48.

[42] SOS in CBI, pp. 48–52.

Nor was there yet the general recognition of the importance of the Assam line of communications which came later.[43]

In summer 1942 the British interest in the Assam line of communications was dominant. The line of communications served not only the American airfields which supported Chennault but the British 4 Corps in Manipur State and the tea industry. The tea gardens played the same role in sustaining the British civilian population that the coffee plantations of South America did for the American people. Whether the air raid warden in a London suburb would have his cup of hot tea after a difficult night with the German bombers depended in large measure on the tonnage allocations made by civilian agencies responsible to the Government of India, which sometimes gave short-commons to the Americans.[44]

First Plans and the Karachi Area

The first American troop units in CBI were the air force personnel diverted from Java by General Brett. They arrived at Karachi on 12 March 1942 with 28 trucks, some bombs, and some small arms ammunition, and needing 619 trucks with other items in proportion. Stilwell's task force received overseas shipment of ten months' rations for 1,000 men, 155- and 105-mm. howitzers, rifles, machine guns, ammunition, a few vehicles, some communications equipment, and six 50-bed hospitals. The first SOS troop units—the 393d Quartermaster Battalion (Port) and the 159th Station Hospital—arrived at Karachi on 16 May 1942.[45]

The initial War Department supply plan of 28 February 1942 directed that everything possible be procured locally, that six months' supplies of food and clothing be kept in India for all troops, and that an additional nine months' level be kept in China for 1,000 men. The directives of summer 1942 retained the six months' level for India and defined it as including supplies at the port of embarkation and in transit. Because India was so far from the United States the supply position was therefore precarious. The War Department ordered further that requisitions had to be for actual rather than projected strengths; since CBI personnel increased 500 percent between March and December 1942, the SOS had to run hard just to stay in place.[46]

Base Section No. 1 at Karachi was activated on 27 May 1942, Col. Paul F. Yount commanding, its initial area comprising 360,000 square miles. Present

---

[43] History of CBI, Sec. II, Ch. X, p. 1.

[44] MS, History and Development of the Assam LOC, pp. 1–3, Movement and Transportation Div, Hq SACSEA. Gen Ref Br, OCMH.

[45] Strength Rpts, USAF CBI, Feb–May 42, OPD Green Book (Asiatic Sec). Gen Ref Br, OCMH.

[46] Rpt on Activities of Quartermaster Serv, Col Harvey Edward, Theater Quartermaster, 15 Aug 42. Misc Corresp Folder (Mar–Dec 42), CT 23, Dr 2, KCRC.

in the area were 1,033 U.S. personnel, almost half of them medical. Because Wheeler had opened SOS headquarters at Karachi a few days before, offices, barracks, and staging areas had been obtained from General Headquarters (India).[47]

Most deficiencies in supplies were filled by reverse lend-lease (henceforth, reciprocal aid) from India, some by open-market purchase. Often, ingenuity was needed. One hundred and two sedans were bought in Karachi; 172 truck chassis were found in Bombay and wooden beds and cabs were made for them in Lahore. Cargo diverted from Rangoon and Singapore yielded much signal equipment, office furniture, and tools. The Chinese agreed to the transfer of many supplies from their lend-lease. Subsistence came from local firms on a contract basis.

Building was accomplished by submitting requests to SOS headquarters, which passed them to General Headquarters (India), which in turn gave them to the Royal Engineers for performance. Sometimes as long as three months was needed to obtain sanction, and the actual construction, when finally begun, was done by primitive methods under the supervision of the Base Section engineer. The picture was one of U.S. engineers supervising work and handling heavy equipment, aided by great numbers of Indian laborers. Under these handicaps, work went forward, and by the end of 1942 the Karachi base had a staging area at North Malir cantonment, with accommodations for about 20,000 men, barracks for about 2,000, a well-equipped air base with several landing fields, a depot area with railway spurs, and the other physical equipment of a functioning base.

Some 1,500 Indian employees of all types, from typists to dock coolies, were employed on a reciprocal aid basis, with a consequent economy of U.S. manpower and funds.[48]

In addition to procuring and distributing supplies for the U.S. forces, the Karachi base had 20,000 long tons of Chinese lend-lease to safeguard. These vital supplies had been casually dumped at Karachi with no attempt to inventory, classify, or safeguard them, or even to clear them from the docks, while the Chinese in Washington were demanding that more supplies be shipped to India immediately. The SOS obtained 1,000,000 square feet of open storage plus 100,000 square feet of covered storage, and in three months 15,000 long tons of Chinese lend-lease were cleared off the docks and properly stored by SOS. In performing its duties of receipt and distribution, Base Section No. 1 unloaded 130,342 long tons at Karachi between March and December 1942 and shipped forward 54,140 long tons to other parts of the theater. A large portion of lend-lease ordnance was sent to Ramgarh for training purposes.[49]

[47] GO 6, Hq SOS USAF CBI, 27 May 42.
[48] (1) Rpt cited n. 46. (2) SOS in CBI, App. 12, pp. 5–21.
[49] SOS in CBI, App. 2, Base Section No. 1, Sec. I, pp. 1, 2, 5, 8–13, 21.

SOS Expands Across India Into China

Base Section No. 2, with headquarters at Calcutta, began slowly and haltingly because of its exposure to air attack from Japanese bases in Burma. Its existence was authorized on 27 May 1942. The first commanding officer, Lt. Col. Edwin M. Sutherland, took up his duties on 22 June 1942, with a total personnel of four officers, and the section's first troops, Company E, 45th Engineers with attached medical personnel, arrived on 20 September 1942 from Karachi. The first cargo arrived on 24 September, and by the end of the year a total of 9,686.5 tons was unloaded.[50]

Farther down the coast of India and out of range of all but the four-motored Kawanishi flying boats and raiding carrier aircraft were the ports of Madras and Vizagapatam. Unfortunately, these had but nine shipping berths between them, and moving cargo from them to Assam would mean more strain on the creaky rail system. Calcutta's facilities were excellent, and as soon as the threat of Japanese air attack lifted it was the obvious choice for a base to support the American effort in Assam.

By authority of expediency the engineers were used as a port company. Americans were used as guards and checkers, and Indians were used for the other posts. Fourteen vehicles were on hand for all purposes. By the end of the year, when the engineers were sent to Assam to resume their normal role, Base Section No. 2's strength dropped to eleven officers and eighty-nine enlisted men.[51]

There were, however, obvious indications that this was only a lull. It had always been apparent that Karachi was poorly sited to be the main U.S. base, so in late summer 1942 SOS urged that the United States accept the hazards involved in making Calcutta the principal American base in India. Stilwell approved of Calcutta's use on 31 August 1942 and planning for the change began.[52]

There were many obstacles to be overcome before Calcutta could be an efficiently functioning base. The city, India's largest, was overcrowded; its people were strongly nationalist, and pro-Japanese sentiment was present; the food situation, soon to lead to a great famine, was already precarious. There were grave civil disturbances in Bengal Province during August 1942 when nationalist extremists sabotaged communications and attacked police stations. Strict neutrality was enjoined on the U.S. forces. Nevertheless, Calcutta was the logical base for Assam, so planning and preparation proceeded.[53]

Advance Section No. 1 under Maj. Henry C. Willcox, with headquarters temporarily at Agra, and later Allahabad, was activated on 27 May 1942 to "serve Air Force units within its area, to take delivery from British depots, and

[50] SOS in CBI, App. 3, Base Section No. 2, Sec. I, pp. 1–3, 5, 6, 8–13, Table 4.
[51] *Ibid.*
[52] SOS in CBI, App. 3, Secs. II, IIIA.
[53] (1) Document, p. 117, cited n. 33(3). (2) CM–IN 5162, Stilwell to Marshall, 13 Aug 42.

to expedite shipments to forward areas."[54] Its first depot operated at Allahabad from July to December. The second depot opened at Gaya in November, assumed the responsibility for handling airfreight to China in December, and was redesignated Air Freight Reception and Discharge Depot No. 1.[55]

Advance Section No. 2 under Maj. Henry A. Byroade, activated on 27 May 1942, in northeastern India, had for its principal mission support of Tenth Air Force units flying cargo to China and the supplying of cargo to be carried by them. "It controlled the changeover from rail and river transportation to air transport of all supplies and equipment going in to China." Its Advance General Depot No. 2 was the railhead for supplies received and the supply point for troops within the area of the section.[56]

The SOS established itself in China with the activation of Advance Section No. 3 on 11 June 1942, with headquarters opened at Kunming soon after. Its supply levels were dependent on what could be flown in from India. The supply situation in China differed from the customary in that the Chinese Government undertook to provide food and shelter for the Americans in hostels run by its War Area Service Command, thus substantially limiting the sphere of the SOS. To supervise and control lend-lease for the Thirty Divisions, Stilwell established an Eastern Section, SOS, under Col. Fabius H. Kohloss, which would have no territorial boundaries but would operate like a G–4 section in maintaining liaison between SOS and the Chinese in regard to lend-lease questions. Colonel Kohloss was also charged with the planning for rehabilitation of the Chinese section of the Burma Road in preparation for any offensive into Burma that might be launched from China.[57]

Local Procurement

By August 1942 Wheeler could report to Stilwell "that the U.S. Forces were practically living off the land."[58] In India this involved a major feat of administration, based on the generous help of the Government of India, which in turn rested upon the real sacrifices of the Indian people. The basis of agreement between the U.S. Forces and the Government of India was given in a cable from the Secretary of State for India, from London, on 7 February 1942:

[54] GO cited n. 47.
[55] The airfreight reception and discharge depots were conveniently located near the chain of Tenth Air Force fields across India and China. SOS operated these installations, which were not depots in the general sense. Airfreight priority shipments were received, checked, and routed to the ultimate consignee within forty-eight hours. In this respect, the airfreight depots were merely clearing stations. Circular 12, Hq SOS USAF CBI, 3 Jul 42, and Memo 35, Hq SOS USAF CBI, 11 Jul 42.
[56] GO cited n. 47.
[57] (1) Ltr Order, Wheeler to Kohloss, 26 Nov 42. Hq Y–Force Operations Staff Files, KCRC. (2) Colonel Kohloss ordered his engineer, Maj. Louis Y. Dawson, to work with the Chinese in rehabilitating the Burma Road from Kunming to Pao-shan. The estimated cost for restoring and widening the highway amounted to CN (Chinese Nationalist currency) $117,424,400. Rpts 1, 2, Dawson to Kohloss, 26 Jan 43, sub: Yunnan–Burma Highway. AG (Y–FOS) 611, KCRC.
[58] (1) SOS in CBI, p. 132. (2) Rpt cited n. 46.

The U.S.A. authorities have called to our attention the importance of arrangements being made as soon as possible regarding the facilities and articles which the United Kingdom and Dominion Governments can furnish the U.S. Present and future dispositions of the U.S. Forces make prompt consideration of these questions of what may be described as "Reverse Lend Lease" desirable for practical purposes and we wish to approach the matter in a generous spirit. However, to give complete reciprocity is impossible. One of the main objects of Lend Lease has been to obtain from the U.S.A. those munitions and materials for which we could not pay out of our dollar resources and current dollar earnings. We still have considerable dollar commitments in the U.S.A. arising from pre-lend lease contracts and not all our requirements are being obtained under Lend Lease. We cannot therefore afford to reduce our current dollar earnings by foregoing payment of raw materials and commercial supplies. We should then transfer to the U.S.A. on Lend Lease terms war munitions and military stores (and analagous services such as servicing or repairing such stores) whether these are issues from stores or involve the placing of a special contract in this country. We should include machine tools in munitions for this purpose. We should sell stores to contractors working for the U.S. Raw materials and commercial supplies we would continue to sell for cash.[59]

On receipt of this cable an agreement became a matter of defining terms to mutual satisfaction. It was agreed on 22 March 1942 that "raw materials and commercial supplies" meant those articles normally exported by India to the United States, such as mica, jute goods, hog bristles, manganese, shellac, and chromite, of which only jute for sandbags and sacking would figure in SOS's calculations. "Military stores" were agreed to include everything the Army used, including timber, cement, steel, and coal, though the Indian representatives pointed out to Wheeler that steel was in extremely short supply.[60]

Provision of rations was questioned by the Government of India because of the bad local food situation, but Generals Brereton and Wheeler pointed out that food could be imported from the United States only by sacrificing badly needed arms and that the Quartermaster General (India) had stated he could supply 50,000 U.S. troops. The trend of discussion revealed that the Indian authorities with whom Wheeler was negotiating were disposed to place a liberal interpretation upon the 7 February cable from London and to do their best to supply the Americans. In this favorable atmosphere negotiations prospered, and on 8 June Wheeler with Somervell's approval informed the Government of India that he accepted their most recent proposals, which were then distributed as a letter of instructions from the Government of India to all Indian Army agencies.[61]

The agreement provided that the SOS would obtain the bulk of its requirements by requisition on the Government of India. Demands would be placed through SOS headquarters rather than through the section commanders. A priority board would consider the supply aspects, and a lend-lease committee, the eligibility for transfer of the items sought. Actual procurement would be

[59] SOS in CBI, pp. 124–25.
[60] SOS in CBI, pp. 123–28.
[61] Ibid.

through normal Government of India channels. In requisitioning construction, U.S. forces would accept the usual Indian Army scale of office or housing accommodations or pay cash for desired additional facilities. Supplies not obtained on reciprocal aid could be bought in the open market or imported from the United States. In regard to open-market buying, it was agreed that American commanders would not bid against one another or against the Government of India, nor would they embarrass the price and supply position prevailing. In practice this meant the co-ordination of all purchases over 1,000 rupees ($330.00) by SOS headquarters.[62]

Reciprocal aid was also extended to the Chinese Army in India, which was paid, fed, clothed, and housed thereby. Much of its ordnance came from U.S. lend-lease to China as did approximately 75 percent of its medical requirements.

Because of these agreements, by fall 1942 all rations were being procured locally except for canned fruits and vegetables which came from the United States and raw coffee which was bought in Brazil and ground in India. Indian coffee, without the chicory usually present, was later substituted. Specifications and patterns for clothing and web equipment were obtained from the United States, and contracts let to Indian factories. Aviation gasoline and motor fuel were being procured from local sources, which in turn were supplied from Iran. As a rule, lubricating oils and greases came from the United States. Office, signal, and electrical supplies were obtained locally, and many such items came from frustrated cargo originally bound for Southeast Asia.[63]

Unable to obtain data from the Government of India, SOS estimated that the U.S. forces received $36,000,000 reciprocal aid in 1942. The Government of India was unwilling to set a value on reciprocal aid. Repeated requests to India for such information were met with the argument that this would impose an administrative burden which India was not prepared to assume. The Americans were also told that the Government of India was not keeping any records showing the value of goods or services supplied to the United States under reciprocal aid. Since a postwar settlement of lend-lease accounts was expected in which the United States would be badly handicapped were it compelled to accept countering claims at face value, the SOS created its own system for appraising every item received and let its existence be known.[64]

The Reciprocal Aid System at Work

As both parties to the reciprocal aid agreement began to operate under it, difficulties soon arose from its application. There were two major areas in which differences were fairly numerous: SOS reluctance to accept Indian Army

[62] SOS in CBI, pp. 128–30.
[63] (1) SOS in CBI, pp. 132–34. (2) MS, pp. 159–61, cited n. 40.
[64] SOS in CBI, pp. 160–63.

standards of accommodation, and the reluctance of U.S. officers in the field to use the slow reciprocal aid machinery as against more rapid purchases in the open market. On the question of standards SOS contended that any requisition for the U.S. forces in India was by definition in furtherance of the war effort and so should be approved. The Government of India contended that additions to the Indian Army scale should be covered by American cash purchases. So many differences arose on this point that Wheeler was moved to draft a cable to the War Department summarizing the situation, which he then showed to the Quartermaster General (India).[65]

Conferences with the Government of India immediately followed. One point at issue was solved by the initiative of General Headquarters (India) in bringing their troops to a higher ration scale, while they yielded to Wheeler on the matter of woolen clothing, another disputed point. The matter was finally settled by a compromise agreement that U.S. requests would be considered on their own merits, that the United States would not ask for imported items, that differences would be resolved in India if at all possible, and that SOS would, on request, withdraw requisitions which might embarrass the Government of India.[66]

Local purchases offered even more complex problems. To American ways of thought, the supply mechanism of the Government of India was slow, but India could retort that in many cases local U.S. commanders did not preplan their requirements and allow enough time for procurement. Further, if rapid delivery was required, the local supplier was quite ready to exact an exorbitant price, and this the Government of India was unwilling to pay. There was also a general suspicion of the whole lend-lease process on the part of the Indian public, of which manufacturers and suppliers were part. The SOS was not always innocent, for at times it failed to take delivery of an item which it had earlier asked be procured. SOS fully shared India's views on the undesirability of SOS's operating in the open market, with all that such operations implied of bidding against the Government of India. So SOS set up a Procurement Section in fall 1942 to provide central control of all open-market purchases.[67]

The Procurement Section investigated Indian supply sources, screened requisitions on the United States from local commanders to make sure supplies could not be obtained locally, and examined, in the light of known market conditions, requests which India had rejected. In time the Procurement Section's efforts to cut local market purchases for the American forces met with real success.

The Procurement Section also improved the functioning of reciprocal aid. Close liaison was maintained with American diplomatic and consular agencies

---

[65] SOS in CBI, pp. 137–40.
[66] Ibid.
[67] (1) SOS in CBI, pp. 142–47. (2) GO 27, Hq SOS USAF CBI, 1 Sep 42. (3) Cf. Mohandas K. Gandhi in Harijan, 26 April 1942: "We know what American aid means. It amounts in the end to American influence, if not American rule added to British."

to gain the fullest knowledge of Indian resources and to expand them through nonmilitary lend-lease if local production might be increased thereby. Thus, tire-making equipment was ultimately lend-leased to Indian factories to permit them to supply SOS with automobile and aircraft tires under reciprocal aid.[68]

Lend-Lease Responsibilities

The SOS was an executive and not a policy-making organization for Chinese lend-lease and was charged with receiving, storing, and transshipping matériel in accord with directives from above. Because SOS had clerical and warehousing facilities, on 1 September 1942 the Chinese agreed to have SOS handle all the different varieties of matériel destined for China that had been diverted to India during and after the First Burma Campaign.[69]

These may be differentiated by the program under which they were procured or by the procuring agency.

1. By program:

a. Those items procured for the use of Ministries of the Chinese Government and for Chinese Troops other than those under American sponsorship or supervision. . . .

b. Those items procured for Chinese Troops under American sponsorship or supervision. . . .

2. By procurement:

a. Items procured by the War Department. . . .

b. Items procured by the Foreign Economic Administration. . . .

c. Items procured by the Universal Trading Corporation . . . a corporation set up to purchase for the use of the Chinese agencies non-military or indirect [*sic*] military material with cash loaned by the United States Government. . . .

d. Some small amounts of items procured from the British in India for use of the [U.S.-sponsored Chinese Forces]. . . .

e. Items of Canadian War Supplies under the Canadian Mutual Aid Program . . . the U.S. Army having only custody for purposes of receipt storage and onward movement to China.

Matériel was procured by the War Department and by the Foreign Economic Administration alike for Chinese and American programs, though generally items procured by the Foreign Economic Administration were for Chinese account and were nonmilitary in nature. Since each of the above types of matériel had different legal status, "The difficulties encountered in laying down general rules for the control, handling, and reporting of all types become readily apparent."

Initial handling of Chinese matériel was not systematic. Chinese requests for shipments from War Department procured stocks to China were made orally, and no confirming written directives were issued. Since China National Aviation Corporation flew Chinese matériel over the Hump, the United States was not further concerned once delivery was made to the corporation by the

[68] SOS in CBI, pp. 148–51, 157–59.

[69] Unless otherwise indicated, material in this section is drawn from SOS in CBI, App. 11, China Lend-Lease Section.

SOS. The earliest known tally-out for movement of Chinese matériel from Karachi to Assam is dated 11 June 1942. "No regular periodic reports of receipts and issues were instituted until September 1942. . . ."

The Chinese Board of Transport Control was charged with handling, storing, and transporting all matériel procured by the Chinese, how casually has been noted. Gradually the opinion grew that it would be best if SOS bore the sole responsibility for all goods destined for China, irrespective of their legal status, and that the entire process should be placed on a businesslike basis.

These trends finally crystallized in a new arrangement, which was made on 2 August 1942 between General Wheeler and Commissioner Shen Shih-hua of the Board of Transport Control. On 1 September 1942 SOS took over all lend-lease and Chinese-procured matériel then in India and assumed responsibility for future receipt, storage, and transshipment. This left the Chinese with the responsibility of calling forward matériel intended for Chinese agency programs, as air cargo space for China was available. As a result of the agreement, and of the Board of Transport Control's delegating so much of its responsibility, SOS inherited most of the Chinese commission's employees, over 400 of them in Assam alone.

The duties given to the SOS were a considerable step toward complete U.S. administrative control of the very considerable quantities of lend-lease that were in India and on the way there. As cargoes of lend-lease or related matériel were discharged at Karachi, SOS gave the Chinese a checked manifest and a tally-in sheet, both itemized in detail. As cargoes moved out of Karachi toward Assam and the airfields, SOS gave the Chinese shipping advices and tally-out sheets in complete detail. On arrival at Assam tally-in sheets went to the Chinese, and tally-out sheets were furnished when the goods left for China. Priorities were set by the Chinese for the movement of goods by China National Aviation Corporation transports. Stilwell set priorities for dispatch of cargo by U.S. aircraft.

This latter provision meant that as the proportion of U.S. aircraft flying cargo to China steadily increased, Stilwell's power to determine what cargo went to China increased with it. The Generalissimo's objections to Stilwell's role in the lend-lease field had been made clear in the Three Demands crisis. Now, administrative processes were extending this control. Since there was only so much air cargo space at his disposal, Stilwell, as events showed, was adamant that it should be used only for the effective prosecution of the war, which to him meant arms for the Thirty Divisions and supplies for Chennault's aircraft, in such proportions as Stilwell might determine.

Ramgarh Training Center

In April 1942 the Generalissimo gave his approval in principle to Stilwell's plan to train a Chinese Army in India. As the likelihood of defeat in Burma increased so did the number of the Generalissimo's reservations on Stilwell's 27 April plan, which was now in need of recasting. When the Chinese began to reach India, and the full impact of the Burma debacle was felt, the Generalissimo's initial reaction was to have his troops spend the next three months at the hill station of Darjeeling, from which they might retreat to China via Tibet should the Japanese attack India. On 24 June the Generalissimo went so far as to tell Stilwell he might send 50,000 men to India. On the 29th the Generalissimo approved Ramgarh in Bihar Province as a site, but by that time the Three Demands crisis was under way and so his approval on 2 July went to a much more modest scheme. Stilwell's alternate plan was: to train the 9,000 men as artillerists and heavy weapons specialists; to equip them with lend-lease arms; to organize them into ten artillery and four heavy weapons battalions; to move them into Burma in the wake of a British attack; then, to send them to Yunnan to give fire power to the Thirty Divisions. The Generalissimo agreed that Stilwell would command these troops and would control training and supply, with the Chinese handling discipline and administration.[70]

The facilities of Ramgarh were ample and suggested larger schemes. The camp had held 20,000 Italian prisoners of war and had actual housing facilities for 12,000 men. There was "a healthful climate and a low malarial rate . . . an open and contrasting terrain for training and firing ranges. Central lighting and water systems also had been installed, and messing, washing, and latrine facilities were available." If the sanitary facilities were improved, it was estimated that 20,000 men could be accommodated.[71]

With the improvement in Sino-American relations that followed Currie's visit, Stilwell returned to the idea of creating in India a Chinese Army able to play its part in retaking Burma. The Generalissimo was co-operative and agreed to provide 23,000 more men for Ramgarh, with which Stilwell could create by February 1943 a force of two full divisions, three artillery regiments, an engineer regiment, ten artillery battalions, and 1,500 Chinese instructors for thirty divisions. The plan thus hinged on the Government of India's approval of such an increase in the number of Chinese in India. It appeared a great step forward to Stilwell, who took the Generalissimo's approval as evidence that he was at least partly converted. If such was the case, then the approval was vital, for it would be extremely unwise to anger the Generalissimo at the moment he was consenting to accept U.S. aid.[72]

---

[70](1) CM-IN 0535, Gruber to Stilwell, 2 May 42. (2) CM-IN 0174, Gruber to Stilwell, 2 May 42. (3) CM-IN 7479, Chungking to AGWAR, 28 Apr 42. (4) CM-OUT 5677, Marshall to Stilwell, 29 Apr. 42. (5) CM-IN 5665, Stilwell to Stimson, 17 Jun 42. (6) CM-IN 0570, Stilwell to Marshall, 2 Jul 42. (7) Ltr, Ferris to COS, GHQ (India), 2 Aug 42. Folder, Chinese Army (Ramgarh), Gen Ref Br, OCMH. (8) History, pp. 1–2, cited n. 7(3). (9) *The Stilwell Papers*, p. 117.

[71](1) MS, Ramgarh Training Center, p. 4. Gen Ref Br, OCMH. (2)Ltr, McCabe to Sibert, 2 Jul 42, sub: Reception of Chinese Troops at Ramgarh. Folder, Chinese Army (Ramgarh), Gen Ref Br, OCMH.

[72] CM-IN 10253, Stilwell to Marshall, 22 Sep 42.

The proposal met with objections from Wavell, General Headquarters (India), and the Government of India. At first Wavell approved (27 September), but in two days he asked Stilwell for a formal written request, including the reasons. General Sibert replied for Stilwell, stating that the reason was to aid in the reconquest of Burma, and giving assurances that there was no plan to operate independently. In later discussions Wavell suggested a whole host of administrative difficulties, making the Ramgarh project seem impossible. Asked to intervene by Stilwell, Marshall went into action on the CCS level, placing his case before Field Marshall Sir John Dill of the Joint Staff Mission to Washington. Dill was told that Stilwell had to bear personally the Generalissimo's anger at the presence of Chinese troops in India. Reminding Dill of the original agreement to provide bases in India for Stilwell's operations, Marshall asked him to consider the consequences of an obstructive attitude by the Government of India. Marshall also told Roosevelt of the problem, saying he hoped to handle the matter through Dill but wanted the President to know of it. Dill's answers made it quite clear that the objections of the Government of India caused the difficulty.[73]

That body, possessed of great powers, had developed a policy of its own which did not always accord with the wishes of the War Cabinet. Dill told his American colleague that the British Chiefs of Staff favored the increase but the local authorities objected. The Government of India thought that the Generalissimo had been entirely too close to Indian nationalist opinion. Moreover, they disliked the contrast between a Chinese Army well equipped by lend-lease supplies and the Indian forces that they were then able to raise. Furthermore, the Government of India feared that if domestic troubles came to a head, the Chinese might side with the Congress Party.[74] Soon after, Stilwell was able to radio the good news that there was no further objection to an increase in the Ramgarh force, that the administrative problems had vanished: "Remarkable change. They must have gotten the word from London."[75]

Operation of Ramgarh Training Center

A venture in three-power co-operation, Ramgarh Training Center was formally activated on 26 August 1942. Indian authorities were responsible for providing the Chinese troops with rupees (for pay and local purchases), certain items of ordnance, medical stores and equipment, rations, gas and oil, transportation, and accommodations. Any items in the above categories which the

[73](1) *Ibid.* (2) Memo with Incl, Marshall for President, 10 Oct 42, sub: China-India-Stilwell. WDCSA (China), A45–466. (3) Rad, AMMDEL to AMMISCA, 29 Sep 42. Item 43, Bk 1, JWS Personal File. (4) Rad, Stilwell to Sibert, 30 Sep 42. Item 45, Bk 1, JWS Personal File. (5) Ltr, Sibert to GHQ (India), 1 Oct 42. Folder, Chinese Army (Ramgarh), Gen Ref Br, OCMH. (6) *The Stilwell Papers,* pp. 162–64. (7) Memo, Marshall for Dill, 6 Oct 42. WDCSA (China), A45–466. (8) CM–IN 4048, Stilwell to Marshall, 10 Oct 42.
[74] Ltrs, Dill to Marshall, 13, 19 Oct 42. WDCSA (China), A45–466.
[75](1) CM–IN 11578, Stilwell to Marshall, 27 Oct 42. (2) *The Stilwell Papers,* p. 164.

Indian authorities could not furnish, chiefly heavy ordnance equipment, including vehicles, were bought and charged against British lend-lease to China. The frustrated Chinese lend-lease cargo was a primary source for this latter item. The SOS placed requisitions on the Indian authorities on behalf of the Chinese forces, received supplies, and with them took care of supply and administration for the post, including medical care for the Chinese. The Chinese were responsible for unit administration and discipline and for supplying the men to be trained and equipped. Replacements and fillers provided the next major problem, as once again it appeared that the Generalissimo's formal engagement was not binding on his subordinates.[76]

In September replacements were not forthcoming to bring the 22d and 38th Divisions up to strength to meet the current Ramgarh plan, let alone the greater one that Stilwell was earnestly expounding. Colonel Aldrich, then commanding the Kunming Area Command, had to put the very heaviest pressure on Gen. Ma Tseng Liu, representative of the Ministry of War, to get the flow of troops from China to India via the airline under way. Stilwell's chief of staff, General Hearn, sent some rather strong letters to General Ho Ying-chin, for Stilwell insisted that after the trouble he had had in getting the Government of India's concurrence, the project must not be allowed to die of Chinese indifference. The actual passage of Chinese troops began on 20 October. Some 4,000 flew to India that month, but Stilwell was not satisfied and ordered his Chungking headquarters to remonstrate with Ho once again. This latter effort brought results. The Chinese soon passed the desired 400-a-day figure, and theater headquarters had to limit daily shipment to 650 because Assam transportation facilities were congested.[77]

Water supply was the chief barrier to the expansion of Ramgarh to hold 23,000 more Chinese troops. A camp site near by seemed promising, but it was very close to the Argada and Sirka coal mines. Coal was vital to the war effort; so when the mine operators argued that the Chinese would frighten away the unsophisticated jungle folk who dug the coal, their plea carried the day. The Chinese were then quartered on the south side of the Damodar River. When in 1943 the question arose again, the same objections were raised. This time they were ignored, and the presence of the Chinese had no discernible effect on the miners. Generally, the discipline of the Chinese Army in India was excellent.[78]

There were three headquarters at Ramgarh: the training center, the post, and Chih Hui Pu. Activated on 4 October, the last was headquarters for the Chinese Army in India, charged with administration and discipline of the

---

[76] MS, pp. 7–8, cited n. 71(1).

[77] (1) History of CBI, Sec. III, Ch. VI, Chinese Fillers Fly the Hump, pp. 1–4. (2) Memo, Boatner for Brig Gen William E. Bergin, CofS, Rear Echelon, Chih Hui Pu, 11 Jun 43, sub: Random Notes on Evolution and Organization of Chinese Army in India. Gen Ref Br, OCMH.

[78] SOS in CBI, pp. 490–92.

RAMGARH TRAINING CENTER, 1942. *Chinese troops are taught to use the U.S. Enfield rifle, above. Below, inspecting the troops. Left to right, Maj. Gen. Sun Li-jen, Lt. Gen. Lo Cho-ying, and General Stilwell.*

Chinese soldiers. Its combat role was as yet undecided. Stilwell commanded, General Lo was vice-commander, and Brig. Gen. Haydon L. Boatner was chief of staff. The question of who was actually the superior officer, Lo or Stilwell, arose in September, as it had a few months before in Burma, and in a brief passage at arms Stilwell broke the news to Lo that Lt. Gen. J. W. Stilwell commanded.[79] Stilwell also announced that Lo would not be given any lump sums from which to pay his troops, the customary procedure which permitted large amounts to stay in the commander's pockets.

This announcement was a preliminary skirmish, and battle was joined in October after the activation of Chih Hui Pu. Lo again demanded 450,000 rupees; and when told that 270,000 rupees, the amount actually required to pay the 22d and 38th Divisions, was at hand, he refused to have anything to do with it. His attitude plainly revealed his belief that the Americans were whimsically and arbitrarily blocking a legitimate transaction. Lo had also insisted on diverting replacements for the 22d and 38th into the Chih Hui Pu or Army troops, which he thought of as his. As a result Chih Hui Pu was soon 4,000 men overstrength while the 22d and 38th Divisions were short at this time five to six thousand men each. For Lo to have used replacements to fill the divisions of two generals who were strangers to him and concurrently lose all hope of ever claiming the pay of the 4,000 men would have been completely alien to the accepted Chinese practice. But such customs as these had reduced the Chinese Army to near impotence; Stilwell did not propose to connive at them, and Lo was sent back to China.[80]

The senior officer of the SOS was post commander and functioned in a manner similar to the commanding general of a service command in the United States, with no authority over training. One of the earliest problems faced by Col. William A. Fuller and his successor, Brig. Gen. William H. Holcombe, was the medical treatment and reconditioning of Chinese soldiers. To accomplish this task, they had the services of the Seagrave medical unit, of Maj. Gordon Seagrave, of a British Red Cross Unit, and, after 21 August, of the 98th Station Hospital. According to the SOS history:

> The Chinese were in bad condition. Malnutrition, malaria, dysentery, and Naga sores (large, ulcer-like sores on the limbs) soon brought the Ramgarh hospital population to 1,300, but the Chinese had remarkable recuperative powers when fed plenty of rice and given good medical care. They were soon ready for [sanitary] training which they needed as badly as they needed medical care. They cared nothing about cleanliness or sanitation. . . . They

---

[79] (1) *The Stilwell Papers,* p. 149. (2) Chih Hui Pu Diary, 4 Oct 42. Folder, Chinese Army (Ramgarh), Gen Ref Br, OCMH.

[80] (1) Diary, 16, 20 Oct, 18 Nov 42, cited n. 79(2). (2) Memo cited n. 77(2). (3) For a time at least, Lo had the support of the Chinese War Ministry, which asked that Lo be given 100,000 rupees a month "to meet general office expenses and special disbursements of the headquarters" and 350,000 rupees a month to pay his two divisions plus army troops. Ltr 7511, Ho Ying-chin to Stilwell, 6 Nov 42. SNF-13g. It will be remembered that the expenses at Ramgarh were being borne by reciprocal aid.

were careless about allowing water to remain in containers, with the result that mosquitoes were breeding everywhere . . . [but] by October 1942 there was a "high degree of sanitation at Ramgarh."[81]

In the early days at Ramgarh the rather curious supply system, under which the SOS placed requisitions on Indian authority for the Chinese, often creaked and groaned and sometimes failed to produce. This was not peculiar to Ramgarh for the same thing often happened at other U.S. installations in India as the nations concerned learned to work together. Ramgarh Training Center was commanded by Brig Gen. (then Col.) Frederick McCabe, who was responsible directly to Stilwell. Theoretically, the center was free of Chinese influence, but, as McCabe wrote to Colonel Ferris, "You know how that works with the Chinese with their ability to circumvent whenever they don't wanna." Though the Chih Hui Pu chief of staff, General Boatner, had no formal authority over the training center, McCabe found him a great aid in keeping the Chinese content and busy.[82]

The center originally had infantry and artillery sections, reflecting the plan to train such units. Believing they would enter combat in winter 1942–43, the center tried to train them as rapidly as possible. With the adoption of the plan for a Chinese army corps, the center changed accordingly. From 15 September on it had a headquarters and headquarters detachment, plus infantry and artillery sections. A special units section, added 25 November 1942, gave all specialist training needed in the infantry division. The basic concept of the center was Stilwell's belief that the Chinese soldier could learn his trade and, once taught, be as good as any. Therefore, divisions of such men under a leadership willing to attack should be equal to the reconquest of Burma. Under a program based on the U.S. Mobilization Training Programs, the Chinese were taught to use rifles, light and heavy machine guns, 60-mm. and 81-mm. mortars, rocket launchers, hand grenades, and 37-mm. antitank guns under any conditions. An eight-day course in jungle warfare was given after the soldiers had mastered use of their weapons. The artillery section for six weeks taught the use of pack artillery, 105-mm. and 155-mm. howitzers, and assault guns, with emphasis on jungle operations.[83]

So that Chinese units would be able to give emergency medical care in combat, Chinese medical personnel were trained at Ramgarh. A number of courses were offered, including one of six months intended to train intelligent junior officers to perform a variety of medical services. Chinese line officers got courses in field sanitation to prevent the diseases that had taken such a toll in 1942. Short courses in dentistry and veterinary service were offered, to provide men who could perform certain basic tasks in the field. Field hospitals for the

---

[81] SOS in CBI, App. 16, Medical Section, p. 14.
[82] (1) Ltr, McCabe to Ferris, 10 Nov 42. Folder, Chinese Army (Ramgarh), Gen Ref Br, OCMH. (2) SOS in CBI, p. 486.
[83] MS, pp. 7–10, 29–46, cited n. 71(1).

STAFF DISCUSSION AT RAMGARH TRAINING CENTER, 1942. *Left to right, General Yang, Maj. Gen. Franklin C. Sibert, General Stilwell, General Sun, and Maj. Gen. Liao Yao-shiang.*

Chinese divisions were equipped and trained at Ramgarh and at Ledo. Ultimately, individual training in medicine, dentistry, and veterinary medicine was given at Ramgarh to men from five Chinese divisions.[84]

In providing basic training to individual officers and men, American personnel at the center found that the basic principles of pedagogy applied to Chinese as well as to Americans but that great ingenuity was needed to overcome the language barrier, the concept of face, and the indifference of the Chinese to time. Under the belt-line instruction system, a different instructor taught each phase of a subject. By constant practice the American instructor, with his interpreter, became adept at conveying his meaning to the peasant lads who clustered around the strange products of Detroit and Pittsburgh.

The interpreters were indispensable. Usually members of the student class, they were often highly intelligent but ignorant of military matters and so had to be previously instructed in military phraseology and concepts. Careful super-

[84] U.S. Army Medical Service in Combat in India and Burma, 1942–1945, MS by 1st Lt James H. Stone, Medical Historian, India–Burma Theater, Vol. I, pp. 72–75, 78–80, 83. Gen Ref Br, OCMH.

vision was needed to see that they did not embroider the instruction with their own ideas. It took perhaps three times as long to teach a subject through interpreters as to teach where no language barriers were present.

The concept of face made it hard to train field grade officers with their juniors, commissioned officers with noncommissioned officers, and all holders of rank with enlisted men. Overcoming the preconceived notions implanted by seven years of passive defense was also hard. Chinese with long experience of war as they had known it did not take kindly to the suggestions of men who had never been under fire. Because the Chinese had been weak in artillery, they had fewer preconceived notions in that field and so artillery instruction went ahead faster than infantry.

The time problem was vexing, because in conformity with American cultural patterns classes had to attend instruction at fixed times. This notion was strange to the Chinese, who thought one hour quite as good as another. Consequently, the best efforts of liaison officers were needed to keep the flow of students on schedule.[85]

When Chinese officers and enlisted men of the 22d and 38th Divisions completed approximately six weeks of basic training and indoctrination, the Chinese units were reassembled and began to conduct their own training. This training was guided by directives issued by the training center. The Chinese applied these themselves while American liaison personnel kept the center apprised of the Chinese progress. The training center supplied facilities, training aids, ammunition, and instructors as required. Since the responsibility for meeting the standards set by the directives and by the commanding generals of the 22d and 38th Divisions lay with the Chinese themselves, they set the hours of training, which were long, and the pace, which was steady. The Americans aided and guided; the British and Indians provided food, clothing, pay, shelter, and the bulk of the needed supplies. The basic principle was to help the Chinese to help themselves.[86]

Summary

As it became apparent in the summer of 1942 that the crisis in Sino-American relations precipitated by General Brereton's transfer from India to Egypt would be amicably adjusted, Stilwell gave his expanding forces the organization of a theater of operations. The tremendous geographic expanse involved, the unreliable nature of communications and transport, and the circumstance that the two major portions of Stilwell's theater were under two different Supreme Commanders, Chiang and Wavell, forced a considerable degree of decentralization. Stilwell's principal headquarters, and the one in

---

[85] MS, pp. 5, 11, 29, 83–86, cited n. 71(1).
[86] Interv with Lt Col William B. Powell, Former Opns Off, Ramgarh Training Center, 28 Nov 50.

which he spent most of his time, was at Chungking. This headquarters had a Branch Office at New Delhi.

The two major headquarters under Stilwell's theater headquarters were the SOS under General Wheeler, and the Tenth Air Force under General Bissell. Reflecting the logistic difficulties of operations in China, most of the SOS and Air Force installations and strength were in India. In India, the SOS spent the summer of 1942 in establishing itself, storing Chinese lend-lease, and supporting the Tenth Air Force and the nascent Chinese Army in India. The Tenth Air Force was deploying itself toward Burma. In China, General Chennault was trying to shape an air task force from the remnants of the American Volunteer Group plus a few untried replacements.

CHAPTER VII

The Attempt To Plan a Spring Campaign

The efforts of Currie and Stilwell had been attended by a great improvement in the atmosphere at Chungking. The Chinese attitude suggested a willingness to be satisfied with less than the full letter of the Three Demands.[1] In Washington, too, the prospects for more effective Sino-American co-operation were brighter. The vigor of the Chinese response to sending Brereton to the Middle East was further evidence that the Atlantic First policy had consequences which the United States could not afford to disregard. If the two powers, China and the United States, could establish a working accord, then the success of Stilwell's mission would be more likely and a powerful Chinese Army might play a significant part in the Pacific war.

U.S. Answer to the Three Demands

The answer to the Three Demands which the War Department wrote for the President was based on a changed attitude in the Operations Division of the War Department. Stilwell's request in May for U.S. combat troops had been coolly received. Soon after in June came the great American naval victory at Midway. The sinking of 4 Japanese aircraft carriers and 1 heavy cruiser at a loss of 1 American aircraft carrier had shifted the balance of naval power in the Pacific quite clearly to the Americans. They began to think in more aggressive terms, and so on 2 July 1942 the United States resolved to make an offensive-defensive effort in the Solomon Islands. Several weeks later, the United States and Great Britain decided to attempt the occupation of French North Africa (Operation TORCH). TORCH was given highest priority, thereby limiting what could be sent to the Pacific and, even more so, to Stilwell in CBI.[2] On 7 August Marines landed on Guadalcanal Island.

Four days after the landing, Admiral William D. Leahy, Chief of Staff to the President, suggested to the Joint Chiefs of Staff that a specific commit-

---

[1] See Ch. V, above.
[2] Sherwood, *Roosevelt and Hopkins*, Ch. XXV.

ment be made to open the Burma Road. The Navy adopted this view and often in the days to come urged aggressive Allied action in Burma to support Pacific operations.[3] Leahy's proposal undoubtedly influenced what soon followed in the Operations Division of the War Department.

OPD weighed the Generalissimo's Three Demands against U.S. capabilities and, on 14 August, suggested to General Marshall that U.S. aircraft commitments to China be meticulously discharged, that aircraft replacements be forwarded promptly, and that the Combined Chiefs of Staff be urged to consider retaking Burma after the monsoon rains ended. The Operations Division accepted in full and strongly urged Stilwell's and Magruder's recommendations that lend-lease to China should be contingent on the Chinese Government's meeting certain conditions. Lend-lease to China should not be given as philanthropy but rather on a *quid pro quo* basis, with Chinese military reforms to precede it and Chinese military accomplishments to be the sole acceptable guarantee of its continuance. General Marshall and Secretary Stimson approved this approach to the problems of Sino-American relations and recommended it to the President.[4]

On 25 August Marshall presented to the JCS the OPD proposal that Burma be retaken. In the light of nationalist disturbances then under way in India, he hesitated to advance the subject but thought the Burma operation should be investigated and analyzed to determine what could be done. Admiral Leahy suggested the proposal be placed before the CCS. A specific agreement to open the Burma Road seemed essential to the admiral.[5]

The paper presented to the CCS warned that, unless visible Allied assistance to China was increased, China might make peace with Japan, thus freeing a number of Japanese divisions for service elsewhere. Though the United States was making some air support available for China, it did not believe that such aid, plus the relatively few arms that could be flown into China, was enough to keep the Chinese in the war. Current U.S. commitments, together with the shipping shortage, made it impossible to send any U.S. ground forces to China. The United States, therefore, suggested that the CCS consider the problem of retaking Burma in the next dry season, October 1942–May 1943. Perhaps anticipating that the CCS would adopt the suggestion, the JCS on 19 September ordered Stilwell to tell the Generalissimo that the Combined Staff Planners were studying operations to retake Burma and to reopen the Burma Road, that everything possible was being done to reach a satisfactory solution to the problems involved.[6]

[3] JCS 28th Mtg, 11 Aug 42, Item 6.
[4] Memo, Handy for Marshall, 14 Aug 42, sub: Three Minimum Reqmts For China Theater Submitted by Generalissimo; Memo, Handy for Marshall, 4 Sep 42, sub: Support of China. WDCSA (China), A45–466. Stimson approved the basic memorandum on 27 August 1942.
[5] (1) JCS 30th Mtg, 25 Aug 42, Item 7. (2) Item cited n. 3.
[6] (1) CCS 104, 25 Aug 42, sub: Retaking of Burma. (2) CM–OUT 6610, AGWAR to Chungking, 19 Sep 42.

With Currie's survey of the Chinese situation complete and his report made, with better feeling prevailing in Chungking, and with the machinery of the CCS about to deal with the strategic problems involved in supporting China, the U.S. Government could now prepare its formal answer to the Three Demands.

On 25 September Marshall asked for Stilwell's comments on a preliminary draft. Noting Marshall's references to one hundred transports on the Hump, to an increase in the emergency air transport program from 3,500 tons to 5,000 tons a month, and to the omission of American combat troops, Stilwell thought that the draft meant "nothing more than at present," substantially, a reaffirmation of existing commitments. He was not pleased with it: "I suppose I am to kid them [the Chinese] into reorganizing the Army." In answering Marshall, Stilwell stressed the importance of securing from the Chinese some indication of what they proposed to do to carry out the Thirty Division Program. He suggested a hint from the President to the Generalissimo that if the Chinese did not propose to use American lend-lease there was no point in letting it accumulate in India. The rest of Marshall's draft was covered with the terse comment that it seemed excellent.[7]

The President's answer to the Three Demands, as modified by the Chinese memorandum to Stilwell on 1 August,[8] came during the height of the celebration with which the Chinese marked the anniversary of the end of the Manchu regime. Stilwell presented the President's message to the Generalissimo on 13 October. It was "exactly as I had recommended," noted Stilwell.[9] Pleased with Currie's report and with the more co-operative attitude of the Generalissimo in August, Roosevelt again promised almost 500 aircraft for the China Theater, plus 100 aircraft on the Hump in early 1943. He regretted that American combat troops could not be supported in CBI, thus rejecting one of the Three Demands.

Telling the Generalissimo that the United States would do its best toward creating an American air force and a reorganized Chinese army in India to join in reoccupying Burma, the President went on to say that Stilwell's plan for retaking Burma was being developed by the JCS. Roosevelt told the Generalissimo that Burma had to be retaken to open a practical supply route to China, because the Hump would never carry enough supplies. The President pointed out that because of the limitations of air transport there was little point to simply accumulating stockpiles in India that had no early prospect of receipt in China, whereas reopening the Burma Road would permit deliveries in quantity. Consistent with Currie's advice, the President did not insist that the Chinese reform and reorganize their Yunnan forces; however, he did say that if the

---

[7](1) *The Stilwell Papers*, p. 152. (2) CM–OUT 8582, Marshall to Stilwell, 25 Sep 42. (3) CM–IN 12306, Stilwell to Marshall, 28 Sep 42.
  [8] See Ch. V, above.
  [9] Stilwell Diary, 13 Oct 42.

Generalissimo would do it, "it would be of the greatest importance in obtaining our mutual objectives." [10]

On 12 October, the same day that the President's reply reached Chungking, Stilwell moved to advance the *rapprochement* with the Chinese one step further by submitting his views on China's lend-lease program for the next year. The timing may have been a coincidence or it may reflect Stilwell's belief that the United States could be more generous, a feeling precipitated into action by the terms of the President's 12 October reply. In his message to the War Department, Stilwell asked that the emergency air transport program be continued for another year on a scale that would supply equipment for a second thirty Chinese divisions. He now contemplated a total of sixty re-equipped Chinese divisions. [11] To the Chinese, Stilwell seems to have said nothing about this significant expansion of his program. It may be assumed that he was ready to introduce the topic of a second thirty divisions at some moment propitious to the advancing of his reform program, in accord with his intentions of bargaining with the Chinese. A week later the War Department told Stilwell that his sixty division program would be generally met within the next six months. [12]

The October Negotiations

Satisfied with the President's answer, the Chinese in effect ordered Stilwell to begin negotiations with the American and British Governments on an offensive to retake Burma. General Shang Chen, the National Military Council's liaison with Stilwell, wrote: "My Government would like to know your views on the draft plan. If you concur, it is the desire of the Generalissimo that you will kindly bring this up with both the American and British Governments. As soon as a definite reply is received, please have it submitted to the Generalissimo so that final details for the execution of the plan may be drawn up." [13]

The Chinese general plan gave four reasons why Burma should be retaken: (1) to establish a base from which to start a counteroffensive against Japan; (2) to prevent Germany, Italy, and Japan from joining forces in the Middle East; (3) to open a line of communications from India to China so that large quantities of supplies could be brought into China, "thereby enabling the

[10] (1) Min, Conf, Stilwell and Mme. Chiang, 14 Sep 42, Alexander, recorder. Item 18, Bissell Corresp Folder, CT 23, Dr 2, KCRC. (2) Assisted by Currie, Marshall had drafted the U.S. reply to the Generalissimo's modified demands. On 10 October Roosevelt approved the draft radio. Memo, Hopkins for Marshall, 10 Oct 42. WDCSA 381 China (10-2-42), A46-523. (3) Memo, Stilwell from Roosevelt for Generalissimo, 12 Oct 42. Item 71, Bk 1, JWS Personal File.

[11] Stilwell asked that beginning November 1942 the War Department ship to India for airlift to China: ordnance to bring China's artillery allocation to 720 37-mm. antitank pieces, 720 75-mm. pack howitzers, 360 105-mm. howitzers, 12,000 submachine guns, 13,250 Bren guns, and 30,000,000 rounds of 7.92-mm. ammunition. CM-IN 5524, Chungking to AGWAR, 12 Oct 42.

[12] CM-OUT 6064, Marshall to Stilwell, 19 Oct 42.

[13] Ltr, FAB/NMC 136, 14 Oct 42, signed Shang Chen, with Incl, sub: Gen Plan For Retaking Burma Under Jt Effort of Chinese, British, and American Forces. SNF-84.

Chinese to complete their plan for a general counteroffensive at an early date";
(4) to keep the Japanese too busily occupied to seize the initiative anywhere
else in the Pacific.[14]

The Chinese proposed to put fifteen to twenty of their divisions into an
attack from Yunnan, while the United States and Britain put five to seven
divisions plus paratroops into a frontal attack from India and an amphibious
operation against Rangoon. The Chinese set certain prerequisites to their participation in the campaign. Their allies were to provide three or four battleships
and six to eight aircraft carriers, obtain control of the air and dominate the
China and Java Seas, and attack the Andaman Islands to cover a landing on
Rangoon. Then the overland advance could begin. In essentials, however, it
was Stilwell's July plan coming back with the Generalissimo's qualified approval, so Stilwell hastened to obey the Generalissimo's order to "bring this
up with the American and British Governments." [15] Since the President's reply
made it plain that Stilwell's American superiors were working on his plan, and
so, by implication, on future orders to him, a trip to India for a conference with
Wavell was the next order of business.

The War Department instructions to Stilwell for his talks with Wavell
were given to him orally by Col. Thomas S. Timberman of OPD, sent to
Chungking to give Stilwell the War Department point of view. They were:

> *a.* It is necessary to have Chinese Forces participate with the British in the retaking of
> Burma.
> *b.* Due to the command problem, that such Chinese Forces as are made available by
> Chiang Kai-shek be integrated in the British undertaking as a separate task force under a
> commander acceptable to the Chinese.
> *c.* That the Chinese thrust into Burma, supported by the 10th Air Force, be coordinated
> by Stilwell with the British effort.
> *d.* That the 10th Air Force remain under Stilwell's command and only when, in his
> judgment, the situation warrants, will it be diverted from the support of Chinese Forces.[16]

To the conference table Stilwell brought some tangible assets: the beginnings in India of a Chinese corps trained and equipped to U.S. standard; the
nascent Tenth Air Force;[17] and the Generalissimo's willingness to join in
operations to break the blockade of China.

On 17, 18, and 19 October Wavell and Stilwell met in New Delhi, together
with Gen. Sir Alan Hartley, the Deputy Commander-in-Chief, India; Air Chief
Marshal Sir Richard Peirse, the Air Officer Commanding-in-Chief, Air Forces,
India; General Bissell; and Colonel Ferris. The first two conferences were not
satisfactory from Stilwell's point of view. Wavell objected to any increase in
the number of Chinese trained in and based on India. He also mentioned a

---

[14] *Ibid.*
[15] See Chapter V, page 179, above for Stilwell's July 18th proposal.
[16] (1) Memo, Handy for Marshall, 1 Oct 42. sub: Burma Opns. WDCSA 381 China
(10-1-42), A46-523. (2) Stilwell Diary, 18 Oct 42.
[17] See Ch. VI, pp. 198–201, 212–20, above.

number of logistical difficulties to support his view that any Burma operations should be on the most modest scale.[18]

From Wavell, Stilwell received the first description of British plans for Burma which had been extended to him to date:

General Wavell explained that he had been planning the re-conquest of Burma ever since the withdrawal of the Army at the end of April.

He had originally intended to start operations at the beginning of October but his plans had been upset and retarded by many factors. The chief of these was the low capacity of the railway and river communications to Assam, which had been further accentuated by inefficient working and by breaks in the system due to monsoon conditions. There had also been a very high rate of sickness amongst the troops, due principally to malaria. In addition aircraft, troops and equipment intended for India had been diverted in large quantities to the Middle East. . . . For administrative reasons any advance in force against Northern Burma could not start before March 1st.

He hoped however to advance at an earlier date in the South down the Arakan Coast and he was planning a small combined operation for the capture of Akyab. A decision with regard to the latter had not yet been taken.

An advance on March 1st left only 2½ months campaigning weather [before the monsoon rains] and even if he managed to get two Divisions to the MANDALAY area it would not be possible . . . to maintain them there. He did not want to be forced to withdraw from Burma a second time. He had therefore issued instructions for the initial objective of the Eastern Army to be Northern ARAKAN, the CHIN Hills, and the Upper CHINDWIN. He fully intended however to advance further East should it be possible to do so.[19]

Wavell's goal was not the seizure of Rangoon at which Stilwell aimed, but his plan could well serve as the first phase of a larger operation directed toward Rangoon.

On the last day of the conferences, Wavell's attitude changed. From Washington, Marshall and Dill of the British Joint Staff Mission to Washington had successfully urged the British War Cabinet to direct the Government of India's approval of a sharp increase in the number of Chinese troops in India.[20] This action was promptly reflected in Wavell's attitude and improved the chances for a successful outcome of a limited campaign to retake north Burma. Therefore, when Stilwell produced the Chinese general plan for retaking all Burma and opening the port of Rangoon, Wavell gave his "general agreement with it as a basis for planning." [21] Wavell noted again the obstacles to operations in Burma, such as the difficulty of gaining the air superiority needed, and

---

[18](1) CM–IN 07342, Stilwell to Marshall, 17 Oct 42. (2) CM–IN 08124, Stilwell to Marshall, 18 Oct 42. (3) Rad from Wavell, 28 Oct 42, Tab A, JCS 40th Mtg, 3 Nov 42. ABC 384 (Burma), 6–25–42, Sec 1A, A48–224. (4) Wavell Despatch, March 1942 to December 31, 1942, *Supplement to The London Gazette.* (5) *The Stilwell Papers,* pp. 163–64.

[19](1) Notes, Conf at GHQ, New Delhi, 18, 19 Oct 42, Wavell and Stilwell. Stilwell Documents, Hoover Library. (2) *The Stilwell Papers,* pages 162–63, suggest that the Notes actually refer to the session on 19 October.

[20](1) Memo, Marshall for Dill, 6 Oct 42. WDCSA 381 China (10–6–42), A46–523. (2) CM–IN 04048, Stilwell to Marshall, 10 Oct 42. (3) Memo, Marshall for Roosevelt, 10 Oct 42; Ltrs, Dill to Marshall, 13, 19 Oct 42. WDCSA 381 China, A46–523.

[21](1) Notes cited n. 19(1). (2) CM–IN 11578, Stilwell to Marshall, 27 Oct 42. (3) *The Stilwell Papers,* p. 164.

remarked that the date for "major operations" would have to be indefinite for the moment, but he agreed with Stilwell "that the plans already made by the Commander-in-Chief India and the memorandum from the Generalissimo should form the basis of future planning." [22] Planning between the British and American staffs in India began forthwith, both for the limited operation in north Burma, which could be the first step toward retaking all Burma, and for operations to reopen Rangoon.

General Headquarters (India) promptly invited the American forces to send representatives to sit on a combined planning staff. SOS and Headquarters, Tenth Air Force, each sent an officer, while Lt. Col. Frank D. Merrill represented Stilwell's headquarters. The first meeting on 22 October formed two subcommittees to examine the problems of moving the two Ramgarh divisions to Ledo, from whence they might move into north Burma, and of maintaining them once they were there. [23]

Because of the limitations of the Assam line of communications and the many demands on it, moving the Chinese from Ramgarh to Ledo was far from routine, and many conferences were held on the problem in the next few days. One combined planning session feared nine weeks might be needed for the move, and there was also the problem of stocking the 45-day supply level that was needed at Ledo. [24]

It was also necessary to fix Anglo-American responsibilities in filling gaps in the equipment of the two Chinese divisions. It was agreed that the United States would assume responsibility for movement of supplies from railhead to roadhead and that 200 tons a day would be needed for a Chinese corps and 800 trucks to support two divisions over a 350-mile line of communications. The British very presciently suggested that air supply be investigated.

Summing up the conference on 26 October, Colonel Merrill told Stilwell that the British had offered 500 trucks and many pieces of medium artillery. They were also procuring animals for five battalions of pack artillery. The move forward could start about 1 February 1943. There were two major questions left to be settled between Stilwell and Wavell: what sector was to be given the Chinese Army in India, and what was its mission? [25]

The Anglo-American staff conferences had postulated Ledo as the base for Stilwell's Chinese Army in India and Myitkyina as its goal but, as seen by Merrill's remark, the point had not been settled. In his 29 July proposal to the Generalissimo, Stilwell proposed that the Chinese Army in India advance

[22] Notes cited n. 19(1).

[23] Ltr, Lt Col Frank Milani, Asst AG, Br Office, for Stilwell, to Wheeler, Bissell, Merrill, 21 Oct 42, sub: Jt Planning. SNF-60. The CBI usage of *joint* for *combined* was late in being abandoned.

[24] Min, Conf, 24 Oct 42, sub: Quartermaster Problems Arising Out of Move of Chinese Corps from Ramgarh to Ledo Area. SNF-60.

[25] Min, Second Mtg, Jt British and American Stf Com, 26 Oct 42; Summary of Confs, Merrill, recorder, SNF-60.

into Burma from Imphal via Tamu and Kalewa.[26] Therefore, when he met with Wavell on 27 October, Stilwell suggested that sector for the Chinese. Wavell refused, saying the Manipur Road from the Bengal and Assam Railway to Imphal could not support both the Chinese and the British and assigned the Hukawng Valley of north Burma to Stilwell. That done, the two commanders agreed Stilwell's mission should be to occupy the area Myitkyina–Bhamo to obtain use of the Myitkyina airfield and make contact with Chinese advancing from Yunnan. Since the Chinese were to be based on Ledo and advance down the Hukawng Valley, it was agreed that the Americans should assume responsibility for building the road from Ledo down the Hukawng and Mogaung Valleys to Myitkyina, eventually to link with the Burma Road. Stilwell's contemporary papers do not discuss the project, suggesting that his interest was slight and that building the Ledo Road was assumed as an added responsibility coming from the action by Wavell, who was Supreme Commander, India, in assigning north Burma as Stilwell's sector.[27] Stilwell's solution to China's problem of supply, as he had told the Generalissimo on 29 July, was to reopen Rangoon.

The Generalissimo Will Be Ready

Returning to Chungking with the results of his conferences with Wavell and India Command, Stilwell found he had an unexpected ally, China's Foreign Minister, Dr. Soong. Before his departure from Washington for Chungking on 10 October, Soong had had long, frank talks with Marshall and Stimson. Stimson chose to paraphrase a letter Marshall was planning to send the President and spelled out the Marshall-Stimson thesis for the Chinese diplomat. The situation in Burma, said Stimson, was a tangled one which required zeal and co-operation to prevent misunderstanding. The solution to the problem of mutual co-operation between the three powers required action to open a ground line of communications over which supplies might be moved to China. To open that line of communications required military action. As Soong had remarked, the British and Chinese did not get on well together, hence U.S. action was important and necessary. This meant any American representative had to be a fighting military leader, not just a smooth and diplomatic type of person. Stimson asked Soong to tell the Generalissimo, in homely phrase: "It was a situation in which pepper was required more than molasses."[28]

The Chinese Foreign Minister laughed and said he understood. He assured Stimson he was anxious to "promote harmony" and asked Stimson to assure Stilwell that such was Soong's only purpose. Soong also spoke to Marshall,

---

[26] See Ch. V, pp. 181–82, above.
[27] Ltr, Stilwell to Wavell, 8 Nov 42, again stressing that Stilwell had been "assigned" the Hukawng Valley; Min, Conf, Stilwell and Generalissimo, 3 Nov 42; Notes, Conf, Wavell and Stilwell, 27 Oct 42. Stilwell Documents, Hoover Library.
[28] Memo of talk with Soong, 12 Oct 42. Stimson Papers. (See Bibliographical Note.)

who stressed the same points.[29] After Soong's return to Chungking, Stilwell found an unprecedented atmosphere of co-operation and the Foreign Minister took Stilwell aside and reaffirmed his desire to aid. During the winter of 1942–43 Stilwell worked closely with Soong.[30]

This co-operation from Soong was most welcome to Stilwell, who after the Three Demands crisis was much concerned with the problem of finding someone in authority with whom he might work. During the First Burma Campaign the Generalissimo had sent letter after letter to Stilwell. There were no letters after the campaign, and, as noted, very few of Stilwell's memoranda received any answer. Then came the Three Demands crisis, with its clear indication that the Generalissimo would like to see Stilwell recalled. After the crisis, and until Stilwell left China, conferences between them were few and confined to the business at hand. Memorandums from Stilwell to the Generalissimo were rarely if ever answered, and the Generalissimo did not trouble to address Stilwell on his own initiative.[31]

Therefore, Stilwell sought someone who could play the classic Chinese role of go-between and possibly exercise considerable independent power in the loose-jointed Chungking government. First he thought he had found such a one in General Ho, then in Foreign Minister Soong, and then in the women of the Soong family. So on 28 September Stilwell wrote: "Saw Shang Chen about going to Ho on 30-Div Plan. 'Go-ahead' he says. Encouraging attitude. So J. Liu and I went over at 2.30 and saw him. 'Ch'ing Chiao, etc.' He heard the story and made notes. *Very* pleasant and when we left he said: 'Come over and talk whenever you have any questions and *we can settle everything quickly right here.*' . . . Can it be possible? Maybe this is the way to do it." [Stilwell's italics] [32]

Then Soong came back; the Generalissimo authorized him to help co-ordinate preparations, and Stilwell wrote: "Talk with T. V. [Soong] on general lines. He seems Christianized (watch and lighter presents). Promises all possible help. To replace Madame in dealing with Gmo." [33]

When Doctor Soong arrived in China, and was authorized by the Generalissimo to help co-ordinate preparations, I told General Ho Ying-chin that I was conferring with him; and that I trusted that General Ho would understand that there were matters outside the strictly military sphere, which I would have to handle with Doctor Soong; that I did not wish to appear to be avoiding or ignoring any recognized Chinese authority; that it would be easier

---

[29] Memo, Marshall for President, 5 Nov 42. WDCSA 381 China (11–5–42), A46–523.

[30] (1) Folder, Ltrs and Memos, Stilwell to Soong, 1942–43, Stilwell Documents, Hoover Library. (2) *The Stilwell Papers,* pp. 166–67. (3) Ltr, Stilwell to Marshall. Bk 6, OPD Exec 8. Colonel Timberman hand carried this letter to General Marshall in November.

[31] "To ignore your chief of staff completely [may] be good practice, but I doubt it. Over a period of a year and a half, I submitted memos and studies on various subjects to him. He never deigned to discuss any of them. It was impossible to argue with him. He would simply pass down the decision—always 'No.' And that ended it." *The Stilwell Papers,* pp. 221–22.

[32] Stilwell Diary, 28 Sep 42.

[33] Stilwell B&W, 5 Nov 42.

for me to deal with one agency only; but that I realized conditions required this procedure if the best progress was to be made, and that I would keep him informed of anything I did that had a bearing on military affairs.[34]

Stilwell addressed himself to the task immediately before him and laid the results of his conferences in India before the Generalissimo, Madame Chiang, and Soong, on 3 November 1942, together with a description of the preparations the Chinese would have to make if their share in the Burma campaign was to be a success. The difficulties of the campaign were candidly outlined. Wavell's plans for a limited offensive were presented as they had been given to Stilwell, and Stilwell warned that Wavell was not committed to an amphibious attack on Rangoon that was "being studied." Then, to forestall any attempt to place General Lo's headquarters in command of the offensive down the Hukawng Valley, Stilwell listed the logistical arrangements to be made in India. These ran from "a. Organization of a base at Ledo . . ." to "n. Arrangements with the railway authorities. . . ." In responding the Generalissimo said: "As to General Wavell's inquiry about the size of the Chinese force to be placed in the field for the operation, please inform him that I will employ 15 divisions from the Yunnan side exclusive of the troops to be used against the enemy in Indo-China, aside from the two Chinese divisions in India, and that these troops will be ready for operations before the end of February 1943." Since the Generalissimo was Supreme Commander, China Theater, the readiness of these troops would be his responsibility. To this promise the Generalissimo attached but one condition — Allied sea and air forces must be present in strength to dominate the Bay of Bengal and prevent the Japanese from reinforcing through Rangoon.[35]

In the discussion which followed, Stilwell told the Chinese leaders that the Hukawng Valley was very difficult terrain but that he had not been able to get another sector; that British command would be nominal; and that massive air and naval support might not be forthcoming. The Chinese made their desire for Allied naval control of the Bay of Bengal very clear, and Stilwell promised his best offices. It was agreed by Stilwell and the Generalissimo that it would be diplomatically inexpedient for the Generalissimo to be commander in chief of an Allied effort in Burma. The question of which Chinese officer would command the Chinese forces advancing from Yunnan was left open, but the Chinese Army in India was placed under Stilwell's command for Burma operations.[36]

Stilwell promptly informed Wavell of the substance of the conference with the Generalissimo, stressing his intention to proceed on the assumption that the Generalissimo's requirement of Allied naval and air dominance of the Bay of Bengal would be met. Wavell's reply repeated the essence of Stilwell's

[34] Memo, Stilwell for Soong, 23 Jan 43. Stilwell Documents, Hoover Library.
[35] Min (Chinese version), Conf, Stilwell and Generalissimo, 3 Nov 42. Stilwell Documents, Hoover Library.
[36] (1) Ibid. (2) CM–IN 1965, Stilwell to Marshall, 5 Nov 42.

remarks on the relation of air and sea power to the projected operation, and in
effect the commanders were pledged to make detailed plans, begin preparations,
and take the actual decision later. The code name of this operation to retake all
of Burma was ANAKIM. The limited operation in north Burma took the name
of RAVENOUS.[37]

"How was it all done?" asked Stilwell.

I got the G-mo to see it was necessary. Got his O. K. on the big SW Pacific scheme—
ostensibly proposed by himself. In this he promised to use 15 to 20 divisions. This forced
Wavell's hand and made him agree in principle to an offensive. Then Washington put on
some heat, and the Chinese had to make a plan. This committed CKS, irrespective of the
bigger concept. I got Wavell's plan and put it up to CKS. He agreed if reasonably sure of
naval and air superiority. Then the North African affair began to go well, and we could look
for naval and air reinforcements. Then Soong came in and grabbed my stuff. He evidently
told CKS what the U.S. attitude would be if the Chinese didn't go to bat, so CKS gives the
Chun Lung Pu the word, and they come with the stuff I have been pushing at them since
last June. It looks as if they knew I was getting my way, and they have decided to go along.
If I could have seen this far ahead last spring, I would have had more sleep.[38]

Japanese Plans and Dispositions in Burma

While Stilwell, Wavell, their superiors, and the Generalissimo were weighing the situation caused by the Japanese conquest of Burma, the Japanese
themselves were wondering whether to exploit their successes or to remain on
the defensive. Their intentions, their strength, and their dispositions are the
background to what the British, Chinese, and Americans contemplated doing
in Burma.

Their smashing victory in Burma exhausted the body of prewar planning
that had brought such brilliant successes to the Japanese. Even before the end
of the campaign, *15th Army* was studying plans for an advance into India, but
the necessary troops were not available and overland communications did not
seem able to support an offensive.[39] The first directive from *Imperial Headquarters* to *Southern Army,* under which the *15th Army* operated, was dated 27
June 1942. *Southern Army* was ordered to stabilize its area and make it self-
supporting. Pressure against the Chinese Nationalists was to be maintained
from Burma, French Indochina, and Thailand. Offensive air operations against
China and India could be carried out at the discretion of *Southern Army,* but
while *Southern Army* was to prepare to eliminate strong points on its boundaries,
it was not to undertake operations into India and China without specific orders.
On 22 August, *Imperial Headquarters* took a more aggressive attitude, approved
the suggestions of a Lt. Col. Hayashi on the *Southern Army* staff, and ordered

[37] Ltr, Stilwell to Wavell, 8 Nov 42; Ltr, Wavell to Stilwell, 16 Nov 42. SNF–46.
[38] This passage completes Stilwell's essay on page 168 of *The Stilwell Papers.* Stilwell Undated
Paper. Stilwell Documents, Hoover Library.
[39] Japanese Study 88.

Southern Army to prepare to occupy northeast Assam, the Chittagong area, and cut the air supply line to China.[40]

In compliance, *15th Army* produced Plan of Operation 21 in September 1942, which called for the *33d Division* and part of the *55th Division* to advance to the line Silchar–Dimapur in Assam. A portion of the *18th Division* following them would leapfrog and advance to Golaghat. The rest of the *18th Division* would advance up the Hukawng Valley to Ledo, then swing west to Tinsukia, forming the right prong of a double encirclement. The airline to China would thus be effectively destroyed. Operation 21 was objected to by the commanders of the divisions concerned, Lt. Gen. Renya Mutaguchi and Lt. Gen. Shozo Sakurai, because of the geographic and logistical obstacles. Their views prevailed and the scheme was dropped on 23 December 1942. For the time being, the Japanese stood on the defensive in Burma.[41] The American operations in the Solomons seem not to have determined this attitude, for later events make clear the principal reason for the Japanese decision—the belief that it was impossible even for them to conduct a campaign across the Chin Hills.

In June 1942 *Imperial Headquarters* ordered *Southern Army* to build a rail line connecting the Burmese and Thai rail systems in order to reduce the strain on Japanese shipping space caused by the long haul around Malaya and to meet the needs of the *15th Army* which would be greatly increased by a build-up to meet any Allied counteroffensive or to invade India. Japanese engineers lacked road-building equipment, but one asset they had on which they might freely draw—an asset expendable and replaceable at will—the miserable Allied prisoners of war taken in Southeast Asia, and the coolies the Japanese had come to "liberate." Without medical care, without even the bare minimum of food and shelter, with the simplest and most primitive of tools, a total of 61,806 Allied prisoners of war and 269,948 coolies were driven into the steaming jungles of Thailand and Burma to hack a railway across the Dawna Range. From both sides of the hills the road began to go through the jungles, and the men began to die. Some died of sheer exhaustion, some of hunger, some of dysentery, some of cholera, some of malaria, many of combinations of all. The Japanese drove their prisoners forth in the morning, gibed at their sufferings, and rolled the dead into a ditch. These arrangements placed the very minimum of burden on the Japanese supply lines, and the tracks crept across the hills as more and more prisoners and coolies were fed into the jungle. For every mile completed, 325 men died.[42]

[40](1) *Imperial General Headquarters* Army Order 650, 27 Jun 42, with Apps. I and II, Pt. V, SEATIC Sp Int Bull, 1946, p. 9. MID Library. This order also in GHQ, Far East Comd, Mil Hist Div, *Imperial General Headquarters* Army Orders, Vol. II. Gen Ref Br, OCMH. (2) *Imperial General Headquarters* Army Order, 22 Aug 42, to *Southern Army,* SEATIC Sp Int Bull, 1946, p. 18; SEATIC Hist Bull 240, 9 Jul 46. MID Library.

[41](1) Japanese Study 89. (2) SEATIC Hist Bull 240, 9 Jul 46. MID Library. (3) *Imperial General Headquarters* Army Directive 1381, 23 Dec 42, GHQ, Far East Comd, Mil Hist Div, *Imperial General Headquarters* Army Directives, Vol. II. Gen Ref Br, OCMH.

[42] SEATIC Bull 246, 8 Oct 46, App. B, sub: Burma–Siam Ry, pp. 17–18. MID Library.

The four Japanese divisions that conquered Burma spent the rainy season resting and refitting. Defensive sectors were assigned as follows:

56th Division—Yunnan (Lt. Gen. Sukezo Matsuyama)
18th Division—northwestern Burma (Lt. Gen. Renya Mutaguchi)
33d Division—the Arakan (Lt. Gen. Genzo Yanagida)
55th Division—southwestern coastal area of Burma (Lt. Gen. Ken Kokan)

Forward areas were occupied with a minimum of personnel, and the bulk of the men went back to more healthful areas in Yunnan, the Shan States, and around Pegu and Toungoo to rest, retrain, and re-equip. On 1 December movement back into position began, to be completed by 1 January 1943. The line to be held went through Tengchung, Myitkyina, Kamaing, Kalewa, and Akyab, which left the Hukawng Valley and most of the Mogaung valley—the trace of the road from Ledo—as a sort of no man's land, crossed only by wandering patrols.[43]

Preparations in China for the Offensive

Preparations for a Chinese advance from Yunnan into Burma may be said to have begun with the Generalissimo's statement of 1 August that the Chinese could provide twenty divisions with appropriate artillery.[44] In the days following, the Chinese order of battle and strategic concepts had been disclosed to the Americans, and some troops began moving toward Yunnan. With the Generalissimo's statement of 3 November that fifteen Chinese divisions would drive from Yunnan as authority, Stilwell sought to persuade the Chinese into preparing a second Chinese Expeditionary Force. There were three problems: (1) the detail of efficient Chinese commanders; (2) the reorganization and re-equipment of the participating units; and (3) logistic support of the offensive. Stilwell did not approach his problems in that order. The realities of army politics in China demanded that he have something concrete to show any senior Chinese officer who might be asked to assume command of the Yunnan force, or Y–Force, as it was called thereafter.[45]

There were very considerable ordnance stocks in China. Talking to Currie on 31 July 1942, China's Chief of Ordnance, Gen. Yu Ta-wei, said the Chinese had 1,000,000 rifles, 66,000 light machine guns, 17,000 heavy machine guns, 1,000 antitank guns, 1,000 75-mm. guns and howitzers, 91 105-mm. howitzers, 60 6-in. howitzers, and 8,200 trench mortars. There were 250,000,000 rounds of small arms ammunition, more or less. The Chinese figures cannot be taken at face value. Thus, some weeks before, General Yu told an American lend-lease official that the Chinese had 1,700,000 rifles, while in December 1941

---

[43] (1) SEATIC Bull 246, 8 Oct 46, App. B, sub: Burma–Siam Ry. MID Library. (2) Japanese Study 89.
[44] See Ch. V, pp. 181–82, above.
[45] (1) CM-IN 5176, Stilwell to Marshall, 12 Nov 42. (2) *The Stilwell Papers,* page 191, gives Stilwell's appreciation of the politics involved.

AMMISCA had used the 2,000,000 figure.[46] Moreover, more detailed surveys of unknown origin in CBI Theater files, though agreeing rather closely with General Yu as to over-all totals, suggest that 25 percent of his artillery was obsolete and certainly some of it was in very bad repair.[47] But there was enough Chinese ordnance on hand, as Stilwell's artillery officer, Colonel Dorn, wrote General Handy of OPD, to build up the Thirty Divisions to a very respectable scale:

The 30 Division Plan is sound and feasible; and the Chinese have ample equipment in China today to build up such a force. Instead they scream for planes, disregarding the fact that they have fuel and bombs for no more than a reasonably small force.[48]

Stilwell's task was to persuade the Chinese to assemble an appropriate amount of this equipment in Yunnan and to assign it to a group of divisions that had been brought up to strength and purged of inefficient commanders. Transportation and repair problems plus the ammunition shortage would leave gaps in the Chinese armory, and these lend-lease would fill as the transports flew in supplies.

In March 1942 the National Military Council proposed a Table of Organization and Equipment for the Thirty Divisions. This was accepted as a basis for discussion, and since August Stilwell's staff and the Chinese had worked on their tables. By November these were in fairly complete form and reflected both the needs of the Chinese and the capabilities of air transport. (*Charts 3 and 4*) The tables also reflected Stilwell's long study of the Chinese Army and revealed his desire to increase the base of fire and give added mobility to the maneuvering element of the Chinese regiments and divisions. Fitting the existing Chinese divisions to this pattern revealed at once what reorganization would have to be done and what would have to be flown into China before the Chinese could cross the Salween River into Burma with a fair prospect of success. The next step was to translate the results of this examination into requisitions and steps toward reorganization. (*Table 5 and Chart 5*) [49]

---

[46](1) Memo by J. Franklin Ray, Jr., 9 Aug 42, sub: Notes, Conf, Currie and Yu Ta-wei, Chungking, 31 Jul 42. SNF–159. (2) Ltr, Maj Gen Kiang Piao, CDS Ordnance Off, Washington, to Col John B. Franks, Actg Dir, Def Aid Div, 29 Aug 42. Folder, 7.92-mm. Ammunition, ASF (DAD) ID, A46–299. The Chinese rifles and machine guns were 7.92-mm.

[47] In SNF–159 an otherwise unidentified table, dated 12 August 1942, lists: 750 modern anti-tank guns and 251 obsolete, 274 obsolete pieces of pack artillery, 176 obsolete field guns, etc. (2) In SNF–15 an undated, but detailed, survey gives 1,000,000 rifles, 62,000 light machine guns, 16,000 heavy machine guns, 7,800 trench mortars, 593 modern antitank guns of 37-mm. caliber and larger, 417 modern pack howitzers, and 211 antiaircraft guns of all sizes. If the obsolete pieces are included, the figures in this survey tally closely with those Yu gave Currie.

[48] Ltr, Dorn to Handy, 4 Aug 42. OPD 381 CTO, Sec 3, A47–30.

[49] Stilwell's total lend-lease stockpile during 1942 consisted of the 3,500-ton emergency air transport program, some British reverse lend-lease to China, and the stockpile gathered in India after the fall of Rangoon. The U.S. contribution to the Chinese Tables of Organization and Equipment was to come largely from the six months' 3,500-ton program, or a total of 21,000 tons for thirty divisions. See Chapter V, pages 160–61, above, for the Munitions Assignments Board's decision on the 3,500-ton program.

CHART 3—ORGANIZATION OF CHINESE INFANTRY REGIMENT: 1942 [a]

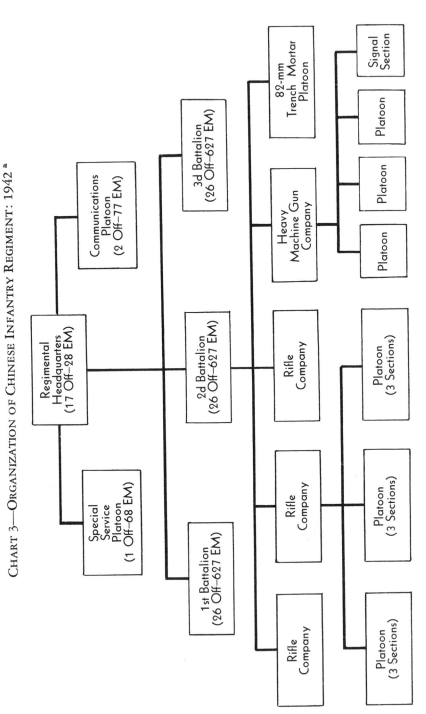

[a] Approved Table of Organization, but not in effect in Chinese Army.

Source: MA Rpt (China) 61, 12 Mar 42. MID Library.

CHART 4 — STILWELL'S PROPOSED REORGANIZATION OF CHINESE INFANTRY
REGIMENT: 1942

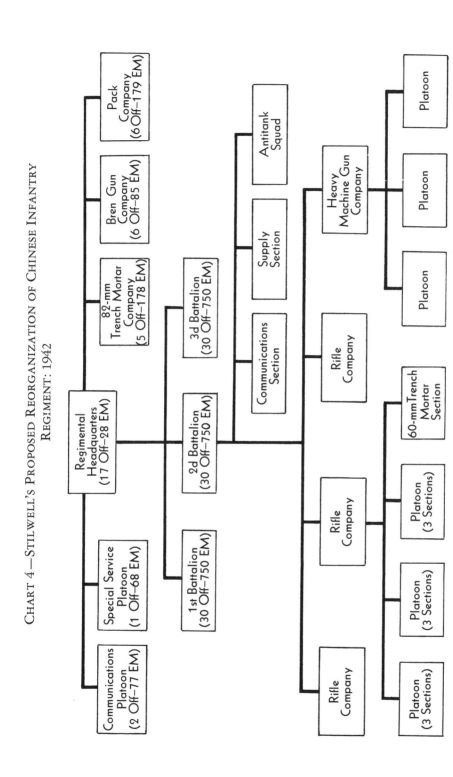

Source: AG(Y-FOS)320.3, HQ, Y-Force Operations Staff, CBI, KCRC.

TABLE 5—INCREASE IN PERSONNEL AND EQUIPMENT UNDER PROPOSED REORGANIZATION OF CHINESE
INFANTRY REGIMENT: 1942

Personnel and Equipment	1942 Organization	Proposed Reorganization	
		Quantity a	Percent Increase
Officers..	98	127	29.6
Enlisted Men.......................................	2,054	2,865	39.5
Horses and Mules..................................	147	441	200.0
Pistols, Small......................................	93	139	49.5
Pistols, Large......................................	206	283	37.4
Rifles..	953	1,097	15.1
Thompson Submachine Guns, .45 caliber.............	0	90	....
Machine Guns, Light................................	54	81	50.0
Machine Guns, Heavy...............................	18	18	0.0
Grenade Dischargers...............................	54	81	50.0
Trench Mortars, 60mm..............................	0	27	....
Trench Mortars, 82mm..............................	6	6	0.0
Boys Antitank Rifles, .55 caliber....................	0	6	....
Bren Guns, .303 caliber............................	0	9	....

a Virtually all increase in equipment was to have been supplied through lend-lease from the 3,500-ton emergency air transport program.

Sources: (1) Ma Rpt (China) 61, 12 Mar 42. MID Library. (2) AG (Y–FOS) 320.3, Hq Y–Force Operation Staff, CBI, KCRC.

CHART 5—LEND-LEASE CONTRIBUTION TO REORGANIZED CHINESE
REGIMENTS: 1942

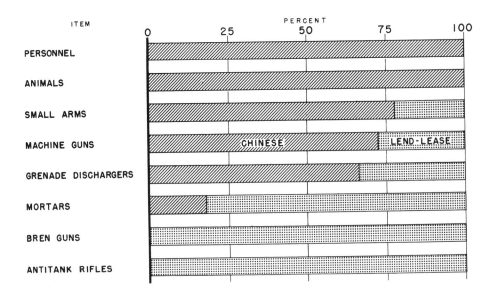

Source: Table 5.

On 7 November Foreign Minister Soong himself mentioned the need of reorganizing the Chinese SOS to support the projected 1943 spring campaign and approved Stilwell's prompt suggestion that Wheeler fly from India to advise on supply matters.[50] Remembering how General Yu Fei-peng had vexed him in the First Burma Campaign, Stilwell asked to have him removed from any supply responsibility in Yunnan. Thanks to Soong, Yu's removal was shortly promised.[51] When Wheeler arrived, Stilwell introduced him to some of the key Chinese military personnel, and then Wheeler began his survey. Stilwell wrote, "With Wheeler to see [Generals] Liu Fei and Ch'en. General walla walla [general discussion]. Told them a few things about getting down to cases. Apparently, preparations are actually under way. Imagine! for a Chinese offensive—Saw T. V. [Soong] and gave him a memo on essentials to be done now." [52]

In his memorandum Stilwell told Soong that a commander should at once be chosen for the Y–Force, that units to participate should be named, that reorganization of these units should begin, that the 269 75-mm. guns available should begin the trip to Yunnan, and that incompetent commanders should be removed. His paper devoted equal space to supply matters. Soong read that an efficient officer should head the Y–Force SOS; that, "transport being the basis of supply," this service should be reorganized at once and the lines of communications repaired; that supply depots should be established and movement forward to the Salween front of sixty days' supplies be initiated at once; that a medical evacuation service should be started; and that "the gasoline, weapons, ammunition, trucks, etc. that are stored away in varying amounts in the hands of individuals and organizations should be called for and produced, under serious penalties for retention." [53]

Wheeler discussed the supply situation at length with his Chinese counterparts—the ordnance, quartermaster, medical, signal, motor transport, engineer, traffic control, and "road improvement" officials. These Chinese asked only enough "to make a fight of it." Their requirements for the initial operations added up to 4,299 tons of air cargo to be flown from India.[54]

Flying 4,300 tons to Y–Force would drastically reduce the tonnage available

[50](1) Stilwell B&W, 7 Nov 42. (2) Rad T–114, Stilwell to Wheeler, 7 Nov 42. Item 92, Bk 1, JWS Personal File.

[51](1) Stilwell Diary, 18 Nov 42. (2) CM–IN 5176, Stilwell to Marshall, 12 Nov 42. Periodically, Stilwell kept Marshall informed of his talks with Soong. The War Department thereby was quite close to his day-by-day progress on the Y–Force.

[52] Stilwell Diary, 21 Nov 42.

[53] Memo, Stilwell for Soong, 12 Nov 42. Stilwell Documents, Hoover Library.

[54](1) CM–IN 12216, Stilwell to Marshall, 28 Nov 42. (2) Memo, Wheeler for Stilwell, 28 Nov 42, sub: Chinese SOS. SNF–55. Wheeler breaks down the ammunition to 15,000,000 rounds of 7.92-mm. and 30,000 rounds of artillery. Quartermaster items included raincoats, mosquito bars, tennis shoes, blankets, and tents. (3) Complete stockpile details on Y–Force's lend-lease build-up are in Yoke Reports, prepared by Eastern Section, SOS, under the direction of Colonel Kohloss. Yoke Reports 1 (13 Dec 42), 6 (7 Feb 43), 16 (18 Apr 43), 20 (1 May 43), 37 (10 Jul 43), and 49 (11 Aug 43) give the status of Y–Force lend-lease stockpiles. G–4, Y–FOS, KCRC. (4) Rpt, Hq Eastern Sec, USAF SOS CBI, 13 Dec 42, sub: Initial Status Rpt of Yoke Force. G–4, Y–FOS, KCRC.

Quartermaster supplies.............2,797 tons (mostly motor gas to bring sup-
                                                plies up).
Ordnance supplies..............1,100 tons (7.92-mm. and 75-mm. ammuni-
                                                tion).
Signal supplies................... 372 tons.
Medical supplies................   30 tons.
                                  4,299 tons.

to Chennault's air task force; Chennault protested as soon as word reached him
in Kunming.[55]

The allocation of tonnage posed a fundamental issue. Unless Stilwell could
divide Hump tonnage between the Chinese Army and Chennault according to
strategic needs as the situation demanded, his influence on ANAKIM would be
limited to what he could persuade the Chinese to do by the devices of rhetoric
and the force of personality. In November 1942 Stilwell, as he told Soong,
expected soon to have one hundred transports on the Hump and looked
forward to the increasing efficiency of the airline. These factors would make
possible a tonnage allocation in quantities more nearly satisfactory both to
Chennault and to Y-Force.

Concentrating Chinese divisions loyal to the Generalissimo in Yunnan
Province affected the whole structure of Chinese domestic politics. The
Governor of Yunnan had to be placated by Soong, while a number of the key
war area commanders convened at Chungking to discuss the projected operation and their contribution to it. Perhaps ominously, Soong warned Stilwell
not to press the Generalissimo too hard with his reforms and urged him to
establish cordial relations with Gen. Chen Cheng (VI War Area, and a potential
Y-Force commander), Lt. Gen. Hsueh Yueh (IX War Area), and Lt. Gen. Hu
Tsung-nan (I War Area). These powerful satraps, who controlled the territory
between Sian and Changsha, would by their attitude largely determine the
resources that the Generalissimo would feel able to commit to Yunnan. But
Stilwell had to assume the Generalissimo would be strong enough to keep
them obedient.[56]

So, looking about him, Stilwell wrote:

We're rolling. Yu Fei-peng is out of the picture. The new [supply] man is Ch'en Chin
Chieh. Cantonese. 45. Originally 4th Army. Shanghai experience. Chang Fa Kwei's [IV War

[55] (1) In *Way of a Fighter*, page 204, Chennault writes that on 20 January 1943 Stilwell cut him
to 700 gallons of gasoline a day to stockpile supplies for Y-Force. (2) Ltr, Col Clinton D. Vincent,
Executive Off, CATF, to Chennault, 22 Jan 43. Replying to Chennault's oral orders, Vincent as-
sumes two cases, A and B. Under A, the worse case, the China Air Task Force would receive 900
gallons of gasoline a day which would allow it only defensive action at Kunming and Chanyi, and
a precarious defense at that. (3) Ltr, Chennault to Lt Gen Albert C. Wedemeyer, CG, USF China
Theater, 6 Jul 45. WDCSA 091 China, 15 Aug 45. Col Vincent's Memo is Item 3, Incl II.
[56] (1) *The Stilwell Papers*, pp. 157, 169-70, 173. (2) Every fall the Central Executive Committee
of the Kuomintang had its annual gathering. Without knowing what the Generalissimo told his
war area commanders, Stilwell assumed that they were kept abreast of the Y-Force build-up though
he worried over the commanders' adherence to the plan. CM-IN 9374, Stilwell to Marshall, 22
Nov 42; CM-IN 12216, Stilwell to Marshall, 28 Nov 42; CM-IN 1197, Stilwell to Marshall, 2
Dec 42; CM-IN 3814, Stilwell to Marshall, 9 Dec 42.

Area] gang. Short and stocky, serious. May be a henchman of Fish-head's but we'll have to risk it. T. V. vouches for him. Associated since 1923.

They've accepted Wheeler as adviser. He's here and conferring with Ch'en. Arranging for meetings with signal, medical, ordnance, and transport services.

I've put Dorn on the artillery. He has seen Yu Ta-wei and latter is with us 100%—many good suggestions. Six-in. trench mortars available. Getting Dorn all the dope on artillery equipment, organization, and assignment. Dorn will see operations people.

Operations Section [Chinese General Staff] state the 30 divisions will be put in and compressed into 20. Formed into 10 corps. Six divisions on Indo-China border, plus four at Kunming. Ten divisions in Y–Force. Peanut said only one on lower line. I want two and so does Liu. We'll probably get them. Of all the points I was after we now have substantially all but the purge [of incompetent commanders]. And even that is working piece meal. (Yu Fei-peng, Tu Yu-ming, Lo Cho-ying).

We have now got both the Limies and the Chinese committed and working at it. If we can keep a fire lit under Wavell and horn in on command and training on this side, the job is in a fair way to get done. . . . And since everybody said it was impossible, naturally I'm pulling for it hard.[57]

Indeed, Stilwell was rolling, for on 1 December the Generalissimo agreed to command Y–Force in person. Stilwell at once told Marshall that since the Chinese had committed themselves, that since practically all the main points Stilwell had argued for had been accepted, the United States would have to be heard from next; for the situation was ". . . approaching the point where it was up to the United States to make good on promises of supply and transport. Chinese realize the seriousness and importance of operation and I believe are prepared for whole-hearted co-operation." [58]

Looking toward the future, Stilwell drafted a long and detailed memorandum for Soong outlining a campaign in China once the Chinese Army was rebuilt. The prerequisite was Burma's recapture. Immediately after it was taken, the Y–Force should move east to Kweichow and Hunan and prepare to attack Hankow. Stilwell suggested immediate stockpiling of supplies in the Changsha area to support the drive on Hankow. After Hankow was encircled from the vicinity of Kiukiang, its fall would be certain. Next would come occupation of Hsuchow, in order to "reach Japan from the air. . . . As soon as there is any prospect for initiating it, a large increase of aviation should be secured to support the operation and at once capitalize on it by starting an intensive and continuous bombing of Japan." [59]

Plans and Preparations in India

Immediately after the 27 October conference with Wavell, Stillwell ordered his SOS to make plans for supporting the Chinese attack down the Hukawng

[57] Stilwell B&W, 19 Nov 42.
[58] CM–IN 1197, Stilwell to Marshall, 2 Dec 42.
[59] Memo, in Stilwell's hand, for Soong. Stilwell Documents, Hoover Library. The memorandum speaks of U.S. instructors for Y–Force leaving the United States "about Dec. 1." There is no record of the memorandum having been presented, but since Stilwell obviously thought it important enough to preserve, it may have been.

Valley. Wheeler announced that he was beginning work at once and showed no doubt of SOS's ability to support an offensive. He planned to have warehouses, sidings, and troop accommodations ready by 1 March in order to receive personnel from the United States. Lend-lease supplies on hand would meet all of his needs except for seventy-two 81-mm. mortars, ordnance maintenance supplies, and medical supplies. The American personnel he needed totaled 540 officers, 256 nurses, and 9,906 enlisted men.[60]

The units Wheeler required illustrate the nature of U.S. support. Requested were one general hospital, three evacuation hospitals, one veterinary company, one medical battalion, one engineer depot company (less two platoons), one engineer maintenance company, one road-construction engineer regiment, twelve dump-truck companies, one quartermaster depot company, one quartermaster truck regiment, one quartermaster truck battalion, one ordnance depot company, one ordnance medium maintenance battalion, one infantry battalion, one military police battalion, and three antiaircraft batteries. Stilwell passed Wheeler's needs on to the War Department, thus facing it with the concrete problem of how far it could go in supporting a campaign in China–Burma–India that involved U.S. troops, matériel, and shipping.[61]

Agreement on some major points of logistical policy was reached by the Joint British and American Staff Committee, sitting in New Delhi, by 4 November. The plans for co-ordinating the movement of supplies to Ledo with the movement of the British 4 Corps to Manipur State were completed. It was agreed that British responsibility for moving supplies to Ledo ended at the railhead and that the SOS would run the Ledo base. Six hundred tons of stores a week were allotted to the SOS in the Ledo area until 4 Corps' concentration was complete. Col. John C. Arrowsmith arrived at Ledo on 5 November to begin reconnaissance of the area, of the road trace, and of the Ledo base.[62] (*Map 7*)

Difficulties on the India side began to appear a fortnight after Stilwell secured the Generalissimo's conditional agreement on 3 November. General Ferris and Brig. Gen. William D. Old, Chief of Staff, Tenth Air Force, attended a meeting of Wavell's chiefs of staff, at which Wavell stated frankly he did not think troops could be trained and supplies accumulated by 1 March. He believed with Stilwell that the reopening of Rangoon was the way to re-establish a supply route to China but did not think the needed resources would be at hand for some time. Nor did naval and air superiority seem likely of attainment. No action resulted from the meeting,[63] but to the Americans Wavell's reluctance to attempt a drive to the Chindwin seemed apparent.

[60] (1) Memo, Wheeler for Hearn, 29 Oct 42, quoting Memo, Stilwell for Wheeler. SNF–60. (2) Memo, Wheeler for Stilwell, 4 Nov 42, sub: Plans for Mission of SOS at X [Ledo]. SNF–58.
[61] (1) Memo cited n. 60(2). (2) MS 428, Army Service Forces Activities in the Supply of China, Burma, and India, 1942–1943, p. 47. Gen Ref Br, OCMH.
[62] (1) SOS in CBI, p. 18. (2) Interim Rpt by Jt British and American Stf Com, 4 Nov 42. SNF–57.
[63] Min, 52d Mtg, COS Com, 17 Nov 42, COS(42)–III. SNF–84.

SERVICES OF SUPPLY BUILD-UP. *Above, construction work in progress, and below, lend-lease supplies are loaded into railroad cars, India, 1942.*

British hesitation to undertake an operation in Burma in March 1943 became more evident during later November conferences between them and officers of Stilwell's headquarters. At a meeting between Colonel Merrill and Wavell's chief of staff, the latter pointed out that the Generalissimo's agreement to Burma operations was so hedged by conditions that it was hardly an agreement. He felt it would be impossible to support the Chinese once they were in Burma, yet ". . . the thought of another withdrawal into India caused everyone to shudder." [64] A three days' conference on the SOS's taking over the Ledo area left the definite impression on Colonel Merrill that the British delegates had sought to persuade the Americans into an admission that an advance into north Burma was impossible. Merrill felt the point had been reached at which the SOS would have to undertake to do what it could with U.S. resources. Therefore, wrote Merrill, the SOS was about to ask CBI Theater headquarters for aid. [65]

Merrill's proposal that the SOS shift its resources from support of the Tenth Air Force to support of road building introduced a major issue in the allocation of American resources within CBI—should the air effort or ground operations be sustained? On behalf of the SOS Merrill suggested that the 823d Engineer Battalion be diverted from the Tenth Air Force to the SOS, on condition that the SOS keep the Assam airfields in shape. Merrill argued that without this battalion the Ledo base and the Ledo Road would be severely handicapped, whereas the Tenth would be merely inconvenienced. He further recommended in his memorandum that the 45th Engineers, then scattered from Agra to Karachi, be concentrated in Assam with a minimum of delay. To both these requests, General Stilwell put "O.K." in the margin. There were more suggestions in the paper for dump-truck companies and Chinese engineers. In short, Merrill proposed concentrating the meager U.S. resources around Ledo and beginning construction of a base for the projected campaign on the most modest basis possible. To the majority of his suggestions Stilwell agreed. [66]

The exchanges in the conferences of 19–21 November with the British suggested to Merrill that Wavell's staff feared that a Chinese attack into north Burma was premature and could not be successfully accomplished but that the British feared to say so because of possible reactions in China and the United States. He told Stilwell that Wavell would probably suggest limiting spring 1943 operations to a British advance to the Chindwin, plus occupation of Akyab, and postponement of more ambitious operations to fall 1943. [67]

Stilwell's needs for the North Burma Campaign were weighed by the War Department, and the answer that returned on 24 November provoked him into one of the strongest communications he, or probably any American com-

---

[64] Memo by Merrill, sub: Notes on Conf, 17 Nov 42. SNF–84.
[65] Memo by Merrill, sub: Summary of Confs Nov 19, 20, and 21. SNF–84.
[66] *Ibid.*
[67] *Ibid.*

mander, ever addressed to the War Department. The radio from Washington told Stilwell that because of other theaters' needs all he could be spared was essential lend-lease matériel, essential engineer items to support the Chinese, U.S. instructors, and the "increasing effectiveness" of the airline to China.[68] All of these items had been promised to him earlier, so according to this radio the War Department could spare nothing more to support the Chinese in their unprecedented offensive. The message was in accord with Marshall's 25 September draft but not with the encouraging references to a Chinese campaign in the reply sent over the President's signature. On 28 November Stilwell sent the War Department a message of blunt and scathing candor, telling it that if nothing could be done for him, he was content; but he would be most obliged if the War Department would not go on telling him of its intent to back him to the limit, for this message from it was the limit.[69] If this radio accurately expressed the United States attitude, it would be extremely difficult to persuade the Chinese actually to go forward in Burma.

More Than JCS Support Required

The attitude Stilwell's military superiors took toward his proposals, and their accompanying feelings on persuading the British and Chinese to endorse Stilwell's proposals, was some months in evolving. On receiving the JCS's suggestions that plans be made for Burma's reoccupation, the CCS had referred them to their planners, who in turn reported in September that means for a major operation would not be available before fall 1943. Wavell's plans for a limited operation in Burma were in a sufficiently advanced stage to be communicated to his superiors, so the Combined Planners examined them along with Stilwell's plans.[70] The scarcity of resources plus the trend of Wavell's and Stilwell's planning for a limited operation to take only north Burma in spring 1943 to be followed later by opening Rangoon apparently impressed the Joint Chiefs of Staff. As a result they were soon considering, for agreed-on Anglo-American strategy, a limited offensive before the 1943 monsoon along lines similar to those suggested by OPD:

1. Take the Japanese airfields in north Burma which were being used as bases for attacks on the airline to China;

2. Dislodge Japanese forces from the India border to enable roads to be built into north and central Burma for a line of communications to support fall 1943 operations;

3. Take Akyab to obtain airfields in order to strengthen the air defense of Calcutta and future operations.[71]

[68] Rad WAR 1724, Marshall to Stilwell, 24 Nov 42. Item 115, Bk 1, JWS Personal File.
[69] (1) CM-IN 12205, Stilwell to Timberman, 28 Nov 42. (2) *The Stilwell Papers,* p. 171.
[70] (1) CCS 104/2, 9 Sep 42, sub: Plan for Recapture of Burma. (2) Min, CPS 31st Mtg, 4 Sep 42. Item 4, Tab L, ABC 384 (Burma), 8–25–42, Sec 1B, A48–224.
[71] Notes, JCS 40th Mtg, 3 Nov 42, sub: Plan for Retaking Burma. ABC 384 (Burma), 8–25–42, Sec 1A, A48–224.

This was on 3 November. Shortly after, Stilwell's report of his conferences with the Generalissimo came to Washington. Indicating approval of Stilwell's views, Marshall made a practice of sending Stilwell's more important communications to the President, and so he sent this on, first explaining how he had made his views on Stilwell clear to Soong:

. . . I forcibly impressed T. V. Soong with the fact that the great issue was Burma (not merely a harmonious group at Chungking); which meant a properly trained Chinese force at Ramgarh, an improved or selected Chinese force in Yunnan and a practical basis of co-operation with the British in such an operation—in other words Stilwell.

General Stilwell apparently has gained ground that I did not anticipate. We have been working in the Combined Chiefs of Staff on an operation into Burma, and of course the great problem pertains to the logistics and the naval support required. Until the situation is clarified in the Middle East and the Caucasus, the calculations could only be on such a vague basis as to have little reality.[72]

On 8 November the situation in the Middle East and the Mediterranean began to clarify as the British and American forces successfully landed in French North Africa. Completion of the campaign would relieve British fears for the Middle East, would open a supply line through the Mediterranean to India, and would permit Wavell more freedom in approaching Burmese problems. Fears over the Caucasus abated as the Soviets began their counter-offensive at Stalingrad on 19 November. Four days later the German Army which had been attacking Stalingrad found itself encircled. The long German retreat was about to begin. The initiative had passed to the Allies.

Stilwell's request for service troops and engineer equipment to support the north Burma operations arrived at a time when the War Department and JCS attitudes toward China and her problems were in the process of crystallizing. The 25 September draft by OPD of an answer to the Generalissimo's Three Demands took the attitude that nothing more than existing commitments could be spared for Stilwell. The President's formal reply of October urged offensive action in Burma on the Chinese. Stilwell had secured their assent to such action. However, on his asking for the means to support the Chinese in the offensive that the President had suggested, Stilwell had received OPD's chilling answer. Plainly, the time to harmonize the conflicting currents had come. And harmony was promptly established; the Chief of Staff supported Stilwell and told him so on 7 December:

MY DEAR STILWELL:

I am keenly aware of the seemingly unsurmountable difficulties that you have faced daily in the creation of an efficient striking force to reopen ground communications with China. You have far exceeded our expectations in securing authority for the reorganization which you are now rapidly putting into effect. We are doing everything in our power to find the ships to carry to you at least the bare essentials you so urgently require. Incidentally, the Chiefs of Staff are taking this up with the President tomorrow.

[72] Memo cited n. 29.

To paraphrase Mr. Churchill's famous statement, nowhere has so much been done with so little as under your driving leadership.

This note carries my Christmas greetings and personal thanks to you and your people. Please feel that we have you constantly in mind. I am certain that if we find ways and means to supply your most essential requirements you will give an historic beating to some Japs in 1943.

Faithfully yours,

(Signed) G. C. MARSHALL.

P. S.   I read your profane message for "Timberman's eye only" and I sympathize with you in your reaction.[73]

As General Marshall wrote, the Joint Chiefs placed the matter before Roosevelt on 8 December. In doing so, they revealed their pleasure at Stilwell's success in bringing the Chinese around. A significant new element was the statement that a limited operation along the lines Stilwell had discussed with Wavell could succeed and result in a land route to China from Ledo to Wanting via Myitkyina. Stilwell's initial proposals to Wavell had revealed no interest in such a route. After Wavell assigned Stilwell to north Burma, Stilwell had used the prospect of a road from Ledo to Kunming as an added argument to persuade the Chinese. Now, the Joint Chiefs were telling the President of the prospect. To give Stilwell road-building machinery and engineer, signal, and medical personnel, Marshall proposed to divert cargo vessels from lend-lease and troop lift from other operations. The JCS observed that if ANAKIM succeeded in opening a land route to China, it would permit basing greater air power in China. Roosevelt approved the JCS's suggestion that Stilwell be given the means for his share of ANAKIM, and Stilwell's modest requirements for the projected operation received a priority second only to Eisenhower's in North Africa.[74]

In accordance with the JCS directive, Army Service Forces examined the problem of filling Stilwell's request. By eliminating every man whose work might be done by an Indian civilian, it believed that a shipment of 6,000 U.S. troops would be enough. These were assembled and rushed to CBI.[75]

Before Marshall's reassuring words were received by Stilwell, the latter was becoming increasingly aware that both British and Chinese were having long second thoughts about operations in Burma. While Stilwell was in Chungking in November working with the Chinese, his New Delhi headquarters under Ferris was in constant touch with Wavell's. General Ferris's reports were disquieting to General Stilwell. It seemed to the American staff that Wavell's India Command and the Royal Navy command for the Indian Ocean and the Bay of Bengal were approaching the operation with reluctance. Since the Gen-

---

[73] (1) Ltr, Marshall to Stilwell, 7 Dec 42. Stilwell Personal Papers. (2) Rad cited n. 68.

[74] (1) Suppl Min, JCS 45th Mtg, 8 Dec 42, Item 6. (2) JCS 162, 7 Dec 42, sub: Opns in Burma, Mar 43. (3) Rpt, Jt Subcom, JPS, 10 Dec 42, sub: Opns in Burma, Mar 43. ABC 384 (Burma), 8–25–42, Sec 1A, A48–224. (4) Ltr, Marshall to Dill, 13 Dec 42. OPD 381 CTO (12–13–42), A47–30.

[75] MS, pp. 46–55, cited n. 61(2).

eralissimo had insisted on Allied naval and air superiority as a prerequisite, British reluctance could suggest to the Chinese leader that he might at any time declare India's arrangements inadequate and withdraw from the operation. The Generalissimo's position was known to India Command, which could easily make use of it by declaring naval strength unavailable, thus creating a situation from which the Generalissimo would be very likely to withdraw.

General Wavell made it quite plain that any operation would have to be a success, and Stilwell wondered how that could be guaranteed. Admiral Sir James Somerville, commanding Eastern Fleet, seemed unable to think of anything that might be used to convince the Generalissimo that the Royal Navy commanded the Bay of Bengal and knew of no forthcoming reinforcements. Wavell's quartermaster-general argued in conference that the recently begun U.S. road-building effort from Ledo was foolhardy and a waste of resources.[76]

Stilwell's relations with Wavell and the Generalissimo were not improved by some actions of the U.S. Naval Attaché in Chungking, Lt. Col. James M. McHugh, USMC. In October McHugh reported to the Navy Department a conversation between himself and the Generalissimo regarding Stilwell's replacement by Chennault and offered his opinion that such a step would be wise. Returning to the United States, McHugh paused in New Delhi and discussed Stilwell's plans and position with Wavell, criticizing Stilwell severely, and discoursing on Chennault's belief that Japan could be defeated by a minute China-based air force. In Marshall's opinion, expressed to the Joint Chiefs on 21 December, this indiscretion caused irreparable harm to the U.S. war effort in CBI and the Southwest Pacific.[77]

The first week of December Ferris was approached privately by Wavell and asked to consent to the elimination of the projected campaign because of the logistic difficulties involved.[78] Wavell also complained to his superiors of the problems Stilwell was causing him. Stilwell was said to be in Chungking planning for Burma operations without consulting Wavell and with little reference to his American staff in Delhi, who were alleged to know little of his plans. Ferris was accused of being afraid to present the "true administrative picture" to Stilwell and of being overawed by him. Wavell's radio was a very long one, cataloguing every logistical and medical problem, from the monsoon to malaria. Earlier, Wavell had hesitated to attempt more than the most limited operations in Burma. Now, he wondered if, in the light of all these difficulties,

[76](1) Rad AMMDEL 516, Ferris to Stilwell, 18 Nov 42. Item 103, Bk 1, JWS Personal File. (2) Ltr, Ferris to Stilwell, 16 Nov 42. Item 209, Bk 3, JWS Personal File. (3) CM–IN 11004, Stilwell to Marshall, 24 Nov 42.

[77](1) Memo, Marshall for JCS, 21 Dec 42, sub: Gen Stilwell. OPD 381 CTO, Sec. 3, A47–30. (2) Suppl Min, JCS 47th Mtg, 22 Dec 42, Item 10. (3) Memo, Handy for Marshall, 12 Dec 42, sub: Rpt by Naval Attaché in Chungking Re Opns U.S. Forces, CBI. OPD 381 CTO, Sec. 3, A47–30.

[78](1) Rad AMMDEL 568, Ferris to Stilwell, 6 Dec 42. Item 136, Bk 1, JWS Personal File. (2) Rad AMMISCA 1494, Stilwell to Marshall, 7 Dec 42. Item 137, Bk 1, JWS Personal File. (3) The Stilwell Papers, p. 176.

the Allies would be wise to attempt the reoccupation of north Burma in spring 1943.[79] Analyzing Wavell's comments, Colonel Roberts of OPD, who had been Stilwell's G-2 in Burma, reported that Wavell had in many ways misrepresented Stilwell's plans and solutions for his supply problems and that Wavell's radio simply indicated he was not an aggressive commander.[80]

Marshall moved to support Stilwell by applying some pressure through Field Marshal Dill. The Chief of Staff pointed out that recent preparations in India might not have been brought to Dill's attention. The Anglo-American planners at New Delhi had estimated that the British concentration in Manipur State could be completed on 15 January, that the stocking of the Ledo base could then begin, and that the Chinese Ramgarh-trained divisions would be there on 1 March with the supply base ready to support them. With the means at hand Stilwell would build a dry-weather, single-track road (for pack train operations beyond the roadhead) as far forward of Ledo as possible. "In the light of the above," asked Marshall, "and as soon as Wavell learns that we plan to send engineer and other service troops and equipment, do you not think that his attitude toward carrying out the British-American-Chinese limited operations against Burma will be less apprehensive?" [81]

On 7 December Wavell told Stilwell directly of his doubts. He was most anxious to see Stilwell because the extreme difficulty of solving the problem of keeping troops in north Burma through the monsoon was now apparent, and reinforcements for India from the Middle East in early 1943 were extremely doubtful. Therefore, a north Burma operation in spring 1943 might be premature.[82]

Stilwell and Ferris met with Wavell and his chiefs of staff in New Delhi on 17 December. Wavell stated that as agreed previously he had continued planning for a combined offensive into north Burma. The problem was logistics. While he had no doubt the British and Chinese could get into north Burma he did not see how they could stay there during the monsoon rains. The supply route to China could only be reopened by taking Rangoon; however, the North African campaign had taken so much shipping that an amphibious operation against Rangoon would be impossible before fall 1943. By implication, therefore, the projected north Burma campaign would accomplish nothing to relieve China. Stilwell replied that the Generalissimo was anxious to open a road from India to China. Inflation was becoming rampant in China, while the Chinese forces badly needed small arms ammunition, artillery shells, and artillery. "Gen. Wavell said that the question really hinged on the possibility of maintaining a force throughout the rains at Myitkyina, and he thought that what was needed was an estimate of the earliest date by which the road

[79] (1) Rad COS W 388, COS to JSM, 9 Dec 42. Folder 22, OPD Exec 10. (2) Ltr, Dill to Marshall, 10 Dec 42. WDCSA (China), A45–466.
[80] Memo, Roberts for Wedemeyer, 12 Dec 42. ABC 384 (Burma), 8–25–42, Sec 1A, A48–224.
[81] Ltrs, Marshall to Dill, 10, 13 Dec 42. WDCSA (China), A45–466.
[82] Rad British MA to Stilwell, 7 Dec 42. SNF–46.

could be through to Myitkyina and brought up to all-weather standards. . . ." [83]

Stilwell then described the U.S. contribution to the Ledo road-building effort and to sanitation, and the Chinese proposal to commit twenty reorganized divisions. Wavell closed the discussion by remarking that he would go on with an advance toward Akyab regardless of what happened in north Burma though he had no plans to advance from Akyab. [84]

Wavell had planned a swift amphibious descent on Akyab, but North African operations had a higher priority on landing craft while a British amphibious brigade, which might have been used, was riddled with malaria as an aftermath of the earlier occupation of Madagascar. Consequently, his advance on Akyab with the 14th Indian Division had to be overland, and it was under way as he spoke with Stilwell on 17 December. [85]

When Dill sent Marshall a British study urging that nothing be done in Burma, the Army's Chief of Staff was moved to offer in rebuttal an exposition of his own views on CBI strategy:

> Our great objective in the China Theater is the build-up of air operations in China with a view to carrying out destructive attacks against Japanese shipping and sources of supply.
>
> To get the plan under way, General Stilwell has, with our approval and that of the Generalissimo, undertaken a program of intensive training and the task of equipping and providing effective leadership for selected Chinese units. This has taken form through the medium of the reorganization of the Yunnan forces and the preparation of an Army Corps at the Ramgarh Training Center.
>
> The concessions made by the Generalissimo were promptly accepted and his promises of action are being implemented by the assignment of American officers with the units of his Yunnan forces, by the decision to have American officers accompany the advance into Burma of the Ramgarh Forces and by the provision of American service troops to back up the Ramgarh advance.
>
> I am confident the individual Chinese soldier will fight, has no nerves, requires a minimum of food, clothing and similar supplies, and should, if properly led, trained and equipped (which has never been the case in the past), give a good account of himself.
>
> The success of limited operations in Burma will afford increased protection to the air freight route to China and help to maintain this slender supply link to our American–China Air Task Force until such time as a land route can be opened. Upon the opening of a land route to China, we propose to move supplies for this air task force in increasing quantities and build up this force to where it will be extremely effective against the enemy.
>
> Our present operations in China are severely restricted by the limitations of the air freight route from India to China, which necessitates early offensive action to facilitate at the earliest possible moment the opening of a land route to China. [86]

The Emergence of the Chennault Plan

Developments in Chungking paralleled those in Delhi. As soon as Stilwell tried to translate the Chinese 3 November promises into action, he met with

[83] Min, 61st Mtg, COS Com, 17 Dec 42. SNF-84.
[84] *Ibid.*
[85] Field Marshal Viscount Wavell, "Operations in the India Command from 1st January, 1943, to 20th June, 1943," *Supplement to The London Gazette,* April 22, 1948, pars. 1–5.
[86] Ltr, Marshall to Dill, 21 Dec 42. WDCSA China (12–9–42), A45–466.

inertia in the Chinese Ministry of War and General Staff and an ever-growing tendency on the part of Chinese in high places to adopt the attitude, against which Magruder and Stilwell had often warned Marshall, that Chennault and his China Air Task Force should do the fighting in and for China.[87] Nothing loath, Chennault was now claiming that with 105 fighters, 30 medium bombers, and 12 heavy bombers he could defeat Japan.[88] The Generalissimo's diplomatic correspondence of 1943 suggests Chennault's claims had decisive effect on the Generalissimo's policies.[89]

Chennault's views on what could be accomplished in Asia by a small but effective air force were often expressed by him in 1941.[90] Then came the First Burma Campaign, in which his American Volunteer Group had performed brilliantly. But instead of becoming the senior American air officer in China Theater, Chennault had become subordinate to other airmen without his combat record.[91] Marshall's and Stilwell's plans contemplated reforming the Chinese Army and clearing north Burma before giving Chennault the supplies for a major air effort in China. These plans were not to Chennault's liking; in July and September 1942 he stated that given about 2,000 tons of supplies a month he could operate aggressively and effectively against Japanese aircraft and merchant shipping.[92]

The absence of comment in Stilwell's diaries suggests that he may have been largely unaware of the trend of Chennault's thinking until mid-October. There is no word of criticism directed toward Chennault until mid-December. Stilwell had been quick to support Chennault in aggressive action. Thus, when a major Japanese convoy dropped anchor at Hong Kong in October 1942 Stilwell was prompt to arrange reinforcements for Chennault to attack it.

Big opportunity at Hong Kong. Discovered on Tuesday, October 6th. On the 10th, still nothing done. Ordered help up from India by rad to Bissell, urgent. 10 P. M. radio from Bissell wanting to "confer" at Dinjan on important project; the birds will have flown. . . .[93]

Bissell got right on the job. The typewriters [B–24's] should be in on Mon (5) and Tues (7). . . .[94]

. . . Birds should be ready to fly Tues A. M. The news is spreading. They can't keep their traps shut. . . .[95]

The real restraint on Chennault was the inability of the Hump to support his operations. In his memoirs Chennault charges Stilwell with studied neglect

---

[87] (1) *The Stilwell Papers,* pp. 179, 180, 183. (2) See Chs. III and V, above.
[88] Chennault, *Way of a Fighter,* p. 214.
[89] (1) Rad AGWAR 31, Chiang to Roosevelt, 9 Jan 43. Item 161, Bk 1, JWS Personal File. (2) Ltr, Chiang to Roosevelt, 23 Feb 43. Item 58, OPD Exec 10. (3) Ltr, Soong to Roosevelt, 29 Apr 43. Bk VII, Hopkins Papers.
[90] See Ch. I, pp. 10, 17–21, above.
[91] See Ch. II, pp. 73, 78–79, above.
[92] See Ch. V, pp. 187–89, above.
[93] Stilwell B&W, 10 Oct 42. Lack of criticism in Stilwell diaries may usually be taken as approval.
[94] Stilwell Diary, 11 Oct 42.
[95] Stilwell Diary, 12 Oct 42.

of the airline to China, but Stilwell, as noted in Chapter V, was always asking for more transports than OPD would allocate.[96] Whether Stilwell should have devoted more time to his relations with the commander of the China Air Task Force is a major question, but, for whatever reasons, Stilwell did not, and Chennault drew his own conclusions.

Administrative problems embittered relations between Chennault's air force and Bissell's staff. Charged with misuse of its radio command net, scolded for using irregular command channels, suspected of harboring a smuggling ring, and disciplined for the misconduct of its personnel, the China Air Task Force felt persecuted. Moreover, Chennault deeply resented a directive which gave Bissell the right to select tactical commanders and staff officers for the China Air Task Force. Correspondence on the subject of appointments and removals of China Air Task Force staff officers revealed animosity between Bissell and Chennault.[97]

The September directive from Stilwell's headquarters made defense of the Hump Chennault's primary mission, but the monsoon rains of October in effect performed that mission for him and left him free to mount a series of attacks on Japanese aircraft and shipping in and near China that brought excellent results at small cost.

In defense of their portion of the ferry route, Chennault's fighters made offensive sweeps over Burma which persuaded him that "With a relatively small effort the C.A.T.F. was able to keep the enemy supply system sufficiently disjointed to make it impossible to accumulate enough matériel in advanced positions for a major offensive. The Japs were never able to support more than a few small patrols on the east bank of the Salween, and their long-anticipated major offensive never materialized despite the weakness of the Chinese defenses." [98] Chennault concluded from this that a small air force could do great things to stop an army. Unfortunately for his deductions, the Japanese *15th Army* had no thought of crossing the Salween, for its gaze was fixed on India; the anticipated offensive toward Kunming was a complete misinterpretation.[99]

When Mr. Wendell L. Willkie came to China in October as the President's personal representative Chennault made another convert. To Willkie, Chennault gave a letter for the President, dated 8 October 1942. In the letter he asked for "full authority as the American military commander in China," and an air force of 105 fighters, 30 medium bombers, and 12 heavy bombers, to be kept up to strength with 30 percent fighter replacements and 20 percent bomber replace-

---

[96] Chennault, *Way of a Fighter,* p. 203.

[97] (1) Memo, Bissell for Chennault, 16 Sep 42, sub: Infraction of Radio Procedure, with Incls and Inds. Misc Corresp Folder (Apr–Dec 42), CT 23, Dr 2, KCRC. (2) Rad SVC 130, Bissell to Stilwell, 1 Dec 42; Rad AG 409, Stilwell to Marshall, 18 Oct 42. Items 128, 78, Bk 1, JWS Personal File. (3) Portions of the bitter exchange of letters between Chennault and Bissell are in CATF 312.9, USAF Hist Div.

[98] Chennault, *Way of a Fighter,* p. 195.

[99] Japanese Study 89.

ments. With this tiny air force he would "accomplish the downfall of Japan," and "destroy the effectiveness of the Japanese Air Force," the latter feat "probably within six months, within one year at the outside." To support this force, the aerial supply line over the Hump should be built up, but the amount of freight to be carried over it was "very small." [100]

How, precisely, would Chennault do this? He told the President:

Japan must hold Hong Kong, Shanghai, and the Yangtze Valley. They are essential to hold Japan itself. I can force the Japanese Air Force to fight in the defense of these objectives behind the best air warning net of its kind in the world. With the use of these tactics, I am confident that I can destroy Japanese aircraft at the rate of between ten and twenty to one. When the Japanese Air Force refuses to come within my warning net and fight, I will strike out with my medium bombers against their sea supply line to the Southwest Pacific. In a few months the enemy will lose so many aircraft that the aerial defense of Japan will be negligible. I can then strike at Japan from Chuchow and Lishui with heavy bombers. My air force can burn up Japan's two main industrial areas—Tokyo and the Kobe, Osaka, Nagoya triangle—and Japan will be unable to supply her armies in her newly conquered empire in China, Malaya, the Dutch East Indies, etc. with munitions of war. The road is then open for the Chinese Army in China, for the American Navy in the Pacific and for MacArthur to advance from his Australian stronghold—all with comparatively slight cost.

While engaged in these operations, I will maintain full ground installations for the eastern terminus of the ferry route in Yunnan, at Kunming, Chanyi, Yunnanyi, etc. If a really major swift aerial movement is made by the Japanese across their staging route into Burma, to attack the India-China air supply lines, then, acting on interior lines of air communications, I can move back and again be within the warning net which I have established in Yunnan, and meet the Japanese over their Burma airfields and then and there destroy whatever force they have sent against us.

My entire above plan is simple. It has been long thought out. I have spent five years developing an air warning net and radio command service to fight this way. I have no doubt of my success.[101]

This then was the Chennault plan: attack military objectives in Japanese-held China; destroy the Japanese Air Force when it tried to defend them; then bomb the Japanese home islands after the Japanese Air Force had been destroyed. The logistic requirements steadily expanded in the years ahead, but the plan itself was unchanged.

Arnold heard that Chennault claimed two hundred aircraft would give him air superiority in China. Apparently, too, Chennault's complaints about lack of support were being heard in Washington. Stilwell immediately answered that Chennault's men had first priority on available supplies, that Chennault had wide latitude under his directive, and denied that any obstacles were being put in the way of awards to Chennault's airmen. Stilwell went on to say that while Chennault was superior in his sphere, his administration was bad. Stilwell doubted that Chennault could achieve air superiority in China, because only a few American aircraft could operate there. In reply, Stimson wrote that if Stilwell accepted Chennault's administrative weaknesses and gave him more

[100] Chennault, *Way of a Fighter*, pp. 212–14.
[101] Chennault, *Way of a Fighter*, p. 215.

support and prestige, the result might strengthen Stilwell with the General-issimo.[102]

In late November Madame Chiang arrived in the United States and was met in New York by Mr. Hopkins. After telling Hopkins that she had come to the United States only for medical treatment and rest, "in the same breath she proceeded to raise many questions relating to China and the United States." [103] In the course of her interview with Hopkins, Madame Chiang made it "pretty clear she does not like Stilwell and expressed the greatest admiration for Chennault." [104] Her expressions found a willing listener, for Hopkins was an enthusiastic supporter of Chennault in the highest Administration circles, which, thanks to Mr. Willkie, the U.S. Naval Attaché, Colonel McHugh, and returning members of Chennault's task force, were now fully aware of Chennault's claims and grievances.[105]

On 9 November 1942 the President wrote to Mr. Joseph W. Alsop, the columnist, then about to join Chennault in China, that he wished he could go with him to Chennault and that he was suggesting as an alternative that Chennault be called back for a short visit if the American airman thought it advisable.[106]

The Chinese Hesitate

In China, December found Stilwell having an increasingly difficult time with the Chinese Ministry of War and General Staff. Continuing his attempt to work through T. V. Soong, Stilwell bombarded the Chinese diplomat with memoranda, frankly discussing the difficulties which were accumulating with every day's delay. On 5 December Stilwell warned Soong that if the Burma operation was to succeed preparations had to begin at once, but "It is not known that these Armies have started to march." After discussing the artillery situation and criticising the dilettante approach that the Chinese had adopted toward it, he wrote: "The time has come when the Chinese Government must decide whether or not it intends to carry out the operation. To date there has been little indication that it considers the matter seriously. Sacrifices must be made. Difficulties must be overcome." [107]

Analyzing the situation he faced, Stilwell wrote, "What the hell will I do if they saddle me with this thing? Ramgarh Force—OK. Y-Force? (unless we

[102](1) CM–OUT 05132, Arnold to Stilwell, 16 Oct 42. (2) Rad AMMDEL AM 409, Stilwell to Marshall, 18 Oct 42; Rad WAR 100, Stimson to Stilwell, 24 Oct 42. Items 78, 79, Bk 1, JWS Personal File.

[103] Sherwood, *Roosevelt and Hopkins,* p. 660.

[104] Sherwood, *Roosevelt and Hopkins,* p. 661.

[105] Bk VII, Hopkins Papers.

[106] *F.D.R., His Personal Letters, 1928–1945* (New York, 1950), Vol. II, p. 1361. Contrast the President's statement of Alsop's mission, dated 9 November 1942, with a memorandum, Stettinius for Hopkins, dated 17 November 1942, in Book VII, Hopkins Papers: "I have today completed arrangements for Joe Alsop to proceed to Chungking about December 1 to become the lend-lease representative there."

[107] Memo, Stilwell for Soong, 5 Dec 42. Stilwell Documents, Hoover Library.

get a tough comdr). Limies? (lukewarm). Naval support—? Air support—? It seems to be mostly question marks!" [108]

But since on the surface at least the Chinese were co-operative, Stilwell adhered to his *quid pro quo* approach and told Marshall in a very strong radio that the United States in turn must honor its promises. After telling the Chief of Staff what the consequences would be if the Air Force was allowed to divert 12 transport aircraft promised earlier for support of the Y–Force, Stilwell went on to say that there should be an immediate increase in aid to China, that 2 fighter groups, 1 medium bomber group, and 50 transports should be dispatched at once to CBI, and that the 3,500 tons a month of lend-lease should be stepped up to 10,000 tons a month regardless of whether it could be moved from India or not.[109]

By 23 December, Stilwell spoke to Soong in terms of urgent warning. The Generalissimo had entrusted plans and preparations to that same General Lo Cho-ying whom Stilwell had forced out of Ramgarh for his attempt to divert 100,000 rupees a month to his own pocket, and the results had not been impressive.

More progress can be made if there is less nonsense. Just one department—the Ordnance—is working efficiently. Everywhere else is delay and confusion. The trouble can be largely corrected, even now, if the Generalissimo will appoint a *real commander,* give him *real authority,* and hold him responsible for results.

Has a commander been appointed for the Y–Force? I do not know yet, and I am entitled to the information. . . .

We have as difficult a task as I can conceive of coming in through the Hukawng Valley— the worst malaria section in the world—building a road over two hundred miles long through the mountains, and taking on a fight for a junction with the Y–Force. . . . Under these circumstances [of major U.S. aid for the project] I must assure myself that the Chinese commander is competent.

I have reported to the Generalissimo that in my opinion Lo Cho-ying and his staff are *not* competent to make the preparations for this operation. They have no conception of the requirements. . . .

If the present neglect of essentials by Lo—who I assume is the candidate for command— continues . . . I shall not feel justified in pushing my own people as I am doing at present. But even Lo could be made to do if the Generalissimo, as he agreed, will take command and insist on action.

As the matter is being conducted now, it cannot be put on at the date set, and may easily break down entirely. . . . The net result might very well be the acquiring by the British of all American resources in this Theater, for use in India under British command. We must avoid such a catastrophe at any cost. To do it, it is essential that the Generalissimo realize that efficient, radical, prompt steps be taken, that the War Ministry be energized, and that the command question be settled.[110]

Over the next few days Soong pondered Stilwell's warning that without drastic remedial action the attack from Yunnan would fail. A solution other

[108] Stilwell B&W, 9 Dec 42.
[109] (1) CM–IN 9374, Stilwell to Marshall, 22 Nov 42. (2) CM–IN 3891, Stilwell to Marshall, 9 Dec 42.
[110] Memo, Stilwell for Soong, 23 Dec 42. Stilwell Documents, Hoover Library.

than remedial action may well have suggested itself to Soong, that is, to postpone the operation until fall. The Chinese Foreign Minister knew of the differences between Chennault and Stilwell, and certainly after a radio from Marshall on 16 December Stilwell was fully aware of Chennault's claim that he could defeat Japan with a tiny air force. If Soong could adjust the relationship between Stilwell and Chennault and pave the way toward the badly needed reform of the Chinese Army and Air Force, he would have made a major contribution to China Theater.[111]

Soong's proposal for a compromise solution was given to Colonel Dorn on Christmas Eve, 1942. On Christmas Day, Stilwell recorded that Dr. Soong had told Dorn of Soong's belief that "we have a chance to do almost anything." Soong suggested Stilwell yield on Chennault in order to obtain what Stilwell cryptically called "the big gravy." Soong, so Stilwell believed, was "firmly convinced Henry [Stimson] and George [Marshall] will do anything I tell them to." [112]

This was a crucial moment in Stilwell's relations with the Chinese. Stilwell's response to Soong's suggestion would reveal Stilwell's attitude and intentions in China Theater. If Stilwell accepted Soong's suggestions, if Soong in turn could deliver "the big gravy," then Stilwell could press forward with reform and reorganization of the Chinese Army, which as Stilwell himself had stated did not depend on matériel, while Chennault could have a free hand with his plans. And, if Stilwell aimed at command of the Chinese Army, his answer would reveal it, for it would have to define "the big gravy," as Stilwell saw it.

Stilwell's answer of 27 December was given orally, possibly to avoid compromising Soong. As was Stilwell's custom, he drafted it carefully beforehand:

1. Long Range Objective:
A powerful independent China, with a modern well-organized Army, in a position to back up all legitimate demands, and with close ties of interests and friendship with the United States. (Under these conditions, peace in the Orient could be assured, and China could take the lead in the organization of an Asiatic League of China, Indo-China, Siam, Burma, and India. The Pacific Ocean would be controlled jointly by the United States and China, with no conflicts of interest in the Dutch East Indies, Australia, or the Philippine Islands.)

2. Immediate Objective:
Re-organization, equipment, and training of the Chinese Army, including the Air Force. The 30-Division Plan can be adapted to the units of the Y–Force, concentrated in Yunnan, where they are accessible for training and supply, and at the same time assure the defense of a vital area. (To assure supply, and convince the United States of China's sincerity, the joint

[111] (1) Stilwell Diary, 16 Dec 42. (2) CM–IN 5640, Stilwell to Marshall, 13 Dec 42.
[112] Stilwell Diary and B&W, 25 Dec 42. The original texts are: "Full day. T. V. called Dorn over last night and gave him a blast. Wants me to give Chennault his way. Wrote out a scheme. Also suggestion for a mission to the U.S. headed by Ho." (Diary) "T. V. thinks we have a chance to do almost anything. He wants me to give in on Chennault in order to get my mitts on the big gravy. He is firmly convinced that Henry and George will do anything I tell them to." (B&W)

operation against Burma is an essential preliminary step. If unduly delayed, doubts will arise in the United States, and the present inclination to assist, even at the expense of other Theaters, will cool off. On the other hand this evidence of China's intentions to make what effort she can with her meager resources, will greatly enhance her prestige in the United States and put her in a position to get further help.)

3. Obstacles:

a. *Time.* Avoidable delays have made it difficult to prepare the operation in time, but it is still possible if red tape can be cut, and if the Generalissimo gets behind it.

b. *Insufficient Means.* We can make up for Japanese superiority in equipment and training by numbers, co-ordination with the British move, and proper leadership.

c. *Cumbersome administration* and obstruction by certain elements with different ideas. The answer to this is a re-organization of the War Ministry, which might in effect, be accomplished by the following plan:

The Generalissimo to form a Mission to the United States to confer on all aspects of the war in the China Theater, in particular on further aid to China. General Ho Ying-ch'in should head this mission. It would take up such questions as the supply for the second 30-Division Plan, tank units, air service, the new Chinese Navy, development of road and rail communications, motor transport, technical assistants, etc. It would tour the manufacturing plants in the United States and serve also as a good-will mission. At least six months would be needed for it to complete its duties.

Meanwhile the Generalissimo would be concurrently Minister of War, and would appoint Dr. T. V. Soong as his *Executive Assistant to co-ordinate American and Chinese activities for the improvement of the technical and supply services of the Chinese Army.* [Stilwell's italics] The Ordnance is no problem, Communications, under Tseng Yang-fu should be no problem. The Air Service can be handled. Engineering and Motor Transport can be handled through Tseng Yang-fu. The medical tangle can be straightened out by the appointment of a strong man to head the service. The present Service of Supply can be developed and perpetuated as the field set-up for the entire Army. The "technical" control can be extended to Infantry and Artillery units through the medium of training schools that can be set up in Yunnan. (The Ramgarh school should continue as a feeder of Chinese instructors to units in China.)

d. The obstacle to the above is principally in in [*sic*] the Chinese General Staff, which for various reasons, is almost completely indifferent to and neglectful of the present low state of training, morale, equipment, supply, and leadership in the Chinese Army. Such minutiae as occasional breakage of supplies in the American Service of Supply in India, or orders for moving picture apparatus, or the status of a few airplane or motor parts, receive the attention that should be devoted to the big and glaring deficiencies in the Chinese Army itself. Some way *must* be found to energize the War Ministry, or such tendencies will continue to nullify all the efforts that are made elsewhere.

The mission suggested above offers a possible means od [*sic*] starting some much-needed changes.[113]

Stillwell's answer had some subtle aspects. On the basis of his great power within the Chinese Government, Soong had offered to mediate between Stilwell and Chennault. Stilwell's answer ignored this offer and countered with a proposal that closely resembled Soong's proposal to Stilwell. Aware that Soong considered him to wield great influence in Washington, Stilwell suggested an

---

[113] In his diary entry of 25 December 1942, Stilwell noted: "Wrote out a scheme. Also suggestion for a mission to the U.S. headed by Ho." The "scheme" is a Memorandum, Stilwell for Soong, dated 27 December 1942, in the Stilwell Documents, Hoover Library. On the typed memo is the note in Stilwell's hand: "Gist to T. V. verbally."

arrangement that would greatly extend Soong's power in China at the expense of Gen. Ho Ying-chin, Soong's colleague.

While Soong and Stilwell conducted their delicate negotiations in Chung-king, Soong's China Defense Supplies, Inc., in Washington, presented its version of China's lend-lease requirements for 1943. General Somervell promptly passed the Chinese bid on to Stilwell, observing that many of the Chinese proposals were beyond U.S. production capacity. Somervell added that the Chinese had assured him that their program was approved by Stilwell. Stilwell hastened to set matters straight and told Somervell that far from having approved the Chinese proposals, he was then in the process of reaching an agreement with Soong, Chen Cheng, and Ho Ying-chin on what the 1943 Chinese lend-lease program was to be.[114]

The Generalissimo Says No

Soong never answered directly, but over the weeks ahead Chinese diplomatic messages and Chinese inaction spelled out the answer. First hint that the Chinese would not cross the Salween in spring 1943 came in a radio from the Generalissimo to the President on 28 December. The Generalissimo claimed that in spring 1942 Churchill had assured the Pacific powers that at the end of the monsoon rains the Royal Navy would have eight battleships, three carriers, and supporting craft in the Bay of Bengal. In the Generalissimo's opinion Burma could not be taken without Allied naval control of the bay. Now, Stilwell had told him the Eastern Fleet had only destroyers and submarines. Moreover, though Wavell had allegedly promised that seven divisions would take part in the operation, the Generalissimo now understood only three would be used. The Chinese would be ready in March but could not attack unless the Royal Navy was ready to dominate the Bay of Bengal.[115]

This radio stirred Washington. Marshall at once told the President that Stilwell had reported no serious matter unsettled save that the Generalissimo insisted on British naval superiority in the bay. The President reacted immediately and sent a strong message, on 2 January 1943, to the Generalissimo through Stilwell. The Generalissimo was told that opening the Burma Road was more important than reoccupying all Burma, and he was promised that at the earliest possible date the President would definitely take up with the highest Allied authorities the matter of reopening the Burma Road without any avoidable delay.[116]

The Joint Chiefs of Staff discussed the naval question with the British Joint

[114] (1) Rad AMMISCA 1924, Somervell to Stilwell, 30 Dec 42. (2) CM–IN 1933, Stilwell to Marshall, 5 Jan 43.

[115] Msg, Chiang to President, 28 Dec 42, sent as CM–IN 12657, Stilwell to Marshall, 30 Dec 42. Item 150, Bk 1, JWS Personal File.

[116] Memo and Incl, Marshall for President, 30 Dec 42. Roosevelt's reply to the Generalissimo's 28 December 1942 message is WAR 1942, Roosevelt to Stilwell for Chiang, 2 Jan 43. WDCSA (China), A45–466, and Item 156, Bk 1, JWS Personal File.

Staff Mission, and Marshall told the JCS: "Advantage must be taken of the willingness of the Chinese to take the offensive. Means must be found to give the Generalissimo the necessary assurance that will enable the attack to jump off." [117]

The means were not to be found. Dill's attitude, consistent with that of Wavell, was cool, and he argued that the Generalissimo was confused about the nature and extent of proposed operations in Burma. There could be no fleet operations in the Bay of Bengal, Dill told Marshall, because Eastern Fleet lacked destroyers to escort the obsolete battleships which were all it had. Thi attitude was made yet more emphatic as the American authorities learne(Wavell had told Dill that Stilwell was aware British naval co-operation coulc not be counted on even though the Generalissimo made it a condition of his joining in Burma operations. [118]

Soong came to Stilwell's house on 4 January 1943 to receive the President's message and assured Stilwell the Chinese would be ready to go on time. On the 6th, Stilwell's hopes of a successful operation fell when he learned the Generalissimo had appointed Lt. Gen. Tu Yu-ming, whose relief Stilwell had requested months before because of his performance at Toungoo in April 1942, as a group army commander of the Y-Force reserve at Kunming. [119]

The Generalissimo's formal withdrawal from the proposed Salween campaign came in the form of a reply on 8 January 1943 to the President's radio of 2 January:

I am deeply grateful for your message dated January 2nd. With reference to it, the following points suggest themselves to me.

(1) The Japanese are fully aware that their final defeat will be accomplished, not by slow and costly reduction of island after island in the southwest Pacific, but by hard blows at the heart of their system of new conquests, on the mainland of Asia.

(2) Their resistance has been extremely tenacious, even when fighting superior numbers for points not strategically vital, as in New Guinea. It is reasonable to assume that when the first hard blow at the heart is struck, they will fight still more obstinately and with infinitely more carelessness of the resources expended. An advance into Burma, even if limited to North Burma alone, would be such a blow. Furthermore, the Japanese have now had ample time to establish themselves and fortify their positions in Burma, and to repair the facilities of the numerous supply lines, river, rail and road, by which they may reinforce and munition their armies. In a campaign in North Burma supply lines which would be available to us both on the Indian and on the Chinese side, are weak and exceedingly restricted.

(3) Therefore I am convinced that the attempt to retake Burma must be a combined overland and seaborne operation. Unless the navy could prevent enemy reinforcements by sea, or enable a landing force to take the Japanese in the rear in South Burma, the enemy will be in a position to concentrate rapidly against our armies in the North. Owing to the weakness of our supply lines, we shall not be able to match the Japanese concentration, whatever

[117] Memo, Marshall for Handy, 5 Jan 43; Memo, Marshall for JCS, 5 Jan 43, sub: Burma Opns. Item 22, OPD Exec 10.
[118](1) Ltr, Dill to Marshall, 2 Jan 43; Memo, Marshall for Handy, 5 Jan 43. Item 22, OPD Exec 10. (2) CM–OUT 2819, Marshall to Stilwell, 8 Jan 43.
[119](1) Stilwell Diary, 5 Jan 43. (2) Stilwell B&W, 6 Jan 43.

strength we may have available in the rear. Thus I consider it possible, and even likely, that in an advance restricted to North Burma our armies would ultimately be exposed to the risk of defeat. I am also convinced that to avoid defeat, the Allied forces must strenuously muster satisfactory numbers and quality on the Indian as well as on the Chinese side, and I consider that the forces which Field Marshal Wavell now proposes to engage are too inadequate.

(4) For these reasons, I regretfully conclude that if the navy is unable to control the Burma seas, it will be better to wait a few months longer, or even until the monsoon season ends next autumn, than to run the risks involved in the suggested North Burma campaign. Keenly as China desires the re-opening of her land communications, ready as I am to do anything in my power to bring the day nearer, I cannot forget that another failure in Burma would be a disaster for China so grave that the results cannot now be predicted. Under the circumstances, the more cautious course appears the only one open to me.

Then, in his next paragraph the Generalissimo struck the note that was to dominate the next eighteen months in China Theater—the acceptance of Chennault's claims and the reliance on U.S. air power.

(5) Although the advance into Burma is temporarily deferred, there is no reason why preparatory measures in this theatre should not be pushed forward as rapidly as is consistent with the Grand strategy of the United Nations. The remarkable potentialities of an air offensive in China have already been demonstrated by a small and ill-supported force. I believe that an early air offensive is feasible, since, owing to the peculiar tactical conditions which prevail here, neither the supply, material and personnel requirements are such as to embarrass the United Nations' air effort elsewhere. The return, I predict, will be out of all proportion to the investment, and by further weakening the Japanese air arm and striking at the sea-borne communications with their new conquests, an air offensive in China will directly prepare for the ultimate general offensive to which we both look forward.

(6) I would also urge that even if the British are not now able to muster sufficient strength, everything be done to induce them to set a definite date by which time they will have already concentrated adequate land and naval forces for a Burma campaign.

(7) On the part of the Chinese Army, I reiterate that we are proceeding with our preparations with all possible speed. We shall be ready to strike whenever our Allies are ready.

I have placed our position before you with the utmost frankness, which the gravity of the situation demands. I repeat, it is with the deepest regret and only after the most careful thought, that I have reached the conclusions herein expressed.[120]

The United States was at first reluctant to accept the Generalissimo's message at face value. For a week or more Stilwell thought the Chinese might yet attack. Roosevelt urged the Generalissimo not to make a final decision until after a forthcoming conference between the President and Churchill, for naval support could be arranged there in ample time for March operations. The Generalissimo would not accept this, and his 8 January message was the final answer. It was regarded by the highest Allied authorities as ending prospects for a Burma operation in spring 1943.[121]

---

[120] Rad AGWAR 31, Chiang to President, 8 Jan 43. Item 161, Bk 1, JWS Personal File. Sent as CM-IN 3980, Stilwell to Marshall, 9 Jan 43.

[121] (1) Rad, Roosevelt to Chiang, 9 Jan 43. Item 19, OPD Exec 10. (2) JCS Min, Casablanca Conf, p. 65. (3) Rads AMMDEL AD 134, 139, Stilwell to Ferris, 23 Jan 43. Item 183, Bk 1 JWS Personal File

A few weeks later Madame Chiang addressed the Congress. A report stated, "The audience shouted unrestrainedly when she said: 'From five and a half years of experience we in China are convinced that it is the better part of wisdom not to accept failure ignominiously, but to risk it gloriously!' " [122]

Summary

The Generalissimo's refusal to risk failure in Burma, and his obvious desire that offensive action in China Theater be the task of American aircraft and American airmen, ended a period in which Stilwell, with the support of the President, had sought to persuade the Chinese into seeking their own salvation by reforming their Army and with their allies making an effort to break the blockade of China. In the course of this effort, Stilwell had presented a plan of action to the Chinese, British, and Americans, had begun organizing and equipping a Chinese corps at Ramgarh, and had sought to persuade the Chinese into assembling twenty reorganized and re-equipped divisions in Yunnan. The Joint Chiefs of Staff approved his plan. His immediate superiors, Stimson and Marshall, approved his suggestion that a bargaining approach be adopted in dealing with the Chinese.

The British revealed reluctance to mount an operation into Burma almost as soon as they had agreed to begin preparations for it. Further complicating matters, General Chennault placed before the Chinese, the British, and Stilwell's superiors his claim that with 105 fighters, 30 medium bombers, and 12 heavy bombers plus replacements he could defeat Japan. The proposition was most attractive to the Chinese. Chennault urged it strongly during the weeks when British hesitations were becoming apparent in Chungking. The Generalissimo accepted Chennault's views. Moreover, he joined those who were urging them on the President, among whom was the President's closest adviser, Harry Hopkins.

Having accepted Chennault's ideas, the Generalissimo called a halt to the operations scheduled for spring 1943. Thereby he moved to a diplomatic position of considerable strength, from which he could urge that the solution of China's military problems lay in the United States sending more and yet more air power to China, rather than in anything the Chinese might do for themselves.

The President was thus confronted with a major issue. Inevitably, he would have to choose between support of Stilwell and Marshall, with their insistence on bargaining with the Generalissimo to reform his Army with a view toward fighting the Japanese, and of General Chennault, whose plan permitted the President to be in full accord with the Generalissimo's wishes.

[122] *Time*, March 1, 1943.

CHAPTER VIII

ANAKIM Marks Time

All things considered, Stilwell was rather relieved by the Generalissimo's refusal to cross the Salween River into Burma. Stilwell's memorandums to Soong had been eloquent in their description of Chinese unreadiness and, as Stilwell believed, unwillingness, so the months ahead could be used to good advantage. Up to the present, Stilwell had enjoyed a good measure of support from his government, and by January 1943 it was plain that he would need it if China were to be rearmed. True, the President at Currie's suggestion had refused to ask anything of the Chinese in return for lend-lease, but on the other hand, and apparently more important to Stilwell, the shrewd and well-informed Soong regarded Stilwell worthy of collaboration. So long as Soong, and such Chinese as thought like Soong, regarded Stilwell as commanding predominant influence in Washington, then Stilwell could apply himself to reform of the Chinese Army without worrying about his position.

The Generalissimo's action could even be made to support the cause of Army reform, so long as Stilwell's superiors appeared to attach importance to his projects. Unity and coherence among American personalities and agencies would be vital in dealing with the Chinese. With unity and coherence, with American technical skill to draw on, the most daringly conceived projects might perhaps succeed despite all that could be urged against them, but "if the trumpet give an uncertain sound, who shall prepare himself to the battle?"

Talks About Reform Continue

Stilwell's initial and personal reaction to the Generalissimo's withdrawal from the projected March 1943 offensive was an indignant one, but, after he had surveyed the new situation and mapped out his course of action, he wrote in his diary on 18 January 1943 that it was a "damn good thing March 1 is off. We'd have been hung." [1] There must have been encouragement for him in a letter from Stimson that he received about this time, even though the Secretary of War wrote it before the Generalissimo's refusal to cross the Salween was known in Washington.

---

[1] (1) *The Stilwell Papers,* p. 183. (2) Stilwell Diary, 18 Jan 43.

Although I have not written you as often as I should have liked to, I have been following your negotiations and actions with the deepest interest and confidence. There is hardly a step you take that is not talked over by Marshall and myself and I know that our feelings for you are similar and deep. You have been sorely tried and I hope you realize how thoroughly we appreciate what you have been through. It is a very real source of gratification to us both that you seem now to be successful in conquering all of the difficulties which have been thrown in your path.

Wherever it is possible, we have tried to smooth your way for we believe in the soundness of your judgment and the correctness of your strategic decisions. We realize the dangers and difficulties of the North Burma campaign which have apparently so disheartened Wavell and his staff, but we agree with you in thinking that it is a necessary prerequisite to any thoroughly satisfactory line of communications to China. We hope that you will be successful in conquering the difficulties of the terrain and the dangers of malaria.

When I offered you this China mission I knew it would be a tough one but I confess I did not realize how very tough it would be; and I wish you to feel now my sympathy and congratulations for the surpassing fortitude, skill, and courage which you have shown in carrying through. I hope that the New Year will give you a full measure of success and the satisfaction that will go with it.

Very sincerely your friend,

HENRY L. STIMSON [2]

In private conversations with the Chinese immediately after the Generalissimo withdrew from the Burma operation, Stilwell adopted the tactics of indicating his extreme disappointment and of prophesying a radical change in U.S. public opinion unless the Chinese took immediate steps to make amends.[3] Stilwell believed the Chinese very likely would try to compensate for their withdrawal and laid his plans accordingly:

If I can report full cooperation on the first 30-division plan and a determination to use this force offensively, I will have a basis for demanding [from the War Department] the equipment for the second 30 divisions and additional personnel for training. If the delays experienced to date are to continue, then it is certainly not too early to start on the second group. These units would not have to be moved for some time. They could, however, be reorganized and groups of instructors sent out to them to begin their training. Much could be done without any new equipment—tactical training particularly—and a great deal of time could be saved. The economy and efficiency in a small, well-equipped, well-trained, mobile force compared with a large, ill-equipped, untrained, immobile one is obvious. With 60 divisions in being, China will have nothing to fear from the Japs.[4]

Stilwell, therefore, drafted an agreement to be presented to the Chinese if they seemed willing to admit a desire to repair the damage that Stilwell expected the Generalissimo's action would have inflicted on Sino-American relations. He hewed to the line of his 27 December 1942 note to Soong and therefore included his now-familiar proposals for reorganization and concentra-

[2] Ltr, Stimson to Stilwell, 6 Jan 43. Stilwell Personal Papers.
[3] CM-IN 5492, Stilwell to Marshall, 12 Jan 43. This radio was relayed to Marshall, then at Casablanca.
[4] Note, in Stilwell's hand. SNF-55. Stilwell's papers in this folder are for January–February 1943. It was Stilwell's custom to analyze his situation and prepare plans in advance of major discussions. It seems safe to date this note as January 1943.

tion of the Chinese Army, service schools, and an efficient SOS. The text of the draft agreement read:

1. *At Ramgarh. a.* Continue the combat training of the New 1st Army [22d and 38th divs.]. *b.* Augment the force by one division. *c.* Set up an armored force school. *d.* Set up a CWS school. *e.* Continue and amplify instruction in artillery, infantry weapons, motor transport, anti-aircraft, signal, engineer, medical, and QM branches. Organize six additional 75-mm. pack howitzer battalions. Continue officers' school.

2. *At the base at Ledo.* Prepare the base, with medical, motor transport, engineer, and supply facilities. Stock it. Work on the road.

3. *In Yunnan. a.* Concentrate, re-organize, equip, and train the units to participate. *b.* Build up stocks of supplies. *c.* Establish in the Kunming area officers' schools for infantry, artillery, and air-ground liaison. Feed instructors from these schools to the armies in Yunnan. *d.* Thoroughly organize the SOS and *all* its services—engineer, medical, signal, motor transport, depots, etc. *e.* Repair and develop the Burma Road, and prepare the communications to the east.

4. *Elsewhere in China. a.* Designate the units for the second 30 division plan. Begin re-organization. Send selected officers to the Kunming schools. *b.* Reorganize the Chinese Air Force.[5]

The proposed agreement had three significant new points. On 6 January Soong had formally asked on behalf of the Chinese Government that the United States assist in the reorganization, training, and future planning of the Chinese Air Force, with "quite a few [U.S. airmen] in order to stiffen the whole force," and for operations under Chennault's control. Stilwell therefore included this major point. The draft also invited attention to the importance of developing a line of communications from the terminus of the Burma Road to east China and made the important proposal that designation and reorganization of the second Thirty Divisions begin at once.[6] Obviously Stilwell felt the time had come to raise the major issue of a second Thirty Divisions.

Completing his personal preparations for further talks with the Chinese, Stilwell listed every proposed step in detail for Marshall's approval, together with his prophecy of a great change in U.S. opinion. Marshall's complete approval came at once on 16 January, and Stilwell prepared to resume discussions and await the opportune moment to give the proposed agreement to the Generalissimo.[7]

For their part, Soong and Chen Cheng continued the discussions with no indication that the Generalissimo's 8 January note represented a change in Chinese policy. The talks covered every aspect of the projected fall 1943 cam-

---

[5] Draft Memo, Stilwell for Soong, sub: Proposed Program In Case X–Y Opn Is Not Carried Out. SNF–55. There is no evidence that the memorandum was ever formally presented to the Chinese Foreign Minister to sign. Instead, its points were discussed with Soong, who recommended that they be laid before the Generalissimo. *The Stilwell Papers*, p. 184.

[6] (1) Soong's request on CAF and quotation in Memo, Dorn for Stilwell, 7 Jan 43. SNF–21. (2) Draft Memo cited n. 5.

[7] (1) CM–IN cited n. 3. (2) Rad WAR 2010, Marshall to Stilwell, 16 Jan. 43. Item 169, Bk 1, JWS Personal File.

paign, and Stilwell's staff had a study at hand for every major point. Soong asked for a list of "outstanding differences, misunderstandings, or difficulties," plus a detailed plan for Y–Force preparations.[8] He also promised to do something about relieving Generals Tu Yu-ming and Ho Ying-chin.[9] Stilwell reported to Washington that he, General Ho, and the local representative of the Chinese supply agencies in Washington had agreed on a 1943 program to procure lend-lease for sixty Chinese divisions, on the basis of completing the equipment of the first thirty and initiating procurement for the second thirty. Within a few days Stilwell and his Chinese colleagues agreed that Chinese requests for 1943 lend-lease supplies would be presented to Stilwell for prior comment.[10]

By 24 January Chen was of the opinion that there were four matters left to be presented to the Generalissimo: (1) Was Chen to have complete authority over the Y–Force? (2) Did the Generalissimo intend to order immediate concentration of the Y–Force and an immediate start on training? (3) When could the concentration be completed? (4) Was everything about the Chinese SOS settled? All other matters, said Chen, could be settled between him and Stilwell "as they were in complete agreement on all main points."[11]

Chen's questions cut to the heart of the matter, for in surveying his position on 20 January and listing an imposing series of his proposals that the Chinese had accepted in preparation for a Burma offensive, Stilwell noted: "BUT no action. Orders delayed and not obeyed. 3 armies exempted from amalgamation. 8th, 93rd, 37th, and 74th not moved. Obstruction in getting schools. Chen Cheng absent [from Yunnan]. Money not appropriated. Lung Yun not controlled."[12]

The area of uncertainty was apparently well defined by Chen, for when a few days later Soong, Chen, and Stilwell met again it was agreed that some points were still unsettled, among them, the central one—when would the orders for the troops to move to Yunnan actually be issued? Chen's command status was still in doubt, but it may have seemed subordinate to the question of whether the Chinese Government would take action.[13]

The Soong-Chen discussions were one of the high points of Stilwell's Mission to China. Stilwell's mood was hopeful because Marshall and Stimson

[8](1) Memo with Incls, Conf, Chen, Soong, and Stilwell, 24 Jan 43. SNF–151. (2) *The Stilwell Papers*, p. 190. (3) Memo, Dorn for Stilwell, 15 Jan 43. Stilwell Documents, Hoover Library.
[9] Stilwell B&W, 10, 11 Jan 43.
[10](1) CM–IN 7220, Stilwell to AGWAR, 16 Jan 43. The principal items on the approved requisitions were 13,500 machine guns, 3,650 trench mortars, 360 75-mm. howitzers, 360 105-mm. howitzers, 96 155-mm. howitzers, 300 40-mm. antiaircraft guns, 120 90-mm. antiaircraft guns, 20,000 submachine guns, 10,000 2½-ton trucks, 10,000 ¼-ton trucks, 35,000,000 rounds per month of 7.92-mm. ammunition, and appropriate amounts of spares for all items. (2) CM–IN 14594, Stilwell to MAB, 31 Jan 43.
[11] Memo, Conf, Chen, Soong, and Stilwell, 24 Jan 43. Stilwell Documents, Hoover Library.
[12] Stilwell B&W, 20 Jan 43.
[13](1) Stilwell B&W, 28 Jan 43. (2) Notes, sub: Essential Points Brought Out at Mtg of Soong, Stilwell, and Chen Cheng, Wednesday, 27 Jan 43. SNF–151.

were supporting him strongly; Soong was co-operating closely, and Ho Ying-chin, while still a disturbing factor, seemed to be on the way out. Word that Madame Chiang needed Soong in Washington did not upset Stilwell. Pleased with Soong's help, Stilwell wrote him, "Mr. Stimson and General Marshall have been informed of the great assistance you have furnished me in carrying out my orders for the best and most efficient aid to China. Please accept my personal thanks for your service." [14]

Just before Soong's departure for Washington, Stilwell gave the Generalissimo the finished product of his discussions with Chen and Soong, and his exchange with Marshall, a memorandum dated 28 January 1943:

> This is our opportunity to equip and train a force that will make China strong and safe. The opportunity must be seized while the supply of weapons is available. If the first 30-Division Plan is carried out and the force used offensively, I will have a basis for demanding the equipment for another thirty divisions. I have already recommended the procurement of this materiel, and if a plan is produced to equip and train them, I can ask for instructors to assist in their training.
>
> I recommend that the program for the Y–Force be pushed; that the concentration of the troops be expedited; that General Ch'en Ch'eng be relieved of all other duties at once; that any necessary changes in Armies for the Y–Force be made at once; that financial arrangements be authorized; and that the training program be approved. Also that the units of the second 30-Division Plan be designated; that their re-organization and re-equipping be started at an early date; and that a plan of training similar to that proposed for the first thirty divisions be adopted.
>
> If these things are done now, by next fall the first thirty divisions should be an efficient field force, and the second thirty divisions should be well advanced in tactical training. With a supply line open, both groups could be equipped promptly with their weapons, and from then on China would have nothing to fear from the Japanese. Without such a definite plan, there will be difficulty in continuing the present flow of supplies from the United States, let alone increasing it materially; as I am trying to do at present.
>
> To me this matter seems of such extreme importance to the future of China, that I bring it again to the attention of the Generalissimo, and hope that he will give it particular consideration. The Generalissimo may depend on all American personnel to exert their best efforts to make the program a success. [15]

Administrative Changes for U.S. Forces

Presumably since no offensive would begin until fall 1943, thus allowing time for extended and elaborate preparations, Stilwell decided in early January to move toward an expanded American organization in CBI Theater. The original 1942 War Department concept had been of a mission, to reassure the Generalissimo of American support. In the next stage, so many projects accumulated that Stilwell formed a task force. Finally, in July 1942 Stilwell set up a theater headquarters. The bent of his thought, though, lay toward the concept

---

[14] Memo, Stilwell for Soong, 22 Jan 43. Stilwell Documents, Hoover Library.
[15] Memo, Stilwell [Actg as CofS] for Generalissimo, 28 Jan 43. Stilwell Documents, Hoover Library.

of an American Mission to China, which term he used to describe his organization in a memorandum to Soong on 3 January 1943. Indeed, the terms *American Mission* and *Stilwell Mission* lingered for a long time in CBI. Late in January 1943 Stilwell took the next hurdle and told his chief of staff that he was thinking of greater American activity organized on a basis that lent itself to expansion. General Hearn passed the word to Wheeler, telling him to submit requirements for an expanded SOS.[16]

American troop strength in CBI as of 31 December 1942 was: [17]

Type	China	India–Burma	Total
Air Force	812	9,664	10,476
Services of Supply	152	4,470	4,622
Ground Forces	96	298	394
Air Transport Command	195	1,404	1,599
Total	1,255	15,836	17,091

Stilwell's force was thus about the size of an infantry division.

Given the green light from Stilwell's headquarters, Wheeler began preparing to discuss his requirements with the Commanding General, Services of Supply (Lt. Gen. Brehon B. Somervell), whose presence in CBI was expected shortly. Stilwell's action was timely, for according to a report from The Inspector General, SOS in CBI was understaffed and undermanned. In order to permit the functioning of SOS offices, officers had been borrowed from troop units, Tenth Air Force, and Stilwell's headquarters.[18]

In contemplating greater American effort in CBI, Stilwell was no longer required to think of the airlift to China as his direct command responsibility. On 1 December 1942, the airlift had become part of the world-wide Air Transport Command (ATC). This step had been directed by the War Department in late October. In that month, Stilwell had set 5,000 tons per month over the Hump as the goal for February 1943 and had accepted the logistical requirements of the target that Bissell and Stilwell's air officer, Lt. Col. Edward H. Alexander, stipulated in July 1942. At that time Washington officialdom had accepted seventy-five as the number of transports needed to reach the 5,000-ton goal.[19]

---

[16] (1) Memo, Stilwell for Soong, 3 Jan 43. Stilwell Documents, Hoover Library. (2) Rad CH 9, Hearn to Wheeler, 22 Jan 43. Item 182, Bk 1, JWS Personal File.

[17] History of CBI, Sec. II, Ch. XIII, Staff and Administration, G–3 Section.

[18] Ltr, Maj Gen Virgil L. Peterson, The Inspector General, to DCofS, 31 Dec 42. WDCSA (China), A45–466.

[19] (1) Ltr, Handy to Stilwell, 31 Oct 42, sub: Transfer of ICFC to the ATC, India–China Wing. Item 348, Misc Corresp Folder (May–Dec 42), CT 23, Dr 2, KCRC. (2) Rad S1135, Bissell to Stilwell, 24 Nov 42; Rad 1460, Stilwell to Marshall, 27 Nov 42. Items 116, 124, Bk 1, JWS Personal File.

Stilwell, Bissell, and Alexander stated that 5,000 tons a month meant 140 aircraft (C–47 [DC–3]) on the Hump during good weather and 300 during the monsoon; 280 crews during the monsoon, and 234 at other times, plus spares and gasoline. In October 1942 Stilwell asked the War Department to provide these aircraft in time to hit the 5,000-ton goal by February. His next communication from Marshall crossed this radio and was not in answer to it.

Marshall's radio took the aircraft and men of the airline to China from Stilwell's command and placed the airline under the Air Transport Command. Henceforth, the airline to China was a semiautonomous organization within the CBI Theater, which theater headquarters had to support but which it could not command. *Semiautonomous* is an awkward word, but it seems to approach the realities of the situation more closely than to say ATC in CBI was actually independent of theater headquarters. Several factors made for this. Item, Stilwell was theater commander; if he expressed a wish, would ATC be politic to refuse? Item, ATC depended on Stilwell for its logistical support, and any wise commander stays on good terms with those from whom he draws his beans and bullets. Thus, when Stilwell learned that food and living conditions in one ATC mess were intolerable, he stepped in with direct orders to ATC to straighten up the place. ATC complied forthwith.

Marshall explained that the step was taken because of accumulating evidence that the transports in India were not being used as well as were those of the ATC in other parts of the world. Marshall believed that diversion of aircraft from the Hump for intra-India transport might have a part in this. He reminded Stilwell of the heavy pressure from the White House to increase deliveries to China.

OPD added its explanation, which was more technical but which mentioned one very pertinent point: that various activities had pre-empted supplies from the ATC on their way across the Atlantic and Africa to the Hump airfields. Now that the Hump was part of the ATC family, thought OPD, it might expect better treatment. Since half of the Hump transports, by Stilwell's own estimate, were grounded for lack of spares, the point was well taken. Stilwell protested the War Department's action on the ground that any lack of efficiency simply reflected a lack of spares, which could not be remedied by simply adding another agency to the already complex CBI picture. His protest was set aside, and India–China Wing, ATC, took over on 1 December 1942, with forty-four aircraft and 866 men at its disposal.[20]

[20](1) CM–IN 09036, Stilwell to Marshall, 20 Oct 42. (2) Rad WAR 87, Marshall to Stilwell, 21 Oct 42. WDCSA (China), A45–466. (3) CM–OUT 07429, OPD to Stilwell, 22 Oct 42. (4) MS, ICD ATC During General Stilwell's Command, Dec 42–Oct 44. History of CBI, Sec. II, Ch. VI. (5) ATC delivered 5,390 tons in September 1943 with 228 aircraft. It must be noted that the new C–46 carried 4.35 tons per flight as against 2.5 tons for the old C–47 which Stilwell had contemplated using. Of these 228 aircraft, 101 were C–46's, so Stilwell's estimate was not far off. Analysis of Transport Opns in India–China Wing, 11 Oct 42, Analysis Sec, 16th Statistical Control Unit, MATS, OSD. Statistical Serv Div, Comptroller, Andrews Field, Washington. (6) Ltr, Merrill to Stilwell, 29 Jun 43. SNF–47.

The Arnold-Somervell-Dill Mission

When the Combined Chiefs of Staff agreed in August 1942 to lay Marshall's proposal for a Burma operation before their planners, in effect they placed Burma operations on their agenda. In retrospect, much of the difficulty which had attended the first attempt to plan a combined operation in Burma seems to be that the proposal to invade Burma in March 1943 was never an operation agreed on at the highest Allied levels. There was no CCS directive setting the scope and objectives of ANAKIM and binding Wavell and Stilwell to work in harmony. There was no JCS directive to Stilwell, who had to find support for his projects. As for the Chinese, they were outside the CCS machinery, and when the Generalissimo pledged himself to attack, he did so under circumstances of which he was the sole judge.

The Joint Chiefs of Staff were now firmly behind operations to break the blockade of China, and so an offensive in Burma was high on the agenda of the next great Anglo-American conference, that of Casablanca, 14–23 January 1943. In preparing to take part in the conference, the JCS listed among desirable operations for 1943 one in Burma to re-open the line of communications to China in order to obtain "bases essential to eventual offensive operations against Japan proper." Here was stated the strategic goal: staging areas and airfields in north China.[21]

The strategic picture in the Pacific war as of January 1943, and indeed for many long and weary months thereafter, lent a peculiar emphasis to the strategic advantages which might be won in China. Along the whole vast arc of the Pacific and the Bay of Bengal the outer defenses of the Japanese kept Allied sea and air power in those sectors far from Japan's vitals. The two campaigns then under way, in the Solomons and in New Guinea, were proceeding slowly and were unsettled. Losses on both sides had been heavy and the Japanese had resisted with great determination. A major Japanese naval concentration just north of the Solomons suggested the Japanese might be preparing a major effort to decide the struggle for Guadalcanal.

But the great arc of Japanese defenses was incomplete. There was nothing comparable to it in China. In China, the Chinese armies lay within a few days' march of such points as Hong Kong. From airstrips in China, Allied bombers could reach Japan itself. Other aircraft could harass the great shipping lane that connected Japan with the Netherlands Indies, and the oil fields there. In China, therefore, it was possible for the Allies to take action that would force the Japanese to fight in defense of Japan itself, rather than for some stinking jungle in the far Southwest Pacific. The prize was so obvious that the Americans strained eagerly after it. The differences among them were over the timing and

---

[21] CCS 135, 26 Dec 42, sub: Basic Strategic Concept for 1943.

sequence of the several courses of action, rather than over the desirability of attacking Japan from China.

As far as the Joint Chiefs of Staff were concerned, Admiral Ernest J. King expressed their view when he told the Combined Chiefs of Staff on 16 January:

> In the European theater, Russia was most advantageously placed for dealing with Germany in view of her geographical position and manpower; in the Pacific, China bore a similar relation to the Japanese. It should be our basic policy to provide the manpower resources of Russia and China with the necessary equipment to enable them to fight.[22]

With this view the War Department heartily agreed, and therefore Stilwell was sent to "increase the combat efficiency of the Chinese Army."

To attack Japan from China on an effective scale required a very considerable establishment in China. Aircraft require spare parts, fuel, and ammunition, and ultimately replacements. Pilots become casualties or earn replacement. The airfields from which they operate must be guarded against a ground reaction by the enemy. Therefore, the professional service element in the American leadership conceived of a major effort to open an effective line of communications into China at the end of which really considerable air power could be sustained. This major effort would be a great left hook to the Japanese jaw, which would then be softened up for the crushing straight right coming across the Pacific.

In the course of the Casablanca Conference the Chief of Naval Operations, Admiral King, and General Marshall were most emphatic in expressing JCS support for ANAKIM. In effect serving notice on the British that the United States would not jeopardize its Pacific interests for anything less than complete Anglo-American concentration on an early and full-scale cross-Channel operation, Marshall on 17 January used strong language in arguing for ANAKIM:

> He said that he is most anxious to open the Burma Road, not so much for the morale effect on China as for the need to provide air support to China for operations against Japan and Japanese shipping. He said the expensive operations in which we are now engaged in the South Pacific react on everything else the United Nations attempt to do whether it be in the Mediterranean, the United Kingdom, or elsewhere. He discussed the situation in the Pacific as being so critical as to make it appear at one time that Operation TORCH [occupation of French North Africa] would have to be called off. He also stated that unless Operation ANAKIM could be undertaken, he felt that a situation might arise in the Pacific at any time that would necessitate the United States regretfully withdrawing from the commitments in the European theatre.
>
> General Marshall spoke of our commitments in the Pacific, of our responsibilities, with particular reference to the number of garrisons we have on small islands and the impossibility of letting any of them down. He insisted that the United States could not stand for another Bataan. He said that he is desirous of undertaking the Burma operation in order to reduce our hazards in the Pacific and thus undertake the campaign against Germany.[23]

---

[22] Ray S. Cline, *Washington Command Post: The Operations Division,* UNITED STATES ARMY IN WORLD WAR II (Washington, 1951), p. 334.

[23] Min, CCS 59th Mtg, 17 Jan 43.

The British Chiefs of Staff advanced the argument that if ANAKIM was undertaken at any time in the winter of 1943–1944 it would, because of its demands on landing craft for operations against the Andamans and Rangoon, seriously curtail the British share in any cross-Channel operations in spring 1944. A compromise was indicated and was made possible by the U.S. Navy. Admiral King stated that he was willing to release U.S. landing craft from the South Pacific for operations in the Bay of Bengal.[24]

On the basis of the above, the CCS reached the Casablanca decisions regarding ANAKIM:

(1) That all plans and preparations should be made to mount ANAKIM in 1943, target date 15 November; (2) that the actual decision to attack would be made by the CCS in summer 1943, not later than July; (3) that if ANAKIM was mounted in 1943, the United States would assist in making up deficiencies in landing craft and naval forces by diversion from the Pacific.[25] The resources committed to Burma and the Pacific, the CCS advised the President and Prime Minister, should be adequate to contain the Japanese and minimize the need of having to rush support there to meet an emergency, but not on a scale so large as to prevent seizing a sudden opportunity to defeat Germany in 1943. The purpose of operations in Burma was to keep China in the war, maintain pressure on the Japanese in that area, and establish and operate air power from Chinese bases on Japanese shipping in Chinese and Indochinese ports and on the flank of Japanese sea communications along the China coast.[26]

After examining the CCS report, the President and Prime Minister replied that they approved it and wished to emphasize four points: (1) The desirability of finding means of running convoys to Russia even during the forthcoming Sicilian campaign, and (2) "The urgency of sending air reinforcements to General Chennault's forces in China and of finding personnel to make them fully operative." The third and fourth points bore on European matters.[27]

The Chinese had not been represented at Casablanca. Stilwell would have been pleased to see them in an institutionalized working relationship with the CCS. On 4 January he had suggested to Marshall that the CCS form a subcommittee for Pacific operations, with Chinese representation. This arrangement would place the Generalissimo in proper relation to the conduct of the war, for he would then operate on the Roosevelt-Churchill level. So situated, he might not be tempted to act as a field commander, directing campaigns from Chungking, while Stilwell would not have to play the diplomat to win

[24](1) CCS 153/1, 17 Jan 43. (2) CCS 154, 17 Jan 43. (3) Min, CCS 60th Mtg, 18 Jan 43. (4) JCS Casablanca Min, pp. 23–24.

[25](1) Min, CCS 60th Mtg, 18 Jan 43. (2) CCS 155/1, 19 Jan 43, sub: Conduct of War in 1943. (3) Min, CCS 65th Mtg, 21 Jan 43.

[26](1) CCS 170/2, 23 Jan 43, sub: Final Rpt to President and Prime Minister, Summarizing Decisions by CCS. (2) CCS 168, 22 Jan 43, sub: Conduct of War in Pacific Theater in 1943. (3) CCS 153, 17 Jan 43.

[27] Winston S. Churchill, *The Hinge of Fate* (Boston: Houghton Mifflin Company, 1950), p. 693.

the Generalissimo's consent to decisions the latter must have regarded as so many *faits accomplis*. The proposal was not accepted by the JCS.[28]

The diplomatic device adopted after Casablanca was to send an imposing delegation to Chungking to win the Generalissimo's adherence to the Casablanca proposals for ANAKIM. Its members were General Arnold, commanding the Army Air Forces and ex officio a member of the JCS; General Somervell, commanding the Services of Supply, and so the principal supply man in the Amercan war machine; and Field Marshal Dill of the British Joint Staff Mission, to represent the Commonwealth's great stake in ANAKIM. Before he left Casablanca, Arnold indicated to Hopkins his skepticism about the CCS decisions on ANAKIM and his support for Chennault:

> Arnold feels that in spite of the plan to open the Burma Road which has been agreed upon here, he is very doubtful that this will be done, and thinks that the only intelligent move immediately is to strengthen Chennault's air force and get at the bombing of Japan as soon as possible. Arnold tells me that he cannot tell exactly how this can be done until he goes to China after this conference is over. He is sure, however, that it can be accomplished. He tells me that General Bissell, the Air Force commander in India, is very antagonistic to Chennault and that that complicates Chennault's supply line. Arnold is very confident, however, that the whole business can be worked out.[29]

Arnold, Somervell, and Dill with their staffs flew to New Delhi to confer there with representatives of Wavell's and Stilwell's staffs. Arnold had with him good news for China Theater: by 1 April 137 transports would be present in the CBI Theater, of which 124 aircraft were for the Hump, and the 308th Bomb Group (B-24) was coming to India.[30] The purpose of the gathering was to prepare a detailed proposal for Burma operations based on the Casablanca decisions. The proposal could then be submitted to the Generalissimo. Since the actual decision to invade would be made later by higher authority, the conferees had no power to bind their governments and kept the record straight by reaching a decision without commitments.

The command problem was attacked by proposing that Wavell command both the British forces and the Chinese Army in India until such time as Stilwell's Chinese met the Chinese from Yunnan. The Y-Force was to be commanded by the Generalissimo, who would assume command of all Chinese as soon as they made their juncture in north Burma. The post of deputy commander of operations based on India was reserved for an American. Another American was to command air operations, with a British deputy. Stilwell was not too pleased with the command proposal, for he feared that the deputy

---

[28] (1) CM-IN 1446, Stilwell to Marshall, 4 Jan 43. (2) CM-OUT 9105, Marshall to Stilwell, 27 Dec 42.

[29] (1) Sherwood, *Roosevelt and Hopkins*, pp. 681–82. (2) Somervell became Commanding General, Army Service Forces, on 12 March 1943.

[30] (1) Memo, Col Horace W. Shelmire, Arnold Mission to China, for Arnold, 6 Feb 43, sub: Logistical Situation in Kunming, China, re CATF. Gen Ref Br, OCMH. (2) Ltr, Arnold to Stilwell, 7 Feb 43. Folder 1 (GMO CKS), Item 58, OPD Exec 10.

CONFERENCE AT NEW DELHI, INDIA. *Left to right, Field Marshal Sir Archibald P. Wavell, Lt. Gens. Stilwell, Henry H. Arnold, Brehon B. Somervell, and Field Marshal Sir John Dill.*

ground force commander, a post likely to be his, would have only nominal powers.[31]

The consensus as to operations was that it was essential to take Burma in the period November 1943–May 1944. The preliminaries would include a submarine blockade of Rangoon, Chinese attempts to seize favorable jump-off positions in Yunnan, limited operations based on Ledo to cover the advance of the Ledo Road, an advance by two Indian divisions from Imphal to secure bridgeheads over the Chindwin, and the capture of Akyab and Ramree. In November 1943 a major effort would begin, with eleven Chinese divisions driving from Yunnan, the Ledo advance would become a two-division effort, and three Indian divisions would drive from Kalewa toward Mandalay. Landing operations at Taungup, Sandoway, and Bassein would follow in December, and in January 1944 would come the climax, direct assault on Rangoon.[32]

[31] Arnold quotes Stilwell to that effect in CM–IN 1641, 4 Feb 43.
[32] (1) CM–IN 70, Arnold to Marshall, 1 Feb 43. (2) CM–IN 1641, Arnold to Marshall, 4 Feb 43. (3) CM–IN 2033, Wedemeyer to Marshall, 4 Feb 43.

At the conferences, remarks by Bissell and Arnold illuminated the purpose of Burma operations. General Bissell said that all efforts should be looked at in the light of their contribution to the main purpose, which must be to get supplies to General Chennault, and thus make possible a direct attack from China on Japan and Japanese shipping and bases. General Arnold confirmed that it was with this end in view, and also to avoid a prolonged advance from island to island in the Pacific, that the Burma plan had been given priority; and he felt that it was now only necessary to state clearly what was required for the resources to be made available.[33]

The Conferences in Chungking and Calcutta

While Somervell remained in India to discuss CBI supply problems with Wheeler, Arnold and Dill went to Chungking to present the proposed operations to the Generalissimo. With him Arnold brought a personal letter from the President to the Generalissimo, which promised that something would be done about more U.S. aircraft for China Theater. This was very gratifying to the Generalissimo.[34]

The Generalissimo had good cause for wanting more American air power in his theater. He had become quite impatient over the lack of promised transports on the Hump. He had brought this to the President's attention in an increasing number of messages since the October 1942 answer to the Three Demands. Moreover, the Generalissimo faced varied excuses from his Chinese Air Force for not conducting their portion of the China Air War Plan.[35] During the past six months, thanks to weather, the Chinese Air Force was relieved of the responsibility of defending Chungking. But during the same period neglect and incompetence had ruined the bulk of its lend-lease aircraft. The Chinese Air Force had failed in its training program and failed to carry out the Generalissimo's paper reforms. Chennault reported that the Chinese Air Force objected to operational control by a foreigner and flatly rejected advice to prepare for the day when the Japanese would return over Chungking with the fine spring weather.

In January Chennault was inquiring if the China Air Task Force was responsible for Chungking's defense. It must be surmised that he was fully aware of the deplorable state of the Chinese Air Force and would naturally conclude that the Generalissimo would demand protection for his capital when the bombers returned. And, since in March 1943 the Chinese Air Force formally informed Stilwell's headquarters that it could not defend Chungking, it may be assumed that in February the Generalissimo was aware that he would

---

[33] COS Com, India Comd, USB/7, 1 Feb 43; Min, First American-British Conf, 1 Feb 43. History of CBI, Sec. III, Ch. VII, Arnold-Somervell-Dill Mission.
[34] Henry H. Arnold, *Global Mission* (New York, 1949), p. 419.
[35] See Ch. V, above.

have to provide some sort of protection for Chungking. Only a reinforced China Air Task Force could assume the mission. This meant the end of the China Air War Plan. Again, the demands on Hump tonnage that would be made by protecting Chungking with U.S. resources could not fail to affect plans to develop the Y-Force.[36]

In discussions with Arnold and Dill the Generalissimo again and again demanded more Hump tonnage, and at once; insisted that Chennault be independent of Stilwell; demanded that Bissell be recalled; and insisted that U.S. aircraft in great number be sent at once to China, without regard to the questions of ground establishment and gasoline supply. Arnold wrote, "The Generalissimo and Chennault glossed over these things with a wave of their hands. They could not, or would not, be bothered with logistics." [37] Arnold reported to Marshall that supply problems made a separate air force in China impractical. Inspection had confirmed Stilwell's view that Chennault did not exercise the administrative and executive control of his force necessary to warrant its independence.[38]

The Generalissimo finally approved the ANAKIM operation on 6 February, and a banquet followed to mark the event. After dinner the Chinese again raised the question of immediately increasing the amount of tonnage being flown into China, and Arnold was again called on to explain and defend the ATC's performance. The next day Arnold was summoned for a private audience with the Generalissimo. The Chinese leader told him bluntly that the conferences had been a failure. The Generalissimo had asked for many things, and all he had received were excuses. Then the Chinese presented to Arnold for approval by the President an enlarged version of the Three Demands of June 1942, accompanied by hints of a separate peace. The Generalissimo now demanded: (a) an independent air force for China Theater, (b) ten thousand tons a month over the Hump, (c) five hundred aircraft in China by November 1943.

Arnold's answer was a blend of tact and firmness, for he had not been impressed by the Generalissimo as a soldier. Pointing out that he had already presented the Generalissimo with proposals to rebuild the Chinese Air Force which the Chinese leader had apparently failed to consider, Arnold added that

---

[36](1) CM–IN 1449, Chiang to Roosevelt, 24 Nov 42. (2) Rad AMMISCA 1769, Roosevelt to Chiang, 2 Dec 42. Item 132, Bk 1, JWS Personal File. (3) CM–IN 12657, Chiang to Roosevelt, 28 Dec 42. (4) Rpt of Visit to Cheng-tu, CAF Hq, 1 Nov 42–1 Feb 43, by Mr. Kenneth M. Warder, Vultee Service Representative, to Stilwell, 1 Feb 43. Tate Folder (Nov 42–Jun 43), CT 40, Dr 3, KCRC. As a factory agent Mr. Warder made a routine survey of lend-lease aircraft at Cheng-tu. This report gives many examples of the way in which the Chinese misused U.S. technical equipment. (5) Memo, Chennault for Stilwell, 21 Jan 43. Folder, CAF Corresp (Mar–Jul 43), CT 23, Dr 2, KCRC. (6) Memo, Chennault for Stilwell, 22 Jan 43, sub: Employment of AAF Units at Chungking–1943. Item 9, Contracts with the Chinese (Jan–Jul 1943), CT 23, Dr 2, KCRC. See attchd Inds and Ltrs, Chou Chih-jou, Dir of Commission of Aeronautical Affairs, to Stilwell. On 19 March 1943 Chou stated that the Chinese Air Force could no longer defend Chungking and called on the United States for air support.

[37] Arnold, *Global Mission,* p. 419.

[38] CM–IN 2040, Arnold to Marshall, 5 Feb 43.

he was trying to increase the tonnage delivered to China, had given the necessary orders, but could not promise 10,000 tons by a fixed date because too many factors not under Arnold's control were involved. Tactfully, Arnold thus sought to persuade the Generalissimo that measures to satisfy his demands were under way and firmly told the Chinese leader that the principal question was whether or not China would join in efforts to retake Burma.

A full dress meeting of the Allied leaders was then convened. At its close the Generalissimo's summary of the meeting's results was so equivocal that Stilwell, still with no answer to his 28 January memorandum, asked him point-blank if China would join in an attempt to retake Burma. The Generalissimo said yes, and confirmed it in a letter to the President: "Finally, I wish to assure you that in the combined plan of operation for the Burma Campaign which was prepared after joint consultation, the Chinese Army will be in readiness to perform its assigned task at the specified time without fail." [39]

From Chungking the discussions moved to Calcutta on 9 February "to ensure that the decisions reached at Casablanca and Chungking should be perfectly clear to all concerned." [40] Present for China were Soong and Ho; for the United States, Arnold, Somervell, Bissell, and Stilwell; for the British Commonwealth, Dill and Wavell.

Invited to describe China's share in the offensive, Ho said that with a grand total of over 100,000 men the Chinese would make three main thrusts toward Myitkyina and Bhamo with seven divisions, and two subsidiary thrusts toward Lashio and Kengtung. If all went well, these would join with Stilwell's Ledo force, and the two subsidiary thrusts would head for Mandalay. Though Ho did not want to set a definite date for this offensive, he promised China would be ready to attack when the monsoon was over. The Chinese agreed with Stilwell that by late October 1943 the Yunnan roads would be dry enough.

Wavell said he would advance from the Chindwin with three divisions (45,000 men) to join the Chinese at Mandalay, plus one division in close support, another in the Arakan, and five divisions in general reserve.

The conference attempted to assay the potential Japanese opposition, which Wavell set at eight divisions, and Ho at ten. The discussion of Japanese air strength produced a varied reaction with Wavell suggesting 350 Japanese aircraft possible; the Chinese, 750. From talk of Japanese air strength the discussion turned to the Generalissimo's demand for 10,000 tons a month over the Hump by fall. Stilwell observed this would require additional facilities at both ends of the line. The Chinese, he said, could construct theirs; would the British be able to match them? It would involve not just additional airfields, but increased road, rail, and river capacity.

[39] (1) Arnold, *Global Mission*, Ch. 23. (2) *The Stilwell Papers,* p. 196. (3) Ltr, Chiang to Roosevelt, 7 Feb 43. Folder 1 (GMO CKS), Item 58, OPD Exec 10.
[40] Wavell's remark, Min, COS Com, India Comd, Chinese-British-American Conf, 9 Feb 43. Stilwell Documents, Hoover Library.

Wavell replied that he had not had time for a staff study of the problem, that his own troops were also dependent on the same line of communications that supported the airlift to China. However, he was confident that the line of communications could bring as much to the airfields as the aircraft could carry forward. The conference then moved to its conclusion: "Field Marshal Wavell summed up by saying that all were in agreement, and it remained only for all to press on with the greatest possible energy their preparations to start the battle immediately after the monsoon." [41]

The President Overrules Marshall and Stilwell

The Generalissimo's pledge to take part in Burma operations was the last paragraph of his letter to the President on 7 February 1943, the balance of which was devoted to the enlarged version of the Three Demands that he gave to Arnold in Chungking.[42] The letter, though, made no threats of a separate peace for China. That the President inclined toward Chennault's and the Generalissimo's viewpoint had become apparent in December. In that month he had suggested Chennault be given a task force of 100 aircraft with which to attack Japanese shipping and that he be made independent of Stilwell. Marshall objected because Chennault's mission was to support the then forthcoming offensive in Burma, so that if the aircraft were available they too should be used there. The success of the Burma offensive, Marshall told Roosevelt, was the absolute and essential prerequisite for expansion of air operations in China, for not until an adequate line of communications had been opened could the air effort be expanded to the maximum.[43]

Arnold at that time considered the proposal to make Chennault an independent air force commander premature, but he did urge that the principle be accepted. The President hinted to Leahy that this was his wish and at Casablanca revealed his desire to double the strength of Chennault's task force and with it to bomb Japan proper "for psychological reasons." [44]

Weighing the indications from White House circles—the President desired Chennault independent, Hopkins was Chennault's strong backer, and Currie wanted Stilwell's recall—Marshall told Stilwell candidly that the problem in Washington had been to support Stilwell against constant pressure from almost everyone interested in China, pressure further increased by a press campaign, to accept the Chennault viewpoint. He wrote, "While such factors are not included in the course at Leavenworth they are pertinent to the conduct of operations

[41] Min cited n. 40.

[42] Ltr cited n. 39(3).

[43](1) Memo, Leahy for Marshall, 30 Dec 42. WDCSA 381 China (12-30-42), A46-523. (2) Memo, Marshall for Leahy, 4 Jan 43, sub: Chennault. Item 64, OPD Exec 10.

[44](1) Memo, Arnold for Marshall, 6 Jan 43, sub: Establishment and Asgmt of Mission to Separate Air Force in China; Memo, McNarney for Arnold, 18 Jan 43, sub: Separate Air Force in China. WDCSA 381 China, A46-523. (2) JCS Casablanca Min, p. 56.

and particularly so in your theater." [45] To everyone's surprise, Marshall went on, Stilwell had attained most of his goals with the Chinese. Chennault, then, might wisely be given his chance. Stilwell agreed amiably enough and stated that he was willing to be benched, as he put it, if at any time the pressure grew too heavy. It was always, he continued, his secret ambition to be a sergeant in a machine gun company. [46]

Then the Generalissimo's 7 February letter arrived in Washington with its requests, accompanied by a letter from Stilwell expounding again his *quid pro quo* or bargaining thesis. As he sent Stilwell's letter on to the President, Marshall might have recalled that a few weeks before he, Marshall, had approved Stilwell's telling the Chinese that the United States would resent the Generalissimo's failure to cross the Salween in spring 1943, that China must show signs of seriously intending to pull her weight in the struggle.

Stilwell wrote:

Arnold's and Somervell's trip has been very helpful. I am particularly pleased that Arnold had a look at the machinery of Chinese government and a glimpse of the personalities we have to deal with.

We are grateful for your assistance [the B–24's and transports], even if the Chinese are not. Chiang Kai-shek has been very irritable and hard to handle, upping his demands no matter what is given him, and this attitude will continue until he is talked to in sterner tones. For everything we do *for* him we should exact a commitment *from* him.

The next paragraph gave some details of progress on the Y–Force and concluded:

In general, unless other blocks develop, we will get some much-needed training done on the Yunnan force, in time to make it capable of a serious effort, (I hope, I hope). [47]

The issue (Marshall and Stilwell versus the Generalissimo and Chennault) was now before the President for action. His decision was to back the Generalissimo and Chennault. The President directed preparation of a radio to the Generalissimo stating that Chennault would be placed in command of his own air force, the Fourteenth; that this air force would be built up to 500 aircraft as rapidly as Chennault believed he could support them in China; that as facilities improved, the ATC would be built up until 10,000 tons a month were being flown into China. At this point the President acknowledged the views of his service advisers by telling the Chinese that the ATC could never bring in enough, that a road would have to be built. Nor did he accept the Generalissimo's request for a renovated Chinese Air Force supported by 5,000 tons a month. He did suggest Arnold's more cautious plan to rebuild the Chinese Air Force one squadron at a time as pilots and aircraft were available. Marshall on 19 February gave Stilwell advance notice of the radio to the Generalissimo.

---

[45] Rad WAR 1955, Marshall to Stilwell, 5 Jan 43. Item 159, Bk 1, JWS Personal File.

[46] Football phraseology was freely used by Stilwell in his communications. He was once quarterback of the West Point varsity and distinguished himself against a powerful team from the University of Chicago. Rad 25, Stilwell to Marshall, 8 Jan 43. Item 160, Bk 1, JWS Personal File.

[47] Memo, Marshall for President, 18 Feb 43. WDCSA 381 China (2–18–43), A46–523.

Stilwell was directed to set up a separate air force for Chennault, the Fourteenth. Stilwell's superiors now contemplated that Chennault was to receive 1,500 tons a month of the 4,000 which the 124 transports were to bring over the Hump by the end of March 1943.[48]

To Marshall, Roosevelt explained his dismissal of the War Department's approach to the strategic problems of China Theater. In his explanation the President explicitly rejected the bargaining or *quid pro quo* technique of working with the Chinese, displayed a lack of interest in Stilwell's mission of reforming the Chinese Army, and referred to Stilwell's projects as nothing more than local preparations for a Burma campaign. The letter closed with the good-natured reminder that he had overruled the military before and now thought he had been right in doing so.

Thank you for letting me see the copy of Stilwell's letter of February ninth in regard to Arnold's and Somervell's trip. I have read this letter with a good deal of care and my first thought is that Stilwell has exactly the wrong approach in dealing with Generalissimo Chiang who, after all, cannot be expected, as a Chinese, to use the same methods that we do. When Stilwell speaks about the fact that the Generalissimo is very irritable and hard to handle, upping his demands, etc., he is, of course, correct; but when he speaks of talking to him in sterner tones, he goes about it just the wrong way.

All of us must remember that the Generalissimo came up the hard way to become the undisputed leader of four hundred million people—an enormously difficult job to attain any kind of unity from a diverse group of all kinds of leaders—military men, educators, scientists, public health people, engineers, all of them struggling for power and mastery, local or national, and to create in a very short time throughout China what it took us a couple of centuries to attain.

Besides that the Generalissimo finds it necessary to maintain his position of supremacy. You and I would do the same thing under the circumstances. He is the Chief Executive as well as the Commander-in-Chief, and one cannot speak sternly to a man like that or exact commitments from him the way we might do from the Sultan of Morocco.

The other matter relates to the complete omission by Stilwell of any mention of air action in China in 1943. He is thinking of the Burma end of things and he is thinking of the ground forces now being trained in China.

While I am hopeful of the Burma operation, I still believe that important emphasis [should?] be placed on the strategic value of Chennault's air operations in 1943. I am glad to see it being pushed.

I know you will see that the directives sent to Stilwell and Chennault are so clear about our air plans that there will be no misunderstanding of our intentions.

It is essential that Chennault get his share of the supplies, and I believe he should get all above 4,000 tons a month until he gets an amount that will really keep his force operating. I understand from Arnold that is something over 2,500 tons a month on an all-out basis.

The construction and improvement of airfields both in India and China should be pushed to the limit.

I am assuming that the big bomber group now en route will be directly under Chennault's command.

[48] (1) Ltr cited n. 39(3). (2) Memo, Comdr William L. Freseman for Maj Gen William R. Deane, 6 Mar 43; Ltr, Arnold to Stilwell, 7 Feb 43. Folder 1 (GMO CKS), Item 58, OPD Exec 10. (3) Rad WAR 2170, Marshall to Stilwell, 19 Feb 43; Rad SVC 395, Roosevelt to Chiang, 8 Mar 43. Items 212, 239, Bk 1, JWS Personal File. (4) Memo, Marshall for President, 22 Feb 43, sub: Chinese Theater. WDCSA (China), A45–466.

Of more importance is the assurance—the air policy having been fixed in China—that Chennault, with Stilwell's approval, will have complete control over his operations and tactics.

While I am sure the relationship of Stilwell and the Generalissimo has improved, I hope nothing will be done to prevent Chennault from discussing air operations with the Chinese in an appropriate manner.

Our relations with China are important and I wish you would impress on Stilwell and Chennault that they are our representatives over there in more senses than one. Compatible with their military duties, they may well turn out to be the best "Ambassadors" we have in China. I hope they will.

Above all, I am depending on you to see that Chennault gets his chance to do what he believes he can do.

I do not think that the Staff plans either in Casablanca or here have given sufficient weight to the attrition against Japan each week and each month, or that that attrition can be greatly accelerated through increasing air power in China, by the sinking of Japanese ships off the coast of China, the destruction of Japanese aircraft, and the occasional bombing of Japanese cities.

Just between ourselves, if I had not considered the European and African fields of action in their broadest geographic sense, you and I know we would not be in North Africa today— in fact, we would not have landed either in Africa or in Europe! [49]

In answering the President, Marshall raised the principal War Department objection to the timing of Chennault's proposals. It was the argument with which the War Department always replied to Chennault and his adherents. Marshall warned that as soon as Chennault's effort stung the Japanese they would retaliate by attacking Chennault's airfields with their Army. Such an attack would have to be met by the Chinese Army, still untrained and without lend-lease arms. He also warned the President that many influential Chinese wanted the United States to fight China's battles for her.

I have given a careful reading to your private memorandum of March 8th regarding the relations between the Generalissimo and Stilwell. I should like your permission to quote to him [Stilwell] the second and third paragraphs of your memorandum, omitting the direct reference to the Sultan of Morocco (memorandum is attached).

As to the air phase of the matter, Stilwell is cognizant of our planned air effort out of China which will take place immediately upon the establishment of bases. I will further impress upon him to assist Chennault to the maximum, giving Chennault wide latitude in his operations. In this connection, the planes of the heavy bombardment group have already arrived in India; the ground crews will be there in about three weeks.

The supply problem, affecting air operations from China in 1943, is a tremendous one. Chennault requires help in his logistical planning. To this end, we are sending General Glenn this weekend to be Chennault's Chief of Staff, with General Haddon as his Service Commander, together with a selected staff.

However, the problem which we will face later in continuous air operations is ground protection for the China airdromes we use, as well as for the air freight route. We must build for that now. *Here is the most serious consideration* [Marshall's italics]: as soon as our air effort hurts the Japs, they will move in on us, not only in the air but also on the ground. The air situation Chennault can take care of with his fighters, but the ground effort against our bases

---

[49] Ltr, President to Marshall, 8 Mar 43. Item 54, OPD Exec 10.

must be met by men on the ground. Our "bomb Tokyo" bases in Chekiang Province have been destroyed as a result of Japanese ground action. These fields have not been repaired.

The present Japanese advance into north Burma, although not yet in strength, probably has for its purpose the capture of the air warning stations protecting our Assam Air Freight Terminal. One station has already been forced to retire. Stilwell has just ordered a second Chinese regiment from Ramgarh to oppose this Jap move.

The size of an air force that can operate from China is limited by the means that can be made available to Stilwell from the U.S. On the other hand, ground protection for our airdromes in China and the terminals of the air transport route must come from the Chinese Army.

General Stilwell, realizing this, has concentrated on his local problem of creating dependable units in the Chinese Army. His approach to this problem has been fundamentally sound; namely, to assemble into a field force selected units, officered by selected leaders; this force to be equipped with U.S. equipment and trained sufficiently to place dependence on them in combat.

Stilwell has had marked success in assembling a few units (Ramgarh Project) with selected leaders. However, he has met with considerable obstruction and delay in concentrating a larger force in Yunnan. Although recent reports indicate progress is being made, it will be an up-hill fight all the way. It is firmly established that Ho Ying-chin embodies a school of thought now existing in the Chinese Army, that a military "watch and wait" policy should be followed. This is manifested by constantly emphasizing a U.S. air effort against the Japs from China as a substitute for creating and training the necessary Chinese ground forces to make such air effort effective by opening a ground route of communications through Burma.

The comparatively small air effort possible from China in 1943, although of great strategic value, can be only a beginning. With a land supply route through Burma and dependable forces to secure our air bases in China, we can increase our air action against the Japs and really hurt them.

This means Burma must be recaptured. The part contemplated for the Chinese forces in this offensive is extremely important and the time remaining for their preparation is all too short. Accordingly, delay in organization and concentration for training is a serious obstacle to overcome.

At every turn General Stilwell has been faced with the "let the other fellow do it" attitude on the part of the Chinese leaders. This attitude, combined with the present low combat worth of the Chinese Army, must be reversed before we can fully realize the Chinese potential in this war. To correct this must be the primary objective of any representative dispatched to this theater to represent American interests.

General Stilwell has no doubt talked very plainly to the Generalissimo on many of these points in order to secure his assistance in creating conditions where our help would be effective against the Japanese. In doing this, there have been times when he has incurred the displeasure of the Generalissimo. This is unfortunate. However, I do not know of any other officer in our Army who combines Stilwell's knowledge of the Chinese and their language with his ability as a soldier and as an organizer. He is tough, but only such a man would have survived the Burma campaign, battered down British-Indian sluggish resistance to all our plans and made some headway with reorganization of the Chinese Forces. Conditions must be created in China and a land route established to make an all-out air effort continuous and effective.

I am confident that the relationship between Stilwell and Chennault is such that Chennault will be given every opportunity to use his uncanny skill in the air against the Japs (see attached message).

Stilwell radioed me yesterday the following from Kunming:

Chen Cheng is here and I am sticking to him to get a headquarters set-up established. He is our best bet and present indications are that he will go along with us. I hope to open Infantry and Artillery Training Centers here (Kunming) by end of month. Soong's remark about threat on several fronts is nonsense. Japs are foraging near Shasi [western Hupeh], elsewhere there is no activity. Generalissimo is entirely unconcerned about threats on any front.

Chungking cannot or will not enforce its orders in this area [Yunnan]. Our presence threatens to affect the enormous smuggling racket here, and you may expect a campaign of vilification against me personally. I have already been accused of bad faith for keeping military supplies from racketeers. The continued publication of Chungking propaganda in the United States is an increasing handicap to my work. Utterly false impression has been created in United States public opinion. Army is generally in desperate condition, underfed, unpaid, untrained, neglected, and rotten with corruption. We can pull them out of this cesspool, but continued concessions have made the Generalissimo believe he has only to insist and we will yield.

If we can train and equip the Yunnan force, we can save the situation, but I may have to call for backing in case a showdown is necessary. You may think a year of this has had its effect on me. My opinion of the Chinese soldier and the Chinese people is unchanged. It is the gang of Army "leaders" that is the cause of all our grief. With best wishes and hoping for a better picture soon.[50]

On the same day that Marshall gave the President his comments on the Chennault Plan the Chief of Staff approved the award to Stilwill of the Legion of Merit in the degree of Chief Commander. In suggesting to General Marshall on 16 February 1943 that the Distinguished Service Medal be given Stilwell, Brig. Gen. Albert C. Wedemeyer of OPD had remarked: "General Stilwell, according to my personal observation, understands the situation in China–Burma–India Theater better than any of our allies. Nothing should be left undone to convince China that Gen. Stilwell enjoys full American confidence and that we look to him, in matters of importance concerning China, as the chief arbiter." The Operations Division concurred, but suggested the Legion of Merit as Stilwell already had the Distinguished Service Medal. As head of OPD, General Handy wrote to Marshall: "General Stilwell's constancy of purpose has been unfaltering, and events are proving the soundness of his judgment and the effectiveness of his forceful character." [51]

As General Marshall told Roosevelt, he sent the pertinent passages of the President's letter to Stilwell, who interpreted them as a Presidential rebuke.[52] But the message was more than simply a rebuke; it was repudiation without recall. Since 1941 the senior American officers in China—first Magruder, then Stilwell—had worked out the bargaining or *quid pro quo* approach to China's

[50](1) Memo, Marshall for President, 16 Mar 43, sub: Your Note to Me of March 8th re China. WDCSA 381 China (3–16–43), A46–523. (2) Rad 345, Stilwell to Marshall, 15 Mar 43. Item 261, Bk 1, JWS Personal File.

[51] Memo, Handy for Marshall, 18 Feb 43, sub: Proposed Award of Legion of Merit (degree of Chief Comdr) to Lt Gen Joseph W. Stilwell. OPD 201.52, WDCSA 201 (S). Marshall's stamp of approval is dated 16 March.

[52](1) Rad WAR 2373, Marshall to Stilwell, 27 Mar 43. Item 278, Bk 1, JWS Personal File. (2) Stilwell B&W, 19 Apr 43.

problems. Marshall and Stimson had approved it. Now the President announced that they had exactly the wrong approach. Without the President's support, Stilwell could not negotiate with the Generalissimo, and for about the next twelve months Stilwell was painfully aware that his position as Chief of Staff, China Theater, was largely formal.

After the war, as he looked back on the great argument over air power versus reform of the Chinese Army, the Army's Chief of Staff, General Marshall, commented that subsequent events had proved Stilwell to be right, but unfortunately much too outspoken and tactless. On still another occasion he observed that Stilwell had scorned attempts to counter the backstairs influence so damaging to his cause at the White House.[53]

After April 1943 Stilwell's exchange of memoranda and conferences with key Chinese officials dwindled sharply. Chennault was to have his chance, and results would speak for themselves. In seeking these results, Chennault would be under a handicap not apparent at first, for the President and Hopkins had been influenced by enthusiastic private letters from China. Chennault would have difficulty living up to the promises made for him.[54]

Moving Toward an Expanded Air Effort in China

Henceforth, preparations in China proceeded in two separate and often conflicting areas. Chennault worked to increase his air force and fly more missions with it. Stilwell sought to reform the Chinese Army and prepare for a campaign in Burma. Preparations for a greater air effort and a campaign in Burma each required Hump tonnage, and there Stilwell and Chennault began to clash ever more strongly in March and April 1943. Their differences revolved around a fractional number, one fourth of the Hump tonnage entering China, for each desired five eighths of Hump tonnage in any one month for his project. (*Chart 6*) Clashes between the two men over command and policy continued.

On 22 February Chennault presented a revised version of his plan to Stilwell, asking a little more in means and omitting the sweeping claims of the letter to Willkie. He stated that the Arnold-Somervell-Dill mission and Madame Chiang's appearance before Congress had probably warned the Japanese of forthcoming Allied offensive action, and that the Japanese were about to launch a major offensive to clear the Canton–Hong Kong line, drive the Chinese from the area between Nanchang and Changsha, and perhaps even go on to Wuchow and Kweilin, where lay some of the key east China airfields.

Could such a massive Japanese drive be stopped? Chennault stated: "It is believed that the Japanese cannot obtain their military objectives if opposed by

---

[53] (1) Statement, Marshall to Robert E. Sherwood, 23 Jul 47. Sherwood interviewed Marshall while writing *Roosevelt and Hopkins.* A record of Marshall's statement is in the Hopkins Papers. (2) Interv with Marshall, 13 Jul 49.

[54] Bks VII, IX, Hopkins Papers.

CHART 6—HUMP TONNAGE CARRIED BY ALL CARRIERS IN
INDIA–CHINA: 1943

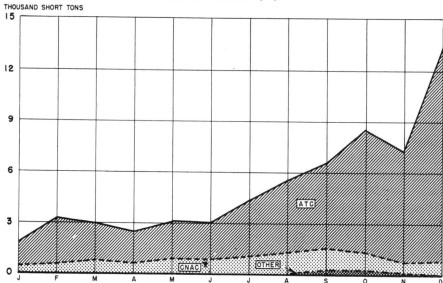

THOUSAND SHORT TONS

* China National Aviation Corporation.
Source: History of the India–Burma Theater, 24 Jun 45–31 May 46, Vol. II, p. 300. Gen Ref
Br, OCMH.

an effective Air Force. It is assumed that the Chinese Ground Armies will offer
resistance similar to that offered in previous years and that, given support of an
effective air force, they will be able to block the Japanese advances in the
directions indicated." [55] There was no suggestion that the Chinese Army needed
lend-lease arms or training. Chennault then went on to say that given 150
fighters, 32 medium bombers, some more men, and 2,500 tons a month over
the Hump (in February a total of 3,000 tons was flown in) he could not only
protect the Hump air terminals but conduct consistent and effective operations
in the central and coastal areas. In conclusion, he warned again that the
Japanese were about to move and that early action was needed.

Chennault's proposals were approved by Stilwell's chief of staff and his air
officer. While Chennault's letter was being considered by Stilwell's headquarters, word came from Marshall that Chennault was to be a major general
commanding the new Fourteenth Air Force, which invested his proposals with
the added significance that they would be his suggestions for the exercise of his
new command. The Fourteenth Air Force was activated on 11 March 1943.[56]

[55] Ltr, with Inds, Chennault to Stilwell, 22 Feb 43, sub: Estimate of China Situation. Item 18,
U.S. Opns, China Folder (Sep 42–Jul 43), CT 23, Dr 2, KCRC.
[56] (1) *Ibid.* (2) Rad WAR 2120, Marshall to Stilwell, 19 Feb 43. Item 212, Bk 1, JWS Personal
File. (3) GO 9, Hq USAF CBI, 11 Mar 43. Chennault was named a major general, AUS, on 3
March 1943.

At this delicate juncture the February 15 edition of *Time* magazine appeared in CBI, with an article stating that Chennault was willfully violating Stilwell's orders in an attempt to bring his case before higher authority, and further stating that opportunities to destroy key Japanese air bases were being lost through alleged obstructionism on the part of General Bissell. Chennault denounced the article as a complete fabrication and denied he had ever violated Stilwell's orders:

> The implication of disrespect for your judgment in any military matters or in matters concerning the Chinese is a contortion of the truth. You are the only Regular Army General I know of who has long observed the Chinese, served with the Chinese Army, and in whom the Chinese have had sufficient confidence to entrust the command of their forces. . . . All the American Forces in China have got to work in closest harmony under the designated American Commander. Any officer who declines to do so should be summarily removed. In time of war, the greatest disservice that any soldier can do is to undermine in any way the relations of our Government with our allies.[57]

In this instance, Stilwell's indorsement to Chennault's 22 February proposals reflected his anger over *Time*'s statements. Chennault was told that his primary mission was to protect the Hump airline and that he would get more supplies as circumstances permitted. The indorsement ended with a sarcastic appreciation of Chennault's interest in theater problems. To prevent Chennault's gaining command of both the Tenth and Fourteenth Air Forces and ultimately replacing him as theater commander, Stilwell suggested to Marshall that a theater air officer be brought in and set up over both Bissell and Chennault. Marshall replied that it would be impossible to put another air officer over Chennault; indeed, it might be better if Bissell went home. Stilwell objected strongly, for he feared that if the Chinese forced Bissell's recall there would be no end to such maneuvers.[58]

Stilwell received another shock when Chennault's new chief of staff, Brig. Gen. Edgar E. Glenn, reported on 31 March that Arnold had said Chennault "should" have complete control of the Hump and had asked that Stilwell be told of his "desires" in the matter. The language was curiously equivocal, and Stilwell promptly asked Marshall for confirmation. Marshall replied that there was no change of status and that Arnold had assured him that this was in accord with Arnold's statements to Glenn and Chennault.[59]

After cautioning Stilwell by inference against anything that might hinder Chennault or anger the Generalissimo, Marshall told him explicitly to support Chennault's operations and give Chennault free rein to see what he could do

[57] (1) *Time,* February 15, 1943. (2) CM–IN 1651, Stilwell to Marshall, 4 Mar 43. (3) CM–IN 1749, Stilwell to Marshall, 4 Mar 43. (4) Ltr, Chennault to Stilwell, 2 Mar 43, sub: Article in *Time* magazine. Item 233, Bk 1, JWS Personal File.

[58] (1) Ltr cited n. 55. (2) Rad AMMISCA 249, Stilwell to Marshall, 20 Mar 43; Rad WAR 2373, Marshall to Stilwell, 27 Mar 43. Items 268, 278, Bk 1, JWS Personal File.

[59] (1) Ltr, Glenn to Stilwell, 31 Mar 43. Item 512A, Bk 2, JWS Personal File. (2) *The Stilwell Papers,* p. 202. (3) Rad AMMISCA 362, Stilwell to Marshall, 20 Apr 43; Rad WAR 2541, Marshall to Stilwell, 21 Apr 43. Items 512, 514, Bk 2, JWS Personal File.

with a firm allocation of 1,500 tons a month. Stilwell was also ordered to submit reports on the administrative planning and preparation for Chennault's air effort. Marshall's radio giving Chennault a priority on 1,500 tons a month centered attention on the Hump tonnage question.[60]

Stilwell's policy, announced on 1 March, was to allocate 1,000 tons a month for Chennault as a target, and to be willing to give Chennault another 1,500 tons a month, to a total of 2,500 tons a month, if Stilwell could also give 2,500 tons a month to the Chinese ground forces in lend-lease. In effect, Stilwell intended to split Hump tonnage evenly every month and try to give Chennault the 2,500 tons he wanted. If bad weather or a shortage of spare parts cut the amount flown in, then Stilwell intended that Chennault would still share equally with everyone else, regardless of what the shortage did to his air operations.[61] Chennault's anger was aroused by this attitude, which he regarded as willful blindness to what might be done by air operations in China. He wanted a first priority on Hump tonnage, with enough transports put on the Hump to guarantee that every month he would get enough to fly and fight. His 1,000-ton allocation was in practice proving to be between 600 and 800 tons a month, not enough for his operations.[62]

Studying the problem of Hump tonnage distribution, Stilwell's chief of staff recommended that Stilwell give Chennault an absolute and fixed priority of 1,500 tons a month, so that the Fourteenth Air Force would be sure to have enough, even though other theater activities suffered. General Hearn warned that if this was not done, political pressure would increase in Chungking. The detailed allocation of Hump tonnage among American and Chinese activities as recommended by Hearn was:[63]

	Tons
Fourteenth Air Force, including Chinese Air Force	1,500
SOS, Kunming	50
Gas and oil for Kunming headquarters	46
Chungking headquarters	9
ATC at Kunming	200
Raw materials for Chinese arsenals	300
Passengers and baggage	25
Y–Force preparations	1,870
	4,000

Stilwell did not accept this proposal. Noting that 1,500 was three eighths of 4,000, and fearing the effect on other activities in China if Chennault had an absolute priority, he asked Marshall if giving Chennault three eighths of

[60] Rad WAR 2373, Marshall to Stilwell, 27 Mar 43; Rad WAR 2047, Roosevelt to Chiang, 1 Apr 43. Items 278, 288, Bk 1, JWS Personal File.
[61] Ltr, Stilwell to Wheeler, 1 Mar 43, sub: Policies and Estimates of Minimum Tonnages to be Moved Over Hump During Next Six Months. Secret Corresp Folder, Headquarters Y–FOS, KCRC.
[62] (1) Chennault, *Way of a Fighter*, p. 217. (2) Ltr, Chennault to Wedemeyer, 6 Jul 45. WDCSA 091 China, 15 Aug 45.
[63] Rad AD 537, Hearn to Stilwell, 29 Mar 43. Item 285, Bk 1, JWS Personal File.

whatever came over the Hump would meet the President's wishes.[64] No immediate answer came from Marshall, for the Stilwell–Chennault problem was again about to receive the President's attention.[65]

Reinforcements for Chennault and added cargo capacity on the Hump to support his operations had been under way since March. The 308th Bombardment Group (B–24) landed in India on 18 March. The concept behind it was that the group would carry its own supplies from India to China until it had accumulated enough for an operational sortie on targets in China, and then begin a process of periodically accumulating and expending its stocks. In agreeing to this plan for the 308th Group, the President had been under the impression that one bomber on one passage from India to China could carry gas and ammunition enough for four sorties. Having discovered his error he then asked Marshall to put thirty more transports on the Hump to support the 308th, which had been assigned to CBI on the premise that it would be self-supporting.

General Marshall argued against assigning these thirty transports. He pointed out that cargo planes were so few that these thirty aircraft could only come from those assigned to support the forthcoming invasion of Sicily, that there were then more transports assigned to the Hump than there were crews to use them to the full, and that adding thirty more to the Hump might jeopardize the success of the Sicilian operation and still not aid China. The President did not accept these views, and the transports were assigned.[66]

Roosevelt also asked that consideration be given to a coolie route across Burma to China. He had been advised by Chinese sources that such a route was practicable for men carrying fifty pounds each, that in some places man-drawn carts could be used, and that China could supply all the coolies needed. In answer, the War Department observed that Burma was currently occupied by the Japanese, which would force the coolies to march across the mountains of Tibet. The Tibetans were hostile to the Chinese, though the latter claimed suzerainty over Tibet, and might well object to such a project. Since no food depots were available in Tibet, the coolies would have to carry their own rations. The food requirements for a coolie trudging from India to China across Tibet were rather more than his carrying capacity, so the project did not appear practicable.[67]

The suggestion for the coolie route and the pressure for more and still more aircraft on the Hump came from Soong and his associates. The Chinese assured the President that the answer to all problems of Hump operations, and

[64] Rad AG 271, Stilwell to Marshall, 31 Mar 43. Item 308, Bk 1, JWS Personal File.
[65] For an account of the TRIDENT Conference, see Chapter IX, pages 327–33, below.
[66] (1) Memo, Leahy for Marshall and Arnold, 24 Feb 43; Memo, Marshall for President, 27 Feb 43, sub: Reply to Generalissimo's Memo. Folder 1 (GMO CKS), Item 58, OPD Exec 10. (2) Ltr, Brig Gen John E. Hull, Actg ACofS, to Marshall, 14 Apr 43, sub: President's Message to Chiang, 31 March 1943. WDCSA (China), A45–466.
[67] (1) Memo, 24 Feb 43, cited n. 66(1). (2) Memo, Marshall for Leahy, 30 Mar 43, sub: Coolie Route from India to China. Item 56, OPD Exec 10.

indeed of strategy in Asia, lay in the simple assignment of more transports to the India–China Wing, ATC. Two messages from the Generalissimo to Roosevelt in March urged that more combat aircraft be assigned to Chennault and that Hump traffic be increased sharply. The President replied in full to each, listing what was being done to aid the Fourteenth and the Chinese Air Force and expressing the hope that the Hump would carry 6,000 tons a month by early summer.[68]

Within China, the Chinese were energetically building four airfields for Chennault's projected operations. Chennault's plans were to the Generalissimo's liking, so he received considerable co-operation from the Chinese. All plans for airfield construction were approved by the Generalissimo, and the Ministry of Communications was told to begin work on them. Liuchow was chosen as the air terminus in east China, and preliminary plans for it were submitted. Stilwell reported to Marshall that everything possible was being done to hasten operations, and that Chennault would not be restrained in any way unless what he proposed was obviously undesirable.[69]

Obstacles in Chennault's Path

In overruling Marshall and Stilwell and directing that Chennault have his way, the President directed that U.S. Army Forces, CBI, implement a strategy for which the logistical foundation had not been laid. Within theater headquarters' possible sphere of action were two major problems, only one of which was to receive corrective action in the near future. The first, which was left unsolved and indeed unapproached for months, was that of moving Chennault's supplies 880 miles from the Yunnan airfields to his bases in east China. (Map 7) There were two reasons why this problem was unsolved in 1943. These were the command structure of China Theater and the lack of American resources in China. For the first, the Generalissimo as Supreme Commander, China Theater, was the responsible officer for all operations in that theater. Stilwell as Chief of Staff, China Theater, was responsible for bringing problems and their suggested solutions to the Generalissimo's attention. Since the Chinese had been unwilling to set up a combined staff for China Theater there was no G–4 to give supply problems his continuing attention. In January 1943 Stilwell had called Soong's attention to the line of communications to east

---

[68] (1) Memo, Soong for President, 25 Feb 43, sub: Memo re Air Opns in China. Bk VII, Hopkins Papers. This memorandum is one of the most extreme communications from Soong, but during the spring of 1943, he was indefatigable, as the Hopkins Papers show, in carrying out his objective of getting more of everything for China. (2) Memo, Leahy for Marshall and Arnold, 1 Apr 43; Memo, Marshall for Stratemeyer, 18 Mar 43; Memo, Hull for Marshall, 14 Apr 43, sub: President's Msg to CKS, 31 Mar 43. WDCSA (China), A45–466.

[69] Rad WAR 2373, Marshall to Stilwell, 27 Mar 43; Rad AMMISCA AG 271, Stilwell to Marshall, 31 Mar 43; Rad AG 536, Hearn to Stilwell, 28 Mar 43. Items 278, 308, 281. Bk 1, JWS Personal File.

China. His files reveal no further attempts in the first six months of 1943 to place the matter before Chinese authority.

As for the Generalissimo and Chennault, there is no indication in the first six months of 1943 that either felt any concern about the problem of moving supplies from Kunming to the air bases; indeed, in April 1943 the General-issimo formally assured the President that "no obstacle" existed to putting the Chennault Plan into operation.[70] Had an attempt to delegate responsibility to him been made, Stilwell would have been extremely embarrassed. Aside from Chennault's few thousand men, only a few hundred Americans, mostly Y–Force instructors, were in China Theater. Every ton of supplies coming over the Hump was divided between Chennault, the Chinese Government, and prep-arations for ANAKIM, to which last operation the Generalissimo's representa-tives had agreed at Calcutta in February 1943. Nothing was left for an American line of communications over the hundreds of miles between Kun-ming and the east China airfields. Therefore, the U.S. SOS at Kunming necessarily relied on Chinese Government agencies to transport supplies eastward to Chennault.[71]

The second problem lay in the fact that on the Indian side of the Hump the Assam airfields were not capable of supporting the aircraft now assigned to the ATC. To be sure, ATC efficiency still left much to be desired, but after December 1942 ATC was independent of Stilwell. The allocation of SOS and Indian resources had not taken into account the possibility of a greatly enlarged Hump effort; the President was ordering the assignment of transports to air-fields not yet completed. When Stilwell in January 1943 told Wheeler to think in terms of an expanded SOS, Wheeler in turn discussed his projects and prob-lems with Somervell during the latter's visit to India with the Arnold-Somer-vell-Dill mission. These discussions were significant. Stilwell's Mission in CBI centered about the reform of the Chinese Army. Problems of supply he left to the experts in logistics: Wheeler, who was of course Stilwell's supply adviser, and Somervell, who played the same role for Marshall. Their recommendations would determine the attitude their superiors took on supply problems. In Stilwell's case, he was happy to leave supply and engineering problems to Wheeler and to concentrate on his efforts to persuade the Generalissimo to reform the Chinese Army. Stilwell's personal papers rarely mention the Ledo Road, and such casual references to the project as do appear indicate no great interest. On the other hand, references to the problems he met in attempting to reform the Chinese Army are extremely numerous, lengthy, and detailed.

Somervell directed Wheeler to propose a plan for the support of 100,000 U.S. troops in China and ultimately 500,000. This Wheeler did, assuming that

---

[70] Ltr with Incls, Soong to Hopkins, 29 Apr 43. Bk VII, Hopkins Papers.
[71] In SOS in CBI, China Section, Appendix C, is a story of the first American SOS people in China. With no pocket guide or reference book to assist them in dealing with the Chinese, they "had to learn the hard way." P. 1.

enough of north Burma would be taken by 1 February 1944 to permit work on the Ledo Road as far south as Bhamo, and that all of Burma would be reoccupied by the beginning of the 1944 monsoon. By fall of 1944 he hoped to be able to support 100,000 American ground troops in Yunnan. Until the Irrawaddy River was reopened to barge traffic, Wheeler proposed to use the Ledo Road as his principal supply route. After this brief initial period of a few months, supplies would begin moving up the Irrawaddy River from Rangoon to Bhamo, from there to go by truck into China. Wheeler planned to unload 87,750 tons a month at Rangoon, and but 18,000 tons a month at Calcutta, of which 89,250 tons would be laid down monthly at Kunming. Therefore, the plans of CBI Theater called for supporting about 90 percent of the U.S. effort in China by means of a line of communications via Rangoon. Wheeler's proposals to Army Service Forces were related to the projects involved in this planning, rather than to direct support of Chennault's current operations.[72]

In spring 1943 SOS in India had two major engineering projects, but was directly concerned with only one of them. This was building the Ledo Road, which was to be paralleled by a 4-inch, thin-walled pipeline carrying fuel from the Digboi refinery area of Assam. The pipeline received high priority from the CCS on 26 February 1943, but its completion would take months. The other project, building airfields in Assam to support the Hump, was sponsored by the SOS but was being executed by the British in accordance with the War Department directive that local resources would be used to the utmost. Of SOS's engineering activities and requests, all that would contribute to Chennault's operations in China was the construction of some plants in India to make steel drums in which to haul oil and gas over the Hump.[73]

In January 1943 ATC warned Bissell that the Assam airfields were not being completed on schedule. In replying, Bissell accepted full responsibility for their completion. Under the circumstances, this could only mean that Bissell accepted responsibility for prodding the appropriate Indian agencies. In March Stilwell listed for Marshall the failure of Wavell's engineers to complete the airfields as one of several examples of lethargy in India. Stilwell made the significant remark to Marshall that this failure was one of the factors not under United States control which materially affected American operations. Marshall then warned Dill that ATC was receiving aircraft in India faster than they would be employed, because of the bad airfield situation. Marshall would be grateful for anything Dill might do to expedite their completion. There was therefore no surprise in the War Department when on 19 April the commander of the India–China Wing, ATC, Col. Edward H. Alexander, reported that the

---

[72] Memo, Wheeler for Somervell, 8 May 43, sub: Restoration of Communication Facilities in Burma. Folder, Burma—Restoring Communications, Gen Ref Br, OCMH.
[73] (1) MS 428, Army Service Forces Activities in the Supply of China, Burma, and India, 1942–1943, pp. 50–54. Gen Ref Br, OCMH. (2) Rpt, Col Frederick S. Strong, Jr., Chief Engr, SOS CBI, to Somervell, 13 Nov 43. Somervell File, Vol IV, Hq ASF, Theaters of Opns, CBI 1944, A46–257. (Hereafter, Somervell File, –) (3) Min, CCS 73d Mtg, 26 Feb 43.

unpaved, incomplete runways in Assam were unusable because of rain. He had but two runways and fourteen hardstandings from which to operate 146 aircraft. The detailed survey of the progress on the airfields which he included in his letter revealed the Assam airfields would not be able to support Chennault for many months to come.[74]

The condition of the airfields angered Stilwell. Far from complacent about the misfortunes of the ATC, he wrote: "The base was in sorry shape. A sea of mud. No hardstandings. No access roads. Very bad storage. Forage ruined by rain. (———, the QM storage man, incompetent.)" [75] So Stilwell put pressure on Wavell: "Rushed to Delhi to squawk to Wavell, and we got action. In two days, 5,000 were at work on each airfield. . . ." [76]

In explanation, the SOS reported to Somervell:

> Construction has for the past year been extremely slow due to British failure to place priority on task, even though during this period the U.S. was assured that such priority existed. Target dates have never even been closely approached. The airdromes, supposedly with sufficiently high priority so that materials and equipment would be forthcoming, have been deprived of both for British projects of Eastern Army. Specific instances would be ascertained only after damage was done. British assurance was always forthcoming that entire field project would be complete before the monsoon of 1943 and with such being the case American Engineers were placed in a position of waiting until completion of project did not appear possible with available resources before effective action could be taken.[77]

Under these conditions, Hump tonnage to China not surprisingly fell from 3,200 tons in February to 2,500 tons in April, and Chennault's allocation, of course, fell with it just when the President was directing he be given a free hand. In March, according to Stilwell's announced Hump policy, Chennault was to have received 1,000 tons. Chennault protested that he actually received only 615 tons (though ATC claimed the true figure was 807 tons). Chennault also believed that in defiance of the President's wishes Stilwell was not giving his supplies high priority. A further element of discord had been introduced by SOS in India. With such heavy political emphasis being placed on the amount of tonnage over the Hump, SOS airfield personnel frequently disregarded the priorities set by Chennault's staff and loaded aircraft as quickly as possible with whatever lay at hand, regardless of priority. Thus, when Chennault asked that 81 percent of his 1,000 tons be gasoline, of the tonnage he actually received, he

[74] (1) CM–IN 430, Stilwell to Marshall, 1 Apr 43. (2) Memo, Marshall for Dill, 8 Apr 43, sub: Program for India–China Wing. Item 66, OPD Exec 10. (3) Ltr, Alexander to Arnold, 19 Apr 43, with Incl, Rad NR J1339, Bissell to Alexander, 30 Jan 43. Folder, New Airdromes in India Corresp (Dec 42–May 43), CT 23, Dr 2, KCRC. (4) CM–IN 11827, Stilwell to Marshall, 27 Mar 43. (5) Ltr, Col Robert F. Tate, Air Off, Hq USAF CBI, to Stilwell, 12 Feb 43, sub: Airdrome Housing and Operational Facilities. Folder, New Airdromes in India Corresp (Dec 42–May 43), CT 23, Dr 2, KCRC.
[75] Stilwell B&W, 19 Apr 43.
[76] The Stilwell Papers, p. 202.
[77] Notes, Lt Col Henry A. Byroade, Engr, sub: Notes for Record on Airdrome Construction and Cargo Availability for India–China Freight Line, 23 Jun 43. Somervell File, Vol III, CBI 42–43.

claimed only 50 percent was gasoline. ATC disputed this, but set the figure at 68 percent, still short of the 81 percent desired by Chennault.[78]

U.S. Forces Establish Training Centers for Y–Force

Preparation for ANAKIM in China continued at a fair pace in February–March 1943. Soong's departure for Washington and his work there on behalf of Chennault did not seem to interfere with Stilwell's progress in China. It was one of those rare and halcyon periods in wartime Sino-American relations when the Chinese were co-operative and reform of the Chinese Army was in progress. It may be surmised that, pending clarification of the American attitude, the Generalissimo co-operated with both Chennault and Stilwell.

In January 1943 after the talks with Soong and Chen indicated enough progress, Stilwell, anticipating final agreement, ordered U.S. instructors to move to Yunnan and to set up in Kunming a branch office of his Chungking headquarters under Colonel Dorn as a deputy chief of staff. Dorn's mission was to represent Stilwell in all matters involving Y–Force training and in administrative matters involving U.S. personnel. Since the Y–Force was under Chinese command, the American responsibility was limited to training and supply of lend-lease equipment.[79]

Stilwell's training program for Y–Force was:

1. *Training.* Training is to be carried out in training centers and in the units themselves. Officers are to attend courses of about six weeks each at the training centers of the Kunming area. After graduating, they go back to their units and become instructors in the unit schools. The unit schools are to be organized and conducted by American instructors permanently stationed with armies and divisions. This will ensure that training is continuous, progressive, and uniform. A group of American instructors will be placed with each army, and can organize the unit schools in the divisions belonging to the army, supervise instruction, and keep the army commander informed of progress.

2. *Training centers.* Training Centers for Artillery, Infantry, and signal communications are to be set up in the Kunming area. Courses should begin in February, and run for six weeks each. Graduates go back to their units and act as instructors. Each artillery class should be about 300 officers, each infantry class about 450, and each signal communications class about 150. The artillery training class will train battery officers in methods of fire and all other subjects pertaining to the battery; the infantry training class will give a thorough course in weapons and the tactics of minor units; and the signal communications training class will give a thorough course in radio, telephone, panel and air-ground communications. These training classes will be staffed and conducted by American instructors.[80]

The Chinese War Ministry was anxious to have direct control over the U.S. instructors and desired to disperse them among the different armies and head-

---

[78] Memo with Incls, Chennault for Arnold, 4 May 43, sub: Factors Which Limit Opns of 14th Air Force. OPD 381 CTO, III, A47–30.

[79] (1) Rpt, Hq Y–FOS USAF CBI, 10 Jul 44, sub: Hist Rpt for 1943. History of CBI, Sec. II, Ch. III, pp. 4–5. (2) *The Stilwell Papers*, p. 198.

[80] Notes, Training for Y–Force, with Incl, Chinese text. SNF–151.

quarters in Yunnan, the Generalissimo's headquarters, and the Chinese military academies. They further desired that these man be under "command" of the unit commander and the "guidance" of his chief of staff, who would approve all training undertaken. The War Ministry would control all their movements and assignments. Stilwell replied urbanely that because the number of these men was so few it would be best to use them at schools in the Kunming area, whose Chinese graduates could go forth as instructors. Stilwell disclaimed any desire to use this program as a means of interfering with Chinese organizations. The training program would be controlled by General Chen under War Ministry directives.[81]

Preliminary orders for the Artillery Training Center went out on 19 January. Chen's appointment as Commanding General, Chinese Expeditionary Force, was finally and formally announced on 17 February, after a period in which General Ho attempted to persuade the Generalissimo to reconsider. The Infantry and Artillery Training Centers opened their doors on 1 April 1943.[82] In the case of the Artillery Center at Kan-hai-tze, of which a detailed account is extant, the doors opened after a brisk struggle with local Chinese authority and Chinese workmen that illustrated some of the difficulties in the way of giving aid to China.

The only buildings Governor Lung Yun was willing to give the Americans were bomb damaged, and a construction and remodeling program was required. Adjoining the compound was an unused Chinese airstrip under command of a Chinese air officer with the title of Station Master. This dignitary complained of the workmen's crossing his field and arrested the contractor's subforeman. His obstructive attitude was supported by his superior in the Chinese Air Force. Wrote Brig. Gen. Jerome J. Waters, charged with organizing the Artillery Center:

> Finally the contractor revealed to me that the Station Master had been insisting that he purchase all building materials from him at ridiculously exorbitant prices. As soon as I learned about this "shakedown" I informed the Station Master in no uncertain terms that the building operations would continue without interference from him even if it became necessary for armed American personnel to guard the contractor's men. The entire incident was reported to General Stilwell, and shortly afterwards Colonel Yien called to inform me that the Station Master was being removed for his stupidity.[83]

His successor blew out the entire electric light circuit in the center "with a crude galvanized iron wire which he ran to his house in Kan-hai-tze in the

---

[81](1) Stipulations Concerning the Employment of the American Instructors. SNF–55. Couched in legal terms, the paper appears to be based on contracts for hired instructors. (2) Draft Memo in Stilwell's hand, for Shang Chen, NMC. SNF–55.

[82](1) *The Stilwell Papers,* p. 190. (2) CM–IN 8392, MA Chungking to MILID, 17 Feb 43. (3) Rad C–8, Dorn to Stilwell, 9 Feb 43. Item 207, Bk 1, JWS Personal File. (4) CM–IN 3365, Stilwell to Marshall, 6 Apr 43.

[83] Rpt, Gen Waters, History of Field Artillery Training School, Incl 6, App. III, Y–Force Hist Rpt, p. 10. AG 314.7. (Hereafter, Waters Report.)

expectation of cadging a little American electricity to light his house. Of course he merely succeeded in blowing out the entire circuit. . . ."[84]

The closest supervision was necessary to prevent the workmen from making off with gasoline, motor oil, and spare parts from the center's few vehicles, for the grinding poverty of China's masses, and the flourishing black market, made this very profitable. On one or two occasions drivers even drained the fluid from their trucks' brake systems and sold it in town. It was necessary to count the nails issued to carpenters and account for each one driven. When the Artillery Center opened on 1 April, gaping holes were still in the roofs and walls, but ANAKIM could not wait on that. Wrote General Waters:

> The original organization of the FATC was patterned after the Field Artillery School at Fort Sill, Oklahoma. As such, it contained a small staff for administrative purposes, a Tactics Department, and a Gunnery Department. . . . When the school opened, American liaison officers were assigned to work with the various units of the school troops, and the Director of the Tactics Department was put in charge of school troop activity.[85]

Waters regarded the organization as very satisfactory. Twenty-three interpreters were on hand when the center opened. Considering themselves members of the superior scholar class and trying to live on fixed incomes at a time of rampant inflation, these men were a problem for the center. Fifty-six American officers and enlisted men were present for duty as classes began. Twelve Chinese officers were present also to act as assistant instructors; two of them were competent and were retained.[86]

School troops were to be provided by the 71st Army Artillery Battalion, with 40 officers and 348 enlisted men who arrived for duty just before the center opened. "The entire organization was undernourished and badly in need of medical attention." Center personnel at once began training the battalion, and efforts were made to bring it up to par physically. The 2d Battalion, 2d Army Field Artillery, arrived on 13 April. It was in comparatively good physical condition. The principal obstacle to training this battalion was the disinterest of the battalion commander, whose removal was finally arranged through Chinese channels. The animals of school troops were in poor condition. "The Chinese are very reluctant to graze their animals for fear of losing both the animals and the soldiers through desertion."[87]

When the Artillery Center began its first class on 5 April, eighty-seven Chinese officers were present as students. This number introduced "the most serious problem" of the center, which was the "failure of the Chinese to furnish students equal to the capacity of the schools. . . . The Artillery Training Center operated at approximately ¼ of its capacity. . . ." in 1943.[88]

---

[84] Waters Report.
[85] Waters Report, p. 28, quotation on p. 14.
[86] Waters Report, pp. 18, 69.
[87] Waters Report, pp. 53–54, 66.
[88] (1) Waters Report, p. 10. (2) Quotation from History of CBI, p. 138.

The course of instruction covered eight weeks. Subjects taught were:

	Hours
Observed Fires	96
Firing Battery	42
Massed Fires	56
Animal Transport	36
Matériel	28
Tactics	56
Motor Transport	12
Communications	52
	378

Instruction in observed fires stressed forward observer techniques, but some instruction in precision methods was given for use against pillboxes. Instruction in massed fire ran counter to the Chinese habit of using pieces singly and without attempt at cover and camouflage. The scarcity of motor transport made it advisable to concentrate on animal transport techniques.[89]

Brig. Gen. (then Colonel) Thomas S. Arms received a personal directive from Stilwell on 12 March 1943 on the training program for the Infantry Training Center. The center's mission was to train officers of the Y–Force in the use of infantry weapons and in tactics up to and including regimental level. Signal instruction was also to be provided for signal officers. General Arms was to be vice-commandant, in charge of training, while a Chinese colleague controlled discipline and administration. Classes of one hundred infantry and twenty-five signal officers were to enter weekly and biweekly respectively.[90]

The former Airplane Factory 1 at Kunming and the area adjoining were received for use by the Infantry Training Center. Opening ceremonies were held on 4 April attended by Chen and senior Chinese and U.S. officers. School troops were furnished by the Chinese authorities. General Arms described their physical condition as appalling. Seventy percent of them suffered from trachoma, scabies, colds, and intestinal disease. Ten of them died in the first three weeks of the center's existence. Analyzing the situation, Arms reported that this condition was due primarily to long-continued malnutrition and lack of medical care. Moreover, the impressment system which passed for conscription brought in only the sweepings of the villages—the men without friends, money, or influence. General Arms reported that conditions in the Chinese Army were so bad that any man who could avoid service did so.[91]

The first two classes received at the Infantry Training Center were not officers, for whom the instruction was designed, but officer candidates who had been attending General Tu's 5th Group Army Training Center for junior officers. Their attitude was satisfactory, but General Arms believed that, in view of

[89] Waters Report, pp. 22, 30, 73–78.
[90] Directive, Stilwell to Arms, 12 Mar 43. AG (Y–FOS) 353, KCRC.
[91] (1) Jour, 1943, Hq Infantry Training Center. Gen Ref Br, OCMH. (2) Progress Rpt 1, 25 Mar–22 Apr 43, Arms to Stilwell, dated 22 Apr 43. AG (Y–FOS) 354.6, KCRC.

the U.S. effort involved in providing a highly qualified American instructional staff, the Chinese should be called upon to provide a representative group of qualified officer students.[92] These officer candidates were receiving only two meals a day from the Chinese authorities responsible for administering the center, and at Arms' insistence meals were increased to three a day. American insistence also changed Tu's plan to send 600 of these officer candidates through the center before Y-Force officers attended, and later classes were more capable of receiving instruction. Consistent with the Chinese attitude toward the Artillery Training Center, the Chinese Army in 1943 never sent enough students to operate the Infantry Center at above five eighths capacity.[93]

Describing his experiences at a Chinese Army training school, Col. Walter S. Wood, commanding a U.S. liaison team with XI Group Army, wrote:

> The school had all the outward aspects of a school. It had adequate buildings. It had ample training areas. It had a rifle and machine gun range. There was a Commandant, Assistant Commandant and faculty. An elaborate training schedule was on hand. There was an opening exercise and a graduating exercise and ceremonies each Sunday morning. The sad thing was that it did not *teach*. No one fired on the ranges. No one maneuvered on the training areas. Haphazard lectures or, to be more accurate, speeches were the order of the day. When the school was inspected by visitors there was a series of "set pieces" which were put on to convey the idea of scheduled and progressive training.
>
> The feeling seemed to be that, so long as the opening ceremony went well, the student body remained in attendance and the graduation ceremony and banquet went smoothly, then the school was a success.[94]

Marshaling the Yunnan Force

By mid-March 1943 the Generalissimo's failure to create a sound command structure for Y-Force and to concentrate its divisions was the major missing portion of the Soong-Chen-Stilwell program of 28 January.[95] On 7 March Stilwell reported these issues to Marshall. He explained that malnutrition, sickness, corruption, and lack of equipment made the troops in Yunnan a "terrible indictment of China's leaders." [96] Of the eleven armies on hand or expected, five were good by Chinese standards, three were fair, and three were worthless. The war lord situation in Yunnan seriously hindered the logical evolution of an over-all command structure for Y-Force. (*Chart* 7) Neither the Indochina border armies, with their important holding mission, nor the Y-Force strategic reserves around Kunming were under General Chen's command. Instead, his Chinese Expeditionary Force faced the Burma border without any control over what happened in its rear. The only semblance of unity was Chen's influence over the Y-Force training program.

[92] *Ibid.*
[93] (1) Rpt cited n. 91(2). (2) History of CBI, p. 138.
[94] Wood, Copy of Rpts, Tali Mil District, Yoke Force, CBI Opns 43–44, p. 4. Gen Ref Br, OCMH.
[95] Memo cited n. 15.
[96] CM–IN 4217, Stilwell to Marshall, 9 Mar 43.

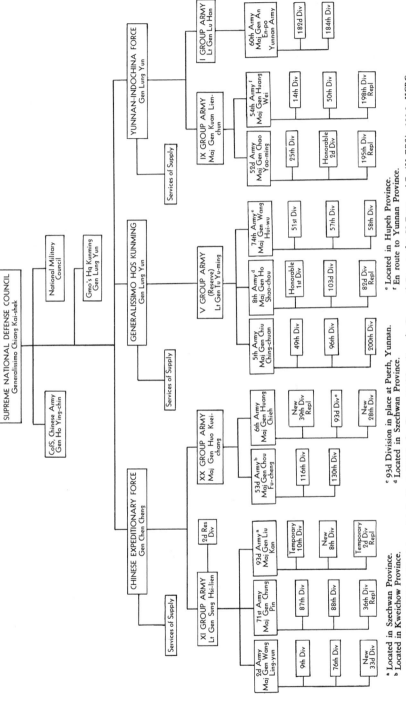

CHART 7—ORGANIZATION OF CHINESE YUNNAN FORCE (Y-FORCE): MARCH–APRIL 1943

SUPREME NATIONAL DEFENSE COUNCIL
Generalissimo Chiang Kai-shek

CofS, Chinese Army
Gen Ho Ying-chin

National Military
Council

Gmo's Hq Kunming
Gen Lung Yun

CHINESE EXPEDITIONARY FORCE
Gen Chen Cheng

GENERALISSIMO HQS KUNMING
Gen Lung Yun

YUNNAN-INDOCHINA FORCE
Gen Lung Yun

Services of Supply

Services of Supply

Services of Supply

XI GROUP ARMY
Lt Gen Sung Hsi-lien

2d Res Div

XX GROUP ARMY
Maj Gen Huo Kuei-chang

V GROUP ARMY
(Reserve)
Lt Gen Tu Yu-ming

IX GROUP ARMY
Maj Gen Kuan Lien-chun

I GROUP ARMY
Lt Gen Lu Han

2d Army
Maj Gen Wang Ling-yun

71st Army
Maj Gen Chung Pin

93d Army[a]
Maj Gen Liu Kuan

53d Army[b]
Maj Gen Chou Fu-cheng

6th Army
Maj Gen Huang Chieh

5th Army
Maj Gen Chiu Ching-chuan

8th Army[d]
Maj Gen Ho Shao-chou

74th Army[e]
Maj Gen Wang Hui-wu

52d Army
Maj Gen Chao Yao-ming

54th Army[f]
Maj Gen Huang Wei

60th Army
Maj Gen An En-po
Yunnan Army

9th Div

87th Div

Temporary 10th Div

116th Div

New 39th Div Repl

49th Div

Honorable 1st Div

51st Div

25th Div

14th Div

182d Div

76th Div

88th Div

New 8th Div

130th Div

93d Div[c]

96th Div

103d Div

57th Div

Honorable 2d Div

50th Div

184th Div

New 33d Div

36th Div Repl

Temporary 2d Div Repl

New 28th Div

200th Div

82d Div Repl

58th Div

195th Div Repl

198th Div Repl

[a] Located in Szechwan Province.
[b] Located in Kweichow Province.

[c] 93d Division in place at Puerh, Yunnan.
[d] Located in Szechwan Province.

[e] Located in Hupeh Province.
[f] En route to Yunnan Province.

Source: Memo, Wang Wen-hsien, Admin Dept, NMC, for Dorn, 23 Mar 43, sub: Personnel Reqmts for Y-Force. AG (Y-FOS) 320.2, KCRC.

The Chinese Services of Supply situation was also confused. The General-issimo's Yunnan headquarters had its own SOS. Gen. Yu Fei-peng, whom Stilwell branded "a rascal of the first water," had the area SOS. General Chen controlled his Chinese Expeditionary Force SOS. In order to bolster Chen, Stil-well was able to obtain control of Burma Road transport and engineering organizations. This control, Stilwell hoped, would permit some restriction of the smuggling that wasted precious gasoline and debauched Chinese soldiers and politicos. Then, he proceeded to one of the larger aspects of China Theater: "From all fronts come consistent reports of fierce fighting. From observation and investigation I am convinced that they are at least 90% false. I note that they get widespread publicity in the United States. This makes my job more difficult, of course. If the Chinese Army is so full of fight and so well led, what am I here for?" [97]

Though he had issued orders previously for the concentration of the Y–Force, the Generalissimo once again on 23 March ordered troops and re-placements to Yunnan. A week later Stilwell radioed Soong that the next problem was to have the replacements with their divisions by 31 May. Stilwell had raised the replacement issue with Soong earlier, reminding the Chinese statesman that the consolidation of troops was to have begun on 21 January but had not yet started. Stilwell pointed out that the basis of the Sino-American wartime relationship was that the United States was to contribute weapons while the Chinese were to furnish men. Then came a gentle hint pinning this reminder to the lend-lease question. If Chinese manpower was not forthcoming, said Stilwell, then munitions supplied would be largely wasted.[98]

Meanwhile, much to Stilwell's astonishment, the Chinese War Ministry adopted the American-proposed Tables of Organization and Equipment and ordered replacements to the units of Y–Force. The War Ministry's 23 March plan embodied:

1. Eleven Armies (corps) [in terms of U.S. Army strength] containing thirty-one (31) divisions are assigned to Y–Force.

2. a. The 2d Reserve Division will remain an independent division.

b. Two divisions of the following Armies will be brought to the new proposed strength of 10,300; the third division in each of these Armies to retain only enough weapons to train, and in effect to become a replacement unit:

71st Army	6th Army	54th Army
93d Army	52d Army	8th Army

Thus the above Armies will consist of two "assault" divisions and one replacement division each.

c. The two divisions of the 53d Army will be brought up to the new proposed strength of 10,300 for each division. [Stilwell did not propose to alter the composition of Army troops (8,400) at this time. Unlike the U.S. practice, Chinese artillery remained under Army com-

---

[97] *Ibid.*
[98] (1) CM–IN 16435, Stilwell to Soong, 30 Mar 43. (2) CM–IN 10597, Stilwell to Soong, 20 Mar 43. (3) Cases 122, 126, 127, OPD 381 CTO, A47–30.

mand, and was attached to organic divisions at the order of the Army commander. When it was possible to bring some 75-mm. pieces into China, Stilwell recommended personnel changes in the artillery units of the Army command].

d. The three divisions of the following Armies will be brought up to the new proposed strength of 10,300; each army to contain three assault divisions:

2d Army   5th Army   74th Army

e. The two divisions of the 60th Army (Yunnan Provincial troops) will be brought up to the present Table of Organization strength (1942) of 7,800 each. [Army troops numbered 4,200 men].

3. a. With re-organization and replacement the Y-Force will consist of twelve (12) new-type assault divisions and three (3) replacement divisions on the Western Front [Salween front]; four (4) new-type assault divisions and two (2) old-type assault divisions, and two (2) replacement divisions on the Southern Front [Indochina border]; and eight (8) new-type assault divisions and one (1) replacement division in general reserve [Kunming area].

b. Thus the Y-Force will consist of a total of: [See Chart 7.]

> 24 new-type assault divisions
> 2 old-type assault divisions
> 6 replacement divisions.[99]

Y-Force was understrength by 185,255 men. Nevertheless, the Chinese War Ministry's plan to provide 122,753 replacements by 10 June met with Stilwell's approval. (*Table 6*) Why were divisions so far understrength in a country Westerners always thought of as teeming with men? There were two reasons: First, in a peasant, small-holding economy only so many farmers can be removed from the land without causing famine. By 1943 Chinese manpower reserves were badly depleted, hence Stilwell's proposals to fill up the better-trained divisions by taking men from the poorer. Secondly, the Chinese supply and impressment systems were very bad. The central government gave cash allowances to unit commanders with which to buy rice.

Naturally a certain amount of "squeeze" is inevitable in the course of the various transactions, and the amount of food that a soldier receives [is] in direct proportion to the honesty and business acumen of his immediate commander. Often in order to secure sufficient food for his men a commander will deliberately pad his strength report. Tactically this causes considerable confusion when the unit arrives at the fighting front with only a fraction of its "paper strength." On several occasions troops at the FATC [Field Artillery Training Center] were not fed for as long as three days because the borrowing ability of the Battalion Commander was exhausted in the local villages and in several instances we were forced to despatch our own trucks for the purpose of obtaining rice, so that units stationed here would not starve to death.[100]

On paper, at least, with the acceptance of the Tables of Organization each Chinese army would be able to meet a Japanese division with a reasonable chance of success. Stilwell proposed during the initial phase of ANAKIM to send two Chinese armies against the lone Japanese *56th Division* barring the way into

---

[99] Memo, Wang Wen-hsien, Admin Dept, NMC, for Dorn, 23 Mar 43, sub: Personnel Reqmts for Y-Force. AG (Y-FOS) 320.2, KCRC.
[100] Waters Report, pp. 65–66.

Table 6—Chinese Personnel Requirements for Y–Force: 23 March 1943

Organization and Deployment	Strength 23 March 1943		Shortage	Replace-ments En route	Planned Strength by 10 June 1943
	Authorized	Actual			
Total.....................	412,600	227,345	185,255	122,753	350,098
Chinese Expeditionary Force....	196,500	86,150	110,350	64,000	150,150
XI Group Army.............	128,200	55,550	72,650	49,000	104,550
2d Army...............	39,300	25,600	13,700	17,000	42,600
71st Army.............	39,300	18,750	20,550	9,500	28,250
93d Army.............	39,300	8,200	31,100	17,000	25,200
2d Reserve Division.....	10,300	3,000	7,300	5,500	8,500
XX Group Army...........	68,300	30,600	37,700	15,000	45,600
6th Army...............	39,300	14,700	24,600	10,500	25,200
53d Army...............	29,000	15,900	13,100	4,500	20,400
Yunnan–Indochina Force........	98,200	54,500	43,700	21,484	75,984
I Group Army...............	19,600	15,650	3,950	4,650	20,300
60th Army.............	19,600	15,650	3,950	4,650	20,300
IX Group Army.............	78,600	38,850	39,750	16,834	55,684
52d Army...............	39,300	20,450	18,850	7,544	27,994
54th Army.............	39,300	18,400	20,900	9,290	27,690
Reserve.........................	117,900	86,695	31,205	37,269	123,964
V Army Group..............	117,900	86,695	31,205	37,269	123,964
5th Army...............	39,300	33,860	5,440	18,984	52,844
8th Army...............	39,300	21,050	18,250	7,300	28,350
74th Army.............	39,300	31,785	7,515	10,985	42,770

Source: Memo, Wang Wen-hsien, Admin Dept, NMC, for Dorn, 23 Mar 43, sub: Personnel Reqmts for Y–Force. AG (Y–FOS) 320.2, KCRC.

Burma. The basic principle behind the new tables was that all Y–Force units down to the smallest should be able to operate as self-contained combat teams. (See Chart 3.) The Salween Front was over 100 air miles long, the 56th Division would be spread very thin, and the Chinese could simply flow through the inevitable gaps.

Under the new Tables of Organization, Chinese infantry regiments increased from 2,052 men to 2,922. Each rifle company would have 90 rifles and 9 machine guns, with a total of 81 machine guns in the regiment. Each company, battalion, and regiment was given increased allotments of mortars to build an adequate base of fire to support its maneuver. Some of these mortars would be the handy and light 60-mm. American weapon, new to the Chinese. Each battalion would have an antitank squad with the Boys .55-caliber rifle, a British weapon quite capable of dealing with the thinly-armored Japanese tanks. Artillery for the Y–Force would be equal, weighed by number of weapons, to nineteen battalions, mostly with pieces of 75-mm. This force was far more than the Japanese defenders would have.

The lend-lease contribution to the Y–Force would not be great for most of the weapons were in China. The Chinese would furnish the rifles, the light machine guns, the grenade dischargers, the 82-mm. trench mortars, and 5,000 submachine guns. The United States was to fly in 2,200 submachine guns, 576 Boys antitank rifles, 900 60-mm. mortars, 558 Bren machine guns, 40 75-mm. pack howitzers, and 430 rocket launchers. These supplies, plus ammunition, totaled 6,900 tons of ordnance. Then it would be up to China to find the soldiers.[101]

In mid-April Stilwell was confident China would find them. He was partially satisfied with the progress being made in Y–Force. The Artillery and Infantry Training Centers for brushing Y–Force officers into shape were in operation. General Chen Cheng was co-operative beyond Stilwell's highest previous hopes. Concentration of divisions in Yunnan was proceeding. Then on 18 April 1943 Stilwell met with the Generalissimo, who "acted scared. Morale at low ebb." [102] Japanese activity in central China, on the direct path to Chungking, was increasing. The result of this activity was irresistible pressure to drain men and supplies from Yunnan to the I-chang gorge area of the Yangtze, and much of the January–March progress with Y–Force was lost.

In the winter of 1942–1943 the Japanese *11th Army,* garrisoning the Hankow area, had expanded its defense perimeter in the Tung-ting Lake area at the expense of Chinese Communist forces there. Using sixteen battalions, by the end of March 1943 the Japanese had scored local success at the cost of 354 dead and 890 wounded, occupied a "fertile [rice] region," and held good positions for future operations.[103] At this time the Japanese shipping situation on the Yangtze, which is navigable by ocean-going ships, became acute because of reverses in the Southwest Pacific. Estimating there were some 20,000 tons of river shipping on the upper Yangtze, which had fled there to escape them, the Japanese determined on a large-scale raid to trap these vessels at their moorings and move them down river. After this, the Japanese would withdraw. The concentration of three divisions plus three detachments of approximately regimental strength began on 16 April and concluded on 4 May. These stirrings, noted in Chungking and accompanied by increased Japanese aerial activity, alarmed the Chinese and disturbed Chennault's staff. On 15 May Y–Force

---

[101] The General Plan of ANAKIM (Y–Force Project), 19 May 1943, is a staff study of the Y–Force role in projected Burma operations during the 1943–1944 dry season. It also contains the general scheme for re-equipping the Y–Force divisions from Chinese and U.S. contributions. Gen Ref Br, OCMH.
[102] Stilwell Diary, 18 Apr 43.
[103] Japanese Study 77, pp. 95–97.

suffered a blow when the Generalissimo ordered Chen Cheng to return to defend his VI War Area.[104]

British Operations and ANAKIM

In summing up the Calcutta discussions of February with the Arnold-Somervell-Dill mission, Wavell said that it was agreed to prepare for the fall offensive with all possible speed. His preparations were greatly influenced by the failure of his December attempt to seize the Akyab airfields.[105] Wavell had wanted to make a quick amphibious seizure of Akyab to forestall Japanese reaction, but landing craft were not available, and so he had settled on an overland advance. The scheme was not hopeless, for Wavell's staff correctly estimated that but two Japanese battalions held the area. Speed in taking it before the Japanese could react was essential. Operations were under Eastern Army, Lt. Gen. N. M. S. Irwin.

The Japanese fell back before the advancing 14th Indian Division, and on 27 December a patrol actually reached the southern tip of the Mayu peninsula directly opposite Akyab. Then, an unfortunate delay of ten days for administrative reasons halted the advance. The pause was fatal, for when the division was set to advance again, elements of the Japanese *55th Division* had dug in and were defending themselves with the accustomed stubborn valor of the Japanese. Terrain that might have been taken by marching had to be conquered.

The effort went on for months, with Indian and British brigades being fed into the Arakan district in sequence. Casualties were the only immediate result. The Indian and British soldiers could not know it, but their sacrificial courage once caused the chief of staff of the *55th Division* to urge abandoning the Japanese foothold on the Mayu Peninsula to safeguard the landing of the main body of the *55th Division* on Akyab. He was overruled, and the Japanese company garrisoning the key point clung to its defenses.

While 14th Indian Division was engaged on the Mayu peninsula, to its left and rear a battalion of the Japanese *33d Division* was completing a long march overland from the Irrawaddy valley. Its appearance in the Kaladan valley which ran roughly parallel to the coast signaled the beginning of the end. Now present in strength, *55th Division* began a series of encircling moves which took full advantage of the superior experience of its veteran troops and repeatedly cut off elements of 14th Indian Division and of 26th Indian Division, which replaced the 14th. After successive actions, during which among other reverses 6th Brigade headquarters was overrun and its commander captured and killed, in May, 14th and 26th Divisions were back in their original positions on the

---

[104] (1) *Ibid.* (2) MA (China) Rpt 417, Tai-Heng Fighting, 16 Apr–28 May 43. MID Library. (3) Headquarters, USAF, CBI, was not officially informed of the seriousness of the I-chang fighting until 11 May 1943. CM–IN 12914, Hearn to Stilwell, 20 May 43.

[105] See Ch. VII, p. 250, above.

Indian border. The effort cost 2,500 battle casualties. Sickness took a dreadful toll. When the first Arakan campaign was ended, observers agreed that the morale of its veterans was badly impaired.[106]

Well to the north of the Arakan, in central Burma, the celebrated British soldier, Brigadier Orde Charles Wingate, led an experimental foray into Burma from February to June, 1943. Wingate had been sent to Burma at Wavell's request during the First Burma Campaign. His varied career had taken him to Palestine and Ethiopia, where he had acquired a profound knowledge of guerrilla warfare and an ability to apply the principles of war to novel situations. His arrival in Burma had been too late to affect the first campaign, but he did perceive the solution to the Japanese tactical system.

The Japanese encirclement tactics were habitually directed against their enemies' lines of communications. They themselves, carrying many of their supplies in their packs, depending to a large degree on animal transport, and being trained to move swiftly through the jungle, were not road bound like the Indian divisions. Since the latter depended heavily on motor transport, the road block was a deadly hazard to Indian troops.

Wingate proposed to form units stripped of all purely formal equipment, organized into small columns with a base of fire and a maneuvering element and supplied entirely by air. Such units in the jungle would have the mobility of ships at sea, and road blocks would hold no terror for them. Indeed, they could attack Japanese lines of communications at will. The mission of these units, Wingate suggested, would be to spread disorganization behind the Japanese lines, which could be exploited by pressure from standard infantry divisions. Obtaining Wavell's approval, Wingate organized his 77th Indian Infantry Brigade. Its members were not handpicked. Rather, the brigade was made of units then available, 2d Battalion Burma Rifles, 13th Battalion the King's Regiment, the 3/2d Gurkha Rifles, and the 142d Commando. If the Generalissimo's troops had gone into Burma in March 1943, 77th Brigade would have been used to cut the Japanese lines of communications to Myitkyina and Lashio. Thus were born the famous Chindits, as they were later nicknamed after the legendary guardian of the Burman shrines.

After the Generalissimo withdrew from the March 1943 operation, the ardent Wingate asked for a chance to test his men and theories against the Japanese. Wavell agreed, and Wingate's men crossed the Chindwin in seven columns on 18 February without opposition to attack the rail line to Myitkyina in the Irrawaddy valley. Extensive damage was done to the railway, and Wingate resolved to press on across the Irrawaddy, deep into Burma.

Once across the Irrawaddy, the Chindits' operations went less smoothly, and in attempting a return to India the force had to use a prearranged method of breaking up into small groups. One of these groups went northward and

[106] (1) Owen, *Campaign in Burma*, pp. 31–38. (2) Wavell Despatch, January 1 to June 20, 1943, *Supplement to The London Gazette.* (3) Japanese Study 89, pp. 5–8.

came out via Fort Hertz; another went eastward and emerged at Pao-shan in Yunnan. The 77th Brigade had spent four months in Japanese-occupied territory. At a cost of about 30 percent casualties it had gained considerable experience in the art of making deep penetrations into enemy territory. The force had done no damage to the Japanese that bombers could not have done more cheaply, but great results were to issue from Wingate's expedition.[107]

On the Allied side, commanders henceforth recognized that units on air supply could move in strength in Japanese rear areas. This opened a variety of interesting tactical and strategic possibilities. Not only India Command and China–Burma–India Theater, but also the Japanese headquarters in Burma, *Burma Area Army* as they now were, studied the operation. In 1942, the Japanese had concluded that the hills on India's border were impenetrable. Now they re-evaluated the problem in the light of Wingate's achievements and concluded that India could be invaded. They failed to observe that armies in the jungle could be supplied by air.[108]

The Arakan failure plus the need to prepare for ANAKIM led to some drastic changes in Wavell's India Command. The officers charged with military training and with the immediate conduct of operations in Burma were relieved. Halting all activity and training based on the defense of India, Wavell ordered concentration of effort on offensive training. The former deputy chief of staff for operations became chief of staff of an expeditionary force headquarters, with orders to organize his staff and begin training. On 31 March General Sir George Giffard assumed command of the new expeditionary force, with orders to restore the Rangoon–Lashio line of communications by 1 May 1944. General Giffard had commanded in west Africa where he had trained two African divisions with the thought that they might be used in Burma. When Giffard came to India to arrange details of the movement, Wavell, under whom he had served in 2d Division at Aldershot in England, offered him the post of army commander.

American observers in India differed in their reaction to these preparations. Col. Russell A. Osmun and his American Observer Group in New Delhi, an independent body, took a highly favorable view of them. President Roosevelt's personal representative in India, Mr. William Phillips, former Under Secretary of State, did not. Mr. Phillips was highly critical and reported to the President that it was hard to find any sign of an aggressive spirit in India, that the authorities seemed to feel their responsibilities ended at the border of Burma. General Stilwell agreed with the President's special representative.[109]

[107] (1) Wavell Despatch, January 1 to June 20, 1943, *Supplement to The London Gazette.* (2) Wingate's Rpt. Library, Hq Infantry School, Ft. Benning, Ga.

[108] (1) Wavell Despatch, January 1 to June 20, 1943, *Supplement to The London Gazette,* pars. 24–28. (2) SEATIC Bull 240, 9 Jul 46, pp. 3–5. MID Library. (3) Japanese Study 89, p. 12.

[109] (1) Ltr, Col Osmun to Brig Gen Hayes A. Kroner, Chief of Mil Int Serv, 17 Apr 43. ABC 337 TRIDENT (May 43) Sec E, A48–224. (2) CM–IN 2540, Ferris to Marshall, 4 Apr 43. (3) CM–IN 5915, Stilwell to Marshall, 10 Apr 43. (4) CM–IN 11837, Stilwell to Marshall, 23 Mar 43. (5) *The Memoirs of Cordell Hull,* Vol. II, p. 1494.

India's matériel needs for ANAKIM, many of which were to be met by lend-lease, were set by Wavell's staff as 182,000 tons a month for six months. When these figures arrived in Washington they were challenged by the Logistics Group, OPD, who believed that the Indian requirements submitted as the bill for ANAKIM were actually those needed to equip the forty-four divisions contemplated by India's long-range plan. For example, armored forces on the scale of those required for ANAKIM would need 165 medium tanks and 89 light tanks. There were then in India 195 light tanks, 1,320 cruiser tanks, and 315 infantry tanks, yet Wavell asked for 4,400 long tons more of tanks as a prerequisite to ANAKIM. Operations Division believed that of the 182,000 tons monthly requirement set as a prerequisite for ANAKIM, 69,000 tons were for civilian requirements in India and Ceylon, and the rest were on a scale more appropriate to forty-four divisions than to the relatively minor ANAKIM operation.[110]

Somervell's first reaction was that, of the 182,000 tons a month requested, 88,000 tons were definitely not needed. Then he reconsidered the next week, arguing that support of India's civil economy was equitable because of the very considerable amounts of reciprocal aid the American forces stationed there received, and because the United States was currently maintaining a very high standard of civilian living. He also observed that the American practice was to support commanders in the full with their requests for equipment even when those seemed high.[111]

Acidly, Stilwell compared what Wavell and himself were to receive for their parts of ANAKIM. It worked out to 180,000 tons a month for Wavell and 3,200 tons for Stilwell (for the Y–Force); an unknown number of tanks for Wavell and five for Stilwell; 12,000 trucks for Wavell, 500 for Stilwell; 3,000,000 U.S. troops for the European Theater of Operations, 1,000,000 for the Southwest Pacific Theater, and for CBI, 3,000.[112]

Since the 182,000-ton figure was Wavell's prerequisite for ANAKIM, there was the obvious possibility the operation might not be mounted, for in spring 1943 the German submarine offensive came closest to separating the Old

[110](1) Rad AMMDEL 305, Stilwell to Marshall, 10 Apr 43. Item 316, Bk 1, JWS Personal File. (2) Memo, Maj Gen LeRoy Lutes, Dir of Opns, ASF, for Somervell, 19 May 43, sub: Monthly U.S. and UK tonnage for Projected Opns in India; Memo, Chief, Strategy Sec, OPD, for Wedemeyer, 17 May 43, sub: Estimate of Tonnage Required for ANAKIM Opn; Memo, Brig Gen Patrick H. Tansey, Chief, Logistics Gp, OPD, for Wedemeyer, 17 May 43, sub: British Reqmts for India. ABC 337 TRIDENT (May 43) Sec E, A48–224.

[111] Memo, Somervell for Marshall, 14 May 43, sub: Memo on Monthy Tonnage of Shipping Space Required from North Africa and UK for ANAKIM; Memo, Somervell for Wedemeyer, 23 May 43, sub: Memo on Shipts Required for Opns in India. ABC 337 TRIDENT (May 43) Sec E, A48–224.

[112] In Stilwell Undated Paper 21, Stilwell continued this note by saying that the United States and China were to do things "50-50," but that "equip., instr, and $$ and backing equalled 0 plus obstruction," that of 324 divisions, 60-odd brigades, and 89 guerrilla units on the Chinese Order of Battle, the Generalissimo had been able to spare three for Stilwell. The paper probably belongs to the fall of 1943, because of its reference to the 3,000 U.S. combat troops, undoubtedly the GALAHAD Project, or Merrill's Marauders. Stilwell Documents, Hoover Library.

World and the New. With shipping space at a premium, Churchill observed in a minute to the British Chiefs of Staff that ANAKIM had "receded" because of the shipping shortage. In accepting an American offer to supply twenty ships for ANAKIM supply accumulation, the British Chiefs of Staff stated explicitly that their acceptance implied no commitment to do ANAKIM, that they accepted only because preparations had to be made if ANAKIM was ever to be a fact.[113]

American Preparations in India–Burma

As of January–April 1943 American preparations in India for Burma's reoccupation included continued training of the Chinese Ramgarh troops, air defense of the Assam Hump terminals, air harassment of the Japanese in Burma, construction of a base at Ledo, construction of the Ledo Road into Burma, and provision of medical aid to the Chinese. Training the Chinese at Ramgarh proceeded along routine lines. The air effort will be described in Chapter IX as one of the factors leading to the decisions on U.S. policy of May 1943.

The 45th U.S. Engineer Regiment and the 823d Engineer Aviation Battalion were assigned to Ledo in December 1942. With substantial and indispensable aid from the British, these troops, Negroes with white officers, prepared the warehouse areas' housing, hospitals, and roads necessary for a base area. Initially, tea sheds were used for the few supplies on hand. The new warehouses and hutments (the hutments were the famous "bashas") had bamboo frameworks with thatched roofs. The only signal facilities at first available were the commercial lines and small switchboard linking a few of the more prosperous residents of Ledo.[114]

In late December the 823d Engineers took over construction of the Ledo Road from the British, in accord with the Wavell-Stilwell agreement of October 1942 and consistent with Wavell's assigning the north Burma area to Stilwell. Between the road builders at Ledo and the Hukawng Valley of Burma lay 103 miles through the juncture of the Patkai and Naga Hills. (*Map* 7) The Patkais rise to a peak of 4,500 feet and drop to 700 feet at Shingbwiyang in Burma. They were crossed by the Refugee Trail, so called because of the unfortunates who had fled from Burma over its narrow, malarious, and leech-ridden stretches. The final report on the Ledo Road described the area as

. . . mountainous terrain, canyon sections, and narrow terraces along torrential streams. This area was unsettled and relatively unexplored. Existing maps were found to be highly inaccurate in their portrayal of ground conditions under the 150 feet of vegetation cover. . . . The soil is largely clay over a weak sedimentary rock structure broken by innumerable fault

---

[113] (1) Incl to Memo, Leahy for JCS, 7 Apr 43. Item 63, OPD Exec 10. (2) Memo, Lt Gen G. N. Macready, JSM, for Marshall, 13 Apr 43. Item 60, OPD Exec 10. (3) Ltr, Macready to Marshall, 20 Apr 43. Case 131, OPD 381 CTO, A47-30. (4) Rad AG 305, Stilwell to Marshall, 10 Apr 43. Item 316, Bk 1, JWS Personal File. (5) Morison, *Rising Sun in the Pacific*, p. 344.
[114] SOS in CBI, App. 6, Advance Section No. 3.

planes and subject to frequent earth tremors. The total annual rainfall through this mountain section amounts to 150 inches but it is concentrated in the monsoon season, May to September inclusive, and the observed intensity reached 14 inches in 24 hours.

The temperature was not uniformly hot. There were "periods of penetrating cold during the winter months"; the monsoon brought "intense heat." [115]

General Wheeler estimated that 103 miles of an all-weather, one-lane road with turnouts could be built to reach Shingbwiyang on the far side of the Patkais by June 20.[116] Wavell's engineer-in-chief was rather skeptical, estimating that forty-five miles by 1 March 1943 would be the best possible. He could not believe that the road could be through Shingbwiyang by 1 May 1943. The British engineer also observed that 600 of his own coolies had died in that area the April before, suggesting some of the medical hazards Wheeler faced. With building the road, Wheeler also assumed responsibility for defending it on 18 February 1943.[117]

British authority furnished swarms of laborers: Indian Pioneer Units of the Indian Army, Indian Tea Association Units organized by the tea planters of Assam, Indian State Labor Units contributed by the quasi-independent Indian States, the Civilian Transport Corps local tea garden workers, and contract labor. "At first these groups were not registered in the Base, and were responsible only to various organizations fortunate enough to get their services. It was a case of catch-as-catch can. Any organization lucky and quick enough to 'acquire' laborers got its work done." These people were used for construction, malaria control, widening and clearing the road, and handling supplies.[118]

Construction equipment belonged to the 45th and 823d Engineers, plus additional items transferred from the Chinese lend-lease stockpile. By 20 January construction was on a 24-hour-a-day basis. "The Road head was pushed at the expense of access roads, and maintenance operations, for it was deemed advisable to make as much forward progress as possible before the monsoon rains." [119] The rate was three quarters of a mile a day of all-weather, single-track roadway with turnouts. Equipment and spare parts were in short supply, and the experience of the Christmas rains suggested that the monsoon would stop construction.

Road construction crossed the Burmese border at 1706 on 28 February 1943, about ten months to the day since the fall of Lashio. There was a little ceremony and Col. Ferdinand J. Tate, commanding the 823d Engineer Aviation Battalion, fired his pistol as the lead bulldozer lurched into Japanese-held

---

[115] (1) History of CBI, Sec. II, Ch. II, The Ledo Road, pp. 1–9. (2) Rpt, Maj Gen Lewis A. Pick, CG, Hq Advance Sec, U.S. Forces, India–Burma Theater, 9 Aug 45, quotation on pp. 5–6. Gen Ref Br, OCMH.

[116] Rad TORCH A679, Wheeler to Stilwell, 9 Jan 43. Item 163, Bk 1, JWS Personal File.

[117] (1) Ltr, Engr-in-Chief, sub: Notes on Ledo Road Project. SNF–84. (2) Ltr, Gen Holcombe, Actg CG, SOS USAF CBI, to Somervell, 19 Feb 43. Somervell File, Vol III, CBI 42–43.

[118] History of CBI, Sec. II, Ch. II, The Ledo Road, p. 11.

[119] Ibid.

Burma. Protecting the roadhead was a regiment of the Chinese Army in India, one day's march ahead of the road builders.[120]

The ceremony, held at mile 43.2 from Ledo, unknowingly marked what was practically the end of forward progress on the road for months to come. The roadhead was beyond practical supply distance from the base. Every means of supply, from tribal porters to elephants, was tried, but to no avail. The engineer, medical, and supply personnel that the JCS had directed sent to Stilwell back in December 1942 arrived at Ledo in March, but these reinforcements were not the solution. By 11 May the monsoon halted all forward progress, about forty-seven miles from Ledo.[121]

The medical problem in the border of Assam and Burma had been expected to be very serious. Inspecting the area in February, 1943, Col. John M. Tamraz, the SOS surgeon, gloomily observed: "I believe the sick rate amongst the Chinese troops will run into 50–75% and amongst the Americans 20% or more." British medical authorities predicted in 1942 that the malaria rate in Assam would be 25 percent. Prewar medical experience offered much support for these forebodings. Malaria and enteric diseases are the two great sanitary problems in the hills. In Burma as a whole there were thought to be some 100,000 cases of bacillary dysentery a year. Exclusive of the Shan States, there were 120,904 deaths ascribed to "fever" in 1939, at least half of them malarial. Rounding out the picture, plague was endemic and the contamination of all water had to be assumed.[122]

Senior Surgeon (Lt. Col.) Victor H. Haas, of the U.S. Public Health Service, who with a number of his colleagues had been sent to Burma before Pearl Harbor to aid in building the Yunnan–Burma Railway, became Surgeon, Base Section No. 3. The 98th Station Hospital moved to Margherita, Assam, in January to care for Ledo Road personnel. It was relieved in April by the 20th General Hospital. The 98th had done yeoman work in medical rehabilitation of the Chinese veterans of the First Burma Campaign, and so was no stranger to CBI. With the 20th General Hospital there arrived the 48th and 73d Evacuation Hospitals, the 151st Medical Battalion, a platoon of the 7th Medical Depot Company, and the 1st Veterinary Company (Separate). Due to the competence and devotion of medical personnel, the precampaign malaria rate was held to 1 percent for Americans and 5 percent for Chinese.[123]

While road building and sanitation were going on, guerrilla activity by Kachin tribesmen of north Burma, who remained loyal to British rule, was annoying the Japanese. General Mutaguchi, commanding the Japanese *18th*

---

[120] (1) History of CBI, Sec. II, Ch. II, The Ledo Road, p. 13. (2) Rads RA–68 and T–92, Stilwell to Wheeler and Boatner. Item 186, Bk 1, JWS Personal File.

[121] History of CBI, Sec. II, Ch. II, The Ledo Road, pp. 13–14.

[122] (1) Col Tamraz, Diary entry of 21 Feb 43. Office, Surgeon Gen, Hist Sec. (2) Memo, Handy for Marshall, 15 Aug 43, sub: Digest of Cables Recd from Stilwell re Burma Opns. Item 51, OPD Exec 10. (3) TB Med 77. Office, Surgeon Gen, Hist Sec.

[123] (1) SOS in CBI, App. 16, Medical Section, pp. 7, 20–21. (2) Memo cited n. 122(2).

Division, resolved to send small columns to Sumprabum, a British outpost some eighty air miles north of Myitkyina, and to the banks of the Tanai River in the Hukawng Valley to deal with it. Beyond Sumprabum lay the small post and airstrip of Fort Hertz, whose loss would threaten Ledo and the Hump air route. On 1 March British civil authority evacuated Sumprabum, and five days later the situation was called "serious." The Kachin tribesmen sensibly dispersed before the veteran *114th Regiment,* and for some anxious days it seemed nothing could keep the Japanese from taking Fort Hertz.[124]

On 12 March, Stilwell ordered Chinese reinforcements to the Ledo area to meet this Japanese threat.[125] Meanwhile, the other Japanese expedition was moving through the Hukawng Valley and soon struck the Indian and Kachin garrison at Hkalak Ga, ten miles northwest of Shingbwiyang, screening the building of the Ledo Road. There was great excitement; the garrison and the U.S. radio team with it burnt its supplies and withdrew. General Wheeler ordered the Seagrave medical unit some miles behind at Tagap Ga, in the Patkai Hills, to pack up and be ready to evacuate. The Chinese outposts held firmly at Nathkaw south of Tagap Ga, but radio contact with them was lost at the end of March.

The Headquarters, Rear Echelon, then buzzed with excitement and activity for the menace seemed progressively greater as the headquarters concerned was farther from the scene. Stilwell stepped in to pour some vinegar on the troubled waters, and the turmoil subsided when the Japanese fell back from the Tagap area and Fort Hertz, never taking Fort Hertz.

Allied airmen were daily strafing and bombing the trails over which the Japanese moved, making their supply situation difficult. Moreover, Wingate's 1943 expedition was now alarmingly active behind the Japanese in central Burma. The Japanese had no units readily available to meet Wingate's men; they feared he might be reinforced, and so the Japanese columns were ordered back.[126]

North Burma is a vast area in itself, and one Japanese division could not of course garrison all of it. Consequently, the Chinese 2d Reserve Division in Yunnan, acting on unknown motives or orders, was able to occupy Shatag Ga on 24 February and to send a regiment down the Nmai Hka Valley to within forty miles of Myitkyina. The Chinese advance was discussed among Stilwell, Wavell, and Ferris, but the occasion was not exploited, and the Chinese withdrew as quietly as they had entered Burma.[127]

---

[124] SEATIC Bull 247, 22 Apr 47, p. 2; Incl (B) to Naval Ln Off, Rangoon, Conf Rpt 49–46, 16 May 46. MID Library.
[125] Rad AGWAR 233, Stilwell to Marshall, 12 Mar 43. Item 251, Bk 1, JWS Personal File.
[126] (1) Gordon S. Seagrave, M.D., *Burma Surgeon Returns* (New York, 1946), p. 31. (2) G–2 Rpts, Forward Echelon, Chih Hui Pu, 1, 6, 9, 13, 22 Mar and 20 Apr 43; Sitrep, 2 May 43. Northern Combat Area Command Files, KCRC. (3) Bull and Incl cited n. 124.
[127] Rad AMMDEL 151, Ferris to Stilwell, 1 Mar 43. Item 225, Bk 1, JWS Personal File.

Summary

Despite the Generalissimo's withdrawal from the spring 1943 campaign, Stilwell's hopes of preparing a powerful Chinese force able to play its part in breaking the blockade of China were not dashed. Working closely with T. V. Soong and General Chen Cheng, he was able to persuade the Chinese to set up training centers and begin the organizing of a second Chinese Expeditionary Force (or Y-Force as it was commonly known). Logistic preparations in India moved slowly, hampered by terrain, weather, and the paucity of available resources. The ultimate goal of this activity was the reopening of the line of communications from Rangoon to Kunming.

Meanwhile, the President in Washington was inclining ever more strongly to General Chennault's views. In March, he overruled his military advisers, telling General Marshall that their views on the diplomacy and strategy of coalition war in Asia were in error, that nothing should be asked of the Generalissimo in return for American support, and that Chennault should have "his chance to do what he believes he can do." The impact of this on activities in CBI was not felt immediately, for the President's decision did not affect Hump priorities.

PART THREE

U.S. AIR POWER GIVEN THE STELLAR ROLE IN CHINA THEATER

CHAPTER IX

Air Power Rather Than Army Reform

In the months May 1942–April 1943, in compliance with War Department and JCS directives, Stilwell busied himself with plans and preparations for breaking the blockade of China and reforming the Chinese Army. While requiring a great deal of effort and preparation by Chinese, British, and Americans, these two projects had one thing in common—their results would not be apparent until 1944 if an offensive was actually begun in late 1943. True, the long-term consequences of establishing a powerful Chinese Army under the Generalissimo were incalculable, but Chennault was claiming significant achievements in the present. For example, China Air Task Force with only the most meager logistical support claimed that in 1942 it had sunk 49,600 tons of Japanese shipping and probably had sunk 11,200 tons more.[1] With Stilwell's efforts showing nothing to match Chennault's claims, with his most trusted adviser pleading Chennault's case, there is little wonder that Roosevelt, in a letter to Marshall on 8 March 1943, indicated his willingness to see how much Chennault could accomplish with top priority on Hump tonnage.

In the early months of 1943 Chennault had to base his promises on what he had done in 1942, for the failure of the Hump to deliver quantities of supplies, plus Stilwell's attempt to stockpile munitions to supplement the equipment of the Y-Force divisions, meant that little reached Chennault, and his operations suffered accordingly. His aircraft were badly in need of maintenance and no replacements came forward. His supplies of gasoline, ammunition, and spare parts were low. Bad weather was a factor. The Chinese Government also contributed to Chennault's problems. In the eight months ending February 1943, 9 percent of all tonnage over the Hump, or 837 tons, was Chinese paper currency, engraved in the United States under lend-lease and flown to China.

---

[1] Probably the air task force sank only 7,000 tons of shipping in 1942, but this could not have been known at the time. U.S. Strategic Bombing Survey, *Air Operations in China–Burma–India, World War II* (Washington, 1947), page 70, gives China Air Task Force and Fourteenth Air Force claims in full and makes no attempt to correct them against Japanese sources. Two other surveys of USSBS–Joint Army-Navy Assessment Committee Report, *Japanese Naval and Merchant Shipping Losses During World War II by All Causes* (Washington, 1947), and *The War Against Japanese Transportation, 1941–1945* (Washington, 1947)—use Japanese sources.

Chennault, chafing at these restrictions, drew back from the east China bases to Yunnan, where he assumed a reluctant defensive.[2]

The Air War Begins Over Burma

Much better supplied, the Tenth Air Force was correspondingly more aggressive. Its mission was threefold: to defend the Hump; to attack Japanese communications and supply installations; to support any attempt to retake Burma. Twice in the fall of 1942 the Japanese *5th Air Division* had revealed itself a dangerous and wily foe. It had attacked the overcrowded Dinjan airfield on 25, 26, and 28 October, destroying 2 U.S. fighters in the air, and 4 fighters and 8 transports on the ground.[3]

In December the Japanese bombed Calcutta, center of the industrial complex which largely sustained the Indian war effort. The attack was alarmingly successful, for 350,000 people fled the city. Had the Japanese persisted in strategic bombing of the Calcutta area they might have achieved major results. At Jamshedpur, 186 miles from Calcutta, were the great Tata steel mills, producing 800,000 tons a year. One hundred and thirty miles from Calcutta, and one hundred miles from the Tata plants, was the Steel Corporation of Bengal, with a 238,000-ton capacity. Crippling Calcutta's dock facilities would have affected the whole Allied war effort in Asia, for supplies went from them to the Assam supply and air bases.[4]

Fortunately for the Allies, *5th Air Division's* appreciation of strategic air bombing was not shared by *Burma Area Army,* which insisted that the *5th Air Division* make tactical air support its primary mission. Moreover, when American successes in the Solomons in November 1942 alarmed the Japanese, they diverted air strength from *5th Air Division.* Indeed, Burma tended to be a low-priority area for both Japanese and Americans. Handicapped by the policies imposed by higher authority, *5th Air Division* had to be content with a series of nuisance raids on Calcutta in January 1943, which RAF Beaufighters made increasingly unprofitable.[5]

[2] (1) Craven and Cate, eds., *The Army Air Forces in World War II: IV, The Pacific: Guadalcanal to Saipan, August 1942 to July 1944,* pp. 518–19, devoted only two pages to these four months. (2) Lauchlin Currie told the President that in the eight months ending February 1943, 9 percent of Hump tonnage, or 837 tons, was simply paper money flown to China for the Chinese. The President sent Currie's note to Hopkins for information, and Hopkins in turn sent it to Soong. Soong replied that Currie was correctly informed, that approximately 840 tons of money had been flown into China, but that the situation called for concern rather than criticism. The Chinese, said Soong, were financing the war by issuing paper money, so that prices were 6,000 times higher than prewar. "If the Burma campaign is not pushed home this year," wrote Soong, "I am alarmed at the consequences." Ltr with Incl, Soong to Hopkins, 12 Apr 43. Bk VII, Hopkins Papers.
[3] (1) History of the India–China Ferry under the Tenth Air Force. USAF Hist Div. (2) SOS in CBI, p. 18. (3) CM–IN 2686, Naiden to Marshall, 7 Jul 42.
[4] (1) Geoffrey William Tyson, *India Arms for Victory* (Allahabad, 1943), pp. 75, 106. (2) Japanese Study 94. (3) CM–IN 650, New Delhi to AGWAR, 1 Jan 43. (4) SOS in CBI, pp. 38–39.
[5] (1) Japanese Study 94. (2) SEATIC Publication 248, Air Hist Bull, 22 Apr 47, p. 38. MID Library. (3) RAF Narrative, The Campaigns in Far East, III, India Command, September 1939 to November 1943, p. 370. USAF Hist Div.

The India-based squadrons of the Tenth Air Force entered 1943 with 67 aircraft operational—38 P–40's, 9 B–25's, and 20 B–24's. By agreement with the RAF the Tenth Air Force assumed responsibility for missions more than 250 miles away from the Allied air bases, all of which were flown without fighter escort. In addition to constant patrol and reconnaissance activity to protect the Assam Hump terminals, the Tenth's fighters gave almost daily ground support to the British 4 Corps on the India–Burma border in the Manipur area, where it was engaged in patrol and outpost warfare.

Using long-range fuel tanks, the fighters also attacked rolling stock, water tanks, repair shops, and bridges from Myitkyina to south of Katha. Lt. Col. John E. Barr found by experiment that the P–40 could stagger into the air with a 1,000-pound bomb, which made of the versatile fighter a formidable new weapon. The B–24's ranged at will from Bangkok to Rangoon and far out into the Andaman Sea to look for Japanese shipping. The medium bombers concentrated on airdromes and rail communications in the Mandalay–Lashio area. For most of this period the mediums staged through the RAF base at Agartala. Headquarters, Tenth Air Force, was unwilling to occupy Agartala and other forward RAF bases because it believed that the Japanese would be able to bomb them at will.[6]

However, the inadequacy of the early-warning system was just as obvious around the American base at Dinjan. On 23 February the Japanese slipped into Assam with 7 bombers and 5 fighters. Scoring surprise, they attacked Dinjan from a high altitude but inflicted only minor damage to 1 transport. Two days later they came in force with about 45 aircraft. This time the Tenth Air Force intercepted with 30 fighters which forced the attackers to jettison their bombs. A heavy toll was taken of the Japanese; only 9 were tracked out of the area by radar. There were false alarms in the following weeks, but no more attacks.

The Japanese air reaction in Burma itself was not much more effective. Operations there cost the Tenth 4 heavy bombers, 3 mediums, and 1 photo reconnaissance craft in the first five months of 1943, a small price for bombers operating alone. In that same period the Tenth's strength almost doubled and became 61 P–40's, 45 B–24's, and 45 B–25's.[7]

In May 1943 the coming of the monsoon failed to halt Tenth Air Force operations, for bomb tonnage delivered on enemy targets in July (750 tons) was 70 percent above June, thanks to the Tenth's meteorological experts, who became skilled in predicting holes in the overcast over profitable targets. But these operations were in a sense routine strategic bombing though the hazards of flight and enemy reaction seemed far from routine to the crews.

[6](1) Obsolescent fighters, inadequate radar, and inadequate air-ground communications sadly hampered the RAF until well into 1943. The RAF Narrative cited note 5(3) has a full description of this heartbreaking early period. (2) MS, History of the Tenth Air Force Headquarters for the Calendar Year, 1942, and from 1 January to 31 May 1943. USAF Hist Div. (3) Brief History of the AAF in India and Burma, 1941–43, pp. 63–64. File 825.01, USAF Hist Div.

[7] MS cited n. 6(2).

AIRCRAFT OF TENTH AIR FORCE, 1942. *Above, medium bombers, B–25's. Note the .50 caliber machine gun mounted to protect the ship from enemy craft approaching from below and back Below, fighter plane, P–40.*

Of future importance was the fact that the British tactical airfield construction program was yielding fruit. Medium bombers were now at Kurmitola, east of Calcutta and closer to the enemy, suggesting that the safety of forward bases was by this time reasonably assured. The Second Troop Carrier Squadron, quietly bringing supplies to Allied outposts in the mountains of the Indo-Burmese border, and Numbers 31 and 194 RAF Squadrons supporting British jungle fighters, were developing techniques of air supply that were to revolutionize jungle warfare. The RAF and the Tenth Air Force had developed such efficiency that bombers could operate in the monsoon.

The effect of the RAF's and Tenth's strategic bombing on the Japanese from April 1942 to May 1943 was small. To cripple a rail system with a small force of heavy bombers is difficult, if not impossible. And few other targets of strategic importance offered themselves in Burma.[8]

Chiang Promises To Hold East China

When the President answered the Generalissimo in March 1943 [9] he had made his support of Chennault and the air arm quite apparent. On 10 April the Generalissimo asked President Roosevelt to call Chennault to Washington to present the plan that he and the Generalissimo had been discussing. Protesting that Chennault was faring no better as commander of the Fourteenth Air Force than he had as commander of the China Air Task Force, Soong urged that Chennault be recalled to Washington to present his case.[10]

The President must have decided immediately on receipt of the Generalissimo's 10 April radio to call Chennault back, for Marshall a day or so later asked Stilwell for comment on the proposed trip. Stilwell replied that he knew nothing of any new Chennault plans, nor did he know why the Generalissimo was bypassing him and dealing directly with Chennault. Stilwell suggested that the United States tell the Generalissimo that the proposal to recall Chennault fitted in well with an American project to bring Stilwell, Bissell, and Chennault to Washington to discuss ANAKIM.[11]

Simultaneously, Marshall wrote to the President:

The attached message from the Generalissimo creates an embarrassing situation. To call in Chennault and ignore Stilwell, which is the probable purpose of the Generalissimo's proposal, would create such a definite division of authority in the China Theater as to necessitate Stilwell's relief and Chennault's appointment to command of ground and air, which so far as I am concerned would be a grave mistake.

---

[8] (1) Narrative Histories of Tenth Air Force for June–July 1943. USAF Hist Div. (2) USSBS, *The Effect of Air Action on Japanese Ground Army Logistics* (Washington, 1947), p. 170. This survey is rather vague on strategic bombing for the 1942–43 period.

[9] See Ch. VIII, pp. 278–79, above.

[10] (1) CM–IN 5919, Chiang to President, 10 Apr 43. (2) Chennault, *Way of a Fighter,* p. 217. (3) Ltrs, Alsop to Hopkins, 1, 3, 5, 26 Mar 43; Ltr, Soong to Hopkins, 24 Mar 43. Bk VII, Hopkins Papers.

[11] Rad AMMRAM 3411, Stilwell to Marshall, 12 Apr 43. Item 321, Bk 1, JWS Personal File.

As a matter of fact we were in process of arranging for Stilwell to come to Washington to talk over the ANAKIM situation. [Marshall then discusses the mechanics of such a conference.]

Under the circumstances I therefore suggest that the request of the Generalissimo be met by including Stilwell and Bissell in the party for a conference here. This would parallel the military Pacific conference just completed, and the conference about to occur in London on the special subject of ANAKIM. A draft of such a message is attached.[12]

Since Stilwell's suggestion was in perfect accord with his own proposal to the President, Marshall at once put it before Roosevelt. Roosevelt was unwilling to include General Bissell but did accept the Marshall-Stilwell phrasing, and the Generalissimo was answered accordingly.[13] Stilwell at once contacted Chennault, who said that he had no new plan and was not aware of what the Generalissimo had in mind. The Generalissimo, therefore, was urging the basic plan that Chennault had laid before Willkie in October 1942—to destroy the Japanese Air Force in China, then attack their shipping and home islands. Chennault and Stilwell parted in anger.[14]

Also, bitterness accumulated between Stilwell and his Chinese superior, the Generalissimo. In 1942 Stilwell's diaries record flashes of anger, as he relieved the tensions of command, but he usually referred to the Chinese leader by name or title. And Stilwell made numerous even more disparaging references to General Wavell, while the Operations Division and the whole War Department were occasionally viewed with something less than admiration.[15] Stilwell's anger increased after the Generalissimo's 8 January refusal to cross the Salween. More and more in his diaries he chose to refer to the Chinese leader by the code name originally intended for use in radio messages, Peanut. To Stilwell, the Nationalist regime appeared a "cesspool" and the Generalissimo simply a "figurehead."[16] In speaking to the Generalissimo, Stilwell was invariably courteous, if candid, but in his headquarters his caustic wit would flash out, and reports of what he had said, with purple additions, would fly back to the Chinese leader.[17]

The exchanges between the Generalissimo and the President, renewed pressure from Chennault's friends, and the growing personal animosity between the Generalissimo and Stilwell immediately preceded a formal bid from the Generalissimo, Supreme Commander of China Theater, for a policy rearrange-

[12] Memo, Marshall for President, 12 Apr 43, sub: Generalissimo's Request For Chennault To Report to Washington. WDSCA 381 (China), A46–523.

[13] (1) Rad WAR 2498, Marshall to Stilwell, 14 Apr 43; Rad WAR 2500, Roosevelt to Stilwell for Chiang, 14 Apr 43. Items 324, 325, Bk 1, JWS Personal File. (2) *The Stilwell Papers*, p. 203.

[14] (1) *The Stilwell Papers*, p. 203. (2) Chennault, *Way of a Fighter*, pp. 217–18.

[15] As the Operations Division was an organ of the War Department, they cannot be officially differentiated. General Stilwell, however, chose to comment on them separately. *The Stilwell Papers*, pp. 120, 152.

[16] In this simple code, the Generalissimo was PEANUT; Stilwell was QUARTERBACK; Madame Chiang was SNOW WHITE. Members of the National Military Council emerged as one or another of Walt Disney's seven dwarfs. See also *The Stilwell Papers*, pp. 190–91.

[17] Interv with Merrill, 20 Apr 48, Washington; Ltr, Hearn to authors, 16 Feb 50. HIS 330.14 CBI 1948, 1950.

ment that would change the whole American effort in Asia. Soong gave the note to Hopkins for the President on 29 April 1943:

I am instructed by the Generalissimo that after careful consideration he has concluded all resources must be concentrated in the immediate future on launching an air offensive in China. Specifically, after weighing the various claims, he now desires that the entire air transport tonnage during the months of May, June, and July be devoted to carrying into China gasoline and aviation supplies, in order to build up the required reserves for decisive offensive action. It is the Generalissimo's view that since initiation of the air effort is both most urgent and presently feasible and since the ground effort has been deferred until next Autumn, military logic demands the requested alteration in schedules.[18]

Parenthetically, it must be noted that 6,900 tons of ordnance, and a total of about 18,000 tons of all supplies, were to be flown into Yunnan as initial equipment for the ground offensive of which the Generalissimo spoke and to which he had agreed. These supplies were all to have been flown in, distributed, and the troops trained in their use by the time the ground dried in late October 1943. The Generalissimo was proposing to stop the import of these arms completely until 1 August. But Chennault would still need supplies after 1 August, so the entire amount of Hump tonnage after 1 August could not in turn be allotted to the ground forces. Only a tremendous increase in Hump tonnage could make up the shortage that the Y–Force would suffer, and only ninety days would be left to receive and distribute the weapons and train the Chinese in their use.[19]

The Generalissimo's note resumed:

It will be recalled that in past conversations the decision was taken to launch a China air offensive at the earliest possible date, and that the only obstacle to prompt action was shortage of air transport tonnage for the purpose. Since the existing capacity of the air transport line is believed to be sufficient to support an air offensive, no obstacle to prompt action now appears to remain. It is hoped, therefore, that the small quantities of needed additional planes and equipment may be allocated; that the needed supplies may move forward at once, and that the offensive may start as soon as preparations for it can be completed.[20]

In this paragraph the Generalissimo thus assured the President that the logistics of the proposed air offensive were well in hand. Singling out the "only obstacle" he then stated that it no longer "appears to remain." The paragraph

[18] Incl to Ltr, Soong to Hopkins, 29 Apr 43. Bk VII, Hopkins Papers.
[19] Between 1 January and 1 October 1943, the Chinese ground forces received 5,541 tons of lend-lease, of which 1,554 were ordnance for the Y–Force, and 3,987 tons were China Defense Supplies for the Chinese arsenal program. This latter was completly under Chinese control; the Chinese used it for the general support of their armies. The tonnage given Y–Force directly reflects the Generalissimo's request that Chennault receive the lion's share. Manifestly this tonnage would not have completed the U.S. portion to Y–Force in time for the offensive that the Generalissimo was promising the President. Stilwell was completely aware of the fact that the Generalissimo's request made equipment of the Y–Force extremely difficult. (1) *The Stilwell Papers*, p. 204. (2) See p. 301, above. (3) Ltr, Lt Col Frank H. Erhart, Pres, Board of Investigation, U.S. Forces, China Theater, to CG, U.S. Forces, China Theater, 1 Nov 45, sub: Hump and Hump Tonnage; Exhibit "G," sub: Tonnage Delivered to China by Type of Cargo and Consignee, 42–45. CT 40, Dr 4, KCRC.
[20] Incl cited n. 18.

would seem to include the eastern line of communications from Kunming to Chennault's east China air bases.

The Generalissimo proceeded to discuss the relationship of the air and ground efforts in his China Theater:

> Such a concentration of present resources on the air effort need not, in the Generalissimo's opinion, interfere with the program of ground action. The question is not whether the ground effort is to be finally sacrificed to the air effort, but whether ground supplies or air supplies are to be carried into China in the months just ahead. It will be understood that after the required reserves for the air offensive have been accumulated, the percentage of air transport tonnage into China allocated to aviation supplies can be reduced to the total needed merely to maintain the air effort. The capacity of the air transport line into China is planned to expand very rapidly; and as this expansion occurs, all needed ground supplies may also be carried into China in ample time to be on hand when called for. Indeed, the Generalissimo believes that the air offensive will not only have great strategic results, in and of itself; but also, and perhaps more importantly, will serve as a direct preparation for the ground effort by weakening the enemy air strength and attacking his main line of communication to the Southward.
>
> The Generalissimo also wishes me to transmit to you his personal assurance that in the event the enemy attempts to interrupt the air offensive by a ground advance on the air bases, the advance can be halted by the existing Chinese forces.
>
> The Generalissimo requested that General Chennault return to the United States to acquaint you with the detailed plans for the proposed air offensive. As General Chennault has now arrived in the United States he can explain what a relatively small number of planes and amount of equipment is needed for this purpose.[21]

The paragraph next to the last in the Generalissimo's message suggests his attitude toward his Army, the Japanese, and Stilwell. It implies that the Generalissimo was satisfied with his Army as it was. There was no need to rearm, reorganize, or retrain it, for the "existing Chinese forces" could stop the Japanese if they tried to seize Chennault's airfields. If the Chinese were capable of stopping up to eleven Japanese divisions, Stilwell's mission of "improving the combat efficiency of the Chinese Army" was unnecessary.

Chennault and Stilwell Present Their Cases

Between 30 April and 2 May the President interviewed the leading personalities in the controversy over the timing of a major U.S. air effort in China. It was the eve of the TRIDENT Conference of the President, the Prime Minister, and the Combined Chiefs of Staff, convened in Washington to discuss the problems raised by the victory in North Africa and the approach of the date by which, under the Casablanca agreements, a decision would have to be reached on ANAKIM.

Chennault, as he told Stilwell, had no new plan. On the transport aircraft as it flew to Washington he occupied himself in making a new estimate of what he would need to carry out the proposals he had laid before Willkie the

---

[21] *Ibid.*

previous October. The Fourteenth's commander estimated his requirements in tonnage per month, described the strength in aircraft he desired, assigned tentative dates to the different phases of his plan, and made an intelligence estimate of the Japanese intentions in China.[22]

Chennault's 30 April appraisal of the Japanese plans differed radically from that of February. Then, he had warned that a major Japanese drive in China was imminent.[23] Actually, *China Expeditionary Forces* was contemplating only the minor Tung-ting Lake affair.[24] Now, in April, Chennault reversed himself and stated, "Japan does not desire to fight in China, particularly in the air. . . . Since Japan does not desire to fight in the air over China, every effort should be exerted to make her fight there." [25]

The Chennault plan in its April 1943 version was closely geared to seasons when good flying weather might be expected in east China. Beginning in July 1943 his fighters would start a two months' attack to wrest air superiority from Japan's *3d Air Division*. Late in August, the B-25's would move to a new field at Kweilin to begin an antishipping campaign along the Yangtze, over Haiphong harbor, off Hainan Island, and over coastal ports. During September the B-25's would widen their sweeps by covering the Formosa Strait and the South China Sea. Strategic bombing of Japanese lines of communications, especially the Indochina railways pointing toward Kunming, would follow.

Then, the B-24's would move to east China to pound Formosa and the Shanghai–Nanking–Hankow triangle. By the end of the year, Phase III, the bombing of Japan, would get under way. Aircraft requirements for the Chennault plan were now 75 P-40's, 75 P-51's, 48 B-25's, 35 B-24's, and some photo reconnaissance craft. For supply he requested 4,790 tons each month from July through September and 7,129 tons monthly thereafter.[26]

Chennault acknowledged the possibility of a powerful Japanese offensive to occupy central China but did not think it would be more successful than similar efforts in the past. If it was made, he thought, it would have to be in such force as seriously to reduce Japanese strength in other theaters outside China. The paper in which he presented his plan said nothing about the line of communications to his forward air bases, nor did it mention supplying lend-lease arms to the Chinese divisions in east China. Chennault's supply requirements would in any event absorb almost all Hump tonnage and, moreover, he may have shared the Generalissimo's belief that the "existing Chinese forces" could defend the east China airfields.[27]

In conversations with Stimson and Marshall, and in a later letter to

[22] (1) Chennault, *Way of a Fighter,* pp. 217–22. (2) Certified true copy of Chennault's Plan of Operations in China, 30 Apr 43, Ltr, Chennault to Wedemeyer, 6 Jul 45. Item 2, Incl II of WDCSA 091 China, 15 Aug 45.

[23] See Ch. VIII, pp. 283–84, above.

[24] Japanese Study 77.

[25] Chennault Plan cited n. 22(2).

[26] *Ibid.*

[27] (1) *Ibid.* (2) Quotation from Incl to Ltr, cited n. 18.

Marshall, Chennault filled in the bare bones of his plan and offered his views on the war in China. He believed that the Japanese would fight to the end to hold the Chinese coastal cities and Formosa, but that they would withdraw from the Yangtze valley after the Fourteenth Air Force had destroyed much of the river shipping on which they depended for their supply in that area. He believed that he could hope to sink 500,000 tons of Japanese shipping in six months, after which the Japanese would begin to withdraw from their outlying holdings. Chennault told Stimson that he needed only 4,700 tons a month over the Hump and Stilwell 1,800 tons more, with which to equip Chinese divisions. He indicated great skepticism as to the worth of the new Ledo Road. Stimson's recollection of what Chennault thought he could do to stop a Japanese advance on Kunming from Indochina was: "He asserted that they had never yet been able to advance more than 100 miles against land obstacles. All of their big advances have been made with the support of rivers and railroads." [28]

To Chennault's presentation of his case to Marshall, Stilwell replied:

What Chennault says about available targets is quite true. The Japs could be done considerable injury. Just one point about the whole thing and that is, as we found out last spring [Chekiang Expedition], any attempt to bomb Japan is going to bring a prompt and violent reaction on the ground and somebody has to decide how far we can sting them before that reaction appears. The Japanese army could make available for a major campaign in China one or a half million men. If we start an air campaign, they may decide they are being hurt to the extent it would be advantageous for them to take Chungking and Kunming. If that is done, we will have to fold up out there.

We have to have China to get at Japan. If we are going to bomb Japan, we will have to have the China bases. I see no way except by development of a ground force. The solution is to build up the Chinese army to the point where they can do the job. That will take considerable time. It won't be a matter of 30 or 60 divisions. I figure there should be 120. At that time the Chinese army, if supplied with proper weapons, can move into central China and maybe take a port and then seize these bases and hold them against a very serious Japanese reaction. If we go and sting them into retaliation before ready, the whole thing will fold up. It is, I admit, tempting to take advantage of these targets and hurt them if we can. I think that will have to be decided in the higher echelon here.

We are not prepared to seize the bases we need to bomb Japan. How long are we going to wait before we attempt to do it? It depends upon what we can build up in China. The Chinese might be able to hold the area outlined by General Chennault with what they have plus air support against what there is there now. In the face of an augmented Japanese force from Hankow or Canton I doubt if they could.[29]

Then Stilwell and Chennault had their interviews with the President. On one major point, Chennault recalled: "I replied [to the President] that if we received 10,000 tons of supplies monthly my planes would sink and severely

[28](1) Quotation from "Notes By SW After Conf At Woodley With Chennault, May 2, 1943." Stimson Papers. (2) Conf, CofS, Stilwell, and Chennault, 10:30 A.M., 30 Apr 43. Item 27, Msg Bk 9, OPD Exec 8. (3) Chennault's letter to Marshall is an inclosure to a letter, Stilwell to Marshall, 17 May 1943. WDCSA (China), A45–466. Stilwell saw nothing new in Chennault's letter and remarked: "Air coverage over nothing is in my opinion of little value."
[29] Conf cited n. 28(2).

damage more than a million tons of shipping. He banged his fist on the desk and chortled, 'If you can sink a million tons, we'll break their backs.' " [30]

The President then approved two objectives for the Fourteenth Air Force. They were, "first, to draw into China and there destroy a crippling proportion of the enemy's total air strength, and second, to sink a minimum of 500,000 tons of the enemy's shipping during this summer and autumn by attacking his main sea lane along the South China coasts." [31] The President also asked Chennault to write to him directly outside of military channels. This Chennault did, corresponding with the President whenever it was convenient for someone to carry a letter back to the United States. Chennault could thus address the Commander in Chief on military matters without Stilwell's or Marshall's knowledge or consent, a singular position for a subordinate commander. A copy of each letter went regularly to Hopkins. [32]

Stilwell's presentation of his case, which Marshall had arranged, was not effective. As at his first meeting with Stimson in 1942 Stilwell said little in his own behalf and slipped into the reserve that came so naturally to him in meet- a stranger, even though in this case it was the President and Commander in Chief on whose support so much depended. He did present orally the gist of a message from the Generalissimo to the President. The Generalissimo and the Chinese people, the message ran, could not understand why so few U.S. aircraft went to China. The Chinese were discouraged and disheartened. The prompt arrival of three fighter groups would immediately restore the situation. The Generalissimo feared that the Japanese Navy might sail right up the river to Chungking. The three groups of fighters would not only stop the Japanese but would enable the Chinese to assume the offensive. If they did not come to China, the Army might desert to the Japanese. [33]

Stilwell prepared a memorandum to the President, but the existence of the signed original in his papers suggests that he presented the gist of it orally.

1. My mission is to increase the combat effectiveness of the Chinese Army. We are attempting it progressively through (1) The Ramgarh training scheme (three divisions and corps troops) (2) The first 30-division plan (troops now in Yunnan, with training started at Kunming) and (3) The second 30-division plan (approved by CKS but not yet under way).

2. I consider it of prime importance to continue the program without interruption. Unless a strong ground force is developed, we shall be unable to seize and hold bases from

[30] Chennault, *Way of a Fighter,* pp. 225–26. General Chennault describes his recollections of the interviews at length in this volume.

[31] Ltr, Chennault to President, 5 Sep 43, restates these two points. Bk VII, Hopkins Papers.

[32] (1) Chennault, *Way of a Fighter,* p. 226. (2) Ltrs, Alsop to Hopkins, 29 May, 2 Jul 43; Ltrs, Chennault to President and Hopkins, 5 Sep 43, 26 Jan 44. Bk VII, Hopkins Papers. Frequently the same returning officer of the Fourteenth Air Force would carry both Alsop's and Chennault's letters to the President and Hopkins. Alsop's letter of 1 September to Hopkins and Chennault's letter of 5 September to the President were carried by the same officer.

[33] (1) Msg, Stilwell's hand, Generalissimo to President. SNF–61. (2) Interv with Marshall, 13 Jul 49. HIS 330.14 CBI 1949.

which Japan can be attacked from the air. A continuing flow of supplies to the Y–force is necessary to ensure that it will be ready for the ANAKIM operation. If this flow, which is on an extremely modest scale, is interrupted for three months, Chinese participation in ANAKIM will be impossible before January, 1944.

3. The Chinese show an increasing tendency to neglect their obligation of furnishing the man-power which we are to equip and train, and to emphasize the desirability of confining activity in China to the air area. If the latter course is followed, the effort will be entirely American and our arrival at our goal in China—the possession of bombing bases—will be indefinitely deferred. We will cause some damage, but it will not be vital to the war effort.

4. The only short-cut to Japan is through China. The Chinese know this and are disposed to extract from the situation every advantage possible. Unless we are prepared to accept indefinite delay, they must be held to their commitments as fully as we are holding ourselves to ours.

5. I strongly recommend: (a) That CKS be reminded of the reason for our presence in China and his agreement to furnish man-power and accept our assistance in training. (b) That he be urged to fully support the present training plan and arrangements for the second 30-division plan. (c) That both the British and the Chinese be held to their commitments for the retaking of Burma, as the necessary first step. (d) That the present allotment of [Hump] tonnage—3/8 for aviation, 5/8 for all other needs—remain unchanged, and that the air effort be limited to these facilities until after ANAKIM, when it can be materially increased without the great risk involved at present. (e) That a statement be made to CKS explaining to him that the military channels must be maintained and that no independence of any portion of our military establishment [*i.e.,* the Fourteenth Air Force] will be countenanced. (f) That a corps of U.S. troops be made available as soon as possible for future operations. (g) That a general strategic plan be prepared and tied in with operations in the SWP [Southwest Pacific Area].[34]

Eighteen months later, Stilwell recalled warning the President that the Japanese would react to Chennault's offensive and gave the President's reply as: "In a *political fight* [Stilwell's italics] it's not good tactics to refrain from doing something because of something your opponent may do in return." [35]

The President's Decision

The issue, increasing the combat effectiveness of the Chinese Army or approving Chennault's program, was now squarely before the President. In making his decision, he could not be guided by the Joint Chiefs of Staff, because they did not agree among themselves. Of the four members, Admiral Leahy inclined toward Chennault, Admiral King, General Marshall, and General Arnold toward Stilwell.[36] Consistent with his earlier inclinations, the President made his decision, and Marshall gave it to Stilwell on 3 May:

[34] Memo, Stilwell for President, 1 May 43. SNF–61.

[35] Stilwell's Data Notebook is of the ring-bound type in which Stilwell kept his diary of the Cairo Conference of December 1943 and the recall crisis of October 1944. The complete entry is: "Now it will come out that everything went to air. And the U.S. is to blame. FDR in May 1943 decided it. My warning was turned down. 'In a *political fight. . . .*'" Stilwell Documents, Hoover Library.

[36] William D. Leahy, *I Was There: The Personal Story of the Chief of Staff to Presidents Roosevelt and Truman Based on His Notes and Diaries Made at the Time* (New York, 1950), p. 158.

I talked to the President yesterday regarding China matters and found him completely set against any delay in Chennault's program. He had drawn the conclusion from his interview with you that the air activities were in effect largely to be suspended while the more tedious ground build-up was being carried on. . . .

The President accepted the proposition that necessary supplies for the Yunnan Force should be sent in, that he would handle Chiang Kai-shek on that, but stated that politically he must support Chiang Kai-shek and that in the state of Chinese morale the air program was therefore of great importance.

Your oral message and Chennault's oral message from the Generalissimo to the President, and the written message from Dr. Soong to the President, all have made their impression. The important thing is to keep out in the clear the fact, as we see it, that all communication with China will be terminated if Chinese troops in Yunnan are not adequately prepared to resist the Japanese.

As to ANAKIM the President was for this on a modified basis, that is, in the north, but not to the south, at Rangoon. Also I think he felt that nothing for ANAKIM should delay Chennault's air operations.[37]

Stilwell's reaction to the trend of the President's thinking, as sketched in a memorandum for Marshall, was:

1. Total misapprehension on the part of the Commander in Chief of the character, intentions, authority, and ability of Chiang Kai-shek.

2. British and Chinese complacency, delay, and obstruction. Each, for their own reasons, content to drift. Both attempting to shift all the burden to our shoulders.

3. CKS' desire to make it almost entirely an air war will delay the formation of an efficient ground force without which the war *cannot* be carried to Japan.

4. Any increase in air activity *may* draw the Jap reaction which will not only close to us all possible future bases, but also the ones we are using now.

5. If strategic decisions are left to CKS, the most fantastic decisions are to be expected.

6. CKS may attempt to exercise full control over all U.S. troops.

7. CKS may attempt to get rid of a U.S. representative who says "no" and put in one who will say nothing but "yes." At the least, he will probably try to have the air arm in China entirely divorced from any control but his own.

8. The Chinese will use the situation to milk the U.S. for CDS [China Defense Supplies, Inc., *i.e.,* lend-lease] supplies and pile up an enormous tonnage for post-war purposes, while ignoring the needs of the present.

"Prevention Measures": 1. Insist on the military channel for all dealings with all U.S. units.

2. Back up decisions of representatives in China on all CDS matters. Close the White House back door.

3. Give the U.S. representative in China [Stilwell] a chance to bargain.

4. Make the U.S. Representative the personal representative of the President, and keep the Curries' and Willkies' at home.

5. Curtail CKS' authority over U.S. troops.

6. Form strategic plans in a committee that sits in Washington, with a Chinese representative, but with American control. Present a general strategic plan by steps with dates and commit CKS to it.

7. Put an American corps in India, but get prior commitments on its use.

8. Adjust the rate of exchange.[38]

[37] Memo, Marshall for Stilwell, 3 May 43. Item 33, Msg Bk 9, OPD Exec 8.
[38] Draft Memorandum, Stilwell for Marshall, SNF-61, possibly never presented; it gives Stilwell's reaction: "Dangers in the Situation."

In speaking to Marshall of a modified ANAKIM, the President reflected an earlier exchange of views in April between himself, General Marshall, and Admirals Leahy and King. The President had wondered if reducing ANAKIM might not permit accelerating preparations for European operations. The President's service chiefs agreed that canceling ANAKIM would materially increase U.S. strength in Europe, but at heavy cost in Asia. They warned that abandoning ANAKIM might cause a reverse that would force a heavy diversion of resources to the Pacific from Europe, and that a vigorous Japanese reaction to Chennault's air offensive might have disastrous effects in China. They did, however, concede that modification of ANAKIM might be essential. This might be the occupation of north Burma only, down to the Mandalay line, which Maj. Gen. Thomas T. Handy of the Operations Division estimated would permit the Ledo Road plus ATC to deliver 20,000 tons a month to China. Thus, and once again almost casually, the Ledo Road, whose construction Stilwell had undertaken as a consequence of Wavell's assigning him to the Hukawng Valley, increased in importance as a possible substitute for the line of communications north from Rangoon that Stilwell had originally proposed.[39]

The President's decision to give formal approval to the Chennault plan was not communicated to the Chinese at once. In answering the Generalissimo's 29 April note, the President on 4 May said that Chennault could not have all Hump tonnage and added that the matter as a whole was under study.[40] Madame Chiang promptly called Assistant Secretary of War McCloy to the White House and insisted on full compliance with the Generalissimo's 29 April memorandum, pointing out that, after all, he commanded China Theater. Soong added his plea in a handwritten letter to the President on 12 May.[41] That the President meant business became apparent on 9 May when he directed that Wheeler take personal charge of the U.S. part of the Assam airfield project, called the situation "extremely serious," and directed Wheeler to rush construction.[42] But no hint of the decision was given to any Chinese until after Soong appeared before the Combined Chiefs of Staff on 17 May and said that China would make a separate peace with Japan unless wholehearted operations to undertake its relief and discharge the post-Casablanca "commitments" began. The Generalissimo, said Soong, commanded China Theater. So long as he was responsible, his view should prevail.[43] The next morning, a week before the

---

[39] Memo, Marshall for President, 3 Apr 43; Memo, Handy for Marshall, 31 Mar 43, sub: ANAKIM vs. BOLERO. ABC 384 Burma (8-25-42), Sec II, A48-224.

[40] Msg, Roosevelt to Chiang, 4 May 43. Item 58, OPD Exec. 10.

[41] (1) Memo of Interv, McCloy and Mme. Chiang, 4 May 43, OASW. ABC 336 (China), 26 Jan 42, Sec 1A, A48-224. (2) Ltr, Alsop to Hopkins, 7 May 43; Ltr, Soong to President, 12 May 43. Bk VII, Hopkins Papers.

[42] CM-OUT 4042, Marshall to Wheeler, 9 May 43.

[43] (1) Summary, CCS 86th Mtg, 17 May 43. (2) Summary, White House and CCS Mtgs. ABC 337 TRIDENT (26 Apr 43), A48-224. (3) Pertinent Notes Sent to the CofS on CCS 86th Mtg. ABC 337 TRIDENT (May 43) Sec B, A48-224.

end of TRIDENT, Soong was called to the White House. Reporting his conversation to the Generalissimo, Soong said:

I saw the President today, who told me he fully understands and is concerned over the military and economic crisis confronting you and is anxious that the air force be immediately strengthened to support you. He has accordingly made the following decisions:

(1) Starting July 1, 1943, the first 4,700 tons of supplies per month flown into China over the India–China route shall be for General Chennault's air force; after this priority is fully satisfied, the next 2,000 tons per month shall be for all other purposes including ground forces; thereafter the next 300 tons per month shall also be for the air force.

(2) President has ordered that starting September 1, the original goal of 10,000 tons per month shall be reached and even stepped up.

(3) I asked the President for all the tonnage for the remainder of May and June 1943 on both Air Transport Command and CNAC planes for air force supplies for the 14th Air Force. The President replied that certain small exceptions might be needed for ground forces and asked me to work out this problem with the Deputy Chief of Staff of the United States Army [McNarney].[44]

Soong and McNarney worked out an arrangement covering Hump tonnage until 31 October 1943. In dividing the 2,000 tons a month mentioned in Soong's paragraph (1) above, 500 tons a month were allotted to the ground forces, and 1,500 tons for all other Chinese and American activities supported by ATC, such for example as the Chinese arsenal program for manufacture of small arms ammunition.[45] There was no suggestion in this correspondence or in that which immediately ensued between the War Department and the White House that this was a decision by the Combined Chiefs of Staff or by the President and the Prime Minister; all spoke simply of "the President's decision."

TRIDENT Decision To Take North Burma

Because the ARCADIA and Casablanca Conferences had given the Americans an appreciation of effective presentation at a full-dress international conclave, the Joint Chiefs on the eve of TRIDENT (8 May) presented a formal statement to the President in order that he might enter the conference fully acquainted with their views. In regard to ANAKIM, they said it "should be undertaken and pressed to a successful conclusion." If this was impossible, and if no adequate substitute could be agreed on, then the United States would have to expand its Pacific operations to counteract the advantage the Japanese would gain through Allied failure to support China.[46]

[44] Ltr and Incls, Soong to Hopkins, 18 May 43; Memo, Marshall for Hopkins, 19 May 43. Hopkins Papers. Copies of Ltrs and Incls in OPD 381 CTO, Case 124, A47–30. To make sure there was no misunderstanding, Soong sent a draft letter to the Generalissimo with inclosures to Hopkins, who in turn asked Marshall to comment on it. Marshall's only objection was to some comments in Soong's paragraph (5) of the same letter in regard to the extent of the Anglo-American commitment to ANAKIM, which at this date had not been settled by the TRIDENT conferees.

[45] Memo, CofS for President, 18 May 43, sub: China Tonnage. WDCSA 381 (China), A46–523.

[46] (1) Ray S. Cline, *Washington Command Post: The Operations Division,* UNITED STATES ARMY IN WORLD WAR II (Washington, 1951), Ch. XI. (2) Memo, Leahy for President, 8 May 43, sub: Recommended Line of Action at Coming Conf. ABC 337 TRIDENT (26 Apr 43), A48–224.

Two days later, 10 May, the Joint Chiefs resolved to lay before the Combined Chiefs of Staff proposals for a modified ANAKIM along the lines Roosevelt had been shown to favor. This was a move toward a compromise with the views of the British Chiefs of Staff, for OPD surmised the British would not want to go ahead with a full ANAKIM in the winter of 1943–44.[47]

The much smaller version of ANAKIM was part of the JCS Strategic Plan for the Defeat of Japan, which thanks to long months of work by their planners the JCS were now ready to present. In the JCS proposals, air bases in north China played a vital part. The basic concept was of American forces from the east, and British and Chinese from the west, converging on the Canton–Hong Kong area, then forcing a way into north China. From north China a massive air bombardment of Japan would be launched. So heavy an attack on Japan's industries might well decide the war. If it did not, then Japan would be invaded.[48]

The British confirmed the JCS's estimate of their probable intentions with the paper they circulated on 12 May, the day of the conference's opening. The British Chiefs of Staff remarked that they had proposed TRIDENT because they thought it time to carry the Casablanca views one stage farther. Expressing their adherence to the principles laid down in January 1943, the British Chiefs believed application of the Casablanca decisions needed review. They wondered if the experiences of the last few months had not led the Joint Chiefs to change their views.

The British Chiefs of Staff did not believe that the full ANAKIM operation should be undertaken in the winter of 1943–44. They presented their reasons: ANAKIM would be a major commitment at a critical period of the war with Germany; its feasibility was doubtful; no long-term plans for the defeat of Japan had been agreed upon by the CCS, so there could be no accurate estimate of how ANAKIM fitted into such long-term plans. Furthermore, if ANAKIM succeeded, it would not open a road to China before the middle of 1945.

However, though it appeared impossible to execute ANAKIM in 1943, the British Chiefs believed everything possible should be done to keep pressure on the Japanese. They suggested examining more closely long-term plans for Japan's defeat, so that the commanders-in-chief in India could plan and prepare accordingly.[49]

The American participants in the 12 and 14 May conferences between the President, the Prime Minister, and their service advisers plainly revealed the growing divergences in U.S. policies in China. Reform of the Chinese Army

[47] (1) JCS 297, 10 May 43, sub: Opns in Burma, 1943–44. (2) Suppl Min, 79th JCS Mtg, 10 May 43, Item 17. (3) Memo, Wedemeyer for Marshall, 10 May 43, sub: Notes on a Shift from ANAKIM to the SW Pacific; Memo, Brig Gen Carl A. Russell for Wedemeyer and Admiral Charles M. Cooke, Jr., JPS, 5 May 43, sub: ANAKIM. ABC 384 Burma (8–25–42) Sec II, A48–224.

[48] CCS 220, 14 May 43, Strategic Plan for the Defeat of Japan. The paper was discussed at the JCS 78th and 80th Meetings, 8 and 10 May 1943.

[49] Memo, prepared by British COS, 12 May 43, sub: Conduct of the War in 1943–44, App. B, pars. 9–11. ABC 337 TRIDENT (May 43) Sec E, A48–224.

was a War Department project; the President's lack of interest was now on the record though he had not ruled against it. ANAKIM, as a means of drawing Japanese strength from the Pacific, was the JCS's and Stilwell's suggestion for strategy. The Chennault plan was the President's favorite. The President gave formal support to ANAKIM—but the burden of the Chennault plan on the line of communications in CBI, the possibility of its prematurely provoking the Japanese, and the fact that the Chinese Government viewed U.S. air power as a desirable substitute for a powerful Chinese Army would go far to make ANAKIM impossible and would impede Stilwell's reforms.

At the 12 and 14 May conferences the President made it plain that he wanted action *now* in China, which could only be by air power. He feared that China might collapse and did not think the continual Chinese calls for aid were "crying 'wolf, wolf.' " The President returned to the themes of his 8 March 1943 letter to Marshall by proclaiming his great faith in the constant attrition of Japanese shipping and aircraft, and by revealing again his concern for maintaining the position and prestige of the Generalissimo. The latter, said Roosevelt, was both Chief of State and head of the Armed Forces; in a sense both Stilwell and Chennault were under him, and so, said the President, it was psychologically difficult to tell the Generalissimo that his allies did not agree with all of his ideas.

Roosevelt approached the JCS's point of view when he disagreed with Churchill's describing the bypassing of Burma to land on Sumatra as analogous to TORCH—but then the President had earlier told Marshall that he thought the Chennault plan was like TORCH.

In earlier combined discussions of ANAKIM, the principal opposition had come from Wavell's staff, whose arguments had been mostly administrative. At TRIDENT the Prime Minister, Wavell, who was now a field marshal, his subordinates, and the British Chiefs of Staff unveiled a comprehensive body of arguments against an attack on Burma based on strategic grounds as well as on the administrative difficulties of campaigning there. Churchill was eloquent in his arguments. He had once been keen on action of the ANAKIM type, but the more he weighed Wavell's plan against the results of action in Burma to date, the less did he like it. Then Churchill brought forth the idea that dominated British strategy in Asia for the next two years.

Could not Burma be bypassed? Was it really necessary to wallow about in swampy jungles where operations could be conducted only five months a year? He suggested leaving Burma to the Japanese, and instead seizing the northern tip of Sumatra as a step toward Singapore. Churchill having introduced this theme, Wavell and his commanders-in-chief for sea and air followed with elaborations on various aspects of it. The merits of the plan were obvious. The United States was about to develop its technique of bypassing major Japanese concentrations in the Pacific; the same thoughts were stirring in London. The Japanese war effort depended on the oil brought over the line of communications that stretched from the Netherlands Indies to Japan, and here was a step toward cutting it.

The formal presentation of the British Chiefs of Staff pointed out that of the four pre-ANAKIM operations stipulated at Casablanca those in the Arakan and from Manipur State had failed. True, the Hump operation had been somewhat improved, but the British Chiefs of Staff accepted as fact that it was impossible simultaneously to build the Hump to its full potentialities and also to support ground operations into Burma. Therefore, on examining ANAKIM, the British Chiefs of Staff opposed it for the winter of 1943–44. It was a commitment they could not accept while the war against Germany was reaching its climax; they doubted its feasibility if undertaken at this time in a land so well suited to Japanese tactics; they could not assume that Burma's reconquest was essential to Japan's defeat, and they feared that even if ANAKIM succeeded, it would not reopen the Burma Road before the summer of 1945. As an alternative to ANAKIM, the British Chiefs of Staff suggested greater emphasis on U.S. air power in China. They proposed first priority for building up the Hump to support a larger Fourteenth Air Force, for they felt the Hump would bring more into China than could the Ledo Road. They favored limited land operations in Assam to contain Japanese forces, but not on a scale to compromise the Hump build-up.[50]

During the exposition of these views on 14 May, Stilwell and Churchill crossed swords over whether the good faith of the British Commonwealth and the United States was pledged to executing ANAKIM that coming winter, and Stilwell went on to predict that not for six months would the Hump materially better the 3,500 tons a month figure. These exchanges, though revealing, did not advance matters, and General Marshall closed the discussion by remarking that all were agreed that ANAKIM in its present form was impracticable.[51]

Examining the proposals of the British Chiefs of Staff to bypass Burma, the Operations Division of the War Department for General Marshall and the Joint Strategic Survey Committee for the Joint Chiefs of Staff recommended that the British proposals not be accepted. Four reasons were advanced. Operations against Sumatra offered no help to China. The British suggestions appeared to be a tactical device to draw attention from operations in Burma, even as, in the opinion of the U.S. staff, Mediterranean operations were always being proposed to take attention from the cross-Channel assault. The resources for ANAKIM were substantially at hand in India; what little more was needed would not interfere with operations against Germany. OPD did not believe the British Chiefs of Staff could argue that the Hump route would ever support both the Fourteenth Air Force and the Chinese guarding the airfields, nor did building up the Hump route answer the problems posed by the very real

[50] (1) TRIDENT Revised Min, First, Second White House Mtgs, 12, 14 May 43. (2) CCS 225, 14 May 43, sub: Opns from India, 1943–44.
[51] Min cited n. 50(1).

possibility of a Japanese ground attack against the Assam or Yunnan terminals from which the ATC operated.[52]

While these staff studies were being prepared, the President's decision to back Chennault began to shape CCS action. Without discussion, the Combined Chiefs directed the commanders-in-chief in India to give first priority to building the Assam airfields so that 7,000 tons a month could be transported to China beginning on 1 July 1943. The first of September was set as target date to increase the flow to 10,000 tons a month. Reflecting the JCS's fears of what the Chennault plan might bring in its wake, the CCS ordered Stilwell and Wavell to provide adequate defenses for the Hump airfields.[53]

General Marshall summed up the conclusions of the American military agencies at the final ANAKIM meeting on 20 May:

A great increase in the air route alone [the Hump] without offensive ground operations would produce a strong Japanese reaction. . . . (1) The retention of China as a base for the defeat of Japan is a vital necessity; (2) we must, therefore, maintain the flow of supplies into China, both by air and, as soon as possible, by a land route, and, therefore, it is essential that these routes be protected; and (3) aggressive action in Burma is extremely important to the success of our operations in the South and Southwest Pacific.[54]

The British views were restated by Gen. Sir Alan Brooke: the proper course was to expand the air route to the maximum in order to increase the strength of the air forces operating in China and provide limited maintenance of Chinese ground forces. Land operations in Burma would limit the supplies which could be transported to the airfields.[55]

In the discussions which followed, Marshall conceded the force of Wavell's arguments on the difficulties of fighting in Burma but countered that operations in New Guinea under very similar conditions had been successfully accomplished. He realized too that ground operations would limit what could be laid down at the Assam air terminals for shipment to the Fourteenth Air Force, but the Japanese had to be threatened on the ground and this meant hard fighting. By this time the principal fear of the Joint Chiefs of Staff with regard to Asia had clear expression: if the Allies adopted in China a policy of provoking the Japanese by an air offensive and did not match it by vigorous action on the ground—in China through training, reorganizing, and re-equipping, and in Burma by actual attack—the aroused Japanese would probably sweep over the bases in China from which the air attack was mounted and the bases in India from which it was supplied.[56]

[52](1) Notes, CCS 84th Mtg, 14 May 43. ABC 337 TRIDENT (26 Apr 43) Sec E, A48–224. (2) Memo, Joint Strategic Survey Committee for Wedemeyer, 12 May 43, sub: Notes on British Proposals or Statements; Memo, Wedemeyer for Marshall, 17 May 43, sub: Comments on "Conduct of the War in 1943–44" (see n. 49); Memo, Wedemeyer for Marshall, 14 May 43, sub: British Policies as Indicated by Remarks of Prime Minister. ABC TRIDENT (26 Apr 43) Sec B, A48–224.
[53] CCS 85th Mtg, 15 May 43, Item 4.
[54] Notes, CCS 90th Mtg, 20 May 43. Folder 1, Item 10, OPD Exec 5.
[55] Ibid.
[56] Ibid.

With this expression of the JCS's apprehensions on record, the exchange of views was well-nigh complete, and the Combined Chiefs of Staff could proceed to the final consideration of their recommendations to the President and the Prime Minister. As a step in the evolution of a plan for the defeat of Japan, they approved the JCS suggestion, CCS 220, Strategic Plan for the Defeat of Japan, as a basis for study and later decision, and ordered the Combined Staff Planners to prepare a plan for the defeat of Japan based on CCS 220.[57]

Then, to complete the exchange of views on the problems of Asia and the Pacific, the Combined Chiefs went into closed session and agreed on the TRIDENT recommendations on China, Burma, and India:

    a. The concentration of available resources as first priority within the Assam–Burma [*sic*] theater on the building up and increasing of the air route to China to a capacity of 10,000 tons a month by early Fall, and the development of air facilities in Assam with a view to
        (1) Intensifying air operations against the Japanese in Burma;
        (2) Maintaining increased American air forces in China;
        (3) Maintaining the flow of airborne supplies to China;
    b. Vigorous and aggressive land and air operations from Assam into Burma via Ledo and Imphal, in step with an advance by Chinese forces from Yunnan, with the object of containing as many Japanese forces as possible, covering the air route to China, and as an essential step towards the opening of the Burma Road;
    c. The capture of Akyab and Ramree Island by amphibious operations;
    d. The interruption of Japanese sea communications into Burma.[58]

The gist of the CCS recommendations on China, Burma, and India was communicated to the Generalissimo after their approval by the President and Prime Minister, with the added pledge: "No limits, except those imposed by time and circumstance, will be placed on the above operations which have for their object the relief of the siege of China." [59] Since the scope and objective of Mediterranean operations were at last fairly well defined by TRIDENT, it was now possible to estimate with fair accuracy what would be available for operations in Southeast Asia.

ANAKIM was therefore modified into a smaller operation which did not provide for taking Rangoon in 1944. This meant the line of communications north from Rangoon to China would not be opened in 1944, and theater supply planning was adjusted to what could be brought across north Burma by air, road, and pipeline.[60] Stilwell's planning for reform of the Chinese Army would not be adversely affected by this development alone if he could control Hump priorities.

What Stilwell wanted for his own plans in China was 675 tons initial equipment for each of the thirty U.S.-sponsored Chinese divisions plus 180

[57] (1) Min, CCS 90th Mtg, 20 May 43, Item 3. (2) CCS Paper cited n. 48.
[58] Min, CCS 91st Mtg, 20 May 43.
[59] Ltr, Incl A, Arnold to Hopkins, 29 Sep 43. Case 224, OPD 381 CTO.
[60] Rad AG 1055, Stilwell to Marshall, 24 July 1943, points out that since the communication facilities of Burma will not be in Allied hands in 1944 as contemplated in the CBI Theater before TRIDENT, an additional pipeline from India to China to supply the Fourteenth Air Force is needed. Item 689, Bk 2, JWS Personal File.

tons monthly maintenance.[61] He was now aiming at sixty reformed Chinese divisions, a force whose equipment needs of artillery and ammunition were well within the capacity of a road across north Burma. The balance of the tonnage brought into China could go to Chennault.

Reactions to TRIDENT

Reactions to the TRIDENT decisions were varied, but no one seemed enthusiastic about them. Stimson thought the TRIDENT decisions meant nothing effective. He noted that the monsoon was delaying construction of the Assam airfields, so that the Hump was not likely to carry 6,000 tons a month, let alone 10,000 tons by early fall. This obstacle meant nothing for Stilwell, nothing for the Chinese Army. The Generalissimo, thought Stimson, would not attack Burma unless the others did, and the Generalissimo could not rebuild his Army on the basis of the trickle of 500 tons a month that the President's decision had left for the purpose.[62]

Churchill and General Stilwell discussed the TRIDENT decisions with candor. Churchill asked Stilwell bluntly if he thought the British in India dilatory and lacking energy, and when Stilwell told him "yes" just as bluntly, the Prime Minister agreed. Then the Prime Minister asked if Stilwell was satisfied with the decisions, aside from the question of Hump tonnage allocation. Stilwell was not, emphatically so—because there was no definite objective assigned, because the advance was not all out against Burma, and because the advance was conditional on being "kept in step." Stilwell added that a really aggressive commander could operate under the plan, but there were too many loopholes for one who did not mean business. Churchill growled that he did, indeed, mean business and was resolved to put every man he could into the battle. But the Prime Minister thought that China needed help now which only the air arm could give, thus furnishing Stilwell the chance to expound his thesis that the Generalissimo meant to sit out the war while U.S. air power won it for him, at the risk of letting his Army deteriorate beyond redemption.[63]

The changes in British command which Churchill's remarks suggested were not long in forthcoming. The impression which Wavell made at TRIDENT was perhaps unfair to that distinguished soldier, for his relief was discussed on the highest levels at TRIDENT. After the war, Admiral Leahy thought the necessity for a change in India's command had been as obvious to everyone as it was to him. Stilwell had long chafed at having to work in harness with Wavell; in Washington and later in London via U.S. Ambassador John Winant, Stilwell had suggested Wavell's replacement by Gen. Sir Claude J. E. Auchinleck.[64] On

---

[61] CM–IN 4167, Dorn to Marshall, 6 Aug 43.

[62] Comments on CCS Decision. Stimson Papers.

[63] Memo, Stilwell for Stimson, 23 May 43. Item 224, Bk 3, JWS Personal File.

[64] (1) Leahy, *I was There,* p. 172. (2) Ltr, Soong to Hopkins, 7 Jun 43. Bk VII, Hopkins Papers. (3) Stilwell Black Book, 18 Jun 43. (4) Stimson and Bundy, *On Active Service,* p. 533.

18 June 1943 the news agencies carried the announcement from the Prime Minister's residence that a new command, as yet unnamed, had been created to relieve the Commander-in-Chief, India, of responsibility for the conduct of operations. It was further announced that Wavell would become Viceroy of India and Auchinleck would succeed him as commander-in-chief.

The Generalissimo's initial reactions to TRIDENT were extremely restrained. Soong was sent to the White House with a list of questions for the President. Was Great Britain committed to engage her Navy in giving effective support to joint action in the Andaman Sea? Was she determined to retake Rangoon? Was the U.S. Navy providing the same support for ANAKIM that General Arnold had indicated at Chungking? How many divisions would the United States provide? Roosevelt replied orally to Soong, but the Generalissimo's formal answer to the President and to TRIDENT was postponed until 12 July.[65]

Reports from the British were not encouraging. Col. Frank D. Merrill of Stilwell's staff told Stilwell that Maj. Gen. A. W. S. Mallaby, Deputy Chief of Staff for Operations, General Headquarters (India), had warned that he could not support his British and Indian troops across the Chindwin River in Burma. Colonel Merrill agreed that without a fundamental improvement of the Assam line of communications General Mallaby definitely could not. The problem was that the ATC and the Assam airfields took so much tonnage nothing was left for anything else.[66]

On his way in August to join the new command whose creation Churchill had announced, General Wedemeyer of OPD stopped in London and in effect repeated Merrill's warnings, this time to Marshall. Wedemeyer wrote that the British would not undertake ANAKIM because they thought an attack on Sumatra the more realistic operation. He added that the new commander, Auchinleck, believed his men could advance only a few miles into Burma.[67]

In India, the contradiction of setting the 7,000–10,000 ton targets for Hump operations and calling for operations into Burma soon became apparent. The joint planners of General Headquarters (India) pointed out that the TRIDENT decisions implied movement of 4,300 tons a day over the Assam line of communications to the airfields which fed the Hump. The Assam line of communications was then carrying 1,720 tons a day. Improvements might lift this to 3,400 tons, but the only way to secure the carrying out of the airfield program to which first priority had been given was to cut the tonnage going to the Chinese troops and the American roadbuilders based on Ledo. There the matter stood, with general agreement between Stilwell's headquarters and General Headquarters (India) that land operations would be more restricted than the TRIDENT decisions directed. Contemplating the 2,500 tons he would receive,

[65] Telg, Chiang to President and Prime Minister, 29 May 43. Case 144, OPD 381 CTO, A47–30.
[66] Ltr, Merrill to Stilwell, 29 Jun 43. SNF–47.
[67] Ltr, Wedemeyer to Marshall, 24 Aug 43. OPD 201 (Wedemeyer, A. C. (0)), A47–30.

Stilwell summed it up tersely: "They made it practically impossible for me to prepare the Y-Force, and then ordered it used in an offensive." [68]

The Generalissimo Weighs TRIDENT

Stilwell presented the TRIDENT proposals to the Generalissimo on 17 June 1943, as soon as the American general returned from the conference via London. As they conferred, it seemed to Stilwell that the Generalissimo was primarily interested in what his allies would supply him and what they would do for Burma's recapture. Chiang's personal reactions were distinctly noncommittal, and it was many weeks before he answered.[69] The Chinese leader had reason to be hesitant. The Japanese *11th Army*'s drive in western Hupeh Province to seize shipping was just falling back after successes that had thoroughly alarmed the Chungking regime. While Chennault in the United States had been saying that the Japanese did not want to fight in China, the Generalissimo in China was telling Maj. Gens. Thomas T. Handy of OPD and George E. Stratemeyer of Arnold's staff that the Japanese were driving straight for Chungking. In accord with this estimate of the situation the Generalissimo ordered General Chen to leave Yunnan and return to his VI War Area near Enshih, diverted 70,000 replacements and two armies from the Y-Force, opened all Chinese Air Force supply stocks to the Fourteenth Air Force, and demanded an immediate major air effort to halt the Japanese. The Generalissimo also raised a delicate question of command by giving direct orders to a squadron of the Fourteenth Air Force. If the Supreme Commander, China Theater, could order a U.S. air unit in this instance, could he also order air support for his operations as Generalissimo against the Chinese Communists? Stilwell's chief of staff, General Hearn, took a serious view of the Japanese drive, as did Chinese and Fourteenth Air Force circles, but Stilwell appraised it correctly as one more Japanese foray.[70]

As the last phase of the Japanese expedition up the Yangtze drew to a close (21 May–13 June), the VI and IX War Areas had committed some seventeen to twenty divisions (102,000 men) against elements of five Japanese divisions (*3d, 13th, 34th, 39th,* and *40th*), plus the *17th Independent Mixed Brigade* and 10,000 Chinese puppet troops. The Fourteenth Air Force was active in bombing and strafing the Japanese. By 3 June the Japanese, their mission accomplished, began to sail their captured shipping down the Yangtze. Abroad, the withdrawal was hailed as "Free China's greatest victory in six weary years of war,"

---

[68] (1) *The Stilwell Papers,* p. 204. (2) History of CBI, pp. 155–57.
[69] (1) Stilwell Diary, 17 Jun 43. (2) *The Stilwell Papers,* pp. 212–13.
[70] (1) CM–IN 10824, Chargé d'Affaires, Chungking, to G–2, WDGS, 17 May 43. (2) CM–IN 11528, Hearn to Stilwell, 18 May 43. (3) CM–IN 12914, Hearn to Stilwell, 20 May 43. (4) Notes of Confs with Generalissimo, 1100, 22 May 43, Bissell, recorder. Contracts with the Chinese (Jan–Jul 43), CT 23, Dr 2, KCRC. Generals Stratemeyer and Handy were on an inspection tour for General Marshall. (5) Rad 559, Stilwell to Marshall, 20 Jun 43. Item 578, Bk 2, JWS Personal File.

but the Generalissimo could have wondered if a fresh assault might not follow soon.[71]

The Generalissimo may also have wished to see how Chennault's new status would affect operations in China Theater, and what the first fruits of the Chennault plan would be. Chennault prepared a report direct to the President as soon as he arrived in China:

Immediately after returning to China, I called upon the Generalissimo in Chungking and acquainted him with the plans for conducting an air offensive in China and for supporting ground troops both in China and in Burma. He was in very good spirits as a result of the decisive defeat of the Japanese forces southwest of Ichang. From the most reliable sources available, it appears that the Japanese employed about 100,000 troops of all services in the drive west of Ichang and that their objective was very probably the mountain stronghold of Shih Pai. Identification was made of the following Japanese units—the whole of the *13th, 39th,* and *40th Divisions,* the whole of the *17th Brigade,* a part of the *3d, 6th,* and *34th Divisions,* and the whole of the *14th Brigade.* The Japanese suffered more than 30,000 casualties, killed, wounded, and captured.[72]

Their defeat was due to the unexpectedly strong resistance of the Chinese ground forces and their losses were augmented by the action of both Chinese and American air forces during the retreat. They now hold very few points south of the Yangtze river and the Chinese are continuing the campaign to drive them north of the river.

I believe that this campaign bears out my statement that the Japanese are unable to supply an offensive effort capable of penetrating more than 100 miles into the interior of China in any area where they are unable to bring up supplies and reinforcements by water. We were unable to operate against their supply lines during the early part of the campaign due to lack of aviation supplies, shortage of aircraft, and unsuitable weather.

I have made a careful survey of the situation here since my return, and I find that we still lack sufficient aircraft and operational units to conduct an offensive in China, while guarding our transport terminals in Yunnan. I have only four fighter squadrons which must operate from Lashio, Burma to Hongkong and Hankow on the eastern front and Haiphong on the Southern Front. I have but one squadron of medium bombers for operation over the same area. The tonnage of supplies delivered by transport planes do not enable the four squadrons of heavy bombers to operate freely. These squadrons are required to bring in their own supplies from Assam.

The tonnage delivered by air transport from Assam is holding up surprisingly well when the difficulties under which they operate are considered. It is this fact which enables me to continue to support the Chinese ground armies in spite of other deficiencies.

My construction program, which includes airdromes and buildings for quarters and operations, in the Forward Area [of east China] has been delayed considerably. The program was prepared about April 1st, before my departure for the United States, and was in good train before I left. Unfortunately, in my absence, the issuance of contrary orders interrupted the work and as a result accomodations [*sic*] for the forces which I propose to send to the

---

[71] (1) MA Rpt 417 (China), 25 Sep 43. MID Library. (2) Japanese Study 77. (3) Leahy, *I Was There,* p. 165, calls it a "serious defeat," for the Japanese. (4) *Time,* June 14, 1943, p. 38, June 21, 1943, p. 34; *Newsweek,* June 14, 1943, pp. 22–23.

[72] Since most of these casualties would have been suffered by the Japanese infantry involved, who are only a portion—even though the major one—of a division, Chennault in effect was claiming that approximately 50 percent of the Japanese infantry regiments engaged were casualties. Postwar Japanese reports show that between February and July 1943, 1,125 men were killed in action and 3,636 were wounded. See Japanese Study 77.

Forward Area will not be ready by the date originally planned. However, I believe the delay will not be longer than two or three weeks.

The effect of all these unexpected delays will be to postpone the opening of my all-out offensive against Jap aircraft and shipping in China. I am most anxious to begin this campaign and endure these delays with the greatest impatience.

It is my hope that I can keep you advised of conditions without asking for supporting action on your part.[73]

Actually, Chennault was better than his word. On 14 June Col. Clinton D. Vincent, formerly Chennault's A–3, established a forward echelon headquarters of the Fourteenth Air Force at Kweilin. Chennault thus moved forward without waiting for reinforcements or an increase in Hump tonnage. Having received fifty late model P–40's in May, Vincent placed one squadron each at Heng-yang, Ling-ling, and Kweilin. The 11th Bomb Squadron (M) also displaced to Kweilin. The reinforcements promised at TRIDENT failed to arrive in India from the Mediterranean area. On 1 July, Chennault directed that shipping and port installations would be primary targets.[74]

Writing to Hopkins on 2 July, Chennault abandoned his claims of a decisive Chinese victory in the Yangtze valley. Though this letter was carried back to the United States with his first letter to the President, Chennault stated that he had not altered the letter to Roosevelt because he had not wanted to add to the President's worries. He wrote: "While the morale of the Chinese people was considerably raised by the recent victories in Western Hupeh, the Japanese were not signally defeated here because they still occupy approximately the same position which they held before that advance. They must, and I believe they can, be forced to evacuate the more exposed points which they have been able to hold for so long." [75]

On 6 July, the antishipping campaign opened off the West River estuary. On 8 July, twenty-two B–24's wasted their precious fuel when they found Haiphong shielded by bad weather. Feeling more secure over Indochina now that Chennault had more fighters in east China to keep the Japanese busy there, the B–24's of the 308th Group made their next two shipping strikes without escort. On 10 and 12 July, the bombers sank two cargo ships of 1,840 and 1,423 tons at Haiphong and Hon Gay respectively. Then they returned to accumulating supplies for the next few strikes.

Meanwhile, the reinforced Japanese *3d Air Division* lashed back at the P–40 bases and temporarily forced the 23d Fighter Group to evacuate Heng-yang and Ling-ling until the damaged airfields were repaired. By mid-July the duel between the Fourteenth Air Force and the *3d Air Division* settled into a pattern. In air combat, the B–24's and B–25's sought Japanese shipping while P–40's looked for Japanese aircraft over the Yangtze valley until the temporary

[73] Ltr, Chennault to President, 18 Jun 43. Bk VII, Hopkins Papers.
[74] History of the Fourteenth Air Force, MS by Ralph G. Hoxie, Frederick Ericson, and Robert T. Finney. USAF Hist Div. (Hereafter, Fourteenth AF History.)
[75] Ltr, Chennault to Hopkins, 2 Jul 43. Bk VII, Hopkins Papers.

CHART 8—COMPARISON OF FOURTEENTH AIR FORCE CLAIMS AND OFFICIAL
ASSESSMENT OF JAPANESE SHIPPING SUNK BY FOURTEENTH AIR FORCE:
AUGUST 1942–DECEMBER 1943 (CUMULATIVE)

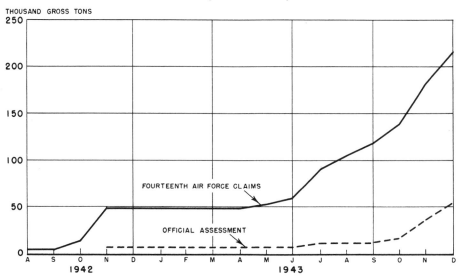

Source: USSBS, Fourteenth Air Force claims, *Air Operations in China, Burma, India, World War
II,* March 1947; Official assessment, Joint Army-Navy Assessment Committee, *Japanese Naval and
Merchant Shipping Losses During World War II By All Causes,* February 1947.

exhaustion of supplies forced a slowdown in operations. Then, *3d Air Division*
would try to bomb the Fourteenth out of its forward airfields.[76] For the shipping campaign, though Fourteenth Air Force claimed 41,389 tons sunk in May,
June, and July, actual sinkings were the 3,300 tons by the B–24's. Fourteenth
Air Force accepted aircrew claims; its shipping claims for the balance of the war
are simply tabulations of what the aircrews said they sank.[77] (*Chart 8.*)

Slowly, the aerial struggle favored the Japanese, despite their heavier numerical losses. The sheer weight of numbers brought the Fourteenth Air Force
down to the dangerously low level of 64 P–40's as July ended. With 33 fighters
in east China and 31 in Yunnan, the Fourteenth Air Force was barely able to
defend the Hump. Chennault's urgent demands for more supplies and more
aircraft reached Stilwell, who told Marshall that no harm would be done in
stopping operations from the forward area fields, for that would simply restore
the situation existing before Roosevelt approved the Chennault plan. (Stopping these operations would, in effect, concede failure of the Chennault plan
one month after the Fourteenth Air Force opened its offensive.) All aircraft

[76](1) Japanese Study 82. (2) Fourteenth AF History.
[77] An examination of daily operational reports, Fourteenth Air Force Files, U.S. Air Force
Historical Division, revealed that the totals claimed by the Fourteenth Air Force were arrived at by
a monthly addition of pilot claims with no discounts for possible duplication or errors.

FLYING TIGERS *of the China-based U.S. Army Fourteenth Air Force run toward their fighter planes, P–40's, after hearing an air raid signal.*

belonging to the Fourteenth Air Force were being sent on into China. If the air offensive was to continue, Stilwell warned Marshall, then Chennault would need heavy reinforcements. In his diary, Stilwell wrote that the Fourteenth had tried and failed, six short months after Chennault had made his promises to drive the Japanese out of China.[78]

Thus, within a few weeks after Chennault opened his offensive in compliance with the President's directive, the Fourteenth Air Force was asking for help. The Fourteenth's setback did not cause abandonment of the Chennault plan, but a second attempt at vindicating Chennault's beliefs would have to wait until the CBI Theater's logistical structure improved to a point where enough tonnage could be flown to China to support a much larger air force.

While the Japanese were counting their gains from the western Hupeh affair and the Fourteenth was making its efforts to cope with heavy odds, Stilwell waited for the Generalissimo's answer to the TRIDENT proposals. It was

[78](1) Fourteenth AF History. (2) CM–IN 18320, Chennault to Arnold, 25 Jul 43. (3) CM–IN 20997, Hearn to Marshall, 29 Jul 43. (4) CM–IN 357, Stilwell to Marshall, 31 Jul 43. (5) Stilwell Diary, 28, 31 Jul 43.

evident that the Japanese *11th Army* drive had thoroughly alarmed the Chinese. Gen. Yu Ta-wei reported his small stocks of ammunition further depleted. General Ho asked Stilwell to send the Y–Force antitank weapons to the central China front. Reports of famine in Honan Province and of a non-Communist peasant uprising there against the Chungking regime began to seep through the Chinese censorship.[79] How all this appeared to the Generalissimo is not known, but he deliberated at length and examined Stilwell on every detail of the Allied contribution to the Burma campaign, while the impatient Stilwell, increasingly bitter over the Chinese leader's methods, fumed and wrote scathing comments in his diary.

Finally, on 12 July the Generalissimo gave his consent to the TRIDENT proposals:

To your [Stilwell's] letter about the Burma operation, which I received on June 19, my reply is as follows. (1) I agree that the air facilities in the Assam area should be developed. At the same time I believe the air strength should be increased so that with complete air superiority the land and naval forces will be more sure to win. According to my judgment, the enemy will be able to put 500 planes into Burma, and increase this number, if necessary, to 800 or even 1,000. I hope at the same time that the shipment of materials into China by the air ferry will not be affected by this operation, and also that the plan of increasing the tonnage will go on as before. (2) With the plan for the use of land and air forces after the rains in attacks from Ledo, Imphal, and Paoshan simultaneously, in order to contain as much enemy force as possible, I am in complete agreement. There is no difference here from former plans. On the India side, I hope the U.S. will send strong ground units to join the effort, for in this way we will be more sure of victory. I trust you will forward this idea to the President. In conclusion, the matter of co-operation between Americans, British, and Chinese in timing the operation and the use of the air force in support of Chinese ground troops, should be discussed between the Americans, British and Chinese, in order to get concrete plans for the operation. (3) I agree with the estimate of three battleships and eight carriers as the basis of the naval force for the control of the Bay of Bengal, and also with the plans for the use of land and naval forces to get control of the Burma coast.[80]

"Red Letter Day," wrote Stilwell.

Now I can begin to prod a bit, and I have already started on Ho Ying-chin (July 13). Told him we'd have to push on preparations or the Chinese would lose face. British would ask embarrassing questions in conference. He insisted he was really pushing. Now I can put it on the ground that I must carry out the Gmo's orders. . . . It's a grand feeling. I am putting it all in writing and handing it to Ho as I leave [for tour of India]. Now let *him* sweat.[81]

Though Stilwell was highly pleased at the Generalissimo's agreement to take part in the Burma operations, which now bore the code name SAUCY, he did not take the Generalissimo's promises at face value. Further, and most signifi-

---

[79] (1) CM–IN 16520, Stilwell to Marshall, 23 Jul 43. (2) CM–IN 17760, Stilwell to Marshall, 17 Jun 43.

[80] Rad AMMISCA 647, Stilwell to Marshall, 13 Jul 43. Item 648, Bk 2, JWS Personal File. The original letter from the Generalissimo has not been found, nor has Stilwell's letter of 19 June survived.

[81] Stilwell Black Book, 13 Jul 43. Stilwell dated this entry 12 July; the Stilwell Diary records the meeting with General Ho on 13 July. It seems safe to call the copybook date a slip of the pen.

cantly, by June 1943 he was prepared to contemplate the exercise of command over Chinese troops in China. In December 1942 when Soong had offered Stilwell "the big gravy," Stilwell's reply said nothing of command.[82] Six months later, puzzling over his problems in his faithful black copy book, Stilwell could see it as a solution.

. . . Incidentally, we have carried out our promises to him. He has *not* carried out his to us. We must get on a working basis now.

The only way to do it is to get tough. If he reneges on SAUCY, tell him: "Too bad. It didn't work out. You can now go to hell. We are stopping all supply to China and putting it where it will do some good. If you had done as agreed, and furnished man-power for weapons, we would have gone along. If you still want to be saved, it will be on the following terms:

"Leave War Ministry and General Staff as is. Make J. W. S. your field Chief of Staff and give him real authority to organize, train, and equip 60 divisions of Chinese troops, at war strength. Deal directly with him, and order the General Staff and War Ministry yourself to implement his decisions. Ostensibly, command will remain with you, and in the field ostensibly with Ch'en Ch'eng. General policy to be decided in a war council to be composed of you, an American representative, and as many non-voting fellers as you wish. Otherwise the U.S. and other interested nations have other plans for prosecuting the war in the Far East."

He can't refuse. It's his neck if we turn him loose. $500,000,000 talks here. And if we don't do it, we are getting nowhere. All we can hope for is a temporary slap at Jap aviation. We'll never get any farther.[83]

As July drew to a close, the divergent trends in U.S. policy were in the open. Reform of the Chinese Army, an augmented air effort, and recapture of Burma conflicted logistically; and though Stilwell's mission was to reform the Chinese Army, to him the Chinese appeared to see U.S. air power as a substitute for a better Chinese army. Stilwell's Commander in Chief indicated little interest in his mission, but it remained unchanged. Further complicating Stilwell's delicate position was that as Commanding General, U.S. Army Forces in CBI, and as chief of staff of the Generalissimo's China Theater he was intimately concerned with each of the three conflicting projects.

Expediting the ATC Airfield Program

A great rearrangement of resources in CBI followed after TRIDENT. The President's decision to back Chennault and to build up the ATC meant American resources had to be shifted from road building to airfield construction. Establishing a more capacious U.S. base at Calcutta was more necessary than ever. Reinforcements for Chennault had to be sent into China. The Generalissimo's approval of the TRIDENT decisions meant that somehow the training and re-equipping of the Y–Force had to be carried forward, and tactical plans for the Burma operation had to be brought up to date.

Following immediately on the President's orders of 9 May 1943 that SOS

---

[82] See Ch. VII, pp. 256–58, above.
[83] Stilwell Black Book, Jun 43.

enter actively upon airfield construction, and that the program be greatly expedited, the President and the Prime Minister put the weight of their great authority behind the project. After the President inquired through Marshall what the SOS might need for the task, so that Roosevelt might insure its reaching General Wheeler, Stimson placed the matter before Churchill. Given first priority, Chabua, Mohanbari, Sookerating, and Jorhat fields would, Stimson thought, be completed by July. (*Map 7*) The reason for expanding Hump facilities, Stimson went on, was to supply arms for the Y–Force. His letter made no mention of the Fourteenth Air Force.[84]

On behalf of the CCS, Marshall gave the formal directive to Wheeler on 22 May. By 1 July, Chabua, Mohanbari, Sookerating, and Jorhat were to be completed in that priority, each with a minimum of twenty hardstandings. Steel landing-mat material could be used if necessary, in order to be sure that the fields could help ATC meet the July Hump goal of 7,000 tons a month. To hit the 10,000 ton target on 1 September, Wheeler was ordered further to complete a minimum of seven fields with forty hardstandings and 6,000-foot runways each. Wheeler was to be free to ask Marshall for help in getting necessary priorities from General Headquarters (India). Weekly progress reports were to be submitted. Wheeler was told to do his best to speed the movement of supplies from Calcutta to Assam, though the actual movement remained a British responsibility.[85]

Wheeler's instructions arrived as General Headquarters (India) was taking action. Stilwell's and Chennault's reports to the War Department at TRIDENT had led to a strong message from the British Chiefs of Staff to India. General Headquarters (India) immediately sent a committee of the Deputy Commander-in-Chief for Air, India, the SOS's Chief Engineer, and a representative of Tenth Air Force to survey the Assam fields. Just as they were completing their survey, orders came from the CCS to put Wheeler in charge.[86]

Remarkable changes swiftly followed as the British and Americans combined to throw their resources into the battle for more Hump tonnage. The airfield projects were removed from the jurisdiction of local British headquarters, such as Eastern Army and 4 Corps, and placed directly under General Headquarters (India). Skilled engineers were placed in key positions. The airfields received the highest priority. The project engineers had a free hand and full powers over transport, matériel, and labor. The requisition of tea garden acreage for airfields had been made easier, and so an improved design of some of the fields with resultant economies had been possible. Trucks, crushers, and rollers were being rushed with all possible speed over the Indian transport network to the airfields and to rock sources.

[84] (1) CM–OUT 5487, Marshall to Wheeler, 13 May 43. (2) Ltr, Stimson to Churchill, 22 May 43. Folder 63, OPD Exec 10.
[85] Rad WAR 2710, Marshall to Wheeler, 22 May 43.
[86] Ltr, Col Strong to Somervell, 15 May 43. Somervell File, Vol III, CBI 42–43. Colonel Strong had just made an engineering survey of CBI Theater.

MAJ. GEN. RAYMOND A. WHEELER, *Commanding General, Services of Supply, U. S. Army Forces in China–Burma–India, 1943.*

The necessary trucks, bulldozers, carryalls, graders, shovels, and men were diverted from the Ledo Road. General Wheeler's role was to assume an active supervisory position, and to support the British with American engineering equipment and personnel. Wheeler, however, did not take complete charge of airfield construction because to do so would cause British withdrawal from the project, which would make its completion impossible.[87]

Despite the increased effort in Assam, not many weeks were needed to disclose that though the airfield facilities could be greatly improved in a short time, the 1 July targets would not be met. On 22 June Wheeler reported to Marshall that only sixty hardstandings would be complete by 1 July, as against the eighty ordered. The first reason was that the Bengal and Assam Railway of the Assam line of communications could not deliver the tonnage needed on time. The second reason was the delays inherent in organizing new procedures, in transferring personnel and equipment from distant points, and in arranging for common labor. But as of 22 June airfield construction was proceeding at a sharply accelerated rate, and matériel was being taken from the Ledo Road to speed it along. The greatest bottleneck, reported Wheeler, emphasizing his words by repetition, was the Bengal and Assam Railway.[88] If Wheeler was overly optimistic regarding the sixty hardstandings for 1 July, the great Allied effort bore fruit within the month. During July the number of hardstandings jumped from 49 to 149. Unfortunately, the Chennault plan had gone into operation thirty days before, and the hardstandings were being completed as the Fourteenth Air Force was being hard pressed in China.[89]

In accordance with the President's February 1943 promise to the Generalissimo of 10,000 tons over the Hump, ATC had received a steady influx of men and aircraft. As Marshall had observed, men and planes came in faster than they could be supported. At the end of April and the beginning of May 1943, thirty C–46's were delivered by a group of the Trans World and the Northwest Airlines' pilots led by five ATC pilots. Others came in so fast that three more transport groups and four airways detachments were activated in India. Key personnel and vital equipment were airlifted, while fillers came by ship. All transport aircraft were being furnished with two crews, and by 4 August forty-six extra crews were on the way. All C–46 spares under construction or available in the United States were being shipped to India. Examining the ATC in India, OPD concluded in early August that maximum effort was being made to increase Hump tonnage, but that the 10,000-ton goal would not be met

---

[87] Memo, Col Byroade for the record, Airdrome Construction and Cargo Availability for Indochina Freight Line; Memo, Col Timberman, Chief, Asiatic Sec, Theater Gp, OPD, for McNarney, 10 Jun 43, sub: Progress Rpt, China Air Freight Project. WDCSA 381 (China), A46–523.

[88] CM–IN 14002, Wheeler to Marshall, 22 Jun 43.

[89] "Existing Agreements With Respect To Future Opns," 10 Aug 43. ABC 381 (Europe), 5 Aug 43, A48–224. This paper contains a broad survey of the existing situation on the eve of the QUADRANT Conference at Quebec in August 1943 and presumably is part of the preconference briefing process.

until all ground facilities, including third and fourth echelon maintenance, and all air transport groups were manned and trained, probably not before December 1943.[90]

Improving Chennault's Position

In July and August some major changes in command plus the arrival of a few reinforcements improved Chennault's position. After the creation of the Fourteenth Air Force, Stilwell had asked for a theater air officer to command both the Tenth and Fourteenth Air Forces, but Chennault's position was such that this was politically impossible. To the War Department, the next best solution was to give Stilwell a senior and very experienced air officer to coordinate CBI's air problems. On 5 July, the President suggested to the Generalissimo that General Stratemeyer, Arnold's chief of staff, be sent to CBI with a small personal staff to "coordinate all air corps matters relating to administration, transportation, logistics of supply, maintenance, and training." [91]

The Generalissimo replied with major proposals of his own: that Bissell be recalled, and that Chennault become Air Chief of Staff, China Theater, on a par with and completely independent of Stilwell. Since Stilwell's views had earlier been rejected by the President, the Generalissimo's request would, if the President agreed, bring the logical result of his having earlier approved the Chennault plan, which now dominated U.S. strategy in CBI. It would give Chennault great freedom in implementing his plan and would so diminish Stilwell's authority as to make his recall inevitable.

The President was agreeable to "an independent command from Stilwell," but when he consulted Marshall, the latter objected that Chennault was not at his best handling logistics, and that he was too closely associated with the Generalissimo to represent U.S. interests.[92] Marshall's loyal support of Stilwell reflected his awareness of the ominous resemblance between the Stilwell-Chennault feud and those between government agencies in wartime Washington.[93] Marshall knew that Stilwell was under constant and heavy attack from political and newspaper sources allied to Chennault.[94] If one theater commander was to be ruined by political intrigue, the precedent thus set would have a damaging effect upon the service, and so Marshall set his face like stone against any suggestions that Stilwell be recalled.[95] The President accepted Marshall's advice and Stilwell's powers were only slightly diminished.

Having decided to follow Marshall's advice, the President approved a com-

---

[90] (1) Oliver La Farge, *The Eagle in the Egg* (Boston, 1949), p. 115. (2) Paper cited n. 89.

[91] (1) Rad AMMISCA 249, Stilwell to Marshall, 20 Mar 43; Rad WAR 2373, Marshall to Stilwell, 28 Mar 43. Items 268, 278, Bk 1, JWS Personal File. (2) Quotation from Memo 601, Stilwell for Shang Chen (from Roosevelt for Chiang), 5 Jul 43. Item 613, Bk 2, JWS Personal File.

[92] (1) Memo, Hopkins for Record, 15 Jul 43. Bk VII, Hopkins Papers. (2) Sherwood, *Roosevelt and Hopkins*, p. 739. Quotation Hopkins'.

[93] Interv with Marshall, 6 Jul 49. HIS 330.14 CBI 1949.

[94] Bk VII, Hopkins Papers.

[95] Interv cited n. 93.

promise of the Generalissimo's proposal. Chennault became Chief of Staff, Chinese Air Force, thus formally obtaining direct access to the Generalissimo. General Bissell was recalled to the United States, where he became Assistant Air Chief of Staff, A–2, Headquarters, AAF, and rose to be Assistant Chief of Staff, G–2, War Department General Staff, in January 1944. Brig. Gen. Howard C. Davidson replaced Bissell in command of the Tenth Air Force on 20 July.[96]

General Stratemeyer, with the Generalissimo's concurrence, received the delicate and responsible position of Commanding General, Army Air Forces, India–Burma Sector. He had to give tactical and strategical air support to Stilwill's projected operations in Burma and logistical support to Chennault's air operations in China. Stratemeyer's missions were: (1) To advise the theater commander on air operations in China, Burma, and India; (2) To conduct, as commander, air operations against the enemy over Burma and in defense of India and the airline to China; (3) To assure the continued and increasing flow of supplies by air to China; (4) To co-ordinate the activities of the Air Transport Command with those of other theater agencies; (5) To train Chinese and American personnel.[97]

On 7 August Stratemeyer arrived in India and gave immediate attention to providing more aircraft for Chennault. The reinforcements were not arriving on schedule, and Madame Chiang had vigorously protested the nonarrival of the promised aircraft and the shortfalls in Hump tonnage. Her letter was detailed and highly technical and closed with Chennault's needs—seventy-five P–51's, a fighter group plus two squadrons, and a B–25 group— if his plan was to be successful.[98] Several weeks before, Stilwell had agreed to add a fourth squadron each to the 51st and 80th Fighter Groups and to assign the former group to Chennault as soon as P–38's arrived from the Mediterranean. Unfortunately, the P–38's arrived in piecemeal fashion.

In mid-August Stratemeyer sent the 449th Squadron, 51st Group (P–38's) to China. Their arrival, however, added a new burden to the supply lines, for the twin-engined P–38 gulped down precious gasoline in quantities. And their presence precluded the activation of a B–25 group until the airlift had been further expanded.

In India, Stratemeyer put new impetus behind long-standing plans for integration into the Fourteenth Air Force of Chinese aircraft and pilots furnished and trained under lend-lease. Later known as the Chinese-American Composite Wing, the unit which resulted could trace its ancestry back to proposals in 1941. For each position in the wing, a Chinese and an American

---

[96] Rad AD 1487, Hearn to Stilwell, 19 Jul 43; Rad 3019, Roosevelt to Chiang, 17 Jul 43; Rad 3024, Marshall to Stilwell, 20 Jul 43; Rad 3034, Marshall to Stilwell, 20 Jul 43; Rad AD 1564, Hearn to Stilwell, 25 Jul 43; Rad 669, Chiang to Roosevelt, 25 Jul 43; Rad AM 1159, Stilwell to Hearn, 28 Jul 43. Bk 2, JWS Personal File.

[97] (1) Ltr, Marshall to Stilwell, 20 Jul 43. Msg Bk 11, OPD Exec 9. (2) History of CBI, Sec. II, Ch. VI.

[98] (1) Fourteenth AF History. (2) Ltr, Mme. Chiang to President, 30 Jul 43. Msg Bk 11, OPD Exec 9.

worked together. On 27 July the War Department had authorized Stilwell to activate the Chinese-American Composite Wing at Karachi, Here, the Fourteenth Air Force assumed responsibility for an operational training unit, and preparations went forward steadily for the expected activation of the new experiment in Sino-American co-operation.[99]

Stratemeyer's initial efforts to bolster the Fourteenth Air Force received a blow when, on 21 August, 14 B-24's of the 308th Group failed to rendezvous with their fighter cover near Heng-yang, prior to a raid on Hankow. The escort had been delayed defending Heng-yang against 33 Japanese Zero fighters. Going on unescorted, the 308th Group lost 2 planes and had 10 badly damaged. Three days later, even though escorted by the P-38's, the B-24's lost 5 more over Hankow. With a third of its strength lost or grounded, the 308th Bombardment Group avoided central China and returned to unescorted missions over Hong Kong and French Indochina.[100]

Flushed with their victories over the heavy bombers, the Japanese *3d Air Division* carried their attack to the 308th's Chinese airfields at Cheng-kung and Kunming in an effort to drive the heavy bombers out of China. Avoiding the P-38's, the Japanese struck with twenty-seven bombers and thirty fighters. The Emperor's airmen held superb flying formation during the bombing runs, but the defenders took heavy toll of the Zeros. As a result, the Japanese began moving better pilots and their latest model aircraft into China.[101] Immediately, urgent pleas for P-51's to match the new Japanese fighters came from every U.S. squadron commander in China. Air action became general over central China, and when the hectic summer ended, the Fourteenth Air Force claimed to have downed 153 Japanese aircraft at a cost of 27 of their own. But Chennault knew that he could not press home the advantage he believed he had, because he lacked the numbers.[102] Thus, the months since TRIDENT—June, July, and now August—had slipped past, and the Fourteenth Air Force still did not have the air superiority its commander had planned to have on 31 October 1943, the day his absolute priority on Hump tonnage expired.

Stilwell Shakes Up the Rear Echelon

Since early spring Stilwell had been concentrating his attention on China Theater and had devoted relatively little time to American affairs in India. Feeling the need of a survey, he sent Colonel Merrill to make a rapid inspection of U.S. activity in India. The report that Merrill submitted on 29 June led Stilwell to make a personal swing around India from 19 July to 15 September, as soon as the Generalissimo was committed to SAUCY.

[99] Fourteenth AF History.
[100] *Ibid.*
[101] Japanese Studies 78, 82.
[102] Chennault, *Way of a Fighter,* pp. 251–52.

The report was alarming in regard to the progress of the Ledo Road. Remarking that the now-revised schedules, which called for the road to reach Shingbwiyang by 15 February 1944, were bad enough, Merrill stated they were actually overly optimistic. The diversion of engineer troops from the road to build airfields and unload ships was a handicap, he went on, but he felt that poor organization of the project was the main fault. Brig. Gen. John C. Arrowsmith, commanding the Ledo base and the road, was severely criticized.

Reading further in Merrill's report, Stilwell learned that the great expansion program for the ATC had inspired the RAF and Tenth Air Force with a desire for more airfields, that unless persuaded otherwise these combat air arms would demand so ambitious a building program that Stilwell's plans would be handicapped.

The human factor in the ATC's inability to reach the tonnage targets set in Washington received searching examination. Merrill wrote that there had been a wonderful improvement in the food and living conditions at the ATC Polo Ground Mess at Chabua, that junior officers and enlisted men were delighted with theater headquarters' intervention to remedy an intolerable situation.

I made a particular effort to talk to as many ATC pilots as possible to get their reactions. . . . "It is not so much the work in flying that gets you but rather getting into a place late at night when you're tired and dirty, and get a dirty plate of greasy food thrown at you, have no decent bathing facilities and finally fight bugs all night and don't get a decent sleep."

I think a planned campaign to improve living conditions all over the Theater for ATC would boost their morale immensely. Nothing elaborate or expensive is required; just cleanliness and ordinary decencies. The ATC higher command are really not soldiers and don't understand these things. They live in comfortable bungalows and don't realize the conditions. It is not pure neglect; they just don't know.[103]

The Chinese troops protecting the Ledo base were receiving training in jungle warfare. Ramgarh had stressed the fundamentals of individual and small-unit training. In the Ledo area, said Merrill, the Chinese received instruction in jungle craft from Naga tribesmen; then company and battalion problems, stressing the infantry-artillery team in jungle combat, were conducted. Every effort was made to instill self-reliance in the Chinese troops.[104]

To confirm these findings and take necessary action, Stilwell after a brief holiday in Kashmir descended on his Indian installations. The Ledo Road project he found at a halt. The monsoon rains were pouring down, and the high priority given to expansion of ATC operations had diverted engineers to work on the Assam airfields, handle air cargo, and unload railway cars. Arrival of the 330th Engineers during April and May did not compensate for this. From the end of March to the middle of August 1943 the roadhead gained only three miles, from mile 47.3 out of Ledo to mile 50.7.

The road builders were constantly wet. Equipment skidded off the road into

[103] Ltr, Merrill to Stilwell, 29 Jun 43. SNF–47.
[104] *Ibid.*

CONSTRUCTION WORK ON THE LEDO ROAD, 1943. *U.S. Army Engineers supervise the building of a bridge by natives, above. Below, a curve on the road is cut into the hillside by bulldozers.*

ravines and ditches. Merely transporting food and gasoline along the road was a major problem. Pack animals and porters could not handle it, and on many occasions air supply had to be used. In July the rains caused such damage that all traffic halted on advance sections of the road. The men of the Ledo Road had the misery of the battlefield, plus a considerable element of danger from malaria, dysentery, and accident, but they had none of the compensations, small though they are, of occasional excitement and a sense of defeating the enemy. Existence was a grim monotony of rain, damp, heat, mud, mildew, mould, insects, isolation, boredom, and physical effort in an obscure corner of the world previously known only to Naga headhunters and an occasional wandering trader.

After inspecting the road, Stilwell was dissatisfied with its progress. Thoroughly aware of the difficulties facing the builders, he nevertheless felt that more dynamic leadership was needed. Stilwell believed that the slowness with which the road was moving forward was jeopardizing the success of SAUCY and so he asked Wheeler to propose a replacement for Arrowsmith.[105]

Visiting the ATC fields in Assam, Stilwell was critical of the ATC's administration, but the ATC's semiautonomous status left little that he could do to affect its internal affairs. Checking the Chinese troops of the 38th Division in training at Likhapani, Stilwell considered their jungle training insufficient and their marksmanship below average.[106] The staff of the Chinese Army in India was inspected, and the Chinese deputy chief of staff, who had put his relatives in such key positions as the radio room, and who had then begun ambitious intrigues for decoration and rank, was removed in the decorous fashion recommended by the sages and classics of Chinese antiquity.[107]

Apathy in Yunnan

On returning from TRIDENT, Stilwell had consolidated all American organizations working with Y-Force into a single command, YOKE–Force Operations Staff.[108] Stilwell assumed command and named Colonel Dorn chief of staff. Dorn's mission, announced 18 June, was: in training, to furnish instructors for the Yunnan training centers and for certain group armies; in supply, to obtain lend-lease from SOS and turn it over to the proper Y–Force commanders; in operations, to assist Chen Cheng and Lung Yun in their planning.[109]

By the end of June the YOKE–Force Operations Staff reported that agreements on training and supply had been reached with the Chinese. These were

---

[105] (1) Rad, Stilwell to Wheeler, 21 Aug 43. Item 581, Bk 2, JWS Personal File. (2) *The Stilwell Papers*, p. 218.

[106] (1) *The Stilwell Papers*, pp. 216–17. (2) Stilwell Black Book, Aug 43.

[107] *The Stilwell Papers*, p. 218.

[108] These organizations included Eastern Section, SOS (Colonel Kohloss), Infantry Training Center (General Arms), and Artillery Training Center (General Waters).

[109] GO 9, Hq USAF CBI, 18 Jun 43.

based on the staff's G–4 plan, which provided: (a) that Americans would advise the Chinese SOS organizations; (b) that 2 base depots (Kunming and Yun-nan-i), 3 intermediate depots, and 5 advance depots would be established for Salween operations; (c) that rations and forage, ammunition, gasoline, oil, and alcohol would be distributed to the intermediate and advance depots; (d) that replacements in animals and men would be provided; (e) that an evacuation system would be organized; (f) that the Burma Road would be improved and Chinese trucks provided. This G–4 plan was based on the foundation laid by the SOS's Eastern Section, Colonel Kohloss commanding. Working since December 1942, Colonel Kohloss and his small force had organized and stocked two general depots, and had reached agreement with local Chinese authority on plans for intermediate and advance depots.[110] On 28 June, in addition to continuing the already established training centers, the Chinese agreed to establish and receive Joint Sino-American Traveling Instructional Groups for each of the four group armies in Yunnan. The mission of the groups was to supervise training, to inspect and enforce compliance with Chen Cheng's training orders, and to recommend improvements in training methods.[111]

On 7 August, Colonel Dorn reported that he was not succeeding with his mission. General Chen was very unwilling to return to Yunnan from Enshih to command the Y–Force and refused to accept any American equipment until the forces to use it had been reorganized. As of 7 August only two Chinese armies (six divisions), had begun reorganization (in accordance with the 23 March agreement).[112] General Chen was unwilling to command Y–Force because the Chinese National Military Council had not provided the necessary troops, funds, and rations; and the Chinese Bureau of Operations had not settled on a strategic plan for the Salween operation. Surveying the whole scene in Yunnan, Dorn flatly warned Stilwell that it was very doubtful if the Chung-king authorities would honor their July pledge to cross the Salween, for they appeared to be deliberately delaying their share of the preparations.

In six fields, the Chinese were failing to fulfill their promises: (1) failure to order the armies and artillery assigned to the operations to move to Yunnan; (2) failure to provide replacements; (3) complete failure of all SOS prepara-tions; (4) failure to reorganize the armies as agreed; (5) delay in General Chen's return to Yunnan two months after the end of Yangtze operations; (6) dilatory manner in which students were sent to the Yunnan training centers.[113]

Dorn and his handful of American aides were in constant touch with their Chinese colleagues, and on social occasions the Americans received some interesting impressions:

[110] Incl to Ltr, Col Kohloss to Ward, 3 May 51. HIS 330.14 CBI 1951.
[111] Y–Force Hist Rpt 1943. AG (Y–FOS) 314.7, KCRC.
[112] Rad RA427, Ferris to Stilwell for Dorn, 7 Aug 43. Item 718, Bk 2, JWS Personal File.
[113] Ltr, Dorn to Stilwell, 9 Aug 43. SNF–16.

The serious thinking officers on the Chinese Staff are very worried about the trend of events. We have discussed them frankly, both cause and effect. They are bitter about the way Chungking has let down the whole show. They do not discuss this often but when they do they are bluntly frank. As an example; when informed that members of the visiting delegation of the Ministry of Training were interested in obtaining our assistance in the re-organization of the entire Signal Corps of the Chinese Army, one of the CEF [Chinese Expeditionary Force] staff officers immediately said: "Watch out that they don't lead you on merely for the purpose of getting hold of your equipment. Their only interest is to get it away from Yunnan to scatter in the troops to the north."[114]

Having warned Stilwell of the Yunnan situation, Dorn placed the elements of the situation very candidly and courteously in a letter to Gen. Ho Ying-chin. Dorn pleaded for a unified Chinese command in Yunnan, and for the Chinese Bureau of Operations to make a definite strategic plan so that the Chinese commander in Yunnan might begin drafting his battle order and attack his supply problem.

To honor the 23 March agreement, which has been discussed in Chapter VIII, Dorn asked that two armies be moved from Szechwan to Yunnan. He pointed out that the Generalissimo had promised Stilwell that the Chinese 8th Army would reach Kunming before 15 September, and the 53d Army by 10 October. The latter date, said Dorn, was much too late to train and rehabilitate these forces in time for a fall offensive (to which the Generalissimo had twice consented).[115]

General Ho answered with equal courtesy and illuminating candor. As regarded a commander, nothing was known; as for plans, he extended reassurances. Then he proceeded to one of the major problems of war in China, the degree of control by the Kuomintang regime over the provincial war lords. The Chief of Staff of the Chinese Army stated that it was not possible to move the 93d and 76th Armies from Szechwan Province to bolster Y-Force. That province was ruled by a very powerful war lord. Though most of the nine Szechwanese divisions would take orders from the central government, some of the nine were very hard to control. It was therefore necessary for the central government to keep its loyal 93d and 76th Armies in position to guard the rice traffic throughout Szechwan.[116]

Dorn's warnings brought no response from Stilwell, for in the summer of 1943 Stilwell considered himself powerless to affect the Y-Force situation. The President had decided that Stilwell could not bargain with the Chinese and had indicated a clear preference for Chennault's point of view. So, after a conference with the Chinese Minister of Communications on 6 July Stilwell wrote: "I struck a new low [in spirits] after this conference. It seems absolutely impossible to do anything. The President has undercut me and the Chinese resist manfully

---

[114] *Ibid.*
[115] Ltr, Dorn to Ho, 17 Aug 43. SNF-16.
[116] Memos, sub: Answers of Memo for Ho Ying-chin from Dorn, 2 Sep 43. SNF-16.

every attempt to help them fight."[117] Why did the Chinese obstruct Stilwell's every effort to provide the Nationalist regime with a modern, efficient army of sixty divisions? In July 1943 Stilwell told Marshall that the Generalissimo did not want the regime to have a large, efficient ground force for fear that its commander would inevitably challenge his position as China's leader.[118]

Though the TRIDENT decisions called for major Chinese participation in taking Burma to break the blockade of China, it was apparent by August that the inconsistencies in the decisions were making them of little meaning. Chennault was handicapped because supplies were not reaching him. Stilwell was handicapped because Chennault's priority, though not enough to support major air operations, was large enough to handicap preparations for ground operations, even assuming the Chinese wished to make them.

Japanese Reaction to Allied Preparations

Well served by their intelligence agencies, the Japanese watched the training projects in Ramgarh and in Yunnan with growing concern. The Arakan campaign of 1942–43 suggested that Wavell's forces were growing more aggressive. Then came the Wingate 1943 expeditions, which led the Japanese to re-examine their position in Burma. Weighing the several indications of a changed and more vigorous Allied policy, the Japanese in February 1943 decided that the British, Chinese, and Americans were preparing a vigorous offensive against Burma.[119]

To meet this anticipated offensive, the Japanese changed both their organization and their strategy. *Headquarters, 15th Army,* the victors of 1942, became *Headquarters, Burma Area Army,* and a new headquarters was activated for *15th Army.* Lt. Gen. Shozo Kawabe took command of *Burma Area Army,* which retained control of *55th Division* in the Arakan. General Mutaguchi relinquished command of the *18th Division* in north Burma to assume command on 18 March 1943 of the *15th Army,* which comprised the *33d, 18th,* and *56th Divisions,* reinforced soon after by the *31st Division.*

Mutaguchi's promotion was significant, for he was now the ardent advocate of an invasion of India. When a drive into Assam had been proposed in the fall of 1942, Mutaguchi had objected. The project had been shelved, and the Japanese had relied on the terrain, malaria, and the poor communications behind the Allied lines to defend Burma. Then came Wingate's expedition in February 1943, and the Japanese opinions changed. The Japanese had long been regarded as masters of the art of moving armies through the jungle. Now, the British had performed a feat from which the Japanese had earlier recoiled. Mutaguchi became an advocate of an overland advance on India to seize the

[117] Stilwell Black Book, 6 Jul 43.
[118] CM–IN 16520, Stilwell to Marshall, 23 Jul 43.
[119] SEATIC Bull 240, 9 Jul 46, pp. 1–2. MID Library.

bases from which the Allies would launch an attack on Burma. He found ready listeners in Kawabe's headquarters and in *Headquarters, Southern Army,* the echelon above Kawabe.

Conferences to discuss an attack on India were held at Rangoon from June to August 1943, attended by representatives of *Burma Area Army, Southern Army, Japanese Expeditionary Forces, Southern Region,* (the Japanese Army-Navy headquarters for Southeast Asia at Singapore), and from *Imperial General Headquarters,* Tokyo. War games were played to present the problems involved in such an operation. The Commander-in-Chief, *Southern Army,* gave his support to the project, and early in July sent his assistant chief of staff, Maj. Gen. Masazumi Inada, to lay the proposal before *Imperial General Headquarters.* That body approved preliminary preparations for an attack on Imphal, without committing itself irrevocably to the operation.[120] As part of these preparations the *56th Division* on the Salween front in the summer of 1943 began to fortify its area so that a Chinese drive from Yunnan would not interfere with the forthcoming assault on India. If and when the Chinese finally decided to cross the Salween, these fortifications would be waiting for them.[121]

Summary

The difference between Stilwell and Marshall on the one hand, and Chennault and the Generalissimo on the other, as to whether an air effort in China Theater should precede or follow major reforms in the Chinese Army came before the President for decision in May 1943. The President decided for air power. The TRIDENT decisions, following soon after, called for a reduced ANAKIM to take north Burma and open a land route to China. Without Chinese participation, these operations appeared to be impossible, yet the President's decision confirmed and strengthened them in their unwillingness to take the offensive anywhere in China or Burma. It was a dilemma that would have to be solved if the blockade of China was to be broken, either by land or air. The time had come for a fresh approach to the problems of coalition warfare in Asia.

[120] (1) See the statements by senior Japanese officers as collected by Southeast Asia Translation and Interrogation Center in fall 1945 and early 1946, particularly those by Lt. Gen. Takazo Numata, *Southern Army;* General Mutaguchi; Col. Takushiro Hattori, Chief, *Operations Section, 1 Department, Imperial General Headquarters;* Lt. Col. Iwaichi Fujiwara, who served in both the G–2 and G–3 Sections of *15th Army.* SEATIC Bulls 240, 242, 245, 247. MID Library. (2) Japanese Comments, Sec. 1, p. 3. (See Bibliographical Note.)
[121] Japanese Study 93.

CHAPTER X

Putting Weight Behind the TRIDENT Decisions

When the TRIDENT Conference reduced ANAKIM to a limited operation to take north Burma, CBI Theater and Army Service Forces planners had to readjust their projects for supply of the Fourteenth Air Force and the U.S.-sponsored Chinese divisions down to what could be brought across north Burma. The President's simultaneous decision to back Chennault made it imperative that the flow of supplies into China be immediately and sharply increased. Dissatisfaction with the conduct of Allied operations in Southeast Asia led to the creation of a combined command, SEAC, or Southeast Asia Command.

Drafting a directive for SEAC offered the opportunity of resolving the conflicts in the TRIDENT decisions. Choosing SEAC's commander offered the opportunity of bringing a fresh approach to the problems of war in Asia. To the extent that discussions of SEAC's directive refocused attention on the problems of breaking China's blockade, such developments, from the standpoint of China Theater, would be constructive. On the other hand, if time was permitted to slip by while discussion explored all the byways of strategy in Southeast Asia, time so lost might never be regained. Just as resources allocated to Southeast Asia had to be weighed against the needs of other Allied theaters, so did time have to be handled as carefully as any other resource. Time for re-forming the Chinese Army was almost gone, and time for deciding how to break the blockade of China, before the Japanese clamped it shut for all time, was also limited.

Allied Discussions of Southeast Asia Command

Churchill's proclamation of Southeast Asia Command on 18 June 1943 began a long discussion on the relationship of the new command to the several chiefs of staff organizations and on the choice of the new Supreme Allied Commander. Churchill's original proposals of 19 June were to create an Allied command for Southeast Asia, comprising British, Indian, American, and Chinese forces under an integrated Anglo-American staff. This proposal was a forward step. It would replace the hastily improvised system of 1942, which had placed

Burma under Wavell as Supreme Commander, India, had placed the Chinese troops in neighboring Yunnan under the Generalissimo as Supreme Commander, China Theater, had provided no clear relation between Wavell's and Stilwell's headquarters, and had produced so many misunderstandings and so few results.

In place of this loose coalition of Allied headquarters, Churchill suggested a Supreme Allied Commander, responsible for operations against the Japanese in east Asia and for the development of the air route to China. Churchill believed that the relation of the Supreme Commander to higher authority should follow as closely as possible what Churchill understood to be the MacArthur model. The Combined Chiefs should exercise general jurisdiction over grand strategic policy and over such relating factors as were necessary for proper implementation of that policy, while the British Chiefs of Staff would exercise jurisdiction over all matters pertaining to operational strategy, and all instructions to the Supreme Commander would be issued through them,[1] thus establishing a relationship like that of the JCS to MacArthur.

Replying to Churchill, the President gave the proposed command his general approval but could not agree to three major provisions in the British plan: to placing the Generalissimo and his China Theater under the British Chiefs of Staff; to giving the British Chiefs of Staff the major share in determining the strategy of the proposed theater; and to accepting the Prime Minister's nominee, Air Marshal Sir Sholto Douglas, for the post of Supreme Allied Commander. The President pointed out that the Generalissimo was most unlikely to accept someone else as Supreme Commander over him. Because of the U.S. policy of aiding China, the President suggested that the new command conform to what he called the Eisenhower type of headquarters in the Mediterranean, with the British Chiefs of Staff acting as agents of the Combined Chiefs in transmitting the instructions of the Combined Chiefs of Staff. The President proposed Air Marshal Sir Arthur W. Tedder or Admiral A. B. Cunningham of the Royal Navy as Supreme Allied Commander. He readily agreed that Stilwell should be Deputy Supreme Allied Commander, for that would bring the Chinese into the arrangement, and he further agreed that the British Chiefs of Staff should name the commanders in chief for air, sea, and land, providing only that nothing in such an arrangement affected the Fourteenth Air Force.[2]

Churchill assured the President that the new command would not include the Generalissimo's China Theater but objected to Tedder's and Cunningham's leaving the Mediterranean. The Prime Minister's conception of Stilwell's role was a narrow one—command of the American and Chinese troops in SEAC, not the broad executive authority of a deputy. The British Chiefs of Staff feared

---

[1] Rad 320, Former Naval Person to President, 19 Jun 43. Item 80, Msg Bk 10, OPD Exec 8.
[2] (1) Rad 293, Roosevelt to Churchill, 24 Jun 43. Folder 25, OPD Exec 10. (2) Rad 298, Roosevelt to Churchill, 30 Jun 43. Item 25, Msg Bk 10, OPD Exec 8.

that with Stilwell's frequent trips to China he would be hard put to command part of the land and sea forces in SEAC. It was further revealed that the British Chiefs of Staff did not care for Stilwell in any role but were acquiescing in the interests of Allied unity. The Prime Minister desired that the British Chiefs of Staff should have the same authority in Southeast Asia that the Joint Chiefs of Staff had in the Southwest Pacific.[3]

Insisting on a larger share of American control in Southeast Asia, the President pointed out that as the tempo of the Pacific war increased, operations in Southeast Asia would have to be more closely co-ordinated with U.S. efforts in the entire Pacific. Centralized control in Washington would eventually be required not only to co-ordinate the Allied effort but also to insure the prompt redeployment of Allied resources from Europe to the Pacific after Germany's defeat. Therefore, it seemed unwise to split control of the war against Japan between London and Washington.[4] To this, the British made no direct reply, but on 10 July Field Marshal Dill in Washington learned that the British Chiefs of Staff might decide to create a British Joint Southeast Asia Command, dealing with Stilwell on a simple liaison basis. It was an impasse, and matters were still unsettled when the next great Allied conference, QUADRANT, convened at Quebec in August.[5]

It was unfortunate that these discussions, time consuming as they were, took place after public announcement of the new command. General Headquarters (India) was now on notice that it was to be relieved of further share in the conduct of Burma operations but, until the new commander with his staff should arrive, General Headquarters (India) would be called on repeatedly for major decisions on matters which might have governing influence on the future operations of the new command.[6]

The QUADRANT Conference, Quebec, 19–24 August 1943

The President, the Prime Minister, and their Chiefs of Staff met at Quebec in August 1943 to weigh the situation caused by Italy's surrender. At this gathering the Combined Chiefs of Staff planners were able for the first time to submit a combined plan for the defeat of Japan. The planners believed that China offered the best potentialities for bombing Japan, for attacking Japanese communications to the South Seas, and for mounting an invasion of Japan. The planners mentioned use of B–29 very long range bombers against Japan but omitted any reference to the Marianas Islands. Their plan called for a converging attack from east and west to seize the Canton–Hong Kong area. From the east, the advance would be from island to island by sea, land, and air forces

---

[3] Rad 323, Churchill to Roosevelt, 28 Jun 43; Rad 342, Churchill to Roosevelt, 3 Jul 43. Folder 25, OPD Exec 10.
[4] Rad 311, Roosevelt to Churchill, 9 Jul 43. Folder 25, OPD Exec 10.
[5] Rad, COS to Dill, 10 Jul 43. Folder 25, OPD Exec 10.
[6] Hist Sec (India), India at War, 1939–1943, pp. 179–80. Gen Ref Br, OCMH.

climaxed by an amphibious assault on the China coast; from the west, the Generalissimo's divisions, revitalized by training and re-equipped by lend-lease arms, would drive overland to meet their newly landed allies. Then both forces would unite and march on north China. The year 1947 was set for operations against Japan proper. In preparing the plan, several disagreements between the British and Americans had developed over Burma operations. After the clearing of north Burma, the Americans suggested Rangoon's seizure, while the British favored bypassing Rangoon for Singapore.

The Joint Chiefs of Staff planners thought the general lines of advance in the plan were sound but feared that a struggle conducted at such a pace might result in a negotiated peace that would actually be a U.S. defeat. They therefore recommended that the JCS urge the preparation of a plan for defeating Japan twelve months after the fall of Germany. The principal theme in the exchanges which followed among the planners was the need for a plan leading to Japan's speedy defeat. A major campaign in China was not likely to survive such an approach.[7]

As a contribution toward Japan's speedy defeat, the AAF through General Arnold submitted a plan at QUADRANT to overcome Japan twelve months after the defeat of Germany (which was assumed as fall 1944) by bombarding her with China-based B-29's, beginning with 10 groups of 28 aircraft each, and increasing gradually to 20 groups. The effort would be supported by C-87's based around Calcutta, their number increasing from an initial 2,000 to 4,000. The bombers would be based in east China and would ultimately include all the heavy bombers of the United Nations. The project was called the Air Plan for the Defeat of Japan.[8]

The exchanges at Quebec between the President and his service advisers, on the one hand, and the Prime Minister and his chiefs of staff, on the other, closely followed the lines of TRIDENT. Once again the President and the Joint Chiefs stressed the need for seizing Burma in order to keep China in the war. The President thought that the line Burma–China was the shortest route toward Japan. The Joint Chiefs of Staff feared that operations in Sumatra would deflect the main effort in Southeast Asia from support of China, which was the sole political reason U.S. troops were present in Asia. Churchill agreed that

[7] (1) The elimination of the projected major Allied land campaign in China is covered in Volume II, Stilwell's Command Problems, a work on the 1943–44 period in which this decision was reached. (2) CPS 83, 8 Aug 43, sub: Appreciation and Plan for Defeat of Japan. (3) USSBS, *The War Against Japanese Transportation, 1941–1945,* p. 116. (4) Memo, Jt War Plans Com for JPS, 9 Aug 43, sub: Strategic Plan for Defeat of Japan. Case 192, OPD 381 CTO, A47–30. A copy went to the President via Admiral Leahy. (5) Memo, JPS for JCS, 17 Aug 43, sub: Appreciation and Plan for Defeat of Japan. ABC 381 (Japan), 8–27–43, Sec 3, A48–224. (6) JPS 67/7, 19 Jul 43, sub: Preparations of Plans for Defeat of Japan, was the Joint Staff Planners' directive under which the Joint War Plans Committee began work on CPS 83, being ordered to: give priority to 1943–44 operations; give priority to south Burma operations over Sumatra–Malaya; indicate which operations were to come before Germany's surrender (set for fall 1944) and which after; have plans ready for the CCS on Burma, Marshalls, Carolines, and New Guinea.

[8] (1) CCS 323, 20 Aug 43, sub: Air Plan for Defeat of Japan. (2) CM–OUT 10990, Marshall to Stilwell, 26 Aug 43.

Sumatra was not on the direct line toward China but called its occupation a great strategic coup, whose alternative was nothing but "Akyab, and the right to toil through the swamps of Southern Burma." [9] The significance of these discussions lay in the fact that once again the President and the Joint Chiefs of Staff stressed the importance of the early reoccupation of Burma to reopen the line of communications from Rangoon, and that again there was no agreement among the Combined Chiefs on what operation should follow the reoccupation of north Burma.

The QUADRANT strategic decisions on CBI reaffirmed those of TRIDENT and left open the issue of whether Rangoon or Singapore would be the next step after occupation of north Burma. To American observers, the British seemed reluctant to use their resources in India to retake Burma in order to open the road to a China whose value as an ally they tended to minimize. They seemed far more interested in conserving their means for a mighty thrust at Singapore.[10] Consistent with the dominant role of U.S. air power in CBI, and with the now firmly established priority of the cross-Channel assault over Mediterranean operations, the conferees directed the Combined Chiefs of Staff planners to prepare a new plan calling for defeat of Japan twelve months after Germany's defeat, and to include in this new approach the Air Plan for the Defeat of Japan by B–29 bombardment.[11] The CCS did not attempt to make all decisions for future plans against Japan at QUADRANT, but left some for the next conference. However, they approved the proposals of the Joint Chiefs of Staff to begin an advance on Japan through the islands of the Central Pacific (the Marshalls and Gilberts). This would provide yet more pressure on Japan from the Pacific Ocean side, while steadily increasing Allied air power in China and improving the Chinese Army would complete the ring around Japan, wear down Japanese resources, and put weight on Japan from the direction of Asia. The convergence of the several lines of approach from east and west on the mainland of Asia would ultimately place Allied bombers and landing craft in north China, within easy range of Japan.[12] The emphasis in the plans for the defeat of Japan as of QUADRANT still lay in establishing Allied power in north China. Approval of the JCS proposal for a drive across the Central Pacific did not minimize the importance of Chinese bases, for the part that Pacific islands could play in strategic aerial bombardment of Japan was not yet realized.

[9] (1) Min, QUADRANT Conf, Aug 43, pp. 426–28. (2) CCS 107th Mtg, 14 Aug 43. (3) JCS 107th Mtg, 18 Aug 43, Item 2. (4) Memo, Wedemeyer for Cooke and Brig Gen Lawrence S. Kuter, 18 Aug 43, sub: Sumatra–Singapore *vs.* South Burma. Annex to JCS 107th Mtg, 18 Aug 43. (5) CCS First Mtg, with Roosevelt and Churchill, Quebec, 19 Aug 43, contains Churchill's quotation. (6) CCS 301/3, 27 Aug 43, sub: Final Rpt on QUADRANT Conf. (7) Item 5, CCS 113th Mtg, 20 Aug 43.

[10] For an expression of Churchill's views on China, see *The Hinge of Fate,* pages 133–34. *Roosevelt and Hopkins,* page 405, states that Churchill considered "any policy based on confidence in China was a 'great illusion.'"

[11] Memo, Capt F. B. Royal, USN, Deputy Secy, CCS, 25 Sep 43, sub: Studies on Defeat of Japan. ABC 381 (Japan), 8–27–42, Sec 4, A48–224.

[12] CCS 319/5, 24 Aug 43, Final Report to the President and the Prime Minister.

The QUADRANT decisions making possible a directive and a commander for the new Southeast Asia Command and logistical support for Allied operations in Asia were of the greatest interest and significance to CBI Theater headquarters. The Prime Minister, the President, and the Combined Chiefs of Staff agreed that Vice-Adm. Lord Louis Mountbatten, Royal Navy, former Chief of Combined Operations, should be Supreme Commander, Southeast Asia. The question of his command relation to the CCS was solved by the formula that the CCS would have "general jurisdiction on the strategy of the Southeast Asia Theater."[13] The Joint Chiefs believed that this gave the Combined Chiefs control over which of several courses of action should be adopted, their sequence, and their timing.[14]

Planning Logistical Support

To support his operations Mountbatten would have the benefit of a major effort by Army Service Forces, whose chief, General Somervell, saw the difficulties in CBI as a great challenge to the resources and ingenuity of his organization. On taking command in India and beginning preparatory planning for SAUCY, General Auchinleck had become convinced of the difficulty and futility of operations in Burma and promptly reported as much to the conferees at Quebec. Since it was accepted by the Joint Chiefs that Burma had to be retaken to break the blockade of China, and since TRIDENT had decreed that operations in north Burma would come first, a line of communications to China would have to be created across north Burma. Army Service Forces' engineering and transport experts believed the logistical problems in India and Burma could be solved. Therefore, Somervell rejected Auchinleck's approach, stated that improvement of the Assam line of communications to an acceptable standard was well within American and British resources, and told Wheeler that a land route to China had to be opened as a matter of urgency. General Somervell asked the SOS commander to radio his views to Quebec.[15]

While Somervell was awaiting word from India, Auchinleck sent the conferees at Quebec a long radio surveying the situation as at appeared to General Headquarters (India). Auchinleck and his staff warned that land operations could be undertaken only at the expense of the airlift to China. The Assam line of communications seemed unable to carry stores for its own improvement without handicapping combat operations. If ATC operations received first priority, then the shortfall must be borne either by the Chinese forces based on Ledo or be shared by them and 4 Corps at Imphal. If the offensive from Ledo was canceled, Auchinleck went on, he could improve 4 Corps' positions in the Imphal area, though an advance as far as Kalewa would be impossible.

[13] JCS 582, 9 Nov 43, sub: Future Opns in SEAC.
[14] (1) CCS 390/1, 18 Nov 43, sub: Future Opns in SEAC. (2) CCS 128th Mtg, 23 Nov 43.
[15] Rad BOSCO–OUT 30, Somervell to Wheeler, 15 Aug 43. Somervell File, Vol III, CBI 42–43.

Because floods from the monsoon rains had breached the Bengal and Assam Railway in many places, concentrating resources on a campaign meant that not until March or April 1944 could the line of communications carry any tonnage for its own improvement. If the line of communications was to be doubled in capacity by 1945, then operations should be canceled and allotments of tonnage to improve the line of communications should take priority. Auchinleck did not believe that abandoning the campaign in Burma would involve a prolongation of the war.

Turning to the actual details of operating the lines of communications, Auchinleck believed that a pipeline from Calcutta northward, though of great long-term value, would through its construction throw an increased burden of unknown size on the lines of communications. He conceded that the railway was not operated at British or American standards, but since the cars had to be ferried across the unbridged and turbulent Brahmaputra at several points, such criticism seemed irrelevant. He agreed that military control of the railway from Pandu, Assam (on the east side of the Brahmaputra, over halfway up the line), forward was essential.

Turning to priorities over the lines of communications, Auchinleck assured the British Chiefs of Staff that preparations for 1943–44 operations were being continued on the basis of first priority for Hump tonnage of 10,000 tons and an air offensive against the Japanese, which absorbed resources otherwise available for the improvement of the lines of communications.[16]

These views did not meet the approval of the British Chiefs of Staff. Laying Auchinleck's radio before the Combined Chiefs, they confessed their inability to see how General Headquarters (India) had arrived at its appraisals and asked that the CCS reach a decision on Burma operations. To General Headquarters (India), the British Chiefs replied that since the line of communications was known to be inefficiently operated, the task of remedying the situation should not be beyond the ability of India Command.[17]

The issue of improving the Assam line of communications to a point that would support both Chennault's operations in China and the projected offensive in Burma and the related issue of building a communications system across north Burma to replace the once-contemplated line from Rangoon northward were now before the Combined Chiefs of Staff. The CCS's advisers put the Ledo Road across north Burma first in their staff study:

The opening of an overland route to CHINA will greatly facilitate operations and may well assist in bringing hostilities to an earlier conclusion than would otherwise be possible. In addition to meeting requirements for 1943/1944 operations in BURMA, and the short-term projects which are necessary to make them possible, it is necessary because of the

---

[16] Telg 66688/COS, CinC India for COS (Quebec), 19 Aug 43. Folder 50, OPD Exec 10.
[17] (1) Rad FW 224, COS to CinC, India. Case 224, OPD 381 CTO, A47–30. (2) CCS 327, 23 Aug 43, sub: Opns from India.

Herculean task ahead to make urgent preparations for completing the overland route and ensuring an adequate supply of stores for delivery over the route when opened.[18]

Preliminary studies had revealed differences between the British and American staffs as to possible opening dates and capacity of the Ledo Road. The staff paper explicitly did not try to judge between them but remarked that all agreed the project was urgent and should be executed at the earliest possible date, subject to such operations as the Combined Chiefs might decide upon.

Regardless of the date the Ledo Road was completed, the CCS's advisers stated that it was now time to examine the tonnage to be carried over it and to begin preparing the Assam line of communications to bring forward this tonnage plus that needed to maintain the road. As of 1 November 1943 the Assam line of communications could maintain only minimum air and ground forces in Burma, construction of the road, and 10,000 tons a month over the Hump. Nothing was left for the Ledo Road's traffic or operation. It was therefore necessary to build up the Assam line of communications and it was further observed that the Joint Chiefs of Staff had just agreed to provide men and matériel to build and operate the Ledo Road.[19]

In writing the paper, the CCS's advisers did not draw on the views of SOS CBI, which were dated 22 August. SOS CBI had no doubts whatever that the Assam line of communications could be speedily built up and called the target figure, which had seemed almost impossible to General Headquarters (India), of 3,400 tons per day by 1 November 1943 over the line of communications "insignificant" and, by implication, easy to meet. To men with experience in American railroading, the figure was picayune.[20]

The CCS approved a great increase in the capacity of the Assam line of communications and ordered General Auchinleck to begin the necessary work prior to the arrival in India of the new Supreme Allied Commander. Also, the CCS ordered the Assam line of communications made capable of carrying 220,000 tons a month by 1 January 1946. This great increase would be exclusive of deliveries of gasoline through two 6-inch pipelines ordered built from the Bengal pumping terminals to the Assam airfields. The United States would provide the men and matériel necessary to meet these goals.[21]

Providing the men, the matériel, and the guidance would be the province of General Somervell and the Army Service Forces. Challenged and inspired by the magnitude of the task, Somervell wrote to his staff:

The development of the line of communications from India to China bids fair to be the greatest engineering undertaking of the War and perhaps the major effort insofar as supply

---

[18] Memo for CCS, 18 Aug 43, sub: Supply Routes in NE India. Somervell File, QUADRANT Conf, 1943, A46–257.

[19] *Ibid.*

[20] Memo, Strong for Somervell, 22 Aug 43, sub: Auchinleck's Telg of 19 Aug 43. Somervell File, Vol III, CBI 42–43.

[21] CCS 325, 21 Aug 43, sub: Supply Routes in NE India.

is concerned. It is essential that this subject be given the attention that it deserves and that we are in a position at all times to back up and even anticipate the demands which are made on us in the way of men and materials.

I want an India Committee set up for the A. S. F. composed of outstanding men in their fields.[22]

Since the jurisdiction of the Combined Chiefs of Staff ended at the border of China, nothing was said in the QUADRANT decisions about moving supplies from the ATC terminals at Kunming to the Fourteenth's east China airfields. Responsibility for the solution of logistical problems within China Theater remained with its Supreme Commander, the Generalissimo.

The CCS's approval and Somervell's forceful support were, in effect, a new charter for the SOS in CBI. Men and matériel would now be forthcoming for an effort to create a logistical base capable of supporting major Allied operations. It would, however, be many months before these efforts created the expanded logistical base, and still more months before the better supply situation made itself felt in operations. Here was the time element. Seventeen months had passed since Stilwell arrived in Chungking to improve the combat efficiency of the Chinese Army. More months would pass before the flow of supplies to the U.S.-sponsored divisions in China reached an appreciable level. Into these calculations of space and time an independent element could introduce itself—the will of the enemy.

SEAC's Organization and Directive

Following QUADRANT, Marshall undertook to explain to Stilwell the conference decisions and Stilwell's position under the new Supreme Allied Commander, Admiral Mountbatten. The strategic decisions, Marshall pointed out, were a reaffirmation of TRIDENT, calling for the occupation of north Burma (D Day, mid-February 1944) to establish overland communications with China, and by taking Myitkyina to broaden the air route to China, for its saturation with transport aircraft could now be foreseen. Preparations would continue for amphibious operations in spring 1944 on the scale of those planned at TRIDENT to take Akyab and Ramree. There was no decision on specific amphibious operations, for the British Chiefs of Staff still hoped for a commitment to Sumatra. And the Hump route was to be built up to intensify operations against the Japanese, keep China in the war, maintain a larger Fourteenth Air Force in China, and equip and train Chinese forces.[23]

The QUADRANT conferees had recognized that operations in China, operations in Burma, and long-term projects for improving the Assam line of communications all competed for tonnage being carried over the Assam line of

---

[22] Memo, Somervell for Maj Gen Wilhelm D. Styer, CofS, ASF, 22 Aug 43. Somervell File, Vol III, CBI 42–43.

[23] CM–OUT 11436, Marshall to Stilwell, 27 Aug 43.

communications. The solution was to give the Supreme Allied Commander authority to decide Indian and Burmese priorities, under the principle that he should give preference to operations in north Burma but at the same time keep in mind the long-term needs of the line of communications.[24]

The command relationships within SEAC were of the greatest complexity. Marshall told Stilwell there was no pretense that they represented sound administrative practice but that they had been openly and consciously so arranged by the CCS and their superiors because of the Government of India's constitutional position in the Commonwealth and because of the Generalissimo's position and methods.[25]

Creation of SEAC meant there were now three geographic theaters and one operational, representing the interests of three nations and the three services, all operating in the same area. SEAC was an Anglo-American command which included Burma, Ceylon, Sumatra, and Malaya, but not India. India was under India Command (Auchinleck), with responsibilities toward the Middle East, where Indian divisions were fighting, as well as to the Far East. In China was the Generalissimo's China Theater. The American operational theater, CBI, operated in all three geographic areas. It was not subordinate to SEAC.

The Chinese Army in India, commanded by Stilwell, was based on India Command, and was to fight in SEAC's area under SEAC command. The Fourteenth Air Force was based in China, supplied from India, and formally under the Generalissimo. Although SEAC was given logistic support by India Command, the latter's administration, defense, and internal security were under Auchinleck, who in turn was responsible to the Government of India. As representative of the War Cabinet and as Viceroy of India, Field Marshal Wavell was priorities arbiter between India Command and SEAC, but each could appeal from his decision to the British Chiefs of Staff.

Liaison between SEAC and the Generalissimo was attempted by suggesting Stilwell, one of the Generalissimo's chiefs of staff, as Deputy Supreme Allied Commander. It was Stilwell's task to see that the Chinese played their part; Marshall called the mission "No easy one!"[26] To strengthen the SEAC staff, Marshall offered the services of General Wheeler as principal administrative officer (G-4). Mountbatten accepted with pleasure.[27]

Stilwell and Mountbatten began their relationship on good terms. Marshall had predicted Stilwell would find the Admiral "a breath of fresh air," and Stilwell agreed, noting in the faithful diary: "Louis is a good egg—full of

---

[24] CCS Second Mtg, with Roosevelt, Churchill, Quadrant Conf, 23 Aug 43, Item 6.

[25] Rads 3243, 3259, Marshall to Stilwell, 26, 28 Aug 43. Items 759, 763, Bk 2, JWS Personal File.

[26] (1) CCS First Mtg, with Roosevelt, Churchill, Quadrant Conf, 19 Aug 43. Quadrant Min. (2) CCS 111th Mtg, 18 Aug 43.

[27] Rpt with Suppls, 1943–46, SACSEA to CCS, 30 Jul 47, Pt. A, par. 39. (Hereafter, Mountbatten Report). Gen Ref Br, OCMH.

VICE-ADM. LORD LOUIS MOUNTBATTEN *with General Stilwell in Burma. (Photograph taken in March 1944.)*

enthusiasm and also of disgust with inertia and conservatism." So, Stilwell could approach his work as Deputy Supreme Allied Commander with obedience to a little homily from Marshall in July that there had to be a genuine co-operation with the British, who were the United States' principal ally. Anything that tended to split the two nations had its repercussions around the globe. If the British played "God Save the King," General Handy added, Stilwell should at least stand up.[28]

The QUADRANT conferees ordered some American infantry assigned to SEAC for organization and training along the lines that Brigadier Wingate had devised.[29] Wingate was present at Quebec, where his views, powerfully supported by the Prime Minister, won general acceptance. After his eruption into Burma a few months before, Wingate had meditated long on his experiences and was now convinced that he had the way to baffle and ultimately to ruin the Japanese.

Wingate proposed the establishment of jungle strong points by Long-Range Penetration Groups (LRPG's or Chindits) landed behind the Japanese lines by glider and transport aircraft. From these the Chindit infantry would fan out to raid the Japanese lines of communications. The Japanese, for their part, could dash themselves against the strong points or wear themselves out chasing the raiding parties. Wingate hoped these tactics would be so successful that ultimately all British and Indian divisions in Southeast Asia would be organized for long-range penetration.[30]

Not only did Wingate's projects receive the CCS's blessing, but Marshall agreed to form an American long range penetration group with the code name GALAHAD. He and Arnold bent themselves to the improvisation of especial air units to support the Chindits and GALAHAD. Two young airmen of high repute, Col. Philip G. Cochrane and Lt. Col. John R. Alison, were ordered to SEAC to activate and command No. 1 Air Commando, a custom-made aggregation of liaison aircraft, helicopters, light bombers, fighters, gliders, and transports.[31]

The Prime Minister's directive to Mountbatten for SEAC was:

1. Your attention is drawn to the decisions of the Combined Chiefs of Staff, QUADRANT, which were approved by the President of the United States and by me on behalf of the War Cabinet. Pursuant to these decisions and acting in harmony with them, you will take up your appointment as Supreme Allied Commander, South-East Asia, provided in my memorandum and, within the limits of your command as defined therein, you will conduct all operations against Japan. . . . You will be responsible to the British Chiefs of Staff, who are authorized by Combined Chiefs of Staff to exercise jurisdiction over all matters pertaining to operations and will be the channel through which all directives will be issued to you.

---

[28](1) Rad WAR 3243, Marshall to Stilwell, 26 Aug 43. Item 759, Bk 2, JWS Personal File. (2) *The Stilwell Papers,* pp. 230, 317.
[29] See Ch. VIII, above.
[30](1) Memo, Comdr Sp Force at Imphal for SACSEA, 10 Feb 44, sub: Exploitation of Opn THURSDAY. SEAC War Diary, A46–217. (2) Mountbatten Report, Pt. A, par. 5.
[31] *Ibid.*

2. Your prime duty is to engage the Japanese as closely and continuously as possible in order by attrition to consume and wear down the enemy's forces, especially his air forces, thus making our superiority tell and forcing the enemy to divert his forces from the Pacific theatre—and secondly, but of equal consequence, to maintain and broaden our contacts with China, both by the air route and by establishing direct contact through Northern Burma *inter alia* by suitably organised, air-supplied ground forces of the greatest possible strength.

3. You will utilise to the full the advantage of the sea power and air power, which will be at your disposal, by seizing some point or points which (*a*) induce a powerful reaction from the enemy, and (*b*) give several options for a stroke on your part in the light of the enemy's aforesaid reaction. For this purpose, in making your proposals for amphibious operations in 1944, you will select the point of attack which seems best calculated to yield the above conditions, and will execute the operation approved. You will also prepare plans for the second phase of your campaign in 1944 contingent upon the reaction extorted from the enemy.

4. At least four weeks before your first major amphibious operation you will be furnished by His Majesty's Government with a Battle-fleet. . . .

5. You will proceed to form, as resources come to hand, a combined striking force or circus which will be available as the foundation of whatever amphibious descent is eventually chosen. . . .

6. You will, at the earliest moment, report your plans, dates and requirements, bearing in mind the advantages of speed.[32]

23rd October 1943   10, Downing Street, S.W. 1.

Stilwell Resumes His Chief of Staff Role

While Stilwell waited for Mountbatten to arrive and present himself to the Chinese, he again essayed his role as chief of staff to the Supreme Commander of China Theater and presented the Generalissimo with a series of new proposals—for an offensive to forestall the inevitable Japanese reaction to the Chennault plan, for the creation of sixty first-rate Chinese divisions, and for some impetus behind the Y-Force preparations. These proposals were not presented in an optimistic spirit, for Stilwell was fully aware of his situation. Without power to bargain, without tonnage to equip the U.S.-sponsored Chinese divisions, and without the President's support, he was limited to persuasion and argument. He also expected to be held responsible for defense of the Fourteenth Air Force's east China bases even though that organization had received the bulk of Hump tonnage. Stilwell's comment was:

"Now with PROJECT 8 [for Hump augmentation] in view, the development of the Chinese Army will be a secondary consideration. The air will get all the supplies and we'll be left to struggle along in the mud unaided. But they'll expect us to damn well produce a force that can protect the fancy boys while they do their spectacular stuff."[33]

On 6 September 1943 he proposed "a diversion in the North West to

---

[32] Telg OZ 3331, Prime Minister to SACSEA, 23 Oct 43. Mountbatten Report, Suppl, App. 12, pp. 41–42.

[33] Stilwell Black Book, 12 Sep 43.

forestall a Japanese reaction [to the Chennault plan]. It will be treated with the contempt it deserves, and due to FDR's attitude I am powerless to do anything about it." [34] This proposal was Stilwell's first suggestion that the Generalissimo order Nationalist and Communist divisions both to attack the Japanese and that the Generalissimo give the Chinese Communists something from his own stocks as an incentive for action against the Japanese. Feeling that such a plan would test the sincerity of the Chinese Communists' protestations that they were earnestly fighting the Japanese, Stilwell proposed:

The following plan, based entirely on military considerations, is offered as practicable and desirable.

1. The 18th Group Army [Communist], the 22nd Army and the 35th Army occupy a position deep on the flank of the Jap forces in North China. This force could be used to advantage in creating a threat to the P'ing-Han Railroad, and the Kweihua-Kalgan area. This action would counteract in large measure any plan of the Japs to push up the Yangtze from Ichang, or towards Changsha from Hankow.

2. Such a threat would be greatly strengthened by a move of the troops in the Sian area into Southern Shansi and towards Chengchow. The Jap garrison of Shansi is not big enough to stop a concerted move of this kind. They could stop it at some points, but at others, progress would be almost certain. The effect of a serious threat in this general area would almost certainly prevent the Japs from committing themselves in the Yangtze Valley, and would thus reduce the present serious danger to Szechwan and Yunnan.

3. The plan suggested is as follows:

a. Fu Tso Yi with the 35th Army to operate East along the P'ing-Sui Railroad, interrupting it with Cavalry raids and isolating the Jap garrison at Paot'ou.

b. Teng Pao Shan with the 22nd Army, to operate in conjunction with Fu Tso Yi between Paot'ou and Kwei-hua.

c. The 18th Group Army [Communist] to move into the Wu T'ai area and raid the P'ing-Han Railroad.

d. The Shansi group of divisions to raid the T'ung P'u Railroad. Very little can be expected from them, but at least they can give the semblance of activity.

e. Hu Tsung-Nan to displace several divisions towards the East, crossing the river, at several points and threatening an attack on Chengchow and Sin-siang.

To prevent the Japs from concentrating against them one at a time, the above moves should be simultaneous. If they are, there will almost certainly be holes in the defense, and the Japs will be forced to move troops from other areas to hold their positions. There is nothing to be lost in this arrangement, and much to be gained. If we remain inactive and leave the initiative to the Japs, they will move troops somewhere and force us to shift in order to meet the threat. In our case, it is much more serious to allow this than in theirs, because any diversions will affect our future plans in Yunnan, on which so much depends. Even if no success is gained anywhere, the mere fact of movement will make the Japs hesitant about committing troops until the real nature of our threat is determined. This is what we want—to make the Japs guess and to keep them from throwing *us* off balance by just such diversionary attacks as the one proposed against them.

4. I recommend that this plan be adopted, that the troops in the Northwest be given sufficient supplies to put it into effect, and that it be scheduled for early October. At the worst, it costs nothing in troops and little in supplies, it makes use of units that are other-

[34] Stilwell Black Book, 6 Sep 43.

wise idle, and it will make plain the degree of reliability of the forces in the Northwest. [i. e., reveal whether the Chinese Communists would accept an order from the Generalissimo to attack the Japanese.]

5. If we do not move, the Japs will.[35]

While the Generalissimo was considering this proposal and Stilwell was drafting still more, new allies in China Theater brought fresh hope to Stilwell. Madame Chiang and her sister Madame H. H. Kung, the wife of China's Vice-President of the Executive Yuan and Minister of Finance, invited Stilwell to the Chiang residence and offered their cooperation. Their motives are unknown; however, in the next few weeks it became apparent that there was a breach between Mesdames Chiang and Kung on the one hand and their brother, T. V. Soong, on the other. Madame Chiang's decision to back Stilwell was a major change; six months before she had been ardent in support of Chennault.

Stilwell was quick to seize the proffered help: "Whatever the cause, they mean business [Army reform] now and maybe we can get somewhere." He met Madame Chiang again for lunch, and she revealed a firm grasp of the essentials, that in China armed power and political power were two sides of the same coin.[36] Stilwell began his collaboration with Madame Chiang by giving her copies of the memorandums he was preparing for the Generalisimo, then explaining them to her so that she might present them successfully to the Generalissimo. With them went several brief comments on the problems of war in China. To give background and meaning to his proposals for China Theater, Stilwell capped his presentation by giving Madame Chiang a group of little essays on the art of war.[37]

The memorandums on 5 and 16 September from Stilwell to the Generalissimo and Madame Chiang were covered by a note pointing out that the time for China to do her share in the Burma operations was almost at hand, and that only the most energetic preparations would "put the troops in condition to carry it out." To meet this need, Stilwell asked for a general directive from the Generalissimo to the War Ministry on the first and second Thirty Divisions for Burma and east China, with a hint that the time had come to reach a firm decision on which were the first Thirty Divisions; for directives to the Y-Force commanders in Yunnan; for specific orders on a unified Chinese command in Yunnan; for orders on "SOS set-up, trucks, road repair, replacements, extra units for Kwangsi and Yunnan, ten more divisions for the first thirty, rations, my status, training in second thirty divisions, assignment of a commander for the second thirty, and reorganization of both first and second thirty."[38]

[35] Memorandum 54, Stilwell for Chiang, 6 September 1943, was signed by Stilwell as Lieutenant General, Commanding, U.S. Army Forces, China, Burma and India. This act was later charged against him as an affront to the Generalissimo. Stilwell Documents, Hoover Library.

[36] *The Stilwell Papers*, pp. 224, 226, quotation on p. 225.

[37] Items 226–28, Book 3, JWS Personal File, cover Personnel, Sample of Current Reports, Organization, Units, Infantry Weapons, Tanks and Trucks, Artillery Weapons, Principles of War, Formations, Combat, and Weapons.

[38] Memo, Stilwell for Chiang and Mme. Chiang, 16 Sep 43. Stilwell Documents, Hoover Library.

Specifically, Stilwell asked that preparation of the Y–Force receive first priority, with target date 1 December, and that reorganization of the second Thirty Divisions, in the Kweilin area, start at once. A plan of operations from Yunnan, consistent with the general plan the Generalissimo had already approved, was sketched to illustrate the need for more men in that province. The need for a commander in chief in Yunnan with clear authority over all reserves there was stressed. The last memorandum gave a list of specific orders, covering all vital points, which Stilwell believed the Generalissimo could, if he would, validate with his signature.

1. General Ch'en Ch'eng is designated as commander of all troops in Yunnan and Kwangsi provinces.
2. The C. E. F., S. O. S. will embrace all supply activities forward of Hou Ch'in Pu depots in Kunming.
3. Extra divisions will be designated at once to fill the list of the first thirty divisions.
4. ——— [Space left by Stilwell] is designated to command the second thirty divisions. He will confer with General Ho Ying chin and General Stilwell on reorganization and training, which will start at once.
5. Every effort will be made to bring all units to strength as soon as possible. For this purpose complete units may be transferred from other war zones.
6. Two more armies will be furnished as general reserve in the Yunnan area.
7. The necessary trucks will be furnished at once—civilian trucks may be requisitioned, under a plan to replace them later.
8. The program of road repair will be pushed energetically. Labor may be forced where necessary.
9. The ration for the Yunnan troops will be improved.
10. General Stilwell is directed as joint Chief of Staff to report direct to the Generalissimo on the progress of preparations.[39]

In sharp contrast to his earlier custom of ignoring Stilwell's memorandums, the Generalissimo promptly answered these in affirmative tones on 21 and 28 September. His changed attitude may well reflect Madame Chiang's support of Stilwell. Unfortunately, it was now September 1943 and very late to begin reform even if each of the Generalissimo's statements had been immediately translated into action.

In regard to the all-important question of the Thirty Divisions, Stilwell's memorandum on 5 September had pointed out that "for various reasons, the first thirty division plan has been so changed that now, counting in the 60th Army and the N22d and N38th Divisions, it amounts to only 22 divisions." So Stilwell "assumed" that the Y–Force under Chen Cheng would be considered as the first Thirty Divisions and have first priority on training and equipment.[40]

---

[39] Memo, Stilwell for Chiang, 16 Sep 43. Item 229, Bk 3, JWS Personal File.
[40] Memo, Stilwell for Chiang, 5 Sep 43. Stilwell Documents, Hoover Library. Through a typographical error, the 5 September 1943 memorandum is dated 26 September. A memorandum from the Generalissimo to Stilwell on 21 September 1943 answers Stilwell's 5 September paper point for point and refers to it as dated 5 September.

To this point, the Generalissimo replied with a new and revised list of divisions for re-equipment. In March 1943, he had ordered re-equipping the 2d, 5th, 6th, 8th, 52d, 53d, 54th, 60th, 71st, 74th, and 93d Armies.[41] Between March and September, new orders and counterorders had whittled the total divisions to twenty.[42] Now the Generalissimo raised it back to thirty, by ordering the re-equipping of each division of the **New First Army,** of the 36th Division, plus the two best divisions of the 2d, 5th, 6th, **10th, 31st,** 52d, 53d, 54th, 60th, 71st, 74th, and 93d Armies. (The newly added armies are in boldface.)[43] It was now two and one half years since Soong had requested arms for thirty divisions; Stilwell had to hope that this latest list of the thirty divisions would be more enduring than the previous ones.

Warned by Stilwell that the Chinese had furnished men for only five battalions of American-equipped field artillery, of the nineteen needed for the Y–Force, the Generalissimo replied that the War Ministry had been ordered to prepare plans within the next fortnight for creating the fourteen battalions. The Generalissimo agreed that cadres from the second Thirty Divisions would begin training 1 December 1943. Urged again by Stilwell to cut the unwieldy mass of three hundred-odd Chinese divisions by 50 percent, the Generalissimo replied: "Your suggestion is very important to the China War Theater as a whole" and dropped the subject. With regard to replacements for the Y–Force to bring its units up to strength, the Generalissimo said that he would order General Chen Cheng to do his best to fill the gaps in the Y–Force.

On the ten specific points for immediate action which Stilwell had presented, the Generalissimo took refuge in delay. Unity of command in Yunnan would be established when necessary. The tangled Chinese SOS system in Yunnan would retain its *status quo* until General Chen assumed command of both the southern and western Yunnan fronts. The Ministry of War would find as many replacements as possible and do something about improving the ration. A commander for the second Thirty Divisions would be appointed in due course. One hint of offensive action did appear; preparations would be made for capturing I-chang and Wuhan (the Wu-chang–Hankow area) with the second Thirty Divisions.[44]

Stilwell judged the moment had now come for a formal presentation of his views on China and its problems. After almost twelve months' silence, the Generalissimo was now corresponding with Stilwell and hinting at action. Moreover, from 14 September on, Stilwell knew a campaign for his removal was under way. Surveying the Chungking situation, he decided that General

[41] Memo, Wang Wen-hsien for Dorn, 23 Mar 43, sub: Personnel Reqmts for Y–Force. AG (Y–FOS) 320.2, KCRC. See also Chart 7.
[42] (1) Memo cited n. 40. (2) Memos, sub: Answers of Memo for Ho Ying-chin from Dorn, 2 Sep 43. SNF–16.
[43] Memo, Chiang for Stilwell, 21 Sep 43. Stilwell Documents, Hoover Library.
[44] Memos, Chiang for Stilwell, 21, 28 Sep 43. Stilwell Documents, Hoover Library.

Ho was inspiring the drive.[45] Stilwell also knew that a variety of charges were being launched against him, that he was "haughty," "anti-Chinese," that he would not "permit Chinese officers to approach the British," and that he signed papers as a U.S. officer, not as joint chief of staff to the Generalissimo.[46]

The vehicle for presenting Stilwell's views was a note signed on 29 September by Stilwell as "Joint Chief of Staff for the Generalissimo," and titled Program for China. In it Stilwell pointed out in so many words that sixty reformed divisions "will assure the Central Government of obedience to its orders." Program for China candidly appealed to the self-interest of the Nationalist regime. Madame Chiang received a copy.

PROGRAM FOR CHINA

CHUNGKING, CHINA, *29 September, 1943*

China's main needs at the moment, as I see them, are as follows:

1. A definite policy of reorganization and training, covered by a general directive, issued by the Generalissimo.

2. A simplifying and speeding up of procedure in the War Ministry to permit of quicker action.

3. A reduction, of 50%, of existing units, accomplished by amalgamation.

4. The formation of two field armies, one composed of the first 30 divisions, the other of the second 30.

5. Elimination of unfit and inefficient officers.

(The two armies in paragraph 4 to be the regular Chinese Army, all other units to be second line troops, the best of the second line troops to be used as garrison units and the others gradually inactivated. They can be reduced first to brigades, and then by drafts to police work, gendarmes, anti-smuggling, etc., to be eliminated as troop units.)

China cannot carry the load she is burdened with at present. It is impossible to properly feed and pay her large army. The result is that nearly all units are under strength, full of sickness, immobile, and inefficient. If the army were a person, a surgical operation would be performed at once. I propose such an operation for the army, in the belief that [if] it is not performed, the patient will die.

Bad cases require radical treatment. A reduction of units by 50% would cure many of the ills we are suffering from. The remaining units would be stronger, and a large number of men would be released to go back to the farms. Ten good divisions are certainly better than twenty poor ones.

How many of China's 300-odd divisions could possibly be brought to bear against the enemy? Only those where the enemy chooses to attack, with a few exceptions. Of what use, then, are the others? There are many divisions that have not fought at all, or so little as to be a negligible factor.

The designation of two groups of divisions as the regular army of China has many advantages. These troops can be fully equipped and trained. They can be paid and fed and cared for properly. They will then be at least three times as effective as an equal number of the divisions that now exist. They will have a keen sense of loyalty to the Central Government. They can be made mobile and moved to wherever they may be needed. They can quickly become a strong, efficient striking force, backed up by necessary auxiliary units and supplied by a working S. O. S.

The plan can be put into effect as follows:

[45] Stilwell Black Book, 25 Sep 43.
[46] *The Stilwell Papers*, p. 228.

1. Begin training the remaining divisions in the first 30, and gradually move them to the Yunnan–Kweichow area. If and when the Burma Road is opened, the C. A. I. [Chinese Army in India] can join the group. Meanwhile training should continue, in anticipation of the receipt of equipment. The first 30, after action in Burma, will be seasoned and experienced, and can then be moved to the Hengyang–Kweilin area, where they will be available for further operations. With such a force in that area, all threats to Chungking and Kunming will be removed.

2. Meanwhile, set up a school in Kweilin and train the officers of the second thirty divisions. After graduates return to their divisions, send U.S. instructor groups to supervise training there. Gradually move the divisions of this group, by exchange with divisions now there, to the Hunan–Kiangsi area, to put them into a position threatening Ichang and Hankow.

3. By the time the first 30 have been equipped and moved to the Hengyang–Kweilin area, the second thirty will be ready for their equipment.

4. Build up the services for the second 30 by cadres taken from the S. O. S. of the first 30.

5. Of the best remaining divisions, designate 30 as garrison units and leave them in key defensive areas—Sian, Loyang, Lao Ho K'ou, Chekiang, Northern Kiangsi, Shiukwan, etc. These units will not be expected to move; they will be used on the defensive only; and will not need the equipment that the first and second 30 will get.

6. The remaining divisions should be inactivated in one way or another. They can be cut down to brigades at once, by order, and a maximum strength of 4,000 each can be established. Very few of them have more than that, anyway. Some of them can be used to form S. O. S. for the first and second 30 division groups, and to supply replacements.

7. The problem of provincial loyalty will disappear as soon as the first and second 30 are constituted. These two groups will assure the Central Government of obedience to its orders.

8. The problem of surplus officers will have to be solved. Junior officers can be given the chances [sic] of demonstrating their ability at the schools. Those who cannot qualify should be released from the army. The number can be cut materially in this way. Senior officers can be sent to the garrison units and carried as extra numbers for the time being. For the surplus ones of very high rank, an advisory body, without authority, but with pay, can be established at Chungking, and they can be used here as a planning board.

The above is a radical procedure. Without it, or something similar, the Chinese Army cannot be expected to pay [sic] its part. The eyes of the world are on China, and now is the time to take vigorous action. The manifesto of the C. E. C. [Central Executive Committee of the Kuomintang] states that "It is China's responsibility to undertake the major operations on the East Asiatic continent." This will be impossible without a thorough reorganization. With it, China will be able to do her part and refute her critics, and will emerge at the end of the war with the means of assuring her stability.[47]

J. W. STILWELL,
Joint Chief of Staff for the Generalissimo.

Writing to the Secretary of War on 12 October 1943, Stilwell summarized the above program for Stimson. Stilwell doubted that the Generalissimo would accept it unless the Chinese leader was told he would have to agree to it or lose U.S. support. But, as the Secretary knew, Stilwell had no power to bargain with the Generalissimo. Stilwell saw his work in China as just a struggle to get the Chinese to live up to their promises. Then, most significantly, he told the Secretary that if he succeeded in putting through the second Thirty Divisions program he would have fulfilled his mission to improve the combat effectiveness

[47] This memorandum in Stilwell Documents, Hoover Library.

of the Chinese Army, a mission in which he had had no real support and been constantly plagued by the Chinese Ministry of War.[48]

Soong Attempts To Have Stilwell Recalled

Alarming reports from the Fourteenth Air Force and from the Chinese Army in India reached Soong in early September. The nonappearance of the reinforcements promised to the Fourteenth Air Force at TRIDENT and the vigor of the Japanese reaction depressed Chennault, and on 5 September he reported again to the President and Hopkins, in tones of discouragement. Chennault made no charges against Stilwell but showed in detail how far the Fourteenth Air Force fell short of having the aircraft and supplies originally promised. The Fourteenth's aggressive commander pointed out that his weakness in fighter aircraft put him far behind schedule, because by September 1943 he had expected to have air superiority, and he told the President that he was fighting against heavy odds.[49] The two squadrons of medium bombers promised to Chennault were being held back in India by Stratemeyer, but Stratemeyer had not so informed Chennault or the Generalissimo.[50]

On 16 September the President apologized to Madame Chiang through Stilwell for the shortfalls in the Chennault program. He regretted that bad weather, floods, and failure to complete the Assam airfields on schedule had interfered, but he assured her that replacements and reinforcements for the Fourteenth Air Force were on the way.[51]

From India, Lt. Gen. Sun Li-jen, whose 38th Division was organized from Soong's Salt Gabelle troops,[52] sent an extremely glum report on 10 September. His division, he reported, was 3,000 men understrength; malaria had been dreadful, and his division would probably have 50 percent casualties before it reached its first objective. Sun's request for a tank battalion had been turned down by Stilwell, undoubtedly because the latter could not understand its importance. On the supply side, General Sun commented that air supply would be unable to keep up with his troops, so that two transport battalions (*i.e.,* coolies) would have to be attached to his division.[53]

After receiving these reports from Chennault and Sun, Soong on 15 Septem-

---

[48] Ltr, Stilwell to Stimson, 12 Oct 43. Stimson Papers.

[49] Ltr, Chennault to Roosevelt, 5 Sep 43. Bk VII, Hopkins Papers.

[50] Rad WAR 3644, Arnold to Stratemeyer, 21 Oct 43. Item 1099, Bk 4, JWS Personal File.

[51] Memo, Stilwell for Mme. Chiang, 16 Sep 43, inclosing a msg from Roosevelt to Mme. Chiang. Item 807, Bk 2, JWS Personal File.

[52] The Salt Gabelle, or salt monopoly, was a major item of revenue to the Chinese Government. Constant policing was required to administer it. From the guards carrying out this mission the 38th had been formed.

[53] Sun's letter to Soong was hand carried by a general officer of the Fourteenth Air Force and is very similar to the one from Sun to Stilwell on 17 August 1943, quoted in full on page 64 of General Ho's *The Big Circle.* The latter, being addressed to Stilwell, says nothing of shortages of men and equipment (the 38th Division was then at full strength, equipped and trained to a standard never before attained in China's history), omits the reflections on Stilwell's grasp of tactics, but takes a very dark view of the prospects of waging a successful campaign in north Burma. Ltr, Sun to Soong, 10 Sep 43. Bk VII, Hopkins Papers.

ber submitted to the President a plan for a complete reorganization of the China Theater. His paper called for placing China on the Combined Chiefs of Staff and the Munitions Assignments Board. A Chinese officer would become Supreme Commander, China Theater, and another Chinese would become Chief of Staff of China Theater, thus eliminating Stilwell. These two Chinese officers would have American deputies. "All military units of whatever nationality operating in this theater, as well as the China–India Air Transport Command, should be placed under the orders of the Theater Commander." Mountbatten's appointment, said Soong, forced a re-examination of Stilwell's position:

At present he is Chief of Staff of the China Theater and has independent command of the U.S. Air Force in China, India, and Burma. He also commands the SOS in India and China, Air Transport Command between India and China, and the Chinese Ramgarh divisions, and has some undefined authority over the Chinese Expeditionary Troops now in Yunnan. In addition he had been given authority by the War Department, without the concurrence of China, over the Chinese lend-lease program. The straddling of authority over such multifarious spheres is making for friction which may dangerously imperil future campaigns.[54]

Soong was anxious that the Chinese be brought under the Combined Chiefs of Staff. Such an arrangement was not possible at the present time, he pointed out, because the Generalissimo as Chief of State could not discuss matters as one of the Combined Chiefs of Staff nor could he be subordinate to them.[55]

Referred by the President to General Marshall, Soong met a polite refusal to alter the existing command structure. One excellent reason against making the Chinese privy to all the secret meetings of the CCS was that Chinese codes were not secure. Every disclosure to the Chinese was a calculated risk. By August 1943 the United States knew Japan had broken the Chinese codes, and Marshall so informed Soong. By the nature of the affair, the United States could not be certain how long the Japanese had been reading Soong's radio messages, nor could the United States be sure that later Chinese codes would be more secure. Messages from Soong to the Generalissimo were being intercepted from Japanese broadcasts, some of them originating in China.[56]

Soong then once again brought Chennault's needs to the President's attention, quoting a cable from the Generalissimo which stated that Chennault had on hand only 85 fighters operational plus 20 repairable and 9 medium bombers operational with 7 repairable. The President turned the matter over to General Marshall, expressing his concern, and adding: "I wish you would get behind this again and vigorously push our agreed plans." [57]

[54] Memo, Soong for Roosevelt, 15 Sep 43, with penciled note: "Dear George [Marshall]: Will you talk with Dr. Soong about this? FDR." Bk VII, Hopkins Papers.

[55] Memo cited n. 54.

[56] (1) Rad AM 1229, Ferris to Hearn, 18 Aug 43. Item 737, Bk 2, JWS Personal File. (2) Interv with Marshall, 6, 13 Jul 49. HIS 330.14 CBI 1949.

[57] Memo, Soong for Roosevelt, 27 Sep 43, sub: China Air Offensive in 1943; Memo, Roosevelt for Marshall, 27 Sep 43. Bk VII, Hopkins Papers.

While Soong was seeking Stilwell's recall in Washington, the campaign against Stilwell in Chungking was steadily increasing in violence. The General-issimo was being told some extraordinary things about him by a member of the Institute of Pacific Relations, who was reported to Stilwell as having said that Stilwell "was behind a plan to push Peanut aside, put T. V. [Soong] at the head of civil affairs, and Chen Cheng in command of the Army. So that, in effect, I would command the Army. May [Mme. Chiang] had this dope on 9/28 when I saw her. Of course, the Peanut had it too. The effect on the latter may be imagined." [58] And again:

Ella [Madame Kung] had to go and see a friend so May and I had a conference on our troubles. It seems that Peanut has been all tied up in knots over misunderstandings. The naval strength [in the Bay of Bengal] for instance. Bum interpreters. She says to put in to Peanut the warning about Burma.

Also I was in Dutch over the North-west proposal [for an attack on the Japanese to fore-stall their reaction to the Chennault plan]. I should know the Reds won't take orders. Told her it would show them up to the world if they didn't. (She got it). [59]

Stilwell Restored to Favor

In October 1943 Admiral Mountbatten and General Somervell arrived in New Delhi en route to Chungking. Somervell was a presidential emissary, whose mission was to present the Southeast Asia Command to the General-issimo and secure his formal assent to the new Allied command structure for Southeast Asia. Very soon after Somervell arrived in New Delhi, he encoun-tered Soong, who was also hastening to Chungking. Soong stated that President Roosevelt had agreed to recall Stilwell, of which news Somervell had received no hint in Washington. Soong also warned Mountbatten that relations "be-tween General Stilwell and Chinese troops" were very bad, and that to issue orders appointing Stilwell as Deputy Supreme Allied Commander would have "disastrous irrevocable repercussions." [60]

Mountbatten delayed briefly in New Delhi to attend to the myriad details of setting up a new headquarters, and Somervell went on to Chungking. There he met with the Generalissimo, while Soong interpreted. The Chinese leader left no doubt that he wanted Stilwell's immediate removal. [61] Meanwhile, in Washington Marshall considered recalling Stilwell and naming Somervell to replace him in command of CBI, with Lt. Gen. Jacob Devers to be command-ing general of Army Service Forces. [62] Marshall knew that Stilwell did not have

---

[58] Stilwell Black Book, Sep 43.
[59] Stilwell Diary, 5 Oct 43.
[60] (1) Cable, Soong to Hopkins, 14 Oct 43. Bk VII, Hopkins Papers. (2) Ltr, Somervell to Maj Gen Orlando Ward, Chief, OCMH, 1 May 50. HIS 330.14 CBI 1950. (3) Mountbatten Report, Pt. A, par. 16.
[61] Ltr cited n. 60(2).
[62] (1) Interv with Marshall, 6 Jul 49. HIS 330.14 CBI 1949. (2) Statement, Marshall to Stilwell, 21 Nov 43. Stilwell Diary.

the President's liking or support, and, greatly respecting Stilwell's talents as a tactician and trainer, was now seriously considering his transfer to a post where those talents could have full opportunity.[63]

At this point Somervell received a War Department radio ordering him to stay on in CBI until further orders. The order made Somervell think his position a delicate one, for he feared that if he succeeded Stilwell, he might be considered to have had a share in removing an officer whom he greatly respected and to whose support he was deploying the resources of Army Service Forces. The radio strengthened Somervell's existing resolve to do his best for Stilwell.[64]

Admiral Mountbatten arrived in Chungking on 16 October to establish cordial relations between himself and the Generalissimo. Somervell as soon as possible told Mountbatten of the Generalissimo's formally expressed desire to have Stilwell recalled. The Generalissimo's wish was a rude initiation into the problems of Mountbatten's new command, and the two men discussed it at length. The new Supreme Allied Commander concluded that he had no desire to use Chinese troops if the officer who had commanded them for two years was removed on the eve of active operations, and authorized Somervell so to inform the Generalissimo.[65]

When Somervell described the stituation to Stilwell, the latter was apparently surprised and angered. He had known of the attacks on him, but the Generalissimo had answered his memoranda, which was a great change from the Chinese leader's usual practice, and Madame Chiang was his ally, so that the sudden demand for his recall was a stunning surprise. Stilwell's reaction, his sense of anger and injury, was an enduring one.[66]

On the next day powerful support came to Somervell's attempts to sustain Stilwell when Mesdames Chiang and Kung rallied to Stilwell. So, too, did General Ho! Somervell discussed the crisis with Madame Chiang and the Generalissimo, urging them to keep Stilwell in China. On the evening of 17 October Madame Chiang called Stilwell to the Generalissimo's residence and exhorted him to effect a *rapprochement* with the Chinese leader. She suggested that Stilwell see the Generalissimo and "tell him that I had only one aim, the good of China, that if I had made mistakes it was from misunderstanding and not intent, and that I was ready to co-operate fully." Stilwell agreed with a reluctance consistent with the discouragement and disillusion evident in his diary, for he was "on the point of telling them to go to hell." [67]

Stilwell then saw the Generalissimo and made his bid for the latter's

[63] Interv cited n. 62(1).
[64] Ltr cited n. 60(2).
[65] Mountbatten Report, Pt. A, par. 10.
[66] *The Stilwell Papers*, pp. 231, 237. On 6 November 1943 Stilwell compared the Generalissimo to a rattlesnake, then wrote: "Mistake! Last time he didn't rattle at all—just struck." Stilwell's statement seems to refer to the Generalissimo's action in demanding Stilwell's recall, for nothing else would seem to fit the implied requirements of surprise and personal injury. Also note succeeding November entries.
[67] *The Stilwell Papers*, pp. 232, 235.

friendship. He described his aims and policies to Chiang and told the Chinese statesman that he was now as always prepared to co-operate fully.[68] The Generalissimo's attitude was pleasant, and in reply Chiang made two points: "(1) That [Stilwell] understand the duties of the commander in chief and the chief of staff. (2) That [Stilwell] avoid any superiority complex." Under those conditions, said the Generalissimo, he and the American could work harmoniously together. "All balderdash," wrote Stilwell in his diary, but the two men were formally reconciled and parted amicably.[69]

In retrospect, it seems the Generalissimo was objecting to Stilwell's dual status, with its responsibility to American and Chinese authority.[70] The Generalissimo's first point—that Stilwell understand the respective duties of a commander in chief and chief of staff—possibly reflects a feeling by the Generalissimo that Stilwell should take orders primarily from him. There could be no objection to that, so long as Stilwell's American superiors agreed to the Generalissimo's orders. However, Stilwell was sent to China to improve the combat efficiency of the Chinese Army; the War Department had never altered those orders, and while they stood, Stilwell would be obliged to exhort the Generalissimo to undertake projects in which the Chinese leader had little interest. To the Generalissimo, it must have seemed that Stilwell was ordering him to reform his army. The Generalissimo's second point about the "superiority complex" no doubt reflects the impression that would be left by any reformer on any second party.

At some point during the negotiations Somervell took the opportunity to advise Stilwell on the latter's relations with the Generalissimo, warning him to avoid the acid remarks which so irritated the Chinese leader when repeated to him. Somervell later wrote Stilwell: "I thought it was very unfortunate for you to refer to the Generalissimo in the way you have and to make some other remarks which have caused unnecessary friction." [71]

The reconciliation, which Stilwell entered with such reserve, seemed to Somervell almost immediately to grow in strength. Stilwell, Chennault, Somervell, Madame Chiang, and the Generalissimo gathered together for tea at the Generalissimo's residence on 18 October. There was an air of good feeling among those present, and, as the afternoon wore on, Somervell began to feel that brighter days were in store for the Sino-American effort in Asia. The Generalissimo and Stilwell pledged mutual friendship, and Chennault promised

---

[68] Handwritten notes in Stilwell Documents were prepared between 18 October and 1 November 1943 for a radio to Marshall and Stimson. The notes summarized Stilwell's estimate of the situation as of late October 1943. Portions of them will be quoted later in the text.

[69] *The Stilwell Papers,* pp. 232–33.

[70] See Ch. III, above.

[71] A letter, Somervell to Stilwell, 9 November 1943, Somervell File, Volume III, CBI 42–43, explained that Somervell offered his advice at Marshall's order. On Somervell's return to Washington, Marshall asked him if he had spoken to Stilwell "concerning the wise cracks which have provoked some hostility."

Stilwell his loyal co-operation in the forthcoming campaigns.[72] Long years after the war, it seemed to Stimson that Somervell was the only Presidential emissary whose work had been "truly helpful."[73]

Sensing the improved atmosphere, Stilwell responded to a degree. When Madame Chiang advised him to "give [Chennault] no ground for complaint, so he can't cry to the Generalissimo," Stilwell called her advice "good." [74] The Generalissimo ordered General Ho to be especially cordial to Stilwell, and that was pleasing.[75]

The crisis ended with T. V. Soong's fall from grace. The Generalissimo ordered him to be ill and to seek the quiet of his home. Soong complied and for many months played no part in the military relations of China and the United States.[76]

When Stimson learned that the Generalissimo's attitude toward Stilwell had changed, he appraised it to Stilwell on 25 October as a "very welcome gleam of hope," suggesting he had come to share Stilwell's growing pessimism about his efforts to reform the Chinese Army.

The situation here has been complicated by the short-circuiting process which has constantly been going on between the respective All-Highests in China and the United States. It was so discouraging and made your patient efforts so well-nigh hopeless that we have wondered sometimes whether in fairness to you we should not offer you the chance to be relieved in favor of some less impossible task. Your readjustment with the Generalissimo has brought a very welcome gleam of hope. I write to let you know that throughout it all and whatever bludgeonings of fate which you encounter, I have the utmost gratitude to you for what you have done and confidence in your courage and ability.[77]

Questions of Boundary and Command

Hectic and tangled though it had been, the crisis over Stilwell's position in China had lasted but a few days. With agreement that Stilwell would continue in his several positions and be acting [78] Deputy Supreme Allied Commander, SEAC, the assembled dignitaries could proceed to defining the exact relations of SEAC to China Theater. Admiral Mountbatten's arrival in Chungking introduced a significant new factor—for the first time since the Arnold-Somervell-Dill mission of February 1943 it was not Stilwell's responsibility to persuade the Generalissimo to accept decisions in whose making China had had no

---

[72] Ltr cited n. 60(2).
[73] Stimson and Bundy, *On Active Service*, p. 536.
[74] *The Stilwell Papers*, p. 234.
[75] Notes cited n. 68.
[76] (1) *The Stilwell Papers*, p. 235. (2) Bk VII, Hopkins Papers.
[77] Ltr, Stimson to Stilwell, 25 Oct 43. Stilwell Personal Papers.
[78] For whatever reason, Stilwell was never appointed Deputy Supreme Allied Commander, SEAC. He was very conscious of the fact that he never received orders giving him the post and often alluded to the circumstance in his diaries and papers. For example, see his notes for a talk with Mountbatten on 6 March 1944, Stilwell Diary, Notebook 10 1/2.

share. It was Mountbatten's task to induce the Generalissimo to accept SEAC, and Stilwell was grateful for the respite.[79]

Admiral Mountbatten raised first the question of a unified command in Burma during the forthcoming campaign. The Generalissimo, having now agreed to retain Stilwell, was willing to solve the command question by having the Yunnan Chinese come under Stilwell's authority when they actually entered Burma, Stilwell, of course, being in turn under Mountbatten. The Generalissimo promised that the Y–Force would be ready for action on 1 January 1944. The Chinese again stressed the importance of Allied naval control of the Bay of Bengal, and of Allied amphibious operations in south Burma to support projected operations in north Burma, but these points caused no anxiety since Mountbatten, a specialist in amphibious warfare, was in Southeast Asia to conduct such operations.

Told of the Combined Chiefs' decision at Quebec to place heaviest emphasis on ground and air operations in Burma, the Generalissimo concurred but was most anxious that Hump tonnage into China not fall below 10,000 tons a month when the Burma operations began. This was a trying point for Mountbatten, who attempted to explain the difficulties of raising tonnage over the Assam line of communications to the target figure set at QUADRANT. Somervell believed that the target figure could be met, but Mountbatten made it plain that he did not share Somervell's optimism. He placated the Generalissimo by promising that any drop in Hump tonnage caused by Burma operations would be purely temporary and described such a shortfall as a wise investment in restoring communications to China. The Generalissimo replied, very simply: "I trust you!" [80]

Shortly after the meetings in Chungking Somervell could not remember just how the question of the boundary between SEAC and the Generalissimo's China Theater happened to be raised there. The question came up initially at QUADRANT, where one of the conferees recalled that the Chinese had been told French Indochina and Thailand were in China Theater. The news that the Combined Chiefs wanted to transfer them to SEAC would have to be broken tactfully to the Generalissimo.[81]

On learning that the Combined Chiefs proposed to transfer Thailand and French Indochina to SEAC, the Generalissimo protested vigorously. He feared that if the Chinese Army and people learned these countries had been removed from China Theater and placed under SEAC, Chinese morale would suffer. The question was settled by Mountbatten's proposal of a gentleman's agreement whereby Thailand and French Indochina would remain formally in China Theater, SEAC and the Generalissimo both having the right to operate in them,

---

[79] To his wife, Stilwell wrote on 15 October: "Somebody else is responsible and it's a grand feeling." *The Stilwell Papers*, p. 231.

[80] CM–IN 15127, Somervell to Marshall, 25 Oct 43.

[81] Interv, Handy with Somervell, 5 Nov 43. Folder 23, OPD Exec 1.

and with any area occupied automatically coming under the authority of the occupying command. The Generalissimo accepted, but the compromise was neither accepted nor rejected by the President, Prime Minister, and Combined Chiefs, who preferred to let the knotty problem alone for the time being.[82]

Somervell's Trip to India

After the successful conclusion of the Chungking conferences Somervell returned to India where he and Maj. Gen. Charles P. Gross, Chief of Transportation, conferred with officers from General Headquarters (India), SOS CBI, and the Government of India to find means to improve the Assam line of communications. His mission was in compliance with the QUADRANT decisions, further emphasized by orders from the President through Marshall. Following Soong's and Chennault's protests of September, the President had asked Marshall why Chennault was not receiving the supplies he needed.

Marshall explained to the President that deficiencies in the operation of the Hump and the Assam line of communications were hobbling Chennault. While the number of aircraft assigned to the India–China Wing of the Air Transport Command had increased from 100 in April to 230 in September, only 50 percent of them were operational, because of mechanical troubles with the new C–46 type aircraft, lack of spares and mechanics, bad working conditions, inexperienced flight personnel, and bad weather. Also, difficulties were caused by a decision of General Auchinleck to divert some engineering resources from airfield construction, and by differences of opinion over rail traffic priorities.[83]

Regarding the Assam line of communications, Marshall believed that the source of the trouble lay with the civil officials who controlled the line of communications, and who were extremely rigid and conservative in their operating methods, while the transportation officers of General Headquarters (India) represented a body which had long had no faith in any offensive action by either the Ramgarh or the Yunnan Chinese. These officers were very sensitive to the limitations of the line of communications but unable to see any way of correcting them. Because General Headquarters (India) thought Burma should be bypassed, General Auchinleck was hard put to find staff and line personnel who would give enthusiastic support to CCS decisions that called for an attack on Burma.[84]

Then another strong protest from the Generalissimo arrived in Washington,

---

[82] (1) Mountbatten Report, App. 4, par. 7. (2) Interv cited n. 81. (3) CM–IN 12040, Somervell to Marshall, 20 Oct 43. (4) CM–IN 12672, Somervell to Marshall, 21 Oct 43. (5) Rad SEACOS 83761, 9 Nov 43. SEAC War Diary, A46–217.

[83] Ltr, CofS to President, 4 Oct 43, sub: Air Cargo, India to China. WDCSA 381 China, A46–523. In the opening paragraph, Marshall states that he is writing this letter because of the President's criticisms of ATC's performance.

[84] These views are those of General Ferris. Marshall accepted and relayed them to the President. Ltr, Marshall to Roosevelt, 7 Oct 43, sub: Preparations for Burma. Case 224, OPD 381 CTO, A47–30.

in which the Chinese leader complained that the TRIDENT decision to build up the Fourteenth Air Force was not being honored. Roosevelt sent the radio at once to General Marshall with the covering note:

> I am still pretty thoroughly disgusted with the India-China matter. The last straw was the report from Arnold that he could not get the B-29's operating out of China until March or April next year. Everything seems to go wrong. But the worst thing is that we are falling down on our promises every single time. We have not fulfilled one of them. I do not see why it is necessary to use B-29's. We have several other types of bombing planes.[85]

Moving to correct the situation, the President cabled Churchill and asked that the Prime Minister personally intervene in the Assam line of communications and the ATC airfield program. The President remarked that the ATC had been a great disappointment which was regrettable because the Fourteenth Air Force was the only specific contribution the United States could make in China in the coming few months. The President feared that Burma operations might lead to Chennault's being deprived of supplies and such a circumstance, he thought, would be a great mistake. Addressing General Marshall, the President ordered that the Chief of Staff give the matter his personal attention. Everything had gone wrong with the program of supporting Chennault, the President wrote, but he was certain Somervell could put real punch behind the program when he set his mind to it.[86]

In compliance with the orders from Washington, Somervell surveyed the line of communications and ATC problems in India. He found that Brig. Gen. Earl S. Hoag, who succeeded Colonel Alexander in command of the ATC on 15 October, was attacking his problems with vigor. Colonel Alexander was exhausted after twenty months at his post, but as he turned over his grinding responsibilities, he could take pride in the fact that in October 1943 the ATC flew 7,240 tons over the Hump, China National Aviation Corporation, 1,122 tons, and other agencies 270 tons for a grand total of 8,632 tons. (*See Chart 7.*) The Hump backlog of tonnage accumulated in Assam was 48,410 tons, of which 40,998 tons was ordnance.[87]

Somervell's survey in late October convinced him that the difficulty of properly maintaining aircraft because of the shortage of spare parts, equipment, and personnel was a major handicap. Bad weather and the inherent difficulties of the route across Burma were serious problems. Pilots lacked confidence in the C-46. Motor transportation to the Assam terminals was inadequate. Radio aids to navigation were insufficient. The inner organization of the ATC was incomplete. Untrained pilots had been assigned to the ATC. Somervell showed his report to the senior ATC and SOS commanders in CBI, all of whom concurred. One of the remedies which the Army Service Forces' commander ap-

---

[85] Ltr, Roosevelt to Marshall, 15 Oct 43. WDCSA 381 China, A46–523.
[86] Ltr with Incl, Roosevelt to Marshall, 15 Oct 43. Folder 70, OPD Exec 10.
[87] (1) LeFarge, *The Eagle in the Egg*, pp. 124–26. (2) CM–IN 11981, Ferris to Marshall, 20 Oct 43.

plied was to bring together the key officers concerned with the ATC, whether directly or through SOS, for a series of conferences.[88]

Then General Somervell turned to the problems of the Assam line of communications beginning with the port of Calcutta. Somervell found it badly congested. As of 1 October, eleven ships in harbor had been there ten days or more. All but one had lend-lease for India. Heavy-lift cargo for India Command congested the wharves, some of it having been there from three to five months. The port's capacity, Somervell told Auchinleck and Mountbatten, was adequate for many times the amount of cargo then being received. "The disturbing factor is that no one at the port possesses the authority to overcome the inertia and to move the cargo out. Some stronger figure is demanded." Somervell understood that the appointment of an officer from British Army Movements and Transportation as port director had corrected a similar condition at Bombay; might it not be done at Calcutta? [89]

Railway problems came next. Mountbatten, Stilwell, Auchinleck, Somervell, Gross, and members of their staffs met on 23 October with representatives of the Railway Commission of the Government of India, the controlling body for the Bengal and Assam Railway. At the beginning of the conference, Sir Edward Benthall of the Railway Commission remarked that the reason the Bengal and Assam Railway had never carried more tonnage than the figure earlier offered by Auchinleck's staff as its capacity was because the railway had never been asked to carry more! The question of the assignment of U.S. railway battalions to Assam arose, and Mountbatten remarked that if India could not guarantee a 50-percent increase in tonnage by April 1944 he would have to accept Somervell's offer to supply the railwaymen. Somervell promised an increase of 50 percent were his offer accepted.[90]

The Indian representatives refused to guarantee a 50-percent increase under civilian control, while they strongly opposed any militarization of the rail lines. They also feared that introducing U.S. personnel in key positions could not fail to cause operating difficulties during the transition period. Mountbatten, however, was resolute in his stand, for he believed no aggressive operations in Burma could start until matters were improved.[91]

In this he had Somervell's support, and the latter wrote to General Wheeler: "I am most anxiously awaiting the results of the railway conferences which simply must come out the way we want. I believe that if you have any further conferences on the railroads that you insist on getting in the railway people before giving up, as Benthol's [sic] revelations at the meeting yesterday certainly implied a lack of liaison on all hands." [92]

---

[88] (1) CM–IN 14107, Somervell to Marshall, 23 Oct 43. (2) Ltr cited n. 60(2).

[89] Ltr, Somervell to Auchinleck and Mountbatten, 21 Oct 43, sub: Congestion in Port of Calcutta. Somervell File, Vol III, CBI 42–43.

[90] CM–IN 15125, Somervell to Marshall, 25 Oct 43.

[91] Mountbatten Report, Pt. A, pars. 45–46.

[92] Ltr, Somervell to Wheeler, 24 Oct 43. Somervell File, Vol III, CBI 42–43.

For the present, the issue of militarizing the railways with U.S. railway battalions remained on the agenda of problems that Mountbatten would have to solve before the fall campaign.

Then Somervell returned to Washington, where he reported to the President and Marshall. He told Stilwell on 9 November:

> I want to let you know that I had the pleasure of seeing the President yesterday and that he was delighted with my report on the outcome of the negotiations in Chungking. I think I made it clear to him that the agitation against you was the result of some plotting of some disaffected individuals and that it did not stem from any real reason. . . . I believe that you can count on full support from this end. General Marshall of course seemed delighted with the outcome. . . .[93]

"What More Can I Do?"

In late October 1943, Stilwell concluded that he was at the end of his resources as far as the mission to China he had been given in January 1942, the task of "improving the combat efficiency of the Chinese Army," was concerned. His decisions marked the end of two and one quarter years in which first General Magruder and then he himself struggled against every variety of obstacle to provide China with an effective modern army. The time for preparation had been consumed by obstruction in Chungking and divided counsels in Washington, and now the time for great events was at hand. The monsoon rains were at an end, and the campaign season in Burma was beginning while in China spring would open the time for battle. Stilwell believed that there was nothing more he personally could do to prepare the Chinese armies in China for what lay before them. The Generalissimo was markedly conciliatory and affable in late October and early November, but Stilwell attached small importance to it and considered that for the present his work in China was at an end. Such Chinese preparations as were under way would continue; he could not hurry them. The post of Chief of Staff, China Theater, was nominal. The joint Sino-American staff that might have made it effective had never been set up. Months before Stilwell had dropped the subject in an effort to placate General Ho Ying-chin.[94] For many months to come Stilwell spent little time in China and left matters there largely to his subordinates.

These conclusions—foreshadowed by the increasingly pessimistic tone of his diary entries for September and October as well as the 12 October letter to Stimson, and firmly adhered to in the months ahead—Stilwell set forth in the draft of a report to Marshall and Stimson, written in the third week of October 1943. He began by summing up the "net result of air offensive in China. A few Jap planes knocked down [but] Japs are still in China. The Y–Force left without weapons." He told of the October command crisis in a few terse sentences, blaming his troubles on the "mud campaign" directed against him. Then

---

[93] Ltr cited n. 71.
[94] (1) History of CBI, p. 101. (2) *The Stilwell Papers*, pp. 237–39.

Stilwell described his position in China Theater, the accomplishments of the last eighteen months, and closed with the statement that he could think of nothing more to do in China.

The Gmo has given orders to Ho to be especially cordial to me. Of course he could do that personally and still fail to cooperate wholeheartedly in backing up the Y-Force, but at least my position has been improved. If this had happened a year ago, we'd be better off now. As it is, I have about reached the limit of what I can do.

Everything connected with the 1st 30 [divisions] is under way. I cannot hurry the preparations already en route. Training teams are with armies in Yunnan and training has started in some units. The President's orders for the first 4,700 tons over the Hump each month to go to air force has [*sic*] resulted in depriving Y-Force of weapons and ammunition urgently needed for the campaign. By hook or by crook I have gotten over some 75's, Boys [antitank rifles], Brens, TM's [trench mortars] and part of the ammo. A fair lift in Oct, Nov, and Dec will give us most of the vital items. The agreement to mold units has not been kept. Result will be reduced strength divisions. Second 30 is [illegible]. School will open in Kweilin Nov 1, 1st class is there, and by May 1944 bulk of officers should be through course. From indications in 1st 30, demands from units for teams of instructors to carry on unit training will solve problem of putting our personnel with the units. Equipment will depend largely on opening the road. Third div for X–Force [Chinese Army in India] now assembling and training in Ramgarh. Should be ready by Jan 1. Two tank bns in training, ready by Dec 1. . . . Chinese have fallen flat on promise of [illegible] personnel for Y-Force. Road repair going well. Truck situation deplorable, etc. What more can I do? Have put out plan for future [operations in SEAC].[95]

Stilwell's appraisal of his position and duties in China meant that henceforth his attention would be focused on his duties as commanding general of the U.S. forces in China, Burma, and India and as acting Deputy Supreme Allied Commander, Southeast Asia Command. As U.S. theater commander he would be responsible for carrying out the variety of projects that had been set in motion to support the Chinese and U.S. operations in the Pacific, such as the reopening of land communications to China, the storage and transfer of lend-lease, the Ramgarh Training Center, and the others which have been described. As acting Deputy Supreme Allied Commander his task had been defined by Marshall as seeing to it that the Chinese Army in India played its part in the retaking of Burma. Preparing to turn his attention to these duties, which lay beyond China's borders, Stilwell flew from China to India on 21 October 1943 to present his proposals for SEAC's coming operations. The days of the Stilwell Mission, the days in which General Stilwell personally sought to prepare the Chinese Army for the ordeals ahead of it, were ended.

Summary

The U.S. Army's interest in China can be traced to the early 1900's when U.S. troops fought to relieve the foreign missions besieged by the Boxer rebels

[95] (1) In his own hand, Stilwell began this page: "George [Marshall] and Henry [L. Stimson]. Net result of air offensive in China. . . ." Stilwell Documents, Hoover Library. (2) *The Stilwell Papers*, pp. 235–36.

in Peking. After those events, a small U.S. garrison was kept in China to support Chinese nationalism against other powers, and young U.S. officers took their turns serving as its officers, among them George C. Marshall and Joseph W. Stilwell. American military attachés were maintained on the staff of the U.S. Embassy and sent back detailed studies of the Chinese forces.

As the Republic of China grew in strength in the late 1920's and early 1930's, Generalissimo Chiang Kai-shek was aided by a German Military Mission which brought approximately thirty divisions loyal to the Generalissimo to an efficiency previously unknown in China. In 1937, the Japanese Army provoked hostilities with China. The German-trained Chinese divisions, reinforced by provincial levies and war lord armies, fought valiantly but ineffectively. Their fighting was watched with great interest and studied in minutest detail by Col. Joseph W. Stilwell, then U. S. military attaché.

In 1938, the Japanese attained their strategic goals in China, and an undeclared peace prevailed, broken by Japanese rice raids and training expeditions. Seeking foreign aid, the Chinese turned toward the United States, which was traditionally sympathetic to Asiatic nationalism. With the passage of the Lend-Lease Act in 1941 the United States was in a position to give some munitions and communications equipment to the Chinese. The Chinese secured U.S. sponsorship of a program to equip thirty Chinese divisions, a 500-plane air force, and a line of communications to China.

Past experience with Chinese methods and the Chinese Army, plus the manner in which the Chinese presented their requests for lend-lease aid, suggested to members of the War, Treasury, and State Departments that a U.S. military mission should be sent to China to advise and assist the Chinese in procuring and using lend-lease supplies. Brig. Gen. John Magruder and his staff arrived in Chungking in October 1941. After arriving, Magruder and his staff reported to the War Department that the Chinese Army was not merely poorly equipped, but poorly trained, poorly organized, and not engaged in active hostilities with the Japanese.

After war began, a series of diplomatic incidents and military reversals caused fear in Washington that China might make a separate peace with Japan. The President was anxious to send a high-ranking U.S. officer to reassure the Chinese. The Chief of Staff, Gen. George C. Marshall, believed that if the Chinese were properly led, fed, trained, and equipped, they would be equal to any soldiers in the world. If they actively opposed the Japanese, the latter would be kept from adventures elsewhere in the Pacific, and American strength would not be dissipated among a number of theaters but concentrated for a decisive blow in the principal theater, Europe. The Generalissimo, newly appointed Supreme Allied Commander, China Theater, asked that an American be sent to act as chief of his Allied staff. The President's wish, Marshall's belief, the Generalissimo's request, led to the decision to send Lt. Gen. Joseph W. Stilwell to China Theater.

The War Department ordered Stilwell to increase the effectiveness of U.S. aid to China and to improve the combat efficiency of the Chinese Army. He was given four posts: Joint Chief of Staff to the Supreme Commander, China Theater; Commanding General of a U.S. task force, "U.S. Forces in China–Burma–India"; U.S. representative on an Allied military council in Chungking; representative of the President on lend-lease affairs.

When Stilwell arrived in China, the Generalissimo sent him to Burma to command the Chinese 5th, 6th, and 66th Armies. His efforts there were rendered futile by the lack of co-ordination in the Chinese effort. However, the period was fruitful in that it gave him an introduction to the local scene.

After walking out of Burma to avoid capture, Stilwell in his capacity as Chief of Staff, China Theater, presented major proposals to the Americans and to the Chinese. These plans to meet the situation caused by the now-complete blockade of China called for reform of the Chinese Army and a converging attack on Burma to liberate that country and restore the lines of communications from Rangoon to Kunming. His efforts to secure their acceptance were greatly handicapped by a June 1942 decision in the White House to transfer U.S. aircraft from India to the Middle East, thereby greatly angering the Chinese and causing the Three Demands crisis.

While waiting for the crisis to abate, Stilwell proceeded to create a U.S. theater of operations in China, Burma, and India. Under his command was a handful of aircraft, the Tenth Air Force, of which one portion, the China Air Task Force, served in China under Brig. Gen. Claire L. Chennault. A Services of Supply under Brig. Gen. Raymond A. Wheeler, with its principal base at the Indian port of Karachi, supported the Tenth Air Force, received, stored, and transshipped Chinese lend-lease, and received and distributed supplies given by India as reciprocal aid. As directed by the War Department and through the generous co-operation of Indian and Chinese authority, the Americans lived off the land as far as food, clothing, and shelter were concerned. The Chinese divisions which had escaped from Burma to India were being brought back to strength and trained at Ramgarh in Bihar Province. Stilwell hoped that driving from Manipur State into Burma they would be one part of his converging attack on Burma of which the reformed Chinese Y–Force would be the other part. Tying together the Indian and Chinese halves of this great expanse of Asia were about fifty transport aircraft which flew between the Assam and Yunnan airfields, the whole operation known colloquially as the Hump.

After compromise of the Three Demands by the President and the Generalissimo, Stilwell secured conditional Chinese assent to his plan to retake Burma. His proposals fitted in well with those of Gen. Sir Archibald P. Wavell, Commander-in-Chief, India, for a similar operation, and the two men went forward with plans and preparations. Wavell, as Supreme Allied Commander, India, assigned Stilwell and his Chinese Army in India to the Hukawng Valley of north Burma. A road from India to China was being built there, and to simplify administrative arrangements, Stilwell agreed to assume responsibility for it. Returning to China, Stilwell secured assent in principle to the arrangements he had made with Wavell.

As fall 1942 wore on, Stilwell was conscious that Chinese co-operation in operations to retake Burma was being given slowly and reluctantly, that the Chinese were greatly interested in the views being expounded by General Chennault. The Generalissimo took no interest in Stilwell's repeated suggestions, plans, and proposals that the Chinese Army be reformed by being cut down from 300-odd so-called divisions to a smaller force capable of being equipped and maintained in the presence of the enemy. Repeatedly, Stilwell exhorted China's Foreign Minister, T. V. Soong, saying that China must bestir herself and play her part. To meet the problems created by Chinese indifference to their Army and by their reluctance to introduce any military reforms, Stilwell urged that the United States adopt the approach earlier suggested by Magruder, that neither lend-lease nor credits should be given to the Chinese until they manifested willingness to help themselves. Marshall and Stimson approved this suggestion.

General Chennault was one of the very few Allied commanders to win distinction in the early months of the war. He had the prestige of victory and the weight of long experience behind his assurances to the President that given 105 fighters, 30 mediums, and 12 heavy bombers he could "accomplish the downfall of Japan." The Generalissimo was greatly impressed by descriptions of what U.S. air power could do in China. In January 1943 he stated that he would not cross the Salween River into Burma the following March and invited the President's attention to what a small air force could do. In April 1943 the Generalissimo as Supreme Commander, China Theater, requested that General Chennault receive first priority on all supplies flown to China and have a free hand in his operations. The President agreed.

A few days later the TRIDENT Conference decided that the clearing of all Burma was not feasible, that only north Burma was a near possibility. This elevated the Ledo Road to a new importance as a potential supply route to China. Competing with it was the Hump route, which under Chinese pressure was being constantly augmented. Following the TRIDENT Conference, it became apparent that Allied resources in Asia could not support both ground and air operations on the scale called for by TRIDENT and the President's decision. Stilwell was also aware that the President supported Chennault and explicitly rejected all suggestions that the Chinese be required to do anything in return for lend-lease, dollar credits, or U.S. air power in China. The President's decision not to ask anything of the Chinese meant that Stilwell lacked all bargaining power and could use only persuasion to interest the Chinese in Army reform.

That the Chinese Army would very probably remain at its current level of efficiency cast a shadow on those Allied plans for the defeat of Japan which were discussed at the great Allied conferences of May and August 1943. These plans called for an offensive by the Chinese Army supported by Allied air power on the Canton–Hong Kong area and synchronized with an Allied amphibious assault from the Pacific. Following capture of the great ports, the combined forces would make their way into north China, from which Japan would be bombed into submission, or at least be so weakened as to make successful invasion a certainty. Manifestly, success of such a plan would require co-operation of an effective Chinese Army.

Dissatisfaction with the conduct of the war in Southeast Asia and realization that the Allied effort in Asia needed more logistical support led the British and Americans to create Southeast Asia Command (SEAC) under Vice-Adm. Lord Louis Mountbatten as Supreme Commander. A major logistical effort was scheduled for CBI, to be powerfully supported by the U.S. Army Service Forces under Lt. Gen. Brehon B. Somervell. If Mountbatten's superiors gave him the resources to succeed in his new post, SEAC by retaking Burma and reopening the line of communications from Rangoon to Kunming would make possible a greatly increased flow of arms and ammunition to the Chinese Army, and that in turn would be a long step toward opening a port on the China coast.

Somervell and Mountbatten made the long trip to China to present SEAC to the Generalissimo. When they arrived, it appeared for a while that Stilwell's enemies might succeed in having the Generalissimo ask Stilwell's recall, but Somervell's diplomacy and Madame Chiang's support persuaded the Generalissimo to keep Stilwell as his joint chief of staff.

Following the creation of SEAC and the reconciliation between Stilwell and the Generalissimo, the future of the Allied war effort in Asia appeared to be at its brightest. Stilwell, however, concluded that he could do nothing more to improve the combat efficiency of the Chinese Army: "I have about reached the limit of what I can do." It was the end of his military mission to China. Thenceforth, he concentrated most of his attention on his duties as U.S. theater commander—charged with a list of projects to aid China or support Pacific operations—and as Deputy Supreme Allied Commander, SEAC.

Bibliographical Note

The sources for this volume are in four main categories:

Official records (contemporary)

Private papers

Manuscript histories, many of which were compiled in the Asiatic theaters by U.S. Army historians

Published works, including books and official dispatches and reports

Official Records

The major source of information for this volume is official records.* These include: (1) Papers and minutes of the Combined Chiefs of Staff and the Joint Chiefs of Staff and their planners; (2) Records of the Operations and Plans Division, War Department General Staff; (3) Records in the custody of Departmental Records Branch, Office of The Adjutant General; (4) Radiograms in the Staff Communications Office, Office of the Chief of Staff, Department of the Army; (5) Records located in the files of the Office of the Chief of Military History, Department of the Army, at the time they were consulted, but which eventually will be retired to the Departmental Records Branch, Adjutant General's Office; (6) Enemy Records. Other depositories of official information consulted in connection with this volume were the Military Intelligence Division Library, the Office of Naval Intelligence, the State Department radio files, and the National Archives.

(1) The papers and minutes of the Joint Chiefs of Staff (JCS) and the Combined Chiefs of Staff (CCS) can be located by the numbers on the papers that were assigned by the JCS and the CCS Secretariats. The papers are cited in footnotes by number, date, and title; for example, JCS 582, 9 Nov 43, Future Operations in the Southeast Asia Command. These papers are in the custody of the Joint Chiefs of Staff.

(2) The Army's set of JCS and CCS papers were kept by the Strategy and Policy Group, Operations Division, under the heading of ABC files. The ABC files are organized by subject and date of the first paper in the file; for example, ABC 381 Burma (3-10-42). They have now been retired to the Departmental Records Branch, Adjutant General's Office. The Army's set of Joint Board

---

* The date on all documents is determined by the time zone at the point of origin; the exception is classified messages, which are dated upon their receipt in Washington.

Papers, which may be identified by their Joint Board subject number and serial, are in the custody of G–3 Registered Documents Section.

The records of the Operations Division and of its predecessor, War Plans Division, are in the Historical Records Section, Departmental Records Branch, Adjutant General's Office. The War Plans Division file is identified in footnotes by the symbol WPD followed by the numerical designation of the subject file in which a particular paper appears and—if there is one—by a case number indicating the position of that paper within the file; for example, WPD 4389–20. The Operations Division central file is identified by the symbol OPD, preceeded by the case number within that file and followed first by a decimal number referring to the specific subject file, and second by the theater area; for example, Case 82, OPD 381 CTO (China Theater of Operations).

The Executive Group file of the Operations Division is an informal collection of papers compiled in the Executive Office of the Operations Division, primarily for the use of the Assistant Chiefs of Staff. These papers have been divided into ten major categories and an arbitrary serial number assigned to each item (book, folder, envelope) in each category. Papers in this file are identified in footnotes by the abbreviation *Exec,* which appears in each citation of item number and category number, as Item 4, Exec 1; Bk 2, Exec 8.

In the field of strategy and policy the Operations Division's files are the most important single collection of World War II documents in the custody of the U.S. Army.

(3) The custodian of all Army records is the Departmental Records Branch, Adjutant General's office, with depositories in Washington, D. C., St. Louis, and Kansas City, Missouri. With the exception of the Adjutant General's files (AG files), numbered according to the War Department decimal file system, all records of other offices or headquarters are maintained intact according to their original file systems, and each major block of records has been given accession numbers by which they may be located. The accession numbers listed below appear in this volume and represent the major blocks of accession relating to CBI documents. The A stands for accession; the first number stands for the year of accession and the last number designates the numerical order of accession within that year.

Accession Numbers:	*Agencies that deposited files*
A43–3	G–4, War Department General Staff
A45–466 . . .	War Department, Chief of Staff, Army
A46–215 . . .	Office, Secretary of War
A46–217 . . .	War Department Special Staff (SEAC War Diary)
A46–257 . . .	Army Service Forces (Somervell File on CBI)
A46–299 . . .	International Division, Army Service Forces (Lend-Lease to China)
A46–523 . . .	War Department, Chief of Staff, Army
A47–30	War Plans Division and Operations Division
A47–68	War Department, Chief of Staff, Army

A47–136 . . . War Department General Staff (Plans and Operations Cables)
A48–102 . . . Stilwell Personal Radio Files
A48–139 . . . War Department, Chief of Staff, Army
A48–179 . . . General Staff, United States Army (OPD)
A48–224 . . . American-British Conversations—Papers from Plans and Operations
Job–11 . . . . U.S. Missions (AMMISCA Files) in Army Service Forces (Defense Aid Division),International Division

Of particular interest to students of the CBI Theater are General Stilwell's personal message books (A48–102, Record Group 800), which have been cited arbitrarily in footnotes as JWS Personal File. There are nine of these books, including the OKLAHOMA File, which relates to General Stilwell's recall, and a book of messages sent and received by General Stilwell at Forward Echelon, Northern Combat Area Command. The last book is cited in the footnotes as 6A and at present is located separately at the Records Center in Kansas City, Mo.

Headquarters, U.S. Army Forces, CBI Theater, records and those of all subordinate commands are now filed in the Kansas City Records Center, a depository of the Departmental Records Branch, AGO. Theater records are filed in cabinets by drawer numbers. Thus, the Bissell Correspondence Folder in China Theater (CT) Cabinet 23, Drawer 2, KCRC, will assist the Departmental Records Branch, AGO, to locate this folder in years to come if the KCRC has ceased to be a depository.

On the Southeast Asia Command there is a chronological compilation of pertinent documents in the SEAC War Diary (A46–217).

(4) Radiograms are a rich source of important information for historians. Radios are found not only in subject files with related documents of other types but also in series files. Comprehensive series files containing more than three million messages dated after March 1942 are on microfilm in the Staff Communications Office, Office of the Chief of Staff, Department of the Army. In the Staffcom (Staff Communications) records, messages are filed chronologically so they may be located quickly according to the date and either the originator's message reference number, transmitted as part of the message, or the local reference number assigned by Staffcom to facilitate control. For example: Number 534 in the AMMISCA file of messages received in 1942 from General Stilwell in Chungking appears as CM–IN 4660 in the April 1942 file of incoming messages. Messages sent and received through Staffcom are identified in this volume according to their local reference numbers, the CM–IN or CM–OUT numbers assigned by Staffcom.

(5) The records in the possession of the General Reference Branch, Office of the Chief of Military History, are the manuscript histories, plus a variety of miscellaneous records collected overseas by CBI historians or obtained by cor-

respondence with participants in an event. Among the miscellaneous records are the Magruder Mission papers, cited arbitrarily in footnotes as AMMISCA Folder—, interrogations of Japanese officers, notes from diaries, and documents on the First Burma Campaign, the *Tulsa* incident, and Ramgarh Training Center. These records will eventually be retired to The Adjutant General's Office. The files of the Assistant Secretary of War are in the custody of the Administrative Assistant of the Secretary of the Army.

(6) An extensive account of the Japanese side is found in Japanese Studies in World War II, a series prepared by former Japanese officers in Tokyo under the auspices of the G-2 Historical Section, U.S. Far East Command, and translated by Allied Translation and Interrogation Section, Headquarters, Supreme Commander for the Allied Powers. These Japanese Studies are located in the General Reference Branch, Office of the Chief of Military History, but they will eventually be retired to DRB, AGO. Those relating to Southeast Asia and China are fragments of orders, plans, and diaries, held together by a thread of personal recollections of the author and a few of his former associates. The tone is generally objective. However, an account that will do justice to the Japanese side is still to be written.

Immediately after the war's end, Southeast Asia Command interrogated a number of senior Japanese officers who had served in Burma. The results were published in a number of mimeographed bulletins, under the imprimatur of Southeast Asia Translation and Interrogation Center (SEATIC). They are in the Military Intelligence Division Library. The Japanese spoke freely and showed no particular disposition to flatter the victors. Unfortunately, the interrogators directed questioning to the period 1943–45, and showed little interest in the First Burma Campaign of 1941–42.

An interrogation directing more attention to the First Burma Campaign, the North Burma Campaign, and Japanese planning was prepared by Mr. Sunderland and sent to the occupation authorities in Japan. Thanks to Maj. Gen. Charles A. Willoughby, Assistant Chief of Staff, G-2, very useful information was obtained from: Lt. Gen. Kitsuju Ayabe, Assistant Chief of Staff, *Southern Army;* Lt. Gen. Tadashi Hanaya, Commanding General *55th Division,* later *18th Area Army;* Col. Takushiro Hattori, *Operations Section, Imperial General Staff;* Lt. Col. Taro Hayashi, staff officer, *56th Division;* Lt. Gen. Masaki Honda, Commanding General, *33d Army;* Maj. Gen. Tadashi Katakura, Chief of Operations, *Burma Area Army;* Lt. Col. Minoru Kouchi, staff officer, *Burma Area Army;* Lt. Gen. Momoyo Kunomura, Commanding, *Guard Division;* Col. Husayasu Maruyama, Commanding Officer, *114th Infantry Regiment, 18th Division;* Maj. Gen. Yasuyuki Miyoshi, Chief of Staff, *5th Air Division;* Lt. Gen. Eitaro Naka, Chief of Staff, *Burma Area Army;* Lt. Col. Masaji Ozeki, staff officer, *General Headquarters* (Tokyo), Lt. Gen. Shoichi Sato, Chief of Staff, *5th Air Division;* Maj. Iwao Takahasi, staff officer, *15th Army;* Lt. Col. Masahiko Takeshita, staff officer, *15th Army;* Lt. Gen. Yutaka Takeuchi, Commanding General, *55th*

Division; Lt. Gen. Shinichi Tanaka, Commanding General, *18th Division;* Lt. Col. Taro Watanabe, *Operations Section, Headquarters, Southern Army,* Col. Motohisa Yoshida, staff officer, *15th Army.*

Colonel Kouchi offered the use of a manuscript history of the *55th Division* in the First Burma Campaign, The Vestiges of War. The information in General Tanaka's replies to the questionnaire was unusually detailed. The interrogations and *55th Division* history are in the temporary custody of the General Reference Branch, Office of the Chief of Military History.

The manuscript cited as Japanese Comments was prepared by the Japanese Research Division, Military History Section, Special Staff, of the Far East Command, General Headquarters, in reply to a request from the OCMH for comment by General Tanaka on a draft narrative of the North Burma Campaign of 1943–1944. Included in it are comments by General Tanaka, Cols. Takushiro Hattori and Ichiji Sugita, and Lt. Cols. Shiro Hara and Iwaichi Fujiwara of the *15th Army* staff.

Private Papers

Another source of valuable information is the private papers of participants in the China, Burma and India Theater. These include: (1) Personal Papers; (2) Diaries; (3) Letters.

Personal Papers: Of primary importance are the records of the late Gen. Joseph W. Stilwell, which consist of: his personal journal (which is cited as the Stilwell Diary); essays and analyses kept in two copybooks (which are cited either as Stilwell Black and White [B&W] Book or Stilwell Black Book); a file of undated papers (which are cited as Stilwell Undated Papers); and his collection of theater records and official personal papers (which are cited as Stilwell Documents, Stilwell Numbered Files [SNF] or Stilwell Miscellaneous Papers). These last are official papers and are in the Hoover Library, Palo Alto, Calif.

Since the days of his boyhood, General Stilwell had kept a diary. As the man grew in maturity and responsibility, his diary kept pace with him. By January 1942 his diary was a tool of command. It acted as a little personal file to which he could turn to refresh his memory. In the diary he summarized important radios, telephone calls, conferences, after action reports, and other papers important to a commander in the field or in the headquarters. In physical form, the wartime diaries are small ring-bound notebooks that the general could slip into his pocket. His family knew he kept a diary, but knew nothing of its contents until after his death, when the little notebooks were found among his personal effects. They were not intended for publication.

In addition to the diaries, General Stilwell kept two copybooks, one with a black cover about eight by ten inches in size, and one black and white, such as school children use. In them he wrote his reflections on the day's events, dating almost every one. However, because Stilwell was prone to worry over his problems, the entries tend to blur the clear, terse statements in the diaries. Because the copybook entries are more literary in style than the diaries, Theodore H. White relied heavily on them in editing *The Stilwell Papers*. Of similar nature is the collection of sketches and essays on pieces of copy paper which have been called the undated papers, following Mr. White's usage.

The Stilwell Numbered Files and their contents fall in an entirely different category, and are best described as Stilwell's personal command file. They are official documents, very similar to the Hopkins and Pawley collections discussed below. Some of the papers in the Stilwell command files are official Chinese documents, some are British, most originated in Stilwell's several headquarters and crossed his desk. On General Stilwell's departure from Headquarters, Army Ground Forces, Washington, D. C., in spring 1945 to assume command on Okinawa, the then Chief of Staff, Army Ground Forces, Maj. Gen. James G. Christiansen, directed that these files be assembled and sealed for storage. They were placed in the custody of The Adjutant General, labeled as General Stilwell's personal effects. On his death in 1946 they were shipped to Mrs. Stilwell, who stored them in a warehouse in Monterey, Calif., along with some family possessions. They remained there, unopened and unread, until Mrs. Stilwell in May 1950 permitted the two boxes to be opened and their contents studied by Riley Sunderland. These five linear feet of documents are now in the Hoover Library. For an understanding of events in China in the years 1942–1944 their importance can hardly be overestimated.

Also of great importance are the private papers of the late Harry L. Hopkins, which were temporarily in the custody of Robert E. Sherwood. The Hopkins papers have now been retired to the Franklin D. Roosevelt Library, Hyde Park, N. Y. As a personal friend of Dr. T. V. Soong, the Chinese Foreign Minister, and, in effect, the lend-lease administrator, Mr. Hopkins was actively concerned with Chinese affairs in 1941–1943. There are three major classes of papers regarding CBI in Book VII of the Hopkins Papers: letters from Soong to Hopkins, official correspondence on lend-lease and Sino-American relations, and letters from Joseph W. Alsop and Maj. Gen. Claire L. Chennault. A complete catalogue of all Hopkins' papers was generously given to the Office of the Chief of Military History by Mr. Sherwood. The authors also used Mr. Sherwood's manuscript of *Roosevelt and Hopkins: An Intimate History,* as well as letters from Mr. Sherwood's personal files.

Material on the background of Stilwell's mission and the candidacy of Lt. Gen. Hugh A. Drum for the China post is in General Drum's personal papers. Here, also, is the diary of Col. Charles E. Rayens, a member of Drum's party.

Of great assistance on the origins of Far Eastern strategy were notes and letters from the Stimson papers in the custody of the Office of the Secretary of Defense.

William D. Pawley, Vice President of Curtiss-Wright Corporation and owner of the Central Aircraft Manufacturing Company before World War II, permitted access to his papers on the formation of the American Volunteer Group and the origins of several projects to place U.S. air power in Asia.

Diaries: Maj. Gen. Edward E. MacMorland (then Col.), General John Magruder's chief of staff, kept a diary which is the best single account of the AMMISCA and early Stilwell periods. Col. Harry S. Aldrich's diary is a good source on AMMISCA's operations in Burma and the early days of American activities at Kunming. Extensive notes from the MacMorland and Aldrich diaries are in the custody of the General Reference Branch, Office of the Chief of Military History.

Letters: On file with the Administrative Office, Office of the Chief of Military History, are a number of letters containing specific information on CBI history, as well as a file of comments and criticisms on the draft manuscripts of the authors which were submitted to informed persons. Of particular value is the file marked HIS 330.14 CBI 1947, 1948, 1949, and 1950, which will eventually be filed at the Departmental Records Branch, AGO.

Manuscript Histories

The first attempt to prepare a CBI Theater history was initiated by General Stilwell, then theater commander, when in the summer of 1944 he created a Historical Section, Theater Headquarters, under Col. Mason Wright. The section's mission was to prepare a comprehensive history of the theater for General Stilwell. After General Stilwell's recall, the manuscript prepared under Colonel Wright's supervision was reworked and edited by General Stilwell at his home in Carmel, Calif. Much of the political comment in the manuscript is a close paraphrase of the reports of John P. Davies, Jr., Stilwell's political adviser. The manuscript was then submitted to the War Department as General Stilwell's report. The original copy is in the custody of the Departmental Records Branch, Adjutant General's Office. A duplicate carbon copy is in the Hoover Library.

While the Historical Section, CBI Theater headquarters, was preparing a history of the theater, the Historical Section of Headquarters, Services of Supply, China, Burma and India, under Lt. Col. Harry L. Mayfield, was preparing a history of that organization. The manuscripts prepared by the SOS and Theater Historical Sections have certain physical similarities. Both have a basic narrative, surveying the years 1942–1944, with a host of appendixes, many of them reports by subordinate units. The two manuscripts are a rich source of material, and the footnotes in this volume reveal how deeply the authors are indebted to Colonel Wright, to his successor, Lt. Col. John Mott, and to Colonel Mayfield. These manuscript histories are in the custody of the General Reference Branch, Office of the Chief of Military History.

The fighting in Burma from the American point of view is covered by The

First Campaign in Burma, and from the British side by Col. E. V. C. Foucar's manuscript, Narrative of the First Burma Campaign.

Miscellaneous histories are: 1st Lt. James H. Stone's U.S. Army Medical Service in Combat in India and Burma, 1942–1945; Ramgarh Training Center, 31 June 1942–15 May 1944; and India at War, 1939–1943, compiled by the Historical Section of General Headquarters (India). These manuscript histories are in the custody of General Reference Branch, Office of the Chief of Military History.

Giving the Air Force side of the story are: Army Air Forces in the War Against Japan, 1941–42, History of the CATF (1942–43), History of the India-China Ferry under the Tenth Air Force, History of the Tenth Air Force Headquarters for the Calendar Year, 1942, History of the Fourteenth Air Force, and the Royal Air Force narrative, The Campaigns in the Far East. These manuscripts, written as collaborative works, are now in the U.S. Air Force Historical Division, Air University Library, Maxwell Air Force Base, Ala.

U.S. strategy is described in Capt. Tracy B. Kittredge's draft manuscript prepared for the Joint Chiefs of Staff Historical Section and his narrative, U.S.-British Naval Cooperation, 1940–1945. There is also the unpublished manuscript of Dr. Rudolph Winnaker, Office of the Secretary of Defense, entitled Office of the Secretary of War under Henry L. Stimson.

Published Works

The following works cover the political aspects of the Far Eastern war:

Churchill, Winston S. *Their Finest Hour.* Boston : Houghton Mifflin Company, 1949.

———. *The Hinge of Fate.* Boston: Houghton Mifflin Company, 1950.

———. *Secret Session Speeches.* Compiled, and with introductory notes, by Charles Eade. New York: Simon & Schuster, 1946.

Hull, Cordell. *The Memoirs of Cordell Hull.* New York: The Macmillan Company, 1948.

Leahy, William D. *I Was There: The Personal Story of the Chief of Staff to Presidents Roosevelt and Truman Based on His Notes and Diaries Made at the Time.* New York: Whittlesey House, 1950.

Morison, Samuel Eliot. *The Rising Sun in the Pacific: 1931–April 1942.* Boston: Little, Brown & Company, 1948.

Roosevelt, Franklin D. *F.D.R.: His Personal Letters.* New York: Duell, Sloan & Pearce, Inc., 1948.

Sherwood, Robert E. *Roosevelt and Hopkins: An Intimate History.* New York: Harper & Brothers, 1948.

Stimson, Henry L., and McGeorge Bundy. *On Active Service in Peace and War.* New York: Harper & Brothers, 1948.

United States Congress. *Hearings of the Congressional Joint Committee Investigating the Attack on Pearl Harbor.* Washington: U.S. Government Printing Office, 1946.

———. *Report of the Congressional Joint Committee on the Pearl Harbor Attack.* Washington: U.S. Government Printing Office, 1946.

United States Department of State. *Papers Relating to the Foreign Relations of the United States, Japan: 1931–1941.* Washington: U.S. Government Printing Office, 1943.

United States Department of State. *Peace and War: United States Foreign Policy, 1931–1941.* Washington: U.S. Government Printing Office, 1942.

————. *United States Relations With China: With Special Reference to the Period 1944–1949.* Washington: U.S. Government Printing Office, 1949.

Background on the Chinese Army, political thinking, and philosophy may be obtained from:

Carlson, Evans F. *The Chinese Army: Its Organizations and Military Efficiency.* New York: International Secretariat, Institute of Pacific Relations, 1940.

Chiang Kai-shek. *China's Destiny and Chinese Economic Theory.* New York: Roy Publishers, 1947.

Ho Yung-chi, *The Big Circle.* New York: The Exposition Press, 1948.

Morris, David. *China Changed My Mind.* Boston: Houghton Mifflin Company, 1949.

Peck, Graham. *Two Kinds of Time.* Boston: Houghton Mifflin Company, 1950.

Winfield, Gerald F. *China: The Land and the People.* New York: William Sloane Associates, Inc., 1948.

On more strictly military matters are:

Arnold, Henry H. *Global Mission.* New York: Harper & Brothers, 1949.

Belden, Jack. *Retreat with Stilwell.* New York: Alfred A. Knopf, Inc., 1943.

Brereton, Lewis H. *The Brereton Diaries.* New York: William Morrow & Company, 1946.

Chennault, Claire L. *Way of a Fighter.* New York: G. P. Putnam's Sons, 1949.

Craven, Wesley Frank, and James Lea Cate, eds. *The Army Air Forces in World War II.* Vol. I, *Plans and Early Operations.* Vol. II, *Europe: TORCH to POINTBLANK.* Vol. IV, *The Pacific: Guadalcanal to Saipan.* Chicago: The University of Chicago Press, 1948, 1949, 1950.

Eldridge, Fred. *Wrath In Burma.* New York: Doubleday, Doran & Company, Inc., 1946.

Greenlaw, Olga S. *The Lady and the Tigers.* New York: E. P. Dutton & Co., Inc., 1946.

Hotz, Robert B. *With General Chennault.* New York: Coward-McCann, Inc., 1943.

Hughes, T. L. *The Burma Campaign.* Lahore, India: Northern India Printing and Publishing Company, no date.

LaFarge, Oliver. *The Eagle in the Egg.* Boston: Houghton Mifflin Company, 1949.

Owen, Frank. *The Campaign in Burma.* London: His Majesty's Stationery Office, 1946.

Seagrave, Gordon S. *Burma Surgeon.* New York: W. W. Norton & Company, Inc., 1943.

————. *Burma Surgeon Returns.* New York: W. W. Norton & Company, Inc., 1946.

Stilwell, Joseph W. *The Stilwell Papers.* Arranged and edited by Theodore H. White. New York: William Sloane Associates, Inc., 1948.

Tyson, Geoffrey William. *India Arms for Victory.* Allahabad, India: Kitabistan, 1943.

Watson, Mark S. *Chief of Staff: Prewar Plans and Preparations,* UNITED STATES ARMY IN WORLD WAR II. War Department. Washington: U.S. Government Printing Office, 1950.

Showing the economic effects of the war on Japan are:

United States Strategic Bombing Survey. *The Effects of Strategic Bombing on Japan's War Economy.* Washington: U.S. Government Printing Office, 1946.

————. *The Effect of Air Action on Japanese Ground Army Logistics.* Washington: U.S. Government Printing Office, 1947.

————. *The Campaigns of the Pacific War.* Washington: U. S. Goverment Printing Office, 1946.

————. *The War Against Japanese Transportation, 1941–1945.* Washington: U.S. Government Printing Office, 1947.

United States Strategic Bombing Survey. *Air Operations in China–Burma–India, World War II.* Washington: U.S. Government Printing Office, 1947.

Official despatches and reports by British officers have been published in *Supplements to The London Gazette* or by His Majesty's Stationery Office:

Despatch to the British Chiefs of Staff by Air Chief Marshal Sir Robert Brooke-Popham, 28 May 1942, on Operations in the Far East, from 17 October 1940 to 27 December 1941. *Supplement to The London Gazette,* January 22, 1948.

Despatch by the Supreme Commander of the ABDA Area to the Combined Chiefs of Staff on the Operations in the South-West Pacific: 15 January 1942 to 25 February 1942. London: His Majesty's Stationery Office, 1948.

Despatch for Secretary of State for War by General Sir Archibald P. Wavell, July 14, 1942, on Operations in Burma from December 15, 1941 to May 20, 1942 covering reports by Lt. Gen. T. J. Hutton on Operations in Burma from December 27, 1941, to March 5, 1942, and by General the Honorable Sir Harold R. L. G. Alexander on Operations in Burma from March 5, 1942, to May 20, 1942. *Supplement to The London Gazette,* March 11, 1948.

Despatch for Secretary of State for War by General Sir Archibald P. Wavell, September 27, 1942, on Operations in Eastern Theatre, Based on India, from March 1942 to December 21, 1942. *Supplement to The London Gazette,* September 19, 1946.

Despatch for Secretary of State for War by Field Marshal Sir Claude J. E. Auchinleck, March, 1948, on Operations in the Indo-Burma Theatre Based on India from June 21, 1942, to November 15, 1943. *Second Supplement to The London Gazette,* April 29, 1948.

Report and Supplement for Combined Chiefs of Staff by the Supreme Allied Commander, South-East Asia, 1943–1946, Vice-Admiral Viscount Mountbatten of Burma. New Delhi, India, July 30, 1947.

Glossary

A–1	Personnel section of air staff
A–2	Intelligence section
A–3	Operations and training section
A–4	Matériel and supply section
AAF	Army Air Forces
ABCD powers	American, British, Chinese, Dutch powers
ABDACOM	American, British, Dutch, Australian Theater of Operations covering the area from the Bay of Bengal to Australasia, created at ARCADIA Conference
ACofS	Assistant Chief of Staff
AG	Adjutant General
ALBACORE	Code word for operation to retake north Burma
AMMDEL	American Military Mission, Delhi. Code Name for American Headquarters at New Delhi, India
AMMISCA	American Military Mission to China. Code Name for American Headquarters at Chungking, China
ANAKIM	Plan to retake Burma and open the line of communications to China through the port of Rangoon
AQUILA	Code name for Task Force, Tenth Air Force. Code name for Headquarters, Tenth Air Force, New Delhi
ARCADIA	Washington Conferences, December 1941–January 1942
ASF	Army Service Forces
ASF (DAD) ID	Army Service Forces (Defense Aid Division), International Division
Asgmt	Assignment
ASW	Assistant Secretary of War
Atchd	Attached
ATC	Air Transport Command
AUS	Army of the United States
AVG	American Volunteer Group
B&W	Black and White copybook of General Stilwell
BOLERO	Build-up for the cross-Channel attack
Br	Branch
Bull	Bulletin
Burmarmy Sitrep	Burma Army situation reports
CAF	Chinese Air Force
CATF	China Air Task Force, Tenth Air Force
CBI	China, Burma, and India
CCS	Combined Chiefs of Staff
CDS	China Defense Supplies, Inc
CEF	Chinese Expeditionary Force
CG	Commanding General
CinC	Commander in Chief
CKS	Chiang Kai-shek
CM–IN	Classified Message sent into Pentagon

CM–OUT	Classified Message sent out of Pentagon
CNO	Chief of Naval Operations
CO	Commanding Officer
CofS	Chief of Staff
Com	Committee
Comd	Command
Conf	Conference
Corresp	Correspondence
COS	British Chiefs of Staff
CPS	Combined Staff Planners
CT	China Theater
CTO	China Theater of Operations
DCofS	Deputy Chief of Staff
Def	Defense
Dir	Director
Div	Division
Dr	Drawer
Engr	Engineer
G–1	Personnel section of divisional or higher staff
G–2	Intelligence section
G–3	Operations section
G–4	Supply section
GALAHAD	Code name for American Long Range Penetration Group
Gen Ref Br	General Reference Branch
GHQ	General Headquarters
GMO CKS	Generalissimo Chiang Kai-shek
GO	General Order
GOC	General Officer Commanding
Gp	Group
GYMNAST	Code name for 1941 plan for invasion of North Africa
HALPRO	B–24 Project to bomb Japan from east China
HD SSUSA	Historical Division, Special Staff, Department of the Army
Hist	Historical
Hq	Headquarters
HRS DRB AGO	Historical Records Section, Departmental Records Branch, Administrative Services Division, Office of the Adjutant General
ICFC	India–China Ferry Command, Tenth Air Force
IG	Inspector General
Incl	Inclosure
Ind	Indorsement
Int	Intelligence
Interrog	Interrogation
Interv	Interview
JB	Joint Board
JCS	Joint Chiefs of Staff
Jour	Journal
JPS	Joint Staff Planners

JSM	Joint Staff Mission (British)
Jt	Joint
KCRC	Kansas City Records Center, Kansas City, Mo.
Ln	Liaison
MA	Military Attaché
MAB	Munitions Assignments Board
MAC(G)	Munitions Assignments Committee (Ground)
MATS OSD	Military Air Transport Service, Office of the Secretary of Defense, Statistical Service Division, Andrews Field, Washington, D. C.
MID	Military Intelligence Division
Mil	Military
Min	Minutes
MIS	Military Intelligence Section
MS	Manuscript
Mtg	Meeting
Mun	Munitions
NMC	National Military Council (Chinese)
OCMH	Office, Chief of Military History
OCofS	Office, Chief of Staff
Off	Officer
OPD	Operations Division, War Department General Staff
OPD Exec	Executive Office Files of the Operations Division
Opn	Operation
OSW	Office, Secretary of War
OUSW	Office, Under Secretary of War
OASW	Office, Assistant Secretary of War
POTUS	President of the United States
Prelim	Preliminary
QUADRANT	Quebec Conference, August 1943
RAF	Royal Air Force
RAINBOW	Code name for various prewar plans of military action to meet situations created by Axis aggression
RAVENOUS	Plan for 4 Corps' advance into Burma
Reqmt	Requirement
SAC	Supreme Allied Commander
SACSEA	Supreme Allied Commander, Southeast Asia
SAUCY	1943 code name for north Burma operations
SEAC	Southeast Asia Command
SEATIC	Southeast Asia Translation and Interrogation Center
Serv	Service
Shipt	Shipment
SN	Secretary of the Navy
SNF	Stilwell Numbered File
SO	Special Order
SOS	Services of Supply
Sp	Special

Stf	Staff
SW	Secretary of War
TAG	The Adjutant General
T/O&E	Tables of Organization and Equipment
Torch	North African Operation, November 1942
Tp Conv	Telephone conversation
Trident	Washington Conference, May 1943
USAF	United States Army Forces or United States Air Force
USAF CBI	United States Army Forces, China, Burma and India
USAF Hist Div	United States Air Force Historical Division, Air University Library, Maxwell Air Force Base, Alabama
USA (Ret)	United States Army, retired
USN	United States Navy
USNR	United States Naval Reserve
USSBS	United States Strategic Bombing Survey
WD	War Department
WDCSA	War Department Chief of Staff, Army
WDGS	War Department General Staff
WPD	War Plans Division, War Department General Staff
Y–Force	American-sponsored Chinese division in Yunnan
Y–FOS	Y–Force Operations Staff (American)

United States Army in World War II

The multivolume series, UNITED STATES ARMY IN WORLD WAR II, consists of a number of subseries which are tentatively planned as follows: The War Department, The Army Air Forces, The Army Ground Forces, The Army Service Forces, The European Theater of Operations, The War in the Mediterranean, The War in the Pacific, The Middle East Theater, The China–Burma–India Theater, The Defense of the Western Hemisphere, Civil Affairs, Pictorial Record, The Technical Services, and Special Studies.

The following volumes have been published:*

    * Volumes on the Army Air Forces, published by the University of Chicago Press, are not included.

Index

Adler, Brig. Gen. Elmer E.: 200
Agreements. *See* Treaties and agreements.
Aid to China. *See also* British aid to China.
 agencies procuring: 211
 air force projects: 10–12, 14, 17–21, 23, 24n, 24–25, 31, 48, 78–79, 92–93, 161–62, 163, 386, 387
 air transport: 14, 75, 77–78, 93, 163–67, 272, 387, 388
 aircraft manufacture, repair: 200–201
 allocation procedure: 159–60
 AMMISCA recommendations, responsibilities: 29–30, 48, 49, 386
 benefits held diplomatic: 71
 Chinese paper currency: 313, 314n
 communications projects: 14, 15–16, 30, 47–48, 48–49, 76–78, 89, 90, 163–67, 386, 387–88
 corruption in handling: 60, 60n, 104, 167, 282
 credits: 7, 8, 11
 differentiation by procurement program: 211
 diversions to Middle East: 157–58, 163, 169–70, 171, 387
 factors prompting: 8, 23
 funds approval no guarantee: 16–17
 ground force matériel: 8, 11, 14, 16, 25–27, 31, 37–38, 39, 40–41, 42, 49, 75, 265, 265n, 301, 386
 handling and movement: 211–12
 impracticable requisitions: 26–27
 increase urged by Stilwell: 255
 larger concept: 76–80
 lend-lease funds: 16, 17, 20, 25
 lend-lease initiated: 13, 14, 15–16
 movement priorities: 212
 pilot training: 21n, 24, 41
 policy on diversions: 57, 58, 60, 114, 115, 152
 pre-Pearl Harbor status: 48–49
 program, 1942: 159
 program, 1943: 258, 265, 265n

Aid to China—Continued
 quid pro quo policy advocated: 41, 160, 178–79, 183, 185, 185n, 223, 224, 261, 278, 325, 388
 quid pro quo policy rejected: 41, 185, 185n, 186, 224–25, 262, 279, 282–83, 310, 388
 Rangoon stocks: 57–60, 84
 repossession: 159, 160
 requirements inadequately specified: 13, 15
 shrinkage after Pearl Harbor: 159–60
 Soong's program: 14, 15–17
 SOS responsibilities: 205, 211–12, 387
 Stilwell's role: 73, 159–60, 161, 173, 175, 212, 258, 265, 375, 387
 Stilwell's view, should be greater: 157, 177, 224, 225, 244–45, 255
 stockpiles: 46–47, 48, 159, 160, 160n, 167, 205
 strategic aims: 12, 23, 270
 subordinate to British needs: 8, 12, 15, 24
 title transfer: 48, 57, 161
 tonnage assignments: 160–61, 167–68, 177
 transit tax, Burma: 46
 transfer to British: 53, 56, 57–60, 84, 152, 170
 views, service chiefs, November 1941: 40
 War Department views diverge: 64–66
Air Base Group, 51st: 92, 200
Air Base Squadron, 54th: 200
Air Commando, No. 1: 366
Air Depot Group, 3d: 200
Air Ferry Command: 115, 164, 167. *See also* Air transport; Air Transport Command.
Air operations: 309. *See also* Air transport; Aircraft; Airfields.
 airlift protection: 78, 187, 188, 199–200, 252, 284, 314, 315, 330–31, 338
 American Volunteer Group: 93, 112–13, 130, 134, 143, 146n, 147–48, 251
 B-24 raid on Hankow: 347

U. S. GOVERNMENT PRINTING OFFICE: 1952 O-F—986352